HANDGUNS 96

8th Annual Edition

EDITED BY RAY ORDORICA

DBI Books, Inc.

TABLE OF CONTENTS

FEATURES

CATALOG

STAFF

EDITOR
Ray Ordorica
SENIOR STAFF EDITOR
Harold A. Murtz
ASSOCIATE EDITOR
Robert S.L. Anderson
PRODUCTION MANAGER
John L. Duoba
EDITORIAL/PRODUCTION ASSOCIATE
Holly J. Porter
EDITORIAL/PRODUCTION ASSISTANT
Laura M. Mielzynski
ASSISTANT TO THE EDITOR
Lilo Anderson
ELECTRONIC PUBLISHING MANAGER
Nancy J. Mellem
ELECTRONIC PUBLISHING ASSOCIATE
Larry Levine
GRAPHIC DESIGN
Jim Billy
MANAGING EDITOR
Pamela J. Johnson
PUBLISHER
Sheldon L. Factor

DBI BOOKS, INC.

PRESIDENT
Charles T. Hartigan
VICE PRESIDENT & PUBLISHER
Sheldon L. Factor
VICE PRESIDENT—SALES
John G. Strauss
VICE PRESIDENT/MANAGING EDITOR
Pamela J. Johnson
TREASURER
Frank R. Serpone

HANDGUNS 96

Handgun Trends

Knox views the political climate, page 7.

A round-up of new offerings, page 10.

S&W's Sigma 380 breaks new ground, page 17.

INDUSTRY NEWS

by RAY ORDORICA

THIS BOOK IS dedicated to the cutting edge of today's handgun technology, and to the most advanced issues and developments in the handgun industry. It's a tough task, as you might imagine, to be up-to-date with an annual publication. However, we strive to get an idea of what drives the industry and inform you of the reasons behind new trends. We ask our writers to give you their opinions on where the industry is heading in the future. We don't pull any punches, either. If something is not quite right, we'll tell you about it. We'll pick it apart and find out what's wrong, try to get it changed for the better, and inform you of the results.

Handgun trends are to some extent driven by politics, as was seen in the panic buying in the wake of the Brady Law. However, the election of a batch of pro-gunners in November, 1994 has slowed handgun buying to a crawl. If the Clinton administration gets reelected in 1996 (which currently seems unlikely), you can expect a new batch of gun laws and panic handgun buying again. If Clinton is out, the political scene will probably be somewhat more friendly toward guns and gun owners for the next four years.

With violence on the rise, more than half the states now have concealed carry laws, and sales of defensive/carry handguns are up as law-abiding citizens buy handguns in unprecedented numbers to defend themselves and their homes.

The reduction of allowable magazine capacity has also been a driving force in handgun sales. Industry reports indicate sales of big, heavy 9mm handguns (designed to handle 15-18 rounds of 9mm) are down. Smith & Wesson, for example, says sales of their high-capacity 9mm handguns are sluggish. Instead of accepting the limitation of only ten rounds of 9mms in their magazines, shooters are opting for larger calibers. If you pack a big gun that holds only ten rounds, they might as well be of a bigger caliber. Small guns, however, have their place, and S&W says that their new concealable Sigma 380 is doing very well.

Many new guns are being offered in 45 ACP, and we predict that caliber will be the hottest seller of the late 1990s, with the 40 S&W in second place. That, by the way, goes against most industry predictions, which put the 40 on top.

The nines are evolving into smaller, more compact guns, generally with single-stack magazines. I believe that's a more sensible use for the caliber, and in that guise the 9mms will probably hold their own.

With a restriction on the permissible number of rounds in the magazine, handgunners are again turning to the versatility of revolvers. Shooters are realizing revolvers will digest a great range of types of ammo and are not dependent on perfect ammo, as are semi-autos. Non-gunny householders who want a handgun for home defense are probably better served with revolvers than with semi-autos. Some great new revolvers are coming off designers' drawing boards and are meeting with success. S&W tells me their new Model 640 Centennial five-shot 357 Mag DAO revolver is one of their best-selling handguns.

An old name is again in evidence in the handgun world. High Standard is back in business under their original name, and with many of the same suppliers and personnel. Accuracy and quality are tops.

Sadly, one of the old names is no longer with us. Wesson Firearms Co., Inc., makers of the Dan Wesson revolver line, has bitten the bullet and is out of business. However, we hear there are plans under way that would soon unite Wesson Arms and three other companies—Ithaca Arms, Wildey, Inc., and Charco, Inc.—under one corporate name, to the benefit of all. We wish them the best of luck.

Colt is succeeding in their reorganizational efforts, and sales of their award-winning new 22 semi-auto are doing well. Colt still sells lots of 45 autos, and there's great interest in their redesigned Detective Special 38. Look for a small-frame 357 from Colt, and perhaps another surprise as well, before the end of the year.

Taurus is selling a great many of their innovative revolvers. Ruger's Vaquero and Navy Arms' Schofield are selling well to the cowboy action shooters.

For the most part, the industry is healthy overall and promises to stay so. With every manufacturer vying for your handgunning dollar, you the shooter stand to gain the most with the vast array of available merchandise from which to choose. ●

GUN LAW REPORT '95

by NEAL KNOX

WHAT A difference an election makes!

When the 103rd Congress shut down just before the 1994 election, the press was gleefully reporting that the NRA was on the ropes and the anti-gun crowd was licking its chops over the next step: "meaningful handgun control laws."

Last fall's election had the same impact as an intercepted pass within the 20-yard line. The scoring drive was stopped, but it's been so many years since our team played on offense that almost a year after that historic election we still haven't regained any lost ground in Congress. Progress is being made—particularly in the states—though as the fallout from the Oklahoma City bombing showed, we have such a light grip on a slippery ball that it would be mighty easy to fumble.

The anti-gunners were on a roll up until Nov. 8, 1994. They had hit their No. 1 target—handguns—twice within a year, and imposed the first major restrictions since passage of the Gun Control Act of 1968.

First, the "Brady Act" required a 7-day waiting period, police notification and a background check on all handgun purchasers. Second, the "Assault Weapons Ban" had established the principle of banning production and importation of common military-look guns (most of which are rarely if ever used in a crime, and all Congress knew it). Of even greater impact was the little-noticed provision—carefully ignored by the press—banning all over-10-shot magazines. That cut to the core of the most popular handguns: 13- to 19-shot modern semi-automatic pistols.

What allowed passage of those two laws was a combination of inattentiveness by most gun owners and sleight of hand by President Clinton, his colleagues and accomplices in Congress, and the establishment news media.

President Clinton, et al, were immensely aided by the selfish foolishness of "It doesn't affect me directly, so why should I worry." That attitude, so often visible among trap and Skeet shooters who ignore proposed new handgun restrictions, was even apparent among handgunners. The number one reason why the Brady Bill passed was that two-thirds of the population already lived under some form of waiting period, and most of the handgunners in those states didn't worry about a bill that they wrongly thought didn't have any additional impact on them.

Brady is being hailed as a huge success, having "kept more than 40,000 convicted felons from obtaining handguns." Nonsense. Out of roughly four million handgun purchases, some 40,000-plus sales were stopped or delayed in the law's first year (mostly due to misidentification, non-disqualifying arrests or outstanding warrants for excessive traffic tickets). When Attorney General Janet Reno held a press conference to tout Brady's success, a reporter asked (but few printed) how many of those 40,000 blocked buyers had been prosecuted. The answer: *Four*!

Because the Brady Act became law after a seven-year battle, the anti-gun crowd got an adrenalin boost—in the form of renewed enthusiasm and increased contributions—that made the passage of the so-called "assault weapon" ban possible. Even then, that bill wouldn't have passed if it hadn't been that most handgunners didn't care if there were no more MAC-10s or TEC-9s; didn't own or care to own a military-pattern Colt AR-15, AK47S or Springfield M1A; and forgot that the next-to-be-attacked beloved 1911A1, Beretta 92 and Browning Hi-Power are all military-style guns. Until too late, many handgunners didn't realize that the ban was going to limit their next 9mm Ruger, Glock or S&W to ten shots, and eliminate replacement magazines for existing guns.

GUN LAW '95

Not until after the law was enacted did the full impact of those two laws seep into the consciousness of the huge world of hunters and shooters who rarely read a gun magazine, don't belong to the NRA, or dropped their membership because they got too much mail warning them what was coming if they didn't get off their collective duff. The wake-up call—and the sudden awareness that the NRA had been right—came when newspapers and television triumphantly announced final passage and for the first time described the full impact of the law, including that magazine ban.

Banned guns include "copies or duplicates...in any caliber" of nineteen named models plus a generic prohibition of rifles, shotguns or pistols with certain military characteristics, which describe almost 200 other firearms.

But the final law allows most currently made guns to be produced if renamed and a few minor changes made. That caused Sen. Dianne Feinstein (D-Calif.), who started this mess, to pout on CBS's "60 Minutes" that the manufacturers were not obeying "the spirit" of the law. Faced with the fact that the Colt AR-15 continued to be legally made after renaming and removal of the flash hider and bayonet lug, she tacitly admitted that the differences between banned and unbanned guns were only cosmetic.

She also told "60 Minutes": "If I could have gotten 51 votes...for an outright ban, picking up every one of them, *Mr. and Mrs. America turn them all in*, I would have done it."

Only a generous heart could conclude that she was only talking about a desire to confiscate "assault weapons"—particularly given the (subsequently overturned) San Francisco ordinance banning handguns which she pushed through when she was mayor.

Named guns made after September, 1994 have to show a date of manufacture. So do over-10-shot "feeding devices" (except tubular-magazine 22s), which also have to be serial numbered—which, despite the clear meaning of the phrase, the Bureau of Alcohol, Tobacco and Firearms has thankfully ruled can be complied with by marking the same number on every magazine. Otherwise, the cost of magazines would have been even higher, and the Army would have had to mark a unique serial number on every link that makes up a machine gun belt.

Due to changes made by the House (after the Senate had approved Sen. Feinstein's version), any magazine without a serial number or post-law date will be presumed to have been made before the law. Last-minute House changes also dropped the definition of magazine parts as magazines, and the requirement that over-10-round magazines be treated as "firearms," which would have prohibited your giving a high-capacity magazine to your brother in another state—among other things.

The most significant change from the Senate-passed bill was elimination of the requirement for every current owner of one of the named or described guns to register it with a local dealer, then perpetually keep a modified Form 4473 if the gun were transferred. Similarly, the buyer would have had to receive the original copy of the first owner's registration and records of every subsequent buyer. None of those changes occurred without a great deal of work and worry by NRA lobbyists and others who alerted friendly Congressmen to potential problems.

Probably the most controversial issue as the "ugly gun" ban neared final passage was an attempt by now-former House Judiciary Chairman Jack Brooks (D-Texas) to work a compromise in which the Colt AR-15 would have been dropped from the banned list and the maximum magazine capacity would have been increased to 15 rounds. It has been reported in some of the gun press that such a change could have been obtained with merely "a wink and a nod" from NRA.

That is absolutely false.

Mr. Brooks did attempt to cut such a deal, but he had obtained no agreement from the anti-gun forces. More importantly, it is simply not possible in Washington or anywhere else to trade something for nothing. What NRA would have had to trade was *acceptance of the rest of the ban* and—what the politicians most wanted—an agreement not to use a vote in favor of the gun ban against any incumbent in the November election.

The NRA refused to cut such a deal—to the extreme irritation of a lot of politicians, and not just Democrats. That forced the pols to clearly declare themselves on one side or the other. And that, my friends, is what caused the 1994 election landslide and Bill Clinton's statements to the Cleveland *Plain Dealer*, whose January 14, 1995 banner headline read: "Clinton Blames Losses On NRA." It quotes the President as saying: *"The NRA is the reason the Republicans control the House."*

Because the NRA spent over $3 million directly in the election—and members spent uncounted hundreds of thousands of hours in opposition to anti-gun incumbents, and in support of supporters of gun rights—the NRA has become a major political player. And that's why the President and his minions in the Administration and in the press are doing everything they can to demonize the NRA and its leaders. They don't want the NRA to be able to do it again.

The new House is much more receptive to gun owners' concerns. Forty-seven anti-gunners, twenty-two wafflers and sixteen solid pro-gunners were replaced by a whopping seventy NRA-rated "A's," seven "B's" or unknowns, and eight "F's." If the new House members had voted on the semi-auto ban, which passed 216-214 May 5, 1994, with every pledged newcomer opposing it, and the questionable new Congressmen all supporting it, the same bill would have failed about 185-250.

The picture isn't as pretty in the Senate. Eight Senators who usually voted with the retired Howard Metzenbaum were replaced by seven "A's" and one "C." Considering how the Senators voted on the semi-auto ban (56-43), the net six-vote shift after the election would have made it 50-50—allowing Vice President Al Gore to cast the deciding vote for the ban. However, at least two or three Senators who voted against gun owners in 1993 and 1994 "have felt the heat and seen the light."

We clearly have the votes to pass a repeal of the semi-auto and magazine ban in the House, and could narrowly pass it in the Senate. But no way do we have the sixty votes it would take to bypass Sen. Feinstein's promised "mother of all filibusters"—which she threatened when Majority Leader Bob Dole publicly pledged to repeal the ban.

And we certainly don't have the sixty-seven votes in the Senate plus 291 in the House that it will take to override President Clinton's promised veto and his vow to not allow a repeal "so long as I am President." However, as House Speaker Newt Gingrich has said publicly—and as he has told NRA Executive Vice President Wayne LaPierre, NRA-ILA Director Tanya Metaksa and me privately—there is such a thing as attaching the repeal to the debt ceiling bill or other legislation that the Senate must pass and the President must sign.

Though overshadowed by the Congressional election, a host of anti-gun state legislators went down in flames. That has resulted in minimal new gun laws being adopted by any state, with six more states, as this is written, having passed laws requiring concealed handgun carry permits be issued to people who are not disqualified from gun ownership and who have met certain training requirements. Significantly, one of these was Oklahoma, which passed the law on the very day the sad carcass of the Oklahoma City Federal Building was imploded.

Had it not been for the Oklahoma City bombing—which had nothing to do with guns—the magazine ban repeal bill would have passed the House and perhaps the Senate by the summer of 1995. The bombing probably set that timetable back by six months.

The firearms amendments to the anti-terrorism bill indicated the kind of legislation that the anti-gun crowd thought they might get through the present Congress. The Senate approved the BATF's explosives tagging scheme (long their pet project because of the manpower it would take to administer it), but modified it on the floor to specifically exempt black and smokeless propellants.

Proposed but withdrawn—for the moment; they'll be back—were amendments imposing sweeping new controls on handgun ammunition by requiring licensing of manufacturers and establishing "performance based" criteria. The intent is that any ammo "suitable for use in a handgun" (which would include any rifle ammo chambered in a handgun) couldn't be manufactured or sold if it were capable of penetrating lightweight cloth body armor. *Any* handgun cartridge suitable for big game will penetrate a Type IIA Kevlar vest.

Another amendment—by Sen. Edward Kennedy (D-Mass.)—would eliminate the requirement that local police destroy multiple handgun sales forms and the information they contain within twenty days after receipt from a dealer. Objective: to allow local police to create a registration system. Next step: to strike the prohibition against state and local officials keeping similar information obtained under the Brady Bill background check requirements.

Another would do away with the Director of Civilian Marksmanship program. Another would make it impossible for convicted felons to restore their right to own any gun.

Though not pursued in the Senate, Rep. Charles Schumer (D-N.Y.) and others are pushing for bans on "Black Talon" and other expanding or destructive handgun ammunition. This is an old, old proposal in a flashy new package. For years the anti-gun crowd has attempted to ban "Dumdum"—that is, exposed lead—expanding bullets. On alternate years they push for broadened bans on "cop-killer" non-expanding bullets that will penetrate cloth body armor in relatively low-powered guns.

When Congress gets to its tax bills, we'll again be seeing amendments based on Sen. Patrick Moynihan's (D-N.Y.) theory that "gun control" won't work but "ammunition control" will. He has proposed 50 to 100 percent excise taxes on conventional ammo and as much as a 10,000 percent tax on certain powerful or destructive handgun ammo.

Moynihan has been told that ammo has about a five-year "shelf-life," so chopping down the ammo tree would quickly silence the guns—he thinks. For his information, while cleaning up my junk drawers last year, I ran across some hot 38 Special ammo that I had loaded over 35 years before; it seemed to perform as well as when fresh.

Moynihan, Schumer, et al, have learned about handloading, which is why we will see an unusual interest in "regulating" propellants, loading tools and particularly primers. The primer shortage last year was due to hoarding caused by nonsensical rumors that manufacturers had been "ordered" to produce short-lived primers; the hoarding was triggered by passage of new gun laws and the fear that more were in the works—as there would have been if it hadn't been for the 1994 elections.

Something to watch closely, however, are the "lead-elimination" environmental laws, which not only threaten ranges and the use of lead bullets, but lead-free primers have a much shorter life than conventional primers.

As significant as some of these proposals are, they are nothing compared to the Handgun Control Inc. "comprehensive gun control" package, H.R. 3932/S. 1886, introduced by Sen. Metzenbaum (D-Ohio) and Rep. Charles Schumer in early 1994—and now on indefinite hold.

It includes handgun registration, licensing of owners (after police safety training), and restricts private transfers. It requires a $300 Federal "arsenal license" for anyone who has more than twenty *firearms* and/or more than 1000 rounds of ammo (or primers). Local law enforcement would have to give permission for such "arsenals," and BATF could inspect those homes three times per year to verify all records and security requirements were being met. Not content with Feinstein's ban on magazines over ten rounds the bill bans all magazines over *six* rounds.

The bill's many other provisions include declaring "Saturday Night Specials" (defined to include Colt Single Actions) and handgun ammunition with over 1200 foot-pounds of energy as "prohibited weapons," transferable by present owners only under the same restrictions as machineguns.

Further, all barrels, stocks, magazines and action parts would be considered firearms; it would limit purchases to one handgun per month and forbid dealers from conducting business except at their licensed business—so no dealers could sell at gun shows.

We don't have to speculate about what the gun-banners really want, they've told us. At least, they've indicated what their next step would be. If we let the anti-gunners back into power in 1996 you can bet your last round that they'll again be on the march come 1997. ●

I**N THE WORLD** of automobile merchandising, style is everything. Most of the time there are several trends at work influencing what will be seen on your dealer's showroom floor. A trend toward the square and boxy sport/utility vehicle seems to persist, as does the mini-van. The lines of most modern sedans seem remarkably similar to this inveterate pickup truck driver, and I can't keep track of all the new nameplates as I once did as a working police officer. There are remarkable parallels

AMT's 45 Backup is a compact 5-shot DAO.

NEW HANDGUNS '95

by WILEY CLAPP

between the automobile industry and the world of firearms in general and handguns in particular.

Handgun trends were once exclusively consumer-driven, as when the policeman's demand for more power produced the 41 Magnum cartridge and the S&W revolver to fire it. Just about everybody—and that's worldwide—followed the trend to high-capacity 9mm pistols, and the result was the massive marketing effort affectionately dubbed the "Wonder-nine Wars" by gunwriters. Legislation has also had an effect on trends, as when the Gun Control Act of 1968 banned a number of fine handguns from importation on the basis of size, and drove Walther to produce the PPK/S. Currently, we are looking at a magazine-capacity ban that has sent

shock waves through the automatic pistol business and initiated at least two identifiable trends.

Because of the Crime Bill of 1994, it is illegal to manufacture or sell (in the civilian, not law enforcement, market) magazines with capacities greater than ten rounds. While all existing magazines of greater capacity are "grandfathered" in, this effectively rules out the double-wide magazines which the gun companies laboriously engineered into existence. New production magazines cannot exceed ten rounds, and the manufacturers have already built ten-shot versions by blocking or otherwise irreversibly modifying the fifteen-shot types. This means the harder-to-manage widebody guns that took the double-column magazines have thicker butt sections than necessary. If you can't have the greater capacity, what's the point of struggling with a thick pistol originally designed for lots o' shots?

The loser here is the little 9mm cartridge. The first pistol designed for this round was the Browning Hi-Power and

it's arguably still the best of the breed. But the developmental frenzy that began with S&W's Model 59 in the early '70s is now moot for the civilian marketplace. There are oodles of 9mm handguns in private hands, so the development of ammo will likely continue and the 9mm is a long way from dead. It's just that it won't ever be what is was. We are now seeing a trend toward concealable and effective mini-nines, some of them actually smaller than many 380s.

The big winner is the 40 S&W and there's a pronounced trend to accept this round and its guns as the defensive combination of the future. The 40 was introduced in 1991 and has done very well against the established 9mm in both police and civilian markets. When the major rationale for the 9mm (small cartridges=high capacity) became moot with the Crime Bill, the 40 got a shot in the arm that may boost its popularity to an all-time high. Most 40s are radically modified versions of 9mm pistols and their capacities are most commonly ten or eleven rounds, so the magazine ban had little effect on these guns. The larger 40 S&W is also a vastly superior round in the sense of performance. Look for this mid-size gem of a round to increase in popular usage in the future.

There are further and perhaps more subtle implications to the magazine capacity limitation. Service autos in 45 ACP caliber proliferate, and some of them have cleverly-designed magazines with higher than the typical

effectively stop a criminal attack, there's a trend towards smaller and more powerful handguns, both pistols and revolvers. Ruger, Taurus and S&W now all offer five-shot, small-frame 357 Magnum revolvers weighing about a pound and a half. AMT makes a compact 45 ACP handgun that's actually smaller than a Walther PPK in height and length, if not thickness. Several other plants are cranking out guns that are almost as

time and with which most shooters can stay competent with minimal practice effort.

Innovative manufacturing techniques, also called "high-tech" gunmaking, are really just taking advantage of the best of what modern manufacturing methods have to offer to an industry that's been traditionally very conservative. Whereas guns were—and some still are—made in the walnut-and-forged-steel-school, we now see a shift

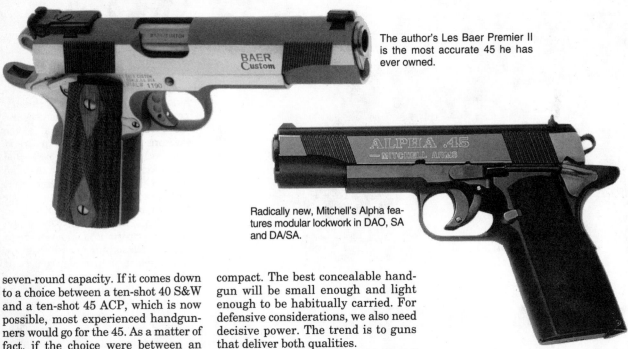

The author's Les Baer Premier II is the most accurate 45 he has ever owned.

Radically new, Mitchell's Alpha features modular lockwork in DAO, SA and DA/SA.

seven-round capacity. If it comes down to a choice between a ten-shot 40 S&W and a ten-shot 45 ACP, which is now possible, most experienced handgunners would go for the 45. As a matter of fact, if the choice were between an eight- or nine-shot 45 versus a ten-shot 40, I wouldn't hesitate to select the bigger caliber. The point is that the 45 is coming back strong, and there are trends to both full-size and mini-gun formats. I view this trend with delight, because the reduction in capacity might just convince a few handgunners that finding and using the front sight will give them a better chance of getting the job done than will emptying those bottomless magazines and hoping the law of averages will work to their advantage.

Many states have enacted, or are in the process of enacting, "mandatory" concealed-carry laws. Under these statutes, the permit cannot be refused without due cause. With more shooters now looking for a gun that can easily be carried on one's person, yet will

compact. The best concealable handgun will be small enough and light enough to be habitually carried. For defensive considerations, we also need decisive power. The trend is to guns that deliver both qualities.

There seems to be a move toward simpler-to-manage operating systems, particularly in semi-autos. I am seeing a great many more DAO (double-action-only) autos, which prompts me to believe that somebody must have shown the gee-whiz engineers who build those new exotics something utterly plebeian like an old-time S&W Model 10. The safety advantages and instant simplicity of a long-arc, dynamic trigger pull (without intermediate manipulation of levers, switches, dials or what-have-you) are now established in the auto-pistol. Every major maker of semi-automatic pistols now has at least a DAO option, and some of them sell complete model lines with this trigger system. It reflects a demand—and therefore a trend—for real-world semi-autos that can be "learned" in minimal

to different materials and techniques. Following the innovative designs of Gaston Glock, whose polymer pistol absolutely swept the country, almost all makers now offer at least one pistol with a moulded plastic receiver. Steel rails embedded in the polymer let the thing work. Investment casting, which gave Bill Ruger great success a number of years ago, is an established facet of modern gunmaking. Even the traditional milled-steel forging has undergone changes in the sense that CNC (computer numeric controlled) machines are doing the milling. Watching one of these beasts at work is like looking into the future, except the future

The newest 9mm and 40 S&W Sigmas are the short-slide compacts.

The newest snubby revolver from S&W is the five-shot 357 Model 640.

In the light of the ten-shot magazine law, S&W's Model 909 makes sense. It's a 9+1 9mm with the graceful grip section of the departed Model 39.

NEW HANDGUNS '95

is here now. Inside spotless sealed cabinets, the big computer-controlled robots cut away at bar stock or forging to build a major component of a gun; they even change their own cutting tool in the process. State-of-the-art technology is upon us in the methods used to build guns, as well as in the designing of the gun itself.

But then, so is low-tech. Some of the most successful movies of recent times have been Westerns. *Unforgiven*, *Wyatt Earp* and *Tombstone*, and a few others, are films made with a sincere effort toward authenticity in costume and armament. Well before the guns hit their peak, many shooters were using frontier-period replicas to shoot in the so-called "Cowboy" matches. It's all great fun, and it has prompted a resurgence of interest in the guns of

the old West. None of these firearms are particularly sophisticated, so it's relatively easy for several small plants in Italy to produce real spittin'-image replicas of Colt, Remington and (most recently) Smith & Wesson Schofield revolvers. Hardly high-tech handguns, but a lot of shooters are having fun with them.

Meanwhile, Bill Ruger, a man who had much to do with bringing back the single-action revolver from obscurity with his Single Sixes and Blackhawks in the 1950s, is still hard at work. He always sold a lot of those brute-strong Blackhawks, but when he pulled the adjustable sights off of them and case-hardened the frame, he just can't make enough of what he calls the Vaquero. Low-tech designs from a high-tech plant—yet another trend.

Finally, and before we travel through a handgunner's alphabet of makers and models, let's remember that all of the great guns are not made by the traditional and still justifiably respected makers. Many smaller firms come and go, and small batches of other handguns are imported by American firms, never to be seen again. Firms like Rossi from Brazil, Tanfoglio from Italy, Astra and Star from Spain and Daewoo from Korea are all making good handguns, and they're being imported in consistent and considerable quantities. Newer nameplates are definitely a part of the American handgun scene. Taurus, for example, was hardly a handgunner's household word 10-15 years ago. They are now making guns fully competitive with anything American makers have to offer and they are scaring the daylights out of some of the biggest names in handgunning in the process. That brings us to list some of the bigger names in handgunning, and their trendy pistols and revolvers.

AMT (Arcadia Machine & Tool)

A small firm located in Irwindale, California, AMT has made a succession of good automatic pistols that sold well, but never really seemed to catch on well enough to reach the mega-numbers. However, I saw an AMT design at the '95 SHOT Show that was the hit of the week with me. Last summer, I was treated to a first-look shooting session with the first 45 DAO to be produced (appropriately enough, serial #DAO-1). This unique little auto may very well turn out to be a supergun in popularity. It's a 5+1 45 ACP, and the smallest 45 auto ever commercially produced. (Yes, I know about the Semmerling, but that wasn't an auto—it was a manually operated repeater). The 45 DAO is a trifle thicker, but no higher or longer than a PPK. That's a small 45, handgunners. The only problem I had was when I tried aimed shots at great distances. The sighting system on the pistol is a simple lengthwise groove atop the slide, and it bothers the devil out of shooters who learned their basic skills looking at Bo-Mars. For the powder-burn, poker-table distances for which this gun was intended, those sights are entirely appropriate. It's a DAO and the trigger pull is very heavy in deference to safety. This is one appealing little pistol which shows a number of our trends at work—DAO, compact power, 45 ACP—and they can't make them fast enough.

Beretta, USA

Beretta is a company that has a very comfortable catbird seat, if you will. Ten years ago they won the contract to make the U.S. M9 service pistol, which put them in a very good position indeed. They'll commemorate that anniversary with a specially marked civilian version of the basic 92F model. They also introduced a strengthened version of the 92 called the Brigadier, intended for shooters who subject their handguns to exceptionally heavy use. A DAO Brigadier in 40 S&W is the new INS handgun, another contract that will mean thousands of handguns. Still, the big news from Beretta is the Cougar, a completely new high-tech design. To be offered in both 9mm Luger and 40 S&W, the Cougar is a locked-breech auto using the rotating barrel principle. It's a pretty simple system which uses an angled cam on the recoil spring guide to turn the barrel in and out of the full battery position. I have fired one of the almost mid-size Cougars with DAO lockwork and it performs quite nicely. This pistol has some interesting innovations, not the least of which is its size. Like few other handguns, the Cougar could just as easily be a service holster handgun as well as a concealed carry piece. Look for delivery soon.

Browning Arms Co.

The 40 S&W version of the Hi-Power is now on the market. This gun was first brought out a few years ago, then taken off the market until some production bugs were worked out. Browning tends to be conservative about bringing out new guns for new calibers, but the 40 S&W version of the Hi-Power was well worth the wait. It's a great gun in a good caliber.

Cimarron Arms

Cimarron is a Texas-based importer of Italian replica firearms. They have an extensive line of fine guns, some of which get custom touches after they arrive on these shores. To my jaundiced eye, the best thing they have is a simple variation on the basic Colt Peacemaker grip shape. Cimarron's Mike Harvey designed a new butt section that comes pretty close to that of the 1877 Thunderer—sort of a bird's-head shape. It shoots very well indeed and seems much faster to me than the traditional plowhandle contour. I thought that the ultra-short-barrel New Thunderers (as the Cimarron folks term them) would be the most popular, but I see the guns in several barrel lengths in the stores, and dealers tell me people like the guns simply because they handle so well. Look for some more innovative guns from the buckskinned folks at Cimarron, as well as some more traditional ones.

Colt's Manufacturing Co.

Out of bankruptcy! The grand old company has a new management team that got it done and now they're turning to modern products that meet real-world needs for the '90s and beyond. They're going to keep things like the venerable M1911 pistol in many variations and the revered Single Action Army in several calibers, but the move is afoot to modernize and improve their revolver line. The first step is a radical update of the Detective Special, now called the SF-VI, which features traditional exterior treatment mated to new transfer-bar lockwork. However, I've been treated to an early look at an even more exciting new product—Colt's as-of-yet unnamed new service auto. The gun is a mid-size, polymer-frame, locked breech, DAO service auto of medium proportions in 9mm and 40 S&W calibers. Holding 10+1 shots, the new pistol has several fancy touches, such as an ambidextrous magazine catch. Of all the polymer-frame pistols on the market, this new Colt has the best feel of them all.

Tiny, *tiny*, *tiny* little 9mm hideout pistol. The Kel-tec P11 is a polymer frame 10+1 9mm that weighs about 15 ounces.

With the UTL (Universal Tactical Light) in place, the H&K USP 45 is a policeman's dream gun.

Another polymer pistol, the Ultra-star, imported from Spain by Interarms.

Beautifully made, the Kahr Arms K9 is a small, DAO pocket nine.

NEW HANDGUNS '95

EAA (European American Armory)

These guys just don't quit. They are importing no less than five different lines of handguns into the United States: Astras from Spain; Tanfoglios from Italy; Weihrauchs from Germany; Benellis from Italy; and Massadas from Israel. It makes for a pretty impressive lineup of handguns. I have been working with a really nice Astra combination pistol—a two-slide 9mm and 40 S&W that uses the same receiver. I also like the Tanfoglio Witness Compact 45, one of the many variations of that line. As this is written, I have just received a Benelli MP95E 22 target pistol, which has all the bells and whistles for international and bullseye target competition; I really want to get to the range to shoot this one. One of the real coups for the EAA crew is obtaining the right to import a version of the Desert Eagle pistol called the Massada. They even import the similarly-styled, but operationally different, Mini-Massada.

Glock

When you sell everything you make, the impulse to develop new models doesn't have to be that strong. The Glock pistol in its several calibers and models is a 20th-century phenomenon and one of the most commercially successful pistols

ever built. They are usually back-ordered, but rumors have abounded for some time about new mini-Glocks. I have seen pre-production prototypes and they're impressive pistols. Beyond that commentary, I cannot say a thing.

Heckler & Koch

The USP pistol of two years ago was a generally successful model for H&K. Intended for the U.S. market, the USP (Universal Self-loading Pistol) has modular lockwork that may be changed for southpaws and which affords a wide variety of lockwork options—decocker with or without safety, DAO or even 1911 style. For '95, the gun has been upsized to accept 10-round 45 ACP magazines. A USP 45 ACP is bound to be a seller in America and the optional UTL (Universal Tactical Light), which mounts in a second to the dust cover area of the pistol, makes it even more attractive. When I let the local sheriff's office wring out my sample copy, they were very positive about this unusual option. That probably means it will be copied. The USP 45 is a very trendy gun with lots of options, polymer receiver and 21st-century lines.

High Standard Manufacturing Co.

After ten years the grand old name of High Standard is back, and they are again producing fine target pistols

using the same tooling, drawings and specifications that made their name famous world-wide. The cover of this book features two of their line, the Victor and the Supermatic Trophy, and the company is also shipping the Citation model at this writing. The Sharpshooter, 10X, and Sport King models will follow soon. The company says their guns are all made to the original specifications. They will be available only in blued form, not stainless, and all will be supplied with the "Military" grip.

JO Arms

This Houston, Texas, based firm imports the Israeli Golan, a blocky, ambidextrous, combat-ready semi-auto that's available in 40 S&W or 9mm. I had a chance to wring it out, and my test report is included elsewhere in this book. The company also imports two other Israeli semi-autos, the Kareen Mk II and Mk II Compact. Both are single-action Hi-Power look-alikes in 9mm caliber.

Lew Horton Distributing Co.

I have included this Massachusetts wholesaling firm for good reason. They have worked very closely with Smith & Wesson's Performance Center in creating several completely different S&W handguns. It's a unique concept that produces some fantastic pistols and revolvers, such guns as the K-Comp 357 and the Shorty Forty. This year, Horton has an exclusive on one of the greatest guns S&W has built in a long time. It's the Springfield Armory Bicentennial Commemorative, essentially an N-frame Mountain revolver in 45 ACP. The laser markings are distinctive, and the gun is a wheelgunner's dream. Horton will also have a special S&W 45 auto, all flossied up for tactical match use, and accurate in the extreme. They even get some pretty interesting Colt special-run guns from the Colt Custom Shop. There's a handgunning trend of sorts to customize or special-feature upgraded guns, and Lew Horton is in the forefront of that movement.

Interarms

The Sam Cummings firm on the Potomoc River imports three handgun lines: Rossi revolvers from Brazil; Star autos from Spain; and Walther autos from Germany. Beyond the immediate horizon, there may be a new—and exciting—Walther pistol, but the '95 catalog shows no new products with the Walther banner on the grip and slide. Rossi has a couple of new guns, including a Lady Rossi stainless steel revolver. For my money, the most interesting new Rossi is a six-shot 357

Magnum on a medium frame with fluted cylinder and fixed sights—a plain gun for serious use. New Star pistols are the 40 S&W and slightly larger 45 ACP Firestar Plus autos. Here's a 6.5-inch long, 30-ounce 45 auto with 10+1 capacity. A lot of American pistoleros are sure to go for the 1911-type controls. Also new from Star is the Ultra Star, a 9mm auto with polymer frame.

Kahr Arms

The single product of this firm has been unavailable so far. After an introduction at the 1994 SHOT Show, the company has been plagued by startup problems in introducing a very appealing new mini-nine. The K9 is a short (6 inches overall, 3.5-inch barrel), light (25 ounces), 7+1 single-column 9mm Luger pistol. The gun is another of those increasingly popular DAOs with simple lockwork. A strong, locked-breech pistol, the Kahr K9 is all-steel and will handle any 9mm ammo, including the +P type. This is a gun that has particularly good balance and feel; just about everybody who picks up the K9 likes it. They are supposed to be available in quantity very soon.

Kel Tec

Kel Tec CNC Industries, Inc., are out with their P11 DAO 9mm, a ten-shooter (10+1) with a plastic frame. This little nine is less than six inches long, has a 3-inch barrel and a decent trigger pull, and weighs 14 ounces empty. It was designed by George Kellgren, who also designed the Grendel handgun a few years ago. The Kel Tec retails for just $300, and they will probably sell a lot of them.

Kimber of America

Among other guns, the Kimber people are offering a high-end 45 of the ever-popular M1911 pattern. Many of the internal parts come from the design genius of famed IPSC shooter Chip McCormick. This guy has experimented with space-age polymers and light alloys to wring the most out of the venerable 45. I haven't shot one of these guns yet, but they look good and have oh-so-beautiful trigger pulls. High-tech at work again.

Les Baer

This isn't a custom gunsmithing operation, but rather a full-fledged gunmaking firm that specializes in the M1911A1 pistol in many variations. I have a Premier II pistol that retails for about $1,200 and has every feature a shooter (other than a top-flight IPSC competitor) could possibly want. That includes Bo-Mar sights, checkered frame and much more. It is the most

Kimber is now producing good-looking 45s called the Classic. Here's their Gold Match model.

Mid-size and efficient, the Beretta M8000 Cougar is upon the handgun scene.

EAA brings in these polished and blued twin-slide Astra 75s in 40 S&W and 9mm.

accurate 45 I have ever had, and Mr. Baer is quite possibly making the best 1911 pistols anyone has ever built. He's justifiably proud of having obtained the contract to build the FBI's HRT (Hostage Rescue Team) pistols. Look to see more of these excellent values in more prestigious hands all the time.

Mitchell Arms

The glossy new Mitchell Arms catalog shows a number of interesting handguns, including the impressive re-

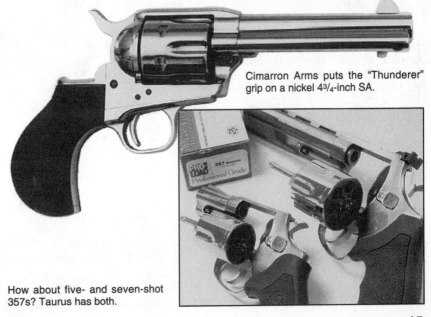

Cimarron Arms puts the "Thunderer" grip on a nickel 4¾-inch SA.

How about five- and seven-shot 357s? Taurus has both.

created P08 Luger and the Sport King II, Citation II and Victor II target pistols. There are new guns in that catalog also, including two completely different series of DA/SA revolvers for police service and/or personal defense. The gems of the line are still the M1911-style 45s, of which the Alpha is the leader of the pack. This gun has modular lockwork which allows the shooter to swap "locks" to make his Alpha a traditional single action, a double-action-only or a double-action/single-action with decocker/safety. If that weren't enough versatility, the Alpha has a widebody frame that takes almost any magazine that can be physically inserted into the well. That's both single and double column magazines. Now how's that for innovation and high-tech?

Navy Arms

An old-line importer, Navy Arms has brought lots of fine surplus handguns into the country in the past several decades, as well as having been in the forefront of the blackpowder replica business. They broke a lot of new ground at Navy, but they absolutely shattered it with the introduction of a replica break-top S&W made by Uberti in Italy. The new Schofield is taking the cowboy gun market by storm. Difficult to produce, the revolver is chambered for modern 45 Colt or 44-40 ammunition and the quality of the replication is first-rate. It took a while, but the guns are in the country in growing quantities.

S&W's SMALLEST SIGMA, THE SW380

Newest gun from Smith & Wesson is the first 380 auto they've ever made, the Sigma Series SW380.

WHEN S&W ANNOUNCED the Sigma pistols in early 1994, they did not refer to them as a fourth generation of autos, but they might as well have. These were radically new handguns in the scheme of things, clearly intended to take on the wildly popular Glocks. In the course of the ballyhoo of a major new product introduction, S&W kept referring to the Sigma *series* of pistols. The first product was a full-size 40 S&W service pistol, closely followed by a 9mm and then short-slide, compact versions of both pistols. But there was also a veiled hint of something else in the mill. The "something else" is now here and I have the feeling it may be *somethin' else*, and will prove to be one of the better-selling products to emerge from the design shops at S&W in many years. The new product is a Sigma-styled blowback 380 auto named the Model SW380. It has many unique design features and is clearly intended to be a pocket auto for defensive purposes.

In the early decades of this century, both European and American designers worked hard at resolving the riddle of the pocket auto—a gun that would fire a powerful cartridge in a package small and light enough to permit routine carrying. After several decades of development, the 380 Auto cartridge emerged as the best compromise, and the typical pistol was something like the Colt Pocket Model or the Walther PPK. The suitability of various pistols in this class for their intended role varied, but they were all subject to the limitations of gun-making technology. In time, the means of manufacturing firearms evolved to include the use of lightweight alloys, investment casting of major components, sheet-steel stampings and eventually moulded plastics. All of these various techniques saw their first use in larger, service-type firearms, but they have now found their way into a true pocket defense auto—the new S&W Sigma 380.

It is a cleverly designed little pistol, one that has no delusions of grandeur to be anything other than what it truly is—a simple, straightforward tool for personal defense. S&W's innovative designers used the best of modern manufacturing techniques to build this handgun, but they showed as much originality in the shape of the gun and in its controls and size/weight characteristics. The SW380 is quite small, measuring 5.8 inches in overall length, 4 inches in height and 1-inch in thickness; the barrel is 3 inches long. Use of a polymer receiver on such a diminutive piece gives it a weight of only 14 ounces. That's about as light as the lightest defensive handgun in the S&W catalog, the alloy-frame Model 37 Chiefs Special. Weight is extremely important in a concealed-carry handgun, because unless the gun is fairly light it may turn out to be concealable but not carryable. If the gun is heavy enough to be a carrying problem, some shooters will simply leave it at home. We all can agree that the first step in winning the defensive gunfight is to have a gun. In this sense, the SW380 is so feathery light that I can't conceive of any reason why it would be left at home.

The newest Sigma also exhibits another vital characteristic of a defense handgun—it's simple and speedy to operate. This gun has the same DAO (double-action-only) trigger system as the larger Sigmas. Trigger pressure retracts the spring-loaded striker in the slide, and pulling the trigger all the way to the rear releases that striker to fire the pistol. The mechanism cannot be cocked as we commonly understand the term. The trigger is the single

SIGARMS

The newest SIG is, in a way, the oldest, since the New Hampshire importing and manufacturing firm nows brings in limited quantities of the justly famous P210 9mm pistol, arguably the best 9x19 ever built. Some of these recent imports have 22 Long Rifle conversion units with them, serialized with the 9mm. P210s are completely Swiss-made and cost like the dickens, but lordy, won't they shoot! A more conventional new pistol is the gun they introduced last year, the P229 in 357 SIG caliber. A necked-down 40 S&W, the 357 SIG round produces high velocity (almost 1400 fps) with 124-grain bullets. The gun is a CNC-slide version of the original P228 and it's plenty strong enough for the 40 S&W and 357 SIG rounds. I'm betting this cartridge will catch on, as it provides some interesting options in the era of 10-round civilian magazines.

Smith & Wesson

That monster catalog is a bit too much to plod through, so suffice it to say the Springfield, Massachusetts gunmaker offers the most diverse line of handguns produced anywhere by anyone. They have two distinctly different guns this year. One is the new Model 640, a Centennial five-shooter with enclosed hammer and short, heavy barrel. Not new, you say? Well, it is in 357 Magnum. That's right, the trim J-frame has been strengthened a lot and lengthened a little, but it now handles the 357 Magnum round. And it is a real handful! Also new is the Model 910, a variation on earlier 3rd generation 9mm pistols. It has the original receiver married to a blocky brand-new upper.

(Below) The new Sigma 380, a 6+1 semi-automatic, is not that much larger than the revered Remington Double Derringer.

(Above) Here's a view of the unique magazine and magazine catch system. In order to remove the mag for loading, the shooter presses inward on the twin buttons.

operative control on the gun and it is also a form of manual safety. If you don't press the trigger, two passive safeties—one on the rear of the trigger and another that blocks striker movement within the slide—prevent the gun from firing. There is only one way to fire the pistol and that's by putting eight to ten pounds of pressure on the trigger. There is no need for manipulation of any intermediate control, a safety or whatever, before the gun may be fired.

After the first shot is fired, the slide cycles for extraction, ejection and feeding of a fresh round. The slide has to cycle to reset the trigger linkage, so a misfire requires (fortunately) a tap-rack-bang drill to get another round in the chamber. There is no other control on the gun, no takedown lever or slide release, because there's no need for them. The magazine catch is unique, and

consists of press-in buttons on both sides of the magazine at bottom. The twin catches are actually spring-loaded extensions of the six-round magazine's base plate. The shooter presses them inward with thumb and forefinger in order to remove the magazine. The mag is not designed to drop free. You have to pull it out of the gun. The magazine follower is white polymer and it doesn't have a provision to lock the slide open after the last round is fired. This simple setup is realistic in view of the fact that few shooters will ever carry a spare magazine for the Sigma 380.

It is in the area of ergonomics where the new S&W really shines. The cast slide is square and blocky, capped by an ingenious sighting system "melted" down into a groove in the top of the slide. You do get a conventional sight picture, but there's no risk of the sights snagging on clothing, etc. Serrations for grasping the slide are fitted into shallow semicircular recesses cast into the rear of the slide. This reduces the snag potential. The polymer receiver is shaped somewhat like that of the bigger Sigma, and includes panels of moulded-in checkering on the front and back. There's a deep recess at the rear of the frame to accept the web of the shooter's hand, and there are shallow trigger-finger relief grooves formed on the sides, just aft of the trigger guard. The pistol feels really good in the hand even though the butt is short enough to accept only two fingers.

I have fired my sample pistol enough to determine that it is 100 percent reliable and more accurate than most 380s. Accuracy, however, is the least important feature of a pocket pistol. This is a blocky little brute of a handgun that has nothing sticking out to snag on clothing in the course of the draw, and an utterly simple operating system that is very easy to use. Recoil is moderate and the pistol manages it well.

The SW380 is a natural for a woman's purse or a jogger's fanny pack. Many will go into the jacket or trousers pockets of police uniforms as second guns. In light of the ground swell of laws allowing more use of the CCW privilege nationwide, S&W really timed the introduction of this handgun well. This is a great little gun, to be regarded something like the Remington Double Derringer of days gone by. The guys from Springfield are going to sell a blue million of them. Bet on it.

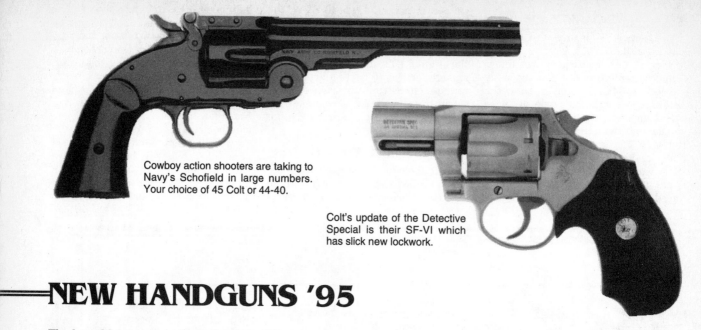

Cowboy action shooters are taking to Navy's Schofield in large numbers. Your choice of 45 Colt or 44-40.

Colt's update of the Detective Special is their SF-VI which has slick new lockwork.

NEW HANDGUNS '95

The barrel has a squared breech that locks into the ejection port. A companion gun is the 909, which has an even better receiver shape. The 909 uses a nine-shot single-column magazine and the 910 uses a blocked double-column ten-shot mag. For one crummy 9mm round, I'd strongly prefer the more ergonomically pleasing butt of the single-column pistol. It is very much like that of the wonderful old Model 39 auto of the mid-1950s.

Springfield, Inc.

The midwestern maker of popular military firearms is alive and well, offering a catalog of great guns for serious shooters. They offer the M1911A1 pistol in more sizes, shapes, finishes and options than you can count. They make alloy, stainless and carbon steel frames, both single- and double-column, and in a variety of capacities. If you like the old service pistol, Springfield is the place to go. The much-awaited ultra-compact V10 pistol is now available.

Sturm, Ruger & Co.

After the furious round of new handgun activity in the past few years (P93, P94, Vaquero, Bearcat), Ruger introduced nothing new in handguns at the '95 SHOT Show. Their existing line is quite wide and varied. Just before deadline I received a press release for a new low-cost version of the polymer frame 22/45 pistol, this one done up in blue steel. That's a popular pistol for M1911 shooters.

Taurus International

This Brazilian gunmaker is on a roll. They're selling a lot of fine handguns by dint of solid quality and modest price.

This year, they surprised a great many people with two unusual 357 revolvers. The 607 begins with the new 44 Magnum frame, a serious platform for heavy-duty revolver use. This frame takes a cylinder much heavier than what you normally see with 357 Magnums, so the Taurus designers used the extra space to drill a seventh chamber. That's right—a seven-shot 357 Magnum revolver. In a similar vein, they have upgraded the small five-shot Model 85 frame to accept 357 loads, creating an ultra-compact but ultra-powerful belly gun. They also have introduced a 44 Magnum, called the Model 44, and it's a big, serious handgun.

Thompson/Center

I've owned a number of Contenders over the years, but the one feature of this amazingly versatile handgun I never liked was the receiver ornamentation. I bought one of the IHMSA smooth-side guns when they were offered in the late '70s, but I am delighted to see the new specs from T/C's Custom Shop include a new plain frame if you want it. They also offer a powerful ejector as an extra-cost option. It's ideal for heavy-duty ground squirrel hunting on, say a 218 Bee barrel. Or maybe a triple deuce?

Voere

This Austrian firm is now producing their bolt-action caseless-ammo handgun, called the VEC-95. Imported by JägerSport, Ltd., the gun is available in either single shot or repeater versions, and in 22 or 24 caliber. Another option is the location of the grip, which may be positioned either at the rear or in the center of the handgun. The gun has electric ignition, so there is no vibration

from moving parts when it fires, which contributes to the gun's extremely good accuracy.

⚫

Casualties

Wesson Firearms Co., Inc., makers of the innovative Dan Wesson revolvers, has closed its doors. No further details are yet available.

Taps sounds over two of the best handguns the American gun industry ever produced. It's the immutable laws of economics at work. If we don't buy them, there's no reason for the manufacturers to make them. The first gun in question is the Remington XP100, a bolt-action pistol that came to be the darling of varminters and silhouette shooters. Originally a single shot, the XP ended up in a number of variations and calibers including a repeater.

Smith & Wesson discontinued their Model 27, the gun that ushered in the magnum handgun era in 1935. Sixty years is a long production history for any product, but the big old N-frame 357 Magnum held a special place in the hearts of many American handgunners. General Patton wore one through WWII, and Ed McGivern did some amazing long-range work with an 8³/₈-inch. They were eclipsed by the somewhat more versatile L-frame revolvers. I managed to hang on to a 5-incher and, no thank you, it's not for sale.

HANDGUNS 96

Handgun Tests

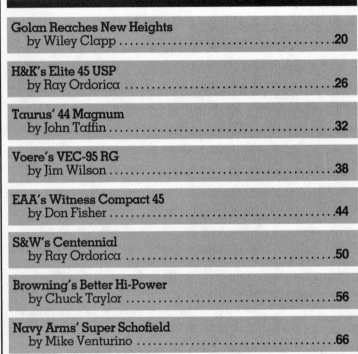

H&K's USP put to the test, page 26.

The case for caseless ammo, page 38.

A Hi-Power(ed) combat course of fire, page 56.

ISRAEL'S HISTORY AND ongoing fight for survival have given birth, out of necessity, to an active arms industry. Under threat of annihilation since its first day of statehood, Israel has developed armed forces capable of holding its enemies at bay and has developed the means to equip them. The famous Uzi submachine gun and the Galil battle rifle were born out of Israel's needs. A new handgun design has recently emerged from Israel, appropriately named the Golan, after the hotly contested escarpment which forms part of Israel's northern bulwark against aggression.

The Golan is an amalgamation of the best features of many other guns in this class, and after several weeks of working with the gun, I find its design virtues outweigh the few disadvantages. Although the Golan will be manufactured in 9mm Luger, my specimen came in the American-popular 40 S&W round. This four-year-old wonder cartridge is sweeping the country, and it's a sensible move on the part of the importers, J.O. Arms of Houston, Texas, to offer the more popular 40 S&W chambering.

The Golan is a locked-breech design working on the Browning short-recoil

GOLAN
REACHES NEW HEIGHTS
With Their Combat-Ready Ambidextrous 40 S&W

by WILEY CLAPP

The clean, squarish profile of a brand-new semi automatic pistol. It's the Golan, made in Israel, and it has a whole bunch of sensible operational features. This is a pistol obviously designed for defensive combat.

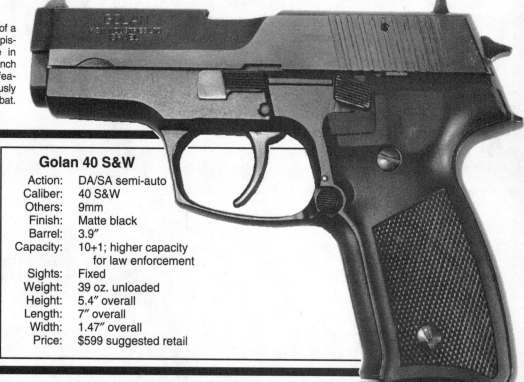

Golan 40 S&W

Action:	DA/SA semi-auto
Caliber:	40 S&W
Others:	9mm
Finish:	Matte black
Barrel:	3.9″
Capacity:	10+1; higher capacity for law enforcement
Sights:	Fixed
Weight:	39 oz. unloaded
Height:	5.4″ overall
Length:	7″ overall
Width:	1.47″ overall
Price:	$599 suggested retail

system wherein various cams cause the barrel breech to drop when the slide starts its rearward stroke. The receiver is of aluminum alloy; the slide and other lockwork parts are of steel. The slide is milled, possibly on CNC equipment, and the magazine is of sheet steel. In 40 S&W, the civilian-issue magazine holds ten rounds in a double row.

By contemporary terminology, the Golan's operating system is DA/SA with decocker and no manual safety, a style pioneered by SIG-Sauer with their P220 of the early '70s that has proven popular with police, military and civilian users worldwide. Though many observers were once aghast at the idea of a magazine-fed pistol with no safety, we have now come full circle and the concept is well established. Safety in a pistol of this sort is inherent in the proper use of the first-shot double-action trigger, which is remarkably like that of a revolver—and every bit as safe.

The Golan is a chunky little brute of a handgun. It weighs approximately 39 ounces fully loaded, about the same as an empty M1911A1 Colt. The overall length is 7 inches, and the barrel length is just under 4. The distributor's literature states the trigger pull is 12 pounds for the first DA shot and 4.5 pounds for subsequent SA shots; my trigger pull gauge tells me these are quite accurate. On the sample gun, some aspects of the trigger action were less than ideal, which we'll discuss presently.

The Golan's passive internal safety ensures the firing pin is locked in its tunnel until deliberate trigger pressure causes a vertical plunger to move out of the way and unlock the firing pin. In essence, it's a drop safety intended to prevent accidental firing in the event the gun is subjected to abusive handling. Externally, the gun is finished in a flat black color, except for the hard-chromed barrel. Grips are black plastic with checkered panels. To further aid grasping the gun, a panel of vertical serrations runs down the grip's front-strap and horizontal serrations on the face of the trigger guard.

With the Golan field-stripped, I find a number of features that suggest it will serve well in extended service. Most locked-breech pistols with alloy receivers run into difficulty locking the steel barrel against aluminum frame surfaces. To solve the problem, they use a steel locking block or insert, rigidly mounted in place. The Golan's hefty hard steel insert extends back far enough to incorporate the feed ramp leading to the chamber. The broad upper flats of the locking insert mate with the corresponding surfaces on the underside of the barrel lug. An angled step on the insert works against the end of the barrel lug to force the barrel upwards into the fully locked position when the slide goes into battery. Like many other modern pistols, the Golan's barrel indexes into the ejection port when the gun is fully locked. As the slide moves rearward, another pair of cams, one on the barrel and one on the locking insert, start the barrel down after it travels a short distance locked to the slide. It's all very modern and conventional. The Golan is engineered in a very robust manner.

Walt Kesteloot helped the author wring out the Golan pistol in hand-held shooting exercises. The gun performed quite well, particularly in the large hands of this lanky handgunner. Shooters with small hands and short fingers might have a problem.

Nice packaging! Golans come in a blow-moulded plastic case that's padded to protect the gun's finish. A cleaning rod is included, as is the all-important spare magazine. An extra magazine should be shipped with every new automatic pistol.

There are other notable points inside the gun. The rails on the receiver, which match up with corresponding grooves on the slide, run almost the entire length of the gun. Increased receiver-to-slide contact is always desirable for increased accuracy and gun longevity. There's extensive use of sheet metal stampings in the various levers, etc., that make up the Golan mechanism, but they all appear to be stamped from some really sturdy stock. One such part is the trigger drawbar, which transmits trigger pressure back to the sear. Many of today's service autos use drawbars mounted on the outside of the receiver and partially cover them with grip plates. On the Golan, the drawbar is inside the receiver in a protected position. Thus there's far less chance of extraneous crud getting into the important parts of the firing mechanism and putting the gun out of service.

The Golan's appearance follows today's trend toward the starkly functional. Flat tactical black in color, the pistol's look is business-like in the extreme. It's very square and blocky in shape, with a more than passing resemblance to the SIG P228/229 guns. The slide has a tapered, pagoda-like cross section and just a hint of a Hi-Power-type step at the forward end. At the other end, the butt is very thick and hand-filling, shaped with a gentle S-curve to the backstrap and a straight line to the front. Both front and rear sights are dovetailed into the slide, which means there's a good range of windage adjustment available. Elevation adjustments require removal of material from the top of the sight. The sights feature the commonly encountered triple dot system. The rear sight notch is square, and appears to be larger than normal, certainly large enough to easily see and align the front sight.

A great deal of what we have covered could apply to many of today's service pistols, but the Golan's other features effectively place this pistol at the top of the heap of practical handguns. There's a problem that plagues a healthy segment of the population all of the time, and all of it some of the time. Combat handguns are made to be carried against the possibility of using them in life-threatening encounters. In this light, the gun must operate in a simple and straightforward manner.

The Golan's controls are remarkably simple. The gun was made to be carried with a round in the chamber and the hammer down. Getting it that way is as simple as inserting a magazine into the pistol with the slide locked back, running the slide forward to chamber a round, and then lowering the hammer. The shooter accomplishes the latter two acts in a manner that differs from almost all other guns.

He does it with a lever located on the left side of the pistol near the top front corner of the grip panel. When the slide is back, a quick downward push on the lever releases the slide

The importer's markings are on the right side of the slide. Also note the serial number on the receiver, slide and barrel. The Golan's finish is a flat business-like tactical black. The gun has an aluminum receiver, steel slide and plastic grips.

(Left and below) Ambidextrous! The grooved catch above the grip panel on both sides of the receiver performs two functions. It will release a locked-back slide and it will drop a cocked hammer. Very few pistols have this desirable complete ambidexterity.

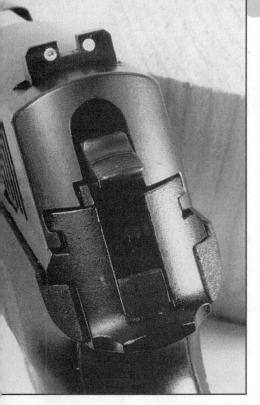

Massive proportions of the rear of the slide and receiver. Also note the dovetailed-in rear sight with large white-dot highlights. The front sight is also mounted in this fashion and has a single dot. The top of the slide is exceptionally broad.

and runs a round into the chamber, leaving the hammer cocked. To lower the hammer, push the same lever again. It is the only operating control on the pistol and its use requires no shifting of the gun in the hand—utter simplicity. This simplicity is important because it's easy to teach and learn how to operate the gun. Another aspect of the gun's system is even more significant. Controls are almost

always set up for the majority of the population, which is right-handed. Watching southpaws struggle with an object not designed for them develops respect for their perseverance and ingenuity. Most semi-automatics may be managed left-handed with reasonable speed once the learning experience is complete. The Golan, however, is completely ambidextrous. The same operating lever we just described is repeated on the right side of the gun in exactly the same relative location, at the top front corner of the grip panel, under the tip of the left-handed shooter's thumb.

The value of an ambidextrous arrangement to *all* shooters is equally great. Tactical circumstances could force a shooter to switch his pistol to his weak hand in order to work around a particular barricade or obstacle. Consider a right-handed police patrol officer who exits his vehicle on the driver's side, comes under fire and must use the door for cover. He needs to shoot left-handed.

What if he has a left-handed partner who comes out of the car on the passenger's side facing the same circumstances? Again the situation requires weak-hand shooting. Also, if a shooter has his primary hand taken out of action due to a wound or injury, he must defend himself using his weak hand. The Golan pistol is every bit as easy to use with one hand as the other.

If the ambidextrous operating levers weren't enough to commend the practical nature of the gun, look at the magazine catch. Inward pressure from either side causes the magazine to drop completely free of the gun. It's not

a reversible catch as on many guns, but rather a totally ambidextrous one.

It makes good sense to have a pistol that works equally well in either hand because of mirror-image controls. Only a few pistols have this characteristic, notably the superb Walther P88, which is, in my mind, the best 9mm pistol made. There's considerable resemblance between the Golan and the P88, as there is between the Golan and a Yugoslavian-designed semi-auto called the CZ 99. All three have a feature that comes as a by-product of their ambidexterity and which somewhat limits their usefulness. They are very thick. The Golan is almost 1½ inches at its widest point.

The gun's designers made an obvious effort to limit the girth of the pistol's butt by using thin grip plates, but there's only so much they can do. The butt must necessarily allow for a wide double-column magazine, but the real difficulty comes from the ambidextrous operating lever. Covered by the uppermost extension of the grip plates, the sheet steel levers contribute to a unusually thick pistol. My hands are not small, but I experienced difficulties shooting the Golan in rapid-fire exercises. Eventually, I resorted to a thin shooting glove with non-skid panels that helped anchor the gun.

Because the Golan is brand new, the Ransom company does not make inserts for the gun for their Ransom Rest, and I was unable to improvise workable inserts from any other type I had on hand. Therefore, I used the established technique of shooting from a sturdy bench with the gun-butt braced on sandbags. I blackened the

Inward pressure on the magazine catch from either side will drop the magazine from the gun. Very few pistols have this system. The magazine catch rotates on a cam arrangement to achieve this end.

In 40 S&W, the Golan magazine for commercial sale holds ten rounds, but you can get eleven into the law enforcement magazine. We found the magazine and the gun to work well, but proper lubrication is necessary.

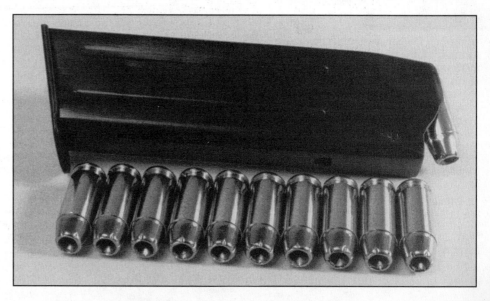

sights with a spray and therefore did not have to work around the extraneous and annoying three-dot sighting system. After aligning the gun with the Oehler chronograph screens and the 25-yard target, I worked through an assortment of fifteen different commercial loads.

All of the shooting was single action, with each shot carefully aimed at a 3.5-inch orange bullseye with a black edge. This system provides a crystal-clear sight picture, and it's about the steadiest and surest way to shoot a pistol for accuracy without the use of a machine rest.

In my experience, the 40 S&W has been troublesome where accuracy is concerned, at least partially because of the internal ballistics of the round. It has a very fast pressure curve and that adds up to a quick-opening pistol. Of all the popular semi-automatic pistol cartridges, the 40 S&W in typical guns seems to be the least accurate. All of this serves to place the rather mediocre average accuracy of the Golan in perspective. The fifteen loads used in the shoot averaged 4.70 inches for ten shots, which is off the pace of typical 40s by almost an inch. The best groups were pretty good—2.58 inches for Winchester's 180-grain JHP and 3.21 inches for Remington's 180-grain Golden Saber. On balance, averaging less than 5 inches is probably all the accuracy a shooter really needs for close-range combat shooting.

That's what the pistol is intended to be—a defensive/combat handgun for short distances. With that I mind, I fired a number of fast, two-shot drills intended to determine the gun's potential as a fighting tool. The trigger was a problem in a couple of ways. Like almost all DA/SA semi-autos, the transition from the first double-action shot to the second single-action one was difficult, even more so because the thick grip section stretches the shooter's hand out to where leverage against the DA trigger is hard to achieve. Further, the DA trigger pull has several distinct stages, producing a "bump-stop" feel that's hard to learn. The single-action trigger pull is full of creep, which made even bench-shooting something of a problem. I would have to rate the trigger action of the Golan about like I'd rate its accuracy.

The weight of a loaded Golan, and its shape, contribute to a pistol that behaves well in recoil, delivering a short, sharp jolt on each shot and allowing

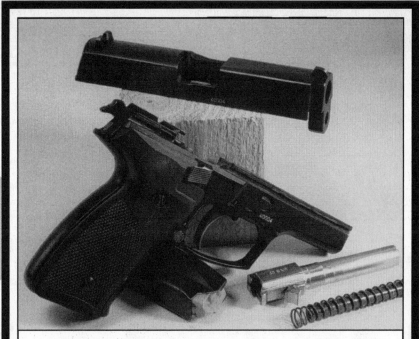

Takedown is very fast and easy. Rotate the catch on the left side of the frame 90 degrees and pull the slide forward off the receiver. The barrel and spring come out easily and the gun is ready for cleaning. It goes back together just as easily.

PERFORMANCE RESULTS—GOLAN 40 S&W PISTOL

Maker	Wgt.Grs.	Type	MV (fps)	SD	Group (ins.)
Pro Load	155	JHP	1172	14	5.66
Winchester	155	JTC Match	1078	7	5.62
Black Hills	155	JHP	1162	23	4.43
Hornady	155	HP/XTP	1175	9	4.82
Winchester	155	STHP	1145	7	5.01
Federal	165	Hydra-Shok	1014	14	4.12
Black Hills	180	JHP	972	8	5.49
Remington	180	BJHP	969	14	3.21
Winchester	180	JHP	996	9	2.58
Remington	180	JHP	957	8	4.90
CCI Blazer	180	PHP	1017	13	5.08
Speer Gold Dot	180	JHP	1029	8	4.92
Winchester DP	180	JHP	954	9	5.38
Master Ctg.	180	JHP	948	7	5.14
Pro Load	180	JHP	961	6	4.16

Accuracy results are based on a ten-shot group fired with the pistol braced on sandbags on a concrete shooting bench. Group size is measured between centers of the most widely spaced pair of shot holes in the group. Velocities measured and standard deviations calculated via an Oehler Model 35P chronograph with skyscreens placed approximately 12 feet from the muzzle.

you to get back on target quickly. After I learned the idiosyncrasies of the trigger system, I found myself able to keep my controlled pairs quite close together and my "hammers" very fast. I also found out that the Golan needs to be liberally oiled; it's one of the pickiest pistols I have ever used if you fail to properly lube it.

What we have here is an unusual and interesting semi-automatic pistol with a number of valuable features and a few glitches that could be a function of the individual specimen I had for testing. The Golan's ambidextrous design rates some very high marks in my book, as does the lockup and rough-service finish. I hope the maker will address the accuracy and trigger pull problems, as they detract from an interesting and worthwhile pistol that fills a definite niche.

THERE IS A steady move in the handgun world away from 9mms to larger-caliber handguns, specifically the 40 S&W and the 45 ACP. This move to bigger calibers is one result of the recent ban on magazine capacity, and it's probably all to the good, because shooters are now forced to realize the truth. Gunfights are stopped not by shooting a lot, but by hitting one's target. Accuracy is needed, not a multiplicity of shots. If you're only allowed to carry ten shots, why not make them more effective? One of the most effective self-defense calibers is the 45 ACP, and there are more and more handguns coming out in that grand old caliber every month.

One of the hottest new 45s is the Heckler & Koch USP (Universal Self-loading Pistol). This gun was designed to compete with the 1911 and its clones, and does a very good job of it. This is the first handgun I've seen that I'd even consider to replace the 1911s I've used for more than thirty years.

H&K's polymer-frame 9mm and 40 S&W USP handguns have proved extremely successful, so it was no surprise that they offered the gun in 45. This, however, is no simple rechambering. The 45 version is bigger than the others, because it got its start on the same drawing board that produced the exotic U.S. SOCOM (Special Operations COMmand) offensive handgun, the pistol of choice for our Army Special Forces, SEALS, Rangers, and other elite U.S. military units.

The SOCOM handgun is designed to be operated with a one-pound suppressor attached. Its polymer frame, after which the USP is patterned, was designed to be stout enough to support

H&K's
ELITE 45 USP
M1911s Move Over!

by RAY ORDORICA

Heckler & Koch USP 45

Action:	Semi-auto, nine variants
Caliber:	45 ACP
Others:	40, 9mm
Finish:	H&K, "Hostile Environment" dull black
Barrel:	4.4"
Capacity:	10+1
Sights:	Fixed
Weight:	40.4 oz.
Height:	5.5" overall
Length:	7.9" overall
Width:	1.45" overall
Price:	$696

The controls of the USP are simple and direct. The slide hold-open lever sits above the trigger. The rear lever is the safety and/or decocker. Normally double action, the gun can be carried cocked and locked. The H&K USP has a ten-round capacity and a polymer frame. The grooves at the front of the frame accept a clip-on light module.

both a suppressor and a laser aiming module (LAM), while still offering complete reliability, long life, and extreme accuracy. In order to "make the cut," the SOCOM weapon had to pass incredibly difficult survival tests, such as firing 30,000 rounds of +P ammunition without repairs, or even being touched by an armorer. It had to provide extreme accuracy while doing so.

The USP's stout frame is very similar to that of the SOCOM gun in terms of material, strength and design. The USP's barrel is only 4.4 inches long, compared with the SOCOM's 5.87-incher, and there are a couple of other subtle distinctions, but the basic designs of the two guns are very close. The polymer frames of both have steel inserts at the points of greatest wear, and they share the buffer that is one of the key design points.

I thought the USP would be big, and I was not disappointed. It is not huge, but it sure ain't no PPK. The shooter sees a somewhat bulkier gun than the 1911 Colt, but the USP doesn't stick up in the air any higher. The new USP is nearly a quarter-inch thicker in the slide than the 1911, and that's going to make some people unhappy, but that's not the whole story. The USP measures only $1/10$-inch thicker at its widest point than my personal custom 1911. The USP looks blocky, but attractive, and definitely business-like with its superb matte black finish. Unloaded, the gun has a slightly top-heavy feel, but that disappears when a loaded magazine is inserted. In weight, the USP is significantly lighter than the 1911 or its clones. More on that later.

The 45 USP is offered in nine flavors, called "variants" by H&K. The buyer has the option of ordering the gun set up for right- or left-hand dominance. In addition, it can be transformed by the maker into double-action-only (DAO). The gun is normally rigged to shoot the first shot double-action, and single-action for all the rest. However, the buyer can carry the gun cocked and locked if he chooses, with no modifications needed. The safety can be a simple safety or, if depressed further, will (in some variants) decock the weapon.

My extensive background with the 1911 meant I would carry the USP cocked and locked. I tend to mash the safety down as if I were back in Alaska setting a fox trap. I press down on the safety-lever *hard* and leave my thumb on it, to make sure the safety goes off and stays off. I missed a few shots some years back in serious IPSC competition when I failed to keep my thumb in place, so I developed a firm technique with the safety-lever. Accordingly, I ordered the USP as a Variant 9. In that configuration, the decocking mechanism is deactivated and the safety comes to a complete and positive stop in the "off" position. I would be able to leave my thumb on top of it as I shoot, and I could press down on the safety-lever as hard as I wanted without decocking the gun.

Unfortunately, due to time constraints beyond anyone's control, H&K didn't convert my test gun into a Variant 9. I got it as a Variant 1, with the decocker still active. As I found out in the first 30 seconds of examining the gun, that simply doesn't work for me. I made sure the gun was unloaded and then cocked the hammer and put the safety on. I quickly raised the USP to the shooting position, slammed my thumb down onto the safety and pressed the trigger. The first time everything worked just fine, and I got the expected "click."

The second time I tried it I sped things up to simulate a hurried, stressful shot, but the hammer didn't drop.

The author's custom 1911 has a belt clip, smooth French walnut stocks, Commander hammer, decent fixed sights and lots of experience. The author feels the totally reliable, '90s-era H&K USP is a more-than-viable alternative to his old Colt.

Dimensions		
	USP vs.	1911
Width:	1.45"	1.35"
Height:	5.5"	5.4"
OAL:	7.9"	8.5"
Weight (loaded):	40.4 oz.	44.6 oz.
Barrel:	4.4"	5"
Cost:	$696 (list)	$707*

*Colt Gov't Model

Pressing down hard on the safety mashed it past its detent and got it well on the way to decocking the hammer. As I wondered why the sear wouldn't release, I pressed even harder on the safety and actually succeeded in decocking the gun instead of firing it.

There is nothing whatsoever wrong with the gun, it works exactly as designed. The problem was me, and the way I've learned to fire a self-defense handgun. However, I'd never own a USP set up as a Variant 1, like my test sample, and I don't recommend this variation to anyone who has ever spent any time with a 1911-type pistol. I am quite sure this gun would get me killed in a panic situation. Just this minute I told myself to "shoot" the closet door as fast as I could, from cocked and locked, with the gun on the desk in front of me. Twice I tried and twice I failed to get the hammer to fall. And I had just spent a lot of time dry-firing it to practice using that safety!

It is possible to fire the gun with your thumb, so to speak. If you press the safety past its first detent in the "F" position and try to fire the gun, it won't go off. If you maintain your firm press on the trigger and then slip your thumb off the safety, the safety will pop back up to the "F" position and the gun will fire.

Other than that problem, my first impression is that the USP is one handsome, er, son of a gun. The polymer—plastic to most of us—frame is light enough that the gun is quite lively. Clip the incredibly light and supremely useful UTL (Universal Tactical Light) flashlight module onto the frame and fill the mag with ten big ones, and the gun is a bit more ponderous, but still totally manageable.

The gun feels really good to me. The gripping surfaces don't have quite enough roughness to make the gun stick to the rather thick skin of my hand. The front of the grip has deep and sharp checkering, but the back of the grip is only serrated vertically, and the gun wants to twist out of my hand when I shoot +P loads, in spite of a strong two-hand squeeze. I need more traction from sharper checkering on the back of the grip. My fingers stay in place in front quite well. The slanted front of the trigger guard is serrated to help keep my digit where it belongs.

My personal 1911 has rather deep and sharp checkering fore and aft, but its grip panels are smooth so I can shift the gun to get at the mag release. The panels on the USP are only slightly roughened, and my mitt almost doesn't know this isn't my 1911. One thing I'd like to see on the USP is a straight backstrap as on the 1911, not 1911-A1 guns. I don't know why that can't be made to happen.

The grip is not too big for my hand, but a normal-size woman's hand had trouble with it in double-action mode. The reach to the trigger, around all those fat double-stacked 45 cartridges, is a long one.

The ambidextrous magazine release on the USP is just at the junction of the trigger guard and the grip. The magazine is released by a downward rocking motion of the lever. I can drop the mag with either my thumb or my index finger. I prefer to use my thumb because I associate pressure on my trigger finger with making loud noises, not with dropping the mag.

H&K beveled the magazine well, but I'd like to see a bit more of a funnel formed into the bottom opening of the frame to aid speed-reloading. This could be done with a simple flared extension moulded into the existing design. As the gun now stands, there are sharp edges where the existing beveling meets the finger grooves at the bottom sides of the grip. They can catch the lip of the magazine as it is jammed into place.

However, the mag is a double-to-single stack design, and it takes some clumsy or panic-induced handling to miss the big hole in a fast reload. Happily, there is no magazine disconnector in the gun. The USP will shoot the last round with no mag in place.

The gun features a dull black finish that H&K calls HE for Hostile Environ-

H&K's SOCOM offensive handgun is the father of the USP. Features include a threaded barrel for a suppressor, longer slide than the USP, and superb accuracy.

ment. It resists incredible abuses from environment, according to their published test data, and I can well believe it.

The double-action pull is smooth, if a bit long, and increases in pressure evenly until it breaks at about 12 pounds. In my double-action firing tests, the gun stayed on target and the bullets struck where intended. In single-action operation, the trigger is two-stage and breaks at just under 5 pounds, though it feels like a lot less. In the first stage, the trigger tip moves rearward slightly more than .2-inch without doing much of anything. It then runs into a soft stop, and then the hammer falls almost before you realize you've done anything. This is not an extremely crisp trigger, but it is an excellent one.

If you're used to a pre-war Walther PPK trigger, you'll like the USP's single-action trigger a lot. It is of a type that is arguably better for rapid engagement of multiple targets than any super-crisp trigger pull. Some of the world's best Olympic rapid-fire triggers are "mushy," not crisp. Some might say the USP trigger has creep, but I like it.

The first time I tried double-tapping this gun I got only one bang. The trouble was that I didn't release the trigger fully to permit it to reset. It requires more motion than a 1911, and once I realized this, the problem disappeared.

You can't "press-check" this gun with 1911 technique. Press-checking is a means of looking to make absolutely certain there is a round in the chamber before you attempt to fire the gun. With a 1911 you hook your thumb into the front of the trigger guard and your index finger just under the barrel at the front

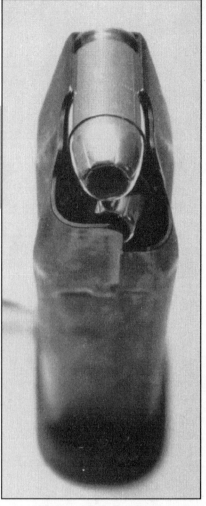

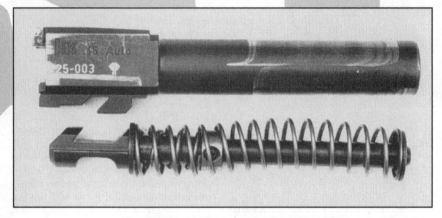

The barrel is locked in battery into the ejection port of the slide. Rearward movement of the slide causes the ramp at the rear of the spring retainer rod to pull the barrel down out of battery. The short buffer spring comes into operation when the recoiling slide contacts the buffer spring's retaining collar. Both springs are captive for easiest disassembly.

The double-to-single magazine holds ten 45 ACP rounds and is easy to insert in a hurry. Typical outstanding H&K construction, and totally reliable.

of the slide, and press the gun slightly open to examine the contents of the chamber. With the USP you have to tug back the slide to look. However, this is arguably a better way, because the slide can be moved rearward for this operation with the safety on, and your finger isn't dangerously close to the muzzle.

Field Stripping

Field stripping the USP is simplicity itself. After ensuring the gun is cleared, totally unloaded, pull back the slide until the window on the bottom of the left side of the slide aligns with the axle of the slide stop lever. Push on the right end of the lever's axle to start its removal, then pull the lever out from the left side of the gun. The slide may now be run forward off the frame.

The recoil spring is captive, meaning that it won't fly across the room. Simply lift it out of the slide, then lift out the barrel. That's really as far as you ought to go. To reassemble the gun, put the barrel in place into the slide, then fit the captive spring in place by poking the front end through the hole at the front of the slide, then press down on the spring. It cams into retention. If it doesn't go, you've got it upside down. Slip the frame into the slide and push the slide stop lever back into its hole, and you're done.

Without any practice, it took me 12 seconds to pull the gun apart and 20 to put it back together again. With very little practice I got these times down to 6 and 14 seconds respectively.

When I had the gun apart, I took a good look at the buffer spring, which is captive like the recoil spring, and concentric with it. The buffer is supposed to reduce the felt recoil and also greatly extend the life of the polymer frame. The SOCOM gun incorporates the same buffer. The SOCOM weapon needs to last at least 30,000 rounds before it goes back to the armorer, so you can see the need for something to keep the slide from bashing the frame into shards of plastic. The buffer works. Its design is so simple that one is inclined to say, "Why didn't I think of that!"

(Left) An offshoot of the incredible SOCOM offensive handgun, designed for elite U.S. armed forces, the USP by Heckler & Koch is an impressively accurate, reliable handgun that can be set up in several different variations. The author's test gun is serial number 003, same gun featured on the cover of H&K's catalog.

(Above) The totally business-like appearance of the USP is enhanced by the performance of the Universal Tactical Light (UTL) module. This is the hot setup for house-cleaning, say cops and the author alike. The focusable and intense light attaches in less than 2 seconds and is totally functional while shooting the hottest loads.

The author feels the pin (arrow) linking trigger to sear is a bit too small for comfort. It measures only .060-inch in diameter.

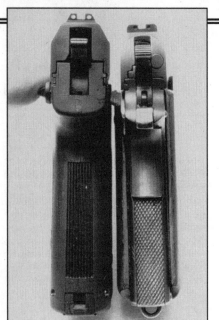

The double-stack magazine makes the USP (left) only slightly thicker in the grip than the author's 1911. The biggest difference is the fatter slide. The guns recoil alike, though the USP is 20 percent lighter.

H&K

The buffer is two systems in one and works like this: The slide rebounds against the mainspring until the slide contacts a collar affixed to the mainspring guide. Then the entire guide moves rearward against the force of a second and somewhat stronger spring, with the result that the slide comes to a low-G stop that the shooter can notice. There isn't any bash because there's no abrupt steel against steel contact, as with a 1911-type gun.

In my shooting tests, I did notice the soft stop to the slide, thanks to the buffer. I could not perceive any significant difference in overall felt recoil between the USP and my Colt 1911. This is remarkable because *the USP weighs 20 percent less than the 1911*! The USP weighs 28.7 ounces empty, versus 36.3 for the 1911. The mass of the USP's slide is somewhat greater than that of the 1911, 20.6 versus 17.6 ounces. The USP frame weighs very little by comparison, 8.1 versus 18.7 ounces for the 1911. The 1911 wins in the empty magazine weight, 2.4 versus 3.5 ounces, but holds only seven rounds, while the USP mag holds ten. The USP is definitely softer on the hand than the 1911, particularly with the hottest +P loads.

One questionable thing I noticed when the gun was apart was that the pin that links the trigger to the trigger bar is mighty small. I'd sure like to see it made larger, if that were possible. It measures only about .060-inch diameter.

The hammer appears to be an investment casting. Most of the visible internal steel parts are stampings, some of them welded. Heckler & Koch is a master of this technique, as evidenced by their famed G-3 rifle of the German army, which is known in civilian form as the HK91.

Before I took the gun to the range, I mounted the UTL (Universal Tactical Light) and wandered around my darkened house to see if it would be of any help in checking out noises in the night. It works so well and is so carefully thought out and executed that I would advise anyone and everyone who owns a USP in any caliber to immediately get one of these incredible lights, and don't consider that you own the whole gun until you have your UTL. In fact, if you don't want a USP, get the light anyway because you can Velcro-attach it to any gun, or use it from its handy belt pouch. It works best on the USP.

The light module attaches or detaches in about two seconds, is totally secure, and has an instant-flash mode for light-burst use in total darkness. Flip the switch the other way and the light stays lit while the gun pounds out round after round. Cops like the Universal Tactical Light for house-cleaning, and after the first time I tried it in a darkened room I vowed never be without one on my house gun.

The light clips and locks to rails on the bottom of the frame in front of the trigger guard. It weighs so little that I was quite sure it came without batteries. I was wrong. It held two lithium batteries that give off a beam strong enough to completely light up a large suburban backyard. The light has two switches, a master switch that turns everything on and off, and an operation switch that can be used to give bursts of light as you flick the switch to the right. Flip it to the left and the light stays on, illuminating your target in a focusable beam of brilliant light.

In use, you aim the gun at the ceiling and tap the operation switch (it lies immediately under the front of the trigger guard and is operated with the weak hand), and in the immediate burst of light you can see if there is a foe in sight. In true tactical use, you would move instantly to avoid any gunfire directed your way. If someone is there, turn the light fully on and engage the target, who is now blinded by the intense beam.

The gun is equipped with drift-adjustable white dot sights fore and aft. Tritium inserts were my first choice, and they're available, but H&K didn't have time to fit 'em before my deadline. I'd rate these fixed sights outstanding. The gun shot where it looked, which for me was center hold at 25 yards.

Accuracy

My firing tests showed the best accuracy was with 230-grain Federal Hydra-Shok loads. It put five into about 1.5 inches at 25 yards, within the limits of my eyes and the range conditions where I did my testing. The USP also particularly liked the 230-grain Hi-Shok ammo and also the 185-grain loads of Cor-Bon. This gun likes any good load, handload or factory. I find it almost unnecessary to say that there were simply no problems with feed or function whatsoever. This gun works.

When it came time to clean the USP, I got another pleasant surprise. The barrel, with its polygonal rifling, was a breeze to clean. There are so few parts

The USP shoots the author's favorite hardball handload right where the sights look. The author shot these ten fairly quickly. The gun is capable of far better, target-grade accuracy.

45 USP CHRONOGRAPH RESULTS

Maker	Wgt.Grs.	Type	MV (fps)	SD	Comments
Federal	185	Classic	966	16	
Federal	230	Hi-Shok	870	6	Very accurate
Federal	230	Hydra-Shok	863	4	Extremely accurate
Cor-Bon	185	JHP	1159	15	
Cor-Bon	200	JHP	1054	5	
Speer	230	Lawman	835	9	
Speer	185	Gold Dot	1004	62	
Speer	230	Gold Dot	898	3	Superb accuracy
Remington	230	Hardball	815	20	Very accurate
Handload	230	Cast, Bullseye	840	12	Good accuracy
Handload	200	Cast, Unique	995	25	

and angles inside that the gun was extremely easy to wipe down, the only problem being how to get at the pin onto which the springs were attached. I solved that problem with a small brush and a rag. The cleaning chores, I must emphasize, are a small fraction of what I usually endure with my 1911.

The USP is a very accurate gun, one of the best I've ever shot. The limited testing I did with the gun indicated that any halfway-reasonable load will shoot less than 2 inches at 25 yards. This came as no surprise because of the gun's design origin, the SOCOM. All thirty of the existing SOCOM guns all *averaged* less than 1.5 inches at 25 meters, for fifty shots with each gun. Obviously, H&K has a good and accurate design concept here, one that I feel will set new standards for 45 ACP handguns. Mine is on order already. ●

WITH THE CONTINUING strong demand for quality 44 Magnums, the Bull has gone big bore as Taurus has now joined the market with a 44 Magnum double-action revolver. Prototypes were first unveiled at the 1994 SHOT Show, but only as this is written have they now finally become available to shooters.

Taurus has long been known for high-quality, relatively low-priced handguns. They also seem blessed with the good sense to bring forth revolvers that should be obvious offerings of other manufacturers, but are not. Such revolvers from Taurus include a 9-shot small-frame 22 LR, an 8-shot 22 Magnum, and a large-frame 357 Magnum with 7-shot cylinder.

This first large-frame 44 Remington Magnum revolver from Taurus is called their Model 44 and it is available in both blued and stainless steel versions, and in 4-, 6½-, and 8⅜-inch barrel

TAURUS'

44 *MAGNUM*
The Bull Goes Big Bore!

by JOHN TAFFIN

lengths. The shortest barrel carries a solid rib, while the two longer-barreled versions both have ventilated ribs. All models have the smooth action common to Taurus guns. The trigger is smooth-faced with no serrations. Both hammer and trigger are of the wide target type.

My test gun was an 8⅜-inch stainless Model 44 and is also good advertising for another Taurus trademark,

Taurus Model 44	
Action:	DA revolver
Caliber:	44 Remington Magnum
Others:	N/A
Finish:	Stainless or blued
Barrel:	8⅜" tested. Also 4" & 6½"
Capacity:	6
Sights:	Adjustable
Weight:	57 oz. unloaded
Height:	5.75" overall
Length:	13.75" overall
Width:	1.75" overall
Price:	$520 suggested retail

Big and handsome is the new Model 44 Taurus in 44 Magnum. A powerhouse with a vent rib, this is a working handgun.

their excellent finish. The bright stainless finish is very nicely polished and the rubber finger-groove stocks make a striking contrast. The rubber grips are certainly more "user friendly" than the wooden grips offered on most revolvers, but I found them too small for this heavy, long-barreled revolver. A call to Pat Hogue of Hogue Grips brought forth a pair of their exotic wood finger-grooved grips that are excellent for controlling such big handguns.

Sights on all Taurus Model 44s are fully adjustable. They have a white outline rear sight and a red ramp front sight. I personally don't care much for either the white outline rear or red ramp front and would prefer a plain black rear with plain black front post, all for the simple reason that my eyes see the latter combination much better than the former. An unusual feature of the Taurus that I really do like are the serrations that run from the front of the rear sight to the back of the front sight. These are not just placed on the top of frame and barrel, but are inside a milled slot. This gives the Model 44 a custom look.

Alongside the front sight on both sides one finds four holes, or ports. This integral compensator system is designed to reduce felt recoil. The ports are aided in their task by the heavy full-underlug barrel that brings the weight of the long-barreled Taurus up to 56 ounces. This is a *heavy* handgun! The combination of weight, ports, and Hogue stocks all combine to make it a 44 Magnum that is as pleasant to shoot as possible and still have a portable sixgun.

The ventilated rib is $6/10$-inch wide and seems to be quite sturdy. Jack Weigand is offering a custom scope mount for the Taurus Model 44 and a call to him brought one by return mail. This mount fits over the barrel rib. Two bars fit through the slots of the rib and are then bolted to the mount with small

Taffin tests the 44 Bull with scope attached. Handgun gave excellent accuracy with all loads fired.

Straightforward lockwork and clean workmanship mark this Brazilian-made stainless revolver.

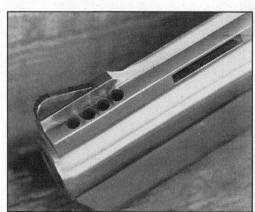

The Taurus Model 44 comes with compensated vent-rib barrel. This big gun tames the 44's kick very well.

Allen screws, resulting in a very secure mount. Weigand's mount extends over the top of the frame to the rear sight and carries three cross slots that accept Weaver rings.

For accuracy testing the Taurus Model 44, I installed a Burris 2x-6x Posi-Lock scope in Weaver rings on the Wiegand mount. All groups were fired with the Posi-Lock set at 4x. The Posi-Lock feature is relatively new from Burris and allows one to sight-in and then lock in that sight setting so there is no possibility of changing impact from recoil.

All groups were fired at 50 yards using the Outers' Pistol Perch as a rest.

THE 44 MAGNUM—A BRIEF HISTORY

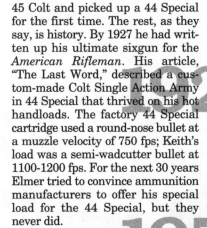

IT IS 1907. America is slowly entering fully into the 20th century. A few automobiles are seen and it is even rumored that a couple of crazy bicycle mechanics in Ohio had actually flown! Rifle shooters were jolted out of the blackpowder era by the 30-30 in 1894, but not until the Rough Riders' 45-70s were hopelessly outclassed by the snipers' flat-shooting and smokeless-powder-powered 7x57s in Cuba did it seem imperative that the U.S. Army be equipped with a more modern weapon. The eventual result was the now-classic 1903 Springfield in 30-06.

Sixguns were still in the blackpowder era and when one of the greatest handguns of all time was unveiled to the public in 1907, nobody really understood what had happened. The magnificent new revolver was the Smith & Wesson

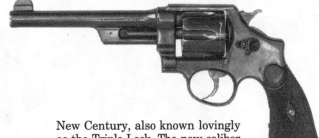

New Century, also known lovingly as the Triple-Lock. The new caliber was the 44 Special.

We move forward to July 4th, 1925. A young Montana cowboy who knows a little about reloading decides to celebrate our country's independence by firing his 45 Colt Single Action Army into the air. That first shot didn't sound right so, just to be sure, he fired another one. Now he knew something was wrong, and in examining his Colt he found that the topstrap and the top half of the cylinder were gone. His load was a 300-grain 45-70 rifle bullet on top of all the blackpowder he could get into the case.

After that experience the young cowboy, Elmer Keith, put aside the 45 Colt and picked up a 44 Special for the first time. The rest, as they say, is history. By 1927 he had written up his ultimate sixgun for the *American Rifleman*. His article, "The Last Word," described a custom-made Colt Single Action Army in 44 Special that thrived on his hot handloads. The factory 44 Special cartridge used a round-nose bullet at a muzzle velocity of 750 fps; Keith's load was a semi-wadcutter bullet at 1100-1200 fps. For the next 30 years Elmer tried to convince ammunition manufacturers to offer his special load for the 44 Special, but they never did.

Keith got a call from Smith & Wesson in December, 1955, telling him that they had brought out a new revolver to handle a new cartridge which was a direct result of Keith's experiments with the 44 Special. Keith had asked for a 1200 fps load; he got a sixgun and load that would do 1500 fps. The 44 Remington Magnum was born.

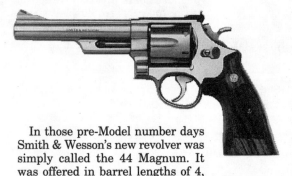

In those pre-Model number days Smith & Wesson's new revolver was simply called the 44 Magnum. It was offered in barrel lengths of 4, 6½, and 8³/₈ inches. Ruger offered their Blackhawk with a 6½-inch

To give both myself and the Taurus the benefit of the doubt, and to also allow for the wind that is always blowing this time of year in southwest Idaho, I fired six-shot groups and measured only the best five shots. I found accuracy with the Taurus exceptional, and one would be hard-pressed to find another 44 Magnum in any price range that would shoot any better than this South American revolver.

Twelve different loads—nine factory loads with jacketed bullets and three handloads with cast bullets—were sent downrange. The *average* group size with all loads, jacketed and cast bullets, factory loads and handloads, light, standard, and heavy bullets, was a very impressive 1⅞ inches. That was at 50 yards. Subsequent firing at 100 yards revealed that it was not at all unusual to keep five shots within 3 inches. There are factory bolt-action rifles that won't shoot that well!

barrel. Within three years Ruger improved their Blackhawk into the Super Blackhawk. For the next two decades serious sixgunners had their choice of any 44 Magnum they wanted as long as it was a double-action Smith & Wesson or a single-action Ruger.

The first 44 Magnums were not great sellers. It was not at all unusual to find a used Ruger or Smith & Wesson with a box of shells with only six rounds missing as many shooters found they really had a tiger by the tail.

However, along came Clint Eastwood's "Dirty Harry," and the immortal uttering of the words, "Make my day!", which created an instant and unbelievable demand for 44s that put a black-market spin on their sale. It was not unusual to pay 50 percent or more above retail to get a Smith 44 Mag in the 1970s. The S&W factory worked overtime turning out as many 44 Magnums as possible, but it was not until other manufacturers, first Dan Wesson and then Ruger, offered double-action 44 Magnums that the prices stabilized. The first Ruger Redhawk to hit my town sold for an astounding $800!

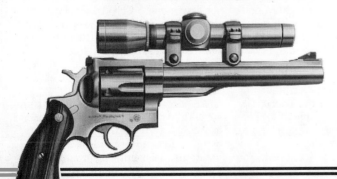

Foreign manufacturers started offering double-action 44 Magnums, and the Astra and Llama versions surfaced. Iver Johnson imported a Uberti-made single-action 44 Magnum, the Buckhorn, and even High Standard at least advertised their 44 Magnum Crusader. Just when handgun hunting and silhouette shooting were both coming on stong, the shortage ended.

Colt, who had not produced a big-bore double-action sixgun since be-

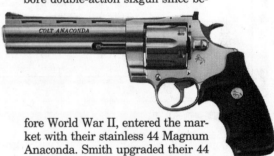

fore World War II, entered the market with their stainless 44 Magnum Anaconda. Smith upgraded their 44 and went from the sleek Model 29 to the workhorse DX series with heavy underlug barrel. Ruger took the strongest 44 ever made, the Redhawk, and made it even stronger with an extended frame Super Redhawk. Dirty Harry may have started a phony demand for 44s, but it became real over the ensuing years as more and more sixgunners became serious handgun hunters and silhouetters. To cater to the silhouette shooter and hunter, the newest 44 handguns are all larger and heavier than the original S&W 44 Mag. The new Taurus Model 44 is no

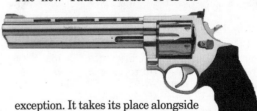

exception. It takes its place alongside the classics and their evolved brethren as a big, solid, working 44 Magnum. It is a welcome addition to today's 44 handgun market.

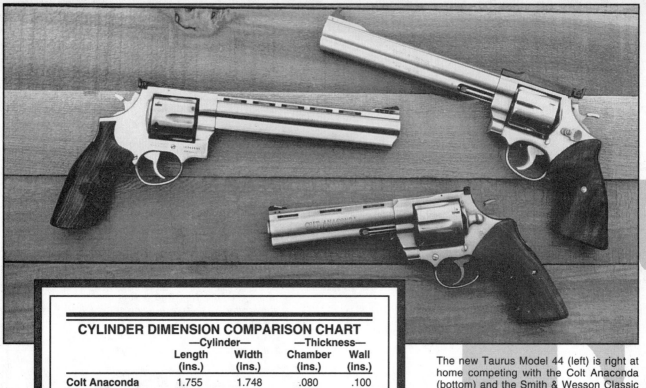

CYLINDER DIMENSION COMPARISON CHART				
	—Cylinder—		—Thickness—	
	Length (ins.)	Width (ins.)	Chamber (ins.)	Wall (ins.)
Colt Anaconda	1.755	1.748	.080	.100
Ruger Redhawk	1.750	1.779	.116	.125
S&W Classic	1.704	1.710	.084	.080
Taurus Model 44	1.695	1.750	.104	.092

The new Taurus Model 44 (left) is right at home competing with the Colt Anaconda (bottom) and the Smith & Wesson Classic heavy 44 Magnum handguns. Taurus offers value for money spent.

TAURUS

Some sixguns will shoot heavy bullets well. Some will shoot light bullets well. And some do their best with standard weight bullets. If you get a gun that will handle two out of three of the weight ranges well, one has an exceptional handgun. Find a 44 Mag that shoots 180-, 240-, and 300-grain bullets all equally well and one might be led to say that gold has been discovered! The Taurus handles all weight ranges of 44 Magnum bullets exceptionally well. The best 50-yard group for five shots was registered by Federal's 240-grain JHP with a measured 1 3/8 inches. This accuracy was approached closely by Black Hills 240-grain JHPs at 1 1/2 inches and CCI's 240-grain Lawman JHPs at 1 5/8 inches. A quarter-inch difference at 50 yards from first to third place is definitely a photo finish.

Going to both ends of the bullet weight spectrum, namely using 180-grain and 300-grain JHPs, resulted in the same excellent performance. Both Hornady's 180-grain XTP and 300-grain XTP JHPs measured out at 1 1/2 inches, while Black Hills' 300-grain load assembled with Hornady XTPs was right

there with a group of 1 5/8 inches.

Two of my favorite 44 Magnum loads are the Lyman #429421 Keith bullet over 10.0 grains of Unique (a duplication of Keith's heavy 44 Special load in Magnum brass), and the same powder charge using BRP's 295-grain gaschecked Keith-style SWC. These clock out at 1192 fps and 1162 fps respectively over Oehler's 35P skyscreens. These are potent loads but still very pleasant to shoot in light 44 Magnums. Both of these loads are certainly adequate for deer-size game and for those who may be recoil shy. They not only make the Taurus handle like a 38 Special, but also shoot 2-inch groups at 50 yards.

With extensive firing, two problems arose, problems well known to anyone who has spent much time with a double-action big-bore sixgun with heavy loads. First the ejector rod backs out and makes it difficult to open the cylinder. In the past, manufacturers have addressed this problem by using a reverse thread so the rod tightened as the gun was fired. With the Taurus the judicious use of a small amount of Loc-Tite on the threads of the ejector rod solved the problem.

The second problem is one that for years was notoriously evident in Smith

& Wesson 44 Magnums. That was the tendency of the cylinder to unlock and rotate backward when the gun was fired. The first shot was no problem, but attempting a second shot would have the hammer dropping on a fired round. Smith & Wesson solved the problem with the addition of a heavier cylinder bolt spring. When I first tested the Dan Wesson 445 SuperMag, the same problem cropped up; a new bolt spring was required to solve it. If this backward rotation is normal with all Taurus Model 44s and not just this particular test example, a newly designed and heavier spring may be required. Curiously, backward rotation only occurred with 240-grain bullets and never with the heavier-recoiling 300-grain bullets.

As a final test, the Taurus cylinder was compared size-wise with three other cylinders from stainless 44 Magnum double-action revolvers. Comparison revolvers were the Colt Anaconda, Ruger Redhawk, and Smith & Wesson Classic. The cylinder of the Taurus is heavier than both the Anaconda and Smith & Wesson 44 Magnums, larger in diameter, and of greater chamber thickness and outside wall thickness.

We can invent long-range shooting games and try to come up with all kinds of reasons for owning a 44 Magnum, but it is first and foremost a hunting handgun. As a hunting handgun the Taurus Model 44 competes with the

Smith & Wesson Classic, the Colt Anaconda, and the Ruger Redhawk. I believe it will give a good accounting of itself.

In fact, as a hunting handgun the Taurus Model 44 does not need to take a back seat to any other double-action revolver. One major plus is the fact that it shoots all bullet weights exceptionally well. Whether the quarry demands the fast-stepping 180-grain jacketed hollowpoints such as needed for varmints or small deer, or the slower but deeper penetrating 300-grain bullets for elk-size animals, or the all-around 240-grain bullet for anything in between, the Model 44 will shoot all weights with better than hunting accuracy.

In testing the various weight bullets, I was pleasantly surprised to find that the 180-grain bullets and 300-grain bullets both shot to the same point of aim. However, 240-grain jacketed bullets in the three different factory loads I tried formed three groups that produced the vertices of a triangle, with each group approximately 3 inches from each other. That's right, light and heavy bullets shoot to the same point of aim, but 240-grain bullets in different factory loadings don't even come close to each other. Very strange.

As mentioned, the Model 44 is a heavy handgun, and my favorite method of packing any heavyweight, long-barreled sixgun is in a good shoulder holster. I like a fancy carved belt and holster and usually employ such an outfit for most uses, but for practicality with the Taurus 44 Magnum I have been using a shoulder holster manufactured locally by Idaho Leather. This nylon holster features a leather lining, and is first quality all the way. Heavy though the Taurus may be, it packs easily for long periods of time in a shoulder holster that divides the weight between shoulders and waist, as this one does. Any holster that fits the heavy-barreled 8³/₈-inch Smith & Wesson N-frame should also fit the Taurus Model 44.

The importance of a good shoulder holster for foul-weather hunting was driven home to me this winter when I spent the better part of two hours climbing straight up a mountain in snow that was waist deep. When I got tired, I simply lay down in the snow with nary a worry about my 44 Magnum Taurus because it had maximum protection in the nylon holster under my vest.

Balance of a sixgun is a most subjective thing, but I find that the heavy-barrel Model 44 Taurus feels right. Most shooters find that a heavy barrel seems to make the sixgun hang

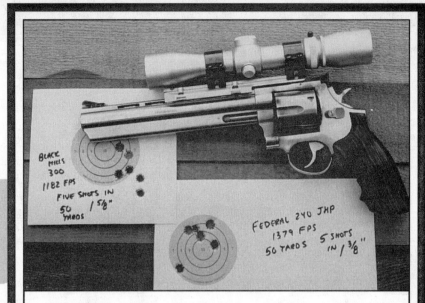

These targets were fired at 50 yards with the scoped Taurus Model 44. The big gun liked all loads.

TAURUS MODEL 44 PERFORMANCE TEST

Cartridge	Wgt.Grs.	Type	MV (fps)	Group (ins.)
Black Hills	240	JHP	1316	1¹/₂
Black Hills	300	JHP	1182	1⁵/₈
CCI Lawman	240	JHP	1341	1⁵/₈
Federal	180	JHP	1657	2
Federal	240	JHP	1379	1³/₈
Hornady	180	XTP JHP	1577	1¹/₂
Hornady	300	XTP JHP	1083	1¹/₂
Remington	240	JHP	1446	2
Winchester	240	JSP	1372	2¹/₂

Bullet	Load (Grs./Powder)	MV (fps)	Group (ins.)
Lyman #429421	10.0/Unique	1192	2¹/₄
Lyman #431244GC	22.0/#2400	1508	2³/₈
BRP 295GC	10.0/Unique	1162	2¹/₄

*All groups were fired at 50 yards.

steadily on one's target much easier. Whether the revolver be a Dan Wesson, Smith & Wesson DX, Colt Anaconda, or now the Taurus Model 44, I find I can hit much easier offhand with a heavy barrel at longer distances than I can with a standard-barrel sixgun. This is fine for fun shooting but of no great importance in a hunting situation, because I am a firm believer in using a tree limb, a rock, a day pack, anything I can find for a rest when shooting at any distance much past 50 yards. The heavier barrel, of course, makes the Taurus Model 44 a little slower to get into action than a standard weight sixgun, but I don't find this a hindrance when hunting. Fast draw has no place in the game fields and the handgun should already be in the

hand when game is encountered.

I had planned to actually use the Taurus Model 44 for hunting this spring at the Third Annual Shootists Spring Sixgun Safari in Texas. But as a wise man once said, the best-laid plans of mice and men oftimes go astray. This instance was worse than most in that our outfitter, Frank Pulkrabek, with whom I have hunted twice a year for the past five years, was killed in a traffic accident. I cancelled my hunting trip to Texas. He was a special friend and is greatly missed.

The stainless Taurus Model 44 looks quite good to the budget-minded buyer. The Taurus sells for $87 less than a Colt Anaconda, and $143 less than a Smith & Wesson Classic. The Taurus Model 44 has a lot going for it. ●

THE EVOLUTION of hunting handguns sometimes leaves a few of us old soreheads continually trying to play catch-up. I'm a handgunner who thinks that the various single-action sixguns are just about as good as can be had. Iron-sighted handguns offer the kind of hunting challenge that I really enjoy.

However, I have consciously avoided one of the traps that seems to get a lot of handgun writers in trouble. This par-

VOERE's

VEC-95 RG
A Case For The Caseless

by JIM WILSON

ticular trap is that of painting yourself into a corner. Like a lot of you, I get pretty tired of reading pieces that proclaim revolvers to be the only "true" handgun hunting weapons. "Pocket rifles" is the usual term of derision aimed at all bolt-action and single shot hunting pistols.

Well, darn it, that just ain't so! Handgun hunting is a solitary sport, and a man ought to be able to use whatever tools happen to suit him. A hunter owes it to his fellow hunters to be proficient in the use of his chosen tool. He owes it to the rest of us to be careful to match his cartridge to the game that is to be taken. He also ought to be committed to adequate practice, so that he can reasonably expect to make clean kills. Beyond that, it's his day off and his money.

By adopting this democratic view, I've managed to stay out of the various controversies that often adorn the pages of the gun publications. It has also offered me the opportunity to test, and hunt with, some mighty interesting handguns, not the least of which is the Voere VEC-95 pistol, imported by JägerSport, Ltd.

I first became aware of the Voere guns about two years ago when my friend Gary Sitton did one of the first

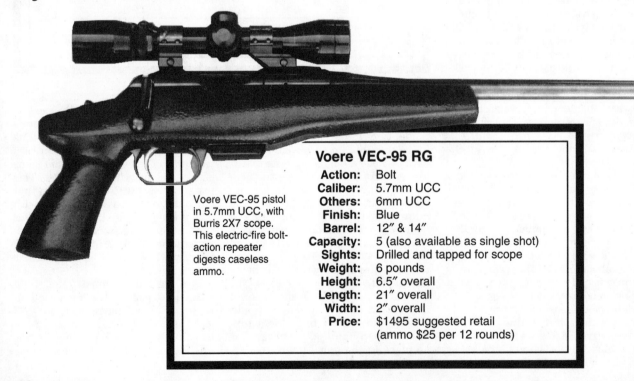

Voere VEC-95 pistol in 5.7mm UCC, with Burris 2X7 scope. This electric-fire bolt-action repeater digests caseless ammo.

Voere VEC-95 RG

Action:	Bolt
Caliber:	5.7mm UCC
Others:	6mm UCC
Finish:	Blue
Barrel:	12" & 14"
Capacity:	5 (also available as single shot)
Sights:	Drilled and tapped for scope
Weight:	6 pounds
Height:	6.5" overall
Length:	21" overall
Width:	2" overall
Price:	$1495 suggested retail (ammo $25 per 12 rounds)

reviews of Voere's new caseless-ammo rifle. Sitton traveled to Austria, toured the plant, and shot some of the first game taken with the new high-tech gun. Since that time, Voere has incorporated this revolutionary concept into a bolt-action handgun that is plenty impressive.

Imported and distributed by Jäger-Sport, Ltd., the Voere VEC-95 is a bolt-action pistol that utilizes a caseless cartridge that is fired by an electronic ignition process. While the gun looks like a conventional bolt action, nothing could be further from the truth. There are no moving parts in the entire firing system. Two 15-volt camera batteries are stored in the butt of the pistol, and these provide the electrical power nec-

essary to charge a capacitor which, when discharged through the primer, fires the gun. The trigger and safety are essentially on/off switches. The capacitor holds its charge until the trigger is depressed, and then it delivers that charge to the caseless round.

Because there are no moving parts to the firing mechanism, there is no vibration of a firing pin, cartridge or other action parts, and no impact against the primer. The trigger is also adjustable, down to 7 ounces. All of these factors allow for an extremely fast lock time and plenty of accuracy.

All of this is possible because the ammunition is far from being conventional. There is no cartridge case used, or needed, with this ammo. Upon exam-

ining a round, we see that the bullet is embedded in a solid white substance that is shaped much like a cartridge case. This entire substance is the propellant itself. It is, in fact, made of hardened nitrocellulose (smokeless powder) without the graphite additive that gives gunpowder its dark color.

Upon further examination of the ammunition, we see what at first glance seems to be a conventional primer in the base. That's what I thought, but I was wrong again. Located in the base of the cartridge is a semi-conductive resistor which receives the electrical charge from the capacitor. The design is so sophisticated that it must receive just the right amount of electrical charge to detonate the propellant. Too much, or

Author chronographing the Voere VEC-95 pistol, using a PACT Professional chronograph. The accuracy and velocity were astounding.

The bolt face of the Voere pistol. What looks like a firing pin is actually an immovable rod which delivers the electrical charge to the caseless cartridge.

The bolt of the Voere pistol showing the stainless steel collar on the bolt face.

The butt of the Voere pistol houses the battery compartment and the two batteries that power the gun.

VOERE

too little, electrical charge will not fire the handgun. This resistor is completely consumed during firing, so that after firing absolutely nothing is ejected when the bolt is opened. When the cartridge is ignited, the propellant burns instantly and cleanly. Its design is such that 12 to 14 inches of barrel is all that is needed to attain velocities that compete with what we have come to expect from many commercial centerfire rifles.

Steve Todd, sales rep for JägerSport, arranged for me to get one of the few Voere pistols to test for this journal. The particular gun that he sent is the VEC-95 RG, in 5.7mm UCC (comparable to the 223 Remington cartridge). The pistol features a five-round box magazine and a synthetic stock. The pistol grip is in the conventional rear position, thus the "RG" designation. The Voere is also available as a single shot, and the stock can also be ordered

with the grip located in the center of the gun, a total of four configurations. The weapon is also available in 6mm UCC caliber. The particular handgun that I tested was mounted with an excellent Burris 2-7x scope in Weaver rings and bases.

My first impression, upon unpacking the Voere pistol, was that of a conventional bolt-action pistol. The safety is mounted on the tang, right behind the action. The magazine release is located in the front of the trigger guard, immediately behind the magazine. A bolt release on the left side of the action

allows the bolt to be removed. These conventional features give one the very correct impression that this is a serious firearm, not some Star Wars gimmick.

The synthetic stock seemed a bit bulky to me. However, the pistol grip felt good and was well designed. The pistol was well balanced and comfortable to shoot from the off-hand position. Still, any handgun is only as good as it shoots. The most important tests would come at the range and in the hunting field.

Penn Baggett, our resident expert on all things having to do with bolt-

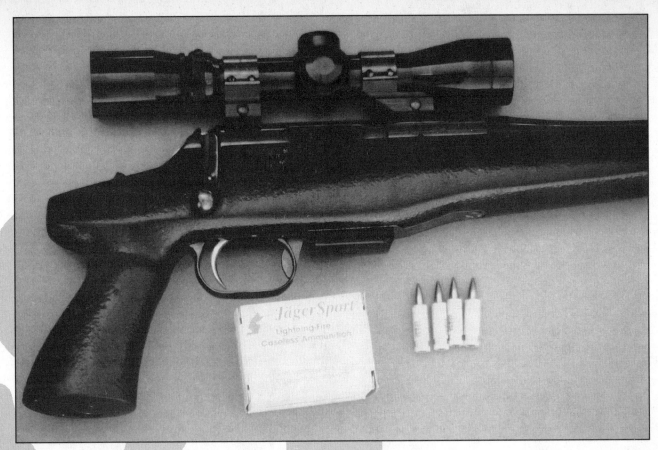

The Voere VEC-95 pistol and its 5.7mm UCC caseless ammo from JägerSport, Inc. The ammo is assembled in the U.S.

action, and single shot, pistols, happens to own and run TrophyHeart Outfitters in Ozona, one of the best hunting ranches in Texas. I decided to test the Voere VEC-95 at the Baggett Ranch. First, we ran accuracy tests and checked the velocity of the 5.7 UCC cartridge.

The ammunition provided by JägerSport utilized a 55-grain Sierra spirepoint bullet. Steve Todd said this load had been tested in Austria and gave a muzzle velocity of 3000 fps, comparable to a conventional 223 cartridge fired from a rifle. There was so little felt recoil and muzzleblast that I was sure these figures were overly generous. I figured Steve was swinging a wide loop, as we Texas boys would say.

Accordingly, we set up my PACT Professional Chronograph and ran velocity tests. The ammunition averaged a muzzle velocity of 3014 fps. The standard deviation was 36 with an extreme spread of only 65 fps. Voere and JägerSport, Ltd., were not exaggerating the performance capabilities one bit. According to these instrumental tests, we figured the gun and ammunition would be one accurate combination.

During my initial firing of the Voere

VEC-95 pistol, I noticed the bolt was just a little tough to close on the downstroke and slightly difficult to open, compared with a conventional bolt-action gun. A phone visit with Steve Todd confirmed my suspicions as to the cause. A conventional brass cartridge expands to seal the chamber and this contains the resultant explosion when the trigger is pressed. Because the UCC caseless ammo has no brass case, the chamber must be tightly sealed so the gas can't escape around the bolt face. In the Voere pistol, this is accomplished in two ways. First, the "cartridge" is crush-fit into the front of the chamber, essentially zero headspace. Second, a stainless steel collar on the face of the bolt seals the chamber at the rear. Once this is understood, the slight tightness of opening and closing the bolt can be overlooked. In my field testing and hunting with the Voere pistol, this tightness was never a problem.

Next we shot the Voere VEC-95 for accuracy. Ordinarily, this is best done using something like the Ransom Rest, so the human factor can be completely removed from the equation. However, the only Ransom Rest I had access to did not have attachments that would

allow for firing the Voere. Plain old sandbags would just have to do.

On the day I shot the Voere, we had a brisk south wind crossing Baggett's range. Ordinarily, one cannot expect to do his best work under such conditions. However, the Voere continued to surprise me. At 60 meters, the 55-grain Sierra spirepoints continually grouped near the half-inch mark. The best group of the day was just a hair under 3/8-inch. This is more than adequate accuracy for the average handgun hunter. Under more favorable conditions, I am sure that the Voere is capable of even better performance.

With the gun sighted in and with its accuracy verified, it was now time to run it through the kind of field test I most enjoy—hunting. Our spring turkey season was in full swing by the time the Voere VEC-95 arrived at my homestead. I figured that the 5.7mm UCC cartridge ought to be just about right for that challenge. In addition, Penn Baggett's ranch has an abundance of Rio Grande turkey.

This, of course, brings up another prejudice among hunters. Many of our Eastern turkey-hunting purists absolutely look down their noses at hunting with anything other than a shotgun.

eral hundred yards from a turkey roost across a valley. Before good light, I heard the turkeys raising Cain as they came off the roost. Unfortunately, they wandered up the valley away from me, and I didn't see a single feather. It was too late in the breeding season for calling to be effective, assuming that my turkey calling is ever effective. My lone visitor was a small javelina, a young sow that wandered by.

(From left) Voere 5.7mm cartridge, conventional 223 cartridge and Voere 6mm UCC cartridge.

VOERE

Pistols and rifles are just not sporting, don't you know. Well, welcome to Western hunting. Turkeys are often taken with rifles and pistols throughout the Western states. With a pistol, it can offer all of the challenge and sport one would want.

Naturally, a softpoint bullet can tear up a lot of meat when the aiming point is center-of-turkey. For this reason, the handgun hunter must wait until the bird is inside good shotgun range, say 40 yards or less, and must aim for the head, the neck, or the junction of the neck and body. To compound the challenge, the head and neck of the big bird are seldom ever still. Frustrating misses are common, and one rarely gets a second shot at a wild turkey. Accurate pistols are a boon to the turkey-hunting handgunner.

During the several days that I hunted, I made a concerted effort not to baby the Voere VEC-95. I left the protective case in the Jeep, and I carried the gun in my hand, as I would one of my Ruger single actions, or my Thompson-Contender. When I arrived at a hunting location, I laid the pistol on the ground beside me, for the same reason. I wanted to see how well the electronics functioned when exposed to the dust and abuse of normal hunting conditions. I carried extra ammunition in my shirt pocket so that it would have every opportunity to pick up lint and dampness, or become damaged.

The first morning found me sitting with the Voere pistol on a hillside, sev-

Author Wilson's patience paid off with a big Rio Grande tom turkey, taken with the Voere VEC-95 pistol in 5.7mm caliber. The caseless-ammo electric-fired bolt-action repeater gave outstanding performance under real hunting conditions. This is one of the first head of game of any type taken with the caseless-ammo handgun.

My sheriff duties took me away from the turkey hunting for a few days, but I finally managed to get back out to Baggett's for a second try. This particular morning found me sitting on the edge of a draw in some cedars just north of the main roost. My theory was that the birds would wander up the draw after coming off the roost.

Before good light, I heard the turkeys squawking and gobbling in preparation to leaving the trees where they had spent the night. Shortly thereafter, two nice gobblers moseyed up the draw right in front of me. Only trouble was, it was way too dark to get a good shot and besides that, these two birds never stopped, obviously having a much better destination in mind. One of my handgun hunting rules is to never try a shot you don't feel comfortable with. I followed that rule.

One of the curses of gun writers is that they have a new gun to test, a deadline to meet, a ranch full of game, and nothing works like it's supposed to. I sat in the cedars looking at my un-

bloodied Voere and feeling absolutely sorry for myself. That, of course, is when I happened to look up and notice a nice tom turkey feeding along about 30 yards in front of me. Stop sniveling, fool, pick up the new pistol and shoot the nice turkey, if you please.

Another of my handgun hunting rules is to always use a shooting rest whenever possible. Even at 30 yards, a turkey neck is a pretty small target, and a solid rest is mighty comforting.

Accordingly, I rested the Voere on a cedar limb and found the bird in the pistol's scope. His position was such that I couldn't try for a clean neck shot, so I aimed for the crop, just above the breast, and hit the bird where his neck joins the body. The fast lock time of the Voere pistol allowed me to see the actual impact of the bullet as the tom folded. I seriously doubt if he ever knew what hit him.

My trophy, one of the first ever taken with the Voere, was a 4-year old with 1½-inch spurs and an 11½-inch beard. The 55-grain Sierra spirepoint had

expanded dramatically, as expected, but my aiming point avoided any damaged meat.

Throughout my tests I was impressed with the performance of the Voere. As I mentioned before, I purposely did not baby the gun, preferring to let the dust and elements cause it to malfunction, if it would. Quite often, new concepts are often too delicate for field use and, I figure, it's the gun writer's job to find these little failings. Our West Texas dust did not cause a single malfunction, and the pistol fired every time the trigger was pressed. The ammunition also passed my field tests with flying colors. Although I didn't try it, Steve Todd tells me the ammunition will still fire even after it has been soaked in water for some time.

As good as the Voere pistol seems to be, I would still offer a few suggestions for improvements. To my way of thinking, the stock ought to be trimmed down considerably, particularly in the area of the forend. A tapered forend, with a rounded end, would make a much more pleasing package. I would also urge JägerSport to make sling swivels a standard item, so the weapon can be comfortably carried on a short sling.

While the 5.7mm UCC cartridge is quite accurate, it is not useful for anything but the smallest game. Even the 6mm UCC would not be our first choice for anything but small whitetail deer. I would urge that the company get a 30-caliber cartridge on the market as soon as possible, something with at least 308 ballistics. Thirty-caliber has long been the mainstay of American hunters, and Voere needs a comparable cartridge to compete as a serious hunting proposition.

One interesting concept of the caseless ammunition is the fact that it comes into this country in components. American bullets are inserted in the propellant after it arrives. For this reason, it will be no problem for JägerSport to offer the propellant for sale, separately, and allow the shooter to insert the bullets of his choice. You can expect this option in the near future.

As it is, the future looks plenty bright for the Voere VEC-95. By the time you read this, the pistols ought to be ready for delivery to dealers around the country. JägerSport, Ltd., is a subsidiary of Swarovski America, Ltd., importers of some of the finest optics available anywhere. These folks are dedicated to providing quality shooting products to the American sportsman. The Voere VEC-95 pistol is just that sort of quality. ●

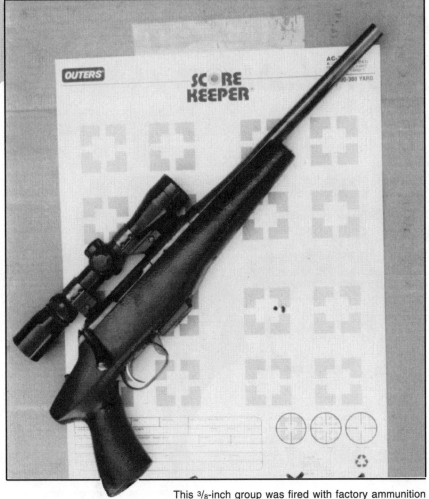

This ³⁄₈-inch group was fired with factory ammunition using 55-grain Sierra spirepoints. The unit's lack of vibration aids accuracy.

I JUST HAD my eyes opened. When I thought about compact carry guns in the past, I used to think in terms of small guns chambered in rounds that don't make me feel real secure if I have to go downtown late at night. Little things like 25 autos, 380s and other calibers I don't want to trust my life to on a dark street at night. Consequently, I was glad of the chance to test a compact carry gun in a decent caliber, 45 ACP, for this book.

I like the EAA Witness Compact 45 so much that, when I get my concealed carry permit, I have a good idea what I'll be buying myself for Christmas.

The first thing I noticed about the Witness Compact 45 is that it fits the hand extremely well for a double-stack magazine gun. A lot of double-stack guns, the Para-Ordnance gun comes to mind, are not real comfortable in the hand. The frames are too thick and

EAA's
WITNESS COMPACT 45
Street-Smart And Reliable

by DON FISHER

EAA Witness Compact

Action:	DA/SA semi-auto
Caliber:	45 ACP
Others:	9mm, 40 S&W
Finish:	Blue or Hard chrome
Barrel:	3.75"
Capacity:	8+1
Sights:	Fixed
Weight:	34 oz. loaded
Height:	5.1" overall
Length:	7.6" overall
Width:	1.35" overall
Price:	$523 suggested retail

The EAA Witness Compact 45 is accurate and very reliable, and can be carried cocked-and-locked. The gun holds eight rounds in its mag.

they feel too big. Before you think I'm complaining because I have small hands, I should let you know that I stand 5 feet, 11 inches and have normal-size hands. I have been shooting a 1911 Colt for twenty years and a CZ-75 for ten years in IPSC competition, all guns with pretty large grips. So it's not my hands but rather the size of some frames that're uncomfortable.

The second thing I noticed was the 550's weight. It has a nice solid feel to

tion. This gun has a solid feel to it that will let you shoot it a lot and won't give you a sore hand after a day at the range.

The Witness comes with a three-dot sight system. Frankly, I'd just as soon have black sights, or some of the aftermarket sights that glow in the dark. If you're one of those who like white-dot sights, these should make you happy. If not, you can paint the dots out with black paint, and you'll have a set of

large ejection port. Now I know you shouldn't have to reload a carry gun in a hurry very often, but it is nice to see the large mag-well opening and the narrow top of the magazine. Even the most experienced shooter can fumble the reload when shots are being fired his way, and a large magazine well can make a big difference. The large ejection port helps ensure reliable ejection and eliminate dented brass, in case you reload. With the high price of today's factory ammo, I would think those who shoot a lot will like the fact that their brass won't all be dented.

The frame has what amounts to a beavertail tang that fits nicely into the web of the hand. Serious shooters of the Colt Government model *sans* beavertail safety probably have a scar in the web of the hand from shooting it. The beavertail effectively keeps the hammer from biting you every time you pull the trigger. A second benefit of the tang is that it helps spread out the pressure in the web of your hand and makes the gun more comfortable to shoot. A third benefit is that the gun doesn't tend to have as much muzzle flip when you shoot. The wide tang spreads out the downward pressure so the tang doesn't sink into your hand, and this keeps the muzzle from rising as much. A tang such as this is a $65 custom feature for the Colt. It comes standard with the Witness Compact.

The Witness Compact 45 (bottom) is notably smaller than the earlier Tangfolio TA 90 9mm. Author Fisher feels this is one of the best carry guns.

it, not the top-heavy feel of plastic guns. This gun feels like something you can depend on. Now I don't know about you, but I think a carry gun, one that may be called on to save my life, should be shot a lot. That doesn't mean you sight it in, run a couple hundred rounds through it, find a holster that fits, and think you're all set for an emergency. What I mean by *a lot* is that you shoot the gun more than any other one you have, except perhaps for specialized competi-

sights that give an excellent sight picture, one you can work with in most lighting conditions. It was nice to see, however, that if you *do* use the dots, when you line up these dots the top of the sights are also lined up. This is not always the case. At least with this gun the point of impact will be the same whether or not you use the dots, making your life a little easier.

Two more things I like about the gun are the magazine well opening and the

Tanfoglio had the good sense to go back to the original CZ-75 hammer safety a few years ago. This allows the option of carrying the gun *cocked and locked* like a 1911 Colt 45, or with the hammer down on a live round. Some people just don't feel safe carrying a gun with the hammer back, even with the safety engaged. And, if you don't feel safe carrying the gun, it may be left at home just when you find you need it most. If you have trouble reaching the trigger in the double-action mode, you can cock the hammer to the half-cock position, and that decreases the distance to the trigger by about a quarter-inch. That's enough to make a big difference for a woman, or anyone with a small hand and short fingers.

The controls of the gun are in the same positions as on the Colt 1911. If you are used to the Colt, you won't have to learn a new set of finger movements. The safety is large enough for ease of operation and has good solid detent

The Witness Compact compares favorably with the Colt Commander and has features that cost extra with the Colt. Both guns can be carried cocked-and-locked.

EAA

clicks that let you know when it goes on or off. A nice little red dot on the frame is exposed when the safety is in the off position, letting you know the gun is ready to shoot. The dot shows up quite well and should make the world a little safer place to live. There is also an ambidextrous safety available if you're left-handed. The slide stop is large enough for easy release when reloading the gun in a hurry, but not so large as to get in the way during normal shooting, as some long slide stops do.

The magazine release is in the same place as that on the Colt, and as an added bonus it can be reversed for left-hand shooters if need be. I think the mag release on the Colt is better suited for the left-handed shooter. I see no reason for a left-handed shooter to reverse the safety's position, but it can be changed on the Witness if you want. I've always felt it easier to hit the mag release with the left trigger finger than with the right thumb. For one thing, you don't need to flip the gun in your hand to reach the button, and then reset your grip. Your choice.

Before heading to the range for the fun part of this job, I decided to take the gun apart and give it a once-over. Field-stripping couldn't be easier. There are two small dots on the left side of the gun at the rear, near the thumb safety, one on the frame and one on the slide. Simply move the slide back until the dots line up, and pull the slide stop out. You may find it easier to remove if you first push it out part way from the right side, as it is a fairly tight fit. Once the slide stop is out, pull the slide and barrel toward the front, off the frame. A full-length guide rod holds the recoil spring in place, so you don't have to worry about springs and things blowing up in your face as can happen with a Colt if you're not careful.

The double-action trigger reach around the double-stack magazine is rather long for most women's hands.

The solution is to place the gun on half-cock. This permits easier access to the trigger.

Takedown is easy. Just line up the dot on the slide with that on the frame and press out the slide-stop lever.

The double-to-single stack magazine slips into the maw of the grip easily for quick reloads.

The back of the guide rod fits into a detent in the barrel under-lug, holding things in place. Move the rod toward the muzzle slightly, pull down, and the rod and spring come right out. The barrel moves down and backward to finish the job. Believe me, it took a lot longer to write up this procedure than it took to field-strip the gun.

That's about as far as you need to disassemble the Compact for cleaning, except maybe to remove the grips for cleaning the inside of the mag well. The trigger and sear and all other internal parts are best cleaned in position in the gun with a spray can of cleaner, a rag, and maybe a toothbrush.

Now that the gun is apart, clean the inside of the barrel, add a little oil to the slide rails and the outside of the barrel, and the gun is ready to be put together. You don't need to oil the rest of the parts; they'll work fine if you leave them dry. Excess oil in the lockwork of the gun will collect more dirt and do more harm than it will ever do good. Re-assembly is just as easy as taking the gun apart. Do the same

things you did before, except in backwards fashion.

I shot over 500 rounds of ammunition though the gun with zero failures of any kind. Well I did have one failure...my thumb broke down reloading the magazine. Test ammo ranged from 185-grain JHPs to 250-grain lead reloads. All the jacketed ammo were factory loads, both standard and +P high-pressure loads. The Witness Compact 45 handled everything with equal ease. While the loads didn't all shoot with equal accuracy, they all shot within 4 inches of the point of aim at 25 yards, with most of the loads hitting between dead on and 2 inches high left. I think that's pretty good for nine factory loads and three reloads. The only thing I can't explain is why there was no correlation between point of impact and the weight of the bullet fired. Some 230-grain bullets shot to the same point as some 185-grain bullets, while the 230-grain American Eagle FMJ (by Federal) shot 1/2-inch high and the Federal 230-grain JHP shot 1 1/2 inches high and 2 inches left. I guess that's what makes shooting

and working up reloads such an interesting and sometimes frustrating pastime.

The testing process started with a 300-round reliability test. I fired a random selection of both lead and jacketed ammo, choosing from all of the ammo available. Sometimes I fired a full magazine of the same ammo and other times I mixed up one of each until the mag was full. The fun part of all this was trying to get the gun to malfunction so I'd have something to write about. I shot the Witness right-handed, left-handed and two-handed. It didn't seem to matter what I tried, the rounds went in and the empty brass came out. *Boring*, with a capital B. And my thumb was starting to hurt from loading the magazine. (I guess I could get lazy and buy one of those magazine loaders, but then I wouldn't have anything to complain about.)

The only thing that kept me awake was when I touched off one of the +P Hornady Custom rounds, since it is more than 14 percent hotter than their standard load. Then there were the lighter and noticeably quieter 185-grain rounds to lull me to sleep just before the +P round showed up again. I'm not sure what was more noticeable, the increased recoil or the louder noise from the +P rounds.

The primers of the +P ejected brass looked flat. I have seen flatter primers in my time, and I doubt the pressure was anywhere near maximum, but you could tell the pressure was higher than the rest of the rounds. Would I shoot the +P rounds in my own gun? Yes I would, with no fears at all. But only if the gun shot better with them than what I now use. I plan to try some as soon as I get a chance, and the weather warms up to freezing or so.

Those of you who shoot in IPSC competition will notice that the 200-grain +P load makes Major power factor

The same small hand has an easier time yet with the Witness cocked and locked.

The EAA Witness Compact breaks down easily for cleaning into these parts. It's a simple design with no surprises.

EAA

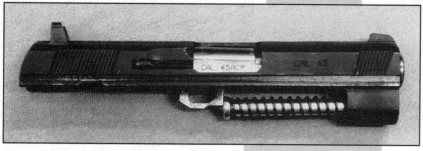

The slide has grasping grooves at front and rear. Note that the recoil spring is captured by the barrel to ease takedown procedure.

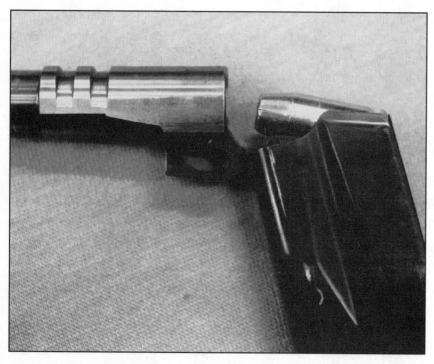

The alignment of the magazine to the barrel is shown here as they are situated in the gun. This is the main reason for the superb reliability of this gun.

(176.6) in the Witness' 3³/₄-inch barrel. The 230-grain +P load is even hotter at 186.3 power factor. In case you don`t understand what IPSC power factor is, you multiply the velocity in fps times the bullet weight in grains, than divide that number by 1000. The minimum power factor for Major is 175.

The second part of the range test was to see if the Witness Compact 45 was accurate enough for its intended purpose. Because this is a carry gun by design, I didn't set as high an accuracy standard for the gun as I would for a match gun. Two-inch groups at 50 yards was not what I was looking for. I was hoping for a group I could cover with my fist at 25 yards.

Out of thirty-six groups fired, there was only one larger than 4 inches, that one being 4.85, an inch worst than the next largest group. I think the 1.37-inch group shot with the Winchester 230-grain STX showed a lot better accuracy than most people would expect from a carry gun. It was more than I expected to see, and it made me very happy with the gun's performance. If you look at the average size of the groups—Hornady 230 +P at 2.28 inches; Winchester 230 STX at 2.10 inches; Federal 185 JHP at 2.51 inches—I think you can find a factory load that will shoot quite well in this gun. The Legend Bullets 200-grain SWC and the 225-grain FN shot better than the jacketed stuff, so you can practice with accurate reloads and save money at the same time. This gun, in all honesty, is accurate enough that if you get a bad group it's your fault, and good groups are tight enough that you know you're learning to shoot better as you practice.

The final range test was to see how the gun handled in the real world. For this I set up an IPSC target at 10 yards, filled the magazine with some 200-grain SWC reloads and allowed myself to play with the Witness. I chose the 200-grain reloads because that's what I normally shoot rapid-fire in my 45. Starting with the gun at the ready posi-

EAA WITNESS COMPACT 45 TEST RESULTS

Cartridge	—Bullet— Wgt.Grs.	Type	MV (fps)	SD	—Group @25 yds. (ins.)— Smallest	Largest	Avg.
Federal	185	JHP	836	5	1.5	3.3	2.5
Federal	230	JHP	762	7	2.5	4.8	3.5
Federal	230	Hydra Shok	780	7	2.5	3.2	2.7
American Eagle	230	FMJ	749	5	2.1	2.4	2.2
Hornady	200	JHP XTP	770	11	2.2	3.9	3.1
Hornady	200	JHP XTP+P	883	16.1	2.1	3.6	2.8
Hornady	230	JHP EXP+P	810	9	2.0	2.5	2.3
Winchester	230	JHP Subsonic	737	10	2.5	3.3	2.9
Winchester	230	JHP SXT	747	10	1.4	2.8	2.1
Legend*	200	SWC	803	10	1.6	2.4	1.9
Legend*	225	FP	729	5	1.8	2.4	2.1
Legend*	250	RN	649	8	2.3	3.6	3.1

*Handloads. All lead bullets, W-231 powder

A rapid-fire burst at 10 yards as fast as author Fisher could empty the gun resulted in this group. The author plans to acquire one of these for himself.

Fisher tested 500 samples of all these factory loads and handloads in the EAA Witness Compact and had zero malfunctions.

tion, I brought the gun up and emptied the magazine as fast as I could see the front sight. I didn't take time to see the back sight; I just hoped it was close to being lined up with the front one. The result was an eight-shot group measuring 6.5 inches, nicely centered on the target. The first shot was a little higher than the rest, or I would have had a 4.5-inch group dead center. I was quite happy with the result, knowing in my mind that I could do a lot better if I took time to practice with the gun and get used to its different feel.

All things considered, this is an excellent gun well suited to its purpose. The fit of the slide and frame is quite good, with very little play. This tight fit is one reason the gun is easy to shoot well. One of the things I learned a long time ago building competition semi-automatics is that a gun with a tight slide-to-frame fit is more comfortable to shoot. It feels like it has less recoil in your hand. The reason (as I see it) is that if the slide is tight, it moves straight back and forth. If it's loose, it moves up and down and left and right as it cycles. That makes the gun bounce around in your hand, making it appear to recoil more than if the slide only moved smoothly back and forth. In any case, the Witness is very comfortable to shoot.

All of the parts appear to be well made and finished, and of good quality. About the only thing I would change if it were mine would be to blacken the white dots, and that's strictly a personal preference. It feels better in the hand than some other guns like the Glock and the SIG. The only gun that approaches the feel of the Witness is the Colt Officer's Model, but it holds two fewer rounds and doesn't give me the options of carrying cocked-and-locked, or double-action with the hammer down. So I guess if my state government does pass the impending concealed carry law, I'll have to start saving my money. ●

IT'S NOISY and obnoxious, kicks a bit, is extremely versatile yet somewhat limited—and I like it. It's the new stainless S&W 640 Centennial.

Today's Centennial is a descendant of those guns brought out in 1952 during the 100th anniversary of the company. This gun, however, is chambered for the 357 Magnum, not the lowly 38 Special with its usual cautions about using +P ammo at your own risk. Smith calls this little rod the smallest 357 on the market, and it'll handle any 357 load you think you're man (or woman) enough to handle.

The noise wasn't much of a surprise. When you shoot light bullets in a short barrel, lots of the powder charge is burned in the air in front of the gun. With some loads, the muzzleblast hurt my ears, even though I was wearing good ear protection. A guy at the range told me he heard the blast nearly a quarter-mile away and correctly guessed it was a 357. When I showed him the gun, he couldn't believe the small size of the package.

It *is* small. It nestles comfortably in the hand, and you can almost hide it there. With its 2⅛-inch medium-weight barrel and round butt, it's short enough

S&W's
CENTENNIAL
World's Smallest 357 Mag

by RAY ORDORICA

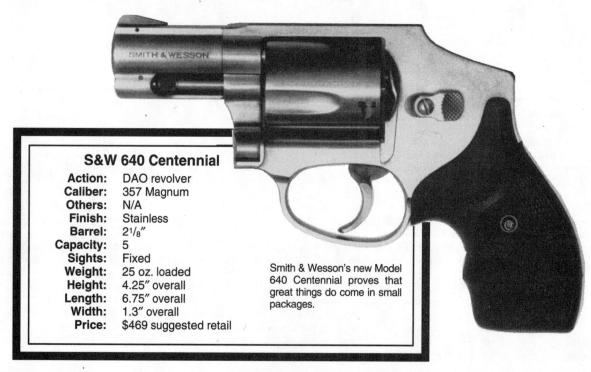

S&W 640 Centennial

Action:	DAO revolver
Caliber:	357 Magnum
Others:	N/A
Finish:	Stainless
Barrel:	2⅛″
Capacity:	5
Sights:	Fixed
Weight:	25 oz. loaded
Height:	4.25″ overall
Length:	6.75″ overall
Width:	1.3″ overall
Price:	$469 suggested retail

Smith & Wesson's new Model 640 Centennial proves that great things do come in small packages.

to fit into nearly any pocket, and thanks to its lack of an external hammer, it comes out of that pocket as slick as anything.

The Centennial conceals better than just about any other handgun. The irregular shape and odd bulges of the gun help it blend with the wrinkles in one's clothing, where a flat semi-auto would give itself away by its sheer regularity. In a dire emergency, the Centennial can be fired from inside one's pocket. True, it might set your clothing on fire...but who cares, if it means saving your life. Other guns with exposed hammers, or even with shrouded hammers, can and will snag the hammer on your pocket lining, and won't fire.

The kick of the 640 is nothing a well-

The longer underlugged barrel of the Centennial 357 Magnum permits a longer extractor rod—manna to snubbie lovers.

(Left) The smallest 357 available today, Smith's Model 640 will handle the hottest 357s or lightest 38s equally well. The gun comes with Uncle Mike's Boot Grips.

seasoned pistol shooter can't handle. It's designed for close-up and personal use, not long-range target shooting. The recoil from a few shots in a dire emergency won't be noticed. I had no problems with even the hottest 158-grain loads at around 1100 fps. Yet the recoil is there and will need to be learned by the novice.

Felt recoil is, to some extent, a function of the grip shape and gun frame, and also the type of grip material. Smith Centennials come well-fitted with Uncle Mike's Boot Grips, and while these don't extend quite to the top of the frame, I didn't find that to be a

problem. The recoil is delivered to the hand through the significant bulge at the rear of the grip frame. The gun doesn't rotate from recoil like a single-action thumb-buster, but stays in place. The only sensation is a rap to the center of the hand.

I computed the recoil at 16.5 foot pounds with the hottest loads, not including the weight of my hand. A 4-inch Model 19 S&W has 9.3 foot-pounds with the same load. By contrast, a Linebaugh 475 Maximum revolver with its 420-grain bullet at over 1500 fps generates about 51 foot-pounds of recoil energy.

To reduce felt recoil, one could install grips with greater surface area at the back. I wouldn't, because bigger grips would reduce the concealability of the gun, and thus its main purpose in life. However, one modification I would consider is replacing the rubber grips with smooth wood panels. Rubber can stick to clothing when you make a fast grab for the gun.

I said the Smith was versatile. That means the 640 will accept any 38 Special or 357 Magnum load. If you can't find your favorite brand, you can surely get *some* ammo that'll fit. In spite of its versatility, this gun is limited by not having an external, cockable hammer, so you can't take it hunting unless you're an exceptional double-action shot.

Centennials over the years have taken on a variety of forms and have been fitted with 2- and 3-inch barrels. My friend, fellow gun writer and Centennial aficionado Wiley Clapp, tells me he has fired Centennials in 32 H&R Magnum, 9mm, 38 Special, 356 TSW, and now 357 Magnum calibers.

Prior issues of S&W Centennials have had grip safeties, though the current reincarnation leaves that "lemon-squeezer" item off the gun. Current barrels are nominally 2 inches in length, though the length of the 640's is nearly 2³/₁₆ inches.

I began this test with the intention of comparing the 38 Special Centennial Airweight with this new stainless 357. I believe the incredibly light Airweight is the best choice for a 38 Special carrying revolver, but I quickly lost interest in the comparison. I had to keep asking myself if the ammo I was about to drop into the Airweight was acceptable; some brands and types, including all those labeled +P, are not recommended. With the 640

Centennial, however, you can drop *any* load into it and you're in business.

Still, the Airweight version, finished in either matte black or nickel, is slightly smaller and significantly lighter than the Model 640 (15 versus 25 ounces), and it might be just what you need.

To upgrade the new 640 from the old 38 Special Centennial, Smith installed a slightly longer and heavier barrel with a full lug, a slightly longer cylinder that'll accept any SAAMI-specification 357 ammo, and a lengthened ejector rod to help clear cases. The most significant difference is that this gun is machined to extremely close tolerances through the use of state-of-the-art CNC (computer numeric controlled) machining. This reduces handling steps and costly hand fitting.

S&W Project Engineer Norm Spencer says that the Model 640 is "...the most accurately machined gun anywhere." S&W personnel consider the Model 640 Centennial 357 to be the best revolver they've ever made. It is very smoothly machined, inside and out. The frame has well-rounded corners at the cylinder cutout in the frame, with a larger radius to the fillets than on previous guns. If you're not an engineer, you may not know that sharp corners are stress risers, and the sharper the corner in the frame

the quicker local stresses can escalate, which means the gun can come apart with hot loads if it's not properly filleted.

I noticed those nicely rounded corners as soon as I got the gun into my hands. In addition, there is a thickening, or enlargement, on the outside rear of the frame just in front of the cylinder latch that reminds me of the bulge on the side of the action of a best quality Holland & Holland double rifle. In both cases, the bulge serves to strengthen the frame at its weakest point.

I recently visited John Linebaugh in Missouri. John builds very powerful handguns that make the performance of 44 Magnums seem like child's play, and he has an extensive background in manufacturing custom cylinders that are designed to operate at very high pressure. John took a good look at the new 640 Smith & Wesson, measured it here and there, and said, "This is probably the most radical step S&W has taken in its entire history."

I asked him to explain, and he said he thought the cylinder was mighty small for hot 357 loads. However, the bolt cuts on the J-frame Smiths are located between the five cylinders, not over them as on S&W six-shooters, so there is no stress riser where the pressure is the highest.

The 357 Model 640 Centennial (left) has a more massive barrel than the 38 Special 442 Airweight (right). More weight up front helps to block the kick.

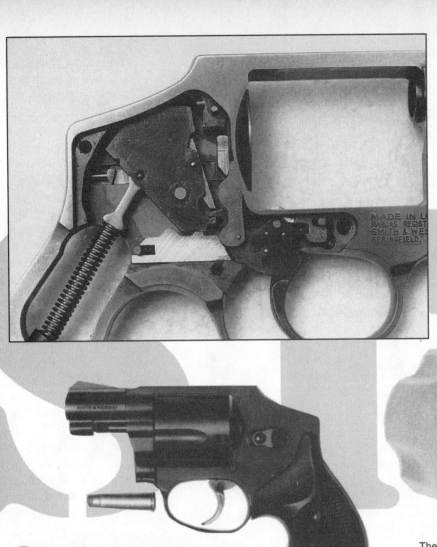

Very smooth machining is evident inside the stainless Centennial 357 as well as outside. Nothing much new here, just good workmanship and excellent materials.

The cylinder walls of the M640 are thick enough. Note that the bolt cuts fall between chambers. The new Smith features very smooth, precise machining overall.

Newest from S&W is their Model 640 in 357 Magnum. The Airweight (black, above) will still be offered, but in 38 Special only. The 640 features heavier barrel and precise CNC machining to let it handle the stress of the hottest loads.

Although those cylinder walls are mighty thin, they are apparently thick enough. When I got done chronographing a variety of hot loads through the little gun I was surprised at the power available in such a small package. The heaviest bullets I shot weighed 158 grains; loads with heavier bullets exist, but I didn't try them. I asked the ammo makers to send me what they would recommend for use in a short-barrel gun, and shot what they sent.

Lightweight bullets are useless in the 640. The 110-grain bullets don't offer enough resistance to the push of the expanding gasses for the powder to burn completely in the barrel. Without a long enough barrel time, the result is great muzzleblast without a lot of velocity, compared with what you could get firing the same load through a longer barrel. This is also true of the 125-grain loads. Some of the most horrendous muzzleblasts imaginable come from 125-grain loads. The blast nearly lifted my hat off. Some of the 140-grain loads, notably Federal's fine Hi-Shok JHPs, have lots of blast, but that load in particular achieves about 1150 fps. You get more performance out of snubbies when you shoot heavier bullets. Those loads are quieter, too.

The 158-grainers are the real sleepers, especially the Gold Dot load from Speer/CCI. It felt less abusive to my hand than the incredibly loud 125-grain CCI Gold Dot, was much quieter, yet went adequately fast (158/1135 fps versus 125/1290). The 158-grainer, in fact, is what I'd carry in the gun.

Accuracy with the 640 is dependent on how firmly you can hold the gun and

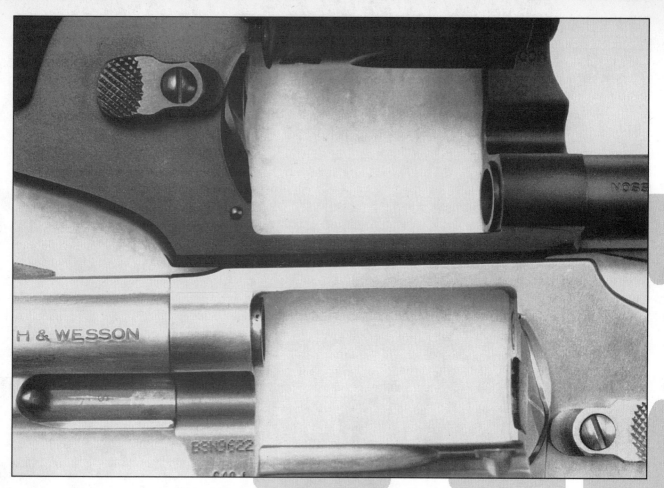

Fillets at the corner of the stainless Model 640 frame cutout are of larger radius than those on the aluminum-frame Airweight (top).

S&W

how smoothly you can pull the DAO trigger. Though this revolver is not designed to be a target gun, it's capable of decent accuracy. It'll shoot well over long ranges, but can't deliver its best performance unless the trigger is immaculately clean and lightly oiled. John Linebaugh and I tried the 640 at a range of about a half-mile, and with heavy bullets we could spot hits and walk them onto the target. We didn't spot any hits when we tried light 110-grain bullets.

Some time back, I shot my very slick Model 36 Chiefs Special double-action at a target 150 yards away, using hot 38 Special handloads. I was able to hit a man-size target at that range with that gun, but I'd need to do a bit of work on the trigger pull of the Model 640 357 before I could shoot it that well. The accuracy potential is surely there, though. From a machine rest, the Smith 640 will shoot with the best of them.

The little 640 withstood some horrifically potent loads and kept on ticking. I

am extremely impressed with the gun. I might occasionally appreciate the presence of a hammer if I had to use this gun for plinking, hunting or occasional long shots, but this was never intended to be that kind of gun.

I tried shooting quickly at a sheet of 8½x11 paper at 15 yards and quickly found that hits were greatly dependent on smoothness of trigger pull, firmness of hold (the harder I grabbed it with both mitts, the better it shot) and the impact point of various weights of bullets. With the 110s that I thought would shoot well, I missed every other shot. With the very hot and loud Federal 140-grain Hi-Shok, I hit thirteen out of fifteen shots. I was trying for fast hits, not maximum accuracy.

The fit and finish of this gun are excellent throughout. It is smoothly polished, without glare. The blued steel front sight is pinned in place so it can be replaced as needed or desired. The ⅛-inch front blade is adequately wide, but the rear notch in the top of the frame is a bit too narrow for my eyes. I can't see enough light on the sides of the front blade. There were some complaints about the slimness of the front

sight on early Model 36s and Model 60s, so Smith made it wider.

The trigger surface is smooth enough for me. The pull, although slick, could be made a bit smoother by a competent gunsmith, but I doubt if it could be made much lighter. It's really quite good as it is.

The ejector rod is much longer than that on other Smith snubbies, but still fails by ¼-inch to completely clear 357 cases. Cases are, however, ejected adequately with one whack on the rod. Gone is the half-hearted ejection of older snubbies, one of their more aggravating habits. The full-length underlug permits an ejection stroke of nearly an inch, compared with just over half an inch on previous S&W 38 snubbies.

I pulled off the sideplate and found that the innards were as slick and well-made as the outside of the gun. The Centennials use a wedge-shaped hammer, but the only other significant difference between the guts of this gun and my old snub is that the diameter of the front sideplate screw is larger in the 640. All three sideplate screws have nylon inserts to help keep them in place.

The bottom line is that if I wanted a versatile pocket or backup gun in a small, concealable package I'd opt for this Smith & Wesson Model 640, which is offered at the same price as its predecessor in 38 Special. The 357 chambering means I can choose from a great variety of self-defense ammo and easily keep the little gun well fed. The 640 Centennial has lots of power and is a well-made, versatile performer. ●

A thick boss behind the frame opening adds strength where it's most needed.

Accuracy of the Centennial is limited only by the shooter. The smooth double action ensures decent groups at 15 yards, this one rapid-fired by the author, aimed at the top of the black.

SMITH & WESSON MODEL 640 CENTENNIAL 357 TEST RESULTS

Cartridge	Wgt.Grs.	Type	MV (fps)	SD
Cor-Bon	110	JHC	1292	37
Cor-Bon	125	JHC	1280	32
Speer	125	Gold Dot	1294	32
Speer	158	Gold Dot	1134	23
Federal	110	Hi-Shok	1245	35
Federal	140	Hi-Shok	1141	26
Fed 38+P+	140	Hydra-Shok	889	37
Handload (38)	125	JHP	953	20
Handload (38)	158	JHP	830	40

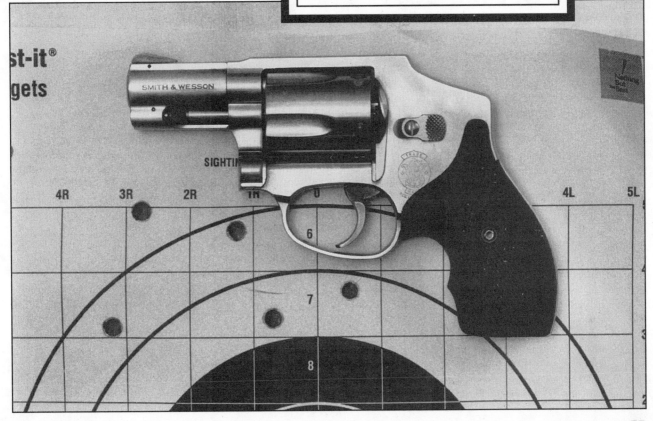

AFTER MUCH ballyhoo and two years of delays while the bugs were worked out of it, it's finally here. At last—the 40-caliber Browning Hi-Power! We've waited a long time for a gun like this—longer than you think; thirty years, to be exact. The idea goes *way* back, to the early 1960s, when some of the boys at *Guns & Ammo* successfully converted the ubiquitous P-35 Browning 9mm to 40-caliber.

They called it the 40 G&A, the idea being to upgrade the venerable 9mm Browning to a more potent caliber while retaining its legendary handling qualities and functional reliability. And it was a good choice, too, for the P-35 Browning did indeed have a superb reputation—good enough to cause more than fifty nations to adopt it as their standard service pistol.

But first, some history. The last design of John Moses Browning, the P-35, was patented in 1927 and first ap-

BROWNING's
BETTER HI-POWER
The 40 S&W!

by CHUCK TAYLOR

Browning Hi-Power 40 S&W

Action:	SA Semi-auto
Caliber:	40 S&W
Others:	9mm
Finish:	"Military" matte black
Barrel:	4.75"
Capacity:	10+1
Sights:	Fixed
Weight:	35 oz. unloaded
Height:	5.0" overall
Length:	7.75" overall
Price:	$525 suggested retail

Outwardly nearly identical to the standard 9mm P-35, the slide of new 40 version is slightly heavier and thicker, as is evidenced by the groove in left side for slide stop clearance (arrow).

peared commercially in 1935, its first version going to the French army. Built at Fabrique Nationale (FN) of Belgium, it has had several additional designators, the most famous of which have been "HP," "Model 88" and, of course, "Hi-Power." And, like most self-loaders of that period, it was originally offered with an adjustable tangent rear sight and grip frame slotted for a shoulder stock/holster.

From the outset, the P-35 utilized a large-capacity magazine (thirteen rounds) and was the result of Browning's attempt to simplify his basic Model 1911 design. In some ways, he was successful—the detachable barrel bushing of the Model 1911 was eliminated. However, in return for the large-capacity magazine, a trigger linkage considerably more complex than that of the M1911 was required.

Curiously, Browning also reduced the size of the thumb-safety tab to the point where it was essentially useless, a puzzling act until one realizes he intended the loaded weapon to be carried either "cocked and *un*-locked" or with the chamber empty and a loaded magazine in place (Condition 3), requiring the slide to be cycled to load, a common military carry configuration both then and now.

Because the P-35 is primarily a military sidearm, it features a tiny front sight and an equally diminutive rear

The Browning 40 Hi-Power looks familiar, but features more power and an ambidextrous safety.

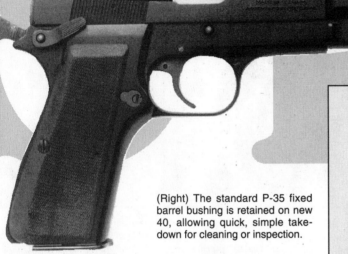

(Right) The standard P-35 fixed barrel bushing is retained on new 40, allowing quick, simple takedown for cleaning or inspection.

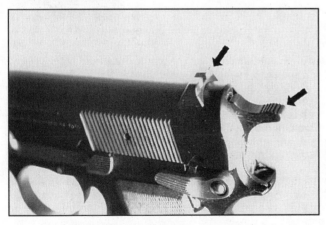

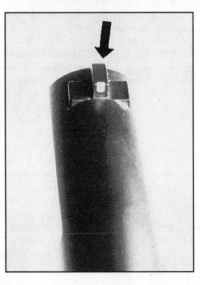

The high-visibility fixed sights of the latest model P-35 are also evident on the 40-caliber version. However, vertical grooves, within which white lowlight squares are located, are disconcerting in normal light, especially when shooting at high speed. The sights would give better service, in the author's opinion, if replaced with sights having a simple horizontal white dot pattern. The spur hammer, while serviceable, has sharp edges which abrade skin and clothing. These should be removed, or the hammer could be replaced with a burr type, the author's choice.

(Right) The 40 Hi-Power has the same slide stop, magazine release and ambidextrous thumb safety as those found on the newest version of the 9mm P-35. The gun also sports a smooth, black-matte military finish.

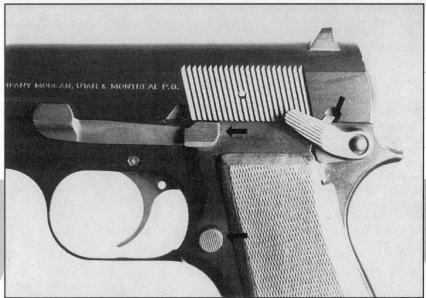

The tried and true Browning-designed pivot/pinned extractor is retained on new 40-caliber model, although it's a bit bigger to handle the potent 40 S&W cartridge.

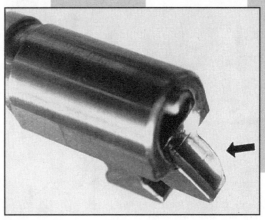

The feed ramp of the test gun had some tool marks, although feeding was unimpaired. Nonetheless, the author recommends polishing the ramp to assure positive feeding of all conventional bullet shapes.

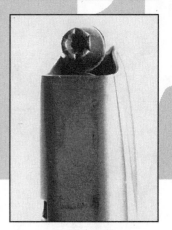

The staggered, double-into-single-column magazine concept of the regular P-35 is used, but in larger form, holding ten rounds. Winchester Black Talon 180-grain JHP (shown) proved to be the most accurate ammunition in the test gun.

BROWNING

sight notch, making rapid sight acquisition under stress impossible. Thus, many complain that the P-35 isn't as accurate as the 1911 and requires serious gunsmithing to upgrade its "human engineering" to acceptable levels. From an academic standpoint, both criticisms are legitimate. However, my experience has been that a little conscientious gunsmithing and the installation of decent sights does indeed cure the problem. All of my 9mm Brownings shoot into 4 inches at 50 meters, making them more than adequate for any function for which I might use them.

Careful ammunition selection, too, does much to improve the P-35's accuracy, because much of the issue is *ammunition*, rather than gun, related. The 9mm Parabellum cartridge is notorious for its tremendous variations in case-wall thickness, overall length, bullet diameters and propellant burning rates, all of which critically affect accuracy.

The diminutive thumb safety and "thumbnail" sights, too, are no longer an issue. About six years ago, Browning began fitting the P-35 with a large-tab, ambidextrous thumb-safety and high-visibility fixed sights, a process that continues to this day. This modernization was further enhanced by a rugged new black military enamel finish, making the venerable P-35 fully equal to the newer SIGs, Berettas and Smith & Wessons that now dominate the police and civilian marketplace.

Back to the 40-caliber cartridge. As mentioned earlier, the idea behind the 40 G&A was to utilize a more powerful cartridge than the 9mm, while retaining the compactness and other positive characteristics of the P-35. In fact, the selection of a 40-caliber cartridge was predicated entirely upon the fact that it was the largest caliber possible in the P-35 without a major upscaling of the gun's basic size.

Although the project was completely successful, no U.S. or European ammunition manufacturer began producing 40 G&A ammo. With no commercial source of 40-caliber ammunition, no one—including Browning—was interested in building 40-caliber P-35s. Sadly, the idea died on the vine, even though it was a fine one, indeed.

In 1979, Jeff Cooper and I revived the concept and expanded it to include not only the P-35, but the newer BRNO CZ-75 as well. After careful consideration, we decided that to provide the best mixture of weapon control, penetration and

The recoil of the 40 S&W Browning is sharp, but not objectionable. Fast two-shot bursts are no problem. The author's overall impression is that this gun recoils about the same as a 1911 Colt 45 ACP.

This five-shot, *50-meter* Ransom Rest group was shot with Taylor's 40 Browning, out of the box. Obviously, accuracy is excellent!

stopping power, the new cartridge, *which we called the 10mm*, would drive a 180- to 200-grain bullet at 900 fps and utilize a case approximately the same overall length as the 9mm.

However, at this juncture, I parted ways with Jeff to pursue other interests, and somewhere along the line, some negative changes in our concept surfaced. First, the handgun that emerged from the project, the Bren Ten, was an upscaled CZ-75 and thus large and heavy. In fact, it rivalled the 1911 45 in size and weight—an abandonment of the original requirement to keep the gun compact.

Second, the new "10mm" cartridge, initially produced by Norma, propelled a 200-grain JTC bullet from a cartridge too long for efficient use in a self-loading pistol at a whopping 1200 fps—*with chamber pressures in excess of 30,000 psi*! Even in a pistol as large and heavy as the Bren Ten, muzzleblast and recoil were brutal, penetration excessive and weapon service-life, therefore, *very* short. Clearly, my idea of keeping the cartridge in the same size-range as the

9mm or 45 ACP and maintaining gun control/acceptable penetration capability had also been abandoned.

To no one's surprise, the Bren Ten/10mm was a failure, and the idea of a 40-caliber self-loader *again* died an ignominious death, the unfortunate victim of that most deadly of developmental maladies, loss of purpose.

Then, in 1989, stunning the firearms community with its boldness in a highly competitive marketplace, Smith & Wesson announced a new cartridge they called the "40 S&W." To my delight, their 40 was a dead-ringer for *my* 40, delivering a 180-grain bullet at 933 fps and featuring virtually identical cartridge dimensions. But, before Smith could market a gun for the new cartridge, another coup emerged. Glock, sensing the validity and resulting commercial viability of the 40-caliber concept, beat Smith to the punch, announcing their Model 22 and compact Model 23, both chambered for the 40 S&W.

Within six months, S&W offered their own 40-caliber pistol, the Model 4006. Between 1991 and 1993, SIG,

Beretta, Taurus and the rest followed suit and, by 1994, the 40 auto was—finally—here to stay.

But nothing from Browning, nothing at all. Perhaps—even probably—they were waiting to see if the 40 would make the grade. Long known as a conservative manufacturer, Browning waited a full three years before they entered the 40-caliber race. Then, after one false start and subsequent recall in 1993 and 1994, they made the big jump. Their 40-caliber P-35 hit the marketplace in 1995. The legendary Browning had become a true "Hi-Power" at last.

And what a handsome pistol it is, too. With all the grace and reliability of its well-known 9mm baby brother, the 40-caliber Browning represents a quantum leap in weapon technology and validates the superiority of John Browning's design genius.

But it's more than just another pretty face. It also sports all the modern features: a rich, black military enamel finish; high-visibility fixed sights with white vertical bar inserts for low-light use; large-tabbed, ambidextrous thumb-safety for safe, efficient Condition One (cocked and locked) carry.

But, in comparison to the 9mm P-35, there *are* some differences. The 40 has a ten-shot magazine. That's enough capacity to satisfy those who believe in the "firepower" concept, and it's con-tained in a magazine compact enough to allow effective high-speed handling. The barrel has three recoil lugs, stiff recoil spring and a larger, heavier slide to handle the increased punch of the 40 as compared to the 9mm Parabellum.

To test it, I had my friend and asso-ciate, Kevin McClung, of M-D Labs, make me one of his excellent "Mad Dog" holsters and matching magazine carriers. Then, equipped with the best

The newest service pistol cartridge, the 40 S&W, first appeared in early 1960s as the 40 G&A, then again in 1980 in conceptual form as Cooper/Taylor's 10mm. The author's specifications called for a 180- to 200-grain bullet at 900 fps, almost exact-ly the performance specs of the current 40 S&W. (Left to right) 9mm Parabellum, 40 S&W, 10mm Auto, 45 ACP.

holster now available, to the range I went.

Because it is the acid test of both shooter and weapon, I ran the gun through the extremely difficult Amer-ican Small Arms Academy (ASAA) Combat Master Qualification Course (see sidebar). As expected, due to the stresses it imposes (only nine men other than myself have successfully completed it), a few negative charac-teristics emerged. I failed by a couple of points to make the 90 percent score required to pass the course because of the following deficiencies in the gun:

1. The combination of a white vertical bar insert in the front sight and dual ver-tical bars to each side of the rear sight notch creates too much clutter, thus preventing efficient high-speed sight acquisition and alignment. Therefore, their replacement with a more effec-tive three-dot horizontal pattern is recommended.
2. The standard thumb-groove stocks with which the piece is furnished from the factory are poorly shaped

Taylor and his ASAA test team took the new 40 S&W Browning Hi-Power well past the norm to deter-mine its true capabilities. Included was this stage, in which five knockdown steel silhouettes were engaged under time pressure from a full 100 meters. The new Browning 40 passed with flying colors and received high marks from all who shot it during testing.

ASAA Combat Master Qualification Course

The American Small Arms Acad-emy (ASAA) Combat Master Quali-fication Course was used as the primary evaluator of the new 40 Browning because it is recognized worldwide as the most challenging and difficult course of fire of its kind. As the accompanying text shows, it

tests virtually every necessary com-bat handgun skill, challenging both weapon and firer to the limit.

As such, it quickly discloses both deficiencies in the shooter's ability and design flaws in his weapon. This is intentional, for a true Master has refined his techniques to the highest possible level, causing weapon de-sign, from both a mechanical and

human engineering standpoint, to become a major factor in itself.

Rules and Scoring Combat Master Certification, Handgun

Target: Taylor Combat, mounted so that head is between 5 feet, 10 inch-es and 6 feet above ground surface.

Weapons Eligible: Any *service* handgun that is safe. No match-pre-

Taylor Relative Stopping Power

While I have long been a proponent of General Julian Hatcher's theory of Relative Stopping Power (HRSP), I find his formula excessively complex and time-consuming. So, in 1980, I streamlined it into simpler form. Instead of struggling with this:

$$HRSP = \frac{1}{2}(32.16) \times WV/7000 \times A \times Y$$
(A minimum "score" of 60 is considered "passing.")

We have this:

$$TRSP = W \times V \times B \times Y$$
(A minimum "score" of 20 is "passing.")

The terms used for both formulas are defined as follows: W: bullet weight in grains; V: bullet velocity in fps; A: bullet cross-sectional area in square inches; B: bore cross-sectional area, rounded off to the nearest convenient fractional expression. For example, a 22 is $\frac{2}{5}$-inch, or .039-inch; Y: bullet shape factor, as follows:

FMJRN: Full Metal Jacket Round-Nose	0.90
LRN: Lead Round-Nose	1.00
LFP: Lead Flatpoint	1.05
LSWC: Lead Semi-Wadcutter	1.25
LWC: Lead Wadcutter	1.25
JHP: Jacketed Hollowpoint	1.25*
JSP: Jacketed Softpoint	1.25*

* = These two bullet types receive a 1.25 factor *if* the velocity at which they are driven exceeds 1088 fps, the speed of sound at sea level and generally accepted velocity at which expansion begins. If they are not, then expansion cannot reasonably be expected and they both receive a factor of 1.00, the same as a Lead Round-Nose bullet.

---

pared weapons are allowed, nor compensators, counterweights nor extended barrels unless sound suppressor threads are evident. The gun may have sight improvements, but optical sights (Aimpoints, et al) are prohibited.

Holsters and Ancillary Equipment: A holster must be worn in concealable manner as must all spare ammunition carriers. Exception—police duty rig, *if worn in standard duty configuration*. All retention devices must be active and used during qualification. Friction devices must hold weapon against loss as deemed acceptable by a certifying ASAA official.

Ammunition: Any full-powered service load. IPSC, PPC, target or squib loads, tracer, armor-piercing and incendiary ammunition is proscribed.

Scoring: Hit in X-zone: 5 points. Hit anywhere else on target (Z-zone): 2 points for major caliber and 1 point for minor caliber.

Major caliber is defined as 357 Magnum full-powered load from a minimum of 5-inch barrel, 40 S&W auto, 10mm auto, 41 Magnum, 44 Special, 44 Magnum, 45 ACP and 45 Colt.

Minor caliber is defined as 9mm Parabellum, 38 Special, 38 Super or 357 Magnum fired from barrel of 4 inches or less.

Any bullet that fails to break through the bold green outline of the silhouette shall be considered a miss.

When head shots are specified, a hit inside the Y-zone will earn 5 points. A hit anywhere else on the head (Z-zone) will be scored on major/minor basis. A hit on the silhouette below the dotted line at the base of the head shall be scored a miss.

Possible Score: 400 points

Pass/Fail Cutoff: 360 points (90 percent)

Penalties: All penalties are 5 points per offense, as listed below:
1. Premature start, creeping.
2. Overtime shot. *Special note:* If overtime shot was caused by malfunction and is properly diagnosed and cleared, no penalty will be assessed.
3. Hit on object designated as cover or hostage.
4. Overtime speed, or tactical reload, or stoppage clearance.
5. Procedural error.

Authority: *The certifying ASAA official has final jurisdiction on all decisions.*

Continued on page 62.

Standby...Ready...Fire! Armed with a new 40 S&W Browning, ASAA Senior Instructor Greg Nordyke presents the weapon from holster, drops into kneeling position and engages target at 50 meters, obtaining two center hits on target in 6.0 seconds, the ASAA Combat Master requirement at this range. All who tried it commented that new Browning's smooth grip-frame is a bit slippery, slowing down establishment of grip-index during high-speed holster presentations. Fine checkering or stippling of the frontstrap and backstrap solved the problem and is recommended.

Candidate Confirmation of Rules of Engagement: Once candidate has read and acknowledged his understanding of the above, he will be briefed on the following course of fire and his equipment inspected and placed in whatever condition, as defined above, deemed appropriate by the certifying ASAA official.

Special Note: *Any questions or clarifications required by the candidate must be asked now and are the responsibility of the candidate, not the certifying ASAA official.*

Course of Fire Qualification Course, Handgun Combat Master

Note: *All presentations are from a secured holster.*

Stage 1: Standard Exercises. Single assailant—2 shots. Perform each drill once. Shots fired: 16. Possible score: 80 points.

1. 1 meter: 1.0 second (Speed rock).
2. 1 meter: 1.0 second (Step back).
3. 3 meters: 1.0 second
4. 7 meters: 1.3 seconds
5. 10 meters: 1.8 seconds
6. 15 meters: 2.2 seconds
7. 25 meters: 2.7 seconds
8. 50 meters: 6.0 seconds

Stage 2: Presentation Evaluation. 7 meters. Single target. One shot from holster: 1.0 second. Perform a total of five (5) times. Shots fired: 5. Possible score: 25 points.

Stage 3: Responses Left, Right & Rear. 7 meter. Perform each five (5) times. Shots fired: 15. Possible score: 75 points.

1. Response Left. 1 shot: 1.0 second
2. Response Right. 1 shot: 1.0 second
3. Response Rear. 1 shot: 1.2 seconds

Stage 4: Multiple Targets. 5 meters. One shot on each as listed below. Targets are to be spaced 1 meter apart, center to center. Shots fired: 9. Possible score: 45 points.

1. Two (2) targets: 1.2 seconds
2. Three (3) targets: 1.5 seconds
3. Four (4) targets: 1.8 seconds

Stage 5: Small Targets at Close Range. *Head shot only*, as listed below. Shots fired: 9. Possible score: 45 points.

1. 5 meters. 1 shot: 1.0 second. Perform four (4) times.
2. 7 meters. 1 shot: 1.2 seconds. Perform five (5) times.

Stage 6: Ambidextrous Shooting. 7 meters. Three targets 1 meter apart, center-to-center. Candidate engages each target, strong hand supported, firing one shot on each, then speed loads, transfers weapon to weak hand and reengages targets, *weak hand only,*

BROWNING

for any kind of quick grip index, especially during high-speed weapon presentations from the holster. However, if these are replaced with standard wood or plastic P-35 stocks, the problem is quickly and economically obviated.

3. The heavy recoil spring prevents rapid clearance procedures in the event of a malfunction. Timed Type 1 (Failure to Fire—1 second); Type 2 (Failure to Eject—1 second) and Type 3 (Feedway—4 seconds) clearance drills thus proved to be very difficult and demand extra operator practice to efficiently execute.

4. The spring protruding from the lower-rear portion of the magazine (intended to overcome the pressure of magazine-disconnector spring and literally eject the magazine from the

well when the release button is pressed) is excessive. This causes the empty magazine to exit the gun with considerable force, impacting the ground hard enough to dent the floorplate.

Removal of the magazine disconnector negates the necessity for this feature and allows not only a better trigger pull, but normal magazine ejection during speed loads as well. It is realized that some prefer not to engage in this practice. However, the handgun is quite safe without the magazine disconnect and *much* easier to operate, particularly under stress.

5. While crisp, the trigger was heavy enough to prevent achievement of this gun's considerable potential. Therefore, a trigger job is highly rec-

The 40 S&W and its bigger brother, the 10mm Auto. With a whopping chamber pressure of 30,000 psi, the 10mm is both uncontrollable and abusive to guns in standard factory loadings, and requires downloading to correct the problem. The new 40 S&W duplicates the vaunted 10mm "FBI Load" in a shorter, more efficient case, with far lower pressure.

unsupported, firing one more shot on each. Time limit: 6 seconds—self-loader; 8 seconds—revolver. Shots fired: 6. Possible score: 30 points.

Stage 7: Hostage Situations. 7 meters. One shot, head only: 1.2 seconds each, as listed below. Shots fired: 10. Possible score: 50 points.
1. Shot on head of hostage holder past *left* side of hostage's head. Perform five (5) times.
2. Shot on head of hostage holder past *right* side of hostage's head. Perform five (5) times.

Stage 8: Targets at Odd Angles. 7 meters. Target 60 percent obscured by cover configured as specified by certifying ASAA official. 1 shot: 1.2 seconds, as listed below. Perform each five (5) times. Shots fired: 10. Possible score: 50 points.
1. Target looking around *left* side of cover.

2. Target looking around *right* side of cover.

Stage 9: Speed Reloads. *No shooting.* Perform five (5) times. Time limit: 1.5 seconds—self-loader; 4.0 seconds—revolver. Possible penalty deduction: 25 points.

Stage 10: Tactical Reloads. *No shooting.* Perform five (5) times. Time limit: 4.0 seconds, regardless of weapon type. Possible penalty deduction: 25 points.

Stage 11: Malfunction Clearing. Self-loaders only. *No shooting.* Perform each five (5) times, as listed below. Possible penalty deduction: 75 points.
1. Type 1, Failure to fire: 1.0 seconds
2. Type 2, Failure to eject: 1.0 seconds
3. Type 3, Feedway jam: 4.0 seconds

Editor's Note

Chuck Taylor had a significant hand in the early development of what became the 40 S&W cartridge, so we let him tell some of the history of what many believe is destined to become the most popular handgun cartridge of the late 1990s.

Only a master handgunner can presume to be able to shoot a handgun so close to its absolute potential that design flaws make themselves known. Chuck Taylor is one who can. I shot against him in IPSC competition seventeen years ago and he was one of the best. He's only become better.

As one can see from the description of the Combat Master Certification Course, this is shooting at the absolute razor's edge of controllability. The first two shots, for example, must be fired in less than one second, including drawing the gun from concealment. It just gets tougher from there. Try putting one shot on each of four targets 5 meters away. You have 1.8 seconds. Go! *RMO.*

In this unique motor-drive camera sequence, Taylor has presented (drawn) the Browning 40 Hi-Power from a concealed holster and engages five knockdown steel silhouettes 7 meters downrange, taking them all down with *center hits* in a sizzling 2.2 seconds! Called the ASAA Standard Controllability Test, this exercise pushes both the gun and shooter to the limit, but the new 40 Browning performed well. Try this sometime.

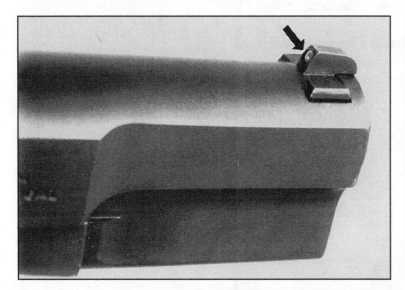

The author recommends the factory sights be replaced with high-visibility tritium sights to enhance high-speed sight acquisition and alignment under low light conditions. These also feature a superior horizontal dot pattern, providing the best results under stress.

ommended, to achieve a pull of about 3.5 to 5 pounds, depending upon the shooter's needs and ability.

Once the above deficiencies were corrected, I again shot the ASAA Combat Master Qualification Course, scoring 384 out of a possible 400 (96 percent, with 90 percent or 360 points required to pass). Prior to trying it with the 40 Browning, I had successfully completed the course with the Colt Government Model 45 (376/94 percent); lightweight Commander 45 (370/93 percent); Glock Model 22 40 (373/94 percent); Browning P-35 9mm (374/94 percent); Glock Model 17 9mm (386/97 percent); Smith

Taylor firing the 40 Browning with his preferred modifications. He feels this new gun is an excellent service pistol and well worth its price.

40 S&W BROWNING P-35 PERFORMANCE
3 SHOTS RANSOM REST @50 METERS

Cartridge	—Bullet— Wgt.Grs.	Type	Load Grs./Powder	Group Size (ins.)	MV Avg. (fps)	Extreme Spread (fps)
Remington	155	JHP	—	2.17	1000	24
Winchester	180	JHP	—	2.68	933	32
Winchester	180	FMJ	—	2.48	954	9
Winchester Black Talon	180	JHP	—	2.25	938	7
Handload	175	SWC	4.8/Unique	2.75	838	28
Handload	190	SWC	4.8/Unique	2.56	868	20

JHP = Jacketed Hollow Point; SWC = Semi-Wadcutter

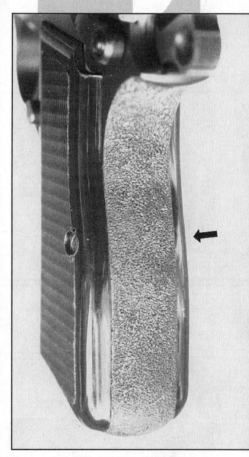

Another Taylor-recommended improvement on the 40 Browning is to round and polish the trigger, and fine-stipple frontstrap and backstrap to give better grip in wet or cold weather. These modifications improve both control and presentation from the holster without abrading skin or clothing.

& Wesson Model 39 9mm (361/90 percent); and S&W Model 10 38 Special (368/92 percent). Thus, I have a good "feel" for how each handgun performs in relation to another.

With its few deficiencies corrected, the 40 Browning is fast, accurate—more accurate than I can shoot it, or care about—mechanically reliable and easy to maintain. In addition, due to the 40 S&W cartridge for which it's chambered, it is a potent manstopper, but without over-penetration or loss of control.

In short, it's a winner and well worth waiting for, even if it did take three decades for the concept to be understood and brought to fruition. I would quite willingly bet my life upon this pistol and feel strongly that, if you need a "social" handgun, you should take a good, hard look at the Browning in 40 S&W. Like me, I think you'll like what you see. ●

COMPARISON OF 40 S&W TO OTHER TYPICAL SERVICE LOADS

Cartridge	—Bullet— Wgt.Grs.	Type	MV (fps)	Hatcher RSP*	Taylor RSP*	KE (ft.lbs.)
Sig P-226						
9mmP	115	FMJ	1068	25	11	302
9mmP	115	JHP	1176	38	17	366
9mmP	147	JHP	942	39	17	296
Colt Python (4" Barrel)						
357 Mag	110	JHP	1090	34	15	290
357 Mag	125	JHP	1416	50	22	578
357 Mag	158	JHP	1070	48	21	405
Browning P-35						
40 S&W	155	JHP	1001	54	26	344
40 S&W	170	SWC**	832	55	23	345
40 S&W	180	JHP	951	60	27	349
40 S&W	180	BT	926	58	25	343
Colt Delta Elite						
10mm	175	JHP	1221	76	33	579
10mm	180	JHP	942	61	27	355
10mm	200	JTC	1226	68	31	663
S&W Model 24						
44 Spl	225	JHP	887	70	33	455
44 Spl	246	RNL	781	62	27	339
Colt 1911						
45 ACP	185	JHP	970	80	37	397
45 ACP	230	FMJ	800	58	27	327

Chronograph: Oehler Model 35P; Elevation: 5800 feet above sea level; Temperature: 70 degrees F; Humidity: 37 percent.
FMJ = Full metal jacket; RN = Round nose; RNL = Round nose lead; JFP = Jacketed flat point; LFP = Lead flat point; JHP = Jacketed hollowpoint; JSP = Jacketed softpoint; SWC = Semi-wadcutter; WC = Wadcutter; BT = Black Talon jacketed hollowpoint.
* = Relative Stopping Power; ** = Select handload, author's favorite. Hard cast 170-grain SWC/4.8 grains Hercules Unique.

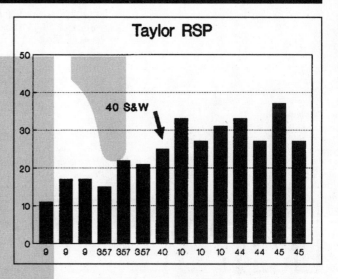

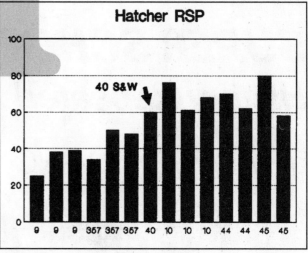

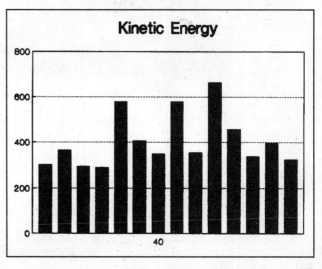

FEW HANDGUN introductions have been as eagerly awaited, nor so long in coming, as Navy Arms' Italian-made replica of the 1870s vintage Smith & Wesson Model #3 revolver commonly called the Schofield. In late 1994, over a year after they were announced, a few shooting samples of these guns began to arrive. I have been fortunate enough to get my hands on two and feel that with minor qualifications they are fine examples of the revolver-maker's art.

There have been some bugs to iron out, as might be expected in such an intricately made piece of machinery, but it certainly seems that the Italian craftsmen are willing to listen to input from American revolver shooters.

Made by the Uberti company in Italy, this revolver is a replica of S&W's Schofield, but it is not an exact clone. It features the same top-break operation, 7-inch barrel, fully blued finish, and walnut grips as on the original. How-

NAVY ARMS'

SUPER SCHOFIELD
History Repeated

by MIKE VENTURINO

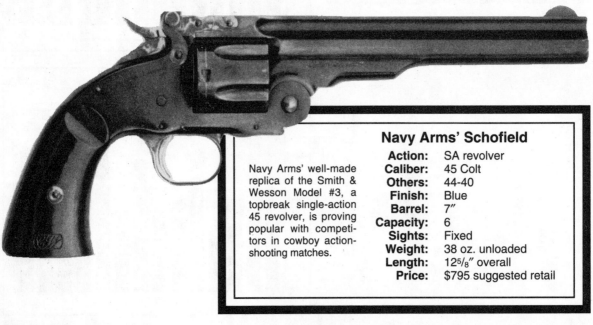

Navy Arms' well-made replica of the Smith & Wesson Model #3, a topbreak single-action 45 revolver, is proving popular with competitors in cowboy action-shooting matches.

Navy Arms' Schofield

Action:	SA revolver
Caliber:	45 Colt
Others:	44-40
Finish:	Blue
Barrel:	7″
Capacity:	6
Sights:	Fixed
Weight:	38 oz. unloaded
Length:	12⅝″ overall
Price:	$795 suggested retail

ever, factory-loaded 45 S&W ammunition has not been made for over 50 years, so Navy Arms chose to have these guns made in 45 Colt caliber. That meant lengthening the cylinder from $1^7/_{16}$ inches to $1^9/_{16}$ inches. The long cylinder also allows 44-40 to be offered as a chambering, but no guns have yet arrived in that caliber.

However, from my experience in firing several hundred rounds of both factory ammo and handloads through two samples, one of the reasons why S&W wanted to avoid the 45 Colt case over 100 years ago is still valid. The star extractor still will not reliably eject the thin-rimmed 45 Colt cases.

Let me explain. Operation of a Navy Arms Schofield is exactly like its predecessor. The hammer is put on the loading notch, the barrel latch is pulled rearward, and then the barrel is pushed downward, which in turn forces the extractor upward. Do this slowly and

all cases will be pushed out. Do it quickly, and chances are the extractor star will slide over the 45 Colt case rims, and one or more will fall back into the chambers. I have a single round of original 45 S&W ammunition in my collection, and it functions perfectly in the new Navy Arms revolver. I have found that if the revolver is turned 90 degrees on its side during extraction the cases will usually fall completely free.

In my collection I have an original S&W Schofield which factory letters indicate as being one of the batch delivered to the government in 1876. Let's compare it to the new Navy Arms version. Starting at the rear, the grip measures exactly 2.01 inches from front to rear on both guns. In thickness, the original's grip is 1.40 inches wide as opposed to 1.415 for the new revolver. Diameter of the cylinders on both guns is 1.67 inches, but as stated above the new Schofield's is $1^9/_{16}$ inches long as opposed to $1^7/_{16}$ inches for the original. That is also the exact difference in overall length between the two revolvers. Width of topstrap at the barrel latch is .75-inch on the old S&W and .765 on the Navy Arms version. On the original Schofield, the barrel diameter at the muzzle is .62-inch, but the new one's is .66-inch. This

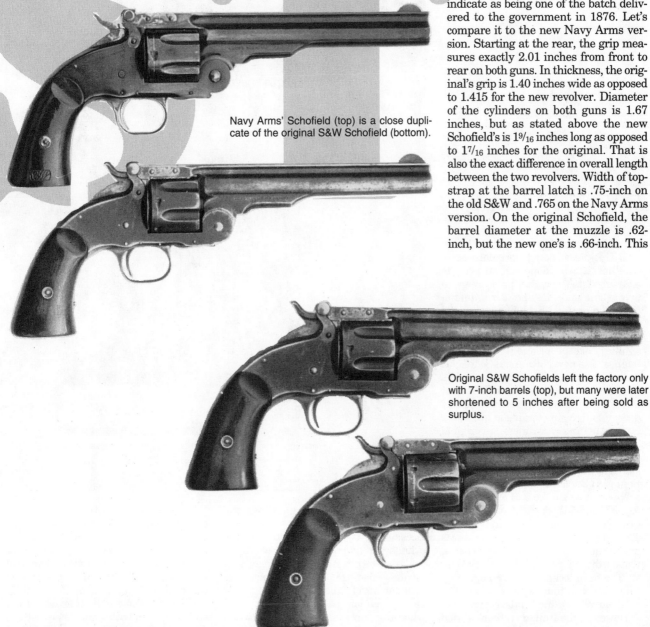

Navy Arms' Schofield (top) is a close duplicate of the original S&W Schofield (bottom).

Original S&W Schofields left the factory only with 7-inch barrels (top), but many were later shortened to 5 inches after being sold as surplus.

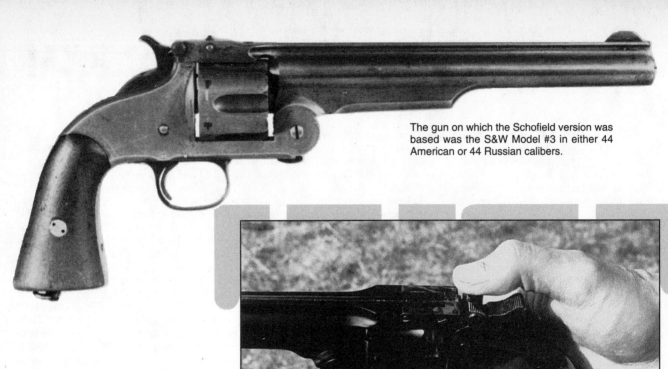

The gun on which the Schofield version was based was the S&W Model #3 in either 44 American or 44 Russian calibers.

The Schofield is opened by pulling the barrel latch rearward with the thumb after putting the gun on half-cock.

NAVY ARMS

is a rather noticeable difference in barrel wall thickness, and I speculate as to whether it was done on purpose to accommodate the higher pressure given by modern smokeless powder ammunition. The original Schofield weighs 34 ounces, and the new one, 38 ounces.

Internally, the two guns function similarly except for one important difference. The new Navy Arms Schofields have a hammer block device inside, which was a necessity for their import into this country. It is not visible and does not affect functioning at all. There is one other internal difference: original S&Ws used 5-groove rifling, while Uberti uses 6 grooves in the new version. Again, this does not affect functioning in the least.

The barrel pivots downward and pushes the empty cases upward.

Now let's compare the two Navy Arms Schofields which I have been testing. The first one, serial numbered 23, arrived in November of 1994 and was one of the first six to reach our shores. Outwardly the gun is of beautiful quality. The fit of lockplate to frame, if anything, is better than on my original. The fit of barrel to frame is utterly tight.

However, the Italian craftsmen tried too hard to keep tolerances tight. For instance, the slot through which the rotating hand fits was too tight. Occasionally, it would bind and the cylinder would not rotate. I took #23 to my gunsmith friend, Ed Webber, and he deepened the slot .005-inch; the cylinder never failed to rotate again. I should mention that this only happened when the gun was loaded; never when it was empty.

The tolerance between the cylinder and the bottom of the frame was also too tight. My original Schofield would accept an .008-inch feeler gauge in that space, while Navy Arms #23 would bind up when only a .001-inch gauge was inserted. This led to some functioning problems as the gun became dirty from shooting; even with smokeless powders. Blackpowder was hopeless. Before I

The Navy Arms Schofield replica even has inspector's cartouches and date on the side of the grips like the originals.

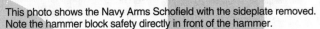

This photo shows the Navy Arms Schofield with the sideplate removed. Note the hammer block safety directly in front of the hammer.

had sorted out what was happening, the cylinder had received several lateral scratches from being rotated with bits of grit lodged between the frame and the cylinder. The trigger pull on #23 was plain awful. It went off the end of my RCBS trigger pull scale which measures up to 8 pounds. I figure it was at least 12 pounds.

Now, one person I told these problems to blamed not the workmanship, but rather the gun design. I disagree. The guns are obviously well built, but they needed function testing. Italy is not a nation of revolver shooters. That is why they sent those initial six samples over here to put into shooters' hands. After my problems with Navy Arms' #23, I wrote a detailed letter and FAXed it to Val Forgett, president of Navy Arms. He in turn sent it on to Uberti in Italy.

My ego is not such that I think my letter was solely responsible for ironing the bugs out, but I'd like to think that it helped. That's because when my second test gun arrived in January, 1995, (serial numbered 52) none of the problems evident with gun #23 were there. I have fired over 400 rounds through this sample with nary a bobble. Its cylinder always rotates when the hammer is cocked, and a .006-inch feeler gauge will fit between the cylinder and the bottom of the frame. To my pleasure, the only scratch on the cylinder is the normal ring which most revolvers develop between locking notches. Trigger pull is exactly 5½ pounds.

Let me give you a detailed description of Navy Arms #52. The fit of the grips to frame is flawless, but they are of a rather porous European walnut with a shiny finish. On the left side of

the grips is stamped "1877" with a facsimile inspector's cartouche bearing the letters "DAL" in script inside. On the right grip panel is another cartouche with "CW" also in script, inside. Barrel-to-cylinder gap is .008-inch, which is slightly large but hardly objectionable.

The hammer, trigger guard, and barrel latch parts are all color case-hardened. The rest of the gun except the front sight is deeply blued. The polishing job was expertly done. The edges are crisp, and none of the screw holes are dished out. The edges of each cylinder flute are nicely beveled, which is the case on the original also.

Except for proofmarks, the only markings on the revolver itself are "CAL .45LC" and "Navy Arms Co. Ridgefield, NJ" on the left side of the barrel, and "A. Uberti—Italy" on the barrel's right side. This is a refreshing change from the paragraph or so found on so many American guns now. Interestingly, #23 has "US" stamped on the butt, just like my original, but that marking was omitted on #52. Navy Arms tells me this is an oversight and will be corrected.

The barrel slugged at exactly .451-inch in the grooves, but to my dismay the cylinder's chamber mouths go .457. This is a continuing problem with the 45 Colt caliber in many makes of revolvers, and it certainly does not contribute to their accuracy. Navy Arms Schofield #52 shoots well enough, as the accompanying chart shows, but I feel that with a better match of chamber mouths to barrel diameter, accuracy would be better. My main complaint about the Navy Arms Schofield, however, is with the hammer. On an original S&W Schofield, the hammer is finely

checkered in a crosshatch pattern, but on the Navy Arms gun, the hammer is only cut with coarse lateral serrations.

Breaking open #52 was slightly stiff in the beginning. My original Schofield nearly opens itself just from the weight of the barrel, but keep in mind it is about 120 years old. The Navy Arms Schofield has smoothed up considerably now with just over a month's use. Something I love saying about these revolvers to my friends who are oriented toward more modern guns is that Schofields are finely fitted, intricately made samples of the revolver-makers art. They cannot just be slapped together from a bucket of parts like some of today's autoloaders.

My original S&W Schofield has the same problem most old top-break S&Ws have. They seem to be sighted-in for 300 yards! It grouped about 18 inches high at 25 yards with 230-grain blackpowder handloads. My friend Ed Webber fitted it with a taller front sight so I could hit something with it. The Italians have done a good job of sighting-in their Schofields. Navy Arms #23 hit about 2 inches low with 250-grain factory loads, but to my joy, #52 hits very near point of aim with no less than a half dozen 250-grain factory loads and handloads.

Perhaps some comments are in order about the purpose for which these new Navy Arms Schofields are intended. That is simply recreational shooting, and I suspect that the cowboy action shooters are the main part of the intended market. If so, Navy Arms has hit the 10-ring, because cowboy matches are buzzing with news about Schofields, and it is my understanding that Navy Arms has over

5000 backorders already. Thus far my only two criticisms about #52 is that the 45 Colt cases sometimes don't eject properly and that the looseness of the cylinder's chamber mouths cost some of the accuracy potential. Those problems have no great bearing on the Navy Arms Schofields as they will be used in cowboy action shooting. A fast reload is not necessary in that game, nor is pinpoint accuracy. In fact with such crude fixed sights, I doubt if accuracy better than 2½- to 3-inch groups

at 25 yards could be seen in handheld shooting, anyway.

Several shooters have asked me if the extra-length cylinder and 4 ounces more weight affect the Navy Arms handling characteristics compared to an original S&W Schofield. To be honest, I must say no. In fact, if you blindfold me and put both guns in my hands I cannot tell which is which. (Until I grasp the hammer with my thumb, that is.)

If I seem enthusiastic about Navy Arms' Italian import, I am. My sincere feeling is that I wish some of our American handgun makers would put such precision into their products. I foresee more S&W reproductions in the

future. For instance: Uberti could make a replica of other S&W Model #3s by restyling the latch and adding one more inch of barrel. S&W made the Model #3 in 44 S&W Russian caliber. Uberti, with this $1^{9}/_{16}$ cylinder could make them up in 44 Special. All they have to do first is catch up on that tremendous backorder for Schofields!

Comparing the Schofield to Colt SAA

As a shooter and amateur historian of the Indian-fighting cavalry, I couldn't help but compare the new Navy Arms Schofield 45s to the Colt SAA. During the same time-frame that S&W was

HISTORY OF THE S&W SCHOFIELD

The S&W Schofield revolver was contempory with Colt's SAA 45 for U.S. cavalry use. The gun at left is a Navy Arms Schofield. The gun at right is a Colt SAA.

What exactly is a Smith & Wesson Schofield revolver? Too often I have heard shooters refer to any Smith & Wesson Model #3 top-break revolver as a "Schofield." That is not accurate. Smith & Wesson made several versions of the Model #3, but only one specific variation is the Schofield.

The Smith & Wesson Model #3 first appeared in 1870, and its initial caliber was the 44 Henry rimfire. The management of Smith & Wesson was primarily interested in a government contract, but the Army told them that a centerfire caliber was necessary. Smith & Wesson changed their revolver design to centerfire, and the new cartridge to be used in it was at

first termed simply the 44/100. It was very close to the 44 Henry rimfire in outward dimensions and has the honor of being the first brass-case, reloadable American revolver cartridge. In 1871, the Army bought 1000 8-inch-barreled Smith & Wesson Model #3 revolvers in this 44/100 caliber; 800 of them were blued, and 200 were nickel-plated.

At the same time, Smith was negotiating with the Russian government about their Model #3 revolvers. The Russians liked the guns, but not the caliber. In 1871, they gave Smith & Wesson a contract for 20,000 revolvers, but stipulated that the cartridge not be the

44/100. They wanted a cartridge in which the bullet fitted totally inside the cartridge case instead of one whose bullet diameter was the same as the outside of the cartridge case. Smith & Wesson agreed, and the new caliber came to be called the 44 S&W Russian; the old one was called the 44 S&W American.

In 1870, a Major George Schofield was serving with the 10th Cavalry regiment in Kansas. He wrote the Smith & Wesson factory requesting one of the new revolvers and asked to become their agent in Kansas and Colorado. Major Schofield must have been a good salesman, because Smith & Wesson factory records show that he had sold sixty-two of the new revolvers by the end of 1870.

However, as a cavalryman he was not totally happy with the design and set about remaking it somewhat. In June of 1871, he was granted a patent for a new latch to fit the Model #3, and in April of 1873, another was issued in his name for an improved extraction system. The first was most important in regard to making the revolver more suitable to a horseback-mounted trooper.

As the S&W Model #3 was first made, two hands were required to open the revolver for reloading. The latch that secured the barrel to the frame was mounted on the barrel. Assuming the user is right-handed, one must pull the hammer back to its loading notch with the right thumb while the right hand holds the revolver's butt. Then the left

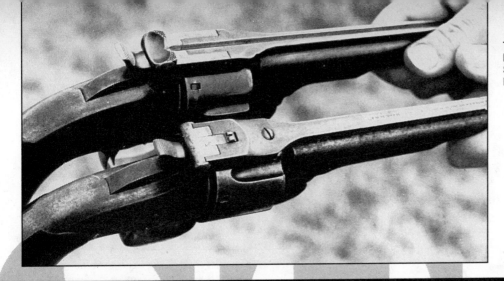

This photo shows the difference between the latches on a S&W Schofield (top) and standard S&W Model #3 (bottom).

hand grasps the latch, lifts it upward, and pushes the barrel downward to eject the empty cases. This is a rather difficult operation for a mounted trooper when one considers that one hand or the other must also be holding onto the reins of a horse.

Major Schofield's improved latch was mounted on the frame rather than the barrel. To operate, one can hold onto the revolver with the shooting hand, pull the hammer back to the loading notch with the thumb, and then open the latch with that same thumb. To eject the empty cases, simply brush the barrel against any object to move it downward. This left the other hand free to control the horse.

In July of 1873, after extensive testing, the U.S. Army Ordnance Board announced the adoption of the new Colt Single Action Army revolver in 45 Colt. Despite this blow, Major Schofield kept lobbying for the Army to try his redesign of the Smith & Wesson Model #3. By September of 1874, his efforts, combined with Smith & Wesson's, paid off. The Army signed a contract for 3000 revolvers using Major Schofield's patents. These first guns were delivered in 1875. Other contracts followed, and further shipments of S&W Schofield-patent revolvers were delivered to the Army in 1876 and 1877. Cost to the government was $13.50 each, with a 50-cent royalty being paid to George Schofield for the use of his patents.

Collectors refer to S&W Schofields as being of first and second model types, but the differences are only minor changes in the latch. Basically, all S&W Schofields were of the

same type. That is, they all left the factory with 7-inch barrels in 45 S&W caliber. All those delivered to the U.S. government have "US" stamped on the butt and were of blue finish. However, slightly fewer than 700 S&W Schofield revolvers were sold to civilians. While all these were still fitted with 7-inch barrels and were of 45 S&W caliber, they lack the "US" stamping and could be either blued or nickel-plated. Counting both civilian and U.S. contract guns, a total of only 8969 S&W Schofield revolvers were made.

When first negotiating with the Army Ordnance Board, Smith & Wesson agreed to make the new revolvers in 45 Colt caliber. However, they quickly found that this cartridge was not suitable for their design. First, it was simply too long for their $1^{7}/_{16}$-inch cylinder length. Second, the 45 Colt's very narrow rim would not function properly with Smith & Wesson's star-type extractor. The extractor would ride over the 45 Colt case rim, allowing the empty cartridge to slide back into the chamber. Smith & Wesson asked the Army to accept a cartridge that used a case only 1.10 inches long as opposed to 1.29 inches for the 45 Colt. Also, the 45 S&W round used a rim diameter .010-inch wider than the 45 Colt's. This gave the S&W extraction system more to push on during cartridge ejection.

The Army agreed to this and ended up having two 45-caliber cartridges in its inventory. The 45 S&W round would function properly through both revolvers, but the 45 Colt cartridge would fit only Colt's revolvers. Incidentally, military

loadings consisted of 250-grain bullets over 30 grains blackpowder in the Colt round, and 230-grain bullets over 28 grains blackpowder in S&W's round.

Naturally, having two kinds of 45-caliber revolver ammunition led to problems. Some units were issued the S&W Schofield revolver, but were sent 45 Colt loads which would not chamber in those guns. Also, from personal experience, I can say that if the shorter 45 S&W cartridge is fired first in the Colt SAA revolvers, the blackpowder fouling in the chambers will not allow chambering of the longer 45 Colt rounds until after a thorough cleaning.

(For years many gunwriters have quibbled in print over the correct name for 45 Colt. They say it should not be called "45 Long Colt" because there never has been a "45 Short Colt." No, there has not, but there was a 45 S&W, which was shorter than the 45 Colt and which could be fired in any 45 Colt handgun. That is why the old timers referred to one as 45 Long and the other as 45 Short.)

Despite glowing reports by some officers, the S&W Schofield's service with the U.S. Army was short; most probably due to the cartridge confusion problem. By 1880, the S&W Schofield model was declared surplus and sold. Many ended up in the hands of arms dealers and had their barrels shortened to 5 inches for resale. One famous purchaser was the Wells, Fargo Express Company. However, it should be noted that 5-inch Schofields were shortened after they left the factory and were not originally produced that way.

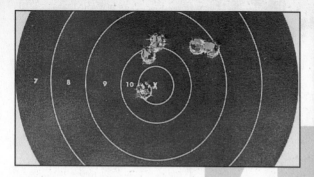

The author's second test Navy Arms Schofield #52 was sighted very close to point of aim with a variety of loads. This group was fired with the new 3-D factory load.

Author Venturino firing Navy Arms' Schofield. He is very fond of them.

The Navy Arms Schofield will be chambered for 44-40 and 45 Colt calibers (left and center). Original S&W Schofields were made only in 45 S&W caliber (right).

LOAD CHART

| —Bullet— | | Load | MV | Group |
Wgt.Grs.	Type	(Grs./Powder)	(fps)	(ins.)
250	H&G #22	8.0/Universal Clays	821	2¼
250	Lyman #454190	8.0/Unique	839	3
230	RCBS #45-225CAV	27.0/Goex FFg	731	2⅞
255		Winchester Factory Load	799	2½
255		3-D Factory Load	779	2¼
225		Federal Factory Load	817	3

All loads were chronographed at 6 feet using Oehler Model 35P.
All loads were fired for accuracy at 25 yards from sandbag rest.
All handloads except the blackpowder load used Winchester brass and Winchester large pistol primers.
Blackpowder load used Starline brass shortened to 1.10 inches to duplicate original 45 S&W cartridge. Primer was Federal #155 Magnum large pistol.

NAVY ARMS

building their Schofields, the U.S. army also adopted the Colt SAA 45 with 7½-inch barrels as the standard sidearm for cavalry troops.

In my collection I have an 1873/1973 Peacemaker Centennial Commemorative. These guns in 45-caliber were built to exactly duplicate the Colt SAA as issued to the cavalry in the 1870s. Grips are one-piece walnut and stamped with inspector's cartouche. A "US" is stamped into the

frame on the left side, just like originals. The frame is of the so-called "blackpowder style" with a screw securing the base pin. Even the sights are the extra-fine style as found on originals.

At my private range, I pitted that Colt SAA 45 and the new Navy Arms Schofield 45 against one another. I found that the Colt is faster for repeat shots than the Schofield because recoil turns the gun upward and places the hammer near the cocking thumb. The Schofield does not turn upward so much during recoil, so the hand must shift position on the butt to cock the hammer.

Also, I feel that the Schofield does not "point" as naturally as the Colt SAA. However, I must temper that statement by admitting that I have 25-plus years of experience in handling Colts, but less than one year with the Schofield.

We now get to what was the Schofield's main positive attribute, quick reloading. Using a PACT Mark IV timer, I clocked myself firing six loads through the Colt SAA, reloading six and firing them all again. Then I did the same exercise with the Schofield. I fired as quickly as possible at 10 yards, and all would have stayed on a human-size target. To get the twelve rounds off with the Colt SAA required 31.35 seconds. I shaved about five seconds off with the Schofield by firing twelve rounds in only 25.96 seconds. It is a faster gun to operate.

Also, it must be noted that loading and unloading the Colt SAA requires two hands. There is just no way to do it one-handed. However, I was able to load and unload the Schofield using only my right hand, my left holding onto a fictional horse's reins. I cradled the revolver under my left arm, and reloading was not a difficult operation. ●

HANDGUNS 96

Self-Defense Scene

Cooper and company lend expertise, page 74.

Distaff doctrine on defense, page 90.

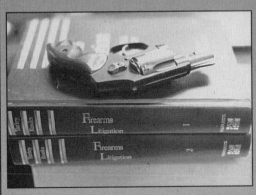

Law, litigation and lethal force, page 95.

THE EXPERTS'
TOP PICKS FOR
HOME DEFENSE

PANEL DISCUSSION

Jeff Cooper

John Dean "Jeff" Cooper is generally considered to be the father of modern combat pistolcraft. The founder of the International Practical Shooting Confederation (IPSC), he was its first president, and is its Lifetime Chairman. At his Gunsite ranch in Arizona, Jeff taught innovative techniques in self-defense handgun shooting to generations of avid shooters.

Born in 1920, Cooper served in the Pacific in the Marines and rose to the rank of Lieutenant Colonel. A former adjunct professor of police science at Northern Arizona University and director of the American Pistol Institute, Cooper is today a member of the board of directors of the National Rifle Association.

His philosophies appear in his many books, which include *Fighting Handguns, Another Country, Principles of Personal Defense, Cooper on Handguns, Fireworks,* and *To Ride, Shoot Straight and Speak the Truth.*

Cooper was handgun editor of *Guns & Ammo* magazine for 20 years and is now editor at large for *Guns & Ammo,* where his sometimes controversial monthly column, "Cooper's Corner," is enjoyed by all avid handgunners.

Massad Ayoob

Massad Ayoob is director of Lethal Force Institute, which offers training to private citizens in the judicious use of deadly force. Ayoob's best-selling book, *In the Gravest Extreme,* offers insight into the private use of handguns in self-defense situations. Ayoob has been national director of firearms and deadly force training for the American Society of Law Enforcement Trainers since 1987, and sits on that association's Ethics Committee. Ayoob completed two terms as co-vice chair of the Forensic Evidence Committee of the National Association of Criminal Defense Lawyers. Ayoob has been a police officer for more than twenty years, serving in all ranks from patrolman to captain. Ayoob is handgun editor for *Guns* magazine.

T wo and a half million citizens defend themselves every year with firearms, according to criminologist Gary Kleck of the University of Florida. Many of these attacks occur in the home, and, as a result, home-owners are buying handguns in unprecedented numbers.

Unfortunately, many of these homeowners are first-time gun buyers and, as non-enthusiasts, make uninformed choices in the handgun they select. Many of us, novice and experienced shooter alike, do not seek instruction on how to effectively use the handgun we have purchased and are ignorant of self-defense law. We thought it would be a good idea to see what the experts recommend.

In the pages that follow, five of the world's top self-defense instructors and competitive shooters give their recommendations for a home-defense handgun and the reasons for their choices. They address their responses to men, women, senior citizens, and families with children. We told them to assume the homeowner is not an avid shooter.

Then, Paxton Quigley, author of *Armed and Female* and *Not An Easy Target,* gives insight into the psychology of self-defense shooting instruction.

To close out our self-defense section, Massad Ayoob, police veteran for more than twenty years, tells how the law views the use of deadly force in self-defense and advises the handgun owner how to deal with the law if involved in a shooting.

Jo Anne Hall

Jo Anne Hall was the former women's shooting editor for *Guns & Ammo* magazine, and currently is field editor for *Women and Guns* magazine.

Ms. Hall first picked up a handgun in September, 1983. The very next year she became the ladies national IPSC champion, and in 1986 was the ladies' champion at the World Speed Shooting Championships.

Ms. Hall was also Texas state ladies champion, winner of the Kansas Indoor Nationals, and in addition to numerous other shooting achievements was third in world standings as a member of the Ladies' Team USA at the 1986 IPSC World Championships.

Mentioned in the 1980-81 "Who's Who of American Business Women," Ms. Hall has represented the National Rifle Association in national TV and print advertising campaigns, has spoken out for women and handguns on national TV on "Geraldo" and "Hard Copy," and in print in *Mademoiselle* and *Glamour* magazines. She was recently a featured guest on "Women in the Outdoors."

Today Ms. Hall lives in the Dallas area with her husband and their 4-year-old daughter.

Chuck Taylor

Chuck Taylor is an adjunct professor of police science, court-recognized expert witness and the first Four-Weapon Combat Master. A decorated Vietnam veteran and qualified for Airborne, Air-Assault and Ranger operations, Taylor is also an NRA-certified rifle/pistol instructor. He is a former world-class IPSC competitor and U.S. IPSC Team member.

He is the founder and director of the American Small Arms Academy and for the last ten years has been credited by the shooting press as being one of the four best trainers in the world. He has been involved in the training of Tactical Response Teams for the Olympic Games, and hundreds of police, SWAT and counter-terrorist law enforcement groups worldwide.

Taylor has had over 800 magazine articles and three books published on weapons and tactics.

Bill Jordan

Bill Jordan, now 84, was a U.S. border patrolman for many years. A big man, his ability to draw his handgun and hit his target in the blink of an eye made him feared and respected all along the border. When he retired, he became field representative at large for the National Rifle Association. He has appeared on national TV many times, representing the Border Patrol and/or the NRA.

He has hunted all continents and has made numerous trips to Africa. His classic book on gunfighting and handguns, *No Second Place Winner*, is still in print, as is his *Mostly Huntin'*. Jordan's new book, *Tales of the Rio Grande*, will be out soon.

A skilled and knowledgeable outdoor and shooting writer, he has been on the staff of various shooting magazines over the years, including *Gunsport, Guns, Peterson's Hunting*, and *Guns & Ammo*. Bill Jordan today is shooting editor of *Shooting Times* magazine.

Home Defense

Jeff Cooper

THE IDEAL PERSONAL arm for house defense is a shotgun—preferably a 12-gauge double with exposed hammers and shortened barrel and stock. Known as the *lupara* in Sicily, this shotgun is easy to use, devastatingly effective, and may be kept at the ready indefinitely in an uncocked condition with no springs compressed. The *lupara*, however, is not likely to be the first choice of a present-day American householder, partly because it is uncommon, and partly because it is less than handy if the householder chooses to go abroad and be armed at the same time. Any shotgun is bulky and awkward to use under conditions of unreadiness. A handgun is much handier, easier to come by, and will serve well for home defense—if not quite as well as the shotgun.

However, the selection of a handgun for home defense should be considered with some care, since the circumstances under which it may be used require different levels of competence of the householder. It is essential to remember that fighting efficiency depends more upon the shooter than on his gun. A first-rate man with a third-rate arm is much more likely to succeed than a third-rate man with a first-rate arm.

It is thus of paramount importance to look first at the householder and only thereafter at the piece he chooses. The handgun is not the easiest weapon to dominate—in fact there is a widespread myth to the effect that nobody can hit anything with a pistol. This, of course, is not true. However, the fact that a vast number of people acquire a handgun without troubling to learn to use it well lends support to that myth. Also, generations of soldiers and policemen have been introduced unsuccessfully to the handgun. They have failed to dominate it partly through ignorance of proper training techniques, but mostly through simple lack of enthusiasm on the part of the student.

No one does anything well unless he enjoys doing it. And so we immediately run into the division between the shooting enthusiast and the "reluctant dragon." One who shoots as a recreation and who regards any given month as incomplete without at least one practice session on the range falls into a different category from one who regards his weapons as burdensome nuisances. There are, of course, degrees of enthusiasm between the hotshot and the timid soul, but at some point along the way, the intelligent choice of weapons encounters a fork in the road. Many years ago when I kicked off the law enforcement revolution from the revolver to the self-loading pistol, I was not aware that most policemen are just not interested in shooting. In those days, the establishment was quite content with the revolver, and if the future could have been foreseen, it should have stayed that way. The self-loading pistol ("auto pistol," "automatic pistol,"

"semi-automatic pistol") is a distinctly more effective defensive sidearm than any revolver. That's simply because it is easier to hit with, and in a lethal confrontation only hits count—a point largely ignored in the public sector. What makes it easier to hit with is its single-action trigger mechanism, which calls for less skill and talented management than the trigger-cocking mechanism of most revolvers. It is also more compact for equivalent power, and its recoil thrust is somewhat mitigated by the operations of the mechanism. The fact that it usually carries more cartridges at the ready than the revolver is of minor consequence. Unless you are repelling a horde of savages armed with spears and clubs, you don't need a lot of shots in a fight. What you do need is a controlled number of hits, and you can obtain these with either the auto-pistol or the revolver. This is obvious in the case of house defense, where burglars do not normally run in packs of more than three or four, but rather are usually solitary (so as to avoid having to divide up the swag, if any).

However, where the revolver is basically very simple in operation, the self-loading pistol is somewhat complicated. It is not *very* complicated—nothing like a typewriter or a guitar—but it is more complicated to use and understand than a revolver, and complexity tends to discourage the non-enthusiast. For anyone who shoots for recreation and is willing to attend school and conduct regular practice, the auto-pistol is an unquestioned first choice. But in this embattled age where large numbers of non-enthusiasts have decided to arm themselves, the minor complications of auto-pistol technique may constitute an obstacle. This has certainly been obvious in the great numbers of police departments which have in the past decade shifted from revolvers to autos—with totally unsatisfactory results.

We may assume that most householders who have resolved to arm themselves in the face of the tidal wave of moral turpitude now faced by our society are unlikely to be shooting enthusiasts. This, of course, may change as these people discover that shooting is not only a defensive technique, but also a delightful entertainment. This attitude may not take hold, however, and for those households in which the pistol is a tool rather than a toy, I think the first choice of weapon should be the revolver. The revolver is simple to operate, its maintenance and manipulation are easy to learn, and while it is somewhat harder to hit with than the auto-pistol, this is not a matter of primary importance when one considers that in most confrontations no shots are fired. And in those cases in which they *are* fired, the range is so short that hitting your target is not an overwhelming chore.

There are those who will maintain that a good man with a revolver hits just as well as a good man with an auto-pistol.

To the extent that this is true, and competition does not suggest that it is, the subject here is that of expert skill. A master of the revolver is impressive to watch and takes no back seat to the semi-auto shooter, but this is the master, and there are not very many of those. Moreover they are certainly not found amongst the non-enthusiasts.

In a lethal confrontation, the overwhelming motive of the defender is to stop the fight. To do this, he must first of all hit his target. He can learn to do this with appropriate instruction and practice. Secondly, he must hit his target *hard*. Pistols, in general, are not very powerful, and there can hardly be a more nightmarish experience than to tag your adversary just below the wishbone and have him pay no attention to the wound. Consequently, when you choose a handgun for house defense, you must consider the matter of stopping power, which is a subject in itself. (There is a substitute for stopping power, and that is extremely precise placement, a subject we will discuss shortly.) The third major consideration is that of speed. The only reason you may have for shooting at another human being is the fact that he is trying to kill you, and that he probably will succeed if you do not stop him. Thus you have to stop him quickly before he can accomplish his purpose. Once the techniques are learned, there is no significant difference between the revolver and the semi-auto in the time it takes to get off the first shot. But if the auto-pistol must be made ready to fire before use, it surrenders a speed edge to the revolver, which is normally kept ready to go with a simple pull on the trigger.

The self-loading pistol is a distinctly more effective defensive sidearm than any revolver. That's simply because it is easier to hit with, and in a lethal confrontation only hits count.

In dividing householders into those who are going to be shooting enthusiasts and those who are not, we should bear in mind that in some households one partner may be a shooter while the other is not. As either may be called upon to defend house and home, it may be unwise to choose a weapon which is only going to be efficient in the hands of one partner. For such households, I have long felt that the answer is two guns—one for the papa and one for the mama. We all realize, from Kipling and others, that the female of the species may be more deadly than the male, but the fact remains that most women do not relish the idea of killing things. Whether most *men* do or not is a subject for a gradu-

ate seminar in weaponcraft. Anyway, the householder need not be a recreational killer in order to become an expert marksman, but when we enter the subject of the combat mindset, we find that one does the job better if one enjoys his work.

There can hardly be a more nightmarish experience than to tag your adversary just below the wishbone and have him pay no attention to the wound.

Back to choice of weapons. I maintain that there is no question but that the most efficient handgun for house defense is the major-caliber single-action self-loading pistol, *assuming that the householder is going to make a hobby of his shooting*. If he is not, he is better advised to avoid the auto-pistol and go to a major caliber double-action revolver. One of the best is the S&W Model 625. Speaking roughly, one can say that a major-caliber pistol is one whose cartridge is of 10mm or 40-caliber, or greater, and fires a projectile of at least 200 grains at a velocity approaching or exceeding 900 fps. Unfortunately, most revolvers that fit this requirement, including the 625, are excessively bulky, but there are exceptions. Additionally, the bulk of a house defense handgun is not a major consideration, since the weapon is going to be kept at home most of the time.

Safety in the selection of a house gun is a subject often brought up by those who have not looked thoroughly into the matter. No firearm can be any more or less safe than another since firearms are designed as lethal weapons, and if they are not effectively lethal they are not useful. As the Russian firearms instructor is said to have said, "*Safe? Eez gon. Eez not safe!*"

Guns may never be characterized as safe or unsafe, but shooters may. A household may well be composed of various sorts of people, some of whom cope, while others do not. This is not entirely a matter of age. Any well-balanced child who is large enough and strong enough to operate a firearm can be taught the principles of firearm safety. If, on the other hand, the household is inhabited by a little monster, or several little monsters, who cannot be taught to do what they are told, certain complications arise. In those houses, the defensive firearm must be kept out of reach of the little monsters. My wife and I never had this problem because we introduced our three children to firearms as soon as they were strong enough to stand up and hold them.

Jeff Cooper

A house defense revolver is normally kept fully loaded and ready. It may be fired either by thumb-cocking it first or by pressing the trigger straight back and cocking the hammer with this same action. (This is why it is called "double action.") This is a safe method of maintenance in the custody of responsible people. General Rule: No instrument is safe in the hands of irresponsible people.

The self-loading or semi-automatic pistol may be maintained in any one of four conditions:

- **Condition One:** Fully loaded, cocked and locked.
- **Condition Two:** Fully loaded, hammer down.
- **Condition Three:** "Half-loaded" with a full magazine in place, but no cartridge in the chamber.
- **Condition Four:** Completely unloaded, magazine out, chamber empty.

Here we have a complexity, and complexity is one of the reasons why we tend to favor the revolver over the self-loading pistol for house defense. Well-educated, fully responsible people will have no trouble with selecting the condition of greatest satisfaction for their needs. It may sound uppity to say it, but it is a fact that "others need not apply."

This raises the matter of gender or age differentiation. If an elderly person is not incapacitated or of reduced manual dexterity, there is no reason to make a special distinction based on age. Most women have smaller bones in their hands and less muscle than most men. If a woman or senior citizen finds that a heavy-duty auto-pistol or a heavy-caliber

---

I have always felt better about the 22 than about the miniature centerfire cartridges because the 22 encourages practice.

---

revolver is uncomfortable to handle or difficult to manipulate, there are some worthwhile alternatives.

One of the first is the minor-caliber, centerfire, compact double-action revolver. There are several of these on the market, and they are dainty enough to be used by women with small hands and light muscles. One of the best is the S&W LadySmith. To achieve compactness, it is necessary to come down a step in power, and this raises questions about the second requirement of a defensive weapon—that of stopping power. Compact revolvers come in cartridges which must be considered compromises. A major-caliber pistol cartridge may be counted upon to cause one's adversary to cease and desist nearly always with one well-placed shot in the center of the chest. The minor-caliber pistol cartridge can be counted upon to do this about half of the time—true of both

the 38 Special and 9mm Parabellum cartridges. However, the discussion need not end here, for there are certain mitigating factors to consider. Nobody wants to get shot with *anything*, and as soon as a handgun is presented to one's adversary, there is a good chance that he will call off the war without any shots being fired. Of course, we cannot count on this, but it is nonetheless an important factor. Secondly, there is the matter of placement. Where a solid hit in the center of mass does not stop one's adversary, a center hit in the eye sockets certainly will. The double-action compact revolver has a certain advantage here in that it can be thumb-cocked and fired with great precision, once the knack has been acquired, and this certainly permits the house defender to stop the fight with at least the second shot with neat placement to the tear duct.

This matter of precise placement introduces the option of the 22. There are a number of well-made compact 22 autopistols on the market. They are usually paralleled by the same weapon in a centerfire cartridge, such as the 380 (9mm Short) or the 32 ACP. I have always felt better about the 22 than about the miniature centerfire cartridges because the 22 encourages practice, whereas the ammunition for the centerfires is much more expensive. A family which opts for a 22 compact auto, for example the Walther PPK, will find it pleasant to take the little piece along on picnics and work with it until all members of the family can hit a pingpong ball at ten paces practically every time. Now then, if the lady of the house (or the gentleman, if we wish to use that term) can *always* hit a pingpong ball at ten paces with her 22, all she needs to save her life and that of her children is *stress control. To win your fight you have to keep your head.* If you can, a 22 will probably do the job perfectly. If you cannot, it is unlikely that a 44 Magnum will do the job any better.

I like the odds to be in my favor. Consequently, I like to use a fight-stopping cartridge as long as I can control it, and I have been working on this for longer than many of my readers have been alive. I prefer the 45 ACP as a defensive pistol round, just as I prefer the 460 Special rifle cartridge, or its equivalent, on Cape buffalo. However, I am an enthusiast, and if I am to advise a non-enthusiast, it might be better to stick with a cartridge you know you can control and rely upon making the head shot if all else fails.

Above all, you must remember that it is the *man* who wins the fight, *not his gun.* And if a woman is reduced by desperate circumstances to engage in the unladylike pastime of lethal combat, it will be the woman and not her weapon that wins the fight. Defensive combat is a deadly serious business and should not be considered lightly. If you do not feel you are up to it, forget the house gun and call 911. The police will show up in due course. ●

Home Defense

Massad Ayoob

IT SHOULD BE understood in all the cases and situations that follow that the advice given is with a view toward a newcomer to firearms. The experienced handgun user can make a lot of high-performance technology stand up and do tricks. The relatively simple and basic handguns suggested here will keep the new shooter alive and safe long enough to become an old hand.

Female

Women's hand sizes generally run smaller than men's, and men designed handguns for themselves. Women's fashions seldom allow for dress gunbelts, meaning that smaller handguns allow them to "carry" when 45s might be left at home. The Colt 1911A1 45 auto and the Browning Hi-Power 9mm work superbly for small-handed women as shooting guns, but many find them too large to carry.

Any good armorer or gunsmith can make any small-frame S&W revolver into a "LadySmith" by taking a couple of coils off the trigger return spring and polishing the serrations off the front of the trigger, but the new LadySmiths come without those serrations anyway. Colt has reintroduced the excellent Detective Special D-frame series of compact six-shooters, and these fit the small-to-medium female hand splendidly. The slightly longer trigger stroke gives a lighter pull. The Colt with its leaf mainspring is easier to shoot well than the slightly smaller revolvers of other brands that work off coil mainsprings.

In the S&W line, the Centennial hammerless is extremely popular among knowledgeable women. Fashions are such that women more often than men need to carry their guns "off body," and a hammerless can fire right through a purse. A standard revolver's hammer can catch its firing pin on a purse or pocket lining as it falls, preventing the shot.

A majority of violent criminals are misogynists who would rather die than surrender to a woman, even at gunpoint, so women are at higher risk of disarming attempts than men. This is an argument for a gun with manual safety and magazine disconnector safety features, such as the S&W Model 3913 9mm series, which is extremely popular as a carry gun among female firearms instructors. However, most women don't care for autoloaders until they've "gotten into shooting." The 2-inch 38 LadySmith makes the most sense in such cases, because it's the hardest gun to take away from someone. There's little for the disarmer to hang onto, and the leverage is mostly with the person holding it by the grip.

Recoil can be nasty with the 158-grain all-lead 38 +P hollowpoints most experts recommend, but it's nothing a small woman in good health, with no hand injuries, can't handle. Once she's fired enough of the +P ammo to develop confidence, she can do most of her practice with lighter loads. In a real fight, she won't notice the recoil.

Male

If you're the "average adult male," congratulations: Almost all the handguns in the gunshop, like the suits on the rack at the men's store, were designed to fit you. Unless you're a lifeguard or work with the Chippendales, your wardrobe probably allows you to discreetly conceal a full-size handgun. What you have to do is remember the one thing Dirty Harry had right: "A man has got to know his limitations."

Average adult males are disproportionately represented in fatal or crippling accidents involving firearms and motorcycles alike, and not just because they're the predominant users of both. In either case, there's something in the male psyche that says, "I have an X chromosome, ergo, I automatically know all there is to know about vehicles, power tools, and firearms." There's a word for people with that attitude: victims.

> **A** majority of violent criminals are misogynists who would rather die than surrender to a woman, even at gunpoint.

Joe Gun-Buyer needs to remind himself, his first time at the gunshop, of something his sister and his grandfather instinctively recognize: One doesn't want to bite off more than one is equipped to chew. The double-action revolver is to the autoloading pistol as the Chevy Caprice is to the Corvette Stingray. The latter can deliver more performance, but its sensitive handling characteristics demand more experienced hands at the controls. Those unwilling to commit the time and effort to master the higher performance machine should stay with the simpler revolver: It will be more forgiving of error or inexperience, and it will still get them where they need to go.

A perceived firepower race with the criminal element has caused American police to switch from service revolvers to semi-automatic pistols. As a result, the used gun market has been flooded with nearly new and generally superbly maintained 38 Special and 357 Magnum revolvers of 2- to (predominantly) 4-inch barrel length. The 357, of course, handles either cartridge, so the person new to the technology can start with 158-grain all-lead +P 38 Special hollowpoints, the recoil of which any average male can handle if he simply stands correctly and holds the gun right. With training and practice, the average man can quickly learn to control 125-grain 357 Magnum hollowpoints, widely conceded to be the ultimate "manstoppers" of the handgun ammo world. With compact "boot grips" of the design pioneered by Craig Spegel and now widely sold by Uncle Mike's and others, and a good, affordable inside-the-waistband holster like the Bianchi #3 or Alessi Talon, a 4-inch medium-frame 357 Magnum can conceal as well under a jacket or sweater as a snubnose 38.

Don't overlook the fact that when cops still had these revolvers, they were winning the vast majority of their gun battles with armed criminals. These traded-in service revolvers sell in my area for $125 to $275 and represent perhaps the best bargain in the handgun market today. You can get a revolver and buckets of training ammo for the price of an equivalent-quality autoloader, and a cool, trained man with a revolver will invariably beat a bozo with an automatic. Remember the last time you discussed the battle of the genders with your significant other and told her how we were the practical ones? Well....

Senior Citizen

When age and arthritis make things difficult to manipulate, the double-action revolver makes the most sense because of its ease of administrative handling (loading, unloading, etc.). However, a revolver requires a trigger pull several times the gun's weight to make it fire, and hands no longer strong or well-coordinated may not be able to deliver the rapid, accurate fire needed in a defensive situation.

An autoloader would be easier to shoot well, but manipulation of the slide will be difficult if the afflictions of age have robbed the hands of strength and agility. After all, many strong, healthy males find double-stack pistol magazines difficult to load, and when strength and dexterity are impaired, "difficult" may become "impossible."

When cops still had these revolvers, they were winning the vast majority of their gun battles with armed criminals.

Enter the Beretta 86, the pistol that solves this particular problem. It is built around the tip-up barrel design popularized by the same firm's little 22s and 25s, but chambered for the 380 ACP (9mm Short) cartridge. Like Beretta's standard Model 85, the 86's grip frame is built for eight-round capacity around a single-stack magazine, allowing even the small or debilitated hand a reasonably firm grasp.

The manual safety is located on the frame, and the design permits four different options of loaded condition. One is

loaded magazine/empty chamber, which will be slow to get into action. Two others are fully loaded with trigger in double-action position, on-safe or off-safe as the owner chooses. However, now we're back to great difficulty in delivering a fast, accurate shot under stress. With debilitated hands, the best bet is something I wouldn't normally recommend for the young and able-bodied: cocked and locked (Condition One) with a round in the chamber.

An intruder at gunpoint might think he had a better chance to disarm a frail pensioner than a man of thirty, so the older armed citizen is probably at more risk of a disarming attempt.

This puts the trigger in a rearward position, easily contacted with good leverage, making it less likely that the shot will go wild. The safety disengages with a simple downward push of the thumb just like a Colt 1911 or Browning Hi-Power.

An intruder at gunpoint might think he had a better chance to disarm a frail pensioner than a man of thirty, so the older armed citizen is probably at more risk of a disarming attempt. The Beretta 86 has two excellent features in this regard. Beretta 380s, unlike the firm's larger-caliber pistols, have magazine disconnector safeties: If the owner feels the gun being torn out of his hand, he can press the magazine release button, dumping the magazine and rendering the round in the chamber unshootable as long as the trigger has not been held back during the process. While the bad guy tries to make the gun shoot, the homeowner has bought time for Plan B.

The manual safety on the frame is also an advantage here. Numerous cops are alive today, along with at least a couple of armed citizens, because criminals got their guns away and tried to shoot them, but couldn't figure out how to release the safety catches.

In terms of stopping power, the 380 is right at the razor's edge of acceptability. However, it also has very light recoil, and this is a major concern in a group where arthritis is common. You can use Cor-Bon's hot 380 +P ammo to bring it up to about the power of the Russian 9mm Makarov, but recoil increases accordingly. Standard hollowpoints like the Federal Hydra-Shok or Winchester Silvertip would be my choice. This is one 380 that feeds wide-mouth hollowpoints flawlessly. The Beretta 86 is also unusually tolerant of being fired with a weak or unlocked wrist, more so than most other auto pistols.

The tip-up design allows the chamber to be loaded without

muscling a slide against a recoil spring. With a magazine loading device like the SuperThumb, its single-stack magazine can be almost effortlessly loaded with even badly disabled hands. Selling for under $400, the 86 is perhaps the ideal defensive handgun choice for a person whose hands and upper body strength have been ravaged by age.

Of course, if the senior citizen is in good shape, he can use a "younger man's gun." I've trained two men of eighty-four. One was near the top of his class with the Colt Government 45 auto he'd used all his life. The other, new to the handgun, did more than well enough to defend his life with an action-slicked S&W Model 686 357 loaded with 38 Specials.

Family

Once the parents decide that an accessible, loaded handgun will enhance their home security against intruders, their real problem now lies with their children, if they are not yet at a responsible age. They must at all costs be kept from accessing the loaded home defense gun.

T he device is called a MagnaTrigger and was patented by an inventor, now deceased, named (no kidding) Joe Smith.

I'm on record as saying that you can't child-proof your guns, you must gun-proof your children instead. Unfortunately, kids not yet at an age of responsibility are too young to be gun-proofed, so we have to make the best effort we can at child-proofing the guns. That best effort, in terms of everything I've turned up in my own research and all that Sandia Labs and the National Institute of Justice have come up with in their quest for a "smart gun"—one that only fires for the designated user—is a concept developed twenty years ago.

The device is called a MagnaTrigger and was patented by an inventor, now deceased, named (no kidding) Joe Smith. His original concept was to create a police service revolver that could not be turned against its user by a gun-snatching cop killer. It turns out to be equally effective for armed citizens, not only for thwarting burglars who get their hands on the gun in question before the homeowner, but also for making the gun virtually unshootable in the hands of a child who has stumbled upon it.

Now available from a single source (Rick Devoid, Boscawen, NH) for $350 including installation and shipping, the MagnaTrigger is applied to a K-frame or larger Smith & Wesson revolver. The bottom line is that the modified gun can only be fired by someone wearing a special magnetic ring.

Devoid charges an additional $35 to render the gun double-action-only, a good idea for reasons that will shortly become apparent.

A segment is cut out of the front of the grip frame, and the MagnaTrigger module is fitted there. It has a part that blocks the internal rebound slide, preventing the gun from firing. However, when a finger wearing the special MagnaTrigger magnetic ring grasps the gun in a normal firing position, reverse polarity from the magnet on the ring interacts with a magnet in the mechanism, flipping the block aside and allowing the gun to fire. As soon as the hand leaves the gun, the module returns to "No Shoot" condition.

The only way it can normally be bypassed is if the double-action revolver were cocked by the designated user before it fell into unauthorized hands; in that case, it can be fired once by anyone who pulls the trigger. This is why I recommend that the modified gun also be rendered double-action-only.

Counting the price of a good used S&W K-, L- or N-frame revolver (the only designs on which the modification can be performed at this time), the completed gun still costs less than a high-tech 9mm new in the box. For a gun no one but you or someone you designate can fire, that's cheap in my account ledger. The ring is worn on the middle finger, and you want one for each hand in case you have to fire weak-hand only. Two rings are included in the $350 package, and additional rings for competent users you designate are $40 apiece.

The MagnaTrigger on my S&W Model 66 Combat 357 Magnum got me through two rug-rats who now own their own handguns. I slept with a loaded revolver near the bed, knowing that unauthorized fingers could not make it shoot, and I slept well. A MagnaTriggered S&W revolver is the best

C ounting the price of a good used S&W K-, L- or N-frame revolver, the completed gun still costs less than a high-tech 9mm new in the box.

recommendation I could make for a handgun owner who wanted to have a loaded sidearm instantly accessible while minimizing the danger of a child doing something awful with it. The MagnaTrigger doesn't make routine firearms safety and storage practices unnecessary; it just adds one more enormously effective and important layer of safety and protection.

Combine the appropriate choice of one of the above simple handguns with good basic training, and you'll be in good shape to defend your home. ●

Home Defense

Jo Anne Hall

IF THERE TRULY were one handgun that would suffice for all individuals, there would not be as many different types on the market. Buying a handgun, like selecting a pair of shoes, is a personal choice based on fit, function and compromise. With the proper gun fit and training, most people are capable of handling a firearm that delivers greater force and stopping power than they might have at first believed. However, your selection probably will be a compromise between what you want to purchase and what you can effectively handle.

Through my experiences teaching self-defense shooting, I have had to become more flexible on my position as to what people should buy for personal safety. My personal choice for self-defense is a 45 ACP, but it is not the right choice for everyone. Special considerations need to be made when selecting a home defense gun: grip strength, size of your hands, physical strength, and willingness to take proper instruction. One thing I would not scrimp on is cost. Your firearm may be more of a life-saver than a dishwasher or a refrigerator, and the purchase should certainly be treated with as much importance.

The number one concern is firepower or knock-down power. You want to select the maximum caliber load you can effectively shoot. Assailants in this day and time are all too often high on alcohol and/or drugs. In many cases even the largest of calibers will not stop them immediately. So I would take a serious approach to caliber selection.

Equally important is making sure you can handle your pistol safely and effectively. If you find it hard to hold a 44 Magnum revolver steady, then chances are you won't be very accurate with it. You must feel comfortable handling, loading and unloading the handgun of your choice and be confident that you can hit your target. I don't agree with the premise that the mere presence of a handgun is a sufficient intimidation factor. Yes, often the appearance of a firearm is enough to ward off an attack, but don't be lured into a false sense of security just because you brandish a big gun. If you point your gun at an assailant, be ready to use it.

Assailants in this day and time are all too often high on alcohol and/or drugs. In many cases even the largest of calibers will not stop them immediately.

I recommend quality firearms in the medium-to-high price range. When you spend a little more for a firearm, you will usually spend less time and money with your gunsmith and more time on the range. The solid, well-built guns I have chosen are ready to shoot with little or no modification. One thing about a high-quality handgun is that it can always be modified to fit specific individual needs later. Because we are looking at home defense, concealability is not a factor. Before anyone buys a gun, I think he should look at all different makes, models and calibers, and then get professional instruction in order to learn the safe and proper way to use it. With these parameters in mind, here are my choices.

Female

If a woman of average physical stature and strength walks in and asks me what handgun to buy, I would tell her to get a Browning Hi-Power. This 9mm semi-automatic has been around a long time and is well made, reliable and easy to fire right out of the box. We want the most firepower we can get in any defensive situation, and the 9mm is a very manageable caliber in a medium-frame design. Petite "pocket" guns are hard to fire accurately, even in the smaller hands of a lady, and are not good home defense guns.

The 9mm cartridge has seen a great upsurge in popularity in the U.S., primarily because our military switched to this caliber in the early 1980s. As a result we have a wide selection of defensive loads. The 9mm is the perfect compromise between the 45 ACP and 380 ACP, and the best choice for a home defense handgun for women.

The Browning is not too heavy to handle, weighing about 4 pounds fully loaded, but has enough weight to keep recoil at a controllable level. The 4¾-inch barrel is long enough to help accuracy and still give good balance. The Hi-Power has a high-capacity ten-round magazine yet maintains a slim grip.

The reason I chose a single-action semi-automatic is due to its ease of operation. Once loaded, it is instantly ready to fire repeatedly. Loading a gun is intimidating for any novice whether you "rack the slide" on a semi-automatic or drop open the cylinder of a revolver. With practice, the operation of pulling the slide back to load or unload the firearm is no more of a problem than opening the cylinder and pushing out the cases on a revolver. If the spring on the slide is too heavy, a lighter spring can be inserted by a gunsmith. About 75 percent of the women I have instructed who had little or no experience in handling pistols prefer a semi-automatic and can fire one accurately after 30 minutes of instruction.

Operating a single-action trigger seems to be the easiest and most accurate method of firing, as well. Using a double-action trigger, especially on a revolver, requires the shooter to maintain a steady grip while pressing the trigger through both the cocking and the firing actions. This is not an easy task for the novice, not if you expect her to fire accurately also. All too often the individual will pull the shots to the right or left of the target. Many will argue that the individual can manually cock the hammer and then fire. This is fine for target shooting, but in a defensive situation it is not practical.

A double-action/single-action trigger is not as difficult, but I don't see the need for it in a home-defense gun. I am not a great fan of the double-action trigger and decocking safety. I prescribe to the K.I.S.S. theory in firearms: Keep It Super Simple. Perhaps it is because of my competition background and love of the Colt 1911. Simply stated, a single-action trigger is easier to fire.

Other factors to consider when buying a handgun are adjustable sights, grip style and gun finish. Sights and finish are not nearly as important as grips. A comfortable grip style is imperative to recoil management and gun control. If the stock is too wide, you can't maintain your grasp under recoil. If it is too slick or narrow, you have the same problem. I have always been partial to the Pachmayr wrap-around grips, which I have on my competition Colt.

It is a toss-up as to which brand and model to choose because I like both the Ruger GP161 and the Colt King Cobra Model 3060.

Gun finish is an important consideration for care and storage. Blued steel is less resistant to adverse conditions than is stainless steel or chrome, and the gun must be wiped down and cared for properly. Even your own body chemistry can be corrosive to gun finishes. If given the choice, it is never a bad idea to go for the chrome or stainless model; the extra $60 or so will be worthwhile.

Adjustable sights are not necessary on a home defense firearm, but they can be helpful. Not all guns hit precisely where you are aiming. Even the choice of ammunition affects accuracy from one model pistol to the other. You might find that your firearm prefers Federal Hydra-Shok over Winchester Sivertips, or vice versa. If your gun already shoots a bit to the right, it may be even less accurate with another brand of ammunition. Adjustable sights give you more flexibility in your choice of ammo, and that can give you confidence your gun will hit where you're aiming.

With the Silver Chrome model Browning Hi-Power, all of the features I would recommend in a handgun come as standard equipment: Pachmayr wrap-around grips, satin-chrome finish and an adjustable sight.

Male

For the male, I recommend a 357-caliber revolver. If the user doesn't feel the need to get instruction (Were men really born knowing how to shoot guns?), this wheelgun is easy to learn and operate. Because it has such good balance and accuracy, a 6-inch-barreled 357 has the versatility to function as both a home-defense handgun and a target pistol. When loaded with magnum loads, it has excellent knockdown power, but it can house 38 loads for target practice, saving wear and tear on both the shooter and the gun. Perhaps it is the romance of the old Westerns, but most men really enjoy shooting revolvers and are more likely to take their six-shooter on a hunting trip or to the range on a regular basis for practice and fun. The 357 gives him these options. The only drawback is the number of rounds the cylinder holds. In a defensive situation, you would like to have as many rounds as possible, but practically speaking, if the job can't be done in six shots, chances are you're in trouble anyway!

It is a toss-up as to which brand and model to choose because I like both the Ruger GP161 and the Colt King Cobra Model 3060. Both are well-constructed, moderately priced revolvers. What I really like is that they are already equipped with a smooth trigger action, fully adjustable rear sight and rubber grips. The grips, which aid greatly in cushioning recoil, take the sharp bite off the magnum loads and make the gun actually enjoyable to fire! The grips on older model handguns were often boxy or awkward and usually had to be replaced with more tailored or more cushioned grips. Not so anymore.

The Colt King Cobra has a neoprene grip with combat-style finger grooves for a more secure grasp. The Ruger has a patented "Santoprene" grip with a walnut insert, not only functional but aesthetically pleasing as well. These "custom" features spare you the time and expense of having your firearm worked over by a pistolsmith. Moreover, the combination results in a multi-purpose handgun. Add a satin stainless finish to one and there really isn't much you need to do but sight-in and go!

Senior Citizen

Depending on the physical limitations of the elderly person, the 380-caliber Beretta 86 with its tip-up barrel feature is my selection. As joint mobility and strength decreases in the elderly, gun maneuverability will be affected. The Cheetah 380 pistol features a tip-up barrel that allows easy, direct loading and unloading without having to operate the slide or remove the magazine. It also lets you safely check for a chambered round. This is not only important for safety reasons, but for ease in handling. Equipped with a 4.4-inch barrel, the Model 86 has an overall length of approximately 7 inches and weighs about 23 ounces, small enough to manage, yet with adequate size and weight to help handle recoil. In the home, you don't have to worry about concealability, but the Beretta is small

Jo Anne Hall

enough to carry if need be. Not a bad idea, actually. Better to know one gun well than to own several that you rarely shoot and may not feel comfortable with.

The semi-automatic blow-back design has many of the features found on the larger frame Beretta 92FS, the model chosen by our military forces. The double-action/single-action trigger fires double for the first shot only and then is single action for the remaining shots, until the safety is activated. This design is better for those who may lack the dexterity to operate a double-action-only trigger. Many elderly persons are afflicted to some degree with arthritis. The Beretta, with its ambidextrous safety and double-action/single-action design, is the best firearm for those persons with limited dexterity.

The semi-automatic blow-back design is better for those who may lack the dexterity to operate a double-action-only trigger.

The 380-caliber is not generally my choice for a home-defense cartridge unless the shooter has difficulty with larger-caliber handguns. Certainly heavy recoil and muzzleblast are concerns to elderly users. Until Beretta chambers this model for the 9mm cartridge, the 86 is the best bet. When used with a defensive load such as the Winchester Silvertip, the 380 can be an effective cartridge.

A blue finish is the only option in the Beretta 86, unless you have it plated. I would most likely stay with the checkered walnut grips that come standard, unless you feel the need for cushioned rubber grips They are available from either Pachmayr or Hogue.

Family

As I name my preference for the family with young children, I must preface my choice with the fact that I am the parent of a youngster who is surprisingly strong and hardheaded to boot. It is chilling to think of accidents involving children and handguns, yet the possibility is always there. Not only should we address the issue of a firearm in the home, but also how it should be stored. An easy solution is a gun locking device, but is it the best? If the key is easily accessible to you, it is just as accessible to a child. If not, then the gun may not be readily available in a life-threatening situation.

Plagued with the seriousness of this scenario, I have determined that keeping my semi-automatic loaded, with the hammer down and nothing in the chamber, is the best answer for me. My home-defense gun is a Colt Gold Cup 45 ACP in "Condition Three," and it is my suggestion for the family.

I don't agree with those who say a revolver is the safest gun, or that a semi-automatic is safer with a double-action trigger. Having witnessed youngsters easily fire a double-action trigger using both index fingers, I will argue that it is much safer to have a single-action semi-automatic in the house, as long as there is nothing in the chamber and the hammer is down. Pulling the slide back on a 45 ACP requires more strength and leverage than most children possess. If they are strong enough, they are more than likely old enough to know better. The major drawback is that the gun must then be readied for action by racking the slide. In an emergency situation the operator must have the presence of mind to remember that. Practice drills are advisable, so that it becomes routine. The time and effort involved are worth the peace of mind.

Until the '80s, the 45 ACP was the government issue handgun. Ballistically, it is superior to its 9mm counterpart, but it got a bum rap as being hard to shoot well. With practice and a few modifications, just about anyone can effectively fire the Gold Cup. The Colt Government Model, though similar (both have 5-inch barrels and essentially the same frame), lacks the extra features that come standard on the Gold Cup: adjustable trigger stop, adjustable sights, and an eight-round magazine. The beavertail grip safety keeps the hammer from "biting," and the neoprene wrap-around grips help maintain a secure grasp.

I don't agree with those who say a revolver is the safest gun, or that a semi-automatic is safer with a double-action trigger.

Further modifications, such as a lighter recoil spring and ambidextrous safety, are options that further customize your handgun, but may not be necessary. It might be wise to select a blue finish because it is less flashy to a curious youngster.

Buying a gun is no small matter and should be taken seriously. Try to find a local range that rents guns and "try before you buy." If you lack the finances to purchase the firearm you want, you might look into buying a used gun in good condition. Consult a gunsmith you trust or a knowledgeable friend to help you make that determination. By all means, take your handgun to the range and brush up on your shooting skills at least once a month. It may save your life one day.	●

Chuck Taylor

PANEL DISCUSSION

Home Defense

HERE YOU HAVE my opinions and choices for each home-defense category. However, I would first state that training is extremely important. While its irrefutably true that some guns are easier to use than others, all defensive handguns require at least some training to allow the shooter to achieve his/her full potential. No gun is better or simpler to use—they all have their idiosyncrasies.

Female

For the average female who has little firearms-handling experience, I recommend a DA (double-action) 38 Special revolver. And specifically, I feel that the K-frame Smith & Wesson Model 10 or 64 (stainless) with a 3- or 4-inch barrel is the best choice. Of sufficient size to allow proper grip and satisfactory recoil control, but small enough to carry and conceal without undue difficulty, either one will give good service.

However, the lady in question should be aware of a few things in order to have a realistic perspective. First, the 38 Special, while a highly accurate and popular cartridge, has a reputation for marginal stopping power. This means that, not only should she should be apprised of its limitations, but also that careful marksmanship and ammunition selection is critical.

Both the Model 10 and 64 feature fixed sights, so zeroing, especially at the ranges at which the gun would be used, presents no problem. Nonetheless, she should still take the time to see where it prints at, say, 15 meters, just to be on the safe side.

All double-action revolvers need some minor modifications to enhance their performance. Among these are: 1) narrowing and smoothing of the trigger surface; 2) breaking the sharp edges on each of the chamber mouths by light chamfering; 3) sharp edge removal; 4) action-smoothing; 5) proper stock selection; and 6) wear- and corrosion-resistant finish.

By narrowing, rounding and smoothing the trigger, the "feel"—and thus trigger control—is greatly improved, especially in conjunction with an action-smoothing job. The double-action trigger stroke is the very heart of the DA revolver, and anything that improves this critical function is worth doing, provided the springs are not cut to the point where mechanical reliability is affected.

Breaking the square edges of the chamber mouths via light chamfering allows fast loading and in no way harms the weapon. Removal of any sharp edges, such as found on the cylinder-release latch, hammer spur, et al, prevents abrasion of both clothing and skin, making the gun more user-friendly.

Some women note that the K-frame Smith is a little too spacious in the area between the frontstrap and trigger guard. Thus, when the gun is fired, the middle knuckle of the middle finger of the firing hand receives a bump. This is also a common finding among males and is easily and economically rectified with either a Tyler No. 3 T-grip or Pachmayr grip-adapter.

Another solution is the installation of after-market stocks by either Uncle Mike's or Pachmayr, the former being my preference. Be careful when considering such stocks because they often result in a reduction of both the weapon's inherent compactness and the shooter's performance. When considering stocks, bigger is not necessarily better.

If the Model 10 (blued) is selected, some form of wear/rust-resistant finish, such as Metalife, Nitex, NP-3, etc., should be applied, especially if the weapon is to be carried daily. The Model 64, however, is stainless steel and requires nothing but bead-blasting to eliminate its reflective potential.

For most self-defense functions, particularly inside an urban dwelling, the Glaser Safety Slug offers minimal penetration and ricochet hazard, and probably the best stopping power one could hope for in a 38 Special. It should also be understood that the Glaser is intended for use against unprotected targets in the open and is virtually worthless if any kind of cover, such as automobiles, vegetation or structures of any kind, are involved. If the weapon is to be used for a more general-purpose function, the best compromise is the 158-grain lead semi-wadcutter or SWC hollowpoint bullet, such as offered by all the major ammunition manufacturers.

Male

The typical male is as capable of handling a single-action self-loader as he is any other kind of handgun. Thus, for him the venerable Colt 1911 series 45 ACP offers by far the best self-defense package. Highly reliable, accurate and potent, the Colt 45 auto has proven itself on a thousand battlefields and in back alleys worldwide for over seventy years, and needs only a couple of modifications to bring it to its full potential.

Among the modifications are: 1) on older models, replacement of the issued "thumbnail" sights with a higher-visibility fixed type, such as offered by MMC. (Current versions come from the factory already equipped with such sights); 2) removal of sharp edges around the grip tang; 3) a "trigger job," a 4- to 4½-pound pull being about right for most shooters; 5) removal of the collet bushing (Series 70 only) and replacement with a standard solid type; and 6) proper finish for the function for which the piece is to be utilized.

The fact that the SA (single-action) auto is carried "cocked

Chuck Taylor

and locked" (Condition One) in order to be readily usable sometimes frightens the novice. However, such fears are unfounded and are easily eliminated with only minimal training. For what I call "ready storage," in a nightstand or automobile glove box, the gun is best kept with an empty chamber, hammer down and a loaded magazine in place. This requires only a brisk cycling of the slide to arm the piece, making it ready for action.

No handgun is faster to the first shot than a Condition One SA auto, and no other type of handgun is as easy to shoot well under stress than the 1911. Add to these points the fact that it is no more difficult to train with than any other handgun, and the picture is complete.

Ammo selection for the 45 ACP is easy: It performs well as a manstopper with virtually any full-powered load. However, some bullet shapes feed better than others in any self-loader, and the 1911 is no exception. Personally, I find standard 230-grain FMJ (ball) to be quite satisfactory, and that is the load with which the 45 built its awesome reputation. That notwithstanding, I must continue to emphasize that an understanding of marksmanship and tactical skills is still required for best results.

Senior Citizen

There are two criteria unique to this category—fixed income and physical capacity. For those who must live on a fixed income, the expense of purchasing a good-quality self-defense handgun is often painfully high. Also, the physical capacity of senior citizens is often less than that found with younger personnel.

Assuming that neither factor is disproportionately prohibitive, I recommend a small-frame double-action 38 Special revolver, modified as discussed in the "Female" category and loaded with Glasers. The Colt Detective Special or Cobra are good choices here, but I personally prefer the Smith & Wesson Model 36 or 60 (stainless) Chiefs Special, due to its extreme compactness. The limitations of the 38 Special and the concept of accurate marksmanship are no less important here.

Guns within this category are generally stored, often in a nightstand or dresser drawer, for long periods of time without inspection or maintenance of any kind. This means that the requirement for a corrosion-resistant finish is especially important. Simpler yet, why not just buy a stainless gun, such as the Model 60, in the first place?

Stock selection is also of special importance, since many senior citizens have limited dexterity due to arthritis, etc. Stock fit to the firing hand greatly influences trigger control, so there is very little latitude here. They've got to fit well or performance suffers greatly, particularly under stress.

Family

This is a tough category, because regardless of the type of handgun selected, any curious child of reasonable intelligence can figure out how to make it fire. So, the best solution is gun education, rather than gun type.

I have two girls, both of whom were brought up around not only handguns, but far more sophisticated weapons, such as submachine guns and assault rifles, as well. Their mother and I ensured that they were exposed to firearms at the earliest possible age. Both girls were allowed to handle and shoot any of my guns they wished, provided a qualified adult was also present. As a result, both of them quickly understood what firearms were about.

The *worst* thing parents can do is to overreact to a child's natural curiosity about guns and institute a policy of prohibition. This only makes the gun *more* attractive and frequently leads to accidents with tragic results. In the child's mind, prohibition means that it must be *wonderful*!

However, were I pressed to recommend one kind of handgun for such a couple, I think I'd prefer the double-action self-loader. The SIG series is, in my opinion, the best. A DA auto is as rugged and accurate as any other pistol, but its heavy DA trigger pull is more difficult for a small child to successfully execute. And, like the single-action auto, storing it with an empty chamber and loaded magazine requires a brisk cycling of the slide, something else that a small child can perform only with great difficulty.

As a defensive arm, it needs many of the same modifications as does the single-action auto, so I'll forgo further elucidation on that point except to state that the weapon should be in the most potent chambering that both husband *and* wife can handle, say a 9mm or 40, although many women find the 45 ACP to be well within their capabilities.

In 9mm, the Glaser ammo is by far the best choice for home-defense or typical civilian self-defense missions. Remember that in standard loadings the 9mm and 40 are both *highly* penetrative and are, therefore, less than optimum choices for typical home-defense scenarios. On the other hand, the 45 ACP is not and might well be a better choice if the lady of the house can also handle it.

Myths are dangerous and can only be dispelled with education, for children as well as parents. Let's not forget the reasons for keeping the gun in the first place, self/home defense. Safe, efficient satisfaction of that mission demands a realistic perspective of the gun, its capabilities and limitations.

Be sure to take the time to learn the capabilities and limitations of the handgun, as well as your own, and how to best utilize them. After all, your life—and perhaps the lives of your loved ones as well—may depend upon it. ●

Bill Jordan

Home Defense

AT FIRST HEARING, this seemed a very simple assignment. I was to list the handgun I would recommend as most suitable for home protection purposes by persons in four different categories: average female; average male; average senior citizen; and average family with young children. Then it struck me that I was faced with a very delicate situation. Over the eighty-four years I have made this planet the place where I do my hunting and shooting, I have never met an average female. If I had, I hope I would have been smart enough not to intimate that I thought she was an average female! So we will rename the first category simply: *female*!

Having shot on the same firing line alongside any number of these capable creatures, I can assure you that, with gun in hand, they are most formidable competition. This is a conclusion I cemented one day on walking up and (inadvertently) noting that the smartest thing I could have done was to swap targets with the lady shooting next to me—when no one was looking, of course! In a recent world-class shooting event, the greatest number of gold medals was collected by an attractive American woman. That was not just the greatest number won by a U.S. Team member; that was by *any team member* in the entire match.

I can get past one stipulation immediately and ignore it for the rest of this discussion. I don't think there is much doubt that anyone with whom I have discussed handguns for use in a serious self-defense situation can have any question as to my conviction about type of weapon. Regardless of the experience, sex, political beliefs, physical condition or any other physical or mental peculiarity of the shooter, my choice has remained the double-action revolver. If something goes wrong, I would rather try to think my way out of the situation than depend on any mechanical contraption to do it for me and further confuse a bad situation.

I will give one example which, although admittedly unlikely to happen, *could*. You, the good guy, are armed with an autoloader. Your opponent, the bad guy, has a plain old double-action revolver, most any make. With gun in hand, you round a corner and find yourself confronted by the "bad guy" who also has gun in hand. You both pull your triggers at the same instant. Both guns fail to fire. Question: How long would you give the "good guy" with the automatic... YOU .... to keep on living? Unlikely to happen? It could and I'll be ready to bet that somewhere, sometime, it has happened.

With that off my chest, let's get on to specific categories. First, we will consider the female. I would think that she would not want to carry any bulky piece of ordnance which might detract from her femininity. Actually, handgun manufacturers as a group seem to have awakened to the fact that women do carry guns these days and decided to cater to this fact. Accordingly, if I mention a firearm by type and use a maker's name, that should not necessarily be construed as a recommendation of that particular gun or maker, but rather of that gun as an example of the points considered pertinent and desirable, with one exception. If there is a choice, buy a handgun manufactured in the U.S.

So for the Female category, my recommendation would be the Smith & Wesson 38 Chiefs Special in either the stainless Model 60 or Airweight Model 37 with 2-inch barrels and overall weight of 19 ounces or 14 ounces for the Airweight model. This small gun, in the 38 Special caliber, has reasonably low recoil and fits nicely in a woman's handbag, or pocket if available. The 38 Special is a very efficient caliber. It was the official handgun of the U.S. Border Patrol for many years (until the 357 was born). It worked quite well, and there were very few disparaging reports issued by Border Patrol opponents.

The S&W Bodyguard Model 38 might be an even better choice. Also light in weight and similar in looks to the Chiefs

---

Regardless of the experience, sex, political beliefs, physical condition or any other physical or mental peculiarity of the shooter, my choice has remained the double-action revolver.

Special or Airweight, it has a shroud covering the hammer which effectively converts it to double-action-only shooting. The gun can be cocked for deliberate fire while the shroud prevents the hammer spur from catching on clothing when the gun is being drawn.

On consideration, I will make no distinction between the female and the male. Their requirements are basically similar, and the types of firearms recommended for her should not be too much for him to handle.

For anyone intimidated by even the reasonable (to a hardened shooter, anyway) recoil of the regular loadings in 38 Special, wadcutter target rounds are available and they have very low recoil. A similar revolver chambered for the 22 Rimfire Magnum (22 WRM) or even the regular 22 rimfire loadings is available.

This brings us to the senior citizen. Unless the senior is truly over the edge, I would have to consider him or her as having somewhere near the capabilities of both the average female and male. Although not likely to be quite as strong, the senior should be able to handle a 38 Special revolver. If not, he should not be living alone.

The elderly person could use the same revolver as the young male or female, with the noise reduced by loading it with 38 Special wadcutters or by selecting a model chambered for one of the rimfire loadings.

Bill Jordan

The shooter should be sure that the gun is kept in a place where it is easily available so as not to lose time wondering where it is. That place should be kept locked, with the key available yet secure if, as so many older people do, they encourage young people to visit.

This works right into the last category—couple with young children. I would consider this the most serious problem of the four. How do you hide *anything* from curious youngsters? The answer is, you can't. You can be sure they will know where the gun is kept. And no matter how well you have trained them or have hidden the gun, they will mention this little secret to their friends. And you can be just as sure that some of those friends are older and stronger and heroes to your kids. They will be able to talk your kids into showing them the gun. Then, when it is in

this dominant kids hands, no matter how well trained your kid is, all bets are off!

First, let's mention the type of firearm for this young couple. Any good, standard double-action revolver will do. There are no problems with the size of the gun. It can be big or small. This does not include caliber. Any caliber, 38 Special or below, should be right.

The only problem for them is how to child-proof it. There are two ways, and I would recommend using both. One is to keep it locked up, with you and your wife both carrying the only (to your knowledge) keys. And second, equip the gun with a hammer shroud *and* a trigger lock so it can be neither cocked nor fired without getting through all that.

Then say a little prayer and trust to providence. Or something. ●

The Panel's Choices

	FEMALE	MALE	SENIOR	FAMILY
COOPER	Colt 1911	Colt 1911	Walther PPK	Walther PPK
AYOOB	Colt Detective Special	S&W Model 686	Beretta 86	S&W Model 66
HALL	Browning Hi-Power	Colt King Cobra	Beretta 86	Colt Gold Cup National Match
TAYLOR	S&W Model 10	Colt 1911	S&W Model 36	Sigarms P220
JORDAN	S&W Model 38	S&W Model 38	S&W Model 38	S&W Model 38

Comparison Chart—Handguns for Females

PANELIST	HANDGUN	CALIBER	WEIGHT OUNCES	BARREL LENGTH	OVERALL LENGTH	NUMBER SHOTS	COST
COOPER	1911 Colt	45 ACP	38	5	8.5	8	$735
AYOOB	Colt Detective Special	38 Special	22	2	6.6	6	$400
HALL	Browning Hi-Power	9mm	32	4.7	7.8	10	$606
TAYLOR	S&W Model 10	38 Special	30	4	9.3	6	$383
JORDAN	S&W Model 38	38 Special	14.5	2	6.3	5	$444

Comparison Chart—Handguns for Males

PANELIST	HANDGUN	CALIBER	WEIGHT OUNCES	BARREL LENGTH	OVERALL LENGTH	NUMBER SHOTS	COST
COOPER	Colt 1911	45 ACP	38	5	8.5	8	$735
AYOOB	S&W Model 686	357	41	6	10.4	6	$528
HALL	Colt King Cobra	357	44	6	11	6	$455
TAYLOR	Colt 1911	45 ACP	38	5	8.5	8	$735
JORDAN	S&W Model 38	38 Special	14.5	2	6.3	5	$444

Comparison Chart—Handguns for Senior Citizens

PANELIST	HANDGUN	CALIBER	WEIGHT OUNCES	BARREL LENGTH	OVERALL LENGTH	NUMBER SHOTS	COST
COOPER	Walther PPK	22 LR	23.5	3.9	6.7	7	$783
AYOOB	Beretta 86	380	23	4.3	7.3	8	$514
HALL	Beretta 86	380	23	4.3	7.3	8	$514
TAYLOR	S&W Model 36	38 Special	19.5	2	6.3	5	$377
JORDAN	S&W Model 38	38 Special	14.5	2	6.3	5	$444

Comparison Chart—Handguns for Families

PANELIST	HANDGUN	CALIBER	WEIGHT OUNCES	BARREL LENGTH	OVERALL LENGTH	NUMBER SHOTS	COST
COOPER	Walther PPK	22 LR	23.5	3.9	6.7	7	$783
AYOOB	S&W Model 66 & MagnaTrigger	357	36	4	9.6	6	$821
HALL	Colt Gold Cup National Match	45 ACP	39	5	8.5	8	$937
TAYLOR	Sigarms P220	45 ACP	28	4.4	7.8	10	$900
JORDAN	S&W Model 38	38 Special	14.5	2	6.3	5	$444

Paxton Quigley (center) tells students to concentrate on the front sight. Her hands-on classes have taught the basics to more than 4500 new shooters. (Photo by Syd Kalcheim.)

ARMED WITHOUT FEAR

Self-Defense Instructions For Today's Woman

by PAXTON QUIGLEY

I USED TO be anti-gun. I feared guns; I never touched them; I came from an anti-gun family. As a matter of fact, my mother used to give money to a national anti-gun organization. But, then, eight years ago, something happened that made me reevaluate my attitude. Early one morning—it was about 2 a.m.—I was awakened by a call from a friend who lived nearby.

"Paxton," she said in a strained voice I'll never forget, "a guy broke into my house. The police are here now. I need to talk to you. Would you mind coming over now?"

When I got there, it was clear that more than a break-in had occurred. My friend's cheek was cut and badly bruised, and one eye was practically swollen shut. Her blouse was torn.

"Did he rape her?" I quietly asked one of the police officers. "Yes," the officer said.

Only later, when we were in the hospital emergency room waiting for a doctor to examine her, did my friend tell me the full story. The attacker, she said, had broken in through the bathroom window on the second floor. She awoke to the sound of glass shattering and, after a moment's hesitation, decided to run downstairs, where she could escape through the front door. But the man was quick. He grabbed her at the top of the stairs and hit her in the face, knocking her to the ground. He kept hitting her and then forced himself on top of her.

"It didn't take long," she said. "It didn't take long at all."

Like me, her self-protection strategy had always been to avoid trouble by being prudent. For much of my adult life, I made little effort to learn how to protect myself against possible criminal attack. I took Kenpo Karate classes, but mainly for sport; listened to a couple of lectures on self-defense; and heeded the advice my parents had given me as a child: Be careful whom you talk to and don't visit certain places alone, especially after dark. It was a simple philosophy and seemingly an effective one, because I'd never been the victim of a serious crime.

Though my friend had fears of being raped, she never believed she could become a victim.

"Part of me always thought that if I didn't have violent thoughts or hurt anybody physically or emotionally, no one would hurt me," she explained to me a few days after the attack. "I just thought, you know, that my good karma would protect me."

Dry-firing begins in class and continues on the range. Quigley, here with black hat, builds confidence in her students before they ever fire a shot. (Photo by Syd Kalcheim.)

Until that day, I, too, often rationalized that my "good karma" would keep me from becoming a victim. But after my friend was raped, I realized my attitude was ridiculous and vowed to take action. Over the next couple of weeks, I installed a better door lock in my home, a house alarm system, and an exterior motion detector lighting system. I also worked up my courage to take private handgun lessons at the Beverly Hills Gun Club in Los Angeles.

Intrigued by my change of attitude brought on by my friend's bad luck, I began to research the subject of women and guns, and found that there were more than 12 million American women who owned guns (by now, they're probably more than 15 million), but virtually nothing had been written on the subject. So I decided to do the writing myself. I sent publishers a book proposal, and after a number of rejections, E.P. Dutton offered me a contract. Eighteen months later, *Armed & Female* was published. Not long after my book came out, I was approached by Ted Stermer, the president of the Orange County Shooting and Training Center, an outdoor range in Santa Ana, California. He asked me if I would instruct women on personal protection and the use of handguns. I accepted his offer, seeing it as a natural extension of my book, and I began to teach a seven-hour "Self-Empowerment for Women" seminar.

Since then, I have taught more than 4500 women personal protection strategies and how to shoot a handgun. Approximately 80 percent of the students who take my seminar have never before touched a gun. They attend because they are concerned about crime and their personal safety, and want to know how to take care of themselves and their families. Nearly all of them are scared about learning how to shoot a handgun, and some are nervous about owning one. One woman stands out in my mind.

Janet, a spirited, hardworking family-practice physician, was quite candid about it. "I don't like guns. I'm frightened of them and I've seen a lot of gunshot wounds, but I've decided to learn how to shoot a gun just to see if I'm comfortable with it. But, basically, I have to say that I'm anti-gun," said Janet.

Although Janet is a tall woman with big hands and could easily hold a 357 Magnum, she insisted that she learn on a "small gun." She was so uneasy that the thought of her handling a large-frame gun was too scary for her. Even holding an *unloaded* snub-nose 38 Special in the classroom made her anxious. She jokingly said that she was sure she couldn't shoot the side of a barn.

Janet was also concerned about the gun's recoil, which she called "the kick." She had been told that she would be knocked off her feet by "the kick." Naturally, I always want to make a student feel as comfortable as possible, so I assured her that she could handle the recoil because I had

New shooters are often afraid of guns, so Quigley gives them warm, caring support in her classes. (Photo by Syd Kalcheim.)

ARMED WITHOUT FEAR

put on special rubber grips—Pachmayr Decelerators—that actually absorb much of the gun's recoil. She seemed dubious, almost testing me, but I told her that if she tried the same gun without the grips, she'd certainly feel the difference.

Her dread of guns combined with her apprehension that she couldn't control a handgun is typical of many first-time shooters. Control is a major issue for women because they believe they won't be able to safely handle a weapon. Part of my job as a gun instructor is to reassure the students that they're all capable of handling and shooting a gun.

I break them in gently. Students first dry-fire their guns about 10 minutes. This gives them some familiarity with the handgun. I continue the dry-fire practice at the range and then we move to actual shooting. We don't talk things over until the students have shot a bit and have had time to assimilate the experience. I find that in most cases the actual act of shooting turns apprehension into confidence. The student feels she (or he) is in control of the situation.

During all my teaching, I never shout at my students. I use a bullhorn and give them positive feedback in gentle tones. I try to be warm and caring in a supportive way, and I find that even for my male students this works best to allay the fears of novice shooters.

Interestingly enough, after students take my seminar, some of them encounter amazing changes in their lives. It happens to the women in particular. Once a woman loses the overriding fear of a gun and knows she can control it, she begins to have more command over other areas of her life.

Unfortunately, some people believe that by owning a weapon, violence will come to them. I've often heard my students say, "violence begets violence." They forget that a gun can be their greatest protector, an effective deterrent against criminals.

One of my former student's experiences provides an excellent example of a gun's great deterrent effect. Six months after the incident, Nancy M. told me the following story:

She was napping on her living room sofa one hot July afternoon when she was awakened by a man yelling obscenities and pounding on her front door, threatening to break it down. She didn't move or say anything, praying that the man would go away, but he didn't leave.

"He banged so fiercely that I thought the door was going to cave in, and then suddenly he stopped," Nancy recalled, still unnerved by the confrontation.

Nancy went to her dresser drawer, where she kept her 38 Special Smith & Wesson, and quickly loaded it. She heard a noise at her bedroom window and realized that the man had pulled off the screen. She knew what to do. She held her gun in the ready position—the way she had learned in my class. She walked to the window and pulled back the drape just as the man started to crawl through. He looked at her in a drunken stupor.

"Is it loaded?" he asked.

"Just try me," she answered.

He slowly backed away as she kept the gun pointed at him, and then he turned and fled down the pathway. Nancy watched him disappear and then quickly closed and locked the window. Still holding her gun, she telephoned the police.

Gary Kleck, a distinguished scholar of criminology and a professor at Florida State University, published a series of studies in which he concluded that guns were used in self-

From shooting, students gain confidence that extends into other parts of their lives.

defense between 800,000 and 2.45 million times a year. Rarely is anyone shot in these incidents. In fact, Kleck reports that the gun-owner fires in fewer than one in four confrontations. In most instances, the mere display of a gun is sufficient to scare off the criminal. Also, Kleck says that one in six survey respondents who had used a gun defensively was almost certain that a life would have been lost if the innocent party had not had a gun—some 400,000 cases of guns saving lives. Kleck, in his book, *Point Blank,* states that people who defend themselves with a gun are more likely to successfully resist the criminals and are less likely to be hurt than those who are unarmed. Supporting Kleck's contentions is the National Crime Survey, 1979-1987, which shows that criminals are successful in only 14 percent of home burglary attempts in which people defend their property and lives with guns, compared with a success rate of 33 percent overall.

Kleck also theorizes that gun ownership has some deterrent effect. Criminals actually admit to not committing a crime because they thought the intended victim was armed.

Over the last five years, I have taught classes in rural, suburban, and urban areas throughout the U.S., and I continually hear my students' stories of why they fear guns, even to the point of being phobic. But, at least those who take my seminar have made some commitment and are open to conquering their fears. Based on my experience, I have found it much simpler for beginning shooters to learn how to shoot revolvers rather than semi-automatic pistols.

It's not that I'm against semi-automatics (I own a few and enjoy shooting them), but they are more complicated to operate than wheel-guns. A novice shooter finds it difficult to load a magazine, especially if the beginner is a woman and has long manicured fingernails. Also, women are usually not as strong as men and therefore have difficulty thrusting the

magazine forcefully enough into the magazine well to ensure good seating. She may also have trouble pulling back the slide and then releasing it.

It's far easier to see if a revolver is loaded or unloaded. With a pistol, to visually verify that a cartridge is in the chamber, you need to do a pinch-check. Again, this is not a simple task for a first-time shooter.

If the semi-auto has a decocking lever or a safety, learning how to manipulate it quickly and successfully is not simple for the beginner. I have frequently watched novice shooters forget to release the safety before shooting. Their inability to recover immediately often leaves them feeling anxious that they can't control the weapon. They believe the weapon controls them.

Furthermore, if a semi-automatic malfunctions, it isn't a simple process to clear the stoppage. It takes practice. (I can't tell you how many times I've practiced clearing a double-feed and a stove-pipe.) A number of lightning-fast steps have to be completed in just the right order to eject the empty case, recock the hammer, and chamber a new round. Also, when I've explained to a beginning shooter that the pistol may malfunction, the student often panics and loses confidence in their ability to control the gun.

Another factor that can't be ignored is the simplicity of cleaning and dismantling a revolver; everyone should understand that after you've shot your gun you need to clean it. Even though a semi-automatic will come with instructions in the box showing how to break the gun down, with many semi-autos it's not easy to follow these instructions. Disassembly requires some dexterity and strength, especially when replacing the slide. The best way to learn is to have someone show you how to do it, and then practice over and over again.

Paxton Quigley, author of *Armed and Female* and *Not An Easy Target*, is one of the foremost teachers of beginning shooters.

Here she instructs a novice in correct grip and sight alignment. Note ear and eye protection. (Photo by Mark Comerford, courtesy Dillon Precision Products, Inc.)

ARMED WITHOUT FEAR

In addition, it's relatively easy to remember the mechanical steps of using a revolver days or weeks after taking a shooting class and then going to the range to practice.

Finally, and unfortunately, many gun owners—female or male—don't practice. They simply put their guns away in a safe, in a drawer, or underneath their pillow, and when they finally do go out to practice, they don't remember how to safely handle them. A revolver is less complicated to load, shoot and unload.

Put together all of the above considerations with a novice shooter's "fear factor," and it makes sense for a newcomer to learn how to shoot a revolver first, rather than a semi-automatic. Of course, once a shooter feels competent with a revolver, if she (or he) wants to learn how to shoot a semi-auto, she (or he) will find that the confidence gained with the revolver makes it easier to learn how to shoot a semi-auto.

Those who have learned to shoot using a revolver and are interested in a semi-auto may want to try the Smith & Wesson Model 3953, a 9mm double-action-only pistol with no decocking lever. This is a good choice for those making the transition from a revolver to a pistol. The double-action-only function requires the trigger be pulled through the complete firing cycle, which is similar to a revolver being shot in double action.

Postscript

You may have wondered how my student, Janet, the anti-gun doctor, fared on the pistol range. The actual shooting of the handgun dispelled her fear. She found that once she confronted her fear of the gun and its "kick," there was nothing there to fear and nothing to hurt her. She was in control of the situation. She quickly moved up to a 357 Magnum Smith & Wesson LadySmith Model 65. She was the best shooter in the class. At the end of the day when we returned to the classroom for graduation, Janet was all pumped up and announced to everyone that she had lost her fear of guns.

The next morning I received the following message from Janet on my answering machine:

"Thanks for yesterday, I had a *great* time. I'm a little bit amazed and a little bit proud of myself, and a little bit hooked on shooting...!" ●

For information on her instruction classes, write or call Paxton Quigley Enterprises, Inc., 9903 Santa Monica Blvd. Suite 300, Beverly Hills, CA 90212, or phone 310-281-1762.

Self-Defense Scene

SELF-DEFENSE HANDGUNS AND THE LAW

by MASSAD AYOOB

THE GROUNDBREAKING research of criminology professor Gary Kleck shows that Americans use guns in self-defense a great many times every year. In most of those incidents, there's no more hassle with "the system" than the filing of routine reports.

Sometimes, however, things get a whole lot heavier. The horror stories go all the way up to include murder charges...and murder convictions. When things get that bad, though, it's a good bet that the otherwise law-abiding citizen who used the firearm did something wrong, or did something ignorant.

The rules are very simple. The intentional firing of a gun in the direction of another human being is an act of "deadly force." The law considers that to be the degree of force a rea-

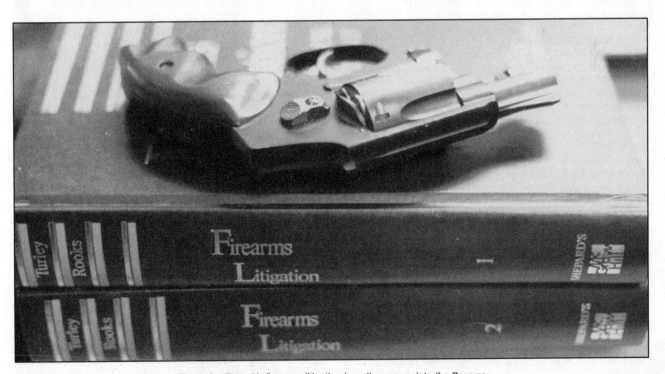

Those familiar with firearms litigation in action appreciate the "lawyer-resistant attributes" of double-action-only handguns like S&W's Model 442 Airweight Centennial 38 Special. Grips on this one are by Final Option.

sonable and prudent person would consider capable of causing death or grave bodily harm. Such an act is justified only when it is done to halt the immediate, otherwise unavoidable danger of death or grave bodily harm to the innocent.

A lot of bad advice is given in these matters. Some is dispensed around the cracker barrel at the gunshop, but some of it has come from cops and lawyers and others who should know better. The person who gives the bad advice isn't the one likely to go to jail; the person who acts on it, however, is likely to end up behind bars.

Let's look at a few examples.

Don't flee the scene of a shooting

"He who flees from trial confesses his guilt," said Publilius Syrus, and that belief holds sway today in the legal maxim, "Flight equals guilt." There are judges who will allow that argument to be made forcefully to the jury that hears your case. The theory is that the honest man who acted correctly will stand his ground to explain his actions, but the man with something to hide will run.

In several years of working as an expert witness and strategy advisor in self-defense shooting cases, I've seen more decent people go to prison for making this mistake than for any other single error, even when they were justified in the shooting. The use of deadly force is literally a larger-than-life experience; a citizen untrained and unprepared for it can easily be overwhelmed; it's not hard to understand why panic induces such a person to flee—unless you're a judge or a juror.

Once the shooting has gone down, and the deadly danger to you and yours is over, holster or otherwise secure your weapon. Immediately call the authorities, requesting ambulance and police, and identify yourself. Your initial statement should not be, "I shot a guy," but something like, "There's been a home invasion and a shooting. The suspect is down. I'm the homeowner." And then give your name and address and physical description.

In rare circumstances, the shooting scene may be too physically dangerous to remain. If you have to leave for your own protection, state loudly, "I'm going for the police." And do it! At least one witness will recall and testify to this evidence of your good faith. You are now in a race to the telephone to call in and become the complainant instead of the fleeing perpetrator. If you have a cellular phone in your vehicle, something I consider to be critical safety equipment, you're ahead of the game.

Don't alter the evidence

Yeah, yeah, I know—Uncle Fred, Casey the cop, and half the gun salesmen you've met all told you, "Drag the dead guy inside and put a kitchen knife in his hand before you call the police."

Decades ago, that might have worked. Not today. Microscopic fiber evidence will show the dragging of the body, and even if you scrubbed the floor with Lestoil until the corpse went into rigor mortis, all the police have to do is sprinkle a little Luminol around, and the bloodstains will show up as clear as day.

You're now *prima facie* guilty of the crime of obstruction of justice for altering the evidence, and something even worse has happened: Your credibility is shot. It's a rule of life: If you lie once, you're a liar forever as far as those you lied to are concerned.

The truth that would have saved you is now gone, and like the little boy who cried wolf, you can expect to be gobbled up. The jaws of the criminal justice machine are not nearly so

Nine millimeter or 45? Ayoob says sixteen 115-grain bullets or eight 230-grain bullets add up the same in the end, but knowing when to use a gun is far more important than issues like this. Pistols are by Sigarms; ammo by Cor-Bon.

mercifully quick as the teeth of a wolf when they close on an innocent person who can be proven to have lied already.

Leave the evidence *in situ*, that is, where it fell. If you acted correctly, the evidence won't be anything to worry about.

Avoid hair triggers

Even as a civilian instead of a cop, you're far more likely to have to take a suspect at gunpoint than you are to have to shoot him. These are high-stress circumstances that have led to a lot of unintentional shootings. Convulsive muscular reaction from being startled or from someone bumping you can cause you to press the trigger unexpectedly.

One answer is to keep your finger off the trigger until the decision to fire has been made. Unfortunately, not everyone can do that in a high-stress, threatening moment. One fallback is a firearm that will require a long, heavy pull of the trigger before firing, at least for the first shot.

You have to understand that the opposing lawyers would rather you had shot him by accident. Convictions are convictions, and it's much easier to convince a jury that you're guilty of manslaughter because you accidentally, carelessly shot the deceased than to convince them to convict you of murder because you killed him maliciously and deliberately, as well as wrongfully. By the same token, a plaintiff's lawyer would much rather convince a jury that you negligently killed the burglar, so they can get into the deep pockets of the insurance company that issued your homeowner's liability policy. If the same jury decides you killed him deliberately, it's a willful tort that is expressly exempt from your liability coverage. All the lawyer can "wet his beak in" here is your personal property. Few of us have as much property as we have household liability insurance.

Therefore, it's in opposing counsel's best interest to mislead the jury into thinking your deliberate self-defense shooting was accidental, and if your gun can be fired with what a layman would call a "hair trigger," you've given him the perfect avenue to create that "big lie" and ruin you. It's not enough for you to simply avoid cocking your revolver when confronting on the suspect; you should have a revolver that cannot be cocked, one that can *only* be fired with a double-action pull! Several double-action-only (DAO) revolvers are now offered that way from the factory, and the rest can be modified by a gunsmith or armorer who removes the single-action cocking notch internally. Bobbing off the hammer spur isn't enough.

This is an argument for the double-action auto pistol, and

for the DAO autoloader. If you insist on using a single-action auto like the Colt 1911 for these purposes, at least make sure that the trigger pull is a minimum of 4 pounds, and 5 is better. If you choose the Glock, it's only about a $15 job to have it fitted with the New York Trigger module, which brings pull weight up to about 8 pounds and gives a firm resistance to the trigger finger from the very beginning of the pull.

Don't deactivate a safety device on your firearm

For years, gun enthusiasts deactivated the grip safeties on their 1911-type pistols and removed the magazine disconnector safeties from their Browning and S&W service autos. In today's civil liability climate, a person who deactivates a safety device on a handgun is seen as the very embodiment of recklessness, and recklessness is the key ingredient in a manslaughter conviction or a civil judgment against you.

The grip safety on the 1911 gets in your way? You can: a) learn to hold the gun properly; b) have an aftermarket grip safety installed that works better; or c) you can buy a Taurus or EAA 45 that doesn't have a grip safety yet still follows your 1911 manual of arms.

If you are afraid that you won't be able to fire the round in the chamber during the few seconds it takes you to reload your auto while the bad guy is rushing you, get a handgun that doesn't have a magazine disconnector. If you remove an

existing safety device, however superfluous, it will make you look bad in the eyes of the law.

Don't use indefensible ammunition

At the time of this writing, a man stands charged with murder because he shot another man with a deep-penetrating handgun bullet. The man he shot wasn't the cause of his troubles. Those started when the bullet penetrated completely through the bad guy and fatally struck another man

behind him. You want a good, street-proven hollowpoint bullet that is likely to stay inside the body of the offender, which is the only safe "backstop" in a shooting situation.

Avoid handloads for defensive shooting purposes. This opens you to an argument by opposing counsel such as this: "Ladies and gentlemen of the jury, regular bullets weren't deadly enough for the defendant! No, he had to make his own 'killer bullets'!" The jury, remember, consists of lay people who aren't shooting enthusiasts and are susceptible to that argument. Besides, few felons are ever shot with handloads. How can you come up with a handload that has a "street record" as a manstopper? Numerous factory hollowpoints have proven themselves in that regard in documented police shootings, some of them hundreds of times.

Your freedom may also hinge on your being able to prove that the bad guy was as close as you say he was when you fired. This may require testfiring of your weapon with "exemplar ammunition," that is, the exact same lot of ammo that was in the gun at the time of the shooting. It's much easier to do this credibly with factory ammo than with handloads.

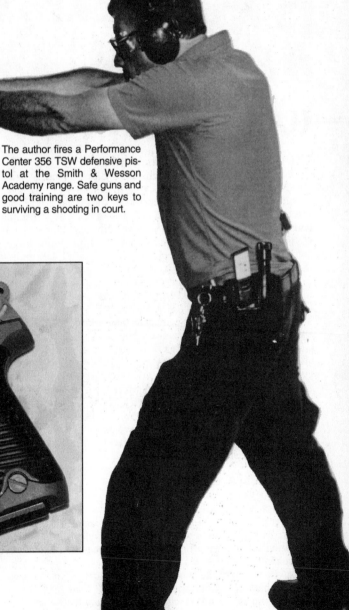

The author fires a Performance Center 356 TSW defensive pistol at the Smith & Wesson Academy range. Safe guns and good training are two keys to surviving a shooting in court.

Because of civil liability concerns in terms of unintentional discharges, police departments have gone heavily toward double-action auto pistols. This is the one issued by the author's department. It's a Ruger P90 45.

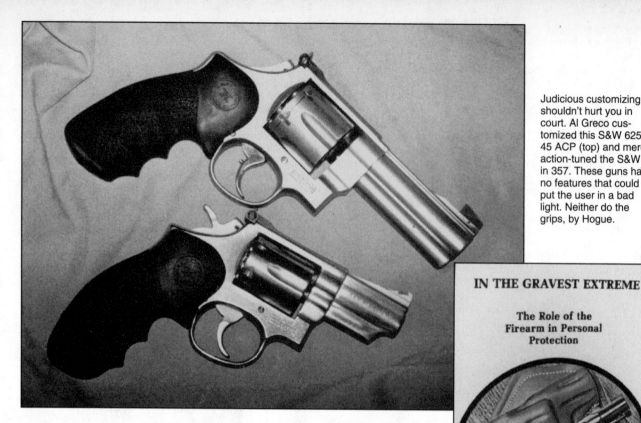

Judicious customizing shouldn't hurt you in court. Al Greco customized this S&W 625 in 45 ACP (top) and merely action-tuned the S&W 66 in 357. These guns have no features that could put the user in a bad light. Neither do the grips, by Hogue.

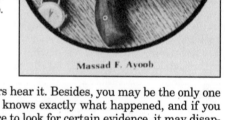

IN THE GRAVEST EXTREME

The Role of the Firearm in Personal Protection

Massad F. Ayoob

Ayoob's book, *In the Gravest Extreme,* has long been recognized as the authoritative text on civilian use of deadly physical force.

HANDGUN LAW

Don't use controversial ammunition

The classic example is Winchester's Black Talon. It was not especially deadly, but it became the focus of media controversy. Not only did Winchester take the round out of the retail mainstream, but even the non-gun-owning public learned to associate the round with bloodthirsty Rambo types who had malicious intent. That was a wrongful image, but it got into the collective mind of the jury pool, and it remains there to haunt you. Not only that, but the effectiveness of the Talon round was overexaggerated. Winchester and other makers produce standard hollowpoints at least as effective as Black Talons for self-defense work.

Using the Talon won't convict you in and of itself, but it sure won't help. The best you can hope for in legal results is that of one of my graduates who killed an armed felon by shooting him with a Black Talon 230-grain 45 slug. The circumstances were such that the prosecutor's office patted her on the back. However, not all shootings are that clear-cut.

Also, she was a law enforcement officer. When you are asked by opposing counsel, "Why did you have to shoot him with a bullet that features razor-sharp claws and a buzz-saw effect?" you won't be able to use her answer: "Sir, it was what my sergeant issued me."

Don't succumb to verbal excesses

This refers to a compulsive need to verbally justify one's actions after something awful has happened...a shooting, for instance. Unfortunately, you're still in the clutch of the "adrenaline dump" and are very likely to find yourself racing your mouth before your brain is in gear. The general advice of attorneys is, "The less said, the better."

However, don't take the attitude of, "I ain't tellin' you coppers nuthin' 'til my mouthpiece gets here!" That may not be the way you say it, but it will most assuredly be the way the responding officers hear it. Besides, you may be the only one at the scene who knows exactly what happened, and if you don't tell the police to look for certain evidence, it may disappear forever before they can find it on their own.

Did the suspect have a weapon? Did he fire at you? Tell them! They won't look for that sort of thing in the rain or the dark if they don't have reason to believe it's there. By morning, the bad guy's spent shell casing has washed down the sewer, or a street person has picked up the knife that was dropped in the grass. That evidence is now gone for good, and so are your chances of anyone but you realizing you were the good guy, not the bad guy.

Let's assume that just before you shot him, the bad guy thrust his hand menacingly into his pocket and screamed in front of three or four other people, "I'll blow yer brains out!" If you say nothing as you're led away to the police car, those witnesses are asking themselves, "Do we want to get involved?" They realize the cops don't know who was there when the shooting went down and who came later to gawk, so they decide this would be an excellent time to melt away into the crowd and stay out of things. The critical corroborating evidence that could have saved you just disappeared.

You need to get critical information into police hands at the scene. It'll sound something like, "This man said he was going to kill me. His knife fell somewhere over there. That person saw it, and so did that one, right over there. A man

Bullets that overpenetrate can cause tragedy and legal nightmares. At least three of these Speer offerings, the ones made for hunting and training, are likely to do so; at least two are likely to stay inside the offender's body, because they were designed to.

and woman in brown raincoats with a blue umbrella saw it, too, and I last saw them heading toward the west entrance of the park."

Then, shut up!

Handle it the way a police union attorney would for an officer who had shot a criminal in the line of duty. Explain to the officers that you are very shaken (that will be the truth), that they know how serious a matter this is (no arguments there), and that you'll give them full cooperation in twenty-four hours, with your attorney present. Stick to that commitment.

I've taught the investigation of the justifiable homicide case to hundreds of experienced detectives at the International Homicide Investigators' Seminars and to hundreds more in Lethal Force Institute's courses. I asked every one of those seasoned detectives two questions.

First, I asked them if they had been trained to interrogate by assuming that the interviewee was lying to them, and that their purpose was to find a chink in the interviewee's armor, peel it open and get him to say something that made him look guilty; and keep him from establishing anything that made him look innocent. All agreed that these were the *core principles* of police interrogation.

I then asked them if they had been trained in how to interrogate someone who had killed justifiably. Had they been taught that fear generated by the near-death experience could cause verbalization and body language that mimic patterns they've been taught to recognize as deceptive? In all these years, *not one has raised a hand.*

I seldom train more than a thousand cops a year. There are more than half a million police officers in this country, so it's unlikely that the one asking you the questions is one of my graduates or has otherwise been taught those subtleties. If the cop gets you talking, shortly after the shooting, you'll remember something out of sequence or leave something out. He'll think you're lying, and the stage has been set for how the rest of it will play out.

Get in an active, dynamic frame of mind (you're the victim, and the guy on the ground is the perpetrator), and let the responding officers and investigators know as soon as possible where the evidence is, and who and where the witnesses are. That's all they need for now. Don't say any more until you've had legal advice, even if you have to wait for your lawyer in a holding cell, which is quite likely to happen.

Don't act, or speak, in anger

A black robber armed with a shotgun terrorized a white victim, using extremely brutal and racist language. The victim was finally able to turn the tables. He ordered the suspect to stop, and when the suspect turned on him with a handgun, he blasted the bad guy with the shotgun. Seconds after the fatal shooting, he allegedly stood over the man who had terrorized him and cried, "How does it feel, you __ __!" The pejorative term he uttered was a cornerstone of the manslaughter charge that was brought against him.

Anger is natural when you face a threat to your very life. However, if only to survive, you must channel the anger into dispassionate, purposeful activity that accomplishes what needs to be done. The other side will argue that you couldn't have been in reasonable fear if you were enraged, because it is axiomatic that when rage comes in, reason goes out. If you called the man a pejorative term that can be seen as racist, a self-defense shooting can suddenly turn into a "hate crime."

We are verbal creatures. Where a frightened animal would growl or roar or bark, we say something hurtful. Fear triggers hate, and the same fear that forced us to shoot in self-defense can impel us to say something we never would have said without the provocation of being threatened with death or maiming. But your words will be twisted by lawyers who never faced the near-death experience that compelled you to fire, and for that reason alone, you need to program yourself now to keep from verbalizing anything that someone who has never faced death could misconstrue as the terminology of hate.

Don't shoot for revenge

The use of deadly force against fleeing felons has been strictly limited by the highest court in the land. It is justifiable only in a situation where the suspect's continued freedom unquestionably presents a clear and present danger to innocent life, and there is no other way to protect that innocent life but to shoot the suspect in the back. The burden will be upon you to prove that it was necessary. It must be known beyond doubt that the suspect has committed not merely a felony, but a heinous felony: murder or attempted murder, or something of similar gravity. A fleeing armed robber has not committed a crime that, in itself, warrants deadly force to stop his flight.

Remember, once the lethal threat to you is over, the right to use deadly force to end the threat has passed as well! If the suspect has broken off the assault, he has effectively broken off your right to shoot him in self-defense. If you shoot him now, you may well be convicted of manslaughter, or worse.

Don't shoot someone who can't really hurt you right now

I've been involved in my share of domestic homicides where the battered wife killed the abusive husband. Two points stand in the forefront of that collected personal experience.

One is that the "battered wife syndrome" defense is a coin-toss. It's an impaired-capability defense based on "learned helplessness" and is seen by the triers of the facts as rather like a temporary insanity plea. Judges and juries don't like to turn people loose after those people admit they lost control and killed people. This defense fails in court about half the time.

A much stronger strategy is pleading straight self-defense, treating it as it would be treated if the woman had killed a stranger who violently assaulted her, instead of a loved one who did the same. However, for this to work, the threat must be immediate. There have been the rare "burning bed" types of cases where a woman was acquitted for killing a man because she was certain he'd terribly hurt her or the kids

If you have to fire weak-hand-only like this shooter, will the evidence show that you were reasonable in believing you could do so without endangering innocent bystanders?

(Below) A 38 revolver you can prove competence with is more defensible than a high-tech autoloader with no documentable qualification. An S&W Model 10 is shown.

HANDGUN LAW

when he woke up, but generally, people who do this can expect to go to prison.

If even the most terrifying stranger tells you he's going to kill you later, it's not justifiable to shoot him now! The danger can't just be certain, it must be immediately present, as the case law now stands.

Interestingly, it is not absolutely essential that the antagonist be armed with a gun, knife, club, or other per se weapon. The three criteria that give him the power to put you in immediate, otherwise unavoidable danger of death or grave bodily harm are: *ability* (the power to kill or cripple you); *opportunity* (his ability to immediately employ that power); and *jeopardy* (actions on his part that create the reasonable and prudent belief on your part that he has manifested intent to do so). The matter of his being armed speaks to the ability factor.

It is understood by law that an assailant has the power to kill or cripple you without a weapon per se if he possesses disparity of force. This means that he is capable of killing or crippling you in a violent assault without recourse to any mechanical instrument. Some examples of disparity of force:

1. An adult violently attacking a child.
2. The able-bodied violently attacking the disabled, the seriously injured, or the frail and/or elderly.
3. An adult male violently attacking a female.
4. A man highly skilled in unarmed combat violently attacking a person without that level of skill. (In this case, however, the defender must *know* that the attacker possesses that skill level).
5. A group of persons violently attacking a lone victim.
6. A very large, strong person violently attacking a much smaller, weaker person.

If none of the above descriptions apply, it is probably not a disparity of force situation. If it's not, and the antagonist has not convinced you that he is armed with a deadly weapon, *don't shoot*!

Don't be misled by the "castle doctrine"

It is a principle of the common law that a person's home is his or her castle, and that if they are attacked there, they need not retreat, but may always stand their ground and defend themselves with force equal to the threat. This is called the castle doctrine. It has been widely misunderstood in many ways.

It doesn't mean that you can kill trespassers. It doesn't mean you can kill any intruder you find in your home. It

merely means you don't have to retreat before shooting them if they attack you. Bear in mind that the castle doctrine does not apply to someone who also lives in the home, i.e., self-defense in a domestic abuse situation. In that case, you'll have to show that you made some attempt to extricate yourself from the situation, or show that it was impossible to get away safely before you fired in immediate self-defense, or in defense of another whom you had the right to protect.

I've about run out of space here, but those interested in studying these disciplines further may wish to read my book, *In the Gravest Extreme: The Role of the Firearm in Personal Protection*. I'm happy it's the best-selling book in its field, but I'm far happier that no one who has read it and has done what I told them has gone down for a bad shooting.

The defensive handgun gives us the power to save innocent lives. However, it also gives us the power to kill, which is why it must always be used with a responsibility equal to its inherent power. ●

I asked Massad Ayoob to write this story because of his experience as a police officer and in dealing with the wheels of justice in the aftermath of shootings. A polive officer for more than twenty years, Ayoob has served in all ranks from patrolman to captain. He has many times been an expert witness in justifiable homicide cases. He has been the National Director for the American Society of Law Enforcement Trainers since 1987. Mas instructs private citizens in the legal use of deadly force through his Lethal Force Institute at various seminars given across the country. We feel his insight into the workings of the justice system and the use of handguns is unique.

Editor.

HANDGUNS 96

Competition Scene

Williams reviews games people play, page 102.

Guns that get the job done, page 108.

Taylor's tips to improve your game, page 112.

HANDGUN

The author in the one-hand Bullseye shooting stance. NRA target shooting permits no other support and stresses the basics of marksmanship.

by DICK WILLIAMS

THERE ARE basically three serious competitive handgun shooting sports today, Bullseye, IPSC, and Silhouette. By serious, I mean they all have recognized sanctioning bodies, international participation, and published rules that are followed at all locations. Over the last 30 years I have had the pleasure of participating in all three events. Here's a look at today's most important handgun competitions.

Bullseye

Bullseye shooting is our oldest organized handgun competition. The National Rifle Association (NRA) became the governing body and sanctioning organization in the 1930s, although NRA sponsored Camp Perry matches had been ongoing since 1903. As the name Bullseye implies, competitors fire at paper targets with circular scoring rings of increasingly smaller diameters. The small, inner ring, marked "X," scores as ten points and is also used as a tie breaker if two competitors shoot identical scores.

A complete match is comprised of these individual matches of 90 shots each for a total of 270 shots and possible point total of 2700. The three individual matches are 22-caliber, centerfire, and 45-caliber. Each match consists of 30 rounds slow-fire (one minute per shot), 30 rounds timed fire (20 seconds for each 5-round string); and 30 rounds rapid-fire (10 seconds for each 5-round string). Distances to targets are normally 50 yards for the slow-fire events, and 25 yards for timed and rapid-fire events. If a pistol range is limited to 25 yards maximum available distance, slow-fire events may be fired at 25 yards with reduced-scale targets. Individual scores from different strings of fire are combined and scored as separate matches, like separating your front nine and back nine scores in golf. This creates more prizes for participants, but it doesn't change the overall match.

The 45- and 22-caliber matches require the use of guns in those respective calibers, reflecting the maximum- and minimum-bore pistol cartridges of the 1900s. The centerfire match can be fired with any caliber from 32 up to and including 45. In earlier days, when revolvers dominated due to their superior accuracy, many competitors used a mid-size caliber in the centerfire event. But as the Model 1911 flourished under the loving touches of several master gunsmiths and became capable of 1-inch groups at 25 yards, 45-caliber autoloaders rose to dominate the game, displacing wheel-guns even in the centerfire event. Matches evolved to a two-gun event: your favorite 22 target pistol and a highly tuned Model 1911 with target sights.

The evolution of Bullseye shooting, both in terms of hardware and rules, is interesting as much for the things that

COMPETITION '95

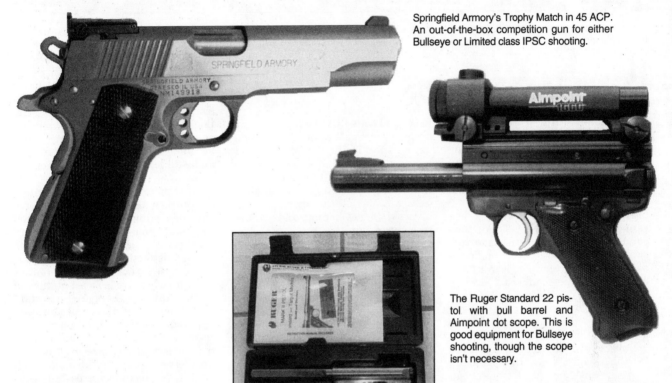

Springfield Armory's Trophy Match in 45 ACP. An out-of-the-box competition gun for either Bullseye or Limited class IPSC shooting.

The Ruger Standard 22 pistol with bull barrel and Aimpoint dot scope. This is good equipment for Bullseye shooting, though the scope isn't necessary.

The Ruger Competitor model in its lockable plastic box with factory-supplied mounting base and rings.

haven't happened as have. Minimum trigger pulls were established as follows: 22 caliber event—at least 2 pounds; centerfire—at least 2.5 pounds; 45 caliber—at least 3.5 pounds. Possibly because all events are fired with only one hand grasping the gun, there is no weight limit set for the gun. Yet there is a barrel length limit of 10 inches which, on a revolver, includes the cylinder. Also, the distance between sights must not exceed 10 inches. After years of "iron sights only," optical sights are now allowed; this excellent idea allows the continued participation of older competitors who have vision problems. Allowable optical equipment includes either scopes or dot sights. Beam projection devices are not allowed.

Most of these rules were in effect during the mid-1960s when I had a go at Bullseye shooting as a young serviceman. I also remember that, while Bullseye offered very little in the way of spectator appeal, it was (and still is) an excellent sport for learning the basic skills and disciplines of accurate pistol shooting. In addition to the need to learn sight picture and trigger control, one needs to learn rhythm and consistency for the timed and rapid-fire events. Action shooters may shrug off 10 seconds as an unrealistically long time for five shots, but it's a very short time to put five shots into a one-inch group at 25 yards. There's no advantage in shaving a fraction of a second off the 10-second limit, but there is that possibility of shooting a perfect score within the allowed 10 seconds. Heady stuff for the participant!

In 1995 the NRA Competition Division shows about 10,000 to 12,000 shooters holding an active classification for indoor and outdoor events, a number that has been fairly stable over the last few years. Each year, about 900 to 1000 enter the Bullseye pistol shooting championship at Camp Perry, and that number has also been pretty consistent for a few years. Other handgun championships that show more than double that number of entries, are events in which the participants register and shoot multiple matches. At Camp Perry, there is only one match to shoot, so 1000 entries mean 1000 different shooters actively participating. The Perry match runs for several days and therefore draws an enhanced social emphasis not found at the usual one-day matches throughout the year.

In keeping with other gun-related trends, I think we'll see a growth in

Different guns and gear are in evidence as IPSC shooters discuss upcoming events.

A couple of competitors visualize and dry-run the event sequence before the shooting starts.

It starts with the draw as Range Officer and scorer watch. Note the typical street gear as Limited class gains increased shooter participation.

COMPETITION '95

Bullseye shooting over the next few years. Americans' concern about crime, or more specifically, of being crime victims is developing into an interest in handguns and a desire to acquire and become proficient in the use of one.

For busy urban Americans indoor ranges are the answer. There they can learn and practice basic shooting skills and become relatively proficient at self-defense. Many indoor ranges offer classes, personalized coaching, and action matches. Almost all of them have the facilities to put on a Bullseye match competition, and most of them are NRA-affiliated.

Bullseye shooting is inherently safer for the shooter than other handgun sports because there is no requirement for quick gun movements or unusual shooting positions that put body parts near the gun muzzle. You simply learn to control a handgun well enough to hit your intended target, and that's a major part of self-protection. Bullseye shooting's growth may not be meteoric, or even particularly rapid, but I do see some growth.

IPSC

Talk about a sport whose time had come! Following WWII, television invaded our homes bringing us nightly doses of the original action-shooting event—cowboy showdowns. There was no escaping the Hollywood influence. Everyone leaped into the fast-draw craze with kids using cap guns and adults shooting blanks in Colt single actions. Never mind hitting anything; we were *fast!*

But making noise quickly wasn't enough for everyone. In southern California, the Southwest Pistol League elevated the leather-slapping events to include use of modern semi-autos, specifically the Model 1911, loaded with real ammunition. It would be unfair to give all the credit for practical handgun shooting to one individual, but one of the driving forces involved in developing and gaining recognition for this new sport that modernized defensive handgunning was an extremely articulate Marine Corps officer named Jeff Cooper. In 1976, when combat-type shooting events were taking place in several countries throughout the world, a meeting now known as the "Columbia Conference" was held in Missouri, and the International Practical Shooting Confederation (IPSC) was established with Jeff Cooper as its first president. Regions were established for participating geographic areas, with the United States Practical Shooting Association governing activities in the U.S.

The USPSA makes a distinction in their recognized shooting categories from those of IPSC. IPSC recognizes Open, Modified, and Standard categories, but USPSA recognizes only two, Open and Limited. The main reason the USPSA has done this is to permit the use of certain revolvers in the U.S. that would be excluded by IPSC restrictions. USPSA Limited is very similar to ISPC Standard.

Within each category there are six classes: Grand Master, Master, A, B, C and D. This lets shooters compete against others of similar proven shooting expertise.

The operative word in IPSC is "practical," and while the sport emphasizes providing participants with realistic training, practical shooting is first and foremost a *sport.* A match must never risk a shooter's safety for realism. And since this is a sport, there is no separation of civilian participants from police or military participants. Distinctions are limited to types of equipment used and skill levels of individual competitors.

IPSC matches are a demonstration of accuracy against the clock. Scores vary depending on hits, misses, and the total time required, but every event is a race against time. One of the unique distinctions of IPSC events is that course layout can be different at every match; there is no set number of shots or targets. There are some standard events that all competitors are required to perform during a year for classification purposes, but just as real-life situations cannot be predicted with certainty, neither can most match events. You have to successfully cope with the situation presented in the shortest possible time or within the allotted time. The accent on multiple targets in minimum time gives the semi-auto handgun a big advantage over the revolver, and the dominating semi-auto has been the Colt Model 1911 and its clones.

As one would expect in a 20th century Open-class sporting event, competitors have developed some high-tech hardware to help solve the variety of problems presented in IPSC matches. The resulting firearms are called race guns—large, heavy semi-autos that function with incredible reliability and possess magazine capacities that allow you to dispatch a score of "bad guys" without reloading. Dot scopes are the optical solutions—large-diameter tubes with a red dot in the center that allow instant target acquisition, have an incredibly wide field of view, don't magnify the shooter's wobble, and withstand amazing amounts of

Shooting from cover, this competitor has sent the first target spinning and is already engaging the next three plates.

Gary Wrigley, vice president of IHMSA shows the hydraulic powered target setting system he designed and built. This is a huge time-saver.

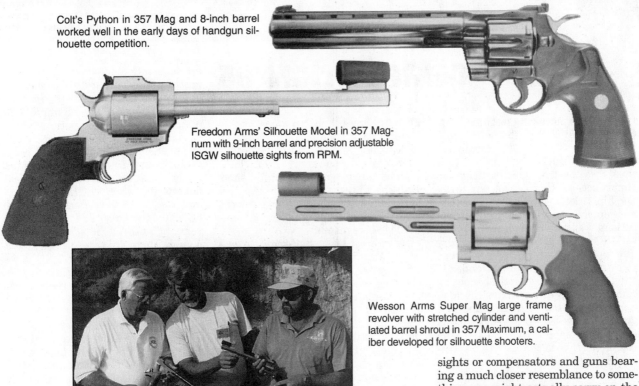

Colt's Python in 357 Mag and 8-inch barrel worked well in the early days of handgun silhouette competition.

Freedom Arms' Silhouette Model in 357 Magnum with 9-inch barrel and precision adjustable ISGW silhouette sights from RPM.

Wesson Arms Super Mag large frame revolver with stretched cylinder and ventilated barrel shroud in 357 Maximum, a caliber developed for silhouette shooters.

Author (center) examines a couple of premier silhouette (and hunting) handguns from Jim Rock of RPM (left) and Randy Smith of Freedom Arms (right).

punishment from the vibration and shock of thousands of rounds per year. To eliminate the muzzle flip of major caliber ammo, IPSC gunsmiths developed compensators that allow the gun to stay locked on target with practically no vertical movement during firing. Race guns from some of the better custom/production houses like Springfield and Wilson come beautifully equipped with every accessory imaginable, and more importantly, equipped with every accessory that has been proven in competition.

There is a down side. Fully equipped guns start somewhere around the $2,000 mark and go up dramatically depending on how close to state-of-the-art you get. Worse, about the time you're getting really good with your big investment, technology advances just enough to leave you a few milliseconds behind the match winners, and you're faced with the expense of upgrading your hardware or settling for other than first place. Worst of all you're doing all your training for a practical event with impractical equipment, equipment you will never carry on the street for self-defense.

USPSA/IPSC's answer to these growing concerns is the creation of the Limited category. Competitors compete with stock guns, meaning no optical sights or compensators and guns bearing a much closer resemblance to something one might actually carry on the street. The creation of this class goes a long way toward easing the debate over *practical* vs. *gamesmanship* that has raged in the IPSC community for some time. More important, Limited seems to be gaining lots of support among participants, judging from the number of entries. The new Crime Bill laws limiting production of magazines to 10-round capacity may be creating some of this increased interest, along with an apparent resurgence of the 45 ACP cartridge. Whatever the reasons, it's probably a good thing for the sport and all competitors faced with restricted budgets.

The USPSA has 14,000 members and is growing. IPSC has 45 to 50 participating countries, depending upon political stability. The numbers run much higher than the 14,000 membership would indicate, because USPSA allows match participation by individuals who are not members of any sanc-

(Below) The silhouette game is fun for everyone who likes to shoot. Twelve-year-old Krista Morris shot a nearly perfect score (78x80) at the NRA Championships with her 14-inch Thompson Contender.

(Above) Ted Zysk of southern California shot a perfect score of 80 at the NRA Championships with a Freedom Arms 44 Mag silhouette revolver.

This wide-frame Springfield with Tasco ProPoint and triple port compensator is chambered for the new 9x25 Dillon, a necked down 10mm case.

COMPETITION '95

tioning or sponsoring organization. Smart move: charge the outsiders a higher entry fee than the members', encourage them to join, but don't turn them away or deny them participation simply because they don't accept membership. A lot of shooters are basically non-joiners, and most shooting organizations tend to bar them from matches. USPSA also attracts many military and police shooters now, whereas years ago, these participants tended to shy away from the practical shooting community. Is this perhaps the ultimate tribute to a better training program? Whatever, IPSC shooting is growing in popularity, and I see no reason for that to change. It's a shooting sport that's almost as much fun to watch as to play, particularly when you see some of the amazing performances of today's professionals.

Handgun Silhouette

This is not a difficult sport to trace. For openers, the first organized, or formal match took place in Tucson, Arizona, only twenty years ago in 1975. And since the match was organized and supported by some very influential people in the shooting industry and media, it received a good deal of attention. Two additional major matches in 1976, one in Los Angeles and one in El Paso, fanned the flames and launched the incredible growth of handgun silhouette shooting.

A handgun silhouette match was, and to some degree still is, an extremely simple event to describe and understand. A handgunner tries to knock down forty metal targets, shaped like animals, at four different distances. There are ten chickens at 50 meters, ten javelinas at 100 meters, ten turkeys

at 150 meters, and ten rams at 200 meters. You get one shot at each animal in sequence, and you get one point for each animal you knock over. Time intervals are two minutes for five shots with short breaks in between the five-shot strings. Winner is whoever knocks over the most animals. That's a standard big-bore match.

As interest grew, half-scale targets at half the distances were introduced. These were for 22-caliber free-style shooting, and for centerfire, straight-wall handgun cartridges fired from the standing position only. While sizes and distances are halved, the matches still consist of forty shots, ten at each type animal, five shots in two minutes. For competitors with super vision and healty egos, there's a forty-round match with half-scale targets at standard distances (50 to 200 meters.) And to determine the winner in the event of tie scores, shootoffs are conducted with half-scale targets at 200 meters. You don't think someone could hit a half-scale chicken at 200 meters using a revolver with iron sights? Check it out!

It has become a little more complicated over the years. Rules evolved regarding classification of competitors based on skill, allowable shooting positions, clothing/padding, sequence of shooting events, alibis, and lots and lots of rules about guns. Weight of guns, calibers, length of barrels, sights, actions, numbers produced, finish, etc., etc. Like some of the other sports, there were some clashes that involved both egos and economics. When the dust settled, there were two sanctioning bodies, the NRA and the IHMSA (International Handgun Metallic Silhouette Association). There

are some differences in rules, but both organizations encourage participation of shooters from the other organization, and some of the championship matches allow the competitor to participate under either banner. That's one of the beauties of identical range layouts and courses of fire. Most importantly, the sport of handgun silhouette has survived the dissention, and the basic forty-round match is basically the same as it was twenty years ago except the scores are a lot higher. There are some excellent reasons for that.

Handgun silhouette was envisioned as a sport to test the long-range power and accuracy of handguns and handgunners. The necessary 200-meter power was available in existing calibers like the 41 and 44 Magnums, but none of the guns then on the market had been designed to deliver that power with the necessary accuracy at 200 meters. Nor could some of them withstand the continued abuse of full-power loads. Even the Thompson/Center Contender had trouble with the sustained pounding, and in 44-caliber, administered a severe beating to the shooter with the then-current grip design. The one gun capable of the required long-range accuracy, Remington's XP-100, couldn't deliver the required power with the 221 cartridge, and it was equipped with totally inadequate sights. Handgun silhouette was a sport that had been designed beyond the existing capability of available hardware. The gauntlet had been dropped, and participants all over the country raced to respond to the challenge.

After thousands of XPs had been rebuilt in more powerful calibers and equipped with quality sights, Remington finally offered the gun in some serious centerfires for the silhouette-shooting community. Thompson/Center introduced new ergonomic grip shapes, offered proper sights, redesigned internal locking bolts, and introduced improved-performance calibers that allowed their guns to shoot perfect scores through 80-round matches and still knock off half-scale animals in the 200-meter shootoffs. RPM redesigned the original Merrill for enhanced performance with new calibers and a "kinder, gentler" effect on the shooter. In the process, they have developed *the single shot* for serious handgun hunters. New single shot guns came on the market from MOA and BF Arms, both featuring tight-locking falling blocks capable of great accuracy.

Wheel-gunners were not ignored. Smith & Wesson beefed up their N-frame and offered it with a 10-inch barrel and precision sights. It's still relatively light for the sustained abuse inflicted by silhouette matches, but it will hold up for some time. And who wants to change the external configuration of one of the most popular big-bore belt-guns in the world? Ruger offered 10-inch standard and bull barrels on their Super Blackhawk, then the Redhawk and Super Redhawk. Wesson hit the market with their large-frame gun with 8- and 10-inch barrels in 44 Mag, plus the 357 Super Mag. Freedom Arms topped it off by making their magnificent 5-shooter in 44 Mag, followed by 357 Mag.

Lest you think the 22 shooter has been ignored, most of the above-mentioned manufacturers have also offered improved hardware for the 22 silhouette game with variations to make weight and dimension limits. And since there are darn few of us who reload 22 rimfire, many of the ammo manufacturers have put some research bucks into developing ammo suitable for the sport. Centerfire ammo for silhouette hasn't been ignored by manufacturers, but since silhouetters shoot so many rounds a year, the emphasis has been on developing bullets for the reloader rather than factory ammo. Yet CCI's lower-cost Blazer ammo has been offered with some fully jacketed rounds for the handgun silhouetter.

Serious handgun silhouette matches typically run longer than one day. Social involvement is encouraged with things like barbecue dinners for those who like to camp out. Family involvement is also encouraged, not just for social purposes, but in encouraging spouses and kids to shoot. Up until recently, only the NRA-sanctioned matches encouraged the senior shooter (those of us with enhanced long-distance vision) through allowance of scopes in certain events. That changed recently, and IHMSA has now adopted a similar policy. There are around

12,000 actively participating silhouette shooters, with attendance fluctuations in certain geographic areas depending on the local economic situation. One of the nice things about a silhouette match that runs longer than one day is that you can participate in multiple events with multiple guns. The flip side is that multiple guns in multiple calibers in multiple matches multiplies your expenses! It's sometimes easier to stay away from a match altogether rather than shoot fewer events, when money's tight. I think that silhouette shooting will enjoy some growth since local clubs actively encourage and solicit new shooters, but participation levels seem to be tied rather closely to economic conditions. After all, this shooting sport is done strictly for fun; motivation is not related to concerns over the rising crime rate.

Unlike action shooting, the silhouette community has doggedly refused to allow monetary prizes for winning matches. They gladly accept donations from the industry to be used in raffles as fund raisers, or to be given away as door prizes, depending on relative value. But in keeping with their philosophy of maintaining a shooting sport for amateurs rather than professionals, no big-buck prizes are allowed. You shoot in a classification based upon your skill against shooters of equal or comparable skill. If you win B class, your trophy looks just like the one given to the winner of Master class. The competition can get serious, but the overall match atmosphere stays pretty light and social.

All the sanctioning organizations have publications that appear monthly or bi-monthly. The NRA has around 3 million members, most of whom don't participate in sanctioned shooting events, so their magazines (*American Rifleman* and *American Hunter*) may not devote as much time and space to your favorite sport as you would like. Regardless, it's still the first organization an American shooter should join. The *IHMSA News* is printed monthly in the summer and bi-monthly in the winter. It focuses on items (guns and shooting equipment) and events (match news and gun politics) of interest to the handgun silhouette shooter. The articles are written by shooters and elected officers, all of whom are quite focused and not in the least shy about expressing their opinions. USPSA publishes a bi-monthly magazine with coverage on items and events relative to its sport and members. There's absolutely *nothing* shy and retiring about the practical shooting community. If you'd like coverage on action or silhouette shooting other than from the official sanctioning bodies, check out *American Handgunner* magazine. They have regular columns on both sports, plus the most widespread coverage of championship matches from all the handgun shooting sports. When you're done with all the reading, go out next Sunday and try one of these handgun sports. Better yet, try them all. I'm betting "you can't eat just one!" •

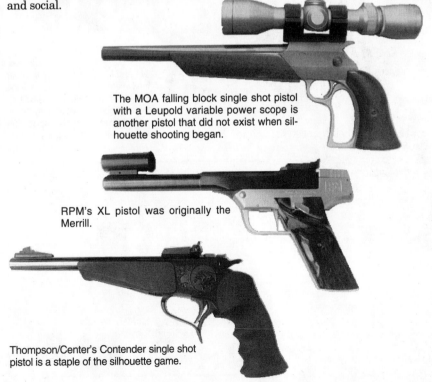

The MOA falling block single shot pistol with a Leupold variable power scope is another pistol that did not exist when silhouette shooting began.

RPM's XL pistol was originally the Merrill.

Thompson/Center's Contender single shot pistol is a staple of the silhouette game.

THE SPORT OF Practical Pistol Shooting began in the late 1950s in southern California and became an amalgam of all elements of pistolcraft including fast-draw, obstacle courses, shoot and no-shoot targets, strong- and weak-hand shooting, multiple targets, short time limits, and a constantly changing course scenario that tested the competitor's street smarts as much as it did his shooting abilities. It was, and still is, one of the finest training methods available to develop top level handgun skills. In fact, many law enforcement agencies, as well as the military, currently incorporate these original principles into their handgun training today.

Unfortunately, once the game became somewhat standardized, the practical aspect began to take a back seat to gamesmanship. Competitors seeking any edge possible engaged in a technological race to develop the ultimate gamesman's gun.

Multi-port compensators were added to reduce muzzle flip and get a competitor back on target faster. Optic LED sights came along and removed the need to properly align front and rear sights, adding even more speed. High-capacity magazines, often holding 20-

GUNS THAT WIN
by CHRIS CHRISTIAN

This Glock 45 ACP is recommended by some instructors as an effective and inexpensive way to enter the Limited class IPSC game. If the gun is ordered with a 5-pound trigger package, all that is really needed to be competitive is a set of high visibility aftermarket sights.

The Limited class is specifically structured to allow a basic law enforcement duty rig, like this U.S. army military policeman's rig, to be competitive. This can be great training for real life situations.

There are a number of readily available rounds that can be used in this new class, but savvy shooters have decided the 45 ACP (left) is the best choice.

plus rounds of high-intensity 9mm wildcat cartridges, became the rule rather than the exception. The resulting guns bore about as much of a resemblance to a "practical" pistol as my Ford pickup does to an Indy 500 race car!

That was also certainly reflected in their price tag. "It reached the point," says international IPSC champion Frank Garcia, "where anyone who wanted to shoot IPSC had to show up with a $3,000 gun just to stand a chance. That is definitely not the way to attract new shooters to the sport."

"The establishment of the Limited Class," he continues, "opened the doors to those who wanted to compete with what could be termed a street gun. It was also seen by some veteran IPSC shooters as an opportunity to return to the original intention of the sport—improving their pistolcraft skills with basic self-defense handguns. Those who wish to shoot the high-tech guns can still do so in the Open class, but I see the Limited class becoming the most popular segment of the IPSC game and I believe it will rejuvenate the sport."

While the Open class allows virtually unlimited modification of the firearm, Limited, as the name certainly implies,

LIMITED IPSC

is considerably more restrictive. The Limited class requires the use of a production gun that is readily available to the public, has been a production item for a minimum of 12 months and has had a minimum production run of 1000 units during that period. Prototype guns are specifically prohibited.

Among the modifications that are specifically disallowed are: optical sights, electronic sights, compensators (either custom or factory supplied), porting of barrels or slides, and any frame modifications other than those specified. (See sidebar.)

In short, all you can do with a Limited class gun is essentially the same things that a custom 'smith would do to create a finely tuned self-defense handgun.

Ammunition requirements are also quite narrowly defined. IPSC relies heavily on the "power factor," which is a mathematical determination of the relative power of handgun cartridges. To determine power factor, multiply the bullet weight (grains) times the bullet velocity (fps) and divide by 1000. For example, a 200-grain bullet launched at a velocity of 900 fps would have a power factor of 180.

To qualify as "major" caliber, the cartridge must have a PF equal to or greater than 175. Anything less is "minor" caliber, and anything that does not make a PF of 125 cannot be used.

(Left) Tack-driving accuracy is not important in an IPSC gun because most targets are shot at relatively close range. Tight-fitting guns can also contribute to malfunctions, which should be avoided at all costs.

(Right) This basic 45 ACP Limited class gun can be assembled for less than $900, and will serve as an excellent self-defense gun. The Limited class is a radical departure from the high-tech, yet impractical, guns often seen in the Open class.

This top-of-the-line Behlert Precision Limited class competition gun features all the trigger work, custom sights, beavertail, grip-enhancing frame checkering, and other practical modifications that win in both Limited class and on the street.

This basic Springfield, Inc., 45 ACP can serve well as an entry-level Limited class gun. Additional modifications can be made as the shooter learns what additions are needed to fit his, or her, shooting style.

GUNS THAT WIN

The minimum bullet diameter allowed is 9mm (.354).

The importance of the power factor cannot be overlooked because rounds hitting outside the "A" zone on the standard IPSC target are scored higher for major than for minor caliber. In the Open class, competitors are allowed to hot-rod 9mm-class cartridges to velocities that will let them make major. Not so in Limited.

The rule book specifically states: "Specialized ammunition that is loaded to make major power factor and that is used to gain a competitive advantage is not in keeping with the spirit of this class and is thereby excluded. This rule will be narrowly interpreted. Therefore, only those calibers that are produced by at least three commercial ammunition manufacturers, that are generally available at retailers across the country and that make major power factor in commercial form may be scored as major. Reloaded ammunition in approved calibers is permitted. Some of the currently recognized calibers meeting the criteria for this category are 357 Magnum, 40 S&W, 10mm, 45 ACP, 44 Special, 44 Magnum, and 45 LC."

The above criteria open the door to a lot of commonly available handguns. However, when it comes to the guns that win, the field certainly narrows.

"The first thing a shooter ought to do in selecting a Limited class gun is to be sure it makes major," notes Garcia. "The scoring advantage of the larger caliber is more than enough to offset

the increased magazine capacity and lesser recoil of the minor caliber. If you take the time to make all A-zone hits with the minor caliber you will score the same, but the time factor will drop your scores overall. Major-caliber shooters can shoot faster because they don't have to make A-zone hits, and for that reason minor calibers are not competitive...in IPSC."

Major calibers can be had in both revolvers and semi-autos, but Garcia notes that revolvers are not competitive either, and are seldom used, primarily because of their reduced capacity and slower reloading time.

For Garcia, the answer is pretty simple. "I definitely recommend a semi-auto in 45 ACP caliber," he states. "It's a low-pressure round that easily makes major, is simple to reload...doesn't prematurely wear out the gun...and is available in almost any gun shop."

For shooters desiring to minimize their cost of entry into the sport, Garcia suggests the Glock 21.

"It's a 13-shot 45 ACP that needs nothing more than a set of Novak or Heinie sights and a five-pound trigger," he feels, "and it is ready to race. You can get into that gun for about $650, and it will last. I have one here at my school that I use as a loaner and it is still purring along after over 100,000 rounds."

Noted pistolsmith Art Leckie favors a different approach.

"It's hard to argue with a Colt Government Model in 45 ACP," he says.

Many Limited class competitors favor a simple, behind-the-hip, high-ride holster over the more exotic competition models. This adds to the sport's value as a training aid for real world confrontations.

"It's a well-designed and highly reliable gun that will provide years of service, and you don't have to spend big bucks to get a quality Limited class gun."

For the new shooter, Leckie suggests the Colt 1991A1, (a no-frills version of their Government Model 1911A1) with a few simple modifications.

"Quality sights are mandatory," he states, "and for fixed sights it's hard to beat the Novak rear sight with a ramp front dovetailed into the frame. If the shooter wants adjustable sights, then I would suggest either the Bo-Mar or the new Pachmayr rear sights. After that, the gun needs a trigger job. I would replace the plastic trigger parts with a metal trigger and either do a simple trigger job by smoothing the existing parts to give about a four-pound pull, or go to a drop-in Behlert trigger assembly that will get you a crisp, safe and long-lasting trigger pull down to three pounds. I would stay away from any-

Although revolvers are legal for Limited class, few savvy shooters use them because a reload is often required in the middle of a shooting stage and the revolver is at a disadvantage to the semi-auto in this respect.

thing lighter than that because they will not last."

Beyond that, he suggests a basic feed and reliability package that includes throating the feed ramp, polishing the breech face, and tuning the extractor.

"With those three basic modifications, which are not expensive, you can add a few 140mm extended (10-shot) magazines and walk right into Limited class all ready to go," Leckie feels.

If a shooter wants to go a bit further, he has some additional suggestions.

"I would add an extended ambidextrous safety, like the Brown Tactical model, or the Wilson or Swenson," he says. "This is definitely an asset in weak-hand stages, and would be a positive factor should the gun do double-duty as a self-defense gun. A full-length recoil spring guide rod is also a plus—it increases reliability and smooths the cycling of the gun. I favor the two-piece models because they make the gun much easier to disassemble and clean than a one-piece unit."

Another very worthwhile addition, especially for shooters who use the high thumb position, is a Brown Memory Groove Beavertail grip safety. This features a raised lump at the base of the safety that not only aids in consistent hand positioning during the draw, but also assures the grip safety will be depressed. Some shooters (the author included) cannot consistently depress the grip safety on the Colt Government model without this device, and many shooters have even resorted to taping down, or pinning the grip safety in order to use the high thumb hand position. Deactivating a safety device is a poor idea in today's legal climate, and the Brown Memory Groove Safety precludes the need to do so. It's well worth the added expense.

"About all that would really need to be added beyond that," Leckie claims, "is some stippling or checkering on the frontstrap to improve the gripping surface—the Behlert weld-on checkering is inexpensive and quite good—and then an add-on beveled magazine well, like the S&A, for speed reloading. Those shooters who use the gun for self-defense often just bevel the magazine well on the gun so as not to add any additional bulk to it. Both approaches work well."

Nothing has been said so far about slide/frame fitting and accuracy work. The reason is pretty simple.

"I don't know if the beginning Limited class shooter really needs to put money into this area," Leckie says. "That would depend upon how well the basic gun shot from the factory. I have seen Colt 1991A1 guns that would shoot 3 inches at 50 yards, and even 3 inches at 25 yards (which virtually all of them will do) which is more than enough for Limited class or street use. Most shooters will be amazed what just a good trigger job and a set of quality sights will do for their shooting. There is no real need for a shooter to spend more than $700-$850 for a Limited class/street gun."

For shooters who insist on accuracy work, Leckie recommends the Accu-Rail system, which uses hardened steel rails positioned within the frame to achieve a tight slide-to-frame fit. All the wear occurs on the rails, and when the fit loosens, the shooter merely replaces the rails with a slightly larger set. This avoids the expense, and time, required to send the gun back to a smith to refit the slide and frame.

Those looking to gain a bit more advantage in the magazine capacity area might consider having the same basic gun made up on a high-capacity Para-Ordnance or McCormick frame. This provides the shooter an additional four to five rounds more than he gets with a single-stack frame, yet the composite materials used in these frames don't result in increased gun weight. All of the other previously mentioned modifications can be incorporated into the double-stacked Para-Ordnance and McCormick frames.

Shooters looking to purchase an effective Limited class gun off the shelf will find firearms with the above features readily available from Springfield Inc., and Kimber of America.

What is the ultimate winning gun in Limited Class? One need only look at the basic Springfield 45 ACP Rob Leatham used to win the 1994 USPSA (United States Practical Shooting Association) Limited Nationals. It was a single-stack Springfield 1911A1 with a set of Bo-Mar sights, extended thumb safety, oversize magazine release button, loading chute, trigger job, and a beavertail grip safety, with a bit of hand checkering on the frontstrap. Leatham opted for the extended magazines, but other than that, his gun isn't much different from those that proved effective when the game was first developed in the late 1950s. It wouldn't be at all out of place in a law enforcement officer's duty holster.

Limited class has brought the game full-circle, and for those who have bemoaned the passing of "practical" from the game of practical shooting, the new class is a welcome return to the sport's original roots.

Limited IPSC doesn't cost big bucks to get into. That's the ultimate practicality of today's practical pistol shooting.●

Limited Class IPSC Handguns Allowed Modifications

1. Replacement of the barrel with one of the same dimensions.
2. Replacement sights that do not extend beyond the end of the barrel or the rear of the gun.
3. Replacement of the trigger; but any alteration of the trigger function is prohibited.
4. Replacement of the safeties, so long as the firearm is still capable of being put into a safe, non-fireable condition.
5. Replacement of springs.
6. Replacement of hammers.
7. Replacement of magazine release buttons.
8. Replacement of slide stops.
9. Enlarging of ejection ports.
10. Enlarging or replacing magazine wells.
11. Replacement or installation of recoil spring guides.
12. Internal finishing to improve the quality and weight of the trigger pull.
13. Internal finishing to improve reliability.
14. The chamfering of revolver chambers and forcing cones.
15. Fitting of slides to frame and cylinders to yokes (including the approval in February of 1995 of the use of Accu-Rails and spherical bushings on semi-autos).
16. Cosmetic enhancements that do not give the competitor a mechanical advantage, such as custom stocks, plating, etc.
17. Checkering of frames to improve gripping surfaces.
18. Alteration of trigger guards.
19. Alteration of grip safety and grip tangs.

Because the FBI Uniform Crime Report has for the last five years shown multiple assailant attacks to be on the increase, simulations of such events should be a part of any practical competition. Here the shooter places one shot on each of two, then three, then four targets 5 meters downrange, 1 meter apart, center-to-center, in 1.2, 1.7 and 2.0 seconds respectively.

PLAYING LIMITED IPSC

by CHUCK TAYLOR

SUCCESSFUL PARTICIPATION in Limited category practical shooting matches requires an understanding that the handgun is, first and foremost, a reactive, *defensive* weapon. Relevant competition minimizes physical movement to no more than a few steps in any direction and avoids undue emphasis on speed-loading. Courses of fire simulate typical handgun confrontations: short time-frames, with only a few shots fired. Moreover, in deference to the tactical requirements of multiple-target scenarios, only one shot, rather

than the usual two, is fired at each target.

Service guns, holsters, spare ammunition carriers and other standard service equipment are required. No specialized equipment is allowed. Full-power ammunition is also needed to insure that the tactical simulation is, in fact, fully presented. After all, muzzle flip and recoil are integral parts of combat shooting, too!

In competition I use the same belt, holster, magazines, mag carrier, gun and ammunition that I carry daily

Since most handgun encounters occur at an average range of 7-10 feet, high-speed presentation and target engagement at such ranges should be an integral part of any serious competition. Here author has, from the holster, engaged a target at 3 meters, hit it twice and is in process of bringing weapon down to Ready. Time limit: 1.0 seconds. Note that his trigger finger is already *off* the trigger.

Nationwide, the trend is toward reasonable concealed carry laws and permits. Thus, concealed carry matches are not only educational, but essential.

on the street. My gun? A "dehorned" (sharp edges removed) Colt Lightweight Commander 45, with fixed MMC high-visibility sights, Metalife finish and a 3.5-pound trigger.

I'm right-handed and prefer a strongside carry. I initially used a Davis #453 Liberty model holster. Later, however, I designed a concealed carry rig, now known as the "Taylor-Omega," and now utilize it exclusively. My mag carrier is a dual-cell unit, also by Davis, as is my belt.

In competition and on the street I shoot 230-grain RNJ hardball ammunition exclusively, since it functions flawlessly in virtually all weather conditions, is quite accurate and demonstrates excellent stopping power. I have no real preference as to manufacturer, but U.S. military ammo produces no discernible muzzle flash, thus providing me with best results in low-light conditions.

One need not be in Olympic form, but a reasonable degree of physical fitness is a good idea, if for no other reason than to help cope with competition stress. Dress appropriately for the weather conditions, not only for com-

fort, but to address the various problems inherent to carrying/using your weapon in that particular environment. This, too, is an important part of realistic competition.

Tactical realism often demands that some stages of the match be shot by only one competitor at a time. Thus, to make maximum use of the available time (and to prevent people from having to sit around inactive too long), most competitions utilize a multi-stage format, with each shooter moving from one stage to the next until he has completed the full program.

When I run a match, I prefer to begin with the first stage being what I call "Standard Exercises." These are stand-up weapon presentations and single-target engagements (two shots) from either the Ready position or with the gun holstered (often concealed), at ranges from 1 to 50 meters. Time limits are based upon the average gunfight times listed in the FBI Uniform Crime Report. This guarantees tactical legitimacy. "Comstocking," an elapsed-time versus score method that is popular in non-tactical, "track meet" type competition, should be avoided.

Usually, ten to fifteen competitors can complete this stage simultaneously, with each then moving on to subsequent tactical stages that must be shot one man at a time. Over the years, I have found that a total of three stages—Standard Exercises and two tactical simulations—offers the best combination of competitive stress, useful information and skill development within the available time.

Tactical stages should represent real-world handgun confrontations in different natural and social environments. Often, I require participants to begin from a seated, or even supine, position. I also use automobiles and knock-down steel silhouette targets as often as possible.

One such tactical simulation, which I call "The Deadly Bedroom," requires the contestant to begin by lying down on a bed, the covers drawn over him, with his pistol located in a nightstand drawer. Behind him and downrange at 7, 10 and 15 meters are three knock-down steel silhouettes, measuring 18x30 inches. Upon the command to begin, the competitor must rise from the bed, throwing off the covers in the

PLAYING LIMITED IPSC

process, obtain his pistol from the nightstand drawer and engage the targets—all within a total of six seconds. There is a penalty for any silhouette still standing after the allotted time-frame expires.

An already stimulating situation, the quick yank on the nightstand drawer by overanxious competitors usually sends the pistol careening to the *rear* of the drawer. The competitor must then dig it out before he can use it against the intruders. Interesting...!

Or, in what I call "The Car," the shooter begins the event seated behind the steering wheel of an automobile, weapon holstered. On receiving the command to fire, he must open the driver's door, exit and, using the car door for cover, engage two knockdown steel silhouettes 7 and 10 meters in front of the car.

Then, using the car body itself for cover, he must move to its left front and engage two more silhouettes 10 meters to the right, knocking them all down. Time limit: 10 seconds. There is a penalty for any silhouette left standing and one for failing to make proper use of available cover.

This event can be made even more interesting by requiring the shooter to move back to the car and remove from it a water-filled dummy representing his "wounded" partner, which he then must drag or carry to a designated position of cover. The 10-second time limit is adjusted accordingly.

One of my favorite tactical simulations is called "The Guatemalan Table," which represents an assassination attempt on the shooter in a restaurant by multiple armed terrorists. In this one, the contestant begins seated at a table with the gun holstered (and preferably concealed), chair pulled up tight. Downrange 7 meters are two knockdown silhouettes, 5 meters apart. Between and behind them at 12 meters is a third silhouette. On the command to fire, the shooter must obtain his handgun and engage the targets, knocking them all down. Time limit: 5 seconds, with a penalty for any target left standing.

This seems pretty straightforward *except for the fact that there are "no shoot" paper or cardboard silhouettes, representing innocent customers, scattered at random between the contestant and the targets!* This means that he will have to briskly move about to get a clear shot at all three. There is, of course, a substantial penalty for hitting any bystanders.

Yet another simulation, called "The Battleground," features a water-filled dummy, dressed as either a soldier or policeman, wearing the appropriate equipment and handgun. Upon receiv-

Tactical simulations offer perhaps the most relevant challenge of all. Here, the competitor began the simulation seated at a table. Upon the signal to begin, he has moved the chair rearward, stood up at his option (he could have remained seated), presented his weapon from under his jacket and has hit each of three targets at 3, 5 and 7 meters once. Time limit: 4.0 seconds.

Tactical necessity requires an understanding of ricochets. Here, shooter has the option of either direct line of fire or ricocheting bullet into target across trunk of automobile.

Truly practical competition is also fun. Here, the shooter must begin lying down in bed, with covers over him. Upon the signal to fire, he must throw away the blanket, leap to his feet, grab his gun from the nightstand (behind range officer) and engage a target 3 meters downrange. Teddy bear is a fun touch, too!

ing the command to begin, the *unarmed* competitor briskly approaches the sprawled-out "body," recovers its weapon, and engages four knockdown silhouettes placed 5, 7, 10 and 12 meters downrange, some of them only partially exposed from behind "cover" composed of stacked wooden logs. Time limit: 10 seconds.

This scenario, while already *quite* stimulating, can be made even *more* interesting by attaching the weapon to the "body" via lanyard, thus making virtually impossible any decent shooting position! Things can be made even more realistic by encumbering the "body" with a full complement of military equipment—rucksack, web gear,

et al—with which the competitor must contend while trying to obtain the gun.

If time permits, the top sixteen competitors from the Standard Exercises and Tactical stages can be paired off in a man-against-man shootoff for final standings. This kind of shooting is crowd-pleasing, often electrifying, and *graphically* illustrates to everyone present what it takes to win.

The accompanying photography illustrates the flavor of truly practical competition. You will note that, aside from each scenario's tactical relevancy, they're also *fun*, another element too long absent from competition. As a professional weapons and tactics consultant/writer/instructor, I discovered long

The snubbie is virtually absent from competitive events, but is routinely encountered as a self-defense arm. This fact is sufficient to include it and courses of fire intended to simulate the circumstances under which it is most typically used.

The unexpected should be a major part of any realistic competition. Here the shooter must approach and roll over a water-filled dummy, obtain from it an unfamiliar weapon and with it, engage five targets downrange at 3, 5, 7, 10 and 15 meters. Events such as this are great fun, promote an understanding of different weapon designs and are excellent evaluators of a shooter's overall skill.

Reactive targets that realistically approximate humanoid shape are both administratively sound and educational. However, care should be taken to avoid irrelevantly shaped and/or excessively large targets. This knockdown silhouette is 25 inches high and 18 inches wide with a 6-inch square head. It is made of 3/8-inch armor plate, making it suitable for not only handgun, but rifle, shotgun and SMG competition, as well.

Action-oriented courses are both fun and educational, but no substitute for "Standard Exercises"—fundamental weapon-handling and shooting drills—from 3 to 50 meters. Be sure to include them as part of any organized competitive event.

PLAYING LIMITED IPSC

ago that people learn more when they're also having a good time.

For "Tactical IPSC" (Limited category practical shooting) competition, the future looks bright—in fact, brighter than it has ever looked during IPSC's 18-year existence. More shooters are now interested in practical shooting than ever before.

In the past, the major firearms and related equipment manufacturers have heavily supported IPSC activities, perhaps because they *weren't* very realistic in scope and were thus "politically acceptable." However, given the current national swing to the conservative side of the political spectrum and widespread concern about self-defense, perhaps the situation will change. It would indeed be nice to see the "Big Boys" sponsoring realistic self-defense competition. Certainly, there can be no argument that such support would virtually guarantee the long-term future of "tactical" competition.

One thing *is* irrefutable—truly *practical* handgun competition is finally back on the right track. If we can keep it that way, it will not only survive, but continue to grow. And maybe, just maybe, we can also save some lives along the way •

Editor's Note

An internationally renowned weapons and tactics writer, instructor and consultant, Chuck Taylor was once a world-ranked IPSC competitor, placing near the top in three consecutive U.S. IPSC National Championships. This feat earned him a place on the famous 1979 IPSC U.S. Team, along with Ross Seyfried, Mickey Fowler, Jerry Usher and Tom Campbell. Taylor was for several years the IPSC Rocky Mountain Sectional Coordinator and was twice Class A Champion.

Tips on How to Win

1. When shooting, remember the fundamentals, e.g., sight picture, sight alignment and trigger control appropriate to the size of the target you're trying to hit. Accuracy and speed must be equally balanced.

2. Develop your gun-handling skills, such as holster presentations (open and concealed carry), to the highest possible level. The less you must think about these mechanical processes, the freer your mind will be to solve tactical problems.

3. Modify your handgun and equipment only to the degree required to bring out their full potential. Excessive alteration reduces functional reliability—a critical factor—and offers little in return. All your defensive handgun really *needs* are:

   a. High visibility sights, not necessarily adjustable.

   b. The removal of sharp edges that abrade skin and catch on clothing.

   c. A crisp, reasonable trigger pull.

4. Your holster, spare ammunition carrier and other ancillary equipment should reflect a pragmatic approach. The rig you select should be governed by your lifestyle.

5. Once you have your gun and equipment in order, get some professional instruction. Learn the *best* ways to perform the various combat handgunning tasks. It is critically important that you learn the *best* way to: 1) present your weapon from both Ready and holster, open or concealed carry; 2) clear malfunctions; 3) speed- and tactical-reload your piece; 4) engage single and multiple, partially concealed or oddly angled, targets; 5) move quickly and smoothly with weapon in-hand; and 6) correctly utilize cover and concealment.

Tactical competition—and gunfight survival—demands a clear understanding of these concepts. Without question, the most efficient way to gain such an understanding is to "go to school." Otherwise, in the long run, you'll spend *far* more time, energy and money in return for *much* less.

6. Practice, practice and *practice some more*. By this, I mean practice the *fundamentals*, for they make all the difference. The better your basic skills—weapon presentation, single and multiple target engagement from different ranges, on different target sizes/shapes and from varying angles—*the better off you'll be*.

Success in practical competition (and real gunfights) is based upon these six simple requirements. Recorded fact and observed history shows that there is really nothing complicated about either event.

HANDGUNS 96

Custom Handguns

The editor gets a line on Linebaugh, page 118.

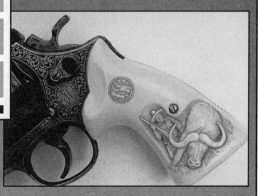

World-class art from world-class artisans, page 126.

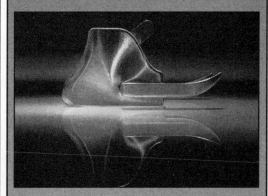

An unfamiliar look at the familiar, page 138.

Editor Ray Ordorica (left) holds a 475 Maximum handgun built by John Linebaugh. Linebaugh holds Ordorica's self-engraved favorite handgun, a 45 Linebaugh.

John Linebaugh

CUSTOM GUNMAKER

The Man and His Genius

*J*OHN LINEBAUGH *makes monster handguns. They have fully twice as much real horsepower as the hottest 44 Magnum, yet they can be packed nearly as easily as, say, a 45 automatic. The 475 and 500 Linebaughs have shot entirely through elephants, been carried alone against Cape buffalo, and in the short span of twelve years have made the name of their maker known around the world.*

Linebaugh came to my attention in 1983 when Ross Seyfried, Shooting Editor for Guns & Ammo *magazine, sicced him onto me with what Ross thought was a really good idea. John called me at my Alaskan digs, explained his revolutionary handgunning ideas to me, and offered to let me shoot his personal 45 Linebaugh conversion so I could see for myself that he knew what he was talking about. Somewhat skeptically, I took him up on his offer, and John sent me the gun and some of his hot loads. I shot it, loved it, ordered one for myself, and wrote a story about it called, "More Power is Possible," which appeared in the 10th edition of* HANDLOADER'S DIGEST. *My 45 Colt Linebaugh conversion is one of the rare Tombstone Sevilles, the twenty-first of John's guns in that caliber. It bears my personal engraving, and it is by far my favorite handgun.*

The world knows of John Linebaugh today because he had a good idea and the integrity and guts to see it through. Working in conjunction with his friend, George Connor, John came up with the idea that if a 45 Colt cylinder could handle the same pressure as the 44 Magnum, the 45 Colt would blow the socks off the 44.

He was right, of course. John had a few 45 Colt cylinders made for Abilene and Seville handguns, shot them, purposely blew some of them up, and proved beyond a doubt that the 44 Mag's domination of the handgun hunting world was over.

That was twelve years ago. Since then, John developed his 500 and 475 Linebaughs, and the "Maximum" or "Linebaugh Long" versions of those two. His guns have been on the cover of Guns & Ammo *magazine twice, in 45 Colt and 500 Linebaugh versions. Handgunners drive hundreds of miles to his shop to meet him and order guns, even though there is no sign on his door.*

If one phrase describes John Linebaugh it is "humble integrity." He keeps his word to the best of his ability and never makes excuses. He tells it like he sees it and speaks straight from the heart in all matters. He has immense respect for the work of other gunsmiths and for the contributions of people who have helped him over the years. As he puts it, "If I had a dollar for every bit of information or help I've been given over the years, I could pay off the national debt."

Always an innovator with a restless sense of purpose, and in spite of odds that some might say he stacked against himself, John continues his experimentation and handgun production in his new shop in Maryville, Missouri. A Westerner at heart, this 39-year-old casts a homesick glance toward the setting sun as he tells his own story. ●

—*Ray Ordorica*

"I was born and raised here in northwest Missouri and moved to Wyoming in 1978. I always had an interest in ballistics and revolvers, and in firearms of all kinds. In Wyoming, I was fortunate enough to meet a few people who shared my interests.

At the time, Wyoming was toying with the idea of legalizing handgun hunting, and when they finally did, they left out the 45 Colt cartridge. They did legalize the 454 Casull and the 44 Magnum. At that time, the 454 Casull was not obtainable; the company was not yet in production.

We decided that since we could not buy a Casull, we would build our own, which fell right in with the ballistic experiments we were playing with at the time. My friend, George Connor, worked hand-in-hand with me on this project for two or three years until we came up with some good results.

We started with early Seville and Abilene frames. Our cylinders were made by a friend at a local tool shop in Cody. At that time we had almost no equipment. We had one small bench lathe and did our own barrel work. We bought our chambering reamers from Clymer and did all of our chambering by hand. We sent our parts to facilities in Phoenix and Texas for heat-treatment.

We did a lot of testing until we had problems or ran out of ideas. We built some devices to test our cylinders and went to the extreme of blowing up some guns to see what our pressure levels and safety factors actually were. At that time, I was corresponding heavily with Dick Casull, Lee Jurras, Homer Powley, Ron Reiber at the Hornady ballistics lab, Tom Brown at Hodgdon, and anybody else who would talk ballistics or pressures with me.

Metallurgical engineers were a big help because they were not biased, they simply wanted to produce the best results. We didn't use exotic steels, we used basically what the industry uses, aircraft-quality steel. We used the best heat-treatment that we could secure for optimum results and strength. Our testing continued.

I had no formal machine shop training at all. I hadn't gone to gunsmithing school. The highest-tech tools I had in 1982 were an electric drill and a bench grinder. I vividly remember going to the bank to try to borrow $900 to buy a flat-bed Atlas lathe that had its date of manufacture etched onto its bed: 1938. I got the loan, got the machine home and trained myself, in very slow and crude fashion, how to turn and thread barrels and fit parts.

George Connor and I continued to experiment. We found that the 45 Colt is basically a magnum-size case. I detest the word "magnum" and everything about it. Magnum, however, means large capacity, and the Colt case is definitely that.

We built several guns in 45 Colt using special, heat-treated steel and oversize cylinders. With the Colt we were able to duplicate anything the 454 Casull did. At that time, all my pistols were chambered for the 454 Casull, and so marked on the barrel. That was so we could legally hunt in the state of Wyoming with 'em.

John Linebaugh. (Photo by Ray Ordorica)

We started building guns in the early 1980s. The first articles on my guns were published around 1984 by John Taffin in *American Handgunner* and Ross Seyfried in *Guns & Ammo*. After those articles came out, business picked up somewhat.

500 Linebaugh

As time went on, we played with the 50-caliber cartridge. That wasn't a new idea. I suspect it would surprise us if we knew how many people have toyed with the 50, at least in their minds. The first people I'm aware of that used it successfully to any extent was an outfit in Salt Lake City named Wheeler and Topping. Bill Topping is dead now of cancer. I met Neal Wheeler and saw some of his early guns. In all honesty, they laid the foundation for a lot of intersting ballistic work with the big 50.

Linebaugh's 475 and 500 handguns require the scarce Ruger Bisley grip for control. Linebaugh now manufactures his own stainless or blued Bisley grip frames, hammers and triggers.

John Linebaugh

Wheeler and Topping never were very successful. I think a lot of the reason was they never got the exposure or were never able to capture the credibility needed, or never had the necessary quality to their work.

They used a cartridge based on the 348 Winchester cut to 1.280 inches, the same length as the 44 Magnum. They used 2400 powder and 50 BMG machinegun barrels, and got some interesting velocity and data.

We built our first 50 in 1984 on a Seville frame supplied by Ross Seyfried. It was originally a 454 Casull. The Seville is a duplicate of the Ruger Super Blackhawk except it has a round-back trigger guard. We put an 8-inch barrel on it and shot it extensively, then we cut 2 inches off the barrel and sent it to Ross with a box of loaded ammunition.

We loaded that first ammo by hand in a homemade die and sized the cases by pressing them into a vise. Then we drove them out by hammer and punch. That first ammo was loaded with 460-grain NEI truncated cone bullets. As I remember, we drove it with H-110 powder at a velocity of 1300 fps out of a 6-inch barrel. Bullet diameter was .510-inch. That gun would rotate in your hand so much the hammer would cut you behind your wrist.

I sent a note to Ross with the gun that read, "I think this is too much gun." In that configuration, it was. He played with it, shot up the ammunition, and was amazed that we could get those kinds of results.

When Ross and I first corresponded about the 50, I said that if we could drive an ounce (430 grains) of lead at 1100 fps I'd be happy and surprised. Little did we know how efficient that huge cartridge would really be. There is tremendous surface area on the base of the bullet, and lots of space for the powder gases to work on, and the 500 is a really fine performer.

After Ross played with the 500 Seville a bit, he asked me if I had ever played with the Ruger Bisley Model. I told him I had not even heard of it, nor had I seen one. He said, "I have a feeling that with that Bisley grip we're going to be able to control this gun a little more. Let's try one."

I had asked if there was a possibility that we could get an article into *Guns & Ammo* on this new cartridge development. Ross thought that was possible, and since I had gained his confidence through the 45 Colt gun and the resultant *G&A* front cover, I then asked if we could get the front cover with the 500. He told me we were gambling with some pretty big odds, but he'd ask.

Now Ross usually isn't one to call you. You usually have to call him to get information. I vividly remember he called me at 9 o'clock the next morning, and said, "If you want the front cover of *Guns & Ammo*, you've got it! They need a gun in their hands in three weeks for pictures."

We didn't have a cylinder, or a barrel, or a Bisley. We didn't even know if we could make it work. Ross said, "I'll secure the barrel and the Bisley, you get the cylinder made."

I waited about a week for this stuff to show up, then called Ross one evening. I said, "Did you find a Bisley and a barrel?"

"Yes."

"Where are they?"

"I shipped them five days ago."

I said, "They're not here."

He said, "I mailed them Parcel Post."

At the time I was living about forty miles from Cody, out in the mountains. Forty minutes before closing I called the Cody post office and asked if they had two packages there for me, from Ross's address. They said yes, and I said, "Don't lock the door, I'll be there in 39 minutes."

I got the packages and came home and worked non-stop for about twenty-four hours. I got the gun into a condition where it would shoot and we could test it. I remember we fired the first shot through that gun late afternoon the next day, and we started chronographing.

When I finished testing, I found we had a revolver that was beyond anything I could

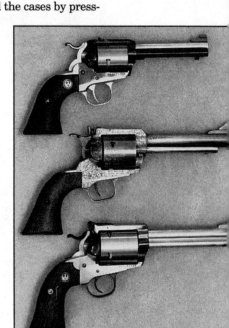

Custom Linebaugh guns include experimental five-shot 357 on small Ruger frame (top); Editor's self-engraved 45 Tombstone Seville (center); and 475 Maximum (bottom).

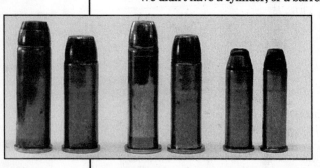

Monster handgun fodder: the 500 Maximum and regular (left), and the 475 Maximum and regular (center) dwarf the 44 and 357 Magnums (right).

comprehend, even though I had built it myself from the ground up. It was unbelievable what it would do and how it would perform. The combination of the Bisley grip with the big caliber made it all work.

I sent the completed gun to Ross, and he shot it a lot. He settled on a load with the 460 NEI bullet at 1330 fps out of the 6-inch barrel. It outpenetrated every handgun he had ever shot, and it consistently stayed in 1½ inches at 50 yards.

Ross delivered the first 500 Linebaugh/Bisley to the *G&A* people at the 1986 SHOT show in New Orleans. That gun was not shown at the SHOT show; it was delivered in secret to the *G&A* people to be flown back to their offices for photography. Information about it leaked out, a few people whispered this, a few whispered that, and before it was all over, a lot of people knew about it. There was a bunch of interest in it. Ross called me and said, "If you've got something you want to do with your life you better do it, because your life is about to change."

The 50 was an instant success. It made the cover of the August, 1986, *Guns & Ammo*, and we had orders for seventy-five to eighty guns the first month thereafter.

To make 500 Linebaugh cases, you can buy your own 348 Winchester brass, cut it to 1.4 inches and form it with RCBS dies, which cost a little over $300, and ream or lathe-turn it; or you can get ready-to-load brass from Lee Landice, Golden Bear Bullets, that is formed, sized, reamed and boxed, for $1 each. That's a bargain unless you love to form cases.

Case life has been excellent. We took three cases and reloaded them until they cracked beyond use, and we got over forty handloads each. Chambers are tight; the case is massive; and we don't work the brass much. The only way to overwork it is to over-crimp. The 50 gives a very gentle, heavy push, not a real sharp, crisp recoil. It's not prone to pull bullets from recoil, with recommended loads. It has never given the problems that the 45 Colt gives.

The 50s have been notoriously accurate handguns. We built a heavy machine rest here and put a high-magnification riflescope on the 500 and resighted it after every shot to assure repeatability. We tested three or four guns considerably, and they all consistently shot under 2½ inches at 100 yards.

I can't guarantee that accuracy with each individual gun, but the majority of the 500s have shot well under 2 inches at 50 yards in most shooters' hands. I'm surprised somebody hasn't put it into production.

Powerful enough to stop a Cape buffalo, the 500 Linebaugh is only slightly larger than a pocket-size S&W M640 Centennial 357 Magnum.

At the time the story on the 50 came out, I was equipped with a flat-bed Atlas lathe and a drill press. I didn't even own a mill. I was in the process of building a shop, and we got behind the eight-ball. I had a problem with cylinder production. I wasn't able to get or make parts, and I didn't have the equipment or the know-how. It's been a roller-coaster ride with this business. We've had good years and bad years.

I didn't start out to be a real gunmaker, I just had an interest in ballistics, and it just got out of hand. I'm not complaining, that's just the truth of it. If I had planned this to happen, it wouldn't have happened.

I never wanted to be known as the man who built the biggest handgun. The purpose of the 50 is not to kill a whitetail deer deader than a 44 could. My 500 Linebaugh won't work better than a 44 on a whitetail deer because you don't have enough animal to use up what the 50 offers.

I'm not saying it's a waste of energy or that we're overkilling them. What I am saying is, if you run over a cat with a Volkswagen he's just as dead as if he got hit with a semi. But when a 2000-pound range bull steps out into the middle of the road, I don't want to be driving a Volkswagen, I want to be in a Kenworth.

This cartridge was designed to allow a man, with the guts and the ability to stop anything in the world, to safely hunt Cape buffalo even under touch-and-go circumstances.

I put my name on the 500 not to boost my ego, but to stop any confusion about the cartridge, and to identify it as the 500 Linebaugh and nothing else. The 270 Winchester and the 30-06 are those and nothing else. There were "500 magnums" out, and a few others. I was the first person to establish the credibility of the cartridge.

About a year and a half after the 50 came out, I was talking with Mike Jordan at Olin.

He told me 348 Winchester brass, on which the 500 Linebaugh is based, was about to be discontinued. I had only two cases of brass and that was it. I checked with every supplier in the country, and they all told me there was no more 348 brass available.

If I didn't come up with another cartridge of some sort, I was going to be making nothing but 45 Colts, and everybody wanted something bigger. Freedom Arms was in production with the 454 Casull and doing fairly well. Their sales were good.

475 Linebaugh

When we could see that there was not going to be any more 348 brass manufactured, I realized that as soon as I made two or three more guns I would be out of the 50-gun business. I needed a new cartridge based on a different case that would use easy-to-get brass and would give lots of punch, and yet be versatile.

Now, I don't want to take full credit for the 500 because a lot of other people had played with the idea before I did. I don't want to be big-headed about the 475, but in all honesty I think I can take full credit for it. J.D. Jones made a full-length 475 that he put in the Contenders, a 45-70 blown straight. I don't think you can call the Contender a practical handgun nor can you call the full-length 45-70 a revolver cartridge. I feel that the 1.4-inch 475 Linebaugh is pretty much an original idea.

I didn't come upon the idea because I'm any smarter than anyone else. I came up with the idea out of absolute desperation. I'd been shooting a 45-70 Marlin lever gun for years, carried it in the mountains a lot on horseback, cowboyin', working in the Wyoming area. I used it with good success. I picked up a 45-70 case one night, measured it, cut it off in the lathe, expanded it, made a crude sizing die, and lo and behold, the 475 Linebaugh was born. It had about a .503-inch base, about .496-inch neck, and a perfect .475-inch diameter mouth.

The next problem was where to get barrels and bullets. I did a lot of calling and asked a lot of questions and finally contacted John Krieger in Germantown, Wisconsin. We obtained one of his 475 barrels and the quality was excellent.

A 475 Maximum cartridge dwarfs the 640 S&W.

Merle Smith started his LBT company at about the time we came out with the 475. He cut some moulds for us and we started testing. Today we recommend his 385- and 420-grain bullets exclusively. They are a flat-nose design that look almost exactly like the original Lyman 45-90 bullets that Elmer Keith loaded in his 45 Colts long ago, a 100-year-old design.

The 475 gave us the advantage of somewhat greater cylinder strength over the 500, which actually wasn't a concern because we've proven the 500 is amply strong. You'll run out of arm or hand before you run out of gun strength. The 475 guns use a cylinder of the same outside diameter as the 500. The 475 operates at a higher chamber pressure. The 50 operates in the mid-30s, and the 475 operates right at 50,000 CUP. We've never had a pressure barrel made to prove this exclusively, but we've tested it against Homer Powley's pressure formula which we have verified very well in our pressure barrel for the 45 Colt. His pressure formula gives uncannily accurate indications of the actual pressure in the gun.

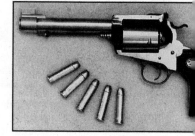

Editor Ray Ordorica found the recoil of this 475 Maximum to be controllable, though its 50 foot pounds of recoil left his hands stinging. This handgun/cartridge combo is capable of shooting through an elephant's skull.

The 475 does everything the 500 does, and it's 100 fps faster with the same bullet weight of a slightly smaller caliber, which translates into increased penetration.

We recommend 385- and 450-grain bullets in the 500, and 385- and 420-grain bullets in the 475. There's not much use going any lighter or heavier. Any heavier you get into unbelieveable recoil, and I think you lose what you gain. If you go any lighter, you've lost the concept of the big-bore handgun. If you want to shoot a little bullet, get a little gun.

Accuracy with the 475 is now fully as good as that of the 500. We had some problems with accuracy with early guns, but that problem is now gone. I've got several targets now that prove to me that the 475 will shoot in the realm of 2 inches at 100 yards.

I don't believe we can make an inaccurate cartridge if the tolerances are right and everything fits. It can be a 465, it can be a 455. If the barrels are the right size, if the barrel fits, if the throats are right, if the powder charge is compatible, if the cases are consistent and if the bullets are right, it will *shoot*. We say in our brochure that most of our guns shoot under 4 inches at 100 yards, but we don't guarantee any specific degree of accuracy.

One thing I have seen consistently is that a revolver will often shoot two groups, just

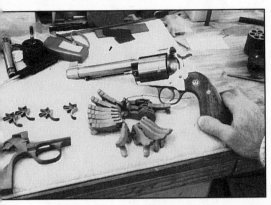

Linebaugh is well into production of his own Bisley parts, necessary to the success of these big handguns. Linebaugh won't comment on the rumor of complete, in-house handgun manufacture under his name.

like a double rifle. If you raise the powder charge a couple grains, the bullets will print right together almost every time. People will think their gun has two bad chambers, or something else is wrong. I advise them to raise the charge two grains, and in most cases the "problem" disappears.

Hunting

Even though I'm not the best shooter in the world, I've managed to kill quite a bit of big game, mostly mule deer and antelope, with a sixgun. I've been fortunate enough to watch my wife do the same with a 45 Colt single action, and I've watched my boys kill some big game with handguns, including bison.

Ross Seyfried used the 475 on buffalo in Australia, and another friend used it extensively in Africa. It'll shoot through a bull elephant's head like it was a block of cheese, using special bullets. Very few hard-cast bullets will do that, because if the bullet is a blink too soft or too hard, it'll go to pieces. Lead cast bullets change their hardness over time, and you can't count on consistent performance at these velocities. The velocity of the 475 is around 1500 fps, and the bullet is subjected to much greater stresses than one at 1200 fps. If you've been getting good results at 1200, you're in for a surprise when you push the same bullet 300 fps faster.

Ross taught me that the best way in the world to test bullets is by shooting big bones in wet paper. You get about a three-foot stack of wet newsprint, and put a big beef knuckle in front of the wet papers, then put about two more inches of wet newspaper over the bone, and shoot your bullet through the bone. A good bullet will blow a hole the size of a golf ball through that bone and will continue to penetrate about two more feet of wet paper, and the bullet nose will still be lookin' downrange.

If the bullet is a little too hard, it'll shatter. It'll blow the bone into a million pieces, as if you hit it with a high-velocity rifle bullet, and you'll find only fragments of the bullet no more than six inches behind the bone. If the bullet is a little too soft, you get the same poor results.

If I were hunting dangerous game, I'd shoot nothing but slightly modified Trophy Bonded Sledgehammer 475 bullets. They have a very thick jacket and a lead core, and they work.

I was approached about three years ago by several custom bullet makers. They suddenly wanted to start making bullets for the 475 and 500. Hamilton Bowen's comment was, "Where were they five years ago when we needed 'em?" I said, "Let's work with them as best we can."

I told them that if I were to make a bullet for these calibers I would make it on a screw machine. Instead of copper I'd use brass. Bowen owned a Corbin swaging system, and he said it would be too costly to make the bullets on a screw machine. He thought that brass is too brittle.

We discussed jacketed bullets, but you don't use a jacketed bullet if you want penetration. You simply use a 10-cent cast bullet if you want it to penetrate. You want a jacketed bullet to blow up, fragment, and expand. That's the theory of 'em. You can't have penetration plus expansion from a handgun bullet, practically speaking.

We came up with a bullet design that offers exactly what I had been looking for, and it is made on a screw machine out of brass. I was right about that, but there are a few trade secrets about my bullet, and I'd rather not have anything more published about them at this time.

Ordorica: If you could only own one of your handguns, which caliber would it be?

For this country, a 45 Colt. For worldwide, it'd have to be a 475 or a 500, I'm not sure which. It's been written a few times that the slug from the 500 is a bit sluggish. I personally don't see anything sluggish about an ounce of lead, a half-inch diameter, at 1300 fps out of a 5½-inch revolver. As Pondoro Taylor said in *African Rifles and Cartridges*, comparing the penetration of the 600 versus the 577 Nitro, some say the 600 is a little sluggish, yet it will stop any elephant, and penetrates completely through the skull, so what more do you need?

I've been asked by lots of folks which handgun to use to hunt worldwide, the 475 or 500. My answer is always, buy one of each, go hunt around the world, send me back the gun you don't want and I'll sell your gun to the next guy who comes along so he can do the same thing. I would say there is no discernible difference. The 475 penetrates a little more, and the 500 gives a little more slap. If I were going to shoot a bear—(by the

John Linebaugh

way, I didn't know until recently that a bear doesn't have hard bones. They're spongy, or springy, unlike a Cape buffalo's bones. A bear's mostly muscle)—I'd use a 50 on big bear because I think it slaps a bit harder.

I killed two bison in Nebraska with the 500. I used a 440-grain Keith-style bullet and 27 grains of H-110 for 1100 fps muzzle velocity. I shot completely through each bison, and also through the corral post behind them. A fellow called me the other day, and he shot his 475 through a bison, through a two-inch iron pipe and completely through the corral post it was attached to. We've got plenty of penetration with either gun.

I guess if I could have a claim to fame it would be the 475 cartridge in its entirety, but I have a soft spot in my heart for that 500. It works. The only real drawback to the 50 is case preparation, but since Browning came out recently with their 348 lever gun, I think we're going to have a good supply of 348 brass available. I recommend all my 500 customers to be sure to store at least 300 cases against the possibility of a shortage. Actually, with lighter loads, it's not necessary to put a crimp on the brass, so it lasts a very long time.

Maximums: The Linebaugh Long Cartridges

I made some experiments for a friend who hunts worldwide and had shot several elephant with these handguns. He wanted a sixgun that he could carry in his pocket and be able to stand in front of elephant and shoot 'em just like he does with his 470 double rifle. I told him I'd build it.

The 475 and 500 Linebaugh Long, or Maximum, cartridges are .2-inch longer than the standards. We jumped the velocity on both the 475 and 500 about 200 fps, but gained less than five percent penetration. That was a shock to me, one ounce of lead at 1500 fps. I have loaded them as fast as 1700, but that's too much. A 500 Max would be dandy for a big bear, but I don't think you gain anything on other dangerous game.

We doubled the price of the gun, doubled the recoil, and gained five percent penetration. The Maximums are not nearly as versatile as the standards. You can't load 'em down as well, there are only a couple powders you can use, but in the standard guns, any 44 Mag powder will work pretty well.

Many folks call and say they want one of my big guns, and I ask them, "What are you going to do with this gun?"

They say they want a gun to shoot monster 150-pound whitetail deer in Pennsylvania, or elk in heavy brush in Montana, and in all such cases I say, "get a 45 Colt [Linebaugh conversion] and load it with a heavy bullet to 1200 fps, and you'll be happy. If you think you need more, the 475 and 500 offer it."

As far as any more performance, I wish I could find someone to answer these questions for me, but I'm finding that at 1300 fps we're penetrating as much material as we do with a 458 rifle at 2100 fps. There seems to be a dead spot for penetration between 1400 fps and 2100 or so. Kind of like slapping water; the harder you slap, the more splash you make, but the less you penetrate. You're trying to move material faster. Until you get over 2200 fps, you can't overcome that slapping effect, the splash. I can't base this on my own findings. I'm not an experienced big game hunter, but I'm getting lots of reports from hunters around the world on the performance of my guns versus rifles.

These handguns shoot through more wet paper than my 375 H&H will with solids and cut a hole that's twice as big. There seems to be a balance around 1300 fps. The 475 regular or Maximum guns are killing everything as well as, or better than, the 375 rifle—buffalo, elephant, you name it. If you shoot them in the same spot, you won't see a difference.

Ordorica: Do you think folks are buying your guns just to say they have the biggest?

About ten percent are ego, or coffee table guns, bragging guns. About seventy-five percent are being used somewhat. A couple percent are being applied as they were intended to be used, by professional hunters. I keep in touch with my customers, and I know many of them personally. They want something bigger and better and different. It's not an ego problem; they just enjoy the thrill and challenge of learning to manage something with this much horsepower.

These guns have also taught us lots about ballistics that nobody ever knew before. One of my best customers who bought an early 45 took a look at the 50 and said, "That's a good idea, but it's only a 50-yard gun." I asked why he thought so, and he thought that the big bullet "just won't carry."

I took him out and we started by shooting at a big rock at a measured 600 yards. I told him, "We'll start there and go further." At the first shot he said, "That puts up more dirt at 600 yards than my 44 does at 100!" Computer programs show that the 500 with a 460-grain bullet at a muzzle velocity of 1300 has more retained energy at 1000 yards than a 44 Magnum does at 100. After 300 yards, it loses less than 50 fps per 100 yards.

I once shot a 44 Mag at a measured 600 yards, Elmer's load. It went through seven inches of white pine. It'd shoot through a man easily at that range, so you can imagine what the 475 or 500 can do at extended range.

Future Projects

I spoke with Frank Barnes shortly before his death and told him that we were going to put a slightly modified form of his 45 Silhouette cartridge into a revolver, and he was quite interested in finding out our results. We call ours the 458 Maximum.

The 458 Maximum uses Winchester 45-70 brass cut to 1.6 inches. Frank's was 1.5. The cartridge tapers from .500-inch at the base to .458-inch at the mouth, and unlike the 475 and 500, this cartridge lives in the realm of pistol powder. H-110 works very well. There is a slight taper to the chambers, and the cylinder is larger for greater safety. The guns are built on the 357 Maximum frame, fitted with Bisley parts and a 6-inch barrel with a barrel band front sight. (That's necessary to keep the ejector rod on the gun. Otherwise they shear off from recoil.) We use 300-, 350-, and 400-grain jacketed bullets and an assortment of cast bullets.

I'd been asked to build a gun for this cartridge several times and refused, because the customers wanted easy bullet availability. That appeal of the cartridge is also its downfall. The bullets currently offered by several makers won't stand up to what the gun will deliver. They are basically a whitetail bullet. The 350 won't expand. It works like a solid. I had great hopes for other bullets, but they failed for a variety of reasons

Linebaugh's well-equipped new shop in Missouri keeps him and two workmen busy nearly 'round the clock.

and gave pressure problems.

We recommend two bullets: the 330 Gould express cast hollowpoint bullet, still available from Lyman, #457122. We drive that bullet at over 1700 fps from a 6-inch revolver. The other is the standard 405 flat-nose bullet. The RCBS flat-nose cast bullet of 420 grains is excellent. We get 1560 fps with it.

The smaller caliber gives a bit of a safety factor, but sacrifices knockout power. Kind of a tradeoff. This cartridge gets about 200 fps over the 45 Colt. It's the "Weatherby" of 45 handguns. The thing that will make the Maximums shine will be when someone comes out with a bullet specifically designed for them, such as a 325-grain soft-nose at 1750 fps, which would simply blow the spots off a leopard.

Philosophy

I believe in the old school of handgunning. Elmer Keith was my hero. I'm accessible, and it's just as well, because people will find you no matter where you set up business. We moved here from Cody partly because of health problems, partly because of a real estate deal gone bad. We just built this new shop and are in production. Our experimentation will continue as we find time.

My toolmaker, Bob Yeager, is busy 13 hours a day. He's very dedicated. We're behind now and always trying to catch up. Regan Nonneman now does all our bluing and takes a tremendous load off of us, and he's a super guy. He's very concerned about the quality of his work and unbelievably conscientious.

So far I have built ten 500 Maximums, eleven 475 maximums, more than 160 500s and over 130 475s. I've built over 600 guns now, all told. We have a very small, less than two percent, return rate for adjustments, which I attribute to Bill Ruger's frame design around which we build the guns. We've had excellent customers and a steady backlog of about a year.

The most common complaint is that the gun is too tight. That's because the customer doesn't follow the recommendations, which are to shoot fifty shots, clean the gun and then lightly oil it. The customer usually ignores the break-in period. We've never had any major problems. Our guns are all guaranteed for life.

We recently had moulds made and we're casting our own Bisley parts now—hammers, triggers, grip frames, all of stainless steel. We also will have them in blued steel. It has been rumored that we have looked into full handgun production of all-stainless Bisleys, and I can't comment further on that at this time. I can only go ahead so fast. ●

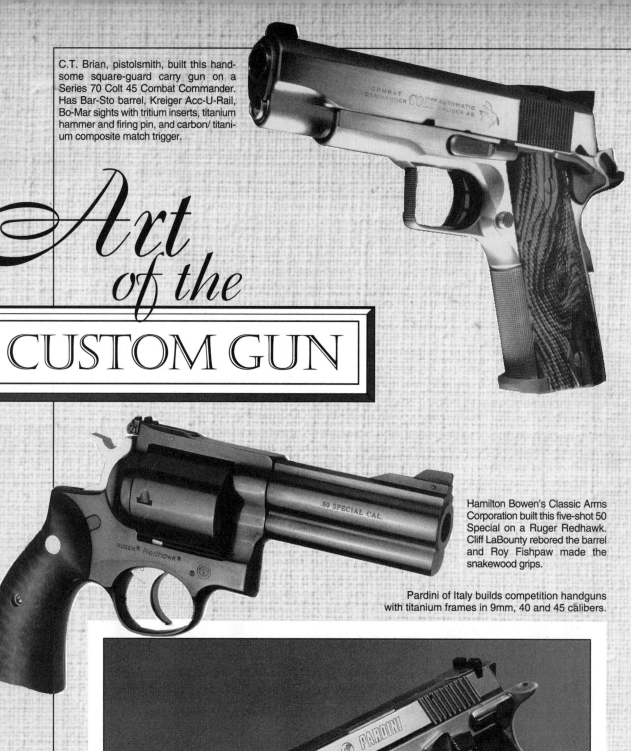

C.T. Brian, pistolsmith, built this handsome square-guard carry gun on a Series 70 Colt 45 Combat Commander. Has Bar-Sto barrel, Kreiger Acc-U-Rail, Bo-Mar sights with tritium inserts, titanium hammer and firing pin, and carbon/ titanium composite match trigger.

Art of the CUSTOM GUN

Hamilton Bowen's Classic Arms Corporation built this five-shot 50 Special on a Ruger Redhawk. Cliff LaBounty rebored the barrel and Roy Fishpaw made the snakewood grips.

Pardini of Italy builds competition handguns with titanium frames in 9mm, 40 and 45 calibers.

Ace Custom 45's tuned this 45 ACP S&W M625 "Texas Special." Has slicked and jeweled action, hammmer spur removed, trigger stop, Millet target sights, modified cylinder latch.

Ten-Ring Precision, Inc., builds nice Ruger 22 pistols with custom compensated barrels that mount scopes and look like this.

Wilson's Gun Shop built this Stealth Defense System 45 on the Springfield, Inc., Compact. It features a tapered cone, match-quality barrel; tritium sights; and fine metal checkering.

Alpha Precision's Master IPSC with exclusive one-piece compensator barrel, extensive metal checkering, Bo-Mar sights, integral mag funnel and high-polish two-tone finish.

LaRocca Gun Works, Inc., did their magic inside this ordinary looking Walther PPK/S. It's ramped and throated, has beveled mag well, trigger job, Trijicon night sights and Pachmayr grips.

Wilson's Gun Shop calls this their Championship Special. Built on the Strayer-Voight frame, it features Accu-Comp "Dot-Tracker" compensator, Tasco Pro-Point scope, and superb workmanship.

G. McMillan and Co., Inc., builds their "Wolverine" around the 1911 Colt frame. It has six interchangeable barrels for 45 ACP, 45 Italian, 38 Super, 38 wadcutter, 9mm and 10mm.

Springfield, Inc., offers their Distinguished Custom Pistol. Features their full-house "Racegun" treatment on single-stack frame and a trigger tuned for 3½ pounds.

D&L Sports put together this striking race gun with vented scope mount, comp, and optical sight. The open slide makes it look racier.

D&L Sports modified a Colt Series 80 into a short, slick carry gun with thumb guard above safety, grooves at the front, and a host of custom features.

(Below) Wichita Arms, Inc. makes serious Silhouette pistols. This is their MK-40, a single shot bolt gun available in all calibers.

(Left) Steven P. Woods did this outstanding checkering on a 38 Super Colt. It's 20 lpi on the grip and slide stop, 30 lpi on the guard and mag button. Kim Ahrends grips and Videki trigger. Photo by Stephen Longley.

LaRocca Gun Works, Inc., does slick J-frame conversions, among other things. Guns feature action jobs, polished triggers and cylinder exteriors, lapped forcing cones, and bobbed hammer on the top gun.

Alpha Precision's 50 lpi checkering on rear of slide; hammer has 30 lpi. This 1911 also features a special wide grip safety.

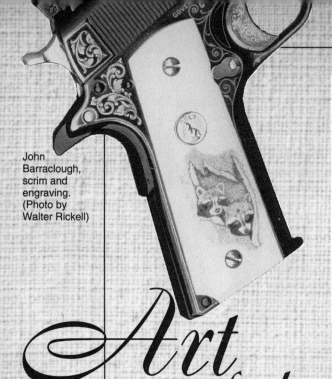

John Barraclough, scrim and engraving. (Photo by Walter Rickell)

Trena Polk

Art of the
SCRIMSHANDER

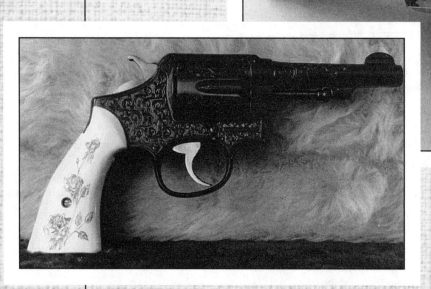

Scrim by Charles Hargraves, Sr. Engraved by Roland Robideau. (Photo by Dennis Hall)

CAM Enterprises (Photo by Russ Williams)

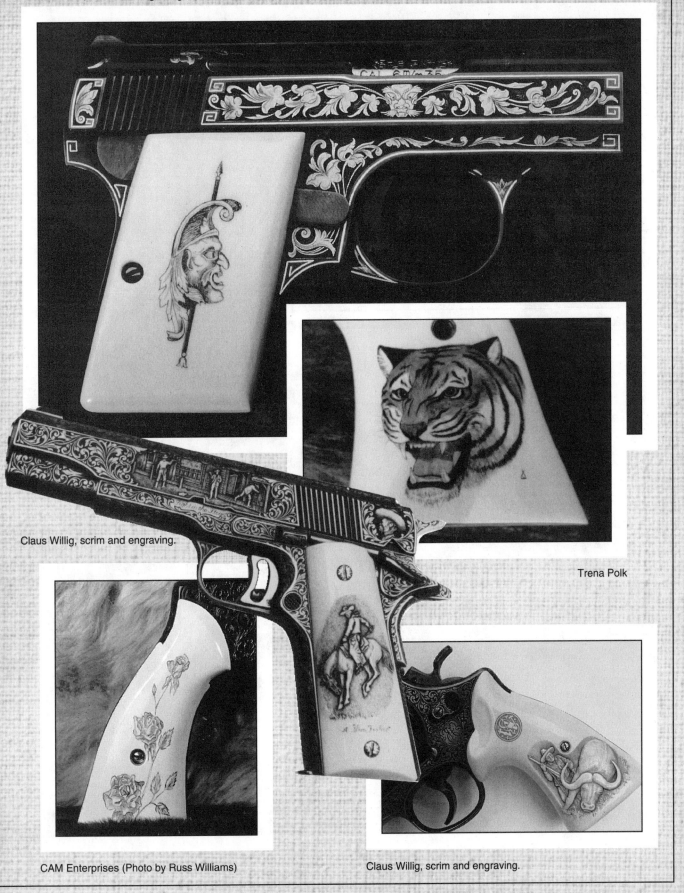

Robert Evans, scrim and engraving.

Claus Willig, scrim and engraving.

Trena Polk

CAM Enterprises (Photo by Russ Williams)

Claus Willig, scrim and engraving.

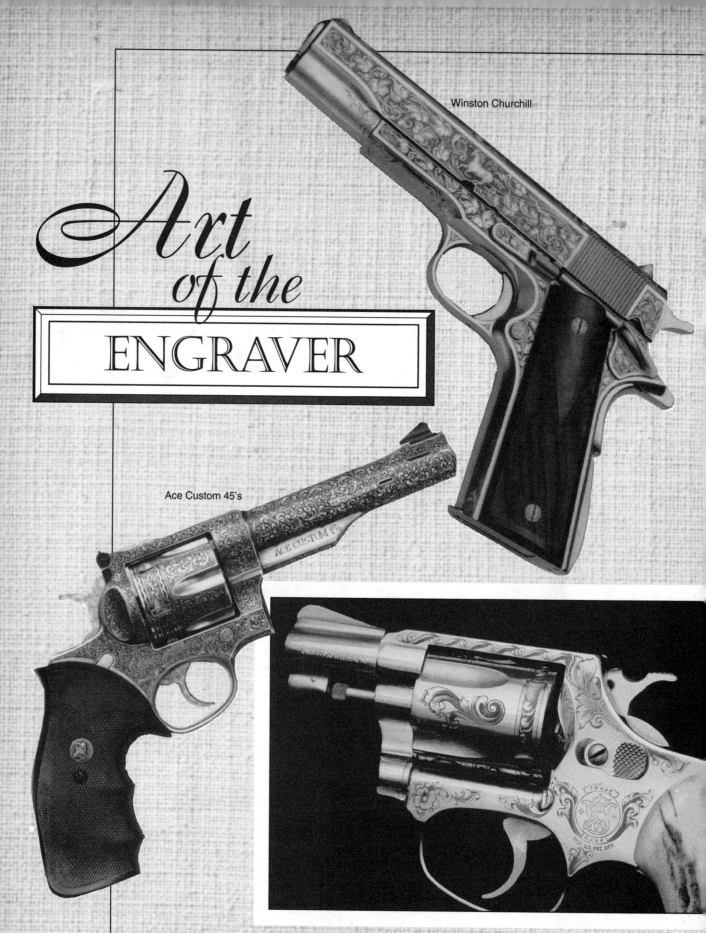

Art
of the
ENGRAVER

Winston Churchill

Ace Custom 45's

Alana R. Cupp

Bruce Shaw

Frank E. Hendricks
(Photo by Bibb T. Gault)

Frank E. Hendricks
(Photo by Bibb T. Gault)

Terry Theis

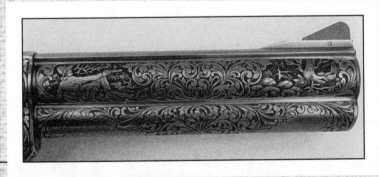

Claus Willig

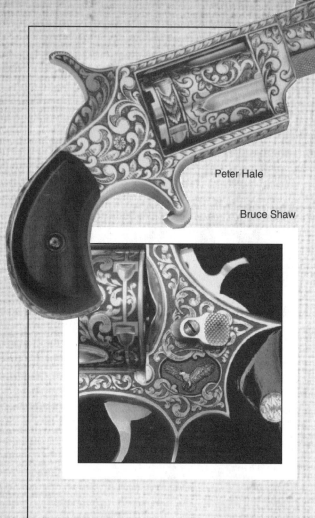

Peter Hale

Bruce Shaw

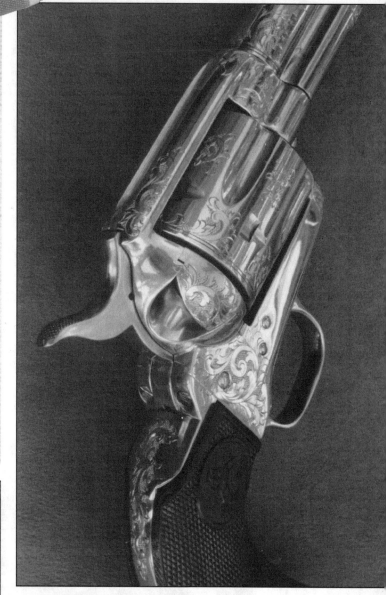

Barry Lee Hands

Peter Hale

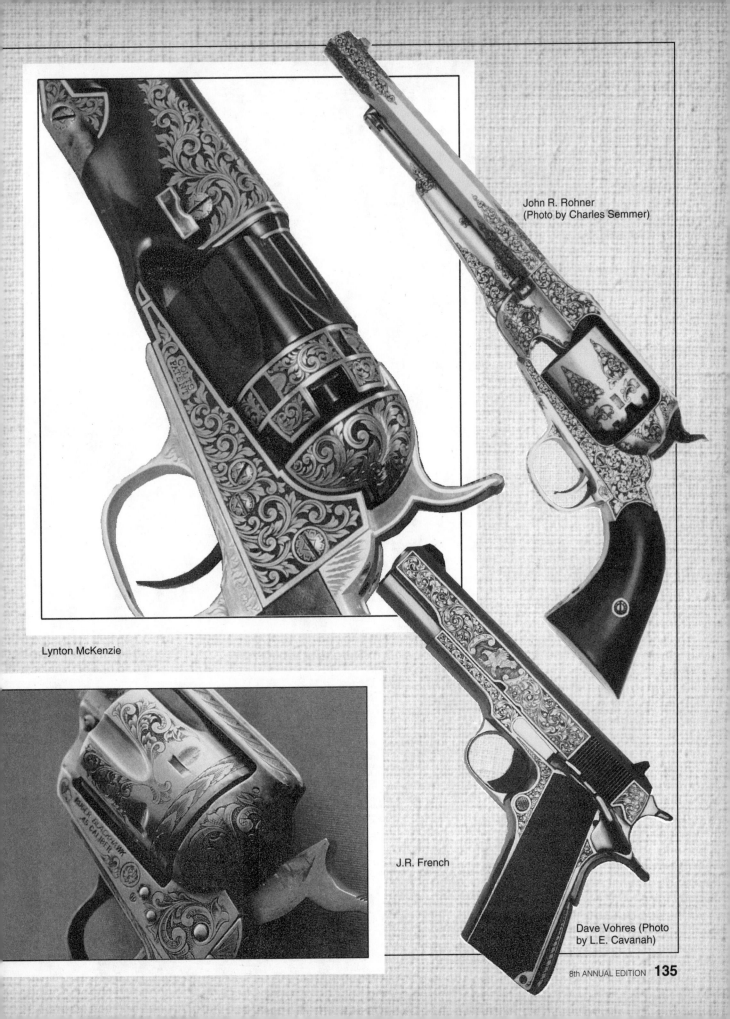

Lynton McKenzie

John R. Rohner
(Photo by Charles Semmer)

J.R. French

Dave Vohres (Photo
by L.E. Cavanah)

Lynton McKenzie

George Sherwood

Scott Pilkington

Claus Willig

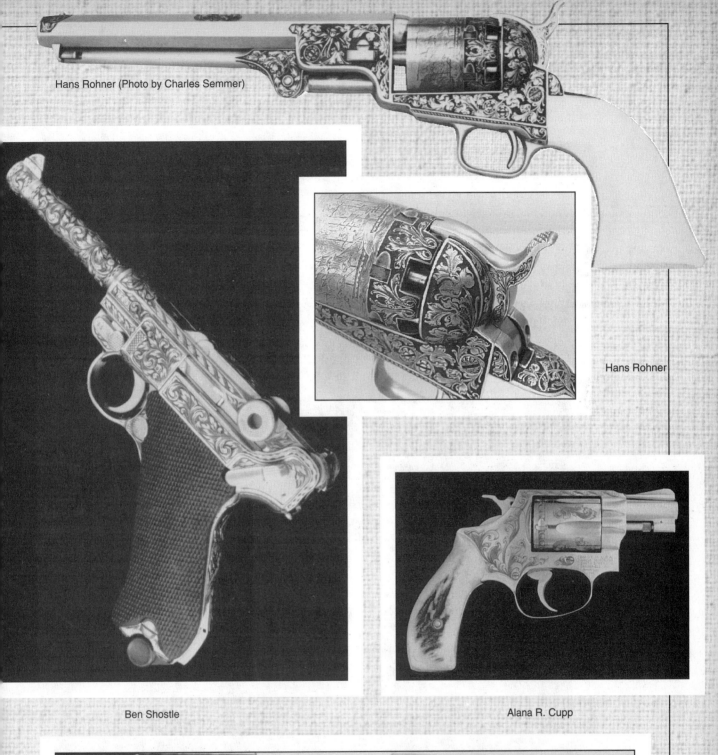

Hans Rohner (Photo by Charles Semmer)

Hans Rohner

Ben Shostle

Alana R. Cupp

Claus Willig

The Art and Soul of
STANLEY LIVINGSTON

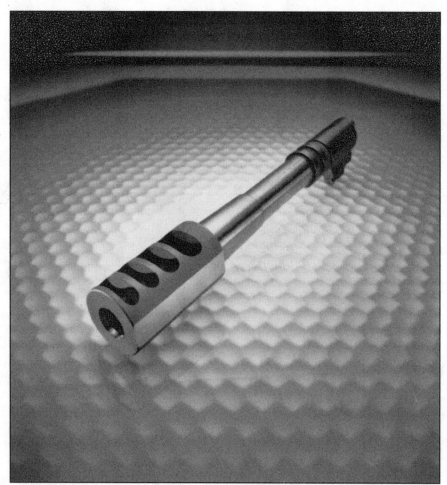

© Stanley Livingston, Ann Arbor, MI

In the preceding pages, we gave you a look at the work of top custom craftsmen and the best engravers and scrimshanders in the world. The individual parts that go into a handgun also have beauty in their sense of purpose.

We asked professional photographer Stanley Livingston, of Ann Arbor, Michigan, to turn his artistic eye onto some handgun components. Stanley, who is also one of the best black and white art photographers in the world, found beauty in the shapes and surfaces of these custom handgun components.

Many thanks to our friends at Brownells, Inc., for providing the parts.

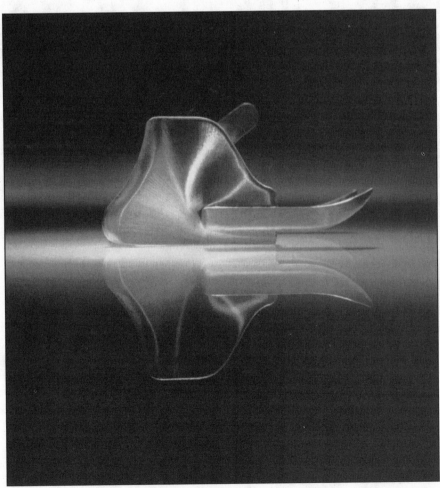

© Stanley Livingston, Ann Arbor, MI

HANDGUNS 96

Ammunition And Reloading Scene

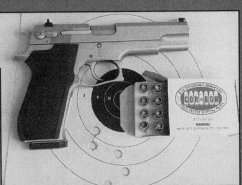

The facts on factory ammo, page 146.

Aagaard compares components, page 152.

The whispering winds of change, page 165.

TRENDS IN FACTORY
AMMUNITION
by M.L. McPHERSON

IN SELF-DEFENSE ammunition the trend is toward high-performance application-specific loads and components. Although already astonishing, performance continues to improve and we can anticipate wider availability of such loads. For the handgun hunter, the variety of use-specific loads, bullets, powders and primers will continue to grow. For the plinker, availability and variety of high-quality inexpensive reloaded ammunition and cast bullets continues to improve. For everyone, "lead-free"—more correctly, lead-pollution free—ammunition and components will become more available.

How good are today's bullets?

We tested a wide variety of bullets and loads by shooting into saturated telephone books, perhaps the best test available to the average handloader. Anyone can do it, and results are repeatable. Certainly this medium does not mimic live targets, but neither does any other substitute. In our experience saturated telephone books reliably provide a relative measure of terminal performance.

Perhaps the ultimate classic JHP bullet is Hornady's excellent EXtreme Terminal Performance (XTP). These affordable component bullets expand uniformly and consistently across a relatively wide velocity range and are also available in a wide selection of loaded ammo from Hornady and other manufacturers. Each different XTP caliber and bullet is designed for realistic velocity applications. Where necessary, e.g., in 158-grain 0.357, Hornady offers distinct versions. One version provides optimum expansion at moderate 357 Magnum revolver velocities, the other at top 357 Magnum velocities.

In author's tests Speer's 125-grain Gold Dot 38 Special +P ammunition stole the performance show. Its terminal performance compared favorably with that of some of the more potent 357 Magnum loadings.

In our tests Hornady's XTP was distressingly dependable. In some instances, as when driven too fast or when impacting too slowly, they didn't expand perfectly. However, they always expanded enough to give a reasonable amount of penetration, retained a high percentage of their initial mass, and stayed in one piece.

Like all expanding bullets, the XTP has one drawback when compared to non-expanding bullets—unavoidable loss of energy associated with expansion. This is an especially significant consideration in cartridges delivering limited impact energy. A jacketed bullet expands because hydraulic forces stress the bullet's nose. This stress expands the nose by tearing and bending the jacket and by tearing and malleably deforming the bullet's core. Energy consumed in this process comes from the bullet's impact energy. Each "unit" of energy thus consumed reduces the energy that can do work on the target by one "unit." We will refer to this as "expansion energy." All *modern* expanding pistol bullets incorporate design features intended to facilitate expansion and reduce expansion energy, e.g., pre-cut jacket noses. Some do better than others.

Consider Speer's Gold Dot (GD). These bullets begin life as a lead-alloy slug of precise weight shaped to approximately the finished contour. The slug is electroplated, molecule by molecule, with a copper-alloy jacket to a precise thickness (of about 0.010). Plating precision contributes to balance and accuracy, but it also affords unmatched jacket-to-core bonding.

After this electro-jacketed slug is resized, a "star" punch creates a precisely shaped rupture of the jacket's nose, cutting both jacket and core. This punch creates either a six- or eight-fluted hole—depending on bullet diameter—as the outside of the bullet's nose is opened to a straight cylinder. Finally, the bullet is sized to final configuration, including forming the hollowpoint's cavity size and shape, which varies, depending upon anticipated impact velocity.

More critically than Hornady's XTP,

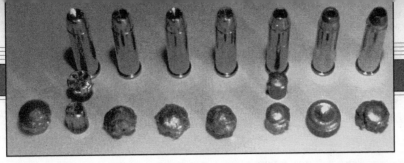

Velocity and bullet design affect expansion and penetration. The bullets are (left to right): three Speer Gold Dot 125-grain; two Speer 158-grain; Federal 158-grain; Zero 125-grain; and Black Hills 158-grain. The bullet at far left, a 125-grain Speer Gold Dot, was fired at 1345 fps. Neither of the second-from-left bullets show any significant expansion, though velocity was 1075 fps. The 158-grain Federal Hydra-Shok, sixth from left, shows marginal expansion in spite of its 1210 fps velocity.

and COMPONENTS

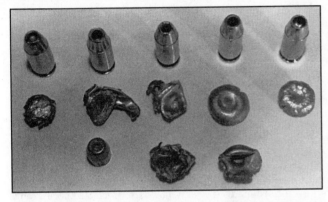

Today's 185-grain 45 ACP bullets show excellent performance in good handloads. The Hornady XTP, Sierra JHP, Remington JHP, Black Hills JHP, and Speer Gold Dot bullets (left to right) were all fired at just over 1000 fps. One of the Sierras failed to expand even though it was launched at 1090 fps.

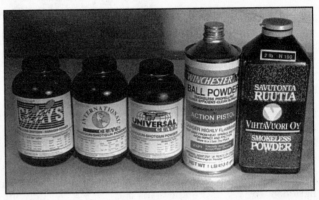

A selection of newer powders, a sign of things to come. Improvements continue, and while we won't likely see increases in ballistics, we can anticipate less muzzle flash, more uniformity and cleaner guns.

each GD is optimized for a specific impact velocity range. Our testing suggests GDs must be loaded to impact within a narrow velocity range to achieve reliable expansion. However, when so loaded, expansion and weight retention are incredibly uniform and consistent.

Because the GD's core is partially pre-cut, expansion results from individual petals bending open with little other malleable deformation. Therefore, expansion energy is reduced. Reduced expansion energy means increased energy for disruption of the target.

Winchester is already offering a "safer" substitute for their politically incorrect Black Talon handgun ammunition. While Winchester's *Supreme eXpansion Technology* (SXT) hollowpoint may not equal the Black Talon in absolute performance, it does meet all FBI performance criteria. Sharing a common thread with the current crop of premium handgun bullets, the SXT is application-specific, and it performed very well in our testing. Unfortunately, it is not yet offered as a component.

Winchester's Silvertip is an interesting variation of the classic JHP. It differs in two significant ways. First, instead of copper alloy, its jacket is aluminum alloy. Second, like the SXT, instead of fully encasing the bullet's base and sides the Silvertip's jacket is a tube folded over the perimeter of the bullet's base.

Silvertip JHPs expand well, perhaps too well. If one of your fears is overpenetration these may be your best conventional bullet choice. In our tests Winchester's 200-grain 44 Special Silvertip penetrated only half as far as some expanding 200-grain 44 Specials and barely two-thirds as far as the 44 Special Glaser load.

Glaser's shot capsule loadings are now widely available filled with either #6 or #12 shot, each having perceived advantages. In our testing, both performed well, delivering the highest energies of any load tested in 38 Special, 44 Special and 45 ACP.

We did have one failure to open, a 44 Special. It is possible that the limited

velocity generated by our 2½-inch-barrel test gun was part of the problem, and, again, no test medium is perfect. For close-range situations the Glaser is still a good choice.

Remington's Golden Sabre features a pre-cut brass jacket with a reinforcing band that is intended to prevent over-expansion, core fragmentation and core/jacket separation. In our test medium this jacket failed to limit its own expansion, but the core remained fully intact. In some instances jacket/core separations occurred. However, overall performance was impressive.

Also on the horizon from Remington are new hunting-specific handgun loadings for 1995, including both 357 and 44 Magnum Core-Lokt loads designed for optimal expansion on deer-size game. This bucks an industry trend, because ammo makers haven't been able to keep up with the demand for what they already offer. Remington is not currently offering any of its high-performance pistol bullets as components.

PMC offers the Starfire. This design

Author's son working hard to match the quality and uniformity of the best modern high-performance factory handgun ammunition—a losing battle.

features a five-flute JHP cavity. Between each flute is a bolstering wedge of lead that deters deformation. Hydraulic impact forces open the jacket into five petals by stretching and tearing the thin lead and jacket between the flutes. Expansion in ballistic gelatin reaches an average of 1.7 in diameter within about 1½ inches of penetration, giving 10-12 inches total penetration with impressive consistency. The 240-grain 44 Magnum Starfire has been heralded—by folks who know—as one of the most accurate 44 Magnum loads ever. It is particularly effective against deer-size game. Like Speer's GD, it consumes little energy expanding and, again, each bullet is application-specific. Unfortunately these are not available as components.

Federal's Hydra-Shok (HS) bullet is another advanced JHP. This is generally a dependable performer that is available in a range of loadings. Our tests showed very good performance in the 45 ACP, but we noted jacket separations with the 357 Magnum loading. The HS has an impressive record in real-world situations. Unfortunately, Federal has never offered component bullets. Several years ago they withdrew their component cases. Fortunately, at this time, they have no plans to withdraw their component primers.

Sierra, like everyone else, has recently found it impossible to meet product demand. New product development is on a back burner there for the next year or so. This does not mean Sierra offers nothing new and worthwhile. Their 150-grain 0.356 Jacketed Full Profile (JFP) is the most accurate pistol bullet Sierra technicians have ever tested: 0.4-inch groups at 50 meters! This, of course, is from a machine rest "rail gun" but it is, nonetheless, incredible pistol-

bullet accuracy. Using this bullet, any target competitor shooting any gun with a barrel designed to handle 0.356-inch diameter bullets should be able to concoct loads that make intrinsic accuracy a non-issue in any realistic target shooting event.

Sierra, like several other manufacturers, also offers bullets designed for the Makarov pistol (95-grain JHP and 100-grain FPJ) and others that work in the Tokarev pistol.

Another fairly new Sierra bullet is the 0.451-inch 300-grain JSP. Effectively non-expanding, with 6 percent antimony and extra tin in the core and with a special hard jacket, this bullet is specifically designed for the 454 Casull. It is intended for hunting the big meanies. Introduction of this bullet portends future developments at Sierra, when they find time, of application-specific handgun bullets for hunting big-game.

Hansen offers a wide variety of Israeli Military Industries (IMI) ammunition. The 185-grain JHP 45 ACP we tested looked and performed very much like an XTP. Hansen does not anticipate new offerings for 1995.

Garret offers an excellent deep-penetration 44 Magnum hunting load featuring a specially alloyed oven-hardened 310-grain cast SWC at a nominal 1320 fps. This load has recently been adopted as the official self-protection load for the Montana grizzly bear control team. They retired their rifles!

Hornady's new Vector line is specialty ammo intended to help the novice gain familiarity and confidence at the range by providing a visible trajectory. At this writing the only available cartridge is 9mm Luger. However, if sales justify, the line will be expanded.

Finally, both Winchester and Rem-

ington are expanding their lines of lead-free loads. Several regional manufacturers have joined in the lead-free game and lead-free primers may soon be available to the handloader. This will become a major issue as more indoor ranges are pressured to eliminate airborne lead pollution.

No other recent innovations compare to the advances in bullets. As a matter of fact, the increasingly litigious environment has led to significant reductions in loading pressure for many cartridges. With modern powders one could see significant increases in delivered energy if peak loading pressures common in the '50s and '60s were employed. However, the reality is that SAAMI pressure specifications and actual factory loading practices keep lowering maximum allowable pressures.

Today, we have better powders than were available a generation ago. Improvements involve not only delivery of more energy at any given peak pressure but also cleaner loads, more consistent velocity and reduced muzzle flash. All significant.

Hodgdon, Winchester, Accurate and VihtaVuori have recently released useful new powders. Because there aren't any significant holes in the burning-rate spectrum, future improvements will involve continued reduction in muzzle flash, improved uniformity and overall cleanliness. The best factory loads currently available are almost unbelievably clean, allowing virtually unlimited shooting without the necessity of cleaning even the most temperamental pistol's action.

Factories are making strides toward muzzle flash reduction. In certain loadings and applications Speer's Gold Dot

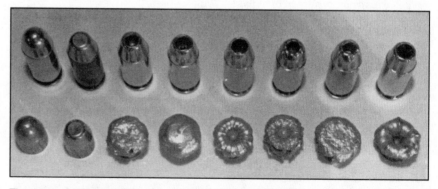

These are all 230-grain 45 bullets. The FMJ Winchester and the Hornady truncated cone slugs at left penetrated more than 11 inches of wet phone books. That's nearly twice as far as the penetration of these hollowpoints (left to right): Black Hills, Federal Hydra-Shok, Speer Gold Dot, Winchester SXT, Zero, and Eldorado. Test velocities ranged from 805 fps for the Gold Dot to 930 fps for the Hydra-Shok.

ammunition produces so little muzzle flash that it practically eliminates the hazard of temporary night blindness during encounters of the worst kind. One exception, however, is their Blazer Gold Dot in 44 Special, fired from a 2½-inch revolver. It produced a blinding strobe-like flash. The champion of all loads tested was Black Hills Ammunition's 357 Magnum 158-grain JHP, which produced no recognizable flash, even from a 2¾- inch-barrel revolver!

Primers, too, continue to improve. Dud cartridges are so rare as to be practically non-issues, and shot-to-shot uniformity can be incredible. There are still factory loadings that are dismal in this latter regard but inconsistent primers are not the cause.

Overall, modern factory ammunition compares quite favorably with the best handloads—even handloads using superior components. Handloaders have been pushing the quality envelope for over a century, but right now the factories may have the edge.

What does the future hold? Probably the biggest thing will be a continuing proliferation of the use of specific high-performance expanding bullets and loads for self-defense and hunting applications. This is partly because of recent innovations in design and manufacturing techniques that, for the first time, allow manufacturers to rapidly design and test a plethora of bullet types without undue costs.

For the hunter, limited delivered energy and reduced shot placement precision—intrinsic features of handgun shooting—make bullet performance all the more critical. Just as in the self-defense arena, expect to see bullets and loads matched to specific applications and labelled to encourage proper use.   ●

SELECTED LOAD PERFORMANCE

Manufacturer (Bullet/Load)	—Bullet— Wgt.Grs.	Type	MV (fps)	SD	Bbl. Lgth. (ins.)	Pen. (ins.)	Ret.Wgt./ % Original	Surface Area (sq. ins.)	Comments
Fiocchi/38 Spc.	148	JHP	730	11	3	7.8	148/100	0.100	No expansion
Hornady/38 Spc.	125	XTP	820	28	3	5.8	123/98	0.137	
Hornady/38 Spc.	140	XTP	720	21	3	7.4	140/100	0.162	
Hornady/38 Spc.	158	XTP	700	5	3	7.5	158/100	0.138	
Speer/38 Spc.+P	125	GD	1010	5	2¾	6.0	124.3/100-	0.238	Very impressive
Glaser/38 Spc.	80	Blue	1420	NA	3	4.4	NA	NA	Maximum destruction: 2-2.8"
Glaser/38 Spc.	80	Silver	1430	NA	3	5.0	NA	NA	Maximum destruction: 3.5-4"
Speer/0.357"	125	GD	1075	31	2¾	8/11.3	124.2/100-	0.145	2nd bullet did not expand, too slow
Speer/0.357"	125	GD	1345	27	2¾	9.5	120.2/96	0.232	
Speer/357 Mag.	125	GD	1370	17	2¾	8.5	124.7/100-	0.242	
ZERO/357 Mag.	125	JHP	1245	27	2¾	6.9	124.7/100-	0.280	Almost incredible expansion
Federal/357 Mag.	158	HS	1210	23	2¾	11.3	115.0/73	0.123	One jacket separation
Speer/357 Mag.	158	GD	1200	11	2¾	10.6	157.9/100-	0.217	
B.H./357 Mag.	158	JHP	1140	23	2¾	9.1	124.9/79	0.201	Muzzle flash undetected!
Speer/0.357"	158	GD	1260	24	2¾	9.6	144.2/91	0.221	
PMC/44 Spc.	110	THP	1120	19	4	6.1	108/100	0.145	A non-expanding bullet
Glaser/44 Spc.	NA	JShot	1410	11	4	4.5	NA	NA	
Glaser/44 Spc.	135	Silver	1240	NA	3	7.5	115.6/86	NA	Bullet failed to fully open
Hornady/0.430"	180	XTP	830	NA	3	6.5	175.3/97	0.212	
Hornady/0.430"	180	XTP	955	NA	3	6.9	171.7/95	0.246	
Hornady/0.430"	180	JHP	1040	22	4	5.5	175.7/97	0.304	
Hornady/0.430"	180	JHP	1115	19	4	4.8	173.0/96	0.341	
Blazer/44 Spc.	200	GD	815	12	3	5.4	199.6/100-	0.327	
Federal/44 Spc.	200	LHP	850	15	4	5.3	198/99	0.251	
Hornady/0.430"	200	JHP	895	16	4	6.8	182.7/91	0.200	
Hornady/0.430"	200	JHP	1035	17	4	6.4	176.0/88	0.278	
Winchester/44 Spc.	200	STip	780	11	4	3.1	199/100-	0.387	
Fiocchi/45 ACP	200	JHP	965	15	5	6.0	167.8/84	0.380	All jackets separated
Glaser/45 ACP	145	Blue	1280	NA	5	5.0	NA	NA	Maximum destruction: 1-4.5"
Glaser/45 ACP	145	Silver	1330	NA	5	4.4	NA	NA	Maximum destruction: 1-4.3"
B.H./45 ACP	185	JHP	1005	12	5	6.1	155.5/84	0.520	Jackets separated, still impressive
Hansen/45 ACP	185	JHP	940	48	5	7.0	176.0/95	0.231	
Hornady/45 ACP	185	XTP	950	20	5	6.2	177.4/96	0.249	
Hornady/0.451"	185	XTP	1055*	—	—	7.5	171.9/93	0.303	
Hornady/0.451"	185	XTP	1135 *	—	—	6.0	176.0/95	0.288	
Remington/45 ACP	185	GS	1050	—	—	7.7	185/100	0.395	One jacket separation noted
Remington/0.451"	185	JHP	1090*	—	—	5.1	185/100	0.483	Bullets ruptured down one side
Sierra/0.451"	185	PJHP	1090	23	5	7.4/11.5	163.4/88 (1st)	0.260	2nd bullet did not expand
Speer/45 ACP	185	GD	1030	24	5	5.3	184.6/100-	0.388	
Hornady/45 ACP	200	XTP	950	20	5	6.0	195.6/98	0.292	
Hornady/45 ACP	200	XTP	980	32	5	6.4	186.9/93	0.243	Compare to above load?
B.H./45 ACP	230	JHP	875	16	5	7.1	229.7/100-	0.326	Hornady XTP bullet
Eldorado/45 ACP	230	SF	860	6	5	5.3	230/100	0.377	
Federal/45 ACP	230	HS	930	11	5	6.8	224.4/98	0.342	A most impressive load
Hornady/45 ACP+P	230	XTP	930	12	5	7.6	230/100	0.372	Very impressive performance
Hornady/0.451"	230	JTC	925	13	5	11.3	230/100	0.16	A non-expanding bullet
Remington/45 ACP	230	GS	890	19	5	7.6	180/78	0.276	Jackets intact but separated
Speer/45 ACP	230	GD	805	18	5	5.1	229.8/100-	0.306	
Winchester/0.451"	230	JRN	800	18	5	11.6	230/100	0.16	A non-expanding bullet
Winchester/45 ACP	230	SXT	880	4	5	5.3	230.0/100	0.332	
ZERO/45 ACP	230	JHP	910	18	5	5.6	228.9/99	0.410	Very impressive load and results

*Estimated

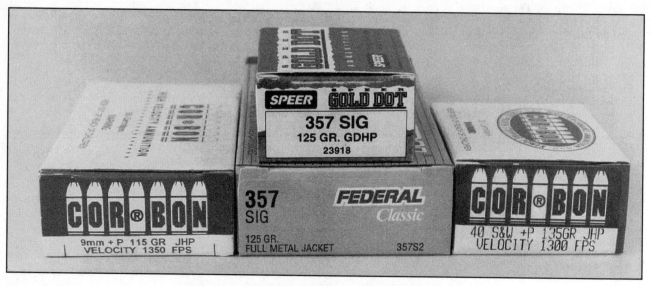

Here are the two brands of 357 SIG ammunition currently on the market flanked by Cor-Bon 9mm and 40 S&W loads that equal or surpass their ballistic performance.

FACTORY AMMUNITION
TESTS '95

by CHUCK KARWAN

The FBI instigated production of 165-grain 40 S&W loads for their use, and it looks like the Federal Hydra-Shok version shown here may be adopted by the FBI. The Cor-Bon company took the 165-grain bullet, applied it to a +P loading and came up with something that the author feels has much more potential.

THIS WAS NOT the year for earth-shattering breakthroughs in handgun ammunition. There were no Black Talon or similar highly promoted bullet technologies introduced. About the only thing along those lines was the introduction of the new 357 SIG cartridge by Federal in conjunction with SIG/Sauer's introduction of a pistol to chamber it. Much to my surprise, Speer also put the round into production in their superb Gold Dot line before any significant number of the SIG/Sauer 357 SIG pistols were in circulation.

The 357 SIG cartridge is little more than the 40 S&W cartridge necked down to take a 9mm bullet. It is extremely similar to the unsuccessful 9mm Action Express, which was the 41 Action Express necked down to 9mm. SIG/Sauer is promoting the cartridge as a semi-automatic ballistic equivalent to the 357 Magnum revolver cartridge. If

it truly were, there is no question that it would be an extremely interesting cartridge with tremendous potential. Unfortunately the 357 SIG cartridge, as introduced, is not the ballistic equivalent of the venerable 357 Magnum and is unlikely to ever be so.

The ballistic data shown in the SIG/Sauer ads for their P229 in 357 SIG show a 125-grain JHP at 1350 fps, with 510 fpe. My gun writer friend Wiley Clapp tested the Federal factory 357 SIG load in a P229 and got an average of 1387 fps. This would indicate that SIG/Sauer's advertised velocity is right on the money.

There are several 357 S&W Magnum loadings on the market that give an honest 1450 fps to their 125-grain bullets, 580 fpe, out of a 4-inch-barrel revolver. This was the load used by such agencies as the Kentucky State Police that gave the 357 Magnum its outstanding reputation for more than 95 percent one-shot stops. The 357 SIG is a full 100 fps and 75 fpe at the muzzle below that performance level. The traditional 38 Super loading until recent times was a 130-grain bullet at 1300 fps and 487 fpe, which comes closer ballistically to the 357 SIG than the latter is to the 357 S&W Magnum. Interestingly, Cor-Bon offers a 38 Super

+P load that produces 1350 fps with a 124-grain JHP that is virtually identical with the 357 SIG, ballistically. The same company also offers a +P 9mm load that is advertised as a 115-grain JHP bullet at 1350 fps for 466 fpe that nips at the 357 SIG's heels rather closely. In testing for this article, the Cor-Bon load gave me an average of 1401 fps out of my Glock 17 for 501 fpe. That is virtually equivalent to the 357 SIG's ballistics.

A look at the hotter 40 S&W loadings on the market reveals that Cor-Bon has a load that uses a 135-grain bullet at an advertised 1300 fps and 507 fpe that is also equivalent to the 357 SIG ballistically, but uses a slightly heavier bullet at slightly lower velocity. I have a couple of years' experience with the older version of this load as my primary ammunition choice for my Glock G23 40, my favorite concealed carry gun. The new version uses a Sierra bullet instead of a Nosler, and out of my compact Glock G23 gave 1336 fps for 534 fpe. Even more interesting is that it produced an average of 1417 fps out of my slightly longer Glock G22, producing a whopping 601 fpe that is true 357 Magnum performance.

Given the virtually identical ballistic performance to the 357 SIG that is available from already established cartridges like the 38 Super and 40 S&W, as well as the outstanding performance achieved by the 9mm +P and +P+, it is really hard for me to see a ballistic role for the 357 SIG that is not already filled by an established cartridge.

Don't get me wrong. The 357 SIG offers an excellent level of performance and should be quite effective as a martial cartridge. Being bottle-necked, it should feed like a champ with most any bullet shape. However, I don't see it as any kind of breakthrough, nor do I see where it has any significant advantage over the 40 S&W cartridge or several other cartridges. It would appear that most of the handgun manufacturers other than SIG agree with me. As this is written I do not know of any other manufacturer intending to chamber the cartridge, even though it would be extremely easy for most of them to do so. In most cases, all that would be necessary would be to rechamber a 9mm barrel to 357 SIG and fit it to one of their pistols that is chambered for 40

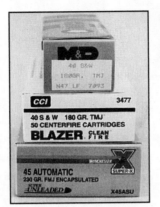

Ammunition designed to remove lead pollution from the shooting ranges is becoming more popular. Typically this consists of a lead bullet covered completely with a tough jacket. Some call it totally metal jacketed or TMJ, while Winchester calls it "encapsulated."

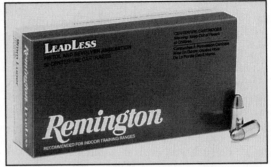

Remington calls its non-lead-polluting ammunition "Lead-Less" and its totally jacketed bullet "Lead Lokt." These loads also feature a lead-free primer.

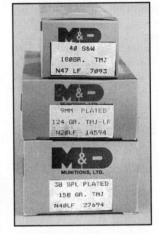

M&D has a full line of non-lead-polluting ammunition. Shown here are just three different loads.

S&W, which is essentially what SIG/Sauer did. Contrast the lethargic response by the industry to the 357 SIG to that which occurred when S&W announced the 40 S&W cartridge. Within *one day,* several other manufacturers announced that they would also be chambering the round, and at least two manufacturers actually beat S&W in getting 40 S&W pistols to the marketplace.

Competition is tough in the field of handgun cartridges, and the huge almost overnight success of the 40 S&W was the exception rather than the rule. A good example is the superb 10mm Auto cartridge that does fill a unique ballistic nitch as the most powerful auto pistol cartridge usable in a normal-size handgun. The 10mm Auto has been chambered by many manufacturers in many guns, and is still being chambered by several. In addition, 10mm ammunition is still manufactured by just about everybody of significance in the ammunition business. In spite of all that, it is beginning to flounder at the marketplace in both gun and ammunition sales, mostly because of competition from the ballistically inferior 40 S&W. The 40 Smith has the advantage of being chamberable in smaller guns with larger magazine capacities. If the superb 10mm Auto cartridge can fail, I am afraid

that the 357 SIG just might go the way of the 41 Action Express, the 9mm Action Express, the 9mm Magnum, the 10mm Magnum, the 9mm Federal, and the 356 Team S&W. All of the latter were introduced in recent years and are for all intents and purposes dead. If you don't believe me, go out and try to buy a new gun chambered for one of those rounds, or try to buy a couple of boxes of ammunition for them. Only time will tell how well the 357 SIG cartridge will fare, but I suspect that it won't be well.

There is no question that the 40 S&W is the cartridge success of the decade. However, all was not always roses for this cartridge. When it first came out and for a good time afterward, virtually none of the ammunition on the market was truly accurate in any auto pistol so chambered. We also had problems with unburned powder, and often there was evidence that the 40 S&W-chambered pistols were trying to extract the case before the pressure in the barrel had a chance to drop off sufficiently. To make matters worse, there were a conspicuously high number of high pressure accidents with 40 S&W handloads all across the country.

Now that the cartridge has had a chance to mature and a great deal of experience with it has been achieved, most of these problems have been worked out. In my opinion, the 40 S&W was fielded a little bit hastily without sufficient testing. Its original ballistic format, a 180-grain bullet at 950 fps or slightly more, was dictated by an FBI requirement for a down-loaded 10mm cartridge with similar ballistics. Going to a shorter cartridge while retaining the same ballistics enabled manufacturers to chamber their staggered-magazine 9mm pistols for this round. This in turn allowed for 40 S&W pistols to have a larger magazine capacity than their 10mm brothers, and in some cases smaller grip frames.

We now know that many of the early problems with the 40 S&W cartridge center on the 180-grain bullet dictated by the FBI requirements. Experiments have shown that a 180-grain bullet load that meets SAAMI pressure limits can have its pressure raised as much as 30,000 psi with some powders if the bullet is jammed back into the case as little as 1/16-inch. I believe that this accounts for the vast majority of the high pressure problems that occurred with handloads. Similarly, small increments of powder added to maximum loads can,

The Eldorado 380 Starfire did not have nearly the expansion of its 40 brother, but this is still good expansion for a 380.

Here are two examples of the PMC Eldorado 40 S&W 155-grain bullets after firing into water. Though the jackets separated from the lead core, author believes this is not necessarily bad since it can make an extra wound channel. The bullets expanded to more than double their original diameter.

with some powders, cause huge increases in pressure, particularly with the 180-grain bullet. In addition, the incidences of the pistol trying to unlock before the pressure had dropped in the pistol's barrel appear to have been caused by the use of certain powders and the 180-grain bullet. With the long 180-grainer in the short 40 S&W case, there is so little powder space that, with some powders, things can get critical in a hurry. What is also interesting is that when lighter bullets are used in the 40 S&W, most of these potential problems disappear or become much less critical. This is probably because the lighter bullets are shorter and allow more airspace in the case behind the bullet, and because the recoil momentum characteristics are more favorable to proper cycling of the pistols.

The FBI quickly recognized many of these problems with the 40 S&W cartridge. After much experimentation, they came to the conclusion that the 180-grain bullet was not the best choice for the 40 S&W. Recently, they have requested that their various ammunition manufacturers do up a 40 S&W load with a 165-grain JHP at 950 fps. At least three of them have complied and are marketing such ammunition. I have it on good authority that the FBI is about to authorize the use of 40 S&W-chambered pistols by their agents and that the official load will be the Federal Hydra-Shok 40 S&W with a 165-grain bullet at a nominal 950 fps. Federal was kind enough to supply us with a small quantity of this load for testing. In my Glock 22 it averaged 1027 fps for a muzzle energy of 386 fpe. It was very accurate, and recoil was quite mild. I believe this will be an excellent load for law enforcement, especially for those who are recoil sensitive.

However, if I give up bullet weight I'd like to get something in return, like higher velocities. Peter Pi at Cor-Bon thinks so, too. He brought out a +P 40 S&W load featuring a 165-grain bullet. This load gave us an average of 1212 fps and 537 fpe in my Glock G22. (Again we have higher energy than the 357 SIG.) To my way of thinking, Cor-Bon is the better ammo choice in this bullet weight as long as the shooter can handle the additional recoil, which I did not find to be uncomfortable.

One of the hot things in ammunition manufacture right now is practice ammo that is designed to not give off any lead pollution in the form of vaporized lead, lead dust or larger lead particles. The most cost-effective way to do

Winchester's new ammunition additions include these two entries, a 45 ACP 230-grain SXT JHP and a 380 ACP 95-grain SXT JHP. These feature bullets designed to expand at the moderate velocities of these chamberings.

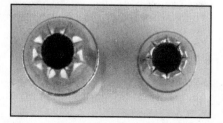

Muzzle view of the 45 and 380 Winchester SXT JHP bullets. Note the striated bullet jackets, which aid expansion.

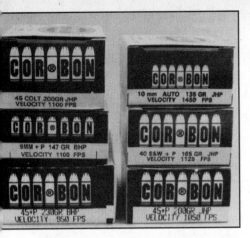

These are some of the new loads fielded by Cor-Bon this year. Some are totally new, while others are upgrades of previous loadings.

this is to use a lead bullet plated on all surfaces to create a jacket that totally contains all of the lead. When this type ammunition first surfaced several years ago, I believe made by CCI/Speer, my old friend Dean Grennell called it totally metal jacketed, or TMJ. That name stuck and is used industry-wide today. With a TMJ, no lead is vaporized by hot powder gases, and the lead is kept all wrapped up after it hits the bullet trap. This prevents any lead dust or particles from entering the atmosphere or getting on the floor of the shooting facility.

This type of ammunition is marketed under a variety of names such as as "Clean-Fire," "Lead Free," etc. Some, like the CCI Blazer and Speer Lawman, go as far as to use special primers that do not use lead, barium, or antimony compounds found in the priming of conventional ammunition. This type of ammunition has enabled many indoor ranges to remain open that would otherwise have been closed because of lead pollution. Those of us who spend a lot of time at such ranges are much better off healthwise than we ever have been in recent history.

We tested three varieties of this type ammunition in 40 S&W with 180-grain bullets. One was the CCI Blazer with non-reloadable aluminum cases, another from the Speer Lawman line, and a third from a smaller manufacturer in Farmingdale, New York, named M&D Munitions. The latter was put up in Winchester brass. As you can see from the enclosed table, the M&D is quite mild stuff, the Blazer is much hotter, and the Lawman hotter still. All shot sub-3-inch groups and would make fine practice ammunition. Because I had more of the Blazer on hand, I fired it in three different lengths of Glocks to see what effect the barrel length had on muzzle velocity. The longer barrel gave

a significant jump in velocity, but not as much as I had hoped. (See test results.)

We also tested M&D's new 9mm 124-grain TMJ low-pollution ammunition in both a Glock G17 and a SIG/Sauer P226 with virtually identical performance, equally low standard deviations and respectable accuracy.

My thoughts were that the hotter ammunition would likely get the most advantage out of longer barrels, so I tested some of the Cor-Bon +P 40 and 9mm loads. I should digress a bit here and explain that Cor-Bon is a small ammunition company that has carved a unique niche in the firearms field. They specialize in high-velocity ammunition of the +P variety, often with lighter-than-typical bullets and often with higher velocities and energies than anything else on the market. They are, in effect, the modern SuperVel for those of you who remember that brand of ammunition from the '60s and '70s. They have excellent quality control and pressure-test their loads in-house using SAAMI reference ammunition for calibration, to ensure their loads meet SAAMI specifications for +P ammunition. They also use special powders that have low flash and are extremely efficient. This means their loads often give higher velocities than those of their competitors even when loaded to the same maximum pressure level. I have had many years of very satisfactory use with Cor-Bon ammunition and recommend it highly. I should also mention that the big ammunition companies are not fond of Cor-Bon.

Regardless, Cor-Bon has the highest-performance ammunition on the market in several different chamberings. One of my favorites for a couple of years was their 40 S&W +P 135-grain load using a Nosler bullet. It gave the single best energy and penetration I could find for my Glock G23. Cor-Bon's new version of this load uses a new 135-grain Sierra bullet and is nominally rated at 1300 fps. In my Glock 23 with 4-inch barrel it gave an average muzzle velocity of 1336 fps and 534 fpe. I can never remember a Cor-Bon load not at least achieving its nominal performance and typically they beat it. It did not let me down in this case either. In the 4.5-inch Glock 22, velocity jumped to 1417 fps and 601 fpe. In the 6-inch Glock 24 it jumped further, up to 1446 fps and 626 fpe. It is interesting to note that the latter two produce more energy than most 357 Magnum loads and nip at the heels of the very best 10mm loads. The big surprise was the huge jump going from a 4-inch to a 4.5-inch barrel. I can only guess that the G22 has a particularly tight bore.

That test was so interesting I did the

same series with Cor-Bon's 40 S&W 150-grain JHP that has a nominal performance of 1200 fps. As you can see from the Velocity/Barrel Length chart, the little G23 got 1229 fps average for 503 fpe. This rose to 1275 fps and 540 fpe in the longer G22, and 1347 fps and 603 fpe in the 6-inch G24. The latter energy figure beats most 357 Magnum loads handily.

The new PMC Eldorado 40 S&W 155-grain Starfire load, fired in a Glock G22, gave an average muzzle velocity of 1171 fps and an energy of 472 fpe. This bullet weight is middle-of-the-road for the 40 S&W. Recoil was mild and accuracy was quite good. The bullet looked so promising we tested it in water, and expansion was enormous. Typically, the jacket would separate from the lead core and proceed on its own. Some

High quality but inexpensive 9mm Makarov-chambered handguns like this East German Makarov have caused this previously oddball round to be in demand here in the U.S. Cor-Bon has the most effective load on the market in this chambering.

would consider that a bullet failure, but I don't. Indeed, I suspect that this bullet would damage more tissue than a similar one that stayed together. All in all it's a very impressive load.

Because I have more 9mm handguns on hand in more barrel lengths than any other caliber, I decided to do a comparison using a variety of pistols with barrels ranging from 3.5 inches to 6 inches using the Cor-Bon 9mm +P 115-grain JHP load having a nominal velocity of 1350. This is the highest velocity 115-grain 9mm load on the market today. A look at the nearby table shows how efficient this ammunition is, as even the shortest barrels gave velocities above the nominal 1350 fps. The veloci-

AMMUNITION '95

The author has shot a great deal of CCI Blazer Clean Fire (lead free) in his trusty Glock G22 and has always found it to be accurate and reliable practice ammunition.

Here is the author's favorite concealed-carry pistol, the Glock G23 shown with the sweet-shooting new 165-grain Hydra-Shok 40 S&W load inspired by the FBI. The lowest shot was the first shot, a common occurrence with semi-autos.

ties climbed with barrel length, the exception being the 4.4-inch-barrel SIG/ Sauer P226 which gave lower velocity than even the 3.5-inch S&W. The 4.5-inch Glock G17 broke the 1400 fps mark and the 6-inch G17L broke the 1500 fps mark. Folks, that's moving right along!

I had two other new Cor-Bon 9mm +P loads to test. Both were shot in a Glock G17. The first is a 124-grain JHP at a nominal 1250 fps. It actually produced 1275 fps for a very respectable 447 fpe. Good but not terribly exciting performance. The other load is unique in that it is a 147-grain JHP bullet normally used in subsonic 9mm ammunition, but in this case pushed to a decidedly supersonic 1101 fps and 395 fpe. If you are one of those guys who insist on heavier than normal bullets, this is the load to use in 9mm.

One cartridge that has been surprisingly successful on the market is the 9mm Makarov. This has been primarily because of the high-quality pistols in this chambering that have been imported in recent years at incredibly good prices. Naturally, a demand developed for good hollow-point defensive ammunition in this chambering. According to most military sources, the 9mm Makarov should have a power advantage over our 380 ACP, but in testing the civilian and military ammunition that is available, this has not proven to be true. The one exception that I have found is the new Cor-Bon 9mm Makarov JHP load. Tested in an East German Makarov and a Hungarian PA-63, it gave significantly better ballistics than the Winchester 380 SXT

and the PMC Eldorado 380 95-grain JHPs fired from a Hungarian R61.

There were two interesting new 45 ACP loads on the market that I was able to obtain for this chapter. The first is the new Winchester 230-grain SXT JHP. This is a standard-velocity load that produced nearly identical performance out of both an M1911A1 Colt and a Glock G21. It is a hollow-point designed to open up reliably at the rather low 45 ACP velocities. Unfortunately, I did not have enough of it to conduct expansion tests, but a couple shots into water certainly indicated that it is promising.

The other 45 ACP load tested was the new Cor-Bon 230-grain +P JHP. Fired in an M1911A1, an S&W 4506 and a Glock 21, performance was impressive, producing over 950 fps and over 460 fpe in all guns. This is a real thumper that would be excellent for use in areas with large animals or where "bad guys" wear heavy clothing. Surprisingly, recoil was not bad in the S&W 4506 or Glock, but it was uncomfortable in the M1911A1 with

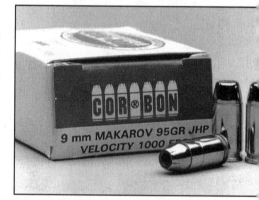

The Cor-Bon 9mm Makarov load appears to be the most powerful in that chambering available today.

The Cor-Bon +P 45 ACP loads shot extremely well in the Glock G21. There are 5 holes here.

The same ammunition as at left did not shoot nearly as well in the S&W 4506.

its narrow grip-safety tang. I highly recommend the installation of a beavertail grip safety on any Colt Government model or clone before I would shoot much of this +P load.

Please realize that the absence of certain loads or manufacturers from this chapter is not a negative reflection on them. The simple fact is that many of the newest loads were not available for testing when this piece went to press.

I came away from this testing session with a greater respect and interest in longer barrels on autos. A long-slide 10mm Glock G21, for example, would probably make an awesome hunting and competition handgun, as would a long-slide 45 ACP with some of the +P loads. I believe that the 40 S&W has matured into one hell of a defensive cartridge that with the lighter bullet high-velocity loads should be about as effective as any handgun can be. I also have renewed respect for the 9mm Parabellum. In its +P format it is quite impressive, in many cases outstripping the typical 110-grain 357 Magnum revolver load quite handily. You will probably note my prejudice toward high energies. While high energy is no guarantee of superior performance, lack of it is a guarantee of inferior performance. Put another way, if the bullet is designed to give adequate penetration and good expansion, then the load with the highest energy has the ability to do the most damage and be the most effective. I know that there are "authorities" who push the idea that energy is not important in handgun ammunition, but in my not so humble opinion they are very wrong!

●

FACTORY AMMUNITION COMPARISON

Make	Cartridge	Wgt.Grs.	—Bullet— Type	Pistol	Barrel Length (ins.)	MV (fps)	KE (ft.lbs.)	Group SD	25-Yd. Size (ins.)
How the 357 SIG Stacks Up									
Fed	357 SIG	125	JHP	SIG P229	3.9	1350	510	—	NA
C-B	38 Super	124	JHP	—	5.0	1350	502	—	NA
C-B	9mm+P	115	JHP	Nominal*	—	1350	466	—	NA
C-B	9mm+P	115	JHP	Glock G17	4.5	1401	501	35	3.2
C-B	40 S&W	135	JHP	Glock G22	4.5	1417	601	8	2.5
Normal vs. +P Ammo									
Fed.	40 S&W	165	JHP	Glock G22	4.5	1027	386	15	2.2
C-B	40 S&W +P	165	JHP	Glock G22	4.5	1212	537	21	3.7
Energy Comparison, 9mm vs. 40 S&W									
M&D	40 S&W	180	TMJ	Glock G22	4.5	879	317	11	2.5
Speer	40 S&W	180	TMJ	Glock G22	4.5	1042	434	16	2.7
CCI	40 S&W	180	TMJ	Glock G22	4.5	998	396	9	2.2
CCI	40 S&W	180	TMJ	Glock G23	4.0	983	385	19	2.8
CCI	40 S&W	180	TMJ	Glock G24	6.0	1039	431	19	2.5
M&D	9mm Para	124	TMJ	Glock G17	4.5	1196	393	12	3.2
M&D	9mm Para	124	TMJ	SIG P226	4.4	1199	395	12	2.4
Makarov vs. 380 ACP									
C-B	9mm Mak	95	JHP	EG Makarov	3.8	1030	223	20	3.5
C-B	9mm Mak	95	JHP	Hung. PA-63	4.0	1032	224	36	3.8
Win	380 ACP	95	SXT	Hung. R61	3.5	891	167	12	4.1
PMC	380 ACP	95	Starfire	Hung. R61	3.5	909	174	20	3.8
Velocity as a Function of Barrel Length 40 S&W and 9mm									
C-B	40 S&W +P	135	JHP	Nominal*	—	1300	507	—	—
C-B	40 S&W +P	135	JHP	Glock G23	4.0	1336	534	14	3.5
C-B	40 S&W +P	135	JHP	Glock G22	4.5	1417	601	8	2.4
C-B	40 S&W +P	135	JHP	Glock G24	6.0	1446	626	28	2.0
C-B	40 S&W +P	150	JHP	Nominal*	—	1200	480	—	—
C-B	40 S&W +P	150	JHP	Glock G23	4.0	1229	503	15	2.7
C-B	40 S&W +P	150	JHP	Glock G22	4.5	1275	540	12	2.2
C-B	40 S&W +P	150	JHP	Glock G24	6.0	1347	603	10	2.2
C-B	9mm Para+P	115	JHP	Nominal*	—	1350	466	—	—
C-B	9mm Para+P	115	JHP	S&W 6906	3.5	1374	481	11	4.1
C-B	9mm Para+P	115	JHP	S&W 5904	4.0	1371	479	47	4.2
C-B	9mm Para+P	115	JHP	Glock G19	4.0	1377	483	33	3.5
C-B	9mm Para+P	115	JHP	SIG P226	4.4	1364	474	32	2.7
C-B	9mm Para+P	115	JHP	Glock G17	4.5	1401	501	35	2.9
C-B	9mm Para+P	115	JHP	Glock 17L	6.0	1502	576	29	1.8
C-B	9mm Para+P	124	JHP	Glock G17	4.5	1275	447	13	2.9
C-B	9mm Para+P	147	JHP	Glock G17	4.5	1101	395	42	3.1
45 ACP 230-Grain Performance									
Win	45 ACP	230	SXT	M1911A1	5.0	868	385	11	3.9
Win	45 ACP	230	SXT	Glock G21	4.6	891	387	14	2.5
C-B	45 ACP+P	230	JHP	S&W 4506	5.0	964	472	13	3.1
C-B	45 ACP+P	230	JHP	Glock G21	4.6	957	466	7	2.8
C-B	45 ACP+P	230	JHP	M1911A1	5.0	954	463	13	3.7

All testing was performed at 75° Fahrenheit temperature and at an altitude of 200 feet above sea level. Velocities were measured with an Oehler Model 33 chronograph with 4-foot screen spacing. Test results are averages of 10 shots.
*"Nominal" is Cor-Bon's claimed velocity, which was *exceeded* in all test results.
JHP = Jacketed hollowpoint; TMJ = Totally metal jacketed; SXT = Supreme Expansion Technology

HANDLOADING COMPONENTS TESTS '95

by FINN AAGAARD

J EFF COOPER OBSERVED that, as a class, shotgun shooters tend to be in good financial health, and riflemen reasonably so, but pistoleros are often a poverty-stricken bunch. Could be—I shoot pistols a lot, rifles some, and shotguns rarely. Though I am rich in many other ways, I do have to count pennies quite carefully. Of course, handgunners usually burn up a lot of ammunition, more than rifle shooters, generally. Regardless of the reasons, pistol shooters tend to be *reloaders*, hence a review of what is new—or at least newish—in handloading components seems meet. We will look into the subject only as it concerns traditional handguns—"belt guns" if you like—leaving aside the "hand-rifle" clan for the nonce. They mostly use rifle cartridge components anyway.

Powders

Charges for pistol cartridges are normally thrown with a measure rather than weighed individually, consequently the ability of a powder to meter consistently is of some importance, especially in high-volume reloading on a progressive press. In general, the spherical-grained powders meter best, while flake powders like Unique tend to show a wider variation between charges. At least in theory, an ideal charge would fill the case just to the base of the bullet, eliminating any air space and making it impossible to accidentally put in a double charge. Some pistol cases such as the 380 Auto and to a degree the 9mm Parabellum are short of powder capacity and can to advantage use dense powders that occupy little room. Others, especially those originally designed to operate at relatively low pressures with bulky charges of blackpowder, such as the 45 Colt and 38 Special, are better served with low density propellants that take up a lot of space for their weight. (The technical term is "bulk density," expressed in

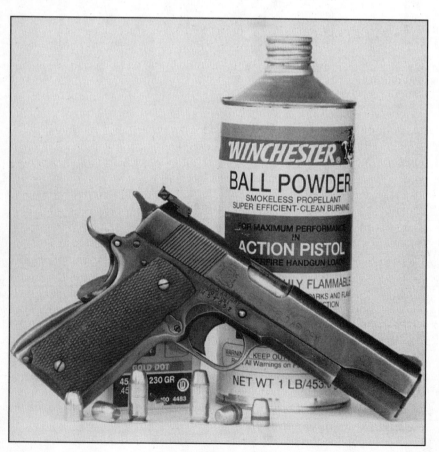

Winchester Action Pistol (WAP) powder gave good results in the Springfield Armory Model 1911-A1, 45 ACP.

VihtaVuori N110 is very suitable for magnums like the author's 44 Magnum S&W 6-inch nickel Model 29-3.

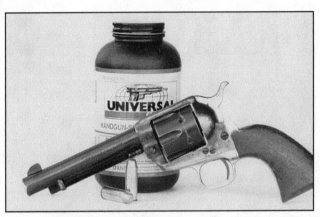

Hodgdon's Universal Clays worked well in the author's Hammerli Virginian SA 45 Colt.

grams per cubic centimeter. The higher the value, the more dense the powder.) Another consideration is the burning rate of the powder. In general, low-pressure and limited-capacity cartridges use "faster" burning powders, while high-performance magnums need "slower" powders to achieve their potential, especially with the heavier bullets. Complete combustion with no unburned kernels or other residue ("clean burning") is a quite desirable characteristic, particularly in revolvers where debris under the extractor star can tie things up at the most inappropriate moments. (Incomplete burning is one reason slow powders are not usually suitable for low-pressure cartridges.) Muzzle flash is undesirable in cartridges that may be used for defensive shooting in low light. Some powders contain flash inhibitors, but as a rough rule of thumb, short barrels and slow powders exacerbate muzzle flash. One advantage of fast-burning powders is that they yield significantly more shots per pound, that is to say per dollar, which matters to many of us.

I ran the powders discussed herein through an old Ideal No. 55 powder measure, set to throw about 6½ grains of Unique. The average weight of ten consecutive thrown charges allows a comparison of the density of the powder to that of Unique, while the maximum variation (extreme spread) in the weights of the individual charges gives some indication of how consistently the powder meters. The least dense—or bulkiest—powder proved to be Hodg-

don's Clays. But it is a fast burner, perhaps slightly faster than Bullseye, so it takes only a little of it to constitute a maximum load. Consequently, with comparable full-power loads, the denser but slower Unique will fill more of the case.

Although they have been made in Finland for over 70 years, and have earned a high reputation for themselves in Europe, the **VihtaVuori** powders are relatively new on the American market. I visited the VihtaVuori Oy plant a few years ago and found it to be a most up-to-date facility. The whole nitration process, carried out in huge, stainless steel retorts, was controlled by a couple of technicians watching an electronic information board in a glass-fronted control room. The product was then piped out to buildings scattered around in quiet woodland (so that fire in one would not spread to another) for further processing. All the VihtaVuori canister powders are single-base, nitro-cellulose propellants (they make double- and even triple-base powders for military applications), mostly in flake or short tubular form, but their ample graphite coating lets them meter through powder measures about as well as spherical powders do, according to the Vihta-Vuori literature. Their pistol propellants start with N310, a fast-burner that is competitive with Bullseye and has similar applications; continue with N320 that is comparable with Winchester 231 or Hercules Red Dot; the medium-fast N340 with a burning rate

close to Herco; and up to the comparatively slow N350 that compares with Blue Dot or Accurate No.7. Their 3N37 was designed, they say, for high-velocity rimfire cartridges. It comes between N340 and N350 in burning rate, and is claimed to be "very desirable for competitive handgun shooting." VihtaVuori N110 is a slow-burner comparable—surprise!—to Hodgdon H110 and Winchester 296. Even slower is N120, whose burning rate lies close to that of IMR or Hodgdon 4227.

VihtaVuori provided me with samples of N340, N350 and 3N37. The kernels of the first two are short, small cylinders, while the latter is in the form of small, perforated cylinders and discs. All three metered quite nicely. N340 gave me the highest velocity with 115-grain bullets in the 9mm Parabellum, and worked well in the 45 ACP. N350 and 3N37 did better than N340 with the 147-grain heavyweight in the 9mm, and proved quite suitable for the 225-grain lead bullet—and probably most jacketed bullets—in the 45 ACP. Despite the VihtaVuori manual's rating of them in both these applications, the test lots of 3N37 appeared to be very slightly slower burning than N350. All three burnt cleanly, leaving little visible residue. Samples of N310 and N110 arrived just before the deadline. Hurried testing suggested that N310 is a little faster than Bullseye, and that it would be equally easy to overlook a double charge. It gave me my best accuracy with wadcutters in the 38 Special. N110 produced good velocities in the 44

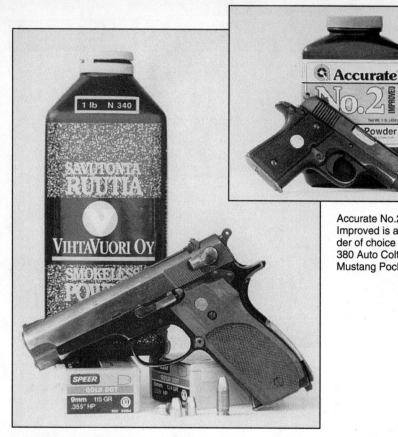

VihtaVuori N340 did well in an old S&W M39-2 9mm Parabellum.

Accurate No.2 Improved is a powder of choice for the 380 Auto Colt Mustang Pocketlite.

COMPONENTS '95

Mag and gave nice accuracy with a 158-grain bullet in the 357 Mag. It should be well worth trying in all cases where H110 and W296 are suitable choices. VihtaVuori claims their powders are designed for "clean, non-corrosive cool burning." These are desirable characteristics, though I had no way of verifying the last two.

Winchester/Olin's latest handgun propellant is Winchester Action Pistol Ball Powder (WAP), for which they claim a low flame temperature that extends barrel life, a not unimportant consideration for those who expend thousands of rounds a year in practice for competition. It meters nicely, and though fairly dense it is a little slower than Unique, so a double charge would nearly fill the case and be quite noticeable with both the 9mm and the 45 ACP. In my necessarily very limited testing it appeared promising in the 9mm, the 45 ACP and in the 40 S&W round. In the 1911-A1 pistol in particular I did notice that it left tiny flakes of a straw-colored residue, but functioning was not affected.

Accurate Arms Co. Inc. have several fairly new reloading powders.

Actually, Accurate No. 2 Improved is merely a bulkier version of the former fast-burning No.2, and its characteristics remain virtually the same. Surprisingly, its granules are smaller than those of the original product. It metered beautifully, giving me an extreme spread in the weights of ten thrown charges of less than .05-grain. It is only slightly slower-burning than Bullseye and is useful in the same applications. Decreasing its bulk density should help make double-charging less likely, though the reloader must always remain alert to the possibility. It is a powder of choice for the 380 Auto, and one I use a lot for lead-bullet practice and plinking loads in several cartridges. Nitro 100 seems to be just a tad faster than No. 2 Improved, but with its flake-like granules it is less dense and takes up more room in the case. I did not get the best accuracy with it in the 45 Colt, for which it is specifically recommended in the *Accurate Loading Guide*, but it did nicely with a 225-grain cast lead bullet in the 45 ACP. Accurate told me to use No. 9 data with their Scot 4100, a powder they acquired with their purchase of the Scot Powder Co. That

seems to be viable advice, as at least in a 357 Mag the same charge of both powders recorded practically identical velocities with a 158-grain bullet, and 4100 gave the better accuracy. XMP-5744 (eXtruded Modern Propellant) is a newly manufactured re-introduction of the discontinued—and missed—MP-5744. It is really designed for reduced loads or blackpowder-velocity loads in rifle cartridges, especially in large-case old-timers like the 50-140 Sharps. It is a double-base powder with a high nitro-glycerin content, and will, it is claimed, give consistent ignition with low-volume charges, without the need for a filler. It is a slow-burner (as far as pistol applications are concerned) that left many unburned granules in both a 44 Mag and a 45 Colt.

Hodgdon's three members of the Clays family of shotgun/pistol propellants are Clays, International Clays, and Universal Clays. Their burning rates vary in that order. Clays is in the same class as Bullseye, while Universal approaches Unique in this regard. They are flake powders with quite low bulk densities, but meter satisfactorily. Hodgdon claims that they are extremely clean burning, which my tests with Universal seemed to bear out. It produced the smallest groups of all in my 9mm Para and 45 ACP and came second only to Unique in the 45 Colt. (In my particular gun, a single-action Hammerli Virginian used mostly for cowboy action shooting, I have yet to find a powder to beat Unique for mid-level lead bullet loads.)

Bullets

Handgun bullets have improved vastly over the last several decades. It used to be difficult to find softpoint or hollowpoint bullets that would feed reliably in autoloaders, or any jacketed bullets that could be counted on to expand. Nowadays every bullet- or ammunition manufacturer provides expanding bullets that feed with 100 percent reliability and will expand, at their designed

KLA 60-grain JHP, with center post, in 38 Special, fragmented in test medium.

The 380 Auto 90-grain Speer Gold Dot Hollowpoint (GDHP) expanded well in test medium.

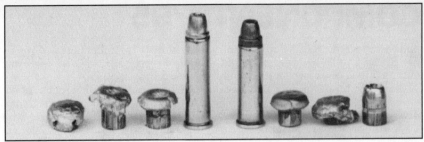

The 357/38 bullets from test medium: (from left) 357 Mag 125-grain Speer GDHP; 158-grain Speer GDHP; 156-grain cast LSWC-HP; 156-grain LSWC-HP loaded 357 cartridge; 38 Special cartridge with Speer 158-grain swaged LSWC-HP; same bullet from test medium; 125-grain Remington JHP from factory load; 125-grain GDHP—no expansion.

(From left) KLA Tri-Pro consists of three 50-grain SWC; same three stacked (and interlocked); loaded in 357; three 50-grain Safeguard Wadcutters loaded in 357 case; same three stacked (they do not interlock); and same three separated. These are designed to spread and limit penetration.

From left: Northern Precision 44 Magnum 275-grain soft lead FN with copper washer "base guard" nicely mushroomed in normal test medium; same bullet unfired; loaded round; Northern Precision Sabr Star 215-grain JHP loaded in case; unfired; and recovered from normal test medium.

Here are 45 ACP bullets from normal test medium. From left: Speer 185-grain GDHP; Hornady 185-grain XTP HP; Speer 230-grain GDHP loaded in case, and from test medium; and unfired, showing hollow cavity.

Rainier TCJ 200-grain SWC penetrated well in test medium. Though battered, the jacket did not rupture to expose any lead. When fired at a steel plate the bullet ruptured and ended up as a flattened disc with much lead visible.

impact velocities, with almost equal certainty. For this report I tried a variety of hollowpoint bullets for expansion and penetration in wet phone books at 15 feet, then hung a double thickness of an old, light, insulated vest (synthetic fibers, not down) over the front of the box of wet books, to determine whether the dry material would pack the cavities of the bullets sufficiently to inhibit expansion. (It didn't.) Finally, I put 1/2-inch of dry book (which is very hard) in front of wet ones to check the performance of those projectiles designed for deep penetration (and some others). I fired a five-shot group on paper with most loads: 21 feet one-handed with the 380 Colt Mustang Pocketlite; from a Weaver stance, fairly fast, at 50 feet with other defensive-type cartridges; and from sitting with cross-sticks at 50

yards (150 feet) with hunting loads in the 357 Mag (though the 4-inch S&W M19 is not really a hunting gun) and the 6-inch S&W Model 29 44 Mag. I was hesitant about including the accuracy results in the tables. A single five-shot group—all I had time for—is indicative of nothing very much. It can suggest that a load may have potential, and that the bullets seem to be arriving nose forward, but that is about all.

Despite progress, many of us still shoot a lot of cast lead bullets, because they are cheaper than jacketed ones, and kinder to barrels. I enjoy casting bullets, but it is time-consuming work for which I can seldom find the time any more, so I buy lead bullets from commercial casters. **Bull-X Inc.** is one of our leading cast-bullet manufacturers, but there are many others, some of

whom supply very local markets. Bull-X sent me samples of a .356-inch diameter 90-grain RN 9mm and a 180-grain .358-inch diameter truncated-cone flat-nose for the 357 Mag. The latter, cast hard, gave the deepest penetration in the 357 Mag, and quite decent accuracy to boot. If I absolutely had to defend myself against large animals with a 357, this is most likely the bullet I would choose. I tried the RN 9mm in the Pocketlite 380, where it proved quite adequate for practice. There was one failure to feed with it, when a round jammed itself up against the roof of the chamber. That was the only malfunction I can ever remember having with this pistol. It was also the only malfunction experienced throughout the testing, which says a lot for the reliability of modern auto pistols, and of modern

COMPONENTS '95

bullets and ammo. Bull-X builds a similar RN lead bullet in 93 grains weight and .365-inch diameter for the 9mm Makarov (9x18mm) pistols that have recently become so commonly available and have a new 98-grain double-ended wadcutter for the 32 S&W/32 Mag. In addition, they list bullets suitable for about every handgun cartridge from the 30 Carbine to 454 Casull.

One drawback to lead bullets is that a sufficient concentration of airborne lead particles and vapor can be extremely bad for one's health. The problem is most acute with indoor ranges, where a lot of pistol practice takes place. Traditional Full-Metal-Jacket (FMJ) bullet design enclosed the nose, but left the lead at the base of the bullet exposed to white-hot powder gases; consequently lead vapor could still be formed. Now both Winchester and Remington have lead-free ammo available, in which the

base of the FMJ bullet is sealed with a brass or copper disc, and a lead-free mix is used for the primer.

CCI/Speer found a different solution. They electroplate the lead core with copper, totally encapsulating it. They call the result their Total Metal Jacket Uni-Cor bullets, and load their Cleanfire target/practice ammunition with them, and also offer them to handloaders.

Others use basically the same technique, including the **Rainier Ballistics Corp.** which specializes in producing a whole range of LeadSafe Total Copper Jacketed (TCJ) plated target bullets, in a variety of shapes and weights, and in calibers from 9mm to 45. Those they sent me showed tiny surface marks and dimples, but the 200-grain SWCs I tried in the 45 ACP shot about as well as anything else in that gun. This bullet also gave me the deepest penetration achieved with the 45, digging slightly

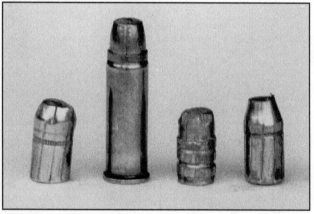

These are 44 Mag penetrators, recovered from resistant test medium. From left: Speer 300-grain JSP; 256-grain cast LSWC loaded in case and as recovered from test; and Northern Precision 300-grain JSP. The cast bullet penetrated as deeply as any of them.

deeper than the Remington factory 230-grain FMJ hardball. When I tried it on a 12-inch steel gong, it smashed itself into a flat lead disc with fragments of embedded copper. Moral: Don't shoot at steel targets when airborne lead is a concern. Rainier tells me that they are now going to put all their bullets through a second swaging process, after the plating, to give them an absolutely smooth surface and a slightly concave base, which should more easily upset to seal the bore. The couple of examples I received were quite pretty.

All our major handgun ammo manufacturers now offer loads with high-performance bullets. **Winchester** recently introduced their Supreme SXT handgun ammo to replace the politically incorrect Black Talon. It comes in black and gold boxes, but does not use black bullets, although they do share the reverse taper jacket design of the Black Talon. **Remington's** premium bullet contender is the Golden Saber, which features a brass jacket with a narrow driving band at the base (which reduces friction), and spiralled cuts in the nose. When asked if they had any plans to make these bullets available to handloaders, both firms said, "No."

Blount's **CCI/Speer** do make their premium Gold Dot (GD) bullets available to us plebeian handloaders, besides using them in their own line of loaded ammunition. The bullets are jacketed by the plating process (they have the smooth finish and concave base that results from being swaged a second time), then have an expansion cavity punched into their noses, which leaves a round dot of jacket material embedded in the bottom of the hole (though it is usually not visible until after the bullet has expanded). These are extremely good bullets. The jackets are totally bonded to the lead; there is no possibility of core-jacket separation, and they typically retain well over 90 percent of their original weight after having penetrated the target. They expand reliably to make big holes, while their high retained weights let them dig deep. The depth of their cavities vary with the weight, and the expected velocities, of the bullets. In the 9mm, for example, the 115-grain bullet has a shallow cavity; the 124-grain has a bigger one; and the slow-poke 147-grain bullet has a very large cavity indeed. As a result, the 115-grain GD actually penetrated deeper than its heavier siblings in every test, while the 124-grain and 147-grain were about equal in this respect. The 90-grain 9mm GD, on the other hand, is meant for 380 Auto velocities and has a cavity nearly as deep as that of the 147-grain bullet. I expect it would be a bomb at full throt-

Table I: Powder Comparison

Maker	Powder	Appearance	Density* (grs.)	Metering** (grs.)
Hercules	Unique	Large flakes	6.55	0.3
	Bullseye	Small flakes	7.81	0.2
	2400	Small discs	11.5	0.2
Winchester Action Pistol (WAP)		Small balls & irregular grains	11.23	0.1
Accurate	Old No. 2	Irregular granules	10.82	0.1
	No. 2 Improved	Fine irregular granules	9.3	0.05
	Nitro 100	Gray flakes	6.17	0.3
	Scot 4100	Very fine balls	13.03	0.1
	No.9	Balls & irregular granules	13.57	0.1
	XMP 57445	Short cylinders	11.42	0.2
Hodgdon	Universal Clays	Small flakes	7.85	0.2
	Int'l Clays	Flakes & pink discs	6.60	0.2
	Clays	Flakes & white donuts	5.77	0.2
VihtaVuori	N310	Very small cylinders	7.16	0.1
	N340	Small, short cylinders	8.20	0.1
	N350	Small, short cylinders	8.65	0.2
	3N37	Small cylinders & discs	9.96	0.1
	N110	Small, short cylinders	10.27	0.3

*Density = average weight of 10 charges thrown with an Ideal No.55 measure set to deliver 6.55 grains of Unique.

**Metering = Extreme Spread (variation) in weight of ten consecutive thrown charges.

Table II: Selected Loads

Cartridge	Barrel Length (ins.)	—Bullet— Wgt.Grs.	Type	Powder	Charge (grs.)	MV (fps)	Accuracy Range (ins.@ft.)	Comments
380 Auto	2.75	95	Bull-X LRN	No. 2 Imp	3.4	813	4.4 @ 21	One failure to feed
		90	Speer GDHP	No. 2 Imp	3.9	922	2.1 @ 21	
		95	Win. FMJRN	Factory load		873	2.1 @ 21	
9mm Para	4.0	115	Speer GDHP	WAP	6.7	1157	3.7 @ 50	
		"	"	Unique	6.3	1218	3.5 @ 50	
		"	"	Universal	5.3	1154	2.0 @ 50	
		"	"	N340	6.1	1231	2.8 @ 50	Compressed load
		124	Speer GDHP	N340	5.7	1150	3.3 @ 50	
		"	"	3N37	6.6	1143		
		147	Speer GDHP	3N37	5.2	936		
		"	"	N350	5.1	954	2.3 @ 50	
38 Spec	4.0	148	Rucker LWC	No.2 Imp	3.2	659	2.1 @ 50	Double load possible
		"	"	Bullseye	3.2	783	1.8 @ 50	
		"	"	N310	2.5	664	1.7 @ 50	
		"	"	Bullseye	2.5	621		
		125	Speer GDHP	No.2 Imp	5.7	930		
357 Mag	4.0	158	Hndy. XTP HP	4100	13.0	1126	3.5 @ 150	Use No. 9 data
		"	"	No.9	13.0	1142	6.0 @ 150	
		160	Hndy. CL-SIL	No.9	13.7	1133	5.0 @ 150	Poor light
		180	Hndy. CL-SIL	No.9	12.3	1055	4.0 @ 150	
		180	Bull-X LFN	No.9	11.7	1149	3.7 @ 150	
		125	Speer GDHP	W296	12.7	1290		
		158	Speer GDHP	W296	17.0	1115		
		"	"	N110	15.0	1166	3.0 at 150	
40 S&W	4.5	180	Speer GDHP	WAP	7.1	1031	3.1 @ 50	
		180	Win. JHP	Winchester load		963		
44 Mag	6.0	300	Sierra JSP	XMP 5744	20.0	956	3.6 @ 150	Many unburned granules
		"	"	4100	17.2	1022	6.0 @ 150 ft	
		"	"	N110	18.6	1130		
		300	Speer PSP	N110	18.6	1119		
		300	North. Prec. JSP	N110	18.3	1162		
		275	North. Prec. CW LFN	N110	19.5	1218	4.6 @ 150	Some leading
		256	Cast LSWC	N110	21.0	1339		
		240	Hndy. XTP HP	N110	21.5	1329		
		240	Hndy. CL-SIL	N110	21.5	1354		
		215	North. Prec. Star JHP	N110	22.5	1423		
45 Colt	5.5	225	Dillon LFN	Nitro 100	6.5	812	5.0 @ 50	
		"	"	Universal	8.6	766	2.0 @ 50	
		"	"	XMP 5744	17.5	775	2.5 @ 50	Many unburned granules
		"	"	Unique	8.0	800	1.4 @ 50	
45 ACP	5.0	225	Dillon LFN	No.2 Imp	5.2	815	2.9 @ 50	
		"	"	Nitro 100	5.0	825	2.4 @ 50	
		"	"	WAP	7.3	811	2.4 @ 50	
		"	"	Universal	6.0	806	1.7 @ 50	
		"	"	N340	6.0	797	2.4 @ 50	
		"	"	N350	7.1	837	2.8 @ 50	
		"	"	3N37	7.1	796	2.6 @ 50	
		200	Rainier TCJ	No.2 Imp	5.8	894	2.4 @ 50	
		"	"	No.7	11.5	997	2.1 @ 50	
		185	Speer GDHP	N340	8.1	1063	2.0 @ 50	
		200	Speer JHP	WAP	8.4	958	2.4 @ 50	
		"	"	N350	7.9	911		
		230	Speer GDHP	N340	6.5	920	3.1 @ 50	
38 Spec	4.0	150	KLA 3x Tri-Pro SWC	Unique	5.1	818	0.85 spread @ 21	
		150	KLA 3x Safeguard WC	Unique	5.1	821	1.12 spread @ 21	
		100	KLA 2x Tri-Pro SWC	Unique	7.0	1254	0.80 spread @ 21	
		60	HP WC	Unique	8.0	1534		
357 Mag	4.0	150	KLA 3x Tri-Pro SWC	Unique	8.5	1183	1.4 spread @ 21; 2.6 @ 50	
		150	KLA 3x Safeguard WC	Unique	8.5	1219	0.55 spread @ 10; 1.5 @ 21; 7.0 @ 50	
			HP WC	Unique	9.0	1790	Strikes 4 low @ 50	

Test guns: 380 ACP = Colt Mustang Pocketlite, 2.75″ barrel. 9mm Parabellum = S&W M39-2, 4″. 38 Special = S&W M15-3, 4″. 357 Mag = S&W M19-4, 4″. 40 S&W = Glock 22, 4.5″. 44 Mag = S&W M29-3, 6″. 45 ACP = Springfield Armory M1911-A1, 5″. 45 Colt = Hammerli Virginian, 5.5″.
Velocities at 10 feet, Oehler 35P chronograph. Ambient temps 65-80°F. Winchester standard large and small pistol primers (WLP and WSP) except for 44 Mag, where Winchester Large Pistol Magnum (WLPM) primers were used. Winchester and Remington cases.
Accuracy = 5 shot groups. 380 tested at 21 feet, one-handed. 9mm, 45 ACP and 45 Colt at 50 feet, Weaver stance. 357 Mag and 44 Mag, 150 feet (50 yds) sitting with cross-sticks.
HP = Hollow Point; SP = Soft Point; SWC = Semi Wadcutter; WC = Wadcutter; FN = Flat Nose; L = Lead; J = Jacketed; P = Plated; GD = Speer Gold Dot; TCJ = Total Copper Jacket.

COMPONENTS '95

Table III: Penetration and Expansion Tests

Cartridge	Wgt.Grs.	Type	Velocity (fps)	Penetration (ins.)	Retained Weight (Grs./%)	Expansion* (ins.)	Comments
Normal Medium: Wet telephone books at 15 feet.							
380 Auto	90	Speer GDHP	956	5.3	90/100	.54	
	90	Sierra JHP	994	5.0	90/100	.60	
	85	Win Silvertip JHP	905	4.5	85/100	.57	
9mm Para	115	Speer GDHP	1248	8.3	115/100	.51	
	115	Sierra JHP	1189	6.8	60/52	.52	Lead core only, jacket lost
	124	Speer GDHP	1148	7.3	124/100	.60	
	147	Speer GDHP	938	7.5	147/100	.57	
38 Spec	60	KLA JHP	1318	3.0	Fragments		1.3″ affected area at 2″ depth
	150	KLA 3x SWCs	927	8.0-8.5			No expansion, no spread
	150	KLA 3x WCs	849	4.5-6			No expansion, 1.3″ spread at 4″ depth
	100	KLA 2x WCs	1106	4.0			Slight expansion, 1.7″ spread at 4″
	125	Speer GDHP	922	11.5	125/100		No expansion
	125	Rem JHP Factory	998	5.5	120/96	.58	
	158	Speer LSWC HP	1080	7.3	156/99	.58	
357 Mag	60	KLA JHP	1704	3.3	Fragments		1.7″ affected area at 2″ depth
	150	KLA 3x SWCs	1229	9.5-10.5			No expansion, no spread
	150	KLA 3x WCs	1270	4.2-5.0			Slight expansion, 1.5″ spread at 4″ depth
	125	Speer GDHP	1300	7.0	124/99	.57	
	125	Rem JHP Factory	1344	6.0	77/62	.55	
	158	Speer GDHP	1113	7.2	158/100	.57	
	156	Cast LSWC HP	1200	7.5	155/99	.60	
40 S&W	180	Speer GDHP	1015	7.5	180/100	.72	
44 Mag	215	N-P Star JHP	1328	6.8	214/99.5	.84	
	275	N-P CW LFN	1196	8.0	270/98	.75	Perfect "mushroom"
45 ACP	185	Speer GDHP	995	7.0	185/100	.66	
	185	Hndy XTP JHP	1050	8.0	174/94	.56	
	200	Speer JHP	976	7.8	134/67	.57	Core & jacket separated, lying together
	230	Speer GDHP	925	7.7	229/99.5	.70	
Insulated Medium: Insulated vest + wet phone books at 15 feet							
380 Auto	90	Speer GDHP	920	4.5	90/100	.53	
9mm Para	115	Speer GDHP	1225	7.5	115/100	.54	
	124	Speer GDHP	1147	6.5	124/100	.61	
	147	Speer GDHP	975	6.5	147/100	.57	
38 Spec	60	KLA JHP	1387	3.0	Fragments		1.5″ affected area at 2″
	125	Speer GDHP	951	11.0	125/100		No expansion
	125	Rem JHP Fact	994	4.5	124/99	.64	
	158	Speer LSWC HP	1038	7.8	156/99	.57	
357 Mag	125	Speer GDHP	1341	8.5	124/99	.52	
	158	Speer GDHP	1140	9.0	158/100	.51	
	156	Cast L SWC HP	1190	7.8	154/99	.62	
44 Mag	215	N-P Star JHP	1368	7.0	129/60	.78	Core/jacket separated, but close
45 ACP	185	Speer GDHP	1005	6.5	184/99	.64	
	185	Hndy XTP JHP	1016	7.2	175/95	.55	
	230	GDHP	935	7.0	229/99.5	.69	
Resistant Medium: 1/2-inch dry paper + wet phone books at 15 feet							
357 Mag	158	Cast LSWC	1201	16.0	156/99		No expansion, nose battered, lost gas check
	160	Hndy CL-SIL	1120	18.0	160/100		No expansion
	180	Hndy CL-SIL	1015	15.0	180/100		No expansion, tumbled
	180	Bull-X LFN	1125	18.5	177/98		No expansion, nose smeared
44 Mag	300	Speer PSP	1117	21.5	300/100	.48	Nose very slightly expanded
	300	Sierra JSP	1136	20.0	300/100		No expansion, nose slightly smeared
	300	N-P JSP	1160	20.0	300/100		No expansion
	275	N-P CW LFN	1181	12.0	240/87	.63	Moderate expansion, lost copper washer
	256	Cast LSWC	1339	21.5	247/96		No expansion, nose battered, lost gas check
	240	Hndy XTP JHP	1329	14.2	233/97	.61	
	240	Hndy CL-SIL	1350	19.5	240/100		No expansion
	215	N-P Star JHP	1400	19.2	215/100	.49	Aperture closed up, riveted
45 ACP	230	Rem FMJ Fact	808	12.5	230/100		No expansion
	225	Dillon LFN	825	9.5	225/100		No expansion
	200	Ranier TCJ	970	13.0	200/100		No expansion, nose battered, jacket intact

*Expansion = Average expanded diameter of recovered bullet.

Aagaard tested the 44 Mag and 357 Mag for accuracy at 50 yards from sitting position with cross-sticks. Here Finn shoots the 6-inch Model 44 Mag.

Author tested defensive pistols, like his 1911-A1 45 ACP, from two-handed Weaver stance at 50 feet.

tle in the 9mm. The 38-caliber Gold Dot bullets are evidently meant for at least 357 Mag velocities, as I could not get even the 125-grain GD to expand from the 38 Special. Here the 125-grain factory-loaded Remington bullet, which has a large lead exposure in addition to its hollow point, proved more suitable.

Actually, my preferred defense load in 38 Special remains the Speer swaged 158-grain lead SWC hollowpoint pushed as fast as is seemly. Its penetration is near ideal, and it always expands. Does it not cause leading? Yes, a cylinder-full will leave noticeable streaks in the bore; for defensive purposes, so what? On the other hand, I believe that in my 45 ACP handguns I will swap from Speer's old 200-grain JHP "flying ashtray" to the 230-grain Gold Dot, which, while giving comparable penetration, expands just as reliably, but to a larger diameter. Penetration can be a problem in the 380 Auto, though some bullet expansion is desirable. The 90-grain GD likely offers the best compromise here. In the 9mm I may change from 115-grain bullets to the 124-grain GDHP. It expanded to a larger diameter than even the 147-grain

GD, while still giving reliable penetration. As to that, I think 6-8 inches of penetration in wet telephone books is probably ideal for defensive pistol cartridges. That's about what the 125-grain JHP in the 357 Mag provides. In the 357 Mag my 156-grain gas check LSWC hollowpoint, cast from 1:20 tin/lead alloy, still looks pretty good.

Speer makes hunting handgun bullets as well, of course. Their latest is a 270-grain Gold Dot softpoint for the 44 caliber cartridges. They were out of them, and could not get a new lot to me in time for this article. They did send me some of their plated 300-grain softpoints. At the velocity to which I was willing to push them in my S&W Model 29, they would not expand to any significant degree, but did penetrate very deeply. It is possible that the new 270-grain bullets could be given enough velocity to show useful expansion, even in my old, somewhat delicate Smith—I just don't know. In passing, Speer also offers a JHP in 325 grains weight for the 50 Action Express.

Reverting to the topic of self-defense, in some circumstances even the minimum "ideal" penetration might be too

much, if it allows a miss to penetrate a flimsy internal wall and injure an innocent person in the neighboring apartment. One way to minimize that possibility is to use a very light, frangible bullet driven to high velocity. Another is to use several light, ballistically inefficient projectiles that will lose energy fast, while creating a shotgun-like effect at close range. Steve Legg of **KLA Enterprises** has developed projectiles to suit both concepts. His Safeguard Max bullet is a straight-walled, jacketed hollowpoint with a center post and a non-lead light-alloy core. It is pre-fragmented, weighs 60 grains in 38-caliber, and can be driven very fast, over 1300 fps even in a 4-inch 38 Special. It seems to fragment every time. In wet paper, fragmentation started at a little over 1-inch penetration, and at 2 inches the fragments had saturated an area 1.3 inches in diameter (1.7 from the 357 Mag). Maximum penetration was around 3 inches, which ought usually to suffice, unless the aggressor is heavily clothed or very fat. A miss might possibly penetrate one typical interior wall if the dry matter inhibited its expansion, but I doubt that it would then have much energy left.

For the multi-projectile concept, KLA makes two different designs. In 38 caliber the Tri-Pro uses up to three jacketed semi-wadcutters of 50 grains each, stacked so that the nose of the lower fits into the hollow base of the upper. The two upper slugs are .357-inch diameter, while the lower one, marked with red ink, is of .354-inch diameter so as not to cause a bulge when seated down where the case walls start to thicken. KLA says that the Tri-Pros are meant for distances out to 25 yards, where they should provide an 8-inch pattern. In my gun they spread to 2½ inches at 50 feet, and 1½

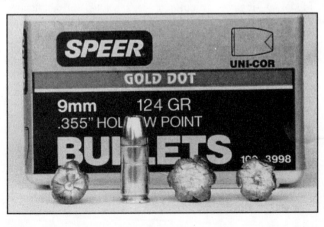

Sample of 9mm Speer GDHPs from test medium. From left: 115-grain; 124-grain (and loaded round); and 147-grain. The 124-grain gave greatest expansion, with adequate penetration.

COMPONENTS '95

Colt Mustang Pocketlite 380 Auto—a true pocket pistol—made a very useful group in fast, one-handed shooting at 21 feet with Speer GDHP.

inches rather than the stipulated 3 inches at 21 feet. For closer ranges KLA advocates its Safeguard Wadcutters, also 50 grains each in weight, but flat on both ends. They disperse faster than the Tri-Pro projectiles, making three separate holes about 1/2-inch apart at 10 feet, while the SWCs are still acting like a single bullet at 15 feet. Both types have serrated jackets to aid fragmentation, but all remained in one piece in my tests. Steve Legg advises using only two sections in the 38 Special, and of course a single 50-grain section could be loaded to rather startling velocities in either cartridge. KLA offers a two-section Di-Pro for the 9mm, with a rounded front section for reliable feeding. He hopes to have Safeguard multi-projectiles available in other calibers eventually.

The **Hornady** folks have seen no need to replace their XTP (eXtreme Terminal Performance) line of expanding premium-type bullets because they were designed to meet FBI criteria and remain as good as anything else being offered, for most purposes. They fairly recently introduced their CrimpLock Silhouette (CL-SIL) bullets, 160- and 180-grain weights in 38-caliber, 210 grains for the 41 Mag, and 240 grains in 44-caliber. Their drawn jackets are initially closed at the base and open at the nose; after the cores are inserted, the nose is closed by crimping the jacket in tightly, rather like a shotgun shell, to produce a flat point. Apart from their designed use, they should also serve well when the deepest penetration is requisite on large animals. In my test, the 160-grain CL-SIL from the 357 Mag penetrated deeper than the 180-grain, the reason being that the latter had tumbled, and was found lying side-on.

Thanks mainly to Dave Corbin, who made jacketed bullet swaging equipment available to the serious hobbyist, a whole host of small (production, not necessarily caliber) commercial bullet makers sprang up. Most failed; a few survived, and have come up with some interesting ideas concerning handgun bullets. Among them are Alpha LaFrank Enterprises and Northern Precision. **Alpha LaFrank** began by specializing strictly in .458-inch diameter rifle bullets of all sorts. Lately they have added handgun bullets in .452, .430 and .357 diameters, mostly heavyweights for hunting large game. They list bullets in weights up to 400 grains in 45-caliber, 370 grains for the 44 and 210 grains in 357, for example. They are available in a bewildering variety of styles, 7/8-length jackets, 3/4-jackets, 1/2-jackets, round, flat or wadcutter noses, softpoints, hollowpoints, or spitzers to maintain long-range momentum for metallic silhouettes. You name it, in heavyweights Alpha LaFrank quite likely makes it. I did not try the bullets they sent me, because at 350 grains in 44-caliber and 375 grains in 45-caliber they were heavier than I care to use in my comparatively light guns. In the stouter Ruger, Wesson and Freedom Arms handguns they should do superbly, however.

Northern Precision also started out specializing in bullets for only one rifle caliber, the 416. Now they have branched out to include .458 and .429 (44-caliber) bullets in their repertoire. Their 44 handgun bullets include weights from 240 grains to 375 grains. They come with thin jackets, with .025-inch tubing jackets, bonded cores or not, various nose designs including the Poly Ball with a plastic tip, and the naked, soft lead Base Guard design that has a copper washer riveted to the base that is meant to scrape out any lead or other fouling from preceding shots. Their 300-grain jacketed softpoint performed almost identically to the Speer and Sierra 300-grain JSPs in my Model 29—it gave 20 inches of penetration with no expansion. The 275-grain lead Base Guard, with its wide, flat nose, expanded nicely and penetrated deeply enough (I believe) to be reliable on medium-size big game. A dozen consecutive shots with it left noticeable lead deposits in the bore, but that again should be of no concern to a responsible hunter. The bullet had no cannelure, but it was soft enough that one could crimp the case into it where he chose, regardless.

The last Northern Precision offering tested was the fast-expanding 215-grain Sabr Star JHP. The jacket, which extends beyond the lead core, is folded in on itself, almost like the beginning of a shotshell crimp, to form half a dozen saw-tooth petals. It expanded dramatically in both my "normal" and "insulated" test media, and would undoubtedly make an effective defense and small deer load. But when I tried it on the "resistant" medium, impact with the initial dry, hard paper closed its nose up, so that it acted more like a "solid." Of course, it is designed for soft targets in the first place. In the end, though, I believe I will just stick with my home-cast, hard alloy, gas-check, 256-grain SWC (Lyman mould No. 429244) for about all purposes in my Model 29. It penetrates as deeply as most, seems easy on the gun, and has proved a reliable killer on the few deer I have taken with it. Furthermore, Elmer Keith would probably approve the choice (except that he did not like gas-checks).

When I asked Randy Brooks of **Barnes Bullets** if he were planning anything analogous to his premium, homogenous copper X rifle bullets for handguns, he just smiled and said he would have nothing ready in time for this report, but that they were already making X-type bullets that worked beautifully at low velocities in muzzleloaders, so....

Brass, Etc.

If anyone needs brass for obsolete handgun cartridges, such as the 7.65 MAS, 41 Long Colt, 7.62mm Nagant, 8mm Nambu, or even the 11.75mm Montenegrin, the Australian firm **Bertram Bullet Co.** might be able to supply him. **The Old Western Scrounger** is also worth contacting when searching for any obsolete, hard-to-find or obscure item. **Starline Brass** makes first-class, very strong cases at competitive prices. In addition to the common cartridges, they can supply brass for the 9x21mm, the 9mm Makarov, and, at the other end of the scale, the 445 Super Mag. The **Midway** catalog lists all sorts of brass, nickel-plated or not, lead bullets, plated bullets and most brands of jacketed bullets, and also presses, dies, calipers, moulds, gauges, scales, and about anything else a handloader could desire. It is worth getting.

Do we need all these goodies? Heck, no! Factory ammunition is so good these days and has all bases so well covered that, except for lead-bullet practice ammo, we really don't need to handload at all. But then, we shoot for pleasure and recreation, most of us, and rolling our own and experimenting with, and fine-tuning, different loads to get the very best out of our guns is a large part of the fun for many of us. The more good stuff we have to play with, the merrier, say I. ●

I STARTED HANDLOADING in the late 1960s and some of my friends were at it before I was born. They report having had problems acquiring components during WWII, but until quite recently, I'd never had a problem finding primers (or any other component) that would work for the application at hand. There were times when I couldn't readily get exactly the brand and type I wanted, but I was never completely stymied; that is, not until early '94.

Despite the fact that I've always been a bit paranoid, I was caught completely off guard when a recent political maelstrom precipitated that shortage. I was fully aware of what was happening, perhaps even more so than the average Joe, but I have *always* anticipated the worst, and I never even considered redoubling my stockpile of ammunition and components.

In early 1994 I visited three of our local sporting goods stores, looking to buy a reasonable supply of powder for each of several rifle/load applications. Innocently, I noticed all three stores—which had previously been relatively well stocked—were completely sold out of primers and most types of powder. Ammunition seemed to be in very low supply, too. Being preoccupied with my

WHERE DID ALL THE PRIMERS GO?

by M.L. McPHERSON

Early '95 saw this welcome sight, back room shelves stocked with all manner of primers because they won't all fit on display shelves. However, these 200,000 primers would have all been purchased in one typical sales day if this retailer hadn't imposed reasonable limits. By fair-handed rationing this retailer was able to keep all his customers shooting—at least a little—throughout '94.

own problems I didn't give the matter a second thought, not on that trip. Just typical off-season poor supply in a small backwoods town, I figured.

A few days later my family and I traveled 200 miles to my old stomping grounds at Grand Junction, Colorado, an area where perhaps 100,000 people live, and a handloading haven. I stopped in at a sporting goods store *knowing* it always had been, and certainly would still be, well stocked with handloading components. Well, so much for what I knew.

Empty shelves now stood in aisles that had always been stocked with components in myriad variety. Then, and for some time thereafter, this shooting-sports-related shortage was not limited to primers but included powder, ammunition and guns.

No use chronicling these shortages in detail; we are all aware of them, at least in local areas, and I suspect most of us have talked with friends and read enough to know that this was a nation-wide epidemic. I have discussed local shortages with local dealers; regional shortages with regional dealers; national shortages with representatives of all the major ammunition producers, all the domestic component-primer producers and every major powder producer or vendor. All tell a similar, though not identical, story.

Starting early in 1994, or even before, there was a serious run on all kinds of handguns nationally and a run on rifles in certain regions. Although demand for handguns remains higher than it had been prior to the Clinton administration, production has now generally caught up. In addition, demand for ammunition of all types was unprecedented throughout early 1994, and demand for handgun ammunition remains very much elevated as this is written, early 1995. There doesn't seem to be any end in sight, although the recent election landslide *may* alter that situation. However, a sudden decrease in demand could devastate the entire industry. Several experts express grave yet reasonable concern that they will be forced to lay off workers—now tending virtual round-the-clock production—and perhaps even close plants, if and when this evident stockpiling hysteria and buying binge subsides. The potential devastation such an eventuality might bring is no small matter. After almost a year of powder supply shortfalls it seems we may finally have seen the end of this shortage. Stocks

Many handloaders faced just this situation: Bullets, cases, powder but no primer.... Without that little 2-cent item, bullets and powder are as useless as an empty case.

When one adds a primer to the equation the outcome is much more satisfactory, let's go shooting!

may not be abundant but most of us can find what we need readily enough, and supplies are likely to continue to improve.

There are two plausible reasons why the powder deficiency problem has been solved faster than the primer shortage. First, folks are more paranoid about primers, and for very rational reasons. We can cast bullets, reuse cases repeatedly and—if worse comes to worse—we can dig and process guano and sulphur and make our own charcoal which are the ingredients required to mix usable blackpowder. However, for all practical purposes, it is simply not possible to make primers at home.

Without the explosive action of primers we would find it virtually impossible to utilize anything resembling modern smokeless powder. All primers contain mixtures which effectively are explosives. This is a fact we can expect to haunt us in the future. Many folks are very concerned that we may wake up tomorrow and discover that primers are suddenly illegal.

Another reason powder appears to have been less hoarded than primers is that there are more sources for powder. Imported primers are scarce and distribution is limited.

You can try, but it just won't work. No primer, no load.

The Primer Shortage

CCI, Remington, Winchester and Federal have been producing virtually all the primers they can since early 1994. Employees have worked overtime, some without a vacation day in months, with production stoppages occurring only for safety inspections and required maintenance.

Manufacturers have been producing what might seem like an endless boun-

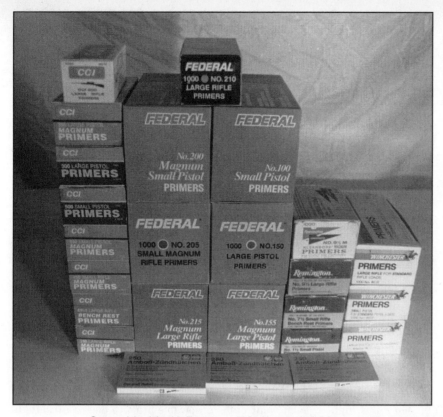

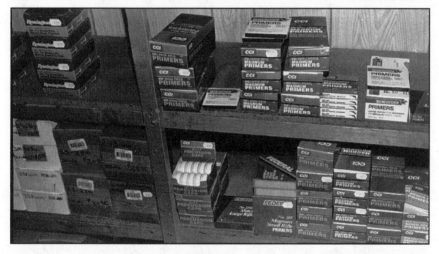

Some might claim this illustrates a "ridiculous stockpile", however, this represents far less than half the primer types readily available. Stocking several thousand of each type of primer that one uses is not unreasonable. There are advantages to keeping to one production lot, which one cannot do buying only 100 at a time.

Just visible is the identifying **B** embossed into the face of the cup of this CCI-BR2 primer, a useful addition. Would that all primers featured such identification.

A good variety of primers, though not many of each type, started to appear on dealers' shelves by early 1995. Though the situation now is pretty much under control, the primer shortage pointed out that a small glitch in the supply/demand equation can make an enormous wave in availability.

ty of primers, something like 30 million primers per week, and over 1.5 billion in the last year. So where in thunder have all the primers gone?

Consider Federal, Remington and Winchester. All three companies have offered primers as components on a continuous basis for decades. However, component-primer distribution has always been subsidiary to ammunition production. In other words, when primer production exceeded the demands of ammunition manufacture, the extra primers were stockpiled and distributed in a manner designed to minimize costs. Obviously, ammunition manufacturers have recently been hard-pressed to fill their own demand for primers. Therefore, in many cases a great percentage of the primers produced were used in-house.

Obviously, manufacturers have to establish priorities. Their businesses are built on ammunition sales, so we can't fault them for putting a priority on continuing to provide ammunition.

Consider CCI, historically the handloader's best primer friend. CCI provides primers for their in-house ammunition (CCI-Speer) but they run things a little differently. In their words: "We have always maintained a separate production capacity to meet ammunition production requirements, and the primers produced for our Blazer line cannot be used for any other application." CCI's new primer facility, opened in 1990, was already running at full capacity before this recent crunch hit.

Obviously, CCI-Speer couldn't simply stop producing ammunition altogether just to fulfill an increased demand for primers. The shortage of CCI-Speer ammunition may have been more severe than the CCI primer shortage; at least this seems to be the case in my part of the country. I haven't seen a single box of CCI-Speer ammunition for sale all year! They are producing ammunition just as fast as they can, but demand continues to far outstrip supply, especially in the Gold Dot line and all 9mm Luger loadings.

As previously noted, producers have stepped up primer production as far as possible without increasing the number of production lines, constructing new facilities, or compromising safety. And, after all, there are only so many hours in a day.

CCI component-primer production in '94 was in the tens of millions per week. Add to this similar contributions by Winchester, Federal and Remington and smaller contributions by Fiocchi,

A variety of suitable primers; some with two legs on their anvils, others with three; some with paper seals, others with a varnish-like substance to seal the pellet. The important point: Use the appropriate primer for the job at hand. Indiscriminate substitutions can be dangerous.

I had RCBS's handy new tool, but I found myself in very short supply of primers to seat with it.

PRIMERS

RWS and other minor importers, and one comes up with an average of perhaps 5 million primers distributed each day. Yet on any given day, most local dealers had none to sell! So, just exactly where have all the primers gone?

Well, first, there are still people loading and shooting. I suspect this activity may actually have increased in '94 for two reasons. First, bad weather over much of the nation in '93 curtailed outdoor activities and sales of related items. This likely created a bit of cabin fever, so when '94 rolled around with good weather, folks simply tried to make up for lost time. Second, paranoia was undoubtedly a factor: "...Better practice while I still can..."

Before this current run, constant demand, along with whatever stockpiling may have occurred, obviously consumed 100 percent of baseline production. Production has been increased about 70 percent over baseline and, therefore, about 41 percent of the primers now produced are actually "surplus." This is still a bunch of primers, on the order of 750 million a year.

However, there are between 4½ million and 6 million active handloaders in the United States. For this discussion we'll assume the latter figure. Therefore, on average, each handloader has stockpiled a whopping *one hundred twenty-five* (125) primers this year. Big deal! It's a miracle the problem hasn't been worse. (Even if we're off on production or the number of active handloaders by a factor of 2, and if only 1 in 10 handloaders has actually attempted to stockpile, we still come up with a very modest 2500 primers stockpiled.)

To get an idea of the volume of primers we're talking about, consider this: If each of six million handloaders

decides to stockpile one thousand of each of the eight main types of primers (standard and magnum, small and large, rifle and pistol) in only one brand that would be forty-eight billion primers. Stacked one on top of the other, that is a stack over 80,000 miles high! If each went out and bought one thousand of each kind of primer offered by each of the suppliers, the stack would reach to the moon and back.

Another aside worth noting is production costs. Primer manufacturers have actually endured reduced profits in the past year. Production, including shift, overtime and "do as you can" work, entails increased costs and reduced productivity. Further, instead of shipping primers by the truckload to distribution centers, manufacturers have been shipping on an "as-can" basis in an effort to minimize the frustration you and I feel.

These efforts are more than just magnanimous, they have cost producers more money than one can imagine. They have nowhere near fully recouped those expenses through increasing prices. Winchester and CCI (at least) have gone far beyond the call of duty in trying to provide handloaders with primers. *All domestic primer producers have borne financial losses, and their employees have endured physical and emotional stress, all on behalf of reloaders. They deserve heartfelt thanks.* There has been plenty of fair profit made, but most of that has been at the retail level.

So far we have assumed every component-primer produced has been made available in retail outlets—which is not the case. One producer has heard from consumers who did a little investigating and discovered that certain dealers, or

their employees, have conspired to withhold primers from standard retail outlets.

These are the primers you or your friends have seen at gun shows selling for twice fair retail price. These primers eventually get to consumers, but this despicable practice does contribute to an exaggeration—at the retail level—of the shortage. Since appearances are so important, this has likely exacerbated the situation by encouraging further consumer stockpiling.

Winchester made a special effort for the Camp Perry event in providing two vendors with a large supply of primers so competitors—many of whom were literally in danger of not being able to compete because they simply could not find primers—would be able to stock up. To those vendors' credit both sold primers at a fair retail price.

One place where primers *have* been disappearing is through semi-custom and smaller ammunition producers. Remember, ammunition sales are up and every primer used in these cottage businesses and smaller industries comes right out of the component-primer pile. Several thousand small manufacturers turning out an additional several thousand cartridges per day would consume a staggering 500 million of the "extra" primers produced in '94! Further, some of the bigger "small producers" report having increased production 50 percent in '94.

When we consider this additional consumption, evident component-primer stockpiling by consumers has been extremely modest. But that is how it is with commodity items. Production always exactly matches demand, and any minuscule unanticipated increase in demand can upset the system all out of proportion to reality. ●

WHISPERS ARE A new concept in guns and ammunition just a few years old. The ordinary modern gun/cartridge combination is capable of a fairly wide range of velocities and bullet weights while producing acceptable accuracy with bullets of moderate weight for the caliber.

The Whisper cartridge/gun combination is designed to produce excellent accuracy with very heavy bullets for the caliber at very low subsonic velocities while producing excellent accuracy all through the spectrum of bullet weights, including very light bullets fired at

publications that a bullet traveling at less than the speed of sound does not make a ballistic "crack." The ballistic crack is the sound made by an aircraft or projectile as it breaks the sound barrier. I can assure you bullets start making an audible sound somewhat under the sound barrier. However, when using a silenced or suppressed gun, it is quite easy to tell when the sound barrier has been broken. The sound is quite distinct from that made by a subsonic bullet as the sound barrier is approached.

The altitude of my shop, SSK Industries, is about 1100 feet. Assuming

BULLETS
THAT WHISPER

by J.D. JONES

(Above) The need for a successful long-range suppressed cartridge led author Jones to develop his Whisper series of cartridges. This suppressed M16-A2 in 300 Whisper has just been fired; the empty case is just above the front sight. No need for ear protection!

moderately high velocities from the same cartridge and barrel.

In the past few years the term "subsonic" has been used as an advertising gimmick to try to denote a cartridge/bullet load of absolutely fearsome capabilities. There is no magic in any of this terminology. "Subsonic" has, in particular, been applied to the 148-grain 9mm loads. Subsonic simply means a velocity below the speed of sound. Normal pistol ammunition such as 38 Special 158-grain or 45 ACP ball falls into this category. When a subsonic load is being hyped as the wonder of all wonders, remember that the lower the velocity the more difficult it is to achieve good terminal bullet performance.

The speed of sound is approximately 1130 to 1160 fps at sea level. Temperature, humidity and altitude all have an effect on it. It has been said in many

my multiple chronographs are correct, the sound barrier usually hovers around 1105 to 1130 fps here. Bullets in flight start making an audible sound at about 1070 fps.

The actual sound of the discharge can be suppressed, but the sound of the bullet in flight cannot be changed. A 50-caliber bullet and a 22-caliber bullet traveling above the speed of sound both sound about the same to me. The shape of the bullet doesn't seem to matter much, nor does velocity once the sound barrier has been broken.

It is widely believed, in 22 LR and long-range high-power shooting, that a bullet in flight that passes through the sound barrier as it slows down will have an accuracy problem. In some 22 shooting the idea is to get the bullet to the target never letting it exceed the speed of sound during the entire flight. In long-range high-power, the idea is to keep the bullet above the speed of sound during its entire flight. I'm not aware of any definitive work on this subject dealing with projectiles, but I'd

300 WHISPER 12" SSK CONTENDER BARREL			
Load (Grs./Powder)	Avg. Vel. (fps)	SD (fps)	Accuracy (ins. @100 yds.)
110-Grain Sierra Hollowpoint #2110			
20.0/H-110	2255	28	1
21.0/H-110	2341	13	½
125-Grain Nosler Ballistic Tip			
19.0/H-110	2109	13	1
20.0/H-110	2212	48	1
13.5/Accurate #9	1839	11	½
14.5/Accurate #9	1931	8	1
130-Grain Hornady Single Shot Pistol #3021			
18.5/H-110	2095	9	1
19.5/H-110	2120	21	½
13.5/Accurate #9	1760	25	1
14.0/Accurate #9	1814	11	
150-Grain Nosler Ballistic Tip			
16.5/H-110	1880	14	2
17.5/H-110	1929	17	½
19.5/Accurate 1680	1854	22	½
20.5/Accurate 1680	1914	21	½
18.5/Reloder 7	1653	25	½
19.5/Reloder 7	1752	15	1
10"/14" SSK CONTENDER BARREL			
168-Grain Match			
8.4/Accurate #9	1013/999		
220-Grain Match			
8.9/H-110	990/958		
Cor-Bon	1067/1089		
240-Grain Match			
9.7/H-110	1065/1072		

Author developed the 300 Whisper (right) by necking up the 221 Fireball case. Result was quiet long-range horsepower in a cartridge the same length as the 223 (left).

BULLETS THAT WHISPER

assume the principle is the same as for an aircraft passing through the sound barrier, i.e., some shapes work a lot better than others.

To have a truly quiet firearm we must suppress the noise of discharge and keep the velocity under the speed of sound. Historically that has been done with 22 rimfires, 9mm pistols and submachine guns, and to some extent the 45 ACP in submachine guns. Notable are some other arms using the 32 ACP, 380 ACP and 458 Winchester in shortened cases, all with mixed results. A great deal of work has been expended on 308 rifles and suppressors. Suppressing the noise of discharge is effective. However, reducing the velocity below the speed of sound in 308 cartridges/rifles generally results in poor accuracy.

The result has simply been that truly *quiet* guns in the past have had very limited power and range. The Whispers make a dramatic improvement in both accuracy and downrange power.

Some time ago I was contacted by a manufacturer who wanted a couple barrels made up to try to extend the "head shot" subsonic capability to at least 200 yards. I assured him what he wanted to do wouldn't work, and it didn't. However, it did get me started thinking.

I first determined I wanted a round that would give at least 200-yard subsonic head shot capability with enough power to get the job done at that range. It had to be easily adaptable to the M-16/AR-15 weapons family, bolt-action rifles, single shot rifles and the T/C Contender, as that is my bread-and-butter business. Increasing its versatility by making it workable at high velocities with lighter bullets seemed desirable and feasible.

The 30 is the major caliber used in long-range shooting by most police/military snipers. The 250-grain Sierra MatchKing was available then and was the experimental bullet of choice. It is accurate and maintains its velocity very

well. Sierra's figures showed it to lose only about 60-65 fps in the first 200 yards of flight if launched at 1040 fps. Although the 30/223 has been used in custom XP-100s and a few custom T/Cs, at least since the advent of handgun silhouette shooting in the mid '70s, a 250-grain bullet in a 223 case wouldn't fit into an M-16 magazine. However, we thought the 221 Fireball case opened to 30-caliber, with the bullet deep-seated to reduce powder capacity, would be perfect for sound suppression. Simply changing the barrel and gas system is all that is required to convert a M-16/AR-15. Remember, our goal was to develop a cartridge that was *quiet*, and all that is required in the way of powder capacity is just enough to propel the heavy bullets to slightly over 1000 fps.

Accordingly, we ordered 1:8 and 1:6-inch barrels and chambered them for the 30/221. We named our new cartridge the 300 Whisper. We made a neck expander to open the 22-caliber case necks to 30, and made some homemade dies. The first barrel was an SSK Contender barrel, the second a Remington Model 700. The third was an M-16 and was used to establish the type, size and location of the gas system. This particular barrel was tested until it finally wore out. Its velocity dropped by 150 fps, but it was still accurate.

Initial powder and bullet testing was done in the SSK Contender barrels. Powder ranging from the fast Bullseye, WW 231 and Accurate #2 burning rates through BL-C2 were tried. We got the best results in subsonic accuracy, uniformity and sound level from WW-296, H-110 and AA9, using 220- through 250-grain bullets. High-velocity light-bullet (up to 125-grain) loads favored WW-296 and H-110. From 135 grains up, superior ballistic performance was achieved with AA-1680 at every bullet weight. Slower-burning powders cannot match the velocities of AA-1680 in this cartridge.

In the high-velocity mode, the deliverable ballistic payload of the 300 Whisper equals the 7.62x39 cartridge with the added bonus of a weapon capable of delivering all bullet weights from the 125-grain at 2300 fps to the 240-grain at about 1400 fps. Armor-piercing and armor-piercing incendiary rounds, as well as many others, have been developed. (Sierra dropped the 250-grain bullet and replaced it with a 240 during our initial testing.)

Accuracy of the 10-inch submachine gun barrel and that of the match grade M-16 upper unit appear to be about identical if the sub-gun is given an equal scope. I don't know of any submachine gun that can compete with the

300 Whisper in accuracy, controllability, power or versatility in the field. It works just as well from a 6-inch-barrel handgun, giving under MOA accuracy with any good match-quality bullet of nearly any weight.

Actual loading of the 300 Whisper is easily accomplished. Simply run the case into the expander die and expand it to 30-caliber. Next run it through the full-length sizing die to straighten out any misalignment of the case neck. Failure to do this operation will result in jams in any gun because the chamber throats are very narrow, and a misaligned bullet will sometimes be impossible to chamber. Prime the case—preferably with the Remington 7½ primer. Any small rifle primer will do, but the No. 7½ has consistently given both SSK and Cor-Bon (who loads the factory ammunition for the Whisper) the smallest extreme velocity spreads and standard deviations with the most suitable powders. It is also a thick-cup primer that resists piercing in high-pressure loads. Charge the case with powder and seat the bullet to a maximum length of 2.240 inches for any SSK or T/C chamber.

That's all there is to it. Since the 300 Whisper and its offspring in 7mm and 6.5mm are small-capacity cases, some seemingly minor differences in lot-to-lot variations are readily apparent. For example, let's say we want a velocity of 1040 fps with a 240, and we can get that velocity with 9.2 grains of H-110. Our extreme spread is 25 fps; 1040 plus half of 25 is 1053. One tenth of a grain of powder is worth 11.3 fps. Now we are up to 1064.3 fps. A 1 percent change in

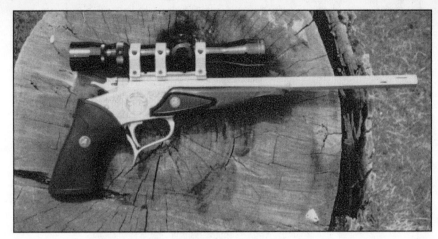

This octagon-barreled 14-inch Contender in 300 Whisper barely moves in recoil, yet has enough punch to deck a deer.

burning rate of a primer occurs and now we are up to 1075 fps and the bullet is making noise. Bump the powder measure slightly and, bingo, jackpot— sonic crack.

Actually, I figure at least a 4 percent lot-to-lot variation in powder as a rough guide. Sometimes it runs more than that. This means if you want to flirt with the sound barrier from below, you better test everything each time you set up. Note I didn't mention the powder scale variables as yet. Of course, if the sonic crack occurs without a silenced gun, it is unnoticed by the shooter.

I feel a good powder measure will give far better accuracy if you use it according to directions—that means uniformly every time—than can be obtained by weighing every powder charge, particularly if you are using a balance-beam scale. Experiment a little

with moving the beam around on the agates and you will find quite a bit of difference in indicated weight. Putting the pan onto and off of a scale, combined with all the bumps the beam takes, is going to result in less accuracy than can be obtained by using a good measure properly. The RCBS pistol powder measure with fixed rotors has worked exceptionally well for me, particularly when we install a set screw into the cavity so minor weight corrections can be made.

The 300 Whisper is not a temperamental cartridge, at least no more so than any other small-capacity case that operates at high pressure, nor any more than the parent 221 Fireball. Certainly we have been loading Hornets, Bees and 9mm pistols long enough to have mastered the simple skills necessary. You cannot, however, be as sloppy with

The beginnings of the quiet concept led Jones to try the 30 Carbine (left) with heavy bullets. Case strength was inadequate, so he went to the 221 Fireball case to get the 300 Whisper (right).

Success with the 300 led to a full line of quiet, supressible cartridges that also perform well with lighter bullets in supersonic modes. Here (left to right) are the 6.5mm/155-grain; 7mm/168-grain; 300/240-grain; 338/300-grain; 458/600-grain; and 500/700-grain Whispers.

Author Jones, who runs SSK Industries, took this record letcherbok on the Y-O Ranch in Texas with the 300 Whisper using a 125-grain boattail out of his 10-inch Contender.

BULLETS THAT WHISPER

the 300 Whisper as you can with a 50-plus-grain capacity 30-06 without it making you aware you are screwing up.

Working up loads in a 30-06 in one grain increments is fine; better cut that in half for the Whisper.

As a recreational cartridge the 300 Whisper has a lot going for it. It uses bullets of high ballistic efficiency and can provide 200-yard MOA accuracy under good conditions with no more noise than a 9mm handgun, unsuppressed. Loaded to its practical maximum, it is an excellent deer cartridge for frontal or broadside shots with the 125-grain Nosler Ballistic Tip, 125-grain Speer TNT, and other 125-grain single shot pistol bullets. It duplicates the velocity of hot handloads in a 30-30 with much less powder and recoil. High-speed video shows about 30 percent less gun movement in recoil with a 10-inch T/C than that of a 30-30, when both are pushing the same bullet to the same velocity. The 30-30 uses almost twice as much powder to get the same velocity. This will vary somewhat from shooter to shooter as the manner in which each of us holds his gun is highly individualistic.

As a metallic silhouette cartridge the 300 Whisper is developing quite a following. It is quite adequate on rams even with 220-grain subsonic loads. The combination of accuracy and light recoil is highly desirable in competition.

Silhouette shooters are experimenting with a wide variety of loads and bullet weights and experiencing success with virtually all they try.

Thompson/Center has been licensed to produce 300 Whisper Contender barrels and has been doing so for some time now. The only other source is from my company, SSK Industries. The T/C factory barrels have a 10-inch twist rate and some will not stabilize 220-grain MatchKings at a velocity under the sound barrier. Virtually all will stabilize the 200-grain Sierra MatchKing subsonic. The SSK barrel blanks are manufactured by Shilen, and my favorite of the

variety available use the hand-lapped 1:8-inch twist match-grade stainless barrel. This is the SSK standard in this caliber from 10-inch Contenders through heavy-barrel counter-sniper rifles and M-16s. The type of rifling in the T/C barrels is quite different from SSK barrels, and starting-load powder charges must be lowered by 10 percent to accommodate the difference.

Frankly, I don't know of any other cartridge capable of filling as many roles as the 300 Whisper. When the cartridge is to be used for sporting purposes, my favorite setup is the 10-inch barrel Contender.

The 300 is ballistically superior to the 6.5mm and 7mm Whispers, although they are interesting cartridges. They are simply the 221 case opened to the proper neck size. They fit and work in any gun the 300 does. There's one area the 6.5 may be superior to the 300—that's as a submachine gun for competitive purposes. With lightly loaded 100-grain bullets and an effective Arrestor muzzlebrake or suppressor the gun is unbelievably fast-handling and accurate. The 6.5 is at its subsonic best with the 155-grain Sierra, and the 7mm with the 168-grain Sierra. The 6.5 will push a 100-grain bullet from a 10-inch SSK Contender barrel at 2150 fps, and it seems quite effective on whitetails at over 100 yards. The velocity of the 100-grain 7mm is about the same, but for hunting purposes the 300 is a far better choice than either of the smaller cartridges.

Going up in caliber, the 338 Whisper uses the 7mm BR case opened to 338. Again, because of its ease of manufacture and accuracy, the T/C Contender was the test mule. The subsonic bullet of choice is the 300-grain Sierra MatchKing, and second choice is the 250-grain Sierra SP. High-velocity loads will do 2200 to 2300 fps with 200-grain bullets. The Hornadys are also good hunting bullets, and so are the Nosler Ballistic Tips.

Here's a handy SSK Contender Carbine with laminated thumbhole stock and 2-8x Bausch & Lomb scope. It also has a suppressor.

The 7mm-08 and 308 are the most popular barrels to convert. The overall length of the 338 is set up to equal the overall length of the 308. If anything, it is more accurate than the 300. Down-range velocity/energy loss is unbelievable. At the muzzle the 45 ACP 230-grain bullet develops 351 foot-pounds energy from 830 fps velocity. At 500 yards the 300-grain 338 Whisper subsonic load is still carrying 437 foot-pounds energy and 888 fps velocity—almost 60 fps faster than the 45 ACP at the muzzle.

A very wide range of powders is useful in the 338 Whisper but the subsonic powder of choice from both the standpoint of accuracy and sound level (with or without suppressor) is WW-231. In my personal test gun under good conditions my worst 100-yard group was $9/16$-inch. The 338-caliber in this cartridge case appears to be optimum. Opening it to 35-375 and larger calibers reduces efficiency and downrange performance.

The 338 Whisper is gaining in popularity with the SSK T/C users, although it is more expensive to shoot than the 300s. Both the 300 and 338 have been given a good workout in Australia from SSK T/Cs in shooting vermin donkeys, which in some areas constitute a severe problem. Frankly, I would be hard-pressed to observe the hit of either the subsonic 240/30 and 300/338 and tell which was which. Both seem to have about the same effect as a close-range hit from a heavily-loaded 44 Magnum revolver with 300-grain bullets. On lengthwise shots the Whispers outperform the 44 unless a 320-grain bullet is used.

Next is the 458 Whisper. Although SSK has been experimenting with every in-between caliber, they all have less potential than either the 338 or 458. The U.S. Army experimented with cut-off 458s years ago with little success. I assume the barrel twist was wrong, suppression not good and the

SSK 338 WHISPER 12″ SSK Contender		
Load (Grs./Powder)	Bullet (Wgt.Grs.)	MV (fps)
8.6/HP-38	200	1060
8.8/HP-38	200	1077
9.5/HP-38	200	1164
8.4/HP-38	250	909
9.2/HP-38	250	991
9.6/HP-38	250	1029
9.6/HP-38	300	895
10.4/HP-38	300	1001
10.7/HP-38	300	1011
10.8/HP-38	300	1050
9.5/N-350	200	1040
10.2/N-350	250	945
10.6/N-350	250	1018
10.8/N-350	250	1040
11.2/N-350	250	1131
10.8/N-350	300	912
11.8/N-350	300	1011
12.3/N-350	300	1066
10.5/H-4227	200	971
11.3/H-4227	200	1061
11.5/H-4227	200	1075
11.2/H-4227	250	899
12.2/H-4227	250	976
12.7/H-4227	250	1020
12.8/H-4227	300	888
13.8/H-4227	300	953
14.8/H-4227	300	1011
15.1/H-4227	300	1055

The 458 Whisper utilizes either the 600-grain low-drag pointed projectile or the 500-grain Hornady round-nose.

This is a recovered 50-caliber 700-grain bullet that was fired from the 50 American Eagle cartridge, another Jones/SSK development.

usual 500-grain RN gave very limited range. Simply cutting the 458 case to 1.740 and loading a 600-grain low-drag, low-friction solid copper bullet gives phenomenal subsonic downrange performance. We don't know the actual velocity loss of this projectile downrange at this time, but we plan to test it soon. Overall length is the same as a 458 Winchester. Loaded with 300- to 400-grain bullets, it is certainly an adequate short-range deer-elk-moose gun.

Some experimentation has been done with the 45-70, 50-70, 348 blown out to 500 Alaskan, and 500 Nitro Express cases in some firearms, primarily Contenders, TCRs and Ruger #1s. Excellent

subsonic and good high-velocity results were noted. SSK chambers the 50-70-750 cartridge in the Contenders and other guns. This uses the 50 BMG bullet in the subsonic mode as well as lighter bullets at higher velocities.

This brings us up to the 500 Whisper. Nothing subsonic matches this one for downrange energy. The 750-grain bullets are the most practical, and 900s are at about the top end of what's available. The 460 Weatherby case is cut to 2.250 inches and opened to 50-caliber. The rim is rebated to standard magnum dimensions so the bolt doesn't have to be reworked. Neck reaming is required to get uniform neck tension. Overall length of a seated 750 is the same as a loaded 460 Weatherby or 416 Rigby cartridge. The Weatherby and Ruger rifles convert to this one, but it's a bit much for handgun use. The most accurate load combination so far has been 44 grains of IMR-3031 under the 750

Sub-guns built around the 300 Whisper, such as this M16, can fire long bursts with no muzzle signature and complete silence. The 6.5mm and 7mm Whispers work well in this type of gun, too.

BULLETS THAT WHISPER

TCCI bullet for about 1030 fps. Last fall I put four consecutive shots into .046-inch at 100 yards. As I felt the recoil of the fifth shot I knew I had screwed up. The stock bulges where the sling is fitted. I had improperly placed the bulge in the sandbag and the shot went out about half an inch. The computers tell us this bullet loses a stunning 25 fps in its first 200 yards of flight. Subsonic or otherwise, the 50 stays under an inch if it's fed decent bullets. GI surplus bullets are good for nothing more than load development or plinking. They simply aren't very accurate. Incendiaries are the most accurate of the bunch and tracers pretty miserable accuracy-wise, but a lot of fun. The 650-700-grain BMG bullets can reach 1800-1900 fps max.

With the right bullets the 50 can do a lot of things the others can't. Its penetration is much greater that the others. At 951 fps impact velocity it penetrated the side of a Kevlar helmet and cut off a $^9/_{16}$-inch bolt that was holding it up. With that kind of penetration and with a little luck, vehicles, radars and missiles can be disabled, fuel dumps fired, and one can just generally cause a lot of mischief under the right circumstances without making any more noise than a cough.

SSK 6.5 WHISPER			
—Bullet—		Load	MV
Wgt.Grs.	Type	(Grs./Powder)	(fps)
10-inch SSK Barrel (1:8 twist)			
100	Hornady	18.4/H-110	2238
120	Bal Tip	16.0/1680	1854
120	Bal Tip	17.0/1680	2001
120	Bal Tip	18.0/1680	2020

This next one isn't a Whisper since it is subsonic only, but the 50 AE case opened to accept the .510-inch diameter 50 BMG bullets over a healthy charge of WW-296 in single shot handguns or bolt-action rifles is very effective. I call it the 50 American Eagle to go with the existing 50 AE headstamp.

The 7.63 Mini Whisper is simply the 30 Mauser. Subsonic, it beats a normal 308 rifle using subsonic ammo in both accuracy and energy. It uses the 200-grain Sierra MatchKing at 1050 fps from an 8-inch barrel T/C and shoots 1 MOA at 200 yards. With an 8-inch barrel and 8-inch suppressor the gun breaks down into an 8-inch package. With 110-grain bullets it will do about 1750 fps. Just for kicks, we built the 7.62 Micro Whisper on the even smaller 30 Luger case. It will handle 180s OK subsonic, but 168s are a little more practical. Accuracy and gun size is identical with the Mini. The 169-grain Hornady or 168-grain Sierra are the most accurate bullets for it. It matches the 168-grain subsonic loads in the 308 and gives far better accuracy than the 308 rifles do with subsonic ammunition. With the 93-grain Norma softpoint it will reach an easy 1800 fps from that little ol' 8-inch barrel, and shoot accurately, too. Load it with the 110-grain Speer flat-nose hollowpoint and it does a creditable job on small game. Neither the 32 H&R Mag case nor the 32 ACP case are as satisfactory in an all-around manner, although both have some specific things they do well.

With all of the subsonic loads, no matter how efficient the bullets are at retaining velocity, the time of flight over any extended distance gives gravity plenty of time to work on the bullet, causing a lot of drop. For even an expert at judging distance, first-shot hits on small objects over 150-200 yards are very, very difficult.

This can be helped in a couple of ways. We have developed scopes with dots spaced on the vertical crosshair to intersect the trajectory every 50 yards

Author J.D. Jones with the first deer ever taken with the 6.5mm Whisper. The 100-grain load did fine at over 100 yards range. This deer was taken at the Y-O Ranch.

from 50 through 300 yards. This even helps a lot at short ranges. The dots themselves can sometimes be used as rudimentary rangefinders. The best way to get a first-round hit is to utilize a laser rangefinder to evaluate the distance and use it in conjunction with the scope dots.

Subsonic bullets don't expand on impact. Generally speaking, the bigger and heavier bullets will be more lethal than smaller ones. This is true in the Whispers, however tumbling bullets create wounds far out of proportion to their diameter. The 30/240-grain and 338/300-grain tumble well. We have no hard data on the 458 and 50s at this time.

Particularly in the T/C the Whispers up through 338 provide excellent low-recoil, low-noise-level, accurate recreational shooting. Turning up the wick under lighter, more frangible bullets increases the cartridge's usefulness to that of a very short lightweight deer gun with a 150-200 yard useful range.

For several years we have tested the sporting capabilities of the Contenders in the various Whispers and have found them to be adequate for animals in the 250-pound category. The Speer TNT 125-grain and the 125-grain Nosler Ballistic Tip give excellent performance in the 300. The usual 150-grain 30-30 bullets do fine for woods hunting, as does the Speer Grand Slam 150.

From past experience I know a number of you are wondering what police/governmental agencies are using one or more of the Whispers. Well, forget it; at this point I'm not going to talk about it! ●

Here are some 30-caliber variations. A 200-grain Sierra boattail bullet and the 7.63 Mini-Whisper loaded with it, plus the 168-grain Sierra and that bullet loaded into the 7.62 Micro-Whisper. These are functional cartridges that have a real niche in the handgunning world.

HANDGUNS 96

Handgunning Today

Showstopping advice on collecting, page 172.

Galan gives the airgun rundown, page 176.

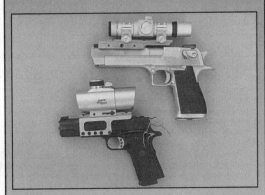

All the latest bells and whistles, page 178.

THE HANDGUN COLLECTING market has undergone some significant swings in the past several years, much of it due to the ever-shifting political climate. The highly touted federal "ban" on so-called "assault rifles" and large-capacity magazines, for example, diverted a lot of gun-buff attention and thus dollars away from older collectibles and into current high-capacity pistols, even though those already in circulation weren't affected by the new legislation. At the same time, the anti-gun sentiment that had created the ban also created concern in some collectors' minds about the future of their firearms investments.

However, the November '94 Republican landslide firmly reversed the downslide in the collector gun market, which was already becoming tempered by time. As a result, the collectors' handgun market in general seems pretty healthy as these words go to print.

With any collectibles, condition and rarity are the prime determinants of value, particularly when the market is weak. A fine Colt single action, Winchester '73, or cased Borchardt will rarely if ever lose value. The same guns in only "good" condition, on the other hand, tend to soar in value when the market is hot, but become hard to sell at any reasonable price when it's not. Auctions are a great place to watch these cycles, as they publicly display what the knowledgeable buyer is willing to pay for a given gun.

As to the current handgun marketplace, U.S. and foreign antiques—muzzleloaders as well as pre-1899 cartridge guns—remain strong if not spectacular sellers. U.S. martial handguns of all vintages have been doing very well, and recently the older large-caliber European revolvers have become a very hot field for U.S. collectors.

Colt handguns of all eras, up to and including the 1950s and '60s, continue to be very active sellers with ever-increasing prices. Smith & Wesson, on the other hand, has been mostly flat, even though some models—for example, the old large-caliber top-breaks, triple-locks and registered Magnums—have been going up at a healthy pace. Other scarce Smiths, such as the LadySmith, 32 auto and steel-frame Model 39, seem to be selling slowly, at about the same prices they brought a decade ago.

Among other U.S. auto pistol makers, both Savage and Remington pocket models are selling well with prices increasing accordingly. Oddly enough, prices of the big 45 Savage haven't been keeping pace with its smaller brothers; they're still being offered at the same prices they brought five years ago. True rarities in the U.S. auto pistol field such as the 25 Savage and the one-of-a-kind pre-1911 Army test pieces have long been and will continue to be very big ticket items, with prices starting in the low five digit area and going up.

As mentioned previously, one of the hot newer handgun fields for U.S. handgun collectors is the larger-caliber European revolvers, particularly martials. This area, long the exclusive province of European collectors, to the point where European dealers could make a living simply by buying them cheaply at U.S. gun shows for resale to their overseas customers, has now turned around to the point where U.S. prices are pretty much the same here as they are in Europe. Pinfires, however, still do not have much following

by JOE SCHROEDER
COLLECTING

Gun shows, like auctions, are always a good place to check the pulse of the collector's market.

in the U.S. Among the European makers, Webley in particular has attracted recent U.S. collector interest with prices increasing accordingly.

German martial revolvers, the Models 1879 and 1883, their commercial derivatives, and the Mauser 1878 "Zig-Zags" have always been strong sellers in the U.S. and should continue to be so. Recent imports of Russian Nagants seem to have sparked an increasing interest in Nagants of all kinds, though prices on the rarer variations haven't yet moved very much, perhaps reflecting lack of collector sophistication.

The market for foreign auto pistols has been a mixed bag at best. Recent imports of large numbers of surplus Mauser broomhandles, Browning and Inglis Hi-Powers from China, and Lugers and P38s from Europe have pounded the low-end market for these pistols rather badly. However, since the condition of these well-used ex-military arms varied from NRA awful to well-worn VG, and many were arsenal refinished, they didn't have all that much effect on the values of their better-quality counterparts that were already in the country. In fact, in some cases they've actually stimulated the marketplace, by making previously high-priced Lugers and Mausers available at "starter" prices to beginning collectors, who then caught the bug and went on into the higher-priced market.

Better-quality collector Lugers, Mausers and P38s are continuing to appreciate despite the surplus competition. Walther PPs and PPKs have also remained popular, though the earlier Walthers have for the most part been flat. Most other German pocket autos including Mausers have also been slow, though Model 1934s and HSCs with Nazi military markings continue to bring a nice premium.

Polish VIS Radoms, not only the pre-war "eagles" with their fine fit and finish, but those made under German occupation as well, have been doing very well. Steyr Hahns and Swedish Lahtis have been slow movers, but Roth-Steyrs, Finnish Lahtis and most Berettas have been doing a bit better. Among the Spanish handguns, Astras and some of the less common Stars are moving pretty well, but the bulk of Spanish 25 and 32 autos generate very little collector enthusiasm.

Most French and Belgian pistols have not shown much appreciation recently either, though the French militaries—the MAS and MAC 1935 and 1950—and Bergmann Bayards are getting a bit scarcer with some increase in pricing. The German Bergmanns—1896, '97, Mars and Simplex—are firmly in the rarity class, and along with auto pistol exotica, like most Mannlichers and pre-1900 self-loaders, are not only very hard to find but very pricey.

Perhaps in anticipation of V-J Day, the more common Nambus and Model 94s have been going up in price recently. However, the less common Japanese autos like the "Papa" and "Baby" Nambus have remained stable or have even dropped slightly, as have the Type 26 revolvers. "Grandpa" Nambus still bring a nice premium, though.

All in all, the market for collector handguns is pretty healthy and—if the Republican promises to halt or even roll back the recent tide of anti-gun-hysteria-generated legislation can be believed—should continue to get better. If the new Congress does indeed relax some current restrictions—particularly the current administration's import ban on Chinese and surplus handguns—we could see a lot of interesting Mauser, Luger, Hi-Power, P38, and who-knows-what-other "curio and relic" handguns on the market in the next few years. Though such imports could, as before, depress some prices, the net effect should still be positive as low end prices induce new collectors to join our ranks. ●

HANDGUNS '95

The big German Model 1879 (top) and 1883 (below) Ordnance revolvers have long been popular with U.S. as well as European collectors.

Older Webley revolvers such as this have become hot items among a growing group of collectors.

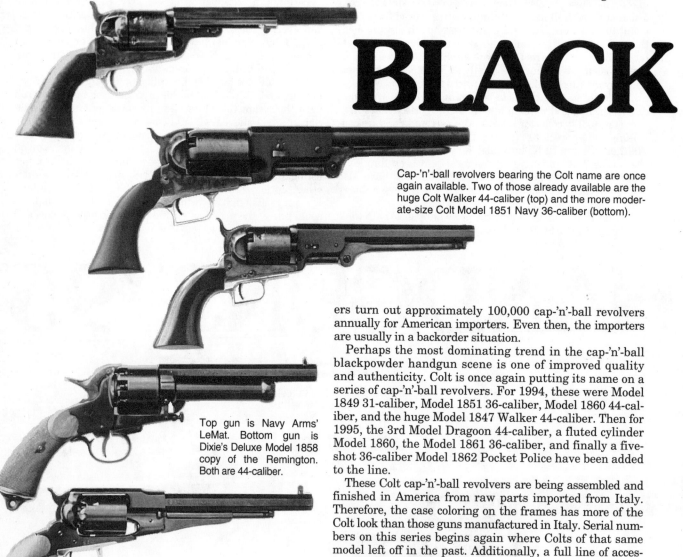

J UST A FEW years ago, when one said "blackpowder hand-guns" it automatically meant cap-'n'-ball percussion revolvers. Those plus a few single shot pistols were the only ones in which enthusiasts went to the trouble of shooting blackpowder.

Not now. Due to the influence of cowboy action shooting, more and more shooters are reloading blackpowder for cartridge revolvers, and furthermore, a couple of gunsmiths are specializing in converting those cap-'n'-ball revolvers to take cartridges, just as Colt and Remington did to their own guns back in the 1860s and 1870s.

All of that does not mean that the cap-'n'-ball percussion revolver scene is dead. Italy is the center of manufacture for those types of handguns, and the northern Italian gunmak-

BLACK

The type of handgun seen more and more commonly at the bigger cowboy action matches is the cartridge conversion. These are cap-'n'-ball revolvers converted to accept cartridges. At top is a Colt Model 1860 Army converted to 44 Colt caliber, and at bottom is Colt Model 1851 Navy converted to 38 Long Colt caliber.

Cap-'n'-ball revolvers bearing the Colt name are once again available. Two of those already available are the huge Colt Walker 44-caliber (top) and the more moderate-size Colt Model 1851 Navy 36-caliber (bottom).

ers turn out approximately 100,000 cap-'n'-ball revolvers annually for American importers. Even then, the importers are usually in a backorder situation.

Perhaps the most dominating trend in the cap-'n'-ball blackpowder handgun scene is one of improved quality and authenticity. Colt is once again putting its name on a series of cap-'n'-ball revolvers. For 1994, these were Model 1849 31-caliber, Model 1851 36-caliber, Model 1860 44-caliber, and the huge Model 1847 Walker 44-caliber. Then for 1995, the 3rd Model Dragoon 44-caliber, a fluted cylinder Model 1860, the Model 1861 36-caliber, and finally a five-shot 36-caliber Model 1862 Pocket Police have been added to the line.

These Colt cap-'n'-ball revolvers are being assembled and finished in America from raw parts imported from Italy. Therefore, the case coloring on the frames has more of the Colt look than those guns manufactured in Italy. Serial numbers on this series begins again where Colts of that same model left off in the past. Additionally, a full line of accessories is being marketed. There will be additional models added in 1996, but information as to exact types is not available at this writing.

Colt-type cap-'n'-ball revolvers are not the only ones being influenced by the trends of quality and authenticity.

Top gun is Navy Arms' LeMat. Bottom gun is Dixie's Deluxe Model 1858 copy of the Remington. Both are 44-caliber.

Navy Arms' replica LeMat revolver has to be one of the most interesting guns of this sort ever reproduced. The LeMat was an American-designed, French-produced, cap-'n'-ball revolver popular among the Confederate cavalry during the Civil War. It had a nine-shot capacity with a 65-caliber smoothbore shotgun barrel mounted beneath the rifled pistol barrel. The Navy Arms replica, made by Pietta of Italy, is a beautifully crafted revolver, functional right down to the pivoting hammer needed to fire the shotgun tube.

Also by Pietta of Italy is a full-size copy of the Remington Model 1858 44-caliber cap-'n'-ball sixgun popular among Federal cavalrymen during the Civil War. Heretofore, copies of Remington-type revolvers were about 7/8-scale as the mak-

'n'-ball revolvers. From the former I have a Colt 1860 Army converted to fire 44 Colt cartridges, and from the latter I have an Italian-made replica of a Colt 1851 Navy converted to fire 38 Long Colt ammunition. Incidentally, John Gren only converts those revolvers supplied to him by the customer. K&D will convert your gun or sell you a pre-converted specimen.

Back in the 1870s, such guns were left unlined and used outside-lubed, heel-type bullets to fit the bores. Both of these modern gunsmiths can build conversions like those, or they can line the barrels down to either .429-inch (for 44s) or .357-inch (for 38s), and the user can then fire ordinary inside-lubed bullets. Both of my guns are the lined versions. Although these are cartridge-firing revolvers, they

POWDER
HANDGUN SCENE '95

by MIKE VENTURINO

ers did not allow for shrinkage when making the moulds. This Pietta revolver, sold by both Dixie Gun Works and Navy Arms, is a dead ringer for the original Remington in size, being about 6 ounces heavier than other types of Remington copies. I have samples of Pietta-made LeMats and Remington Model 1858s on my desk at this writing and consider them to be of as good quality as any American-made revolver currently produced.

I predict we will see more emphasis on quality reproductions in the future, and perhaps some manufacturing of this sort of handgun will begin in the former communist countries of Eastern Europe.

Back in the era between the heyday of cap-'n'-ball handguns and the time when full-fledged production of newly designed cartridge-firing handguns was under way, it was common to see conversions of cap-'n'-ball revolvers to permit them to handle cartridges. These conversions were produced by the big factories such as Colt and Remington, and also by small independent gunsmiths.

For over 100 years, such handguns have been considered merely historical oddities, but now they are becoming popular once again, thanks to cowboy action shooting. At least two gunsmiths, John Gren and R&D Gun Repair, are specializing in building cartridge conversions of cap-

are meant for shooting *with blackpowder only* and are so marked on their barrels.

I predict that in the near future one of the major replica arms importers will pick up on this idea of cartridge conversions and begin offering newly manufactured cartridge conversion handguns. This may not happen in 1996, but it seems eventually inevitable, from my position.

Lastly, we are seeing much more use of blackpowder in reloading cartridges for all sorts of single-action revolvers. Again, this is spurred by the cowboy action shooters, many of whom want the utmost in tradition and authenticity. Colt single actions, foreign-made clones, Navy Arms Schofields, original Model 1875 Remingtons and foreign-made copies of the same are being put to use with blackpowder. Mostly, the calibers used are 45 Colt, 44-40 and 38-40. However, some shooters are also using such calibers as 45 S&W, 44 S&W American, 44 S&W Russian and 41 Long Colt, all in original guns and all with blackpowder ammunition.

Shooting blackpowder in all sorts of handguns is on the upswing, and most of that interest can be traced to the sport of cowboy action shooting. That, coupled with the renewed interest in Civil War guns which we are also experiencing, means that the blackpowder handgun scene in 1996 will be active and exciting.   ●

AIR PISTOL
SCENE '95
by J.I. GALAN

The author puts the superb Daisy 400 through its paces. This BB-firing semi-auto has a reciprocating slide.

THE AIR PISTOL has usually been the "Cinderella" of the airgun world. While nearly everybody who enjoys the shooting sports sooner or later buys an air rifle, air pistols traditionally have never enjoyed the same plateau of popularity as air-powered long guns. This is due, in large measure, to the fact that air pistols just don't produce the same level of raw power—most don't even come close—as many standard-production air rifles, particularly those that fall in the so-called "magnum" class. Fortunately, this general situation is rapidly changing in the 1990s.

Due in large part to the rise in violent crime in recent years and the resulting upsurge in the sale of defensive handguns, air pistols are sort of riding on the coattails of this trend. The political climate also has played a part in all of this. The threat of restrictive gun laws has had a telling effect on the upswing in popularity of air pistols in this country.

There are, therefore, some well-defined trends in the world of air pistols in the mid-1990s. For decades, air pistols looked like, well, air pistols. In most cases they bore only a peripheral resemblance to "real" handguns. This was really unavoidable in many instances, because spring-piston and pneumatic pistols depended upon bulky powerplants that dictated big, longer-than-normal handguns resembling (and only superficially, in most cases) 22 rimfire target pistols and nothing else. One solitary exception in the case of domestic spring-piston pistols is the Marksman 1010, a very close look-alike of the Colt Government Model that shoots pellets, BBs and even darts. But this model has always been aimed primarily at the youth market.

In the case of CO_2-powered pistols, there was far more latitude for manufacturers to design models that came a lot closer in looks to powder-burning handguns, but they tended to be simply more compact versions of the pneumatic (pump-up) pistols produced by the major manufacturers, such as Benjamin and Crosman.

In Europe, such look-alikes were even rarer. The Walther LP-53, a spring-piston air pistol replica of a Walther 22 rimfire target pistol, is one rather unique example.

By the late 1980s, however, the situation changed drastically, and today there's no end in sight. Both Crosman and Daisy—particularly the latter—have been launching a growing variety of CO_2-powered pellet and BB pistols that are spittin' images of world-renown combat and sporting handguns. Daisy's PowerLine series currently carries six different pistol models that are almost identical replicas of real handguns. One of the newest among them is the Model 400, a look-alike of the ponderous Desert Eagle autoloader. Daisy's version is a BB-shooting semi-auto with a reciprocating slide—all operated by CO_2—that recocks the hammer with each shot!

Other stunning replicas in the Daisy lineup include the Model 693, a copy of the 9mm S&W 5906 that is a fifteen-shot BB repeater, and the Model 45, a spittin' image of (what else?) the Colt Government Model. The Model 45 can empty its thirteen 177-caliber pellets real quick and with plenty of accuracy to boot, thanks to a rifled barrel. Daisy's other look-alike pistols in the PowerLine series include the Model 500, a single shot, pellet-firing copy of the Beretta 92F; the Model 1700, a BB repeater that looks like the Glock 17L; and the Model 44, a double-action pellet revolver that would make Dirty Harry proud, because it replicates very closely the look and feel of the 44 Magnum S&W Model 29.

Crosman, for its part, offers the Model 1008 Silver Series, a stunning copy of the big S&W 10mm autoloader. The 1008 spits out eight 177 pellets from a clever rotary magazine in a jiffy with lots of accuracy. Another superb autoloader replica is the Auto Air II. It can handle 177-caliber pellets as a single shot or BBs as a seventeen-shot semi-auto. However, Crosman's top favorite among look-alike handguns is the long-popular Model 357, a dead ringer for the elegant Colt Python revolver that's available in 4- and 6-inch barrels with a black finish or in the stainless-like Silver Series with an 8-inch barrel.

The BSA 240 Magnum has the generic looks of a combat autoloader, but is a single shot pellet pistol that delivers top performance.

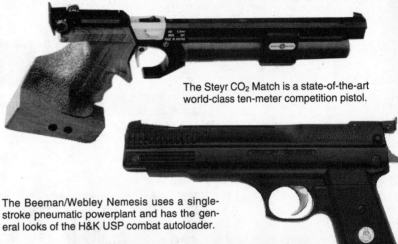

The Steyr CO_2 Match is a state-of-the-art world-class ten-meter competition pistol.

The Beeman/Webley Nemesis uses a single-stroke pneumatic powerplant and has the general looks of the H&K USP combat autoloader.

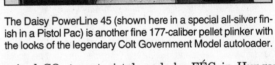

The Daisy PowerLine 45 (shown here in a special all-silver finish in a Pistol Pac) is another fine 177-caliber pellet plinker with the looks of the legendary Colt Government Model autoloader.

The trend is clear. Even traditionally conservative British airgun companies such as BSA and Webley have recently brought out—after more than 15 years—new pellet handguns with the generic lines typically found in combat autoloaders. The BSA 240 Magnum is a fairly powerful spring-piston pistol using a top-cocking system. The Webley Nemesis, on the other hand, has a fairly close resemblance to the H&K USP, one of the recent crop of no-nonsense autoloaders to reach the market. The Nemesis, however, uses a single-stroke pneumatic powerplant that makes this pistol recoilless. It produces around 400 fps in 177-caliber. This latest Webley pistol, the first to utilize the pneumatic system, is available in the U.S. through Beeman Precision Airguns. Both the BSA 240 Magnum and the Webley Nemesis are single shot, by the way.

The training value of air pistols resembling the real McCoy should be obvious. Many folks who own the real thing purchase the BB or pellet-firing look-alike for inexpensive practice right at home.

What about more traditional air pistols? Well, they are also doing just fine, thank you. Ten-meter Olympic-style air pistol shooting is still quite popular, and there is an ever-growing list of models on the market, mostly from Germany, although other countries have also joined the market. The Czech Republic, Hungary and Russia, for instance, have some truly respectable 10-meter competition models available. Daisy, for example, offers the Model 91, an outstanding and affordably priced CO_2 target pistol made by FÉG in Hungary. The Russians introduced the Baikal IZH-46 to the U.S. a couple of years ago. This single-stroke pneumatic target pistol looks a lot like a Walther, but its retail price runs less than half that of the famous German brand. Italy also produces some world-class match pistols, such as the FAS AP604 and AP606, both single-pump pneumatics. The Swiss Morini 162E is another top contender in the lofty world of 10-meter air pistol competition.

Looking into my trusty crystal ball, I can tell you that the future for air pistols looks rather promising. As long as "real" handguns are in high demand, there is bound to be a demand for pellet- or BB-firing look-alikes as well. Should even tougher, draconian gun laws become a fact, the market for air pistols may reach unprecedented heights; sort of a win-win situation for this particular product. Only time will tell, but for the moment, the undeniable fact is that air pistols sure have come a long way in just a few short years. ●

Realistic, yet cost-effective practice at home is a big plus in favor of CO_2-powered replicas, such as the Crosman 1008 Silver Series.

3x9 Burris on XL single shot in 270 JDJ.

HANDGUN ACCESSORIES '95

by DICK WILLIAMS

YOU DON'T HEAR much grumbling from handgunners reminiscing about "the good old days." The reason is, the good old days are happening now. OK, so we're constantly under political attack from the left by those who would abolish private ownership of handguns. And we suffer periodic olfactory assaults from the right by the cowboy shooters who would cheerfully trade hot showers and clean clothes for the joy of seeing everyone dressed in a single-action Colt.

But look at the incredible toys we have! Forget about the handguns for a moment and think about the major accessories that didn't exist, and in some cases weren't even dreamed of, a few years ago. In this report, we'll look at perhaps the three most significant handgun accessories. First, we'll look at today's optical equipment that allows us to shoot better and faster—and us older guys, whose arms aren't growing fast enough to keep pace with our eyes, to just plain *shoot*. Second, we'll look at today's trends in holsters. Third, we'll consider some of today's newest grips that play perhaps the most important role in making the shooter and handgun an integral team.

Optics

My earliest memory of a scoped handgun is from the mid-'60s, when I acquired a used Ruger 357 Blackhawk topped with a small, fragile-looking 1x scope. Those early models had .75-inch tubes and were quite limited in the recoil they could withstand. Because of the small diameter and because I had absolutely no experience with scopes on handguns, I found that acquisition of targets was quite tricky and maintenance of scope alignment, particularly in the offhand position, was extremely difficult. Because I was young and had been blessed with better-than-20/20 vision, I was not

impressed with the scope setup, even though the presentation of the target was much clearer than with iron sights. Actually, with all its limitations, compared to modern hardware, that scope represented a tremendous step forward for its time.

The handgun scope manufacturers continually improved their products, and by the 1970s, Leupold offered us their 2x Extended Eye Relief (soon followed by the 4x EER) handgun scope that set new standards for clarity, brightness and ruggedness. Big game handgun hunters and aging shooters could choose either of these scopes and shoot happily the rest of their lives. However, the needs of varmint hunters and other users of long-range single shot pistols pushed the industry into creating higher-power optics. Burris came out with a 7x Intermediate Eye Relief pistol scope and then their 10x IER. These were extremely large scopes, dwarfing many handguns, but providing unimagined magnification to the handgunner. You could literally shoot bugs off your target with one of these bad boys, and I'm speaking from experience. Recognizing the highly specialized nature and application of these huge magnifiers, Burris came out with variable-power pistol scopes culminating in their masterpiece, a 3-9x that's smaller and lighter than their fixed-power 7x or 10x. Now it was possible for a handgunner to hunt game of any size at any reasonable range with one favorite firearm of adequate power. Dial the power down for fast acquisition of close targets for offhand shots; dial it all the way up to 9x for prairie dogs at 300 yards.

Almost all the U.S. scope companies now offer a complete line of pistol scopes for handgunners. Leupold is closest to Burris at the upper end of the power spectrum with its variable 2.5-8x, but still offers shooters the time-tested and field-proven 2x and 4x EERs. Burris also makes a 2-7x that gives up a couple of x's on the high end, but adds some field of view and eye relief on the low end, while saving considerable weight and size. Simmons and Thompson/Center both offer a 2.5-7x that's remarkably light, compact and rugged. Thompson's version is available with a battery that allows you to light up your crosshairs for the dim hunting conditions of early morning and evening. From Bausch & Lomb/Bushnell comes a pair of downsized variables in 2-6x that represent both the upper and lower end of the price market. These are, respectively, the B&L 3000 Elite and the Bushnell Whitetail Hunter, the latter perhaps the best value in variable-power pistol scopes today. If you don't need a variable (and there's a lot to be said for keeping things simple in the field), check out the fixed-power scopes

available from all these manufacturers. In the lower power ranges, you can save some on weight, bulk and cost. T/C also has their "glowhairs" in 2x, while Burris' answer to dim lighting is a thicker crosshair in their 2x.

The other "optic" developed for the handgunner in the last few years is the non-magnifying 1x "dot scope." This is a tube with lenses and a battery that powers a red dot in the center of your field of view. A rheostat allows the shooter to control the dot's intensity. Whatever you put the red dot on as you look through the tube is what you hit. There is no searching for the intersection of crosshairs and no worrying about alignment as long as you can see both dot and target. Dot scopes were designed for action shooting as an improvement over scopes. They allow precise shot placement with much faster target acquisition. There was no prolonged debate in the practical shooting community over acceptance of this new gadget. When a product starts winning matches, action shooters flock to it.

I had an opportunity to work with a couple of dot scopes from Tasco and Simmons over the last year, and I used them outside the parameters of action shooting. Scopes from each manufacturer were mounted on representative competition guns, a 45 ACP and a new 9x25 Dillon, both built by Springfield. I'm not an active action shooter, but even in my hands the scopes were noticeably faster than iron sights. I also mounted both brands on 44 Magnums, one a Desert Eagle and one an S&W Performance Center revolver. After performing successfully and surviving several hundred rounds on the big boomers, the two scopes took turns on the Springfield 45 on a rabbit safari in the Sonora desert. The 33mm Simmons had a slight advantage on the hunt because it had a small 4-minute dot as opposed to the Tasco's 10-minute dot. Despite Arizona's depleted rabbit populations, both scopes harvested a couple of excellent meals, and a year later the scopes are as good as new. Ok, so Destructo the gun writer dropped the Tasco 40mm and bent the edge of the scope housing, but the scope still works as well today as it did when I received it.

C-More Systems has advanced the dot scope system significantly by eliminating the scope body. They use a small dot-projection system built into the rear of the slide, with a reflecting screen mounted on the forward part of the slide—

Tasco and Simmons dot scopes on a Springfield 45 ACP and Desert Eagle 44 Magnum.

This 2-6x Bushnell rests on a Lone Eagle single shot in 223.

A 2-6x Bausch & Lomb mounted on an XL single shot Hunter pistol in 356 Winchester.

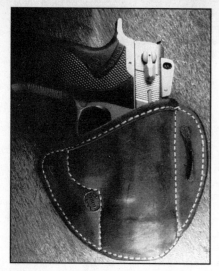

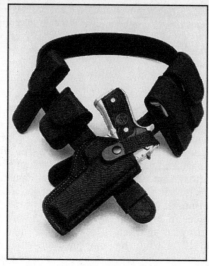

El Paso leather pancake holster with an S&W Model 4006.

Bianchi 7000 Accumold police gear.

Gould & Goodrich horizontal carry "Look of Ostrich" leather holster.

looks a little like a drive-in movie for fleas. New this year is a spring-loaded forward lens that folds down for holstering and pops up when the gun is drawn. It's a slick idea that could put dot-type sight systems in the holsters of on-duty police officers.

Holsters

The advantage of a handgun isn't just that it can be fired with one hand, but that it's always handy, even if both hands are occupied with some other task. The holster serves the function of carrying a handgun somewhere on your person where it is readily accessible yet securely retained during any reasonable activity. We've all seen the pictures of Errol Flynn or Burt Lancaster swinging from the pirate ship to the deck of a richly laden merchant ship with a cutlass in his teeth and a flintlock pistol tucked in his sash. Very dashing, but you don't have to be a rocket scientist to recognize that without better carrying devices, there's a high probability of arriving on board the second ship minus your pistol (and probably one of your hands). It's not that dramatic a problem for the handgun hunter strolling through the woods on his fall deer hunt, but in America today, there are urban arenas where an easily accessible handgun is every bit as important as it was to old Burt and Errol.

In the American West, both handguns and leather holsters were a part of daily life. The accent on holsters then was secure retention and comfort while doing chores, yet still giving reasonable access to the firearm. There was not the general level of affluence in the 19th century that we enjoy today, but judging from the posed portrait-type pictures of the era, those boys were every bit as vain as we are today in terms of personal appearance and equipment condition. I'm not just making a nostalgic journey here. The resurgent interest in cowboy shooting has resulted in a number of manufacturers offering Western belts and holsters for participants in these events. Interestingly, the emphasis is on authentic equipment as opposed to the fast-draw rigs that grew out of the Hollywood Westerns of the '50s and '60s. Some of the most authentic holsters come from manufacturers who specialize in all kinds of Western equipment rather than just holsters, and a trip to any of the big cowboy shoots will help you find sources for all your needs. Bianchi, a holster specialist, offers about three different Western rigs that range from authentic 1880 to 1950 television. Galco International, Ltd., prints a special catalog that is a work of art in itself and features just

Western belt/holster combinations that cover both 19th- and 20th-century designs. The Hunter Company, known for value-priced leather holsters over the years, offers an authentic loop-style holster for just over $30. El Paso Saddlery not only treats the cowboy with authentic belt and shoulder holsters, but also provides two "pancake" holsters for S&W semi-autos that are the most comfortable rigs I've ever worn. If you're feeling the ancestral tug, there's no shortage of well-made, attractive Western leather outfits that will transport you back 100 years in time, or at least to the nearest cowboy shoot.

Leather is still fashionable and readily available for the non-cowboy handgunner whether his carry preference is on the belt or in a shoulder rig. Bianchi's original X15 shoulder holster is a very successful design in terms of comfortably distributing weight over the top of the shoulder in a vertical carry position. Newer "skeletal" designs reduce holster bulk and lighten the load, can be worn on the belt or under the shoulder, and are available in either horizontal or upside-down vertical-carry models. Galco's popular "Miami Vice" horizontal-carry shoulder holster continues to sell well and has led to new models with design features reportedly even more comfortable than the rig made famous by Don Johnson. The first page of the 1995 Safariland catalog acknowledges the company's "...return to genuine leather..." as "...softer and more pliable...." Today's leather holsters built to hold specific guns are form-fitted so well that retention devices are not normally necessary on many models. When such designs are combined with tension screws to control the amount of holster "squeeze" on the gun, one's normal physical movement is virtually unlimited, yet one still has instant access to the gun in time of trouble.

Assessing your own individual body geometry is a critical step in selecting the kind of holster and carry mode that will be both comfortable and useable for you, personally. For example, I'm quite comfortable with a shoulder holster or a strong-side belt carry rig, but my long, used-to-be-really-slim torso that allows a comfortable reach across the chest to a shoulder gun makes it a bit difficult to reach all the way down and across to a cross-draw rig carried slightly below belt level. In a recent exercise that involved equipping my niece for her new job in Africa, I became acquainted with some of the problems unique to properly fitting a holster to a woman. Her small stature left inadequate room to carry an L-frame Smith & Wesson revolver in either a horizontal or vertical shoulder holster, and a strong-side belt holster didn't allow the gun to clear the holster before her hand hit her armpit. Fortunately, both Bianchi and Galco offer dual-position belt holsters allowing either a strong-side or cross-draw carry. She chose the Galco Phoenix model that provides a comfortable cross-draw carry that allows easy access to the gun whether she is sitting or standing. I've had great success with Bianchi's Cyclone model, wearing it on the strong side, but with the belt threaded through the cross-draw loops. This carries long-barreled (like 10-inch) hunting revolvers in a slight muzzle-forward position that permits a reasonable draw, and I can sit down without jamming the muzzle into the ground or ramming the gun up into my armpit. Not what Bianchi had in mind, perhaps, but an extremely workable solution for someone of my height and build.

Belt slides, which are basically two strips of leather sewn together with room for a handgun between them, have become rather popular. The belt goes outside the gun, through two slots on the outer strip of leather, and belt tension holds the gun close against the body and assists in retaining it during strenuous activity. A number of companies make this type of holster, which in some cases is form-fitted to a particular handgun. One of the slickest I've seen comes from knife (and sheath) maker Larry Albach. He offers two sizes of non-fitted gun sheaths that securely hold almost all revolvers and semi-autos. Without the gun, these belt carriers look like they were made for whatever you put in them: a pipe makes you look like a professor, a pair of pliers make you look like Tim Allen, etc. Larry cautions buyers about making sure their pipe is unloaded before re-holstering. Belt slides are inexpensive solutions to concealed carry needs.

In recent years, holster manufacturers have become deeply involved in the use of alternate materials. Many holsters are now made of ballistic nylon, which doesn't come close to the aesthetics of leather unless you're into the SWAT team look, but the buying public realizes substantial savings. Aside from the savings in materials and manufacturing costs, the generic pouch shape of nylon holsters permits shooters to use one holster for a number of different guns. For hunters, nylon belts and holsters feature camouflage patterns that match some of the clothing worn in the field.

In addition to nylon, companies have come up with other synthetic materials designed to do certain things for their selected market niche. Perhaps best known is Safariland's thermally molded Safari-Laminate that has become very popular with police and competition shooters. For uniformed police officers who constantly face the threat of having their handguns snatched and used against them, Safariland makes duty holsters that permit a quick draw by trained officers, but make it extremely difficult for a bad guy to remove the officer's gun. Now Safariland has introduced their new Nylok series Tactical Finish competition holsters to the action shooting community. The "double O" models are already extremely popular with serious competitors.

Having owned the U.S. military market for several years by virtue of their Model M12 holster, Bianchi is going after the police and competition market with two new technologies. Their AccuMold gear provides form-fitting protection to the officer's gun while riding lighter on the belt. Their plastic, moulded Hemisphere Competition Holster has a one-screw adjustment that controls cant, angle and elevation. I had a chance to play with it for a couple of weeks while doing this article and was amazed at the ease of adjusting the rig to an instant, individual fit regardless of its starting position.

In leather, there are a couple of hunting rigs worth noting. Freedom Arms markets their own brand of leather holsters for the big Wyoming five-shooters. Their chest-carry holster for either a scoped or unscoped revolver is quite comfortable and offers relatively quick access whether you're on foot, horseback or jeepback.

The Hunter Co. offers a new leather holster that is draped over the neck and features an open top and a piece of leather to cover the scope. It can be adjusted to fit different gun/scope combinations. It isn't yet available for the longest barrel lengths, and it should be carried inside an outer garment if strenuous activity is anticipated.

Magnum Research also carries a varied line of holsters—leather and nylon, shoulder- and belt-carry—that handle scoped or unscoped Desert Eagles with 6-, 10-, or 14-inch barrels.

One of the neatest developments in handgun carrying packages is the holster/fanny pack. With regular fanny packs being carried by more and more people in urban areas, it's getting difficult for bad guys to know who's armed and who's not. I love it! Several of the holster manufacturers who make ballistic nylon products now make holster/fanny packs. I've tried three of these, one from Uncle Mike's and two from Bianchi. Uncle Mike's opens all across the top seam by peeling Velcro strips apart and pulling down on the front of the pack. The two Bianchi models open (1) by unzipping the top seam and pulling the gun from a rubber holster inside the compartment closest to the body, and (2) by separating the Velcro strips on one end of the pack and withdrawing the gun from the compartment. I found the Velcro Bianchi worked well with a weak-side carry, the zipper Bianchi worked well with a strong-side carry, and the Uncle Mike's worked either way with a preference for weak-side carry. To be honest, I haven't worked with these systems long enough to have drawn any serious conclusions (which, in any case, would probably be applicable only to my personal needs), but I am impressed with this clever development in holsters.

Grips

To semi-quote Master Poo in his last lecture on *Kung Fu*: "Ah, Grasshopper, you must become one with the gun." Unfortunately, this most important teaching was deleted by the liberal TV media when the show went on the air, and Caine was forced to take on the world with nothing but dirty feet. We handgunners, however, know the importance of becoming one with the gun, and good grips that fit our hand help us do that. While some guns just naturally fit some shooters as-issued, all of us need a little help in getting a grip on some guns. If you shoot several different brands and calibers of handguns, you may need different grip solutions for different guns. In addition to achieving the proper fit of hand to gun, some grips provide extra benefits, such as softening felt recoil or positioning your fingers to maintain a consistent grip from shot to shot. Given a reasonable fit and level of comfort with more than one set of grips, your selection of the best of those might be based primarily on aesthetic preferences.

Bullseye shooters realized decades ago that extra points could be picked up by simply installing a set of "target" grips on their competition gun. The result was some of the largest, most elaborately shaped hunks of wood and plastic you've ever seen on a handgun. The concept is just as valid today. If you target shoot, get good grips.

Ironically, it was one of the most popular guns and calibers of the 20th century that forcefully reminded many of us that pain and fun are not synonymous. The Smith & Wesson Model 29 in 44 Magnum with the original Marquis de Sade checkered grips initiated my search for a gentler shooting

Uncle Mike's slip-on grips on a Colt Mustang, S&W Sigma and Glock 17.

setup. I can remember my mixed emotions as I installed that first ugly set of rubber Pachmayr grips on my beautiful Smith and headed for the range. After the first six shots, the Pachmayrs acquired this beautiful, golden aura, and I wondered what fool had ever judged them to be ugly. While I've never lost my feelings for the beauty of wood, I'm still a big believer in rubber grips for softening felt recoil and improving grip comfort.

Alleviating pain isn't the only reason for considering replacement grips. A small, short-barreled revolver does tend to bite when stoked with suitable defense loads, and it's very helpful to tame its behavior so that we're not more frightened of firing the gun than we are of whoever scared us into pulling the gun. We're less likely to practice with a gun that hurts, and if we do practice, pain can teach us bad habits or prevent us from learning good ones. Also of major importance in a self-defense handgun, particularly one being used by a frightened individual with less-than-expert shooting skills, is the natural pointability of the gun in the event only one or two hurried shots can be fired in a crisis situation. For some, concealability is of paramount importance. You have to evaluate your probable situations and prioritize your overall needs when selecting the "best" grip.

Hogue, Pachmayr and Uncle Mike's all make rubber grips for handguns. Pachmayr even makes them for single shot Contenders, and in the really big calibers like the JDJ hand-cannons, they are an essential addition. In my experience with all three brands, I've settled on the Hogue finger-groove grips for round-butt Smith & Wessons, except for 44 Magnums. When the recoil gets that severe, I prefer the bulkier, softer Pachmayrs. On the round-butt J-frame S&W revolvers, the Uncle Mike's finger-groove grips offer the best combination of softening recoil and natural pointability, but sacrifice concealability. If I want to hide a J-frame, I'll use Uncle Mike's rubber boot grip. For K- and L-frame S&Ws, I like Pachmayr's Compac Professionals for a compromise between concealability and comfort. If it's a long shooting session with full 357 loads, I'm back to the Hogue finger-groove grips that I first mentioned. All three brands do what they're supposed to do; you have to determine what works best on your gun in your hand. Both Pachmayr and Uncle Mike's make slip-on grips, a rubber sleeve that slips over the factory grips on a semi-auto, providing instant finger grooves or smoothing the existing grip texture. Pachmayr also combines the worlds of wood and rubber in one grip with their American Legend, a walnut grip with rubber finger grooves on the front and sides.

I've been impressed with the looks of wood grips from Hogue and Eagle. Hogue makes the same finger-groove configuration in wood as is on their rubber grips, except they have checkering and are much prettier. Eagle has a large selection of wood grips in walnut, cocobolo and rosewood for a wide variety of guns. Styles and sizes range from the tiny rosewood Secret Service grips for the J-frame S&W up through target grips with finger grooves for several semi-automatics and the large-frame Wesson 44 Magnum revolver. Eagle also works with some unusual materials like buffalo horn, mother-of-pearl and ebony. Ajax Custom Grips deals in both wood and synthetics with a touch of the exotic in both. Woods include cherrywood and black silverwood, while the non-wood offerings include white and black pearlite, stag and staglite, ivory polymer, pewter and (gasp!) genuine ivory. I thought the Ajax catalog prices were reasonable for everything listed, but they didn't quote ivory; they suggest you call for price quotes on anything made from Tantor's teeth. From what I've heard about the cost of ivory, I suggest you take your medication before calling.

And what of the future? Well, you don't have to be a regular on the 900 psychic network to recognize that *materials* are the name of the game. Magnifying scopes get lighter and more compact while gaining magnification power, and dot scopes get lighter while offering better fields of view. We might see polymer construction in scopes just as we have in pistols, or someone like C-More Systems might design an optic system the size of today's iron sights. Holster manufacturers are already using lots of materials other than leather, and even some alternate types of leather besides the traditional cowhide. Designs will conform to, and even anticipate, the needs of the shooting public, with emphasis and the most attention being devoted to the largest needs. It will be interesting to see if societal changes dictate more police gear or more private carry equipment for a better-armed public. Grips could be made of new materials that literally adapt to the user's individual hand, moulding the gun to the shooter to achieve the proverbial "oneness with the gun." Not that anything would do much for my shooting skills, but self-adjusting grips, perhaps with a memory, are a concept that could become a reality soon and would probably help the vast majority of handgunners.

Anything's possible. And that's why tomorrow will probably replace today as "the good old days" for handgunners. ●

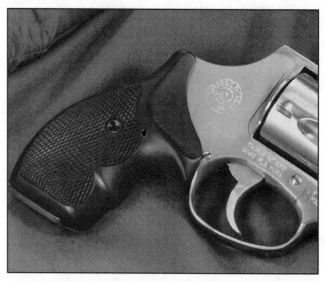

Uncle Mike's rubber boot grip for a small-frame Taurus. The author likes this one on J-frame Smiths, too.

HANDGUNS 96

Handgun Hunting

Swiggett's run for the record, page 184.

Runyan's loaded for bear, page 190.

Sweaty Teddy's always ready, page 193.

Ken French guided Hal to this 51-inch, 16-point, 10½-year-old bull moose. Just before the T/C 45-70 went off, Swiggett heard French say, "He's between 150 and 200 yards." Several witnesses confirmed the range to be at least 180 yards. Hal admits luck played a part.

MAINE'S MONSTER MOOSE
by HAL SWIGGETT

HOW ABOUT BEING number one in the state of Maine handgun record book? For two days, that's where my moose was recorded.

It was truly a l-o-n-g shot, much longer than would have been my choice, especially with a 14-inch Thompson/Center Contender chambered for one of my all-time favorite cartridges, the 45-70. The moose was big, that was obvious. He was far away. That, too, was obvious. He was so far away he looked small through the 2.5x scope riding atop my T/C's 45-70 barrel. However, I used a solid rest to hold the T/C steady. A gentle—make that very soft—gradual pull dropped the pistol's hammer without a quiver, and the 415-grain Garrett SWC sped on its way.

The 122-year-old 45-70 is one of the finest big game cartridges offered today. Born in the 1873 Trapdoor Springfield, it is chambered today in guns like the author's Thompson/Center Contender.

Randy Garrett loads only two cartridges, the 45-70 and the 44 Remington Magnum. His Super-Hard-Cast bullets weigh 415 grains in 45-70 and 310 grains for the 44.

How did this moose hunt come about? It wasn't easy, I guarantee. Over the past good many years I have taken moose in the far northern country of Sweden and, over that same span of time, three in Canada. I took all of them with rifles. However, handguns have been my main items of interest for serious hunting since WWII, and before that fracas I took a lot of small game with rimfire revolvers. I still do, for that matter.

I have brought a good many critters down with the old standard load of 10.0 grains of Unique under Lyman's great #454424 250-grain cast bullet in 45-Colt-chambered revolvers. It worked well enough until Elmer Keith, Smith & Wesson and Remington put their heads together and came up with the 44 Remington Magnum. It was through the continued persistence of Elmer that S&W was convinced of the need to develop the handgun and the Remington-made cartridge. The 44 Magnum was the first honest-to-goodness hunting handgun.

More than two decades back I gave up hunting in any country, state, province or whatever that doesn't let me hunt with handguns. Canada, with lots of moose, was automatically eliminated since they get red-faced and almost violent at any mention of handguns and hunting.

Wyoming has lots of moose and an annual drawing for permits. My postage stamp was put on an entry more years

than I care to look back on. Then I discovered that Maine not only had bigger moose (Canadian as opposed to Wyoming's Shiras), they also let foreigners enter their drawing. You put $10 in the pot and then pay for the permit only if you luck out. Wyoming wants their money up front, $750 the last time I tried, and it is eventually returned if your name not drawn. Maine asks for $250 after your name is drawn.

Ken French, one of the Thompson/Center Arms hierarchy, saw to it annually that I got an application. It had always been returned, accompanied by my personal $10 check.

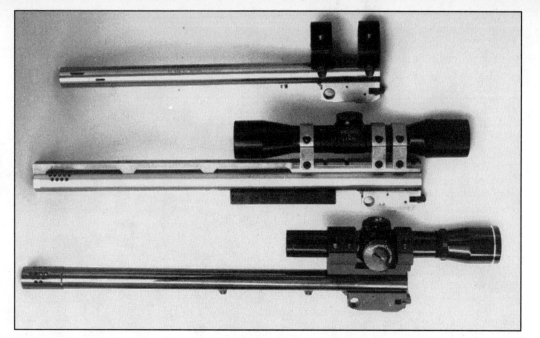

The first 45-70 T/C barrel was a 12-incher by Lee Jurras (top). Then SSK Industries built them with a length of 14 1/4 inches (center), and today T/C offers their own version at 14 inches, including muzzlebrake (bottom).

MONSTER MOOSE

One day, lo and behold, Ken called (he lives in Maine and sees the list soon as it comes out) and told me I was going moose hunting.

I have long been a fan of that 120-plus-year-old cartridge, the 45-70. It was ideally suited to this moose project. Also, the first 45-70 barrel ever built for a T/C Contender frame was built for me. Warren Center well remembers my asking, make that begging, for one way back when. He was afraid his gun might not handle the cartridge.

I approached Lee Jurras, the original owner of Super Vel Cartridges, on the subject, who was, by then, building big single shot pistols from his home base in New Mexico. He and a pair of his buddies put their heads together, and eventually I received a barrel from him. It was Mag-Na-Ported and had one of the first scope mounts produced by Jim Herringshaw. It reads, on the left side, on three lines: "45-70 gov't, created for hal swiggett, by lee e. jurras." All lower-case letters. This was made, as near as I can recall, in the early to mid-1970s. I know I still had an office in the center of downtown San Antonio, on the second floor of the New Moore Building, to be exact.

Back then we had only factory-spec ammo. As I recall, my ammo was Federal. I don't recall what brand scope I installed, but I'm certain it was 2x. As shown in a photo here, there is now no scope in Jim's mount. This barrel is a true, honest-to-goodness original and probably will never be fired again.

I do know I sighted it in and it accompanied me to a sizable (even for south Texas) ranch where a boar javelina gave his all.

Later, another south Texas ranch had a problem—an African oryx that had killed a ranch hand. By the time I came along it was impossible to get close enough for a capture gun (30 yards was max in those days), so I was asked to put him down. That first 45-70 T/C barrel handled the job beautifully, loaded with Federal factory 300-grainers.

Several years later, J.D. Jones and his SSK Industries started producing 45-70 barrels topped with his T'SOB scope mounting system. These barrels were built to withstand almost anything reasonable. I had been a serious

Jim Herringshaw's current production scope mount for the Contender is called the Maxi-Mount. These are seen on more than a few scoped handguns nowadays.

complainer to the Simmons scope company. They finally took me seriously, and one day I received a 2.5-7x from their PR person, Sherry Fears. The specific instructions were, "See if you can destroy this one."

I took her at her word. To this day, I still thank God that I could find only 107 empties. Loaded with 47.5 grains of H-322 under Hornady's 500-grain full metal jacket bullet, it was, to be brutally frank, awesome. I fired all 107 rounds in 90 minutes. My hands were bleeding. My wrists and elbows ached for more than a week. In spite of all this punishment, the scope seemed to be intact.

To find out if the scope was still OK, I installed it on my Anschutz Exemplar 22 Long Rifle pistol, which is a one-holer for certain. At 40 yards it printed three consecutive 1-inch squares—proving its adjustments to be precise. Then I fired six shots, one at each magnification: 2.5, 3, 4, 5, 6, and 7x, all at that same 40 yards. All six were so close to one hole it wasn't otherwise measurable. I was satisfied, and Simmons was satisfied.

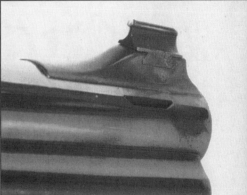

Swiggett's backup Ruger features custom sights by "Trapper" Alexiou. The rear sight is a V-notch.

The front sight on the Ruger SBH is a bead.

This oryx killed a man two days before Swiggett was called in to stop him. Hal used his Lee Jurras custom 45-70 barrel and Federal factory loads. Note the expanded bullet under the neck skin. The mounted head is on display at the Handgun Hunters Museum and Hall of Fame.

You can see that 45-70 ammo in single shot pistols really is *my* thing. Because of that, I felt the T/C Contender in 45-70 was the ideal tool for hanging a Maine Monster Moose on my wall.

I always carry a holster gun, in this case a 4⅝-inch Ruger Super Blackhawk with what I believe to be the first bead front and "V"-notch sights ever put on a sixgun. I got the idea, a long ways back, that such an arrangement might be ideally suited to handguns. I had Lin "Trapper" Alexiou put a rifle bead up front and a handmade "V" rear on my gun. He did a truly magnificent job. My 44 Ruger SBH has backed up many a hunt.

I carry my backup gun in another first. Roy Baker became famous for his "Pancake" holsters. I ordered one for that 4⅝-inch Ruger. I wanted six cartridge loops attached to the outside. Roy said, "Hal, I've never made a holster like that." "No problem," was my quick response. "With your expertise you can do it easily." He did, and added it to his line.

I *do not* carry my hunting handgun in a holster, even though there is one currently marketed by American Sales, with my name on it.

Rifle hunters carry their firearms in their hands, and shotgunners likewise. Why? To get the gun into action faster. Why, then, would any serious handgunner be less needful of that faster shot? Holsters for honest-to-goodness hunting handguns do not make sense, other than for a backup handgun as mentioned earlier.

My loads for both guns came from Randy Garrett at Garrett Cartridges, Inc. Randy got into custom loading a few years back. His 44 Magnum load is the *only* one legal for elk in Washington state. A hunter has to carry a sales slip or the box his ammo came in, or get into deep conversation with a game warden.

Over the years Garrett used a variety of jacketed bullets of several weights in the 45-70. He even tried the 500-grain Hornady. Time, meaning experience, narrowed his needs down, and he developed what he calls Super-Hard-Cast bullets. They are silver-enriched and oven-tempered. His catalog offers only two loads: 45-70 415-grain Super-Hard-Cast flat nose at 1730 fps; and 44 Remington Magnum 310-grain Super-Hard-Cast SWC at 1320 fps. The 415-grain label reads: "Safe Only In Modern Rifles & TC Contenders."

He calls his 44 Magnum the "Most lethal factory load in any handgun caliber," then goes on to list varied big game that includes moose, grizzly and buffalo.

Here is what became #2 in the Maine record book. The 54½-inch, 12-point bull was taken by the author's long-time friend, J.D. Jones, shown here with Jones' wife, Jane. J.D. used his 375 JDJ wildcat in another Contender.

MONSTER MOOSE

Groups? Here again I deal in real hunting facts. I am in no way interested in, nor have I any concern for, how close ten, twenty or fifty bullets come together on a target. My *only* interest is in where that first bullet prints out of a cold barrel. Then I shoot two more semi-soon, to see how well the gun shoots in case I need to put down a wounded animal. More often than not my groups of three are fired thus: shoot 1; 30-45 seconds for 2; then a pause of 60-90 seconds for the last. This simulates real hunting situations.

I did my chronographing in 45-50-degree temperatures and rather dense and very drippy fog. I was amazed at the consistency of Randy's loads. Ten 45-70s averaged 1686 fps with a miniscule standard deviation of 13. His 44s were almost as clean. Ten averaged 1174 with a standard deviation of 19.

Three three-shot groups from the 45-70 at 50 yards averaged about 1½ inches, center-to-center. These strings were fired in the cadence listed earlier, to simulate hunting conditions. With the 44, I shot 25-yard groups because of 73-year-old eyes with implants. (However, a few jackrabbits at 50-60 yards have wished they had been further away). The average of three, three-shot groups was 1½ inches center-to-center. This came about through a fluky three shots that

measured only 9/16-inch, center-to-center. When that happens, I'm not about to shoot it over. Nor, I do believe, would you. With my guns and ammo tested, I was ready for Maine's Monster Moose.

When we first spotted my moose, I looked that big guy over very carefully with my Swarovski 8x30s. He was far enough away to show us no concern other than to acknowledge, by looking, that he knew we were there. A light-limbed bush partially covered his chest. It was certainly not an obstruction for a big, heavy 45-70 bullet.

It was the distance that made me hesitate. He really was a long way down that slope. I knew my pistol was sighted-in to print 4 to 4½ inches high at 100 yards. I knew big, heavy bullets drop somewhere between hastily and very fast. I finally agreed to try the shot and remember saying to myself, as the hammer dropped, "He is between 150 and 200 yards away." I'm not certain where the scope's crosshairs were when the shot broke. Knowing where to hold for 150 yards and allowing another 6 to 8 inches of drop in case it was a full 200 was what I had in mind.

At the shot the big bull never flinched—no sign of a hit—but slowly walked through a bit of cover (we never lost sight of him) and stopped in a narrow clear-cut, maybe 30 yards at the most from where he stood for that first shot. Closing in to about 80 yards I fired two more shots. I was wound up tight and I know at least one shot never touched him. His head was lowered and blood flowed from his nose proving the lung shot, so we eased up quartering from

Hal Swiggett took this world record (handgun) blue wildebeest in South Africa with his T/C fitted with a custom 45-70 barrel by SSK Industries. It launched a 500-grain Hornady bullet at about 1550 fps.

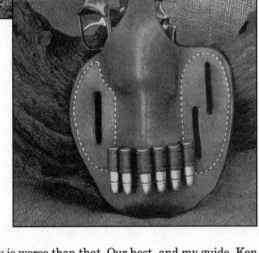

The first Roy Baker "Pancake" holster with cartridge loops was built for the author's customized backup handgun, a 4⅝-inch Ruger Super Blackhawk with Herrett custom stocks.

behind. When we got within 30 yards he suddenly went down on his knees. I tried for a side brain shot, but I had no idea where the brain was located, and missed. (I know now.) He went down on his belly and I moved over near his tail and fired one more 44, this time into the base of his skull. All this happened in about the time it is taking you to read about it.

Randy's big 415-grain Super-Hard-Cast had done its job well.

My first bullet entered half a dozen inches below the top of his lung and exited a few inches lower, passing through near the center of the other lung. There was apparently very little or no expansion. There was definitely, however, more tissue damage to the exiting lung than the other. That brings up my primary life-long shooting sermon: Big bullets do not need expansion. All they need is a flat nose and complete penetration. That concept was positively proved, again, on this magnificent trophy.

No hunter will ever know how big such a moose is until he has one on the ground in front of him, and he's had to climb inside it for the evisceration exercise. Even then, believe it or not, reality won't make itself immediately known, but it'll happen soon. My moose then had to be dragged out to where it was loaded onto a vehicle using a gasoline-powered winch.

We ate lunch and then drove to the check station with the moose. The biologist put the age at a probable nine years. His weight was 825 pounds, which put him at 1072 pounds live weight.

I really was Number One in the Maine handgun record book for two days, October 4 and 5, 1994. J.D. Jones (SSK Industries' head man) put his tag on a bull three points better than mine (155 vs. 158) on October 6. So who cares! J.D. is a long-time friend and in my opinion well worthy of the state record. His, by the way, measured 54½ inches and had 12 points. Mine, 51 inches and 16 points.

It really is worse than that. Our host, and my guide, Ken French had held that Maine state handgun moose record for several years. Now he's third. However, it proves he and his son, Mike, are mighty good moose guides.

We were asked, at the check station, to address a postcard to ourselves and they would let us know the true age of our trophies. I received the postcard today as I was concluding this tale. My moose was officially aged at 10½ years. He was a grand old man, and in moose years actually older than this writer, who was 73 when we met. Had I known that, well.... ●

Some time after Hal turned in this story he learned that his moose was, in fact, number one in Maine's handgun record book. Initial scoring had put Hal's moose as #2 with a score of 155 and J.D. Jones' at 158. After the drying-out period, and official scoring, the situation was reversed. J.D.'s moose was aged at 9½ years and scored 153⅛. Hal's had already been aged at 10½ years, as mentioned in the story, but after the drying period, the official score was 157⅝. We thought you ought to know—Editor.

A BEAR GUIDE'S LOOK AT HANDGUNS

by ANDY RUNYAN

I GOT MY first handgun when I was about 13 years old, and if I remember right it was a 22 Stevens target pistol. It had a little cocking piece on the back of it, and as I remember it was a break action. I had that handgun for many years until just before I came to Alaska.

Of course, I picked up a few handguns over in Europe during WWII, mainly PPK 380s, the occasional Luger, and some P38s. I never really hung onto any of those, so I was out of the handgun business until I came to Alaska in 1946.

Back then there were not a whole lot of handgun options, compared with today. I had a 22 Colt Woodsman at the time, and somehow I ended up with a Smith & Wesson K-38. I carried the S&W quite awhile, mostly when I just didn't want to carry a rifle.

Editor's Note

Master guide Andy Runyan is the holder of the second-ever guide's license issued by the state of Alaska. His hunters have placed more Kodiak bear into the top twenty slots in the record books than any other hunters. Andy is recognized by his fellow Alaskan guides as the most knowledgeable man in the state on caribou. His Exclusive Alaskan Guides operation guides hunters on Kodiak Island and the Alaska Peninsula. Andy lives year-round in Alaska with his wife Ruthie.

Eventually along came the 357 Magnum, but for some reason I never did own a handgun in that caliber. I guess I just wasn't impressed. I carried the 38 until about 1954. Then I got a S&W 44 Heavy Duty[1] and loaded it with Keith loads, using his 250-grain semi-wadcutter bullet. That was quite a successful cartridge, actually, handloaded that way. 'Course we didn't have a chronograph back in those days, so

---

[1]Editor's note: The S&W Heavy Duty was an N-frame gun that was chambered only in 38-44 caliber (plus a dozen in 45 Colt), according to Roy Jinks' *History of Smith & Wesson*. However, the 44 Special S&W Hand Ejector 4th Model 1950 Military looked identical to the Heavy Duty. If Andy's gun had fixed sights, this is probably the model he acquired. If it had target sights, it might have been the 1950 Target (Model 24). S&W made just slightly more than 5000 1950 Targets, and only 1200 of the 1950 Militarys in 44 Special, so Andy was shooting what was destined to become one of the rarer Smith & Wessons.

all we could do was take someone else's word for what we were getting for velocity.

I carried that 44 Special from 1954 to about 1960. It got to the point where you'd shoot it and it'd take half a minute to quit rattlin'. It got a little loose after thousands of heavy Keith loads. The gun just wasn't built to handle that sort of thing.

During those years it gave me good service. I tracked down and killed several wounded sheep while guiding, and got one crippled caribou with it. The caribou was quite a long way away. The fellow shooting at it was using a 300 Weatherby, and he'd probably have done a lot better if he'd left one or both eyes open when he shot. I think he closed both eyes, shot, and somehow hit it. I finally killed it for him with the 44, at about 200 yards. He was impressed. I was impressed, too!

One day a native fellow named Charlie Toby and I were going from Nebesna to Chistochina in my pickup when we saw a moose. I decided we'd gone long enough without any moose meat, so I grabbed my old 44 and went out the pickup door after that bull. I shot him at about 30-35 yards, just behind the shoulder. The bull simply walked around in a big circle and fell over. The performance of the handgun certainly impressed Charlie.

I carried that Smith 44 Special up until the time I got a 44 Magnum. Back then, I don't know just who you had to be to get a Smith & Wesson Model 29. I don't think I knew anybody who actually had one. You just heard stories about them.

I ended up with a Ruger, which, in fact, I liked quite well. It was a good-shooting pistol that had one of the finest triggers of any handgun I've ever had. However, I just didn't care for that long barrel, so I cut it back, even with the end of the ejector rod.

I carried that gun on many hunting trips. I used it to kill several crippled black bear. One time, when I was at my old cabin at Clarence Lake, a big 7-foot black bear had been wounded by a shot from a 7mm Mag rifle, and he disappeared into the thick brush up at the northeast end of the lake. I went looking for him with my 44 Ruger. When I found him, he didn't hesitate—he came for me full-bore! My first shot hit him in the chest but didn't even slow him down. My second shot hit him just above the eye and that did the trick...which was just as well, because at that shot the cylinder rod and a few other pieces fell off the gun.

I retired the Ruger, and by then you could get a S&W 44 Mag, so I did.

Another interesting handgun experience with a bear came when I was guiding some Italian hunters. I went to pack out the moose one of the hunters had shot. I was carrying a 9mm Browning in a shoulder holster at the time.

BEAR GUIDE

There was a bear on the meat, so I had one of the Italian hunters shoot the bear. The bear disappeared into the brush, and when we got to him, there he lay, down in a hole. My Italian hunter was standing off to the side about 50 feet away. I reached down and grabbed the bear with both hands by the back of the neck to drag him up out of that hole so we could get at him for skinning, pictures and such. All of a sudden the bear stood up!

I just held onto the back of his neck with my left hand, grabbed that Browning with my right, stuck it under the bear's ear and touched it off. That put the bear down on the deck right then and there, but the Italian scared the hell out of me. He was waving his rifle all around, trying for a shot at the bear, and he wasn't that good of a shot! You might say I was standing pretty close to that bear at the time! Fortunately, I got his attention in time and he didn't shoot.

Another time at Clarence Lake, Lionel Sullivan was with me and we got onto a moose that was well into the rut. Lionel hit the moose, and I went down into the brush to look for it. (I had my trusty Smith & Wesson 44 Mag by now.) The moose showed up all right and here he came! I shot him right up the nostril. He wasn't very far away at the time. The bullet went right up into the brain cavity and put him on the ground instantly, simply dumped him.

I've had quite a few experiences when packing a handgun while guiding. I've never really considered a handgun to be a hunting weapon as such, but it sure is handy when you've got your hands full doing something else. The handgun is mainly a backup. 'Course, if a guy's carrying a 416 or a 404 around with him, he doesn't really need a handgun. But if you're packing meat in fairly open country, or bowhunting, it pays to have a good healthy handgun along with you. I've had too many run-ins with different critters, and the handgun has often come in handy.

I'd flown two fisherman to my cabin at Clarence Lake and I had no rifle with me. (For cryin' out loud, I didn't even have a gun in the airplane!) We had only been there a short time when a small grizzly came down the beach toward us. I put the fishermen in the cabin and I told them I'd go run off the bear. But the bear didn't run off. In fact it came down the beach my way pretty fast! I jumped back into the cabin and asked, "Do either of you have a gun with you, by any chance?" One of them said, "Well, I've got my 357..." I said, "You better give me that damned thing!"

I went back out there and the bear was just up the beach about 30 yards. I shot into the sand in front of him and the bear turned and looked at me. I shot again into the sand, thinking that another shot would surely get him going on his way. It didn't work. He decided he'd had enough and here he came.

He was about seven or eight feet away, and I tried to hit him down through the top of the head. I missed and instead hit him through the upper lip and knocked a tooth out. The bullet went down under his tongue and came out through his lower jaw, but it didn't break the jawbone. The bear stood up on his hind legs and roared around a bit, and I just kept the gun on him. He was right there in front of me. You don't know what you really ought to do at a time like that. Do you want to try to kill him, or let him go, or what?

He dropped down onto all fours and took off up the beach out of there. I waited a bit to see what would happen, then I put my old dog on him and the dog ran the bear out into the lake. I got into my canoe and paddled out to have a good look at the damage I'd done. I ran the canoe up alongside him, and when he growled and roared at me I could get a good look at the wound inside his mouth. Turned out it wasn't bad enough to justify killing him. His worst problem was that he had a tooth knocked out.

That was one time I wish I'd had a pistol I was more familiar with than a borrowed 357. As I said, I don't hunt with a handgun as such, but it sure pays to have one along.

I don't know much about any caliber but the 44, which I've packed a long time. It's basically about as good as you can get. It's a fairly easy cartridge to shoot, as opposed to some of the things available today. One of the most important aspects of handgun shooting is recovery time. If I can get off two shots with the 44 Magnum in the time it takes to get off one shot with a 454 Casull, I'd take the 44 any day of the week. One shot won't always do the job, and you must be ready to shoot again quickly.

I feel about handgun hunting like I do about bows: They're great within their limits. However, when you start putting a 14- to 16-inch barrel and a scope on a handgun, it's no longer a handgun. If your gun has a 6- to 8-inch barrel and iron sights, I'd consider it to be a handgun. There's nothing wrong with hunting with handguns, even with scopes attached. They certainly do the job when used with discretion.

This past January I was down in California hunting "piggies." A fellow named Gary had invited me out to his ranch to hunt. We were hunting together, and in early afternoon we finally found some wild pigs and made our sneak on 'em.

We made a successful sneak and I shot one; it never got up. Another one jumped into the timber and Gary said something to me into my bad ear. I couldn't understand what he had said, so I didn't shoot. My pig was down, and I figured, one was enough.

Anyway, Gary took off down the hill and through the trees. He was carrying a 14-inch Thompson/Center Contender with scope, chambered for one of the 7mm handgun cartridges. He told me he used it for deer hunting, and it was obvious he knew how and when to use it. About five minutes later I heard a shot. About ten minutes later I heard another shot. I soon found out he, too, had busted a pig with his pistol.

That was about my only real experience in hunting with a handgun as such...except for small game, that is. I used to hunt birds and rabbits with the old Colt Woodsman, and I kept score. If I shot a sitting rabbit, that didn't even count. They had to be running for it to count. If I used a rifle, I had to hit them in the eye before the shot would count. I used to have lots of chances to practice and got to be a decent shot with handgun and rifle.

As I said, I still pack my 4-inch S&W 44 Magnum around, and every now and then a use comes up for it. You never know what it's gonna be, but something will always come up—count on it. ●

Ted hunts with a handgun all over the world, including Africa.

HANDGUN HUNTING ROCK-'N'-ROLL STYLE

by TED NUGENT

I SWEAR, MY whole ponytail was erect! Not just the hair on the back of my neck, like most folks, but the whole wad of ponytail was straight up and skybound. The Spirit of the Wild was once again a runaway freight train of sensual stimuli. My senses were on fire. The counterpoint to the shrill scream of one wild, enraged bull elk, bugling his challenge of dominance over his domain, was the nostril-burning redline overload of clear and scent-saturated mountain

Ted took this elk with his Mag-Na-Ported and action-slicked Model 29 Smith & Wesson 44 Magnum, a handgun he's used many years to "rack and stack" a lot of game. (Photo by Shemane Nugent.)

TED NUGENT

air. Got the picture friends? We're talking *adventure* in its purest form. This is a genuine Ted Nugent shopping spree, and we ain't at the mall!

I was face down, crawling over rock-hell, snaking my way through puckerbrush snagzones, over the likes of which most men never dare tread, and I was closing in on the Ultimate Beast fast. My Lawman leather protected the blue-steel tool-art nestled under my left armpit, and the moment of truth was here and now. The big Smith 29 filled my hand like the handshake of a good old friend. In an instant I was sitting upright as the magnificent 7-point imperial bull emerged from the tangle of impenetrable scrub, 125 yards across the small clearing, still screaming

like a hollowbody Gibson Byrdland guitar in heat. Elbows snugged on knees, my left thumb raked back the hammer, Keith-style. The sight picture materializing before me duplicated my home range practice sessions, and the investment of all those thousands of practice rounds were about to pay huge dividends.

God, I felt wonderful! Life without adventure is death, and all my life, the call of the wild has rung loud and proud in my ears, challenging me to embrace and enhance my instincts to be alive in nature. Raised in a somewhat recreational, casual hunting family environment, I was taught the basics of hands-on cause and effect via woodsman's skills, and how awareness and honesty will steer one to be an asset to himself and to the land. Since birth in 1948, I have missed nary a single fall season in the wilds of America and beyond, and am quite pleased with the balance these outdoor excursions have afforded me and my loved ones.

I was lovingly guided by my parents throughout my youth to safely and responsibly enjoy my bows and arrows, 22 rifles and handguns, and the lessons of our quality family outdoor time together. Though I have been primarily a bowhunter all my life, I am driven to pursue all methods of hunting, fishing and trapping, enjoying all the inherent challenges in various marksmanship and outdoor pursuits. Blackpowder, long-range centerfire rifle, handguns, longbow, recurve, crossbow, compound, atlatl, everything that slings a projectile turns me on. Hell, I bet I could bag game with my Gibson guitar if there was a season!

The deadly efficiency of a 44 Magnum is absolutely a thing of beauty. I've made long-range, in excess of 100-yard, one-shot kills on caribou, bear, elk, whitetail, mule deer, hundreds of wild boar, African impala, waterbuck, warthog, gemsbok, bushbuck, wildebeest, nyala, zebra, tsessebee, hartebeest, and feral critters by the thousands with my old pal, a basically stock 6½-inch blue Smith & Wesson Model 29.

Though upgraded tuning and trigger work over the years by Larry Kelly's select Mag-Na-Port team is a real plus, I have always encouraged new handgun hunters to become familiar and proficient with stock arms first. I have found, on the average, that out-of-the-box Smiths, Freedom Arms, Colts, Rugers, Glocks, Taurus, Contenders and Dan Wessons are ready for long-range big-gaming. Same with factory ammo. Find the right combination and become comfortable with its performance.

For more than twenty years, the handsome Smith was my constant companion. I carried it in the small of my back, in my belt, loaded with Remington 240-grain semi-jacketed hollowpoints, ready to rock. I live on some wild Midwest acres, and a rancher comes to grips, over time, with the practical tools that he keeps on hand. Like guns. Not only that, but there seems to be this streak of independence in the ol' Nuge that runs hot and contrary to the transparent tendencies of the trendy liberal-mentality that is so often overwhelming in the big greasy world of rock-'n'-roll, and in the entertainment industry at large. I defy those folks, always have and always will.

My current baby is a Glock 20, loaded with sixteen of Peter Pi's super efficient Cor-Bon 10mms, that spits a 150-grainer at 1400 fps. Hits like a 41 Magnum. I use it on bowling pins, huge hogs, big feral dogs, deer and bear. The country is experiencing a runaway epidemic of 'coons, skunks, possums, and feral dogs and cats, with rabies and distemper at all-time highs. Not on the Nugent ranch. Population control is a daily maneuver for landowners, and it is the best thing one can do for health and balance in the wild. The only good vermin is dead vermin. The 10mm is wonderful, and it is probably the ultimate carjacker fixer.

Throughout the year, I do a lot of "rough" shooting with various handguns, from small game and varmint hunting to long-range plinking at 100-, 200- and 300-yard ranges and over. I love my Smith K-17s in 22 rimfire and 22 WRM, and shoot lots of squirrels and rabbits over the winter months. From the little rimfires to the 454 Casull and the 375 JDJ handcannons, I love 'em all.

I run my dream Sunrize Acres hunt-ranch from my home in Michigan, harvesting huge whitetails, exotics and mean ol' Russian wild boar, and our many hunts throughout the year provide adventure, excitement, delicious sustenance and real-world ballistic testing. Through a near-daily regimen of target, steel plate and bowling pin practice sessions, I keep my eyes, hands and senses razor-sharp, and my handgun proficiency becomes second nature. It's not only lots of fun, but very important to me as well.

My shooting experience and love of the outdoors led me to

The mighty bull elk is a large animal that is difficult to approach, a trophy worthy of the handgun hunter. Nugent's many hours of practice with a powerful handgun give him the confidence to place his shots carefully.

stalk that 7-point elk we left back at the beginning of this story, big Smith in hand.

The red front ramp was even with the top of the rear sight notch, and the sight picture came up his foreleg as he walked. Shoulder-bound, like a tractor beam drawing heavenly bodies together, the sights rested in just the right spot, and I caressed Larry Kelly's 2-pound silken-steel trigger, igniting the powder and launching the projectile yonder.

Instantly, the elk's huge head dropped, then I heard the *kakwhoomph!* of 240 grains of Remington factory softpoint blasting through heavy leg bone, penetrating the heart, and lodging in the far shoulder. The monster bull lurched forward and vanished into the juniper clump, and all was silent.

As I have with hundreds of big game animals over the years, I whacked that giant bull real good. Quick, clean, humane, a near-instant kill.

My guide and I slowly paced off the 125 yards and we approached the fallen monarch where he lay. He was awe-

TED NUGENT

inspiring. We harmonized in our joyous warwhoops, reveling in the dynamics of this wild encounter. We marveled at the beauty of the beast. Giant, long, wide and heavy ivory-tipped antlers took our breath away. Finally we struggled hard together to roll his mass for the knife work ahead. King backstrap was *mine*.

The Nugent clan proudly feeds ourselves exclusively on wild game, and it represents food for both the body and the soul. To hunt one's own dinner is the purest connection with nature that one can experience. The intimacy of a hand-held arm and its inherent stalking challenge accelerate the overall experience, and that my friends, is handgun hunting and nature at its finest. Go slow, seek expert guidance, always think safety, and learn the joys of outdoor adventure, personal arm in hand.

That's my philosophy on life in general and hunting in particular. It works for me and mine, and I'm proud of all of it. ●

For information on Ted Nugent's book, Bloodtrails: The Truth About Bowhunting *or his bi-monthly* Ted Nugent Adventure Outdoors *magazine, write to: Ted Nugent World Bowhunters, 4133 W. Michigan Avenue, Jackson, MI 49202 or call 517-750-9060.*

The Real Ted Nugent

Rock star Ted Nugent has a remarkable zest for life that extends to everything he touches. Driven by a sense of values that start with his family and extend to an immense love of his country, he has a consuming passion for hunting. Both Ted and his wife Shemane are hunters with handgun, bow, rifle and shotgun. The Nugent family dines almost exclusively on game that they hunt themselves.

Ted's life is incredibly busy as he puts together his latest album, tours with his band, and gives speeches against drug and alcohol abuse to packed houses across the country. Despite his busy schedule and family obligations, Nugent takes time to get personally involved with helping young people. His annual non-profit Kamp for Kids takes about 150 boys and girls, aged 11-15, out of the malls and into the great outdoors. It gives them a hands-on hunting, conservation and outdoor recreation education. As he puts it, "We teach these kids to be assets to their lives, their families, their communities and nature. These kids have gained a new appreciation for the ways of the wild, defying the foolishness of drugs and alcohol."

The fact that Ted finds time to impress his sense of wholesome family values and his love of the outdoors on young people doesn't go unnoticed. Governor John Engler just appointed Ted the spokesman for the Michigan Year of the Family Council and also a member of that state's Hunting Heritage Task Force. Ted was recently named Celebrity of the Year by the Michigan Department of Recreation and Parks. Ted is national spokesman for the Drug Abuse Resistance Education (DARE) program which gives young people a strong message to avoid drugs and alcohol.

Ted has sold more than 31 million record albums, and in spite of what must have been extreme pressure to become a part of the stereotypical rock-'n-'roll scene along the way, he is still rockin'. His peers were musicians like Jimi Hendrix and Jim Morrison. As Ted puts it, "God gave them gifts of talent, but they preferred to poison themselves, and now they're dead. I went huntin' and I'm still Ted."

The Nuge has been rockin' for many years and just gets better. He's sold over 31 million albums. Ted gives his time generously to young people and to his community. (Photo by Lisa Lake)

A strong sense of family values drives Ted Nugent. Surrounding Ted are (clockwise from left) Sasha, Toby, Rocco, Starr and Shemane. (Photo by Robert Alford)

HANDGUNS 96

Nostalgia

Browning doubles your pleasure, page 198.

Great minds think alike, page 209.

Setting the highest standard, page 216.

The Impossible Dream?
FN's DOUBLE-ACTION PISTOLS

by GENE GANGAROSA, JR.

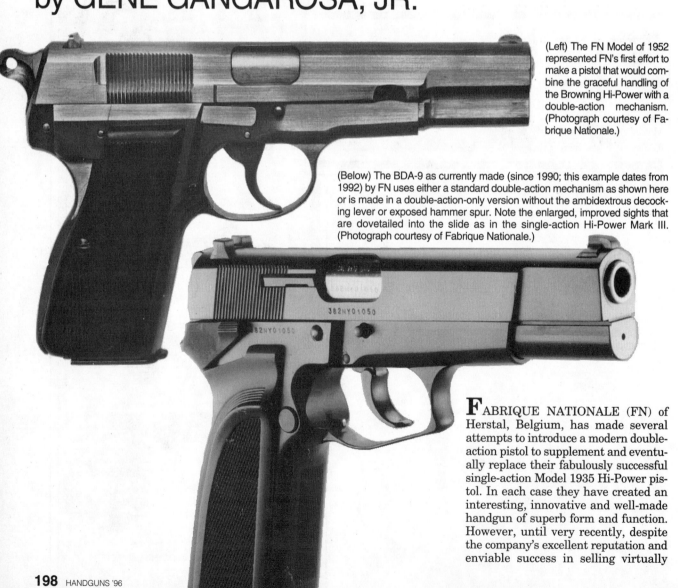

(Left) The FN Model of 1952 represented FN's first effort to make a pistol that would combine the graceful handling of the Browning Hi-Power with a double-action mechanism. (Photograph courtesy of Fabrique Nationale.)

(Below) The BDA-9 as currently made (since 1990; this example dates from 1992) by FN uses either a standard double-action mechanism as shown here or is made in a double-action-only version without the ambidextrous decocking lever or exposed hammer spur. Note the enlarged, improved sights that are dovetailed into the slide as in the single-action Hi-Power Mark III. (Photograph courtesy of Fabrique Nationale.)

FABRIQUE NATIONALE (FN) of Herstal, Belgium, has made several attempts to introduce a modern double-action pistol to supplement and eventually replace their fabulously successful single-action Model 1935 Hi-Power pistol. In each case they have created an interesting, innovative and well-made handgun of superb form and function. However, until very recently, despite the company's excellent reputation and enviable success in selling virtually every other type of firearm, success in this one area has largely eluded them.

FN's first experience with the mass production of double-action pistols was one which, given a choice in the matter, the firm would gladly have done without. In August of 1943, the occupying Nazis compelled the factory to tool up for production of the Walther P-38, the Third Reich's standard military handgun. FN was already making at least two of its own handgun designs, including the legendary single-action Hi-Power, plus several other items of importance to the German war effort, so this P-38 order was simply one added indignity.

The exact extent of FN's P-38 production is not totally clear. We know for certain that, beginning in early 1944, the company made P-38 frames and slides for shipment to Germany for final assembly and is believed to have been tooling up for the manufacture of complete P-38s. Components stamped with the code "140" assigned by the German *Heereswaffenamt* to FN have been observed in several thousand P-38s with 1943 and 1944 dates from Walther, Mauser and Spreewerke, the three primary German manufacturers. (FN-made P-38 frames, in addition to the numerical code 140, often have an "M1" inscription as well as a slightly thicker trigger guard than German-made P-38s.) When the Allies liberated the FN plant in early September, 1944, they found 4700 receivers and 2200 slides waiting to be shipped to Germany for assembly into complete pistols. The Allies also found small numbers of complete P-38s in the FN plant, but in the absence of specialized tooling to make the pistol's additional parts beyond the frames and slides, they concluded that the complete pistols had probably been brought in from Germany as patterns, perhaps to ensure that FN-made parts would fit and function in the German-made pistols. However, it is known that the Germans removed more than 6000 machine tools from the FN plant as they left on September 6, 1944, and it is certainly possible that specialized P-38 tooling was among this equipment. The full story will probably never be known. Whatever the extent of FN's involvement in production of the P-38, this innovative German pistol design unquestionably exerted a lasting influence on FN's own postwar development of double-action pistols.

The remarkable BDA-9C used an extraordinary short grip combined with a seven-round magazine to give a pistol that would fit into a pocket. The sights used on this particular pistol are indentical to those of the single-action Hi-Power Mark II made from 1982-1988. This promising concept needs to be pursued further. (Photograph courtesy of Fabrique Nationale.)

FN sold the BDA-380 in Europe as the FN DA 140. Note the checkered black plastic stocks. (Photograph courtesy of Fabrique Nationale.)

As early as 1952, Dieudonne Saive, perfecter of the prototype single-action Hi-Power which FN had bought from the legendary John Browning in 1922, created a thirteen-shot 9mm double-action pistol. Saive used a standard Hi-Power pistol as the basis of this new weapon, but reworked it extensively, both to incorporate the double-action feature and also to correct some minor deficiencies he felt lurked in the pistol's design. Added to the upper portion of the much-modified frame was an external trigger bar based on that of the P-38. Saive then placed the experimental pistol's double-action lockwork into a modular mechanism like that of the TT-33 Tokarev and SIG P210 pistols.

Saive also took the opportunity in the Model of 1952's design to correct one of the greatest deficiencies of the standard single-action Hi-Power—its undersized manual safety. In the experimental double-action pistol, a much larger safe-

(Right) A 1983-vintage double-action BDA-9S is shown here with the optional twenty-round extended magazine. The standard magazine holds fourteen rounds. (Photograph courtesy of Fabrique Nationale.)

(Left) The BDA-9M used a shortened barrel and slide, but the frame remained the same as that on the full-size BDA-9S. On this particular pistol the standard fourteen-round magazine is fitted. Note the ambidextrous decocking lever. (Photograph courtesy of Fabrique Nationale.)

FN'S DOUBLE-ACTION

ty catch similar to that of the M1911 was located in a prominent spot on the left side of the frame, where it could be easily moved on and off by the shooter's right thumb. Saive also changed the shape of the unlocking cam under the barrel to improve its function.

To judge from extant photographs, about the only parts from the standard Hi-Power that were incorporated into the experimental double-action Model of 1952 without major change were the magazine, the sights, the slide stop and perhaps some small components of the slide. However, there is no questioning the Model of 1952's ancestry. It retained much of the excellent handling of the Hi-Power and would no doubt have been a highly effective pistol.

FN management was said to be greatly impressed with Saive's handiwork. However, the standard Hi-Power was selling extremely well in the early 1950s, and FN saw that the new pistol, if placed into production, would compete with their own product. Therefore, they shelved the design. By the time the desire for a double-action pistol became urgent some twenty-five years later, FN had already modified the Hi-Power pistol to a great extent to reduce its manufacturing costs. Thus it would not have been practical to revive the Model of

1952 even then. Ironically, this elegant pistol would almost certainly have been a major success for Fabrique Nationale, as several armed forces, notably those of Great Britain, were extremely interested in buying a double-action pistol in the early postwar period. Aside from the Walther company, banned from manufacturing the P-38 (or any other firearm) because of its recent association with the Nazi regime in Germany, no other firearms maker had a viable double-action military-caliber pistol set up for mass production. By the time FN developed other double-action pistols many years later, other manufacturers had entered this market and competition was intense.

In the 1960s, the L.W. Seecamp Company of Connecticut, as an experiment, reworked two Hi-Power pistols to add double-action trigger capability, using much the same process as they use in their well-known M1911 conversions. However, the Hi-Power's complex trigger linkage made this conversion much trickier than the process used on the relatively straightforward trigger mechanism of the M1911. The complexity of these conversions caused Seecamp to stop after modifying only two guns. Interestingly, one of the two guns went to FN for study. The other appeared in

an article in the July, 1991, issue of *Gun World* magazine, where owner/author Tom Ferguson expressed his pleasure with the quality of the conversion.

Meanwhile, other gun companies entered the double-action pistol business. Smith & Wesson's Model 39 appeared in 1955. The Carl Walther Waffenfabrik, raised from its World War II ashes, recommenced P-38 manufacture that same year. Both guns saw considerable military, police and civilian sales, and other double-action pistols were to follow over the next two decades.

By the late 1970s, FN saw that the Hi-Power, though still an excellent and popular design, was showing signs of age. So beginning in 1979, FN made attempts of its own to introduce modern pistols with trigger-cocking mechanisms in the hopes of first supplementing the Hi-Power and then replacing it altogether. Initially, FN tried to use as many standard Hi-Power components as possible in its new pistols, but eventually created totally different designs.

While FN worked on its own designs, the company made do with two double-action pistols ordered from outside sources but marked with FN and/or Browning logos. Both were designated BDA, for "Browning Double Action."

The first of these pistols, the BDA-380 or just BDA (U.S. designation), or DA 140 as it was known in Europe and elsewhere, was a 380 ACP caliber pistol closely based on Beretta's Model 84 and made in the Beretta plant in Gardone, Italy. Its importation into the United States by Browning Arms Company, a

The BDA-380 was FN's first attempt to actually market a double-action pistol. Despite its excellent quality, it was only moderately successful and is no longer offered.

(Below) Browning Arms Company's second BDA was the SIG/Sauer P220. This example is a 9mm, although 38 Super and 45 ACP versions also appeared.

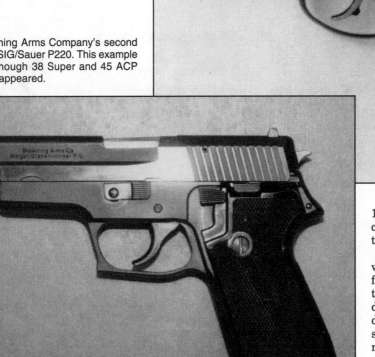

subsidiary of FN, began in 1978. A thirteen-shot pistol like the Model 84, the BDA differed slightly from its Beretta cousin by using an enclosed slide with a small ejection port rather than the Beretta's distinctive open slide. The BDA also differed from the Beretta Model 84 by incorporating a hammer-dropping safety and a revolver-like spur hammer. However, the frames and magazines of the two pistols were virtually identical. BDAs sold in the United States had smooth wooden stocks, while DA 140s sold in Europe and elsewhere had checkered plastic stocks.

Although the BDA was offered for a number of years in FN and Browning catalogs, it was only mildly successful. It was large for a 380, although this was offset to an extent by its smooth contours and great magazine capacity. Eventually the BDA was overshadowed by the similar Berettas, particularly after Beretta updated its Models 84 and 85 to Model 92F standards and undercut Browning's price by the better part of a hundred dollars. Browning finally dropped the BDA from its line in 1993, although some are still available in new, unsold condition from dealers as I write this. The BDA-380's demise is a shame, as it was a well-made and accurate pistol.

Browning's second BDA was a SIG/Sauer pistol made in Eckenförde, Germany. First imported by Browning in 1979, this big gun could be purchased in a choice of 9mm, 38 Super, or 45 ACP calibers. Now sold in the United States with great success as the SIG P220, the BDA as offered by Browning simply did not sell well. Nobody seems to know exactly why; Sigarms, the current importer, has trouble keeping the guns in stock, they sell them so fast. The design and workmanship are outstanding. Perhaps it was just a bit too radical in the early 1980s, when the Colt Model 1911A1, or a close copy thereof, was considered the only "real" 45 ACP pistol.

Meanwhile, as the 380-caliber BDA was struggling and the bigger BDA was failing, FN's 9mm "Fast Action" became the first of FN's new pistol family designed in-house to make it off the drawing boards. Based closely on a standard Hi-Power frame, but with a modified slide, the Fast Action's most notable feature was a clever mechanism which included a two-piece hammer and additional springs. The added Fast Action components allowed the shooter, after loading the gun, to lower the cocked hammer by pushing it forward until it met the rear of the slide. The action of pushing the hammer forward readied the pistol for a "fast-action" first shot. Upon the shooter's subsequently squeezing the trigger, the hammer automatically sprung back quickly to its cocked position and then rapidly fell, firing the chambered cartridge. The trigger pull for the fast-action shot was no heavier than a single-action shot, although the trigger travel itself was considerably longer, more like that for a double-action shot. This first, fast-action shot had the advantage over a traditional single-action pistol of allowing an immediate first shot without the shooter needing to cock the hammer or release the safety catch of a cocked pistol before firing.

The fast action's advantage over a double-action pistol was its light, easy first shot. A double-action pistol's first shot is quite a bit heavier than that of a single-action pistol. A further advantage of the Fast Action was its versatil-

The BDM (top) appears with a current-production Hi-Power Mark IIIS. These two guns make Browning competitive with just about any pistol manufacturer.

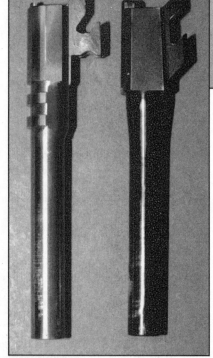

This comparison view of the Hi-Power's barrel (left) and the BDM's barrel (right) shows the differences in manufacture. Since the BDM eliminates the expensive and time-consuming need for locking ribs like those atop the Hi-Power's barrel, the BDM is a cheaper gun to make.

This bottom view of the BDM's magazine shows its checkered bumper pad, which has at its rear edge the integral screwdriver used to change trigger modes. The lanyard loop is also visible just behind the screwdriver blade. The BDM is replete with such clever touches.

In this side view of the BDM's magazine, the pointer indicates the integral screwdriver used to change trigger modes. The lanyard loop is visible just above and behind the screwdriver blade.

FN'S DOUBLE-ACTION

ity—an ambidextrous safety-lever allowed the shooter to carry the pistol cocked and locked, and fire the first shot single action; or to load the gun, lower the hammer and then fire the first shot double action; or to load the gun and prepare it for a fast action first shot as described above. Naturally, every shot after the first one caused the recoiling slide to cock the hammer, making the second and subsequent shots fire in the single-action mode.

The Fast Action's sole shortcoming proved to be its undoing: It required a complicated, delicate mechanism that could not stand up to the rigors of military testing and service. Confidentially tested by the United States Armed Forces in 1979-1980, the Fast Action proved interesting and innovative, but too fragile. Disappointed, FN dropped

In this left-side view of the BDM (top) and Hi-Power Mark III, note the way the single-action Mark III's hammer is cocked and the safety locked up into the slide. The BDA's manual safety, in contrast, moves down, exposing a red dot on the frame as shown, to ready the pistol for firing.

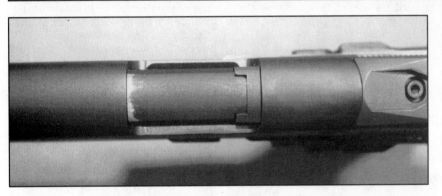

In this top view of the slide, note how the BDM uses the SIG P220-inspired method of locking the rear end of the barrel into the rear edge of the slide's ejection port. The screw used to move the adjustable rear sight is also visible.

In this view of a BDM (left) with a World War II-era Hi-Power (right), the BDM's extraordinarily slim grip is apparent. Note the single retaining screw for the BDM's one-piece grip.

the Fast Action design soon afterward after making only eleven such pistols. (Interestingly, however, the South Korean armed forces' new Daewoo DP-51 9mm service pistol uses a very similar mechanism and has proven quite successful.)

For FN's purposes, the Fast Action's most enduring legacy was that it pioneered the use of both an ambidextrous manual safety and plastic grip panels with moulded thumbrests, features now found on FN's current single-action Hi-Power pistols.

The first true double-action pistol of the new FN pistol family, despite a con-tinuing resemblance to the standard single-action Hi-Power and its use of a slightly modified Hi-Power frame, bore far less similarity to the Hi-Power than had the Fast Action. This first model FNDA (for "FN Double Action") appeared in the summer of 1979. It used an investment-cast slide and frame, a modified extractor, modified ambidextrous safety of different configuration from that of the Fast Action and Hi-Power pistols, and a reversible magazine release. The trigger guard was recurved in front for an easier finger-forward hold by the shooter's support-ing hand. The FNDA's stocks, however, very closely resembled those of the Fast Action and current Hi-Power pistols.

Up to the early 1980s, FN's experimental pistols had retained many of the parts of the Hi-Power, but in 1982 FN decided to break with the past entirely. What resulted was a family of pistols which was completely new and different, without any parts at all in common with the original Hi-Power. The frames of these new pistols were made by the process of investment casting, allowing considerably cheaper manufacture than the forged Hi-Power frame, and also allowing easy switching of parts so that

FN'S DOUBLE-ACTION

fast-action, double-action, and double-action-only lockwork could be installed in the same frame. The slides were investment cast as well. A decocking lever, augmented by a firing-pin lock, replaced the manual safety of earlier models. The rear of the new pistols' skeletonized frames were contained within a new one-piece plastic grip. With minor modifications, FN could make a full-sized service pistol, a medium-sized compact model, or even an extraordinarily abbreviated pocket pistol from the same basic components. Again the savings in material, time and workmanship were considerable.

FN's redesigns, by now in a third generation, added to the company's confidence that they could produce a double-action pistol that would be competitive on the world market. In October of 1982, three decades after Saive had created FN's first experimental double-action pistol, the company finalized the design of a fourteen-shot double-action pistol suitable for police and military service. In September of 1983, the first samples of the new "BDA-9" reached the firearms press.

Initial test results by firearms journalists, notably René Smeets of Belgium, were encouraging, and in late 1983 FN announced the availability of an entire family of pistols in the BDA-9 series. The BDA-9S (Standard), with a total length of 200mm (7.87 inches) and a barrel 118mm (4.65 inches) long was the standard model; the BDA-9M (Medium) had the standard model's frame, but a short-ened barrel (96mm/ 3.8 inches) and slide assembly gave a reduced total length of only 178mm (7.0 inches); and the BDA-9C (Compact) had the 9M's short barrel and slide, and a greatly shortened frame holding a seven-round magazine. The BDA-9C would accept the standard fourteen-round magazine of the larger models, and FN also advertised for the series a lengthened, extended-capacity magazine holding up to twenty rounds. The BDA-9C was only 93mm (3.66 inches) high, compared to 130mm (5.12 inches) for the Standard and Medium models and 3.9 inches for a Walther PPK. Thus, the BDA-9C was extremely short indeed and would easily fit into a coat or pants pocket.

Despite FN's meticulous design work and the excellent product that resulted, the double-action family met with only limited success. In January of 1984, FN sent forty pistols (BDA-9S) to the United States Armed Forces' XM9 pistol trials, but voluntarily withdrew its participation in the test series on May 31. The U.S. Army announced the winning pistol, the Beretta Model 92F, in January of 1985. Meanwhile, FN continued the job of transforming these experimental pistols into series-production models.

Browning Arms Company of Morgan, Utah, FN's American distributor, offered the BDA-9S commercially in 1986-87 as the "Double Action Hi-Power," but few were sold. Browning quickly eliminated the FN double-action pistol from its lineup when it decided, after drop tests, that the pistol was not sufficiently safe from accidental discharges to satisfy its requirements for product liability. Sales in other regions were also disappointing, and so FN decided to discontinue the double-action family in 1987.

Meanwhile, FN's single-action Hi-Power was prospering, some of the improvements introduced in the double-action program actually helping the aging pistol to retain its edge in the highly competitive pistol market. The Hi-Power Mark II, introduced in 1982 and made until 1988, was the first single-action model to incorporate the ambidextrous safety-levers, anatomical plastic grips, and improved, enlarged sights of the early Fast Action and Double Action prototypes. This was followed by the Mark III, essentially the same pistol as the Mark II, but made to a higher standard on improved machinery. The even better single-action Hi-Power Mark IIIS, introduced in mid-1989 and still in production, retained the updated Mark II and III features, but added a firing-pin lock, another feature inspired by FN's double-action family. The Mark III also introduced vastly improved front and rear sights mounted in dovetails and thus easily interchangeable with adjustable target-type sights. This innovation, for the first time ever, gave an FN service pistol a sight picture worthy of the gun.

Although the Mark IIIS rejuvenated FN's pistol business (the company sold 25,000 to meet police orders in Belgium alone in the first six months of production), FN still wanted a double-action

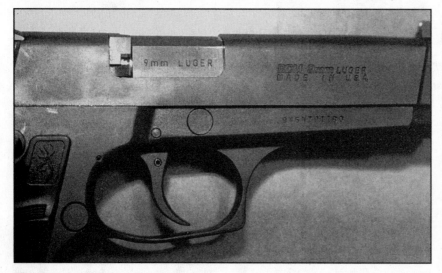

With a round loaded in the BDM's firing chamber, the round is visible, and the loaded-chamber indicator extends slightly to the right of the slide.

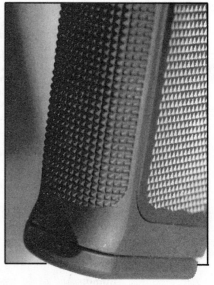

The lower front surface of the BDM's gripstrap and the leading edge of the magazine bottom are both slightly recessed to allow the shooter to use the finger or thumb of his support hand to assist in magazine removal. This is not really necessary, as the magazine release smartly ejects a magazine, but shows the thoughtful finishing touches employed on this interesting pistol.

A disassembled view of the BDM shows its remarkably simple and rugged construction. The one-piece grip is not ordinarily removed in fieldstripping, but has been done here to show the BDM's debt to the Russian Markarov pistol in terms of frame and grip design.

ness with a gun of its own called the Browning Double Mode, or BDM. In the BDM, Browning has succeeded in creating a pistol which is slimmer, handier, and perhaps in some ways even more elegant than the classic single-action Hi-Power, and with an added double-action mechanism that features easy conversion to a revolver-like double-action-only mode.

Browning began the BDM's development in 1986 when Czech-born engineer Peter Sodoma undertook the design of a new double-action 9mm pistol. He did thorough research and canvassed the opinions of a large number of shooters. Sodoma also carefully studied older pistol designs for useful features that could be incorporated into Browning's new handgun. Outside design influences on the BDM include a one-piece wraparound grip modeled on that of the Russian Makarov pistol, a stamped slide with pinned breechblock like the SIG P220-series pistols, and a modified Browning short-recoil system again based on the SIGs. The frame itself is an investment casting. One of the most noteworthy and unusual aspects of the BDM is its mode selector. Located on the left side of the slide, this slotted button offers the shooter a choice of pistol or revolver modes. In pistol mode, the BDM functions as a standard double-action semi-automatic pistol, with the recoiling

pistol to supplement and eventually replace the Hi-Power, and to compete with Beretta, SIG, Smith & Wesson, Walther and other pistol manufacturers on the world market. Thus the company continued developing double-action prototypes and, in 1990, began producing a new BDA-9. Although the new pistol is not offered in the United States, it is said to be modestly successful in Europe and in other parts of the world. Currently, FN makes both a standard double-action model and a similar double-action-only model called

the BDAO. The most obvious difference between the earlier BDA of 1983-1987 and the current models is that the new guns use the improved sights of the Mark III single-action pistol.

Browning Arms Company, as FN's North American distributor and a subsidiary wholly owned by the Belgian firm, has a reference copy of the current BDA at its offices in Utah. However, Browning has absolutely no interest in distributing the Belgian-made gun, the reason being that Browning has itself entered the double-action pistol busi-

With the BDM's selector set in R for "revolver mode," the pistol will fire each shot with a double-action trigger pull, while with the selector set in P for "pistol mode," the BDM's hammer will cock after the first shot, allowing single-action followup shots.

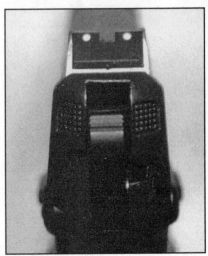

The BDM's rear sight looks much like a Novak unit as found on most modern (Third Generation) Smith & Wesson semi-automatic pistols. In this view from the rear, note also the checkered areas on the slide, intended to support the shooter's thumb while he holsters the weapon.

The BDM (top) is a modern, functional semi-automatic pistol every bit as good as its many excellent competitors. Shown here with it are (center) the Glock Model 19 and (bottom) the Smith & Wesson Model 3914.

The thinness of the BDM's grip (left) is compared with that of Glock's Model 19 (center) and Smith & Wesson's Model 3914 (right). Like the BDM, the Glock holds fifteen rounds in its magazine, while the Model 3914 holds eight.

FN'S DOUBLE-ACTION

slide cocking the hammer after all shots to allow single-action shooting after an initial hammer-down, double-action first shot. In the revolver mode, the hammer follows the slide forward after each shot so that the shooter must pull through on the trigger for a long double-action pull each time. However, in its revolver mode, the BDM, like most modern double-action revolvers, also offers the shooter the option of thumb-cocking the hammer for a single-action shot, after which the hammer again returns to its rest position for a double-action shot. The BDM's hammer is always linked to the trigger, allowing multiple attempts to fire a dud cartridge. This versatility is a step ahead

of the double-action-only mechanism offered on competing guns such as Smith & Wesson's Model 3953, in which the hammer cannot be thumb-cocked and the trigger can only be reset by movement of the slide. Naturally, the BDM can also be manually cocked for single-action shooting while in its pistol mode.

Another unusual aspect of the BDM is its extraordinarily slim grip. It is the slimmest high-capacity 9mm pistol currently offered, slimmer even than the Glock. It is, in fact, not much wider than many eight-shot 9mm pistols, which is a significant accomplishment for a pistol with a fifteen-round magazine. What is more, the BDM is made

completely from steel and is extremely rugged (a legacy of the additional development effort which Browning undertook for the Secret Service bid as detailed below); many competing pistols are not only larger, but also use weaker aluminum alloy frames.

While Browning worked on their new pistol, their parent company FN was purchased by the giant French firm GIAT. Browning, although still owned by FN, is now a separate division of GIAT, and the BDM's early development thus received not only the blessing of the French, but also significant financial backing from the parent company.

After initially announcing the BDM in January, 1991, at the SHOT Show, Browning immediately squelched the resulting enthusiasm by announcing that civilian and police orders would have to wait while they filled a Secret Service order. The Secret Service wanted a BDM without the mode-changing feature and which fired in revolver mode only, thus designated by Browning the BRM for "Browning Revolver Mode." A successful BRM would have given the government an excellent concealable pistol with a large magazine capacity. Unfortunately, Browning's efforts to modify the gun to satisfy the Secret Service was stymied by shifting official specifications and requirements,

The P-38's double-action trigger mechanism strongly influenced postwar FN thinking.

Although the double-action FEG pistols made in Hungary strongly resemble the Hi-Power, they are actually based on Smith & Wesson's Model 39 and resemble the Hi-Power only on the surface. Shown here are (top) the GKK-45, a double-action 45-caliber pistol, and (bottom) the single-action PJK-9HP, a close copy of the Hi-Power.

making Browning not the first gun company to be so treated by the government. The last straw occurred when, quite late in the year-long grace period granted to Browning to perfect the BRM, the Secret Service suddenly upgraded their expectation that the gun be able to handle "occasional" firings with hot +P+ ammunition to a requirement that it be suitably strengthened to handle virtually unlimited use of these high-powered loads. In the end, Browning was simply unable to get a gun to the Secret Service in time, and they bought a different handgun elsewhere. But the improvements made to the BDM during this period have stood the pistol in good stead and will benefit its present and future users.

As currently offered, the BDM is made only in a full-size version with an overall length of 7.85 inches, a barrel length of 4.73 inches, a height of 5.45 inches, a width of 1.5 inches, and an unloaded weight of 31 ounces. It is a good pistol with many factors in its favor. It is well endowed with a host of clever features in addition to those detailed above. For instance, the BDM's

sights are high in profile and generously sized by combat standards, and use the popular three-dot sighting system. They are actually quite competitive with the excellent Novak sights found on most modern Smith & Wesson pistols and, in fact, are even in some respects an improvement over the Novak units. The BDM's rear sight is adjustable, and the front sight is cleverly pinned in place, rather than dovetailed onto the slide, to prevent its coming off accidentally. The BDM's sights are big enough to offer an excellent sight picture, while being well-rounded so as to make snagging virtually impossible. The BDM has a matte black finish which not only holds down the pistol's manufacturing costs (allowing Browning to pass on savings to the consumer), but is also most suitable to a combat handgun. Its trigger is narrow and smooth, making it ideal for rapid double-action shooting. The magazine release is shielded from accidental release by thumbrests on each grip which swell out slightly, and the magazine well is beveled for flawlessly smooth insertion of fresh magazines. Unlike the Hi-Power, the BDM's maga-

zine release smartly ejects the empty magazine, and no magazine safety is provided, allowing the BDM to be fired even without the magazine in place. The BDM has a lanyard loop ambidextrously placed in the center rear of the grip, and in yet another example of this gun's thoughtful ergonomic design, the loop is higher than the bottom of the magazine so that it cannot interfere with the shooter's support hand during rapid reloading. The BDM's grips, front gripstrap, and even the rear of the slide and the magazine floorplate are all well-checkered for a comfortable and secure hold. The checkering on the rear of the slide helps the shooter, when holstering the pistol, to place his thumb there to prevent the slide moving and accidentally cocking the hammer. A passive firing pin safety is only deactivated when the shooter pulls the trigger fully to the rear. A decocking lever/manual safety is provided, as is a clever loaded-chamber indicator that gives both visual and tactile indications of the pistol's state of readiness.

As is common in modern service pistols, the BDM is almost completely

While many FN employees refused to work for the Nazi occupiers, others did and made, among other munitions, parts for the Walther P-38 (top) and complete Hi-Power pistols (bottom).

(Below) The BDM—especially in revolver mode—is easy to shoot rapidly and fairly accurately. Shown here are five shots from 25 feet in a 1.6-inch group. The author used Federal 124-grain Nyclad ammunition for shooting this particular target.

FN'S DOUBLE-ACTION

ambidextrous. All of its operating controls except the slide stop and magazine release are ambidextrous, and even the magazine release is reversible.

The BDM's smooth contours and relatively small dimensions, particularly its narrowness, suit it well to routine carry, even to concealed carry. Kramer Combat Leather and several other firms now offer holsters made to fit the BDM.

The BDM is cleverly thought out and might seem to be the perfect modern combat pistol. It does, however, have a few minor shortcomings. The use of two distinct operating modes could conceiv-

ably cause confusion, and any BDM owner is well advised to thoroughly familiarize himself with the owner's manual before shooting or carrying the pistol (good advice for any firearm). The direction of movement of the safety/decocking lever (called the combination lever by Browning) is up to fire and down to safe, which is opposite to that of the more ergonomic safety used on the Hi-Power. The matte finish is not particularly durable, nor are the magazines. Finally, the BDM's accuracy is only fair, although it is certainly adequate for combat shooting.

Production of the BDM is undertaken at the Browning-owned ATI plant near Salt Lake City, Utah. The rate of manufacture is relatively low, and the BDM is usually backordered. Eventually, Browning hopes to increase production and perhaps to pursue the police market more aggressively, possibly even by reintroducing the BRM of Secret Service testing days, but for now they seem pleased with the pistol's success so far.

Small-handed shooters will find at last in the BDM an ideal high-capacity 9mm pistol which, thanks to its slim grip, is comfortable to handle and fire. This is a truly excellent handgun, one of the best now available, and represents a significant advance in high-capacity 9mm pistol design. ●

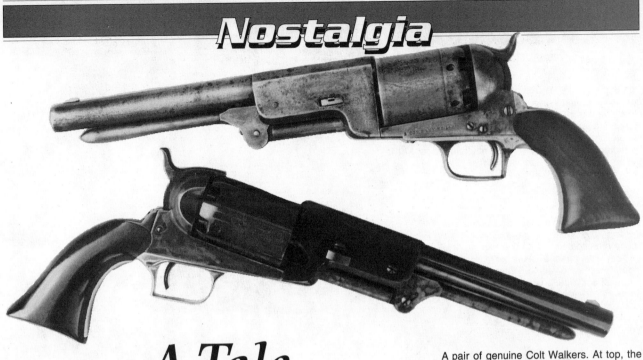

A pair of genuine Colt Walkers. At top, the original 1847 issue which saw service in the Mexican War; note company markings and serial number on frame and barrel. Below it is an example of Colt's blackpowder Signature Series, now in limited production. The modern version is a spitting image of the first issue; serial numbers picked up where earlier production left off.

A Tale Of Two Sams...
THE COLT WALKER
by J. BURKE

Samuel Colt was born July of 1814 in Hartford, Connecticut. He secured his first U.S. revolver patent in February of 1836, and after several disasters went on to found the giant Colt arms empire, after the success of the Walker.

Samuel Hamilton Walker, depicted here as a Captain, U.S. Mounted Riflemen, during the Mexican War. His Texas Ranger service with Colt's Paterson revolvers led to an association with Sam Colt himself, and the production of the largest revolver ever produced by the Colt firm.

IT WAS FEBRUARY, 1847; the hour was late. An accumulation on the window sill of the officer's billet confirmed the heavy blanket of snow settling on Baltimore's Fort McHenry; the same Fort McHenry where Francis Scott Key wrote the "Star-Spangled Banner." Flickering flames from the room's small fireplace cast dancing shadows; light from a single candle illuminated the face of Captain Samuel Hamilton Walker, working intently at a rough-hewn desk. The only sounds were his pen point scratching across coarse paper and the irregular clinking inside a pewter-topped glass inkwell.

The man whose gaze was riveted on each stroke of Capt. Walker's pen was a bit eccentric, having once sold nitrous oxide (laughing gas) highs at 50 cents a hit to further his dreams of business success. But despite his Yankee ingenuity and boundless energy, Samuel Colt had already gone broke in the arms business. However this night,

The Signature Series Colt Walker is not a replica but a continuation of those first Walkers produced in 1847. Fit and finish are excellent, with real Colt case-hardening and the famous "Texas Rangers & Injuns" fight scene roll-engraved around the big six-shooter's 44-caliber cylinder. An empty gun is shown here with the hammer in firing position; "V" notch in top face of the hammer served as an integral rear sight.

The Colt Walker, up close and personal. The roll-engraved "Texas Rangers & Injuns" fight scene runs completely around the massive cylinder. This famous Texas battle involving Paterson revolvers served as proof of the effectiveness of Sam Colt's products. It also helped guard against patent infringements which would later plague the Colt company.

THE COLT WALKER

finally, he was on the trail of perpetual worldwide fame and personal fortune.

In due course, Capt. Walker finished his crude sketch of an event he'd described to Sam Colt a few months earlier and turned the drawing to face the 33-year-old inventor. It was a near-child-like depiction of a horseback fight that took place in 1844. Toting Colt Paterson revolvers, fifteen Texas Rangers under the command of Captain John "Jack" Coffee Hays had faced eighty howling-mad Comanche warriors. Accustomed to greeting invaders who were armed with single shot firepower, the painted redmen had attempted to close the distance to their enemies after the first volley, only to find the Rangers could fire a shot as if from each finger of their shooting hand—without bothering to reload! Half the ranks of the Comanches were either killed or wounded; the Rangers emerged with nary a scratch.

Colt listened again as Walker recounted that historic Texas battle. It took place near the Pedernales River, a portion of which flows through what today is the late President Lyndon B. Johnson's family ranch. On that day in 1844, Capt. Hays' Rangers used Colt's five-shot hand-held revolving invention in battle for the first time, against Texas Indians, as depicted in the sketch. With the details of that white-hot engagement permanently etched in his mind, Samuel Colt—the proud possessor of a newly acquired U.S. government contract—rolled up the sketch and disappeared into the cold dark night. Within days, Colt delivered the drawing of the battle scene to engraver O.L. Ormsby, who created a die used to roll the scene onto the cylinders of the largest revolvers to ever carry the Colt name. This "Texas Rangers & Injuns" depiction identified the guns as Colt products and served to deter patent infringements. The miniature artistic rendering included the likenesses of both Texas Ranger Captain Jack Hays riding a white horse and then-Ranger Sam Walker on a black mount.

What bound these two men together—the inventor and the Ranger—was the need for an improved version of Sam Colt's first revolving pistol, dubbed the "Paterson" by collectors, naming it after the New Jersey city where these history-making weapons were manufactured. However, their zeal for product improvement was fueled by very different motives.

As a young sailor in 1830-31, it's likely Sam Colt saw revolving cylinder firearms—like those produced by Collier—while roaming the British Empire. The prototype that sailor Sam carved from a discarded block of wood on his return voyage, however, was quite unique. It wasn't the multi-loaded firearm cylinder that was revolutionary; what he concocted was the first-ever application of a mechanism to simultaneously rotate the cylinder as the weapon's hammer was cocked. It was soon thereafter that "Dr. Coult of New York, London & Calcutta" took his highly entertaining laughing gas show from pillar to post, determined to finance the production of sample firearms so he could apply for patents on his inventions.

Colt was indeed issued his first U. S. patent in February of 1836, just as the pompous Mexican dictator Santa Anna was surrounding the Alamo, leaving the Texicans without hope of mass escape. The Patent Arms Manufacturing Company was soon launched, with

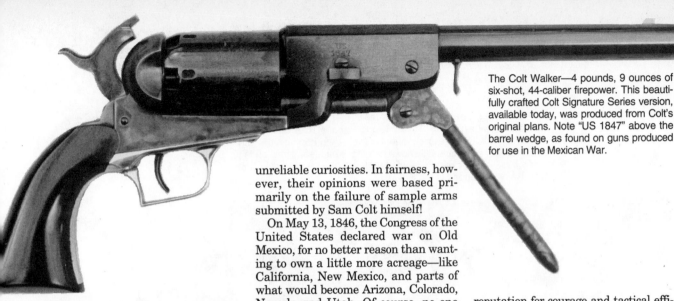

The Colt Walker—4 pounds, 9 ounces of six-shot, 44-caliber firepower. This beautifully crafted Colt Signature Series version, available today, was produced from Colt's original plans. Note "US 1847" above the barrel wedge, as found on guns produced for use in the Mexican War.

production facilities in Paterson, New Jersey, and a big-time Broadway showroom in New York City. At Paterson, some of the rarest of Colt firearms were produced, until a combination of bad timing and limited funding caused the plant to be shut down in 1842. Included in the Paterson production run was the Model Number 5, which publicity hound Sam Colt dubbed the "Texas" Model, once he learned the intrepid Texas Rangers were his biggest fans. But through it all, Sam Colt refused to abandon his dreams of success as a gun manufacturer, even though he faced a military establishment convinced that revolving firearms were nothing more than

unreliable curiosities. In fairness, however, their opinions were based primarily on the failure of sample arms submitted by Sam Colt himself!

On May 13, 1846, the Congress of the United States declared war on Old Mexico, for no better reason than wanting to own a little more acreage—like California, New Mexico, and parts of what would become Arizona, Colorado, Nevada and Utah. Of course, no one cheered louder at the prospects of such a war than the hard-boiled citizens of Texas, who considered the Rio Grande their southern border; Mexico insisted her sovereignty extended much farther north, as marked by the Nueces River. Hostilities soon ensued to the delight of everyone except the government and people of Mexico. Among the Texas adventurers chomping at the bit for war with Mexico was Samuel Hamilton Walker, originally from Maryland.

Born in 1817, Walker was a veteran of the Seminole wars the U.S. waged in Florida. Walker followed that with several hitches with the Texas Rangers. While on the frontier with the Rangers, Walker quickly earned a wide-ranging

reputation for courage and tactical efficiency against both Mexican and Native American foes. He was also a survivor of an earlier failed attempt to conquer Mexican soil known as the Mier Expedition. Absolute folly, it ended in disaster for the outnumbered Texans; seventeen were captured and executed in retaliation for the short-lived campaign—they had picked one of the black beans from a Mexican jar. Walker drew a white bean and lived to serve time in a Mexican prison. From all this and more, Walker was widely famous in 1846, when President Polk put out the call for volunteers to fight on the winning side in the Mexican War.

Just as they would later answer Teddy Roosevelt's invitation to serve with the

The beginning of Sam Colt's success was the Texas-size Walker. It was Colt's first true six-shooter. Sam Colt and celebrated Texas Ranger Samuel Walker collaborated on the design, and Eli Whitney, Jr., produced these hand cannons. Whitney subcontracted many of the individual parts. Author Burke tries a shot with the new Signature Series Walker.

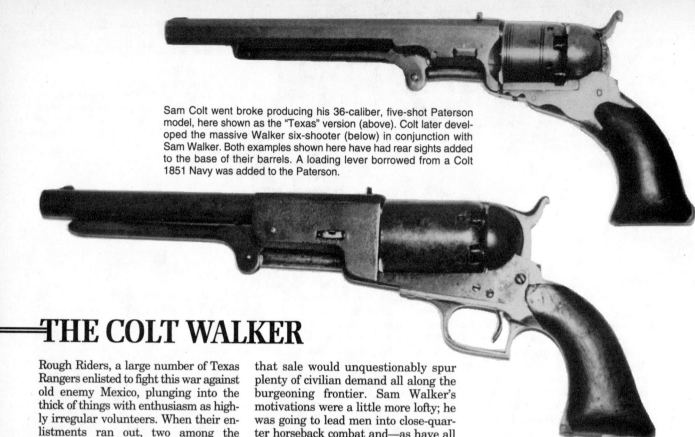

Sam Colt went broke producing his 36-caliber, five-shot Paterson model, here shown as the "Texas" version (above). Colt later developed the massive Walker six-shooter (below) in conjunction with Sam Walker. Both examples shown here have had rear sights added to the base of their barrels. A loading lever borrowed from a Colt 1851 Navy was added to the Paterson.

THE COLT WALKER

Rough Riders, a large number of Texas Rangers enlisted to fight this war against old enemy Mexico, plunging into the thick of things with enthusiasm as highly irregular volunteers. When their enlistments ran out, two among the Rangers, Jack Hays and Sam Walker, were offered regular Army commissions in a regiment of United States Mounted Rifles that was formed to continue the war with Mexico. Hays accepted; Walker, at first, declined the offer.

At the same time, in Washington, D.C., and neighboring locales, Sam Colt was haranguing anyone and everyone he could collar about buying some of his then-nonexistent firearms. When he wasn't hawking pie-in-the-sky hardware, he was trying to wrangle a military commission. When Colt learned Sam Walker had rejected the offered Army commission, he boldly sought that honor and privilege for himself, only to be thwarted yet again when Walker reconsidered and accepted the government's favor. With his usual boundless persistence, Colt decided to contact Capt. Walker, who had arrived in Washington with Hays to recruit men and arms for their regiment. Colt was after a real-life Texas Ranger endorsement from the men who had been putting his wares to such effective use.

Walker obliged Colt with a glowing description of the Paterson's effectiveness. Soon thereafter, the two men began designing an improved version of the 36-caliber Paterson five-shooter. As for Sam Colt, he needed to make a major sale, preferably to the biggest arms buyer of all—the United States government. The publicity spin-off from

that sale would unquestionably spur plenty of civilian demand all along the burgeoning frontier. Sam Walker's motivations were a little more lofty; he was going to lead men into close-quarter horseback combat and—as have all fighting men throughout the ages—wanted the best possible weapons he could get to help him come out on the winning end of things.

After that first meeting, the two men would work quickly and tirelessly to design what Sam Colt named the "Walker" model, get it sold to a skeptical Army Ordnance Board, have it produced in an as yet non-existent factory, and get the big guns to waiting troops—all literally within a few months! The weapon they created, that Colt Walker, was the turning point in each man's life. For Sam Colt, this "improved Paterson" revolver marked the beginning of what would become an arms empire and the acquisition of both a substantial fortune and an equal measure of fame. In the case of the already celebrated Ranger Samuel Walker, the Texas-size revolver which bore his name in all likelihood bought him an early grave.

The closest Sam Colt had ever come to combat was attempting to blow up a raft on a New Jersey pond. Sam Walker, however, had participated in plenty of action and knew what the somewhat pint-sized Paterson (by Texas standards) needed in the way of improvements. Colt was all ears; he'd no doubt have put a rearview mirror on the redesigned pistol if he'd thought Walker wanted one and the government would buy it!

Both men searched for a Colt Paterson to use as a starting point on which to apply their improvements, but to no avail; the few available guns were now in the hands of eager Mexican War volunteers. Undaunted, their deadly work commenced. First, there was the caliber; a 36 didn't have the knockdown power needed to consistently drop an enemy with a single shot. Walker insisted on a weapon firing fifty balls per pound of lead, which translates into 44-caliber. Along with the increased caliber, a larger, longer and now *six*-shot cylinder would provide a significant increase in powder capacity as well as one more shot. The massive cylinder required a beefed-up frame, and Sam Walker also wanted a long, 9-inch barrel so his troopers could take advantage of the extended sighting radius and stabilizing effect of that extra weight out front. As perhaps an unexpected bonus, the new six-shooter was shaping up to be a pretty good "blunt instrument," if a club were required. The trigger on the Paterson presented another problem. Staying out of harm's way when the hammer was fully forward, the trigger swung down from inside the frame as the weapon was cocked. This new Walker revolver would have a fixed trigger and a square-backed trigger guard to protect it.

Now in perfect sync, the two Sams

Colt Walkers break down into three main assemblies: frame, cylinder and barrel. The Walker was the first Colt to have an integral loading lever. The lever, held in place by a clip spring, sometimes came loose from recoil.

began a well-orchestrated campaign to gain a government contract calling for Colt to produce a quantity of the new revolvers. Walker played politics in Washington, D.C. He used his reputation as a military hero to open each and every door. Colt worked behind the scenes; after all, he'd had plenty of run-ins by now with the military brass who still put their faith in single-shot musketry. Without so much as a single tool with which to produce the guns, Colt nevertheless lobbied for Captain Walker—not the military establishment—to retain control of the desired revolver contract.

Perhaps it was America's fervor for Manifest Destiny, but whatever the reason, the team of Sam & Sam prevailed against a stacked deck in record time. The real key was a meeting Sam Walker had with President James K. Polk. Polk made things happen, and Walker got the government to pay Colt's full retail price ($25 per gun). Colt now had the large government contract which had previously eluded him. It was a remarkable sales story. The government contract was acquired *without so much as a sample firearm!* In addition, Sam Colt had already failed as a gun manufacturer, didn't have a blueprint of the improved design, and had neither factory nor machinery with which to produce the weapons. However, a government contract could get the attention of suppliers then, just as now, and Colt soon had a prototypical revolver made. It was based on the initial features Walker wanted in the new blaster and was made by Blunt & Syms of New York City early in 1847.

While the first Walker prototype contained the changes already agreed upon, the gun still didn't suit Capt. Walker. Before actual production began,

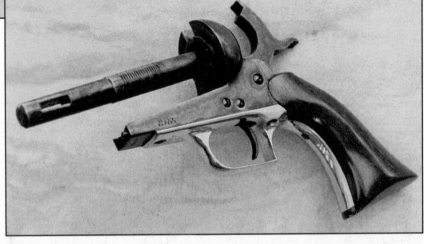

The current run of genuine Colt blackpowder Signature Series Walkers are built from the same drawings as those first manufactured in 1847. The cylinder pin is an integral part of the frame; the grip is of one-piece American walnut; the backstrap is blued iron; the trigger guard is square-backed and made of brass. Note the perfect fit of grip to trigger guard and the dark oval on the grip's frontstrap where the mainspring is attached.

the revolver's grip was significantly lengthened, a Paterson-style loading lever was installed, and numerous other refinements made. The result was an improved weapon with pleasing lines which would affect the look of all single-action revolvers to follow. The lockwork is still in use today on the venerable Colt Single Action Army revolver.

With contract and prototype in hand, Colt now needed a factory. He'd already contacted the son of the man who invented the cotton gin, Eli Whitney, Jr. The younger Whitney was himself an accomplished arms manufacturer, with the capacity for nearly mass production. After some wrangling, Whitney agreed to accept the production assignment for the Colt Walker revolvers, but he subcontracted most of the work literally part-by-part. As a result, Sam Colt didn't actually produce a single one of these revolutionary revolvers, although with the contract that followed, he would ultimately produce the Colt

Dragoon (a scaled-down version of the Walker) in his own facility.

Colt's contract called for production of 1000 Walkers, as well as a powder flask and combination screwdriver/nipple wrench to go with each gun; a significant number of required bullet moulds and spare parts also presented excellent profit potential. However, Sam Colt's next big hurdle would be government inspectors, who took their work seriously. To accommodate Captain Sam's request for a more effective handgun, the Walker's cylinder was $2^7/_{16}$ inches long, presenting an excellent opportunity for overloads. That's just what the inspectors did, testfire the Walker Colts crammed to the gills with powder. The results were predictable. A significant number of Walkers failed with burst cylinders and split barrels.

Such testing procedures weren't unfair; the inspectors were just doing their job. Troops in the field were not likely to carefully measure powder charges.

Two Colt original U.S. government issue handguns of monumental importance in the history of firearms. Top, a cap-'n'-ball Colt Walker; below, a Colt 45 automatic. The guns are photographed to the same scale.

THE COLT WALKER

More probably, in the heat of battle they simply poured powder into empty chambers without looking. After all, there was an enemy to keep an eye on! Then they'd put a ball on top of the overflowing chambers and ram them home. The excessive charges created a virtual bomb in one if not all chambers.

In spite of burst cylinders and the occasional split barrel, production of the Walker Colts moved forward at a brisk pace. Whitney's employees were offered top wages for overtime work, and many former employees who had produced the Paterson Colts were lured into the Walker project by the good money. Whitney's armory was operational literally 24 hours a day, but even that wasn't enough for Captain Walker, who instructed that the first of these largest of Colt revolvers be prepared for Company "C" of the Regiment, the one he would command in battle.

Unlike Captain Walker's men, most of those who fought on the American side in the Mexican War were armed with single-shot *flintlock* muskets. Mexico was still fielding lancers at this point in her history. Walker knew full well the devastating effect the big 44-caliber sixguns would have against an enemy. The Walker Colt gave a velocity close to 1200 feet per second and more than 450 foot pounds of energy with each shot! Instead of a single shot, each man armed with a Colt could deliver twelve, since each was armed with a pair of the big handguns.

As the proposed date for the attack on Mexico drew near, Captain Walker sent increasingly urgent letters to Sam Colt requesting that the big weapons be completed with the utmost urgency. Custom holsters to carry each man's pair of the powerhouse pistols had

already been crafted; Sam Colt himself had developed the pattern. Now on Mexican soil, Walker told everyone in his supply chain to be on the lookout for a shipment with his name on it. Three days before Walker and his men were called to the defense of the American cause at Puebla, a pair of the Walker Colts caught up with Captain Walker. They were not the government-issue sixguns, but a presentation pair, gifts from Sam Colt to Sam Walker. These "Compliments Of Col. Colt" revolvers were among the 100 Walkers produced outside the government contract of 1000 guns. They were identical to the issue weapons, except they lacked the Company markings of "A," "B," "C," "D" or "E"; and, individual serial numbers by Company, as well as government inspector's marks.

The Americans boldly entered the little Mexican town of Huamantla, and the fighting was house-to-house. The Americans were determined to carry the day; the Mexicans fought with uncommon courage. Brave to a fault, perhaps brought on by at last having his revolving hand cannons, Captain Walker led a charge into the town square. When the action was over, Captain Samuel Hamilton Walker, commander of Company "C," U.S. Mounted Riflemen, was dead.

Journalists of the day were rather creative and considerably less accurate than they are now. One report credited Walker with a poetic speech to his men just before passing into the Great

Beyond. An alternate version of his death had him pierced by a Mexican lancer. Another version was that Walker was shot by a relative of a young man the *gringos* had killed earlier in the day. But dead he was, and at least one of the presentation Walkers, serial number 1020, made its way back to Sam Colt. The remains of Captain Walker were interred in a cemetery near the Alamo in San Antonio, and they still lie there today.

Those first Colt Walkers all but disappeared. Fewer than 200 of the 280 issued to Col. Hays' men were surrendered to the government at the end of the Mexican War. Less than half of those Walkers turned in were in working order! Some of the 80 "missing" guns returned to Texas with troopers who "liberated" them from Yankee government service.

I've always wanted to own a genuine Colt Walker, and I've had several opportunities to do so over the years. However, one thing has always kept me from attaining that goal: the $50,000 it would take to acquire one in very good condition. It cost about $25,000 to buy one of those first 1100 Colt Walkers that looks like it's been dragged around behind a wagon since the end of the Mexican War. However, thanks once again to Colt, things have changed. I am now the proud owner of a genuine Colt Walker, and it's in better condition than the finest museum piece you'll find anywhere. The price? Well, it was a little more down-to-earth.

In early 1979, Colt announced the return of this historic cap-'n'-ball revolver. Serial numbers picked up from where original production left off, and somewhat fewer than 2000 cased Colts were made available during the brief run of these "Second Generation" Walkers. The big guns sold out fast and quickly became collector's items. That

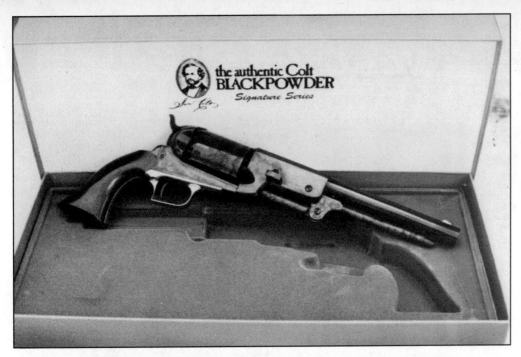

This largest of all Colt revolvers is once more produced to impeccable correctness. The only major difference between the current, limited run of Walkers offered and the ones Captain Walker carried to his death in the Mexican War is the cylinder finish. Original cylinders were left unprotected, "in the white"; today's Colt Blackpowder Signature Series version sports a deeply blued, protective finish.

second production run allowed a number of advanced Colt collectors to complete their collections with the genuine article, even if produced in modern times.

Colt has again authorized production of the Walker model in limited numbers, along with a few other popular blackpowder firearms. These guns—of true Colt lineage—are destined to be called "Third Generation" blackpowder Colts and will take their place in history. Third Generation Walker model serial numbers start at 4100 and will stop at 7600. I have no doubt that many eager buyers will be vying for these terrific sixguns.

This new, limited offering of genuine Colt Walkers is being meticulously produced using the original drawings. They are as beautifully made as any Colt ever produced. Fit and finish are as carefully attended to as if these huge hoglegs were headed for serious close-quarter combat, instead of into the hands of collectors—and a few cowboy action shooters. The "Texas Rangers & Injuns" roll-engraved cylinder gives most handgunners their first good look at that famous scene, just as it appeared on original guns. The front sight is of the correct German silver; and—as on the first Colt Walkers—a small slot on the hammer's face mates with a pin on the back of the cylinder, locking the cylinder between two nipples to avoid an accidental discharge.

Something difficult to find in today's world of "close-is-good-enough" production, the fit of the one-piece walnut grip is beyond reproach. The case-hardening is the genuine Colt article! However, there are two welcome variances from early Walkers. First, a protective coating has been applied to the brass trigger guard, allowing this massive historic beauty to be handled without becoming tarnished. Second, although those first 1100 Walkers were finished with the cylinders "in the white"—raw metal without any protective finish—these are blued. I've seen the "bare cylinder" effect on an original, near-mint-condition Colt Dragoon. It was striking, but vulnerable to rust that would permanently damage the sixgun. Suggested retail on these new incomparable Walker Colts is $442.50, representing a sound investment.

You can order your own Colt blackpowder catalog, featuring the entire limited-edition Signature Series. The smart money will order one of each Colt Signature Series Blackpowder Model and never shoot them. I'm hoping to manage the first part of that concept, but doubt I'll be able to resist shooting these top-of-the-line percussion masterpieces.

The Walker, the largest revolver ever produced by Colt, became a reality at a time when Samuel Colt needed a break in the worst way. His first excursion into the arms-making busi-

ness, producing the Paterson models, was a bust. But those first Colt revolvers were highly prized among Westerners who got their hands on them. Most enthusiastic among Colt's supporters were the famous Texas Rangers. A remarkable man among the remarkable Texas Rangers—Samuel Hamilton Walker—wanted something more than the Colt Paterson for his newly formed Company of U.S. Mounted Riflemen.

Walker knew full well what was needed to improve the "Texas" Paterson. He needed more gun all around, and that's what these two luminaries created. Sam Colt went on to become the most accomplished and renowned arms maker of the 19th century; Sam Walker died in the service of his country, armed with a pair of the revolvers which still bear his name. Although neither man would live to see the term "Peacemaker" applied to a Colt product, it was Sam Walker who first gave Colt that moniker, in a letter to the inventor.

With reintroduction of the Walker revolver in limited quantities, it's obvious today's Colt's Manufacturing Company hasn't forgotten its heritage. The renewed availability of this beautiful landmark revolver will create an increased awareness of the Colt Walker's place in history, as well as in the remarkable accomplishments of the two Sams. ●

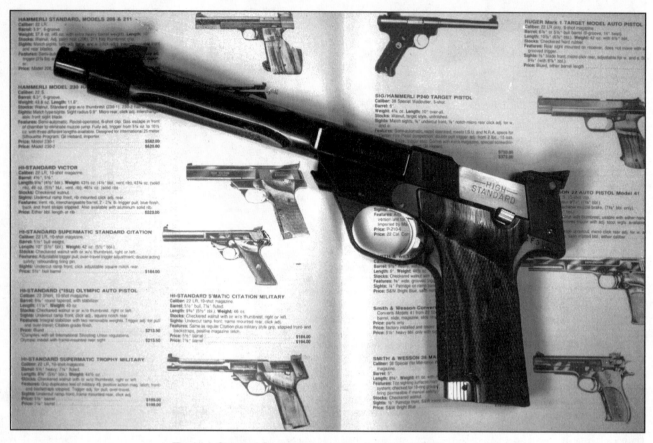

The High Standard Supermatic on a page from the 1978 GUN DIGEST shows the new guns are dead ringers for the original production. Author Anderson reports the new guns shoot just as well as originals.

HIGH STANDARD TARGET PISTOLS
ARE BACK, BETTER THAN EVER

by GARY ANDERSON

SOME MANUFACTURERS' products become universally admired classics. They earn their reputations with their elegant styles, time-tested designs, quality production and decades of user loyalty. Mercedes sedans look remarkably similar to how they appeared thirty years ago, but their reputation as fine automobiles has only been enhanced by time. Leica M series cameras, Rolex watches and other select, time-honored products earned reputations as classics because they

The author used the
new Victor to shoot his personal best
score ever on the 25-meter UIT Sport Pistol Course.
The target is his precision stage record, showing a 97.

look just as good and perform just as effectively today as they did when they were first introduced.

In the field of handguns, High Standard 22-caliber rimfire target pistols enjoy a reputation as classics. The High Standard Manufacturing Co. first entered the pistol-making business in the early 1930s. High Standard's first handgun was a rimfire single shot, but it shortly introduced the very successful Model B semi-auto. That began a tradition of producing popular 22 rimfire competition target pistols that lasted

until the original High Standard company ceased production in 1984.

Whether a person is a High Standard aficionado of long standing or someone just deciding to venture into the romance of using these precision handguns, there are many milestones to appreciate in the history of the High Standard line. Many High Standard owners look back to the particular model they first used or to a model used by a champion they admired. Many 10-, 20- and 30-year-old High Standard target pistols are still active in competition. The High Standard Collector's Association was formed to provide a forum for

interested parties to better appreciate all of these steps in the development of this classic handgun design.

One constant in creating a classic product is establishing a consistent design that distinguishes it through several decades. High Standard rimfire semi-auto target pistols are unique because, even as new models were introduced and new features added, the basic High Standard "look" and function never substantially changed.

There were several milestones in the development of High Standard's tradi-

tion as a "classic" rimfire target pistol. The first was the introduction of the High Standard HD Military Model in the early 1940s. Like the equally timeless Colt M1911 45 ACP semi-auto, the HD had an exposed hammer. The HD had a fabled history apart from its use as a competition gun. Many HDs were purchased by government agencies and fitted with silencers for use in clandestine operations. U2 spy plane pilot Gary Francis Powers carried a silencer-equipped High Standard HD when he was shot down over the Soviet Union in May, 1960.

A second milestone was the introduction of the Supermatic in the 1950s. The Supermatic inaugurated a High Standard hallmark, the removable barrel. The first Supermatics used a lever takedown system. A few years later, the familiar push-button at the front of the frame became the means of releasing the barrel to take the pistol apart. Serious target shooters loved the idea of a removable barrel, not so much because it allowed them to actually change barrels, but because it let them thoroughly clean the pistol after shooting.

A third milestone was an extraordinary competition success with a High Standard pistol. In the 1960 Olympic Games in Rome, U.S. Marine Corps Captain Bill McMillan used a High Standard Olympic 22 Short pistol to win the Olympic gold medal in the rapid-fire pistol event. His win came after he and two other shooters from Finland and the USSR tied at the end of the regular 60-shot event with 587x600 scores. What followed was one of shooting history's most dramatic shoot-offs to decide who would win the gold, silver and bronze Olympic medals. The shoot-off consisted of three series where each shooter fired one shot at each of the five silhouette targets in four seconds. McMillan did not capture the gold medal until the third and final series when the Russian, who was leading, shot his fifth shot a split-second too late and scored a miss.

McMillan used an essentially unmodified, "stock" High Standard. High Standard target pistols were used by lots of shooting champions in the years before 1960 and were among the most popular pistols in the 22-caliber aggregates at the Camp Perry National Matches and hundreds of other impor-

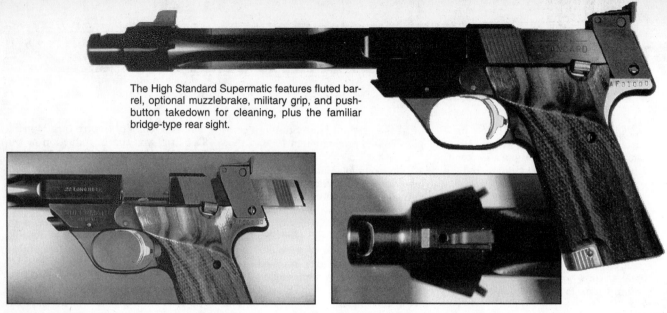

The High Standard Supermatic features fluted barrel, optional muzzlebrake, military grip, and push-button takedown for cleaning, plus the familiar bridge-type rear sight.

The new Supermatic features the familiar bridge attached to the handgun's frame to mount the rear sight. The Victor uses an extended rib to mount both front and rear sights on the same piece of metal. Take your pick, both work very well.

The muzzlebrake is attached by two Allen screws. It's effective in keeping the muzzle down in rapid-fire events.

HIGH STANDARD

tant pistol competitions. With Olympic stardom, however, High Standard's reputation as "the choice of champions" was firmly established. Old-time High Standard executives confirm that sales "took off" after that singularly important competition victory.

With classic products, their elegant styles and recognizable lines remain nearly unchanged even as numerous technical improvements are made. High Standard never altered its basic look, but wisely made improvements that were demanded by champion shooters and based on actual competition experience. High Standard introduced four new rim-fire target semi-autos in 1958. They featured a rear sight mounted on the rear of the barrel instead of on a moveable slide, a detachable muzzle stabilizer, detachable barrel weights, an improved trigger mechanism with a backlash screw in the frame and a trigger weight adjustment in the rear of the frame.

When a gun magazine article about the "guns of champions" was published in 1960, a majority of champion Bullseye and international pistol shooters reported choosing High Standard Supermatics or Citations. They praised High Standard triggers as "crisp and creep-free," and the guns' reliability, high accuracy and affordable prices. The list of champions using High Standards included names like McMillan and six-time national champion Harry Reeves.

Further improvements continued through the 1970s. Supermatic and

Citation rear sights were moved from the rear of the barrel to a bridge over the slide to give a longer sight radius. The trigger backlash adjustment screw was moved from the frame to the trigger itself to give more accessible adjustment. The most significant change was in the grip angle. Traditional highly angled High Standard grips were changed to a straighter "military" grip. They acquired the same grip angle as the popular 45 M1911 semi-autos and 38 Super target pistols that were popular with three-gun Bullseye pistol shooters.

High Standard 22-caliber pistols continued to find their way into the winner's circles in major pistol competitions, but production decisions by the High Standard company threatened to make High Standard pistols another gun of the past. The Hartford, Connecticut, plant closed in 1984.

That decision did not extinguish the lasting appeal of High Standards, however. Older High Standards continued to be the choice of many competition shooters. At the 1994 National Pistol Championships at Camp Perry, 31 percent of the pistols used in the 22-caliber events were High Standards, even though the old High Standard plant had been closed ten years.

The time for the High Standard Phoenix to rise again out of the ashes of a plant closure could not have been better. In 1993, the original High Standard name, trademarks, patents, designs, production drawings and many original

toolings were moved to Houston, Texas. The High Standard Manufacturing Co. was reborn under the leadership of Ron Stilwell, the former President of Colt Firearms, and long-time High Standard executives like Gordon Elliott. In March of 1994, the first of the new line of High Standards were shipped.

Current High Standard Manufacturing Company production is shown in a chart accompanying this article.

All pistols feature the military grips and blue finishes. The 10X pistol is a product of the High Standard Custom Shop under the leadership of Bob Shea.

The question on the minds of both traditional High Standard shooters and shooters who might buy their first High Standard is, "How good are the new High Standards?" Are they really as good as the High Standards that won trophies and medals in the 1960s, 1970s and 1980s?

To answer that question, I began by looking back at my experiences with earlier High Standards and with pistol champions like McMillan, Reeves, Blankenship and other greats. I earned my reputation as a rifle shooter, but like so many shooters who were on U.S. Olympic and World Championship teams or who belonged to the military teams like the U.S. Army Marksmanship Unit, our knowledge of what made great shooters and great target guns was shared among all shooters, whether rifle, pistol or shotgun. We learned a lot about each others' target games and guns. I shot many High Standards during this period and learned much about why champion pistol shooters appreciated their design and accuracy.

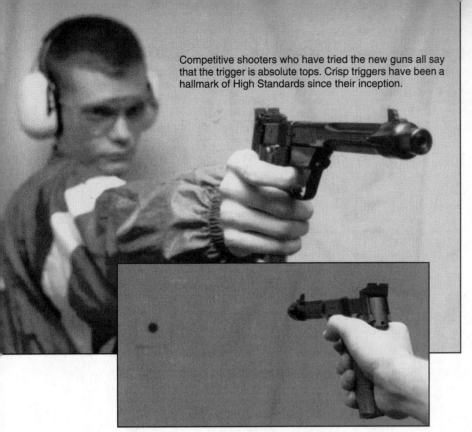

Competitive shooters who have tried the new guns all say that the trigger is absolute tops. Crisp triggers have been a hallmark of High Standards since their inception.

Although the High Standards are designed for one-hand competition, they are also well suited to handgun hunting of small game and for a great variety of other shooting needs.

CURRENT HIGH STANDARD PRODUCTION

Model	Caliber	Barrel Length (ins.)
Victor	22 Long Rifle	4¹/₂, 5¹/₂
Olympic ISU	22 Short	6³/₄
Olympic Military	22 Short	5¹/₂
Supermatic Trophy	22 Long Rifle	5¹/₂, 7¹/₄
Supermatic Citation	22 Long Rifle	5¹/₂, 7¹/₄
Citation MS (Metallic Silhouette)	22 Long Rifle	10
Supermatic Tournament	22 Long Rifle	5¹/₂
10X (Custom)	22 Long Rifle	Optional
10X Victor (Custom)	22 Long Rifle	Optional

Given that personal background, I was excited to have an opportunity to shoot two new High Standards from the Houston plant. A Supermatic Trophy with a 7¹/₄-inch barrel and muzzle-brake, and a 5¹/₂-inch ribbed barrel Victor were available. The Supermatic is a traditional 22 Bullseye target pistol for popular indoor gallery and outdoor three-gun shooting. The Victor more closely resembles the service pistols and centerfire pistols that are such a key part of three-gun competition. The Victor also fulfills the International Shooting Union's dimensional requirements for a standard pistol or sport pistol.

The most important thing is that the new pistols performed beautifully. I took them to two different local clubs, each with several active pistol competitors. All the shooters who tried them remarked about their superb triggers.

Shooters who knew the older High Standards definitely agreed that the new guns embody the qualities they remembered. Are the new pistols as good as the originals? Everyone felt the answer could become "Yes." Their only question was whether the new pistols are better than those that came before.

In my own shooting with the two new pistols, I reached the same conclusion. The triggers are just as crisp and clean as the triggers on any older High Standards I remember. I fired several boxes of new and 30-year-old target ammunition through both pistols without a single malfunction. Their elegant style, checkered walnut grips and clean finishes were every bit as fine as before. I did no formal accuracy tests, but virtually all of my shots in competition courses of fire were "on call" with remarkable precision. The new High

Standards certainly passed my personal "shootability" tests with flying colors.

I do all too little competition shooting nowadays because of job pressures, but I still make occasional trips to the range to shoot different rifle and pistol competition courses of fire to see how close I can come to my personal records. Personal records do not come very often any more for obvious reasons, but I suppose that was what made my own experience with these pistols so satisfying. After several checks to determine how well the pistols were performing, I shot an international sport pistol course with the Victor. I astounded myself with a new personal record, exceeding a score that had been in my personal shooting notebook for over 12 years. One score by an occasional pistol shooter might not prove that a particular pistol is great, but it certainly indicates that it is capable of producing high results.

When I interviewed officials at the new High Standard Manufacturing Company, I began to see why the new pistols may be even better than before. The pistols I tried were true production models. Careful attention was given to adjusting the triggers to break above the competition minimum of 2 pounds but below 2¹/₄ pounds. A third-generation descendant of former High Standard barrel makers makes the new barrels to meet or exceed original expectations. The new plant has original drawings, toolings and gauges dating as far back as 1943. The contention that the Houston High Standards may be better than before is bolstered by the fact that the shop drawings and toolings used for the new production came from the Hamden, Connecticut, plant and not the later Hartford plant where some compromises in quality were made.

The new High Standard 22 rimfire competition pistols continue a classic tradition of excellent design and quality established through 40 years of production and competition successes. Now, chances are good that this distinguished past is only a beginning. High Standard is already working with competition shooters throughout the country to reestablish their dominance at places like the Camp Perry Nationals. In addition, High Standard is working with members of the U.S. Shooting Team to provide pistols that U.S. competitors can use in the 1996 Olympic rapid-fire pistol and sport pistol events. If Bill McMillan's 1960 Olympic rapid-fire pistol gold medal with a U.S.-made High Standard is duplicated in Atlanta in 1996, the new High Standard Manufacturing Co. once again may find it difficult to keep up with the demand for their fine target pistols. ●

CENTERFIRE HANDGUN CARTRIDGES—BALLISTICS AND PRICES

Caliber	Bullet Wgt. Grs.	Velocity (fps) MV	Velocity (fps) 50 yds.	Velocity (fps) 100 yds.	Energy (ft. lbs.) ME	Energy (ft. lbs.) 50 yds.	Energy (ft. lbs.) 100 yds.	Mid-Range Traj. (in.) 50 yds.	Mid-Range Traj. (in.) 100 yds.	Bbl. Lgth. (in.)	Est. Price /box
221 Rem. Fireball	50	2650	2380	2130	780	630	505	0.2	0.8	10.5"	$15
25 Automatic	35	900	813	742	63	51	43	NA	NA	2"	$18
25 Automatic	45	815	730	655	65	55	40	1.8	7.7	2"	$21
25 Automatic	50	760	705	660	65	55	50	2.0	8.7	2"	$17
7.5mm Swiss	107	1010	NA	NA	240	NA	NA	NA	NA	NA	NEW
7.62mm Tokarev	87	1390	NA	NA	365	NA	NA	0.6	NA	4.5"	NA
7.62mm Nagant	97	1080	NA	NA	350	NA	NA	NA	NA	NA	NEW
7.63mm Mauser	88	1440	NA	NA	405	NA	NA	NA	NA	NA	NEW
30 Luger	93†	1220	1110	1040	305	255	225	0.9	3.5	4.5"	$34
30 Carbine	110	1790	1600	1430	785	625	500	0.4	1.7	10"	$28
32 S&W	88	680	645	610	90	80	75	2.5	10.5	3"	$17
32 S&W Long	98	705	670	635	115	100	90	2.3	10.5	4"	$17
32 Short Colt	80	745	665	590	100	80	60	2.2	9.9	4"	$19
32 H&R Magnum	85	1100	1020	930	230	195	165	1.0	4.3	4.5"	$21
32 H&R Magnum	95	1030	940	900	225	190	170	1.1	4.7	4.5"	$19
32 Automatic	60	970	895	835	125	105	95	1.3	5.4	4"	$22
32 Automatic	71	905	855	810	130	115	95	1.4	5.8	4"	$19
8mm Lebel Pistol	111	850	NA	NA	180	NA	NA	NA	NA	NA	NEW
8mm Steyr	113	1080	NA	NA	290	NA	NA	NA	NA	NA	NEW
8mm Gasser	126	850	NA	NA	200	NA	NA	NA	NA	NA	NEW
380 Automatic	85/88	990	920	870	190	165	145	1.2	5.1	4"	$20
380 Automatic	90	1000	890	800	200	160	130	1.2	5.5	3.75"	$10
380 Automatic	95/100	955	865	785	190	160	130	1.4	5.9	4"	$20
38 Super Auto +P	115	1300	1145	1040	430	335	275	0.7	3.3	5"	$26
38 Super Auto +P	125/130	1215	1100	1015	425	350	300	0.8	3.6	5"	$26
38 Super Auto +P	147	1100	1050	1000	395	355	325	0.9	4.0	5"	NA
9x18mm Makarov	95	1000	NA	NA	NA	NA	NA	NA	NA	NA	NEW
9x18mm Ultra	100	1050	NA	NA	240	NA	NA	NA	NA	NA	NEW
9x23mm Largo	124	1190	1055	966	390	306	257	0.7	3.7	4"	NA
9mm Steyr	115	1180	NA	NA	350	NA	NA	NA	NA	NA	NEW
9mm Luger	88	1500	1190	1010	440	275	200	0.6	3.1	4"	$24
9mm Luger	90	1360	1112	978	370	247	191	NA	NA	4"	$26
9mm Luger	95	1300	1140	1010	350	275	215	0.8	3.4	4"	NA
9mm Luger	115	1155	1045	970	340	280	240	0.9	3.9	4"	$21
9mm Luger	123/125	1110	1030	970	340	290	260	1.0	4.0	4"	$23
9mm Luger	140	935	890	850	270	245	225	1.3	5.5	4"	$23
9mm Luger	147	990	940	900	320	290	265	1.1	4.9	4"	$26
9mm Luger +P	115	1250	1113	1019	399	316	265	0.8	3.5	4"	$27
9mm Federal	115	1280	1130	1040	420	330	280	0.7	3.3	4"V	$24
9mm Luger Vector	115	1155	1047	971	341	280	241	NA	NA	4"	NA
9mm Luger +P	124	1180	1089	1021	384	327	287	0.8	3.8	4"	NA
38 S&W	146	685	650	620	150	135	125	2.4	10.0	4"	$19
38 Short Colt	125	730	685	645	150	130	115	2.2	9.4	6"	$19
38 Special	110	945	895	850	220	195	175	1.3	5.4	4"V	$23
38 Special	130	775	745	710	175	160	120	1.9	7.9	4"V	$22
38 (Multi-Ball)	140	830	730	505	215	130	80	2.0	10.6	4"V	$10**
38 Special	148	710	635	565	165	130	105	2.4	10.6	4"V	$17
38 Special	158	755	725	690	200	185	170	2.0	8.3	4"V	$18
38 Special +P	95	1175	1045	960	290	230	195	0.9	3.9	4"V	$23
38 Special +P	110	995	925	870	240	210	185	1.2	5.1	4"V	$23
38 Special +P	125	975	929	885	264	238	218	1	5.2	4"	NA
38 Special +P	125	945	900	860	250	225	205	1.3	5.4	4"V	$23
38 Special +P	129	945	910	870	255	235	215	1.3	5.3	4"V	$11
38 Special +P	147/150(c)	884	NA	NA	264	NA	NA	NA	NA	4"V	$27
38 Special +P	158	890	855	825	280	255	240	1.4	6.0	4"V	$20
357 SIG	125	1350	1190	1080	510	395	325	0.7	3.1	4"	NA
356 TSW	147	1220	1120	1040	485	410	355	0.8	3.5	5"	NA
357 Magnum	110	1295	1095	975	410	290	230	0.8	3.5	4"V	$25
357 (Med. Vel.)	125	1220	1075	985	415	315	270	0.8	3.7	4"V	$25
357 Magnum	125	1450	1240	1090	585	425	330	0.6	2.8	4"V	$25
357 (Multi-Ball)	140	1155	830	665	420	215	135	1.2	6.4	4"V	$11**
357 Magnum	140	1360	1195	1075	575	445	360	0.7	3.0	4"V	$25
357 Magnum	145	1290	1155	1060	535	430	360	0.8	3.5	4"V	$26
357 Magnum	150/158	1235	1105	1015	535	430	360	0.8	3.5	4"V	$25
357 Magnum	165	1290	1189	1108	610	518	450	0.7	3.1	$8\frac{3}{8}$"	NA
357 Magnum	180	1145	1055	985	525	445	390	0.9	3.9	4"V	$25
357 Rem. Maximum	158	1825	1590	1380	1170	885	670	0.4	1.7	10.5"	$14**
40 S&W	155	1140	1026	958	447	362	309	0.9	4.1	4"	$14***
40 S&W	165	1150	NA	NA	485	NA	NA	NA	NA	4"	$18***
40 S&W	180	985	936	893	388	350	319	1.4	5.0	4"	$14***
40 S&W	180	1015	960	914	412	368	334	1.3	4.5	4"	NA
10mm Automatic	155	1125	1046	986	436	377	335	0.9	3.9	5"	$26
10mm Automatic	170	1340	1165	1145	680	510	415	0.7	3.2	5"	$31
10mm Automatic	175	1290	1140	1035	650	505	420	0.7	3.3	5.5"	$11**
10mm Auto.(FBI)	180	950	905	865	361	327	299	1.5	5.4	4"	$16**
10mm Automatic	180	1030	970	920	425	375	340	1.1	4.7	5"	$16**
10mm Auto H.V.	180†	1240	1124	1037	618	504	430	0.8	3.4	5"	$27
10mm Automatic	200	1160	1070	1010	495	510	430	0.9	3.8	5"	$14**
10.4mm Italian	177	950	NA	NA	360	NA	NA	NA	NA	NA	NEW
41 Action Exp.	180	1000	947	903	400	359	326	0.5	4.2	5"	$13**
41 Rem. Magnum	170	1420	1165	1015	760	515	390	0.7	3.2	4"V	$33
41 Rem. Magnum	175	1250	1120	1030	605	490	410	0.8	3.4	4"V	$14**
41 (Med. Vel.)	210	965	900	840	435	375	330	1.3	5.4	4"V	$30
41 Rem. Magnum	210	1300	1160	1060	790	630	535	0.7	3.2	4"V	$33
44 S&W Russian	247	780	NA	NA	335	NA	NA	NA	NA	NA	NA
44 S&W Special	180	980	NA	NA	383	NA	NA	NA	NA	6.5"	NA
44 S&W Special	180	1000	935	882	400	350	311	NA	NA	7.5"V	NA
44 S&W Special	200†	875	825	780	340	302	270	1.2	6.0	6"	$13**
44 S&W Special	200	1035	940	865	475	390	335	1.1	4.9	6.5"	$13**
44 S&W Special	240/246	755	725	695	310	285	265	2.0	8.3	6.5"	$26
44 Rem. Magnum	180	1610	1365	1175	1035	745	550	0.5	2.3	4"V	$18***
44 Rem. Magnum	200	1400	1192	1053	870	630	492	0.6	NA	6.5"	$20
44 Rem. Magnum	210	1495	1310	1165	1040	805	635	0.6	2.5	6.5"	$18***
44 (Med. Vel.)	240	1000	945	900	535	475	435	1.1	4.8	6.5"	$17
44 R.M.(Jacketed)	240	1180	1080	1010	740	625	545	0.9	3.7	4"V	$18***
44 R.M. (Lead)	240	1350	1185	1070	970	750	610	0.7	3.1	4"V	$29
44 Rem. Magnum	250	1180	1100	1040	775	670	600	0.8	3.6	6.5"V	$21
44 Rem. Magnum	275	1235	1142	1070	931	797	699	0.8	3.3	6.5"	NA
44 Rem. Magnum	300	1200	1100	1026	959	806	702	NA	NA	7.5"	$17
450 Short Colt	226	830	NA	NA	350	NA	NA	NA	NA	NA	NEW
45 Automatic	185	1000	940	890	410	360	325	1.1	4.9	5"	$28
45 Auto. (Match)	185	770	705	650	245	204	175	2.0	8.7	5"	$28
45 Auto. (Match)	200	940	890	840	392	352	312	2.0	8.6	5"	$20
45 Automatic	200	975	917	860	421	372	328	1.4	5.0	5"	$18
45 Automatic	230	830	800	675	355	325	300	1.6	6.8	5"	$27
45 Automatic	230	880	846	816	396	366	340	1.5	6.1	5"	NA
45 Automatic +P	185	1140	1040	970	535	445	385	0.9	4.0	5"	$31
45 Automatic +P	200	1055	982	925	494	428	380	NA	NA	5"	NA
45 Win. Magnum	230	1400	1230	1105	1000	775	635	0.6	2.8	5"	$14**
45 Win. Magnum	260	1250	1137	1053	902	746	640	0.8	3.3	5"	$16**
455 Webley MKII	262	850	NA	NA	420	NA	NA	NA	NA	NA	NA
45 Colt	200	1000	938	889	444	391	351	1.3	4.8	5.5"	$21
45 Colt	225	960	890	830	460	395	345	1.3	5.5	5.5"	$22
45 Colt	250/255	860	820	780	410	375	340	1.6	6.6	5.5"	$27
50 Action Exp.	325	1400	1209	1075	1414	1055	835	0.2	2.3	6"	$24**

Notes: Blanks are available in 32 S&W, 38 S&W, and 38 Special. V after barrel length indicates test barrel was vented to produce ballistics similar to a revolver with a normal barrel-to-cylinder gap. Ammo prices are per 50 rounds except when marked with an ** which signifies a 20 round box; *** signifies a 25-round box. Not all loads are available from all ammo manufacturers. Listed loads are those made by Remington, Winchester, Federal, and others. DISC. is a discontinued load. Prices are rounded to nearest whole dollar and will vary with brand and retail outlet. †= new bullet weight this year; "c" indicates a change in data.

RIMFIRE AMMUNITION—BALLISTICS AND PRICES

Cartridge type	Bullet Wt. Grs.	Velocity (fps) $22\frac{1}{2}$" Barrel Muzzle	Velocity (fps) $22\frac{1}{2}$" Barrel 50 Yds.	Velocity (fps) $22\frac{1}{2}$" Barrel 100 Yds.	Energy (ft. lbs.) $22\frac{1}{2}$" Barrel Muzzle	Energy (ft. lbs.) $22\frac{1}{2}$" Barrel 50 Yds.	Energy (ft. lbs.) $22\frac{1}{2}$" Barrel 100 Yds.	Velocity (fps) 6" Barrel Muzzle	Velocity (fps) 6" Barrel 50 Yds.	Energy (ft. lbs) 6" Barrel Muzzle	Energy (ft. lbs) 6" Barrel 50 Yds.	Approx. Price Per Box 50 Rds.	Approx. Price Per Box 100 Rds.
22 Short Blank						Not applicable						$4	NA
22 CB Short	30	725	667	610	34	29	24	706	—	32	—	$2	NA
22 Short Match	29	830	752	695	44	36	31	786	—	39	—	—	NA
22 Short Std. Vel.	29	1045	—	810	70	—	42	865	—	48	—	Discontinued	
22 Short High Vel.	29	1095	—	903	77	—	53	—	—	—	—	$2	NA
22 Short H.V. H.P.	27	1120	—	904	75	—	49	—	—	—	—	—	NA
22 CB Long	30	725	667	610	34	29	24	706	—	32	—	$2	NA
22 Long Std. Vel.	29	1180	1038	946	90	69	58	1031	—	68	—	—	—
22 Long High Vel.	29	1240	—	962	99	—	60	—	—	—	—	$2	NA
22 L.R. Sub Sonic	38/40	1070	970	890	100	80	70	940	—	—	—	$2	NA
22 L.R. Std. Vel.	40	1138	1047	975	116	97	84	1027	925	93	76	$2	NA
22 L.R. High Vel.	40	1255	1110	1017	140	109	92	1060	—	100	—	$2	NA
22 L.R. H.V. Sil.	42	1220	—	1003	139	—	94	1025	—	98	—	$2	NA
22 L.R. H.V. H.P.	36/38	1280	1126	1010	131	101	82	1089	—	95	—	$2	NA
22 L.R. Shot	#11 or #12	1047	—	—	—	—	—	950	—	—	—	$5	NA
22 L.R. Hyper Vel	36	1410	1187	1056	159	113	89	—	—	—	—	$2	NA
22 L.R. Hyper H.P	32/33/34	1500	1240	1075	165	110	85	—	—	—	—	$2	NA
22 WRF	45	1320	—	1055	175	—	111	—	—	—	—	NA	$5
22 Win. Mag.	30	2200	1750	1373	322	203	127	1610	—	—	—	—	NA
22 Win. Mag.	40	1910	1490	1326	324	197	156	1428	—	181	—	$6	NA
22 Win. Mag.	50	1650	—	1280	300	180	—	—	—	—	—	NA	NA
22 Win. Mag. Shot	#11	1126	—	—	—	—	—	—	—	—	—	NA	NA

Note: The actual ballistics obtained with your firearm can vary considerably from the advertised ballistics. Also ballistics can vary from lot to lot with the same brand and type load. Prices can vary with manufacturer and retail outlet. NA in the price column indicates this size packaging currently unavailable.

CAUTION: PRICES SHOWN ARE SUPPLIED BY THE MANUFACTURER OR IMPORTER. CHECK YOUR LOCAL GUNSHOP.

HANDGUNS 96

CATALOG

GUNDEX

Includes models suitable for several forms of competition and other sporting purposes.

ACCU-TEK MODEL AT-9SS AUTO PISTOL Caliber: 9mm Para., 8-shot magazine. **Barrel:** 3.2″. **Weight:** 28 oz. **Length:** 6.25″ overall. **Stocks:** Black checkered nylon. **Sights:** Blade front, rear adjustable for windage; three-dot system. **Features:** Stainless steel construction. Double action only. Firing pin block with no external safeties. Lifetime warranty. Introduced 1992. Made in U.S. by Accu-Tek.
Price: Satin stainless **$317.00**

Accu-Tek AT-40SS Auto Pistol Same as the Model AT-9 except chambered for 40 S&W, 7-shot magazine. Introduced 1992.
Price: Stainless **$317.00**

Accu-Tek AT-45SS Auto Pistol Same as the Model AT-9SS except chambered for 45 ACP, 6-shot magazine. Introduced 1995. Made in U.S. by Accu-Tek.
Price: Stainless steel **$327.00**

Acc-Tek AT-9SS

ACCU-TEK MODEL AT-380SS AUTO PISTOL Caliber: 380 ACP, 5-shot magazine. **Barrel:** 2.75″. **Weight:** 20 oz. **Length:** 5.6″ overall. **Stocks:** Grooved black composition. **Sights:** Blade front, rear adjustable for windage. **Features:** Stainless steel frame and slide. External hammer; manual thumb safety; firing pin block, trigger disconnect. Lifetime warranty. Introduced 1991. Made in U.S. by Accu-Tek.
Price: Satin stainless **$191.00**
Price: Black finish over steel (AT-380B) **$196.00**

Acc-Tek AT 380SS

Consult our Directory pages for
the location of firms mentioned.

Accu-Tek Model AT-32SS Auto Pistol Same as the AT-380SS except chambered for 32 ACP. Introduced 1991.
Price: Satin stainless **$185.00**
Price: Black finish over steel (AT-32B) **$190.00**

ACCU-TEK MODEL HC-380SS AUTO PISTOL Caliber: 380 ACP, 10-shot magazine. **Barrel:** 2.75″. **Weight:** 28 oz. **Length:** 6″ overall. **Stocks:** Checkered black composition. **Sights:** Blade front, rear adjustable for windage. **Features:** External hammer; manual thumb safety with firing pin and trigger disconnect; bottom magazine release. Stainless finish. Introduced 1993. Made in U.S. by Accu-Tek.
Price: Satin stainless **$243.00**
Price: Black finish over stainless **$248.00**

Accu-Tek HC-380SS

American Arms Escort

AMERICAN ARMS ESCORT AUTO PISTOL Caliber: 380 ACP, 7-shot magazine. **Barrel:** 3³/₈″. **Weight:** 19 oz. **Length:** 6¹/₈″. **Stocks:** Soft polymer. **Sights:** Blade front, rear adjustable for windage. **Features:** Double-action-only trigger; stainless steel construction; chamber loaded indicator. Introduced 1995. From American Arms, Inc.
Price: **$312.00**

AMERICAN ARMS MODEL CX-22 DA AUTO PISTOL Caliber: 22 LR, 8-shot magazine. **Barrel:** 3¹/₃″. **Weight:** 22 oz. **Length:** 6¹/₃″ overall. **Stocks:** Checkered black polymer. **Sights:** Blade front, rear adjustable for windage. **Features:** Double action with manual hammer-block safety, firing pin safety. Alloy frame. Has external appearance of Walther PPK. Blue/black finish. Introduced 1990. Made in U.S. by American Arms, Inc.
Price: **$213.00**

CAUTION: PRICES SHOWN ARE SUPPLIED BY THE MANUFACTURER OR IMPORTER. CHECK YOUR LOCAL GUNSHOP.

AMERICAN ARMS MODEL PK22 DA AUTO PISTOL Caliber: 22 LR, 8-shot magazine. **Barrel:** 3.3″. **Weight:** 22 oz. **Length:** 6.3″ overall. **Stocks:** Checkered plastic. **Sights:** Fixed. **Features:** Double action. Polished blue finish. Slide-mounted safety. Made in the U.S. by American Arms, Inc.
Price: $213.00

AMERICAN ARMS MODEL PX-22 AUTO PISTOL Caliber: 22 LR, 7-shot magazine. **Barrel:** 2.85″. **Weight:** 15 oz. **Length:** 5.39″ overall. **Stocks:** Black checkered plastic. **Sights:** Fixed. **Features:** Double action; 7-shot magazine. Polished blue finish. Introduced 1989. Made in U.S. From American Arms, Inc.
Price: $206.00

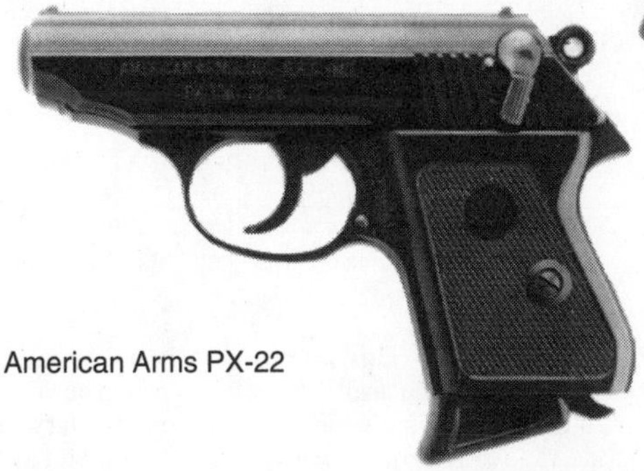

American Arms PK22

American Arms PX-22

AMERICAN ARMS MODEL P-98 AUTO PISTOL Caliber: 22 LR, 8-shot magazine. **Barrel:** 5″. **Weight:** 25 oz. **Length:** 8⅛″ overall. **Stocks:** Grooved black polymer. **Sights:** Blade front, rear adjustable for windage. **Features:** Double action with hammer-block safety, magazine disconnect safety. Alloy frame. Has external appearance of the Walther P-38 pistol. Introduced 1989. Made in U.S. by American Arms, Inc.
Price: $229.00

AMT AUTOMAG II AUTO PISTOL Caliber: 22 WMR, 9-shot magazine (7-shot with 3⅜″ barrel). **Barrel:** 3⅜″, 4½″, 6″. **Weight:** About 23 oz. **Length:** 9⅜″ overall. **Stocks:** Grooved carbon fiber. **Sights:** Blade front, adjustable rear. **Features:** Made of stainless steel. Gas-assisted action. Exposed hammer. Slide flats have brushed finish, rest is sandblast. Squared trigger guard. Introduced 1986. From AMT.
Price: $405.95

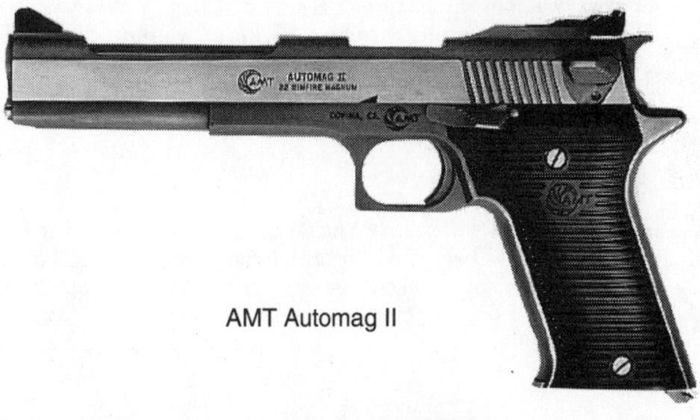

American Arms P-98

AMT AUTOMAG III PISTOL Caliber: 30 Carbine, 8-shot magazine. **Barrel:** 6⅜″. **Weight:** 43 oz. **Length:** 10½″ overall. **Stocks:** Carbon fiber. **Sights:** Blade front, adjustable rear. **Features:** Stainless steel construction. Hammer-drop safety. Slide flats have brushed finish, rest is sandblasted. Introduced 1989. From AMT.
Price: $469.79

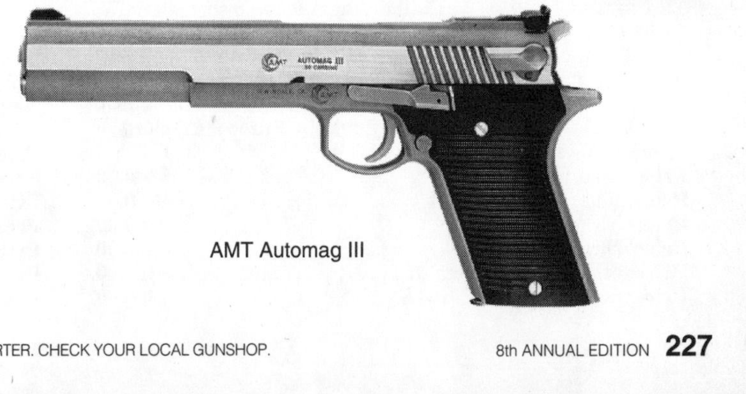

AMT AUTOMAG IV PISTOL Caliber: 45 Winchester Magnum, 6-shot magazine. **Barrel:** 6.5″. **Weight:** 46 oz. **Length:** 10.5″ overall with 6.5″ barrel. **Stocks:** Carbon fiber. **Sights:** Blade front, adjustable rear. **Features:** Made of stainless steel with brushed finish. Introduced 1990. Made in U.S. by AMT.
Price: $699.99
Price: Automag V (50 A.E.) $899.99

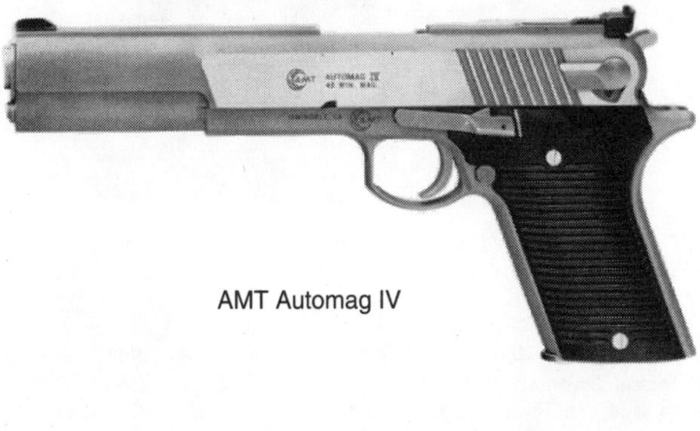

AMT Automag II

AMT Automag IV

AMT Automag III

CAUTION: PRICES SHOWN ARE SUPPLIED BY THE MANUFACTURER OR IMPORTER. CHECK YOUR LOCAL GUNSHOP.

8th ANNUAL EDITION **227**

AMT BACKUP II AUTO PISTOL Caliber: 380 ACP, 5-shot magazine. **Barrel:** 2½″. **Weight:** 18 oz. **Length:** 5″ overall. **Stocks:** Carbon fiber. **Sights:** Fixed, open, recessed. **Features:** Concealed hammer, blowback operation; manual and grip safeties. All stainless steel construction. Smallest domestically-produced pistol in 380. From AMT.
Price: $309.99

AMT 45 ACP Backup

AMT Backup Double Action Only Pistol Similar to the standard Backup except has double-action-only mechanism, enlarged trigger guard, slide is rounded ar rear. Has 5-shot magazine. Introduced 1992. From AMT.
Price: $329.99
Price: 9mm Para., 38 Super, 40 S&W, 45 ACP $449.99

> Consult our Directory pages for the location of firms mentioned.

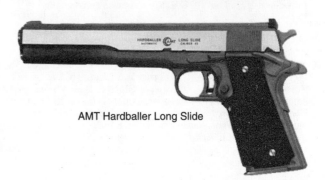

AMT Hardballer Long Slide

AMT 45 ACP HARDBALLER Caliber: 45 ACP. **Barrel:** 5″. **Weight:** 39 oz. **Length:** 8½″ overall. **Stocks:** Wrap-around rubber. **Sights:** Adjustable. **Features:** Extended combat safety, serrated matte slide rib, loaded chamber indicator, long grip safety, beveled magazine well, adjustable target trigger. All stainless steel. From AMT.
Price: $549.95
Price: Government model (as above except no rib, fixed sights) $489.99

AMT 45 ACP HARDBALLER LONG SLIDE Caliber: 45 ACP. **Barrel:** 7″. **Length:** 10½″ overall. **Stocks:** Wrap-around rubber. **Sights:** Fully adjustable rear sight. **Features:** Slide and barrel are 2″ longer than the standard 45, giving less recoil, added velocity, longer sight radius. Has extended combat safety, serrated matte rib, loaded chamber indicator, wide adjustable trigger. From AMT.
Price: $595.99

Argentine Hi-Power

ARGENTINE HI-POWER 9MM AUTO PISTOL Caliber: 9mm Para., 10-shot magazine. **Barrel:** 4²¹/₃₂″. **Weight:** 32 oz. **Length:** 7¾″ overall. **Stocks:** Checkered walnut. **Sights:** Blade front, adjustable rear. **Features:** Produced in Argentina under F.N. Browning license. Introduced 1990. Imported by Century International Arms, Inc.
Price: About $299.95

Argentine Hi-Power Detective Model Similar to the standard model except has 3.8″ barrel, 6.9″ overall length and weighs 33 oz. Grips are finger-groove, checkered soft rubber. Matte black finish. Introduced 1994. Imported by Century International Arms, Inc.
Price: About $310.00

Astra A-75

ASTRA A-70 AUTO PISTOL Caliber: 9mm Para., 8-shot; 40 S&W, 7-shot magazine. **Barrel:** 3.5″. **Weight:** 29.3 oz. **Length:** 6.5″ overall. **Stocks:** Checkered black plastic. **Sights:** Blade front, rear adjustable for windage. **Features:** All steel frame and slide. Checkered grip straps and trigger guard. Nickel or blue finish. Introduced 1992. Imported from Spain by European American Armory.
Price: Blue, 9mm Para. $360.00
Price: Blue, 40 S&W $360.00
Price: Nickel, 9mm Para. $385.00
Price: Nickel, 40 S&W $385.00
Price: Stainless steel, 9mm $450.00
Price: Stainless steel, 40 S&W $450.00

Astra A-75 Decocker Auto Pistol Same as the A-70 except has ambidextrous decocker system, different trigger, contoured pebble-grain grips. Introduced 1993. Imported from Spain by European American Armory.
Price: Blue, 9mm or 40 S&W $415.00
Price: Nickel, 9mm or 40 S&W $440.00
Price: Blue, 45 ACP $445.00
Price: Nickel, 45 ACP $460.00
Price: Stainless steel, 9mm, 40 S&W $495.00
Price: Stainless steel, 45 ACP $525.00
Price: Featherweight (23.5 oz.), 9mm, blue $440.00

ASTRA A-100 AUTO PISTOL **Caliber:** 9mm Para., 10-shot; 40 S&W, 10-shot; 45 ACP, 9-shot magazine. **Barrel:** 3.9″. **Weight:** 29 oz. **Length:** 7.1″ overall. **Stocks:** Checkered black plastic. **Sights:** Blade front, interchangeable rear blades for elevation, screw adjustable for windage. **Features:** Double action. Decocking lever permits lowering hammer onto locked firing pin. Automatic firing pin block. Side button magazine release. Introduced 1993. Imported from Spain by European American Armory.
Price: Blue, 9mm, 40 S&W, 45 ACP $450.00
Price: As above, nickel $475.00

Astra A-100

AUTO-ORDNANCE 1911A1 AUTOMATIC PISTOL **Caliber:** 9mm Para., 38 Super, 9-shot; 10mm, 45 ACP, 7-shot magazine. **Barrel:** 5″. **Weight:** 39 oz. **Length:** 8½″ overall. **Stocks:** Checkered plastic with medallion. **Sights:** Blade front, rear adjustable for windage. **Features:** Same specs as 1911A1 military guns—parts interchangeable. Frame and slide blued; each radius has non-glare finish. Made in U.S. by Auto-Ordnance Corp.
Price: 45 ACP, blue $388.95
Price: 45 ACP, Parkerized $379.25
Price: 45 ACP, satin nickel $405.00
Price: 9mm, 38 Super $415.00
Price: 10mm (has three-dot combat sights, rubber wrap-around grips) $420.95
Price: 45 ACP General Model (Commander style) $427.95
Price: Duo Tone (nickel frame, blue slide, three-dot sight system, textured black wrap-around grips) $405.00

Auto-Ordnance ZG-51 Pit Bull Auto Same as the 1911A1 except has 3½″ barrel, weighs 36 oz. and has an over-all length of 7¼″. Available in 45 ACP only; 7-shot magazine. Introduced 1989.
Price: $420.95

Auto-Ordnance 1911A1 Competition Model Similar to the standard Model 19911A1 except has barrel compensator. Commander hammer, flat mainspring housing, three-dot sight system, low-profile magazine funnel, Hi-Ride beavertail grip safety, full-length recoil spring guide system, black-textured rubber, wrap-around grips, and extended slide stop, safety and magazine catch. Introduced 1994. Made in U.S. by Auto-Ordnance Corp.
Price: $615.00

Auto-Ordnance 1911A1

Baby Eagle FS

Baer Custom Carry

BABY EAGLE AUTO PISTOL **Caliber:** 9mm Para., 40 S&W, 41 A.E. **Barrel:** 4.37″. **Weight:** 35 oz. **Length:** 8.14″ overall. **Stocks:** High-impact black polymer. **Sights:** Combat. **Features:** Double-action mechanism; polygonal rifling; ambidextrous safety. Model 9mm F has frame-mounted safety on left side of pistol; Model 9mm FS has frame-mounted safety and 3.62″ barrel. Introduced 1992. Imported by Magnum Research.
Price: 40 S&W, 41 A.E., 9mm (9mm F, 9mm FS), black finish $569.00
Price: Conversion kit, 9mm Para. to 41 A.E. $239.00
Price: 9mm FS, chrome finish $659.00
Price: 9mm FSS, black matte finish, frame-mounted safety, short grip, short barrel $569.00
Price: As above, chrome finish $659.00

BAER 1911 CUSTOM CARRY AUTO PISTOL **Caliber:** 45 ACP, 7- or 10-shot magazine. **Barrel:** 5″. **Weight:** 37 oz. **Length:** 8.5″ over-all. **Stocks:** Checkered walnut. **Sights:** Baer improved ramp-style dovetailed front, Novak low-mount rear. **Features:** Baer forged NM frame, slide and barrel with stainless bushing; fitted slide to frame; double serrated slide (full-size only); Baer speed trigger with 4-lb. pull; Baer deluxe hammer and sear, tactical-style extended ambidextrous safety, beveled magazine well; polished feed ramp and throated barrel; tuned extractor; Baer extended ejector, checkered slide stop; lowered and flared ejection port, full-length recoil guide rod; recoil buff. Made in U.S. by Les Baer Custom, Inc.
Price: Standard size, blued $1,265.00
Price: Standard size, stainless $1,365.00
Price: Commanche size, blued $1,265.00
Price: Commanche size, stainless $1,375.00
Price: Commanche size, aluminum frame, blued slide .$1,375.00
Price: Commanche size, aluminum frame,stainless slide $1,420.00

Baer Concept IV

Baer Premier II

BAER 1911 PREMIER II AUTO PISTOL Caliber: 45 ACP, 7- or 10-shot magazine. **Barrel:** 5″. **Weight:** 37 oz. **Length:** 8.5″ overall. **Stocks:** Checkered rosewood, double diamond pattern. **Sights:** Baer dovetailed front, low-mount Bo-Mar rear with hidden leaf. **Features:** Baer NM forged steel frame and barrel with stainless bushing; slide fitted to frame; double serrated slide; lowered, flared ejection port; tuned, polished extractor; Baer extended ejector, checkered slide stop, aluminum speed trigger with 4-lb. pull, deluxe Commander hammer and sear, beavertail grip safety with pad, beveled magazine well, extended ambidextrous safety; flat mainspring housing; polished feed ramp and throated barrel; 30 lpi checkered front strap. Made in U.S. by Les Baer Custom, Inc.
Price: Blued $1,428.00
Price: Stainless $1,528.00

BAIKAL IJ-70 DA AUTO PISTOL Caliber: 9x18mm Makarov, 8-shot magazine. **Barrel:** 4″. **Weight:** 25 oz. **Length:** 6.25″ overall. **Stocks:** Checkered composition. **Sights:** Blade front, rear adjustable for windage and elevation. **Features:** Double action; all-steel construction; frame-mounted safety with decocker. Comes with two magazines, cleaning rod, universal tool. Introduced 1994. Imported from Russia by Century International Arms, K.B.I., Inc.
Price: 9x18mm, blue $199.00
Price: IJ-70HC, 9x18, 10-shot magazine, from K.B.I. ...$239.00
Price: As above, 380 ACP (K.B.I.) $249.00

Beretta Model 21 Bobcat Pistol Similar to the Model 950 BS. Chambered for 22 LR or 25 ACP. Both double action. Has 2.5″ barrel, 4.9″ overall length; 7-round magazine on 22 cal.; available in nickel, matte, engraved or blue finish. Plastic or walnut grips. Introduced in 1985.
Price: Bobcat, 22-cal. $244.00
Price: Bobcat, nickel, 22-cal. $254.00
Price: Bobcat, 25-cal. $244.00
Price: Bobcat, nickel, 25-cal. $254.00
Price: Bobcat wood, engraved, 22 or 25 ....$294.00
Price: Bobcat plastic matte, 22 or 25 ....$194.00

BAER 1911 CONCEPT I AUTO PISTOL Caliber: 45 ACP, 7-shot magazine. **Barrel:** 5″. **Weight:** 37 oz. **Length:** 8.5″ overall. **Stocks:** Checkered rosewood. **Sights:** Baer dovetail front, Bo-Mar deluxe low-mount rear with hidden leaf. **Features:** Baer forged steel frame, slide and barrel with Baer stainless bushing; slide fitted to frame; double serrated slide; Baer beavertail grip safety, checkered slide stop, tuned extractor, extended ejector, deluxe hammer and sear, match disconnector; lowered and flared ejection port; fitted recoil link; polished feed ramp, throated barrel; Baer fitted speed trigger, flat serrated mainspring housing. Blue finish. Made in U.S. by Les Baer Custom, Inc.
Price: $1,279.00
Price: Concept II (with Novak fixed rear sight) $1,249.00

Baer 1911 Concept III Auto Pistol Same as the Concept I except has forged stainless frame with blued steel slide, Bo-Mar rear sight, 30 lpi checkering on front strap. Made in U.S. by Les Baer Custom, Inc.
Price: $1,499.00
Price: Concept IV (with Novak rear sight) $1,479.00
Price: Concept V (all stainless, Bo-Mar sight, checkered front strap) $1,559.00
Price: Concept VI (all stainless, Novak sight, checkered front strap) $1,529.00

Baer 1911 Concept VII Auto Pistol Same as the Concept I except reduced Commanche size with 4.25″ barrel, weighs 27.5 oz., 7.75″ overall. Blue finish, checkered front strap. Made in U.S. by Les Baer Custom, Inc.
Price: $1,439.00
Price: Concept VIII (has stainless frame and slide, Novak rear sight) $1,529.00

Baer 1911 Prowler III Auto Pistol Same as the Premier II except also has tapered cone stub weight and reverse recoil plug. Made in U.S. by Les Baer Custom, Inc.
Price: Standard size, blued $1,795.00
Price: Standard size, stainless $1,895.00
Price: Commanche size, blued $1,795.00
Price: Commanche size, stainless $1,895.00

Baer 1911 Concept IX Auto Pistol Same as the Commanche Concept VII except has Baer lightweight forged aluminum frame, blued steel slide, Novak rear sight. Chambered for 45 ACP, 7-shot magazine. Made in U.S. by Les Baer Custom, Inc.
Price: $1,439.00
Price: Concept X (as above with stainless slide) $1,489.00

Baikal IJ-70

Beretta 21 Bobcat

BERETTA MODEL 80 CHEETAH SERIES DA PISTOLS **Caliber:** 380 ACP, 10-shot magazine (M84); 8-shot (M85); 22 LR, 7-shot (M87), 22 LR, 8-shot (M89). **Barrel:** 3.82". **Weight:** About 23 oz. (M84/85); 20.8 oz. (M87). **Length:** 6.8" overall. **Stocks:** Glossy black plastic (wood optional at extra cost). **Sights:** Fixed front, drift-adjustable rear. **Features:** Double action, quick takedown, convenient magazine release. Introduced 1977. Imported from Italy by Beretta U.S.A.

Price: Model 84 Cheetah, plastic grips **$529.00**
Price: Model 84 Cheetah, wood grips **$557.00**
Price: Model 84 Cheetah, wood grips, nickel finish **$600.00**
Price: Model 85 Cheetah, plastic grips, 8-shot **$486.00**
Price: Model 85 Cheetah, wood grips, 8-shot **$514.00**
Price: Model 85 Cheetah, wood grips, nickel, 8-shot **$551.00**
Price: Model 87 Cheetah wood, 22 LR, 7-shot **$493.00**

Beretta Model 84 Cheetah

Beretta Model 86 Cheetah Similar to the 380-caliber Model 85 except has tip-up barrel for first-round loading. Barrel length is 4.33", overall length of 7.33". Has 8-shot magazine, walnut or plastic grips. Introduced 1989.

Price: **$514.00**

Beretta Model 86 Cheetah

BERETTA MODEL 92FS PISTOL **Caliber:** 9mm Para., 10-shot magazine. **Barrel:** 4.9". **Weight:** 34 oz. **Length:** 8.5" overall. **Stocks:** Checkered black plastic; wood optional at extra cost. **Sights:** Blade front, rear adjustable for windage. Tritium night sights available. **Features:** Double action. Extractor acts as chamber loaded indicator, squared trigger guard, grooved front- and backstraps, inertia firing pin. Matte finish. Introduced 1977. Made in U.S. and imported from Italy by Beretta U.S.A.

Price: With plastic grips **$626.00**
Price: With wood grips **$647.00**
Price: Tritium night sights, add **$90.00**

Beretta Model 87 Cheetah

Beretta Model 92D Pistol Same as the Model 92FS except double action only and has bobbed hammer, no external safety. Introduced 1992.

Price: With plastic grips, three-dot sights **$586.00**
Price: As above with Trijicon sights **$676.00**

Beretta Models 92FS/96 Centurion Pistols Identical to the Model 92FS and 96F except uses shorter slide and barrel (4.3"). Trijicon or three-dot sight systems. Plastic or wood grips. Available in 9mm or 40 S&W. Also available in D Models (double action only). Introduced 1992.

Price: Model 92FS Centurion, three-dot sights, plastic grips **$626.00**
Price: Model 92FS Centurion, wood grips **$647.00**
Price: Model 96 Centurion, three-dot sights, plastic grips **$643.00**
Price: Model 92D Centurion **$586.00**
Price: Model 96D Centurion **$607.00**
Price: For Trijicon sights, add **$90.00**

Beretta model 92FS

Beretta 92D Centurion

Beretta Model 92D

CAUTION: PRICES SHOWN ARE SUPPLIED BY THE MANUFACTURER OR IMPORTER. CHECK YOUR LOCAL GUNSHOP.

8th ANNUAL EDITION **231**

Beretta Model 92/96 Brigadier

Beretta Model 92/96 Brigadier Auto Pistol Similar to the Beretta Model 92/96 series except has removable front sight and reconfigured high slide wall profile to reduce felt recoil. Has 10-shot magazine, three-dot sight system, 4.9″ barrel, weighs 35.3 oz. Matte black Bruniton finish. Introduced 1995. From Beretta U.S.A.
Price: Model 92 Brigadier (9mm) . . . .**NA**
Price: Model 96 Brigadier (40 S&W) . . . .**NA**

Beretta Model 96 Auto Pistol Same as the Model 92F except chambered for 40 S&W. Ambidextrous safety mechanism with passive firing pin catch, slide safety/decocking lever, trigger bar disconnect. Has 10-shot magazine. Available with Trijicon or three-dot sights. Introduced 1992.
Price: Model 96, plastic grips **$643.00**
Price: Model 96D, double action only, three-dot sights . .**$607.00**
Price: For Trijicon sights, add **$90.00**

Beretta Model 92F Stainless Pistol Same as the Model 92FS except has stainless steel barrel and slide, and frame of aluminum-zirconium alloy. Has three-dot sight system. Introduced 1992.
Price: **$757.00**
Price: Model 92F-EL Stainless (gold trim, engraved barrel, slide, frame, gold-finished safety-levers, trigger, magazine release, grip screws) **$1,240.00**
Price: For Trijicon sights, add **$90.00**

BERETTA MODEL 950BS JETFIRE AUTO PISTOL Caliber: 25 ACP, 8-shot. **Barrel:** 2.5″. **Weight:** 9.9 oz. **Length:** 4.5″ overall. **Stocks:** Checkered black plastic or walnut. **Sights:** Fixed. **Features:** Single action, thumb safety; tip-up barrel for direct loading/unloading, cleaning. From Beretta U.S.A.
Price: Jetfire wood, blue **$187.00**
Price: Jetfire wood, nickel **$221.00**
Price: Jetfire wood, engraved **$267.00**
Price: Jetfire plastic, matte blue **$159.00**

Beretta Model 92F Stainless

BERETTA MODEL 8000/8040 COUGAR PISTOL Caliber: 9mm Para., 10-shot, 40 S&W, 10-shot magazine. **Barrel:** 3.5″ overall. **Weight:** 33.5 oz. **Length:** 7″. **Stocks:** Textured composition. **Sights:** Blade front, rear drift adjustable for windage. **Features:** Slide-mounted safety; exposed hammer. Matte black Bruniton finish. Announced 1994. Imported from Italy by Beretta U.S.A.
Price: **$636.00**
Price: D models **$611.00**

BERNARDELLI P. ONE DA AUTO PISTOL Caliber: 9mm Para., 10-shot, 40 S&W, 10-shot magazine. **Barrel:** 4.8″. **Weight:** 34 oz. **Length:** 8.35″ overall. **Stocks:** Checkered black plastic. **Sights:** Blade front, rear adjustable for windage and elevation; three dot system. **Features:** Forged steel frame and slide; full-length slide rails; reversible magazine release; thumb safety/decocker; squared trigger guard. Introduced 1994. Imported from Italy by Armsport.
Price: 9mm Para., blue/black **$530.00**
Price: 9mm Para., chrome **$580.00**
Price: 40 S&W, blue/black **$530.00**
Price: 40 S&W, chrome **$580.00**

Beretta 950BS Jetfire

Bernardelli P. One Practical VB Pistol Similar to the P. One except chambered for 9x21mm, two- or four-port compensator, straight trigger, micro-adjustable rear sight. Introduced 1994. Imported from Italy by Armsport.
Price: Blue/black, two-port compensator **$1,425.00**
Price: As above, four-port compensator **$1,475.00**
Price: Chrome, two-port compensator **$1,498.00**
Price: As above, four-port compensator **$1,540.00**
Price: Customized VB, with four-plus-two-port compensator **$2,150.00**
Price: As above, chrome **$2,200.00**

Beretta M8000/8040 Cougar

BERNARDELLI MODEL USA AUTO PISTOL Caliber: 22 LR, 10-shot, 380 ACP, 7-shot magazine. **Barrel:** 3.5″. **Weight:** 26.5 oz. **Length:** 6.5″ overall. **Stocks:** Checkered plastic with thumbrest. **Sights:** Ramp front, white outline rear adjustable for windage and elevation. **Features:** Hammer-block slide safety; loaded chamber indicator; dual recoil buffer springs; serrated trigger; inertia-type firing pin. Imported from Italy by Armsport.
Price: Blue, either caliber $387.00
Price: Chrome, either caliber $412.00
Price: Model AMR (6″ barrel, target sights) $440.00

Bernadelli PO18

BERNARDELLI PO18 DA AUTO PISTOL Caliber: 9mm Para., 10-shot magazine. **Barrel:** 4.8″. **Weight:** 34.2 oz. **Length:** 8.23″ overall. **Stocks:** Checkered plastic; walnut optional. **Sights:** Blade front, rear adjustable for windage and elevation; low profile, three-dot system. **Features:** Manual thumb half-cock, magazine and auto-locking firing pin safeties. Thumb safety decocks hammer. Reversible magazine release. Imported from Italy by Armsport.
Price: Blue $505.00
Price: Chrome $568.00

Bernardelli PO18 Compact DA Auto Pistol Similar to the PO18 except has 4″ barrel, 7.44″ overall length, 10-shot magazine. Weighs 31.7 oz. Imported from Italy by Armsport.
Price: Blue $552.00
Price: Chrome $600.00

Bersa Series 95

BERSA SERIES 95 AUTO PISTOL Caliber: 380 ACP, 7-shot magazine. **Barrel:** 3.5″. **Weight:** 22 oz. **Length:** 6.6″ overall. **Stocks:** Wraparound textured rubber. **Sights:** Blade front, rear adjustable for windage; three-dot system. **Features:** Double action; firing pin and magazine safeties; combat-style trigger guard. Matte blue or satin nickel. Introduced 1992. Distributed by Eagle Imports, Inc.
Price: Matte blue $274.95
Price: Satin nickel $291.95

BERSA THUNDER 9 AUTO PISTOL Caliber: 9mm Para., 10-shot magazine. **Barrel:** 4″. **Weight:** 30 oz. **Length:** 7³/₈″ overall. **Stocks:** Checkered black polymer. **Sights:** Blade front, rear adjustable for windage and elevation; three-dot system. **Features:** Double action. Ambidextrous safety, decocking levers and slide release; internal automatic firing pin safety; reversible extended magazine release; adjustable trigger stop; alloy frame. Link-free locked breech design. Matte blue finish. Introduced 1993. Imported from Argentina by Eagle Imports, Inc.
Price: Matte finish $474.95
Price: Satin nickel $524.95
Price Duo-Tone finish $491.95

Bersa Thunder 9

BERSA THUNDER 22 AUTO PISTOL Caliber: 22 LR, 10-shot magazine. **Barrel:** 3.5″. **Weight:** 24.2 oz. **Length:** 6.6″ overall. **Stocks:** Black polymer. **Sights:** Blade front, notch rear adjustable for windage; three-dot system. **Features:** Double action; firing pin and magazine safeties. Available in blue or nickel. Introduced 1995. Distributed by Eagle Imports, Inc.
Price: Blue $308.95
Price: Nickel $341.95

BERSA THUNDER 380 AUTO PISTOLS Caliber: 380 ACP, 7-shot (Thunder 380), 10-shot magazine (Thunder 380 Plus). **Barrel:** 3.5″. **Weight:** 25.75 oz. **Length:** 6.6″ overall. **Stocks:** Black rubber. **Sights:** Blade front, notch rear adjustable for windage; three-dot system. **Features:** Double action; firing pin and magazine safeties. Available in blue or nickel. Introduced 1995. Distributed by Eagle Imports, Inc.
Price: Thunder 380, 7-shot, deep blue finish $308.95
Price: As above, satin nickel $341.95
Price: As above, Duo-Tone finish $324.95
Price: Thunder 380 Plus, 10-shot, matte blue $367.95
Price: As above, satin nickel $408.00
Price: As above, Duo-Tone finish $384.95

Bersa Thunder 380

Browning Hi-Power Adjustable Sight

BROWNING HI-POWER 9mm AUTOMATIC PISTOL **Caliber:** 9mm Para., 40 S&W, 10-shot magazine. **Barrel:** 4²¹/₃₂″. **Weight:** 32 oz. **Length:** 7³/₄″ overall. **Stocks:** Walnut, hand checkered, or black Polyamide. **Sights:** ¹/₈″ blade front; rear screw-adjustable for windage and elevation. Also available with fixed rear (drift-adjustable for windage). **Features:** External hammer with half-cock and thumb safeties. A blow on the hammer cannot discharge a cartridge; cannot be fired with magazine removed. Fixed rear sight model available. Ambidextrous safety available only with matte finish, moulded grips. Imported from Belgium by Browning.
Price: Fixed sight model, walnut grips **$556.95**
Price: 9mm with rear sight adjustable for windage and elevation, walnut grips **$605.95**
Price: Mark III, standard matte black finish, fixed sight, moulded grips, ambidextrous safety **$524.95**
Price: Silver chrome, adjustable sight, Pachmayr grips .**$619.95**

Browning Hi-Power Silver Chrome

Browning 40 S&W Hi-Power Mark III Pistol Similar to the standard Hi-Power except chambered for 40 S&W, 10-shot magazine, weighs 35 oz., and has 4³/₄″ barrel. Comes with matte blue finish, low profile front sight blade, drift-adjustable rear sight, ambidextrous safety, moulded polyamide grips with thumb rest. Introduced 1993. Imported from Belgium by Browning.
Price: Mark III **$524.95**

Browning Hi-Power HP-Practical Pistol Similar to the standard Hi-Power except has silver-chromed frame with blued slide, wrap-around Pachmayr rubber grips, round-style serrated hammer and removable front sight, fixed rear (drift-adjustable for windage). Available in 9mm Para. or 40 S&W. Introduced 1991.
Price: **$599.95**
Price: With fully adjustable rear sight **$649.95**

Browning HP Practical

Browning Capitan Hi-Power Pistol Similar to the standard Hi-Power except has adjustable tangent rear sight authentic to the early-production model. Also has Commander-style hammer. Checkered walnut grips, polished blue finish. Reintroduced 1993. Imported from Belgium by Browning.
Price: 9mm only **$659.95**

BROWNING BDM DA AUTO PISTOL **Caliber:** 9mm Para., 10-shot magazine. **Barrel:** 4.73″ **Weight:** 31 oz. **Length:** 7.85″ overall. **Stocks:** Moulded black composition; checkered, with thumbrest on both sides. **Sights:** Low profile removable blade front, rear screw adjustable for windage. **Features:** Mode selector allows switching from DA pistol to "revolver" mode via a switch on the slide. Decocking lever/safety on the frame. Two redundant, passive, internal safety systems. All steel frame; matte black finish. Introduced 1991. Made in the U.S. From Browning.
Price: **$594.95**

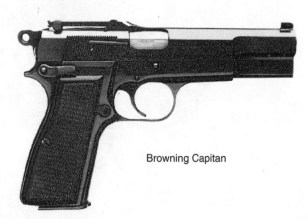

Browning Capitan

Browning BDM

CAUTION: PRICES SHOWN ARE SUPPLIED BY THE MANUFACTURER OR IMPORTER. CHECK YOUR LOCAL GUNSHOP.

Browning BDA 380

Browning BDA 380 Nickel

Browning Buck Mark Plus

Browning Micro Buck Mark Nickel

Browning Micro Buck Mark Standard

BROWNING BDA-380 DA AUTO PISTOL **Caliber:** 380 ACP, 10-shot magazine. **Barrel:** 3¹³/₁₆″. **Weight:** 23 oz. **Length:** 6³/₄″ overall. **Stocks:** Smooth walnut with inset Browning medallion. **Sights:** Blade front, rear drift-adjustable for windage. **Features:** Combination safety and de-cocking lever will automatically lower a cocked hammer to half-cock and can be operated by right- or left-hand shooters. Inertia firing pin. Introduced 1978. Imported from Italy by Browning.
Price: Blue $614.95
Price: Nickel $646.95

BROWNING BUCK MARK 22 PISTOL **Caliber:** 22 LR, 10-shot magazine. **Barrel:** 5¹/₂″. **Weight:** 32 oz. **Length:** 9¹/₂″ overall. **Stocks:** Black moulded composite with skip-line checkering. **Sights:** Ramp front, Browning Pro Target rear adjustable for windage and elevation. **Features:** All steel, matte blue finish or nickel, gold-colored trigger. Buck Mark Plus has laminated wood grips. Made in U.S. Introduced 1985. From Browning.
Price: Buck Mark, blue $249.95
Price: Buck Mark Nickel (nickel finish with contoured rubber
    stocks) $292.95
Price: Buck Mark Plus $304.95

Browning Micro Buck Mark Same as the standard Buck Mark and Buck Mark Plus except has 4″ barrel. Available in blue or nickel. Has 16-click Pro Target rear sight. Introduced 1992.
Price: Blue $249.95
Price: Nickel $292.95
Price: Micro Buck Mark Plus $304.95

Browning Buck Mark Varmint Same as the Buck Mark except has 9⁷/₈″ heavy barrel with .900″ diameter and full-length scope base (no open sights); walnut grips with optional forend, or finger-groove walnut. Overall length is 14″, weight is 48 oz. Introduced 1987.
Price: $379.95

BRYCO MODEL 38 AUTO PISTOLS **Caliber:** 22 LR, 32 ACP, 380 ACP, 6-shot magazine. **Barrel:** 2.8″. **Weight:** 15 oz. **Length:** 5.3″ overall. **Stocks:** Polished resin-impregnated wood. **Sights:** Fixed. **Features:** Safety locks sear and slide. Choice of satin nickel, bright chrome or black Teflon finishes. Introduced 1988. From Jennings Firearms.
Price: 22 LR, 32 ACP, about $109.95
Price: 380 ACP, about $129.95

Browning Buck Mark Varmint

Bryco Model 38

BRYCO MODEL 48 AUTO PISTOLS **Caliber:** 22 LR, 32 ACP, 380 ACP, 6-shot magazine. **Barrel:** 4". **Weight:** 19 oz. **Length:** 6.7" overall. **Stocks:** Polished resin-impregnated wood. **Sights:** Fixed. **Features:** Safety locks sear and slide. Choice of satin nickel, bright chrome or black Teflon finishes. Announced 1988. From Jennings Firearms.
Price: 22 LR, 32 ACP, about $139.00
Price: 380 ACP, about $139.00

Bryco Model 48

BRYCO MODEL 59 AUTO PISTOL **Caliber:** 9mm Para., 10-shot magazine. **Barrel:** 4". **Weight:** 33 oz. **Length:** 6.5" overall. **Stocks:** Black composition. **Sights:** Blade front, fixed rear. **Features:** Striker-fired action; manual thumb safety; polished blue finish. Comes with two magazines. Introduced 1994. From Jennings Firearms.
Price: About $169.00
Price: Model 58 (5.5" overall length, 30 oz.) $169.00

CALICO M-110 AUTO PISTOL **Caliber:** 22 LR. **Barrel:** 6". **Weight:** 3.7 lbs. (loaded). **Length:** 17.9" overall. **Stocks:** Moulded composition. **Sights:** Adjustable post front, notch rear. **Features:** Aluminum alloy frame; flash suppressor; pistol grip compartment; ambidextrous safety. Uses same helical-feed magazine as M-100 Carbine. Introduced 1986. Made in U.S. From Calico.
Price: $359.00

Calico M-110

CENTURY FEG P9R PISTOL **Caliber:** 9mm Para., 10-shot magazine. **Barrel:** 4.6". **Weight:** 35 oz. **Length:** 8" overall. **Stocks:** Checkered walnut. **Sights:** Blade front, rear drift adjustable for windage. **Features:** Double action with hammer-drop safety. Polished blue finish. Comes with spare magazine. Imported from Hungary by Century International Arms.
Price: About $263.00
Price: Chrome finish, about $375.00

Century FEG P9RK

Century FEG P9RK Auto Pistol Similar to the P9R except has 4.12" barrel, 7.5" overall length and weighs 33.6 oz. Checkered walnut grips, fixed sights, 10-shot magazine. Introduced 1994. Imported from Hungary by Century International Arms, Inc.
Price: About $290.00

COLT GOVERNMENT MODEL MK IV/SERIES 80 **Caliber:** 38 Super, 9-shot; 45 ACP, 8-shot magazine. **Barrel:** 5". **Weight:** 38 oz. **Length:** 8½" overall. **Stocks:** Black composite. **Sights:** Ramp front, fixed square notch rear; three-dot system. **Features:** Grip and thumb safeties and internal firing pin safety, long trigger.
Price: 45 ACP, blue $735.00
Price: 45 ACP, stainless $789.00
Price: 45 ACP, bright stainless $863.00
Price: 38 Super, blue $735.00
Price: 38 Super, stainless $789.00
Price: 38 Super, bright stainless $863.00

Colt Government Model

Colt Delta Elite

Colt 10mm Delta Elite Similar to the Government Model except chambered for 10mm auto cartridge. Has three-dot high profile front and rear combat sights, checkered rubber composite stocks, internal firing pin safety, and new recoil spring/buffer system. Introduced 1987.
Price: Blue $807.00
Price: Stainless $860.00

Colt Combat Elite MK IV/Series 80 Similar to the Government Model except has stainless frame with ordnance steel slide and internal parts. High profile front, rear sights with three-dot system, extended grip safety, beveled magazine well, checkerred rubber composite stocks. Introduced 1986.
Price: 45 ACP, STS/B $895.00
Price: 38 Super, STS/B $895.00

COLT COMBAT COMMANDER AUTO PISTOL Caliber: 38 Super, 9-shot; 45 ACP, 8-shot. **Barrel:** 4¹/₄″. **Weight:** 36 oz. **Length:** 7³/₄″ overall. **Stocks:** Checkered rubber composite. **Sights:** Fixed, glare-proofed blade front, square notch rear; three-dot system. **Features:** Long trigger; arched housing; grip and thumb safeties.
Price: 45, blue $735.00
Price: 45, stainless $789.00
Price: 38 Super, stainless $789.00

Colt Lightweight Commander MK IV/Series 80 Same as Commander except high strength aluminum alloy frame, checkered rubber composite stocks, weight 27¹/₂ oz. 45 ACP only.
Price: Blue $735.00

COLT MODEL 1991 A1 AUTO PISTOL Caliber: 45 ACP, 7-shot magazine. **Barrel:** 5″. **Weight:** 38 oz. **Length:** 8.5″ overall. **Stocks:** Checkered black composition. **Sights:** Ramped blade front, fixed square notch rear, high profile. **Features:** Parkerized finish. Continuation of serial number range used on original G.I. 1911-A1 guns. Comes with one magazine and moulded carrying case. Introduced 1991.
Price: $538.00

Colt Model 1991 A1 Compact Auto Pistol Similar to the Model 1991 A1 except has 3¹/₂″ barrel. Overall length is 7″, and gun is ³/₈″ shorter in height. Comes with one 6-shot magazine, moulded case. Introduced 1993.
Price: $538.00

Colt Model 1991 A1 Commander Auto Pistol Similar to the Model 1991 A1 except has 4¹/₄″ barrel. Parkerized finish. 7-shot magazine. Comes in moulded case. Introduced 1993.
Price: $538.00

COLT GOVERNMENT MODEL 380 Caliber: 380 ACP, 7-shot magazine. **Barrel:** 3¹/₄″. **Weight:** 21³/₄ oz. **Length:** 6″ overall. **Stocks:** Checkered composition. **Sights:** Ramp front, square notch rear, fixed. **Features:** Scaled-down version of the 1911A1 Colt G.M. Has thumb and internal firing pin safeties. Introduced 1983.
Price: Blue $462.00
Price: Stainless $493.00
Price: Pocketlite 380, blue $462.00

Colt Combat Elite

Colt Combat Comm. STS

Colt Model 1991 A1

Colt 1991 A1 Compact

Colt Government Model 380

Colt Government Model Pocketlite 380

CAUTION: PRICES SHOWN ARE SUPPLIED BY THE MANUFACTURER OR IMPORTER. CHECK YOUR LOCAL GUNSHOP.

8th ANNUAL EDITION **237**

COLT OFFICER'S ACP MK IV/SERIES 80 Caliber: 45 ACP, 6-shot magazine. **Barrel:** 3½". **Weight:** 34 oz. (steel frame); 24 oz. (alloy frame). **Length:** 7¼" overall. **Stocks:** Checkered rubber composite. **Sights:** Ramp blade front with white dot, square notch rear with two white dots. **Features:** Trigger safety lock (thumb safety), grip safety, firing pin safety; long trigger; flat mainspring housing. Also available with lightweight alloy frame and in stainless steel. Introduced 1985.
Price: Blue $735.00
Price: L.W., blue finish $789.00
Price: Stainless $735.00
Price: Bright stainless $863.00

Colt Officer's ACP

Colt Mustang 380, Mustang Pocketlite Similar to the standard 380 Government Model. Mustang has steel frame (18.5 oz.), Pocketlite has aluminum alloy (12.5 oz.). Both are ½" shorter than 380 G.M., have 2¾" barrel. Introduced 1987.
Price: Mustang 380, blue $462.00
Price: As above, stainless $493.00
Price: Mustang Pocketlite, blue $462.00
Price: Mustang Pocketlite STS/N $493.00

Colt Mustang Plus II Similar to the 380 Government Model except has the shorter barrel and slide of the Mustang. Introduced 1988.
Price: Blue $462.00
Price: Stainless $493.00

Colt Mustang 380

COLT DOUBLE EAGLE MKII/SERIES 90 DA PISTOL Caliber: 45 ACP, 8-shot magazine. **Barrel:** 4½", 5". **Weight:** 39 ozs. **Length:** 8½" overall. **Stocks:** Black checkered Xenoy thermoplastic. **Sights:** Blade front, rear adjustable for windage. High profile three-dot system. Colt Accro adjustable sight optional. **Features:** Made of stainless steel with matte finish. Checkered and curved extended trigger guard, wide steel trigger; decocking lever on left side; traditional magazine release; grooved frontstrap; bevelled magazine well; extended grip guard; rounded, serrated combat-style hammer. Announced 1989.
Price: $727.00
Price: Combat Comm., 45, 4½" bbl. $727.00

Colt Mustang Pocketlite

Colt Double Eagle Officer's ACP Similar to the regular Double Eagle except 45 ACP only, 3½" barrel, 35 oz., 7¼" overall length. Has 5¼" sight radius. Introduced 1991.
Price: $727.00

COLT'S 22 AUTOMATIC PISTOL Caliber: 22 LR, 10-shot magazine. **Barrel:** 4.5". **Weight:** 33 oz. **Length:** 8.62" overall. **Stocks:** Textured black polymer. **Sights:** Blade front, rear drift adjustable for windage. **Features:** Stainless steel construction; ventilated barrel rib; single action mechanism; cocked striker indicator; push-button safety. Introduced 1994. Made in U.S. by Colt.
Price: $248.00

Colt Double Eagle Combat

Colt's 22 Target Pistol Similar to the Colt 22 pistol except has 6" bull barrel, full-length sighting rib with lightening cuts and mounting rail for optical sights; fully adjustable rear sight; removable sights; two-point factory adjusted trigger travel. Stainless steel frame. Introduced 1995. Made in U.S. by Colt's.
Price: . . . . .NA

Colt's 22 Target

Colt's 22 Automatic

COONAN 357 MAGNUM PISTOL **Caliber:** 357 Mag., 7-shot magazine. **Barrel:** 5″. **Weight:** 42 oz. **Length:** 8.3″ overall. **Stocks:** Smooth walnut. **Sights:** Interchangeable ramp front, rear adjustable for windage. **Features:** Stainless and alloy steel construction. Unique barrel hood improves accuracy and reliability. Linkless barrel. Many parts interchange with Colt autos. Has grip, hammer, half-cock safeties, extended slide latch. Made in U.S. by Coonan Arms, Inc.
Price: 5″ barrel $720.00
Price: 6″ barrel $755.00
Price: With 6″ compensated barrel $999.00
Price: Classic model (Teflon black two-tone or Kal-Gard finish, 8-shot magazine, fully adjustable rear sight, integral compensated barrel) $1,400.00

Coonan 357 Magnum Classic

Coonan Compact Cadet 357 Magnum Pistol Similar to the 357 Magnum full-size gun except has 3.9″ barrel, shorter frame, 6-shot magazine. Weight is 39 oz., overall length 7.8″. Linkless bull barrel, full-length recoil spring guide rod, extended slide latch. Introduced 1993. Made in U.S. by Coonan Arms, Inc.
Price: $841.00

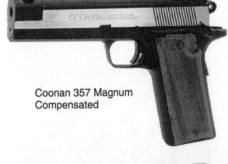

Coonan 357 Magnum Compensated

CZ 75 AUTO PISTOL **Caliber:** 9mm Para., 40 S&W, 10-shot magazine. **Barrel:** 4.7″. **Weight:** 34.3 oz. **Length:** 8.1″ overall. **Stocks:** High impact checkered plastic. **Sights:** Square post front, rear adjustable for windage; three-dot system. **Features:** Single action/double action design; choice of black polymer, matte or high-polish blue finishes. All-steel frame. Imported from the Czech Republic by Magnum Research.
Price: Black polymer finish $539.00
Price: Nickel $569.00

Coonan Compact Cadet 357

CZ 75 Compact Auto Pistol Similar to the CZ 75 except has 10-shot magazine, 3.9″ barrel and weighs 32 oz. Has removable front sight, non-glare ribbed slide top. Trigger guard is squared and serrated; combat hammer. Introduced 1993. Imported from the Czech Republic by Magnum Research.
Price: Black polymer finish $539.00

CZ 75 Semi-Compact Auto Pistol Uses the shorter slide and barrel of the CZ 75 Compact with the full-size frame of the standard CZ 75. Has 10-shot magazine; 9mm Para. only. Introduced 1994. Imported from the Czech Republic by Magnum Research.
Price: Black polymer finish $519.00
Price: Matte blue finish $539.00
Price: High-polish blue finish $559.00

CZ 75 9MM

CZ 85 Auto Pistol Same gun as the CZ 75 except has ambidextrous slide release and safety-levers; non-glare, ribbed slide top; squared, serrated trigger guard; trigger stop to prevent overtravel. Introduced 1986. Imported from the Czech Republic by Magnum Research.
Price: Black polymer finish $549.00

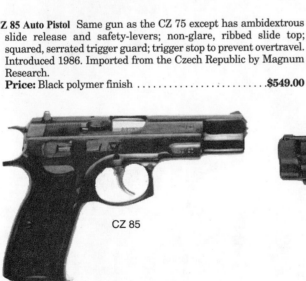

CZ 85

CZ 75 Compact

CAUTION: PRICES SHOWN ARE SUPPLIED BY THE MANUFACTURER OR IMPORTER. CHECK YOUR LOCAL GUNSHOP.

8th ANNUAL EDITION **239**

CZ 85 Combat

CZ 85 Combat Auto Pistol Same as the CZ 85 except has walnut grips, round combat hammer, fully adjustable rear sight, extended magazine release. Trigger parts coated with friction-free beryllium copper. Introduced 1992. Imported from the Czech Republic by Magnum Research.
Price: Black polymer finish **$649.00**

CZ 83 380

CZ 83 DOUBLE-ACTION PISTOL **Caliber:** 32, 380 ACP, 10-shot magazine. **Barrel:** 3.8". **Weight:** 26.2 oz. **Length:** 6.8" overall. **Stocks:** High impact checkered plastic. **Sights:** Removable square post front, rear adjustable for windage; three-dot system. **Features:** Single action/double action; ambidextrous magazine release and safety. Blue finish; non-glare ribbed slide top. Imported from the Czech Republic by Magnum Research.
Price: **$409.00**

Consult our Directory pages for the location of firms mentioned.

Daewoo DP51 Fastfire

DAEWOO DP51 FASTFIRE AUTO PISTOL **Caliber:** 9mm Para., 10-shot magazine. **Barrel:** 4.1". **Weight:** 28.2 oz. **Length:** 7.5" overall. **Stocks:** Checkered composition. **Sights:** $1/8$" blade front, square notch rear drift adjustable for windage. Three dot system. **Features:** Patented Fastfire mechanism. Ambidextrous manual safety and magazine catch, automatic firing pin block. No magazine safety. Alloy frame, squared trigger guard. Matte black finish. Introduced 1991. Imported from Korea by Kimber of America, distributed by Nationwide Sports Dist.
Price: DP51 . . . .**$400.00**
Price: DH40 (40 S&W) **$450.00**

Daewoo DP51C, DP51S Auto Pistols Same as the DP51 except DP51C has 3.6" barrel, $1/4$-inch shorter grip frame, flat mainspring housing, and is 2 oz. lighter. Model DP51S has 3.6" barrel, same grip as standard DP51, weighs 27 oz. Introduced 1995. Imported from Korea by Kimber of America, Inc., distributed by Nationwide Sports Dist.
Price: DP51C **$445.00**
Price: DP51S **$420.00**

Daewoo DP51C Compact

DAEWOO DP52, DH380 AUTO PISTOLS **Caliber:** 22 LR, 10-shot magazine. **Barrel:** 3.8". **Weight:** 23 oz. **Length:** 6.7" overall. **Stocks:** Checkered black composition with thumbrest. **Sights:** $1/8$" blade front, rear drift adjustable for windage; three-dot system. **Features:** All-steel construction with polished blue finish. Dual safety system with hammer block. Introduced 1994. Imported from Korea by Kimber of America, distributed by Nationwide Sports Distributors.
Price: **$380.00**
Price: DH380 (as above except chambered for 380 ACP, 8-shot magazine) **$410.00**

Daewoo DP52

DAVIS P-32 AUTO PISTOL **Caliber:** 32 ACP, 6-shot magazine. **Barrel:** 2.8". **Weight:** 22 oz. **Length:** 5.4" overall. **Stocks:** Laminated wood. **Sights:** Fixed. **Features:** Choice of black Teflon or chrome finish. Announced 1986. Made in U.S. by Davis Industries.
Price: **$87.50**

DAVIS P-380 AUTO PISTOL Caliber: 32 ACP, 6-shot, 380 ACP, 5-shot magazine. **Barrel:** 2.8″. **Weight:** 22 oz. **Length:** 5.4″ overall. **Stocks:** Black composition. **Sights:** Fixed. **Features:** Choice of chrome or black Teflon finish. Introduced 1991. Made in U.S. by Davis Industries.
Price: $98.00

Davis P-380

Desert Eagle Magnum

Desert Industries War Eagle

Desert Industries
Double Deuce

DESERT EAGLE MAGNUM PISTOL Caliber: 357 Mag., 9-shot; 41 Mag., 44 Mag., 8-shot; 50 Magnum, 7-shot. **Barrel:** 6″, 10″, 14″ interchangeable. **Weight:** 357 Mag.—62 oz.; 41 Mag., 44 Mag.—69 oz.; 50 Mag.—72 oz. **Length:** 10¼″ overall (6″ bbl.). **Stocks:** Wraparound plastic. **Sights:** Blade on ramp front, combat-style rear. Adjustable available. **Features:** Rotating three-lug bolt; ambidextrous safety; combat-style trigger guard; adjustable trigger optional. Military epoxy finish. Satin, bright nickel, hard chrome, polished and blued finishes available. Imported from Israel by Magnum Research, Inc.
Price: 357, 6″ bbl., standard pistol $789.00
Price: As above, stainless steel frame $839.00
Price: 41 Mag., 6″, standard pistol $899.00
Price: 41 Mag., stainless steel frame $949.00
Price: 44 Mag., 6″, standard pistol $899.00
Price: As above, stainless steel frame $949.00
Price: 50 Magnum, 6″ bbl., standard pistol $1,249.00

DESERT INDUSTRIES WAR EAGLE PISTOL Caliber: 380 ACP, 8- or 10-shot; 9mm Para., 10-shot; 10mm, 10-shot; 40 S&W, 10-shot; 45 ACP, 10-shot. **Barrel:** 4″. **Weight:** 35.5 oz. **Length:** 7.5″ overall. **Stocks:** Rosewood. **Sights:** Fixed. **Features:** Double action; matte-finished stainless steel; slide mounted ambidextrous safety. Announced 1986. From Desert Industries, Inc.
Price: $795.00
Price: 380 ACP $725.00

DESERT INDUSTRIES DOUBLE DEUCE, TWO BIT SPECIAL PISTOLS Caliber: 22 LR, 6-shot; 25 ACP, 5-shot. **Barrel:** 2½″. **Weight:** 15 oz. **Length:** 5½″ overall. **Stocks:** Rosewood. **Sights:** Special order. **Features:** Double action; stainless steel construction with matte finish; ambidextrous slide-mounted safety. From Desert Industries, Inc.
Price: 22 ....$399.95
Price: 25 (Two-Bit Special) $399.95

E.A.A. WITNESS DA AUTO PISTOL Caliber: 9mm Para., 10-shot magazine; 38 Super, 40 S&W, 10-shot magazine; 45 ACP, 10-shot magazine. **Barrel:** 4.50″. **Weight:** 35.33 oz. **Length:** 8.10″ overall. **Stocks:** Checkered rubber. **Sights:** Undercut blade front, open rear adjustable for windage. **Features:** Double-action trigger system; round trigger guard; frame-mounted safety. Introduced 1991. Imported from Italy by European American Armory.
Price: 9mm, blue $399.00
Price: 9mm, satin chrome $425.00
Price: 9mm Compact, blue, 10-shot $399.00
Price: As above, chrome $425.00
Price: 40 S&W, blue $425.00
Price: As above, chrome $450.00
Price: 40 S&W Compact, 8-shot, blue $425.00
Price: As above, chrome $450.00
Price: 45 ACP, blue $525.00
Price: As above, chrome $550.00
Price: 45 ACP Compact, 8-shot, blue $525.00
Price: As above, chrome $550.00
Price: 9mm/40 S&W Combo, blue, compact or full size ..$595.00
Price: 9mm or 40 S&W Carry Comp, blue $550.00

E.A.A. Witness

E.A.A. EUROPEAN MODEL AUTO PISTOLS Caliber: 32 ACP or 380 ACP, 7-shot magazine. **Barrel:** 3.88″. **Weight:** 26 oz. **Length:** 7³/₈″ overall. **Stocks:** European hardwood. **Sights:** Fixed blade front, rear drift-adjustable for windage. **Features:** Chrome or blue finish; magazine, thumb and firing pin safeties; external hammer; safety-lever takedown. Imported from Italy by European American Armory.
Price: Blue $160.00
Price: Chrome $175.00
Price: Ladies Model $225.00

E.A.A. European

ERMA KGP68 AUTO PISTOL Caliber: 32 ACP, 6-shot, 380 ACP, 5-shot. **Barrel:** 4″. **Weight:** 22¹/₂ oz. **Length:** 7³/₈″ overall. **Stocks:** Checkered plastic. **Sights:** Fixed. **Features:** Toggle action similar to original "Luger" pistol. Action stays open after last shot. Has magazine and sear disconnect safety systems. Imported from Germany by Mandall Shooting Supplies.
Price: $795.00

FEG B9R AUTO PISTOL Caliber: 380 ACP, 10-shot magazine. **Barrel:** 4″. **Weight:** 25 oz. **Length:** 7″ overall. **Stocks:** Hand-checkered walnut. **Sights:** Blade front, drift-adjustable rear. **Features:** Hammer-drop safety; grooved backstrap; squared trigger guard. Comes with spare magazine. Introduced 1993. Imported from Hungary by Century International Arms.
Price: About $312.00

FEG B9R

FEG GKK-45C DA AUTO PISTOL Caliber: 45 ACP, 8-shot magazine. **Barrel:** 4¹/₈″. **Weight:** 36 oz. **Length:** 7³/₄″ overall. **Stocks:** Hand-checkered walnut. **Sights:** Blade front, rear adjustable for windage; three-dot system. **Features:** Combat-type trigger guard. Polished blue finish. Comes with two magazines, cleaning rod. Introduced 1995. Imported from Hungary by K.B.I., Inc.
Price: Blue $399.00
Price: GKK-40C (40 S&W, 9-shot magazine) $399.00

FEG PJK-9HP AUTO PISTOL Caliber: 9mm Para., 10-shot magazine. **Barrel:** 4.75″. **Weight:** 32 oz. **Length:** 8″ overall. **Stocks:** Hand-checkered walnut. **Sights:** Blade front, rear adjustable for windage; three dot system. **Features:** Single action; polished blue or hard chrome finish; rounded combat-style serrated hammer. Comes with two magazines and cleaning rod. Imported from Hungary by K.B.I., Inc.
Price: Blue $349.00
Price: Hard chrome $429.00

FEG GKK-45

FEG SMC-22 DA AUTO PISTOL Caliber: 22 LR, 8-shot magazine. **Barrel:** 3.5″. **Weight:** 18.5 oz. **Length:** 6.12″ overall. **Stocks:** Checkered composition with thumbrest. **Sights:** Blade front, rear adjustable for windage. **Features:** Patterned after the PPK pistol. Alloy frame, steel slide; blue finish. Comes with two magazines, cleaning rod. Introduced 1994. Imported from Hungary by K.B.I., Inc.
Price: $279.00

FEG SMC-22

FEG PJK-9HP

FEG FP9 AUTO PISTOL **Caliber:** 9mm Para., 10-shot magazine. **Barrel:** 5". **Weight:** 35 oz. **Length:** 7.8" overall. **Stocks:** Checkered walnut. **Sights:** Blade front, windage-adjustable rear. **Features:** Full-length ventilated rib. Polished blue finish. Comes with extra magazine. Introduced 1993. Imported from Hungary by Century International Arms.
Price: About **$269.00**

FEG P9R AUTO PISTOL **Caliber:** 9mm Para., 10-shot magazine. **Barrel:** 4.6". **Weight:** 35 oz. **Length:** 7.9" overall. **Stocks:** Checkered walnut. **Sights:** Blade front, rear adjustable for windage. **Features:** Double-action mechanism; slide-mounted safety. All-Steel construction with polished blue finish. Comes with extra magazine. Introduced 1993. Imported from Hungary by Century International Arms.
Price: About **$262.00**

FEG SMC-380 AUTO PISTOL **Caliber:** 380 ACP, 6-shot magazine. **Barrel:** 3.5". **Weight:** 18.5 oz. **Length:** 6.1" overall. **Stocks:** Checkered composition with thumbrest. **Sights:** Blade front, rear adjustable for windage. **Features:** Patterned after the PPK pistol. Alloy frame, steel slide; double action. Blue finish. Comes with two magazines, cleaning rod. Imported from Hungary by K.B.I.
Price: **$279.00**

FEG SMC-918 Auto Pistol Same as the SMC-380 except chambered for 9x18 Makarov. Alloy frame, steel slide, blue finish. Comes with two magazines, cleaning rod. Introduced 1995. Imported from Hungary by K.B.I., Inc.
Price: **$279.00**

GRENDEL P-12 AUTO PISTOL **Caliber:** 380 ACP, 10-shot magazine. **Barrel:** 3". **Weight:** 13 oz. **Length:** 5.3" overall. **Stocks:** Checkered DuPont ST-800 polymer. **Sights:** Fixed. **Features:** Double action only with inertia safety hammer system. All steel frame; grip forms magazine well and trigger guard. Introduced 1992. Made in U.S. by Grendel, Inc.
Price: Blue **$175.00**
Price: Electroless nickel **$195.00**

FEG FP9

Grendel P-12

GLOCK 17 AUTO PISTOL **Caliber:** 9mm Para., 10-shot magazine. **Barrel:** 4.49". **Weight:** 21.9 oz. (without magazine). **Length:** 7.28" overall. **Stocks:** Black polymer. **Sights:** Dot on front blade, white outline rear adjustable for windage. **Features:** Polymer frame, steel slide; double-action trigger with "Safe Action" system; mechanical firing pin safety, drop safety; simple takedown without tools; locked breech, recoil operated action. Adopted by Austrian armed forces 1983. NATO approved 1984. Imported from Austria by Glock, Inc.
Price: With extra magazine, magazine loader, cleaning kit **$608.95**
Price: Model 17L (6" barrel) **$806.67**

Glock 19 Auto Pistol Similar to the Glock 17 except has a 4" barrel, giving an overall length of 6.85" and weight of 20.99 oz. Magazine capacity is 10 rounds. Fixed or adjustable rear sight. Introduced 1988.
Price: **$608.95**

Glock 20 10mm Auto Pistol Similar to the Glock Model 17 except chambered for 10mm Automatic cartridge. Barrel length is 4.60", overall length is 7.59", and weight is 26.3 oz. (without magazine). Magazine capacity is 10 rounds. Fixed or adjustable rear sight. Comes with an extra magazine, magazine loader, cleaning rod and brush. Introduced 1990. Imported from Austria by Glock, Inc.
Price: **$670.41**

Glock 17

Glock 19

Glock 20

CAUTION: PRICES SHOWN ARE SUPPLIED BY THE MANUFACTURER OR IMPORTER. CHECK YOUR LOCAL GUNSHOP.

8th ANNUAL EDITION **243**

Glock 21

Glock 22

Glock 23

Heckler & Koch P7M8

Glock 21 Auto Pistol Similar to the Glock 17 except chambered for 45 ACP, 10-shot magazine. Overall length is 7.59″, weight is 25.2 oz. (without magazine). Fixed or adjustable rear sight. Introduced 1991.
Price: **$670.41**

Glock 22 Auto Pistol Similar to the Glock 17 except chambered for 40 S&W, 10-shot magazine. Overall length is 7.28″, weight is 22.3 oz. (without magazine). Fixed or adjustable rear sight. Introduced 1990.
Price: **$670.41**

Glock 23 Auto Pistol Similar to the Glock 19 except chambered for 40 S&W, 10-shot magazine. Overall length is 6.85″, weight is 20.6 oz. (without magazine). Fixed or adjustable rear sight. Introduced 1990.
Price: **$608.95**

HECKLER & KOCH USP AUTO PISTOL Caliber: 9mm Para., 10-shot magazine, 40 S&W, 10-shot magazine. **Barrel:** 4.25″. **Weight:** 28 oz. (USP40). **Length:** 6.9″ overall. **Stocks:** Non-slip stippled black polymer. **Sights:** Blade front, rear adjustable for windage. **Features:** New HK design with polymer frame, modified Browning action with recoil reduction system, single control lever. Special "hostile environment" finish on all metal parts. Available in SA/DA, DAO, left- and right-hand versions. Introduced 1993. Imported from Germany by Heckler & Koch, Inc.
Price: Right-hand **$636.00**
Price: Left-hand **$656.00**

Heckler & Koch USP 45 Auto Pistol Similar to the 9mm and 40 S&W USP except chambered for 45 ACP, 10-shot magazine. Has 4.13″ barrel, overall length of 7.87″ and weighs 30.4 oz. Has adjustable three-dot sight system. Available in SA/DA, DAO, left- and right-hand versions. Introduced 1995. Imported from Germany by Heckler & Koch, Inc.
Price: Right-hand **$696.00**
Price: Left-hand **$716.00**

HECKLER & KOCH P7M8 AUTO PISTOL Caliber: 9mm Para., 8-shot magazine. **Barrel:** 4.13″. **Weight:** 29 oz. **Length:** 6.73″ overall. **Stocks:** Stippled black plastic. **Sights:** Blade front, adjustable rear; three dot system. **Features:** Unique "squeeze cocker" in frontstrap cocks the action. Gas-retarded action. Squared combat-type trigger guard. Blue finish. Compact size. Imported from Germany by Heckler & Koch, Inc.
Price: P7M8, blued **$1,141.00**

Heckler & Koch USP

HI-POINT FIREARMS JS-9MM AUTO PISTOL Caliber: 9mm Para., 9-shot magazine. **Barrel:** 4.5″. **Weight:** 41 oz. **Length:** 7.72″ overall. **Stocks:** Textured acetal plastic. **Sights:** Fixed, low profile. **Features:** Single-action design. Scratch-resistant, non-glare blue finish. Introduced 1990. From MKS Supply, Inc.
Price: Matte black $139.95

HI-POINT FIREARMS JS-40 S&W AUTO Caliber: 40 S&W, 8-shot magazine. **Barrel:** 4.5″. **Weight:** 42 oz. **Length:** 7.72″ overall. **Stocks:** Checkered acetal resin. **Sights:** Fixed; low profile. **Features:** Internal drop-safe mechansim; all aluminum frame. Introduced 1991. From MKS Supply, Inc.
Price: Matte black $148.95

HI-POINT FIREARMS JS-45 CALIBER PISTOL Caliber: 45 ACP, 7-shot magazine. **Barrel:** 4.5″. **Weight:** 44 oz. **Length:** 7.95″ overall. **Stocks:** Checkered acetal resin. **Sights:** Fixed; low profile. **Features:** Internal drop-safe mechanism; all aluminum frame. Introduced 1991. From MKS Supply, Inc.
Price: Matte black $148.95

Hi-Point JS-40

Hi-Point JS-9MM Compact

HI-POINT FIREARMS MODEL JS-9MM COMPACT PISTOL Caliber: 380 ACP, 9mm Para., 8-shot magazine. **Barrel:** 3.5″. **Weight:** 35 oz. **Length:** 6.7″ overall. **Stocks:** Textured acetal plastic. **Sights:** Combat-style fixed three-dot system; low profile. **Features:** Single-action design; frame-mounted magazine release. Scratch-resistant matte finish. Introduced 1993. From MKS Supply, Inc.
Price: $124.95
Price: With polymer frame (32 oz.), non-slip grips $132.95
Price: 380 ACP $79.95

HUNGARIAN T-58 AUTO PISTOL Caliber: 7.62mm and 9mm Para., 8-shot magazine. **Barrel:** 4.5″. **Weight:** 31 oz. **Length:** 7.68″ overall. **Stocks:** Grooved composition. **Sights:** Blade front, rear adjustable for windage. **Features:** Comes with both barrels and magazines. Thumb safety locks hammer. Blue finish. Imported by Century International Arms.
Price: About...................................$187.00

INTRATEC PROTEC-22, 25 AUTO PISTOLS Caliber: 22 LR, 10-shot; 25 ACP, 8-shot magazine. **Barrel:** 2½″. **Weight:** 14 oz. **Length:** 5″ overall. **Stocks:** Wraparound composition in gray, black or driftwood color. **Sights:** Fixed. **Features:** Double-action only trigger mechanism. Choice of black, satin or TEC-KOTE finish. Announced 1991. Made in U.S. by Intratec.
Price: 22 or 25, black finish $102.00
Price: 22 or 25, satin or TEC-KOTE finish $107.95

INTRATEC TEC-22T AUTO PISTOL Caliber: 22 LR, 10-shot magazine. **Barrel:** 4″. **Weight:** 30 oz. **Length:** 11³/₁₆″ overall. **Stocks:** Moulded composition. **Sights:** Protected post front, front and rear adjustable for windage and elevation. **Features:** Ambidextrous cocking knobs and safety. Matte black finish. Accepts any 10/22-type magazine. Introduced 1988. Made in U.S. by Intratec.
Price: $161.00
Price: TEC-22TK (as above, TEC-KOTE finish) $183.50

Intratec Category 9

INTRATEC CATEGORY 9 AUTO PISTOL Caliber: 9mm Para., 7-shot magazine. **Barrel:** 3″. **Weight:** 21 oz. **Length:** 5.5″ overall. **Stocks:** Textured black polymer. **Sights:** Fixed channel. **Features:** Black polymer frame. Announced 1993. Made in U.S. by Intratec.
Price: About...................................$225.00

INTRATEC TEC-DC9 AUTO PISTOL Caliber: 9mm Para., 10-shot magazine. **Barrel:** 5″. **Weight:** 50 oz. **Length:** 12½″ overall. **Stock:** Moulded composition. **Sights:** Fixed. **Features:** Semi-auto, fires from closed bolt; firing pin block safety; matte blue finish. Made in U.S. by Intratec.
Price: $269.00
Price: TEC-DC9S (as above, except stainless) $362.00
Price: TEC-DC9K (finished with TEC-KOTE) $297.00

Intratec TEC-DC9M Auto Pistol Similar to the TEC-DC9 except smaller. Has 3″ barrel, weighs 44 oz.; 20-shot magazine. Made in U.S. by Intratec.
Price: $245.00
Price: TEC-DC9MS (as above, stainless) $339.00
Price: TEC-DC9MK (finished with TEC-KOTE) $277.00

Jennings J-25

Kahr K9

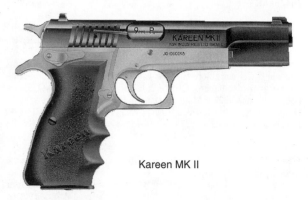

Kareen MK II

Kimber Classic 45 Custom

JENNINGS J-22, J-25 AUTO PISTOLS Caliber: 22 LR, 25 ACP, 6-shot magazine. **Barrel:** 2¹⁄₂″. **Weight:** 13 oz. (J-22). **Length:** 4¹⁵⁄₁₆″ overall (J-22). **Stocks:** Walnut on chrome or nickel models; grooved black Cycolac or resin-impregnated wood on Teflon model. **Sights:** Fixed. **Features:** Choice of bright chrome, satin nickel or black Teflon finish. Introduced 1981. From Jennings Firearms.
Price: J-22, about $79.95
Price: J-25, about $79.95

KAHR K9 DA AUTO PISTOL Caliber: 9mm Para., 7-shot magazine. **Barrel:** 3.5″. **Weight:** 25 oz. **Length:** 6″ overall. **Stocks:** Wraparound textured soft polymer. **Sights:** Blade front, rear drift adjustable for windage; bar-dot combat style. **Features:** Trigger-cocking double-action mechanism with passive firing pin block. Made of 4140 ordnance steel with matte black finish. Introduced 1994. Made in U.S. by Kahr Arms.
Price: $595.00

KAREEN MK II AUTO PISTOL Caliber: 9mm Para., 10-shot magazine. **Barrel:** 4.75″. **Weight:** 32 oz. **Length:** 8″ overall. **Stocks:** Textured composition. **Sights:** Blade front, rear adjustable for windage. **Features:** Single-action mechanism; external hammer safety; magazine safety; combat trigger guard. Blue finish standard, optional two-tone or matte black. Optional Meprolight sights, improved rubberized grips. Introduced 1969. Imported from Israel by J.O. Arms & Ammunition.
Price: ....$425.00 to $575.00
Price: Barak 9mm (has 3.25″ barrel, 28 oz., 6.5″ overall
   length) ....$425.00 to $575.00

KEL-TEC P-11 AUTO PISTOL Caliber: 9mm Para., 10-shot magazine. **Barrel:** 3.1″. **Weight:** 14 oz. **Length:** 5.6″ overall. **Stocks:** Checkered black polymer. **Sights:** Blade front, rear adjustable for windage. **Features:** Ordnance steel slide, aluminum frame. Double-action-only trigger mechanism. Introduced 1995. Made in U.S. by Kel-Tec CNC Industries, Inc.
Price: Blue $300.00
Price: Electroless nickel $330.00
Price: Gray finish $310.00

KIMBER CLASSIC 45 CUSTOM AUTO PISTOL Caliber: 45 ACP, 8-shot magazine. **Barrel:** 5″. **Weight:** 38 oz. **Length:** 8.5″ overall. **Stocks:** Checkered hard synthetic. **Sights:** McCormick dovetailed front, low combat rear. **Features:** Uses Chip McCormick Corp. forged frame and slide, match barrel, extended combat thumb safety, high beavertail grip safety, skeletonized lightweight composite trigger, skeletonized Commander-type hammer, elongated Commander ejector, and 8-shot magazine. Bead-blasted black oxide finish; flat mainspring housing; short guide rod; lowered and flared ejection port; serrated front and rear of slide; relief cut under trigger guard; Wolff spring set; beveled magazine well. Introduced 1995. Made in U.S. by Kimber of America, Inc.
Price: Custom $575.00
Price: Custom Stainless $650.00

Kel-Tec P-11

Kimber Classic 45 Royal Auto Pistol Same as the Custom model except has checkered diamond-pattern walnut grips, long guide rod, polished blue finish, and comes with two 8-shot magazines. Introduced 1995. Made in U.S. by Kimber of America, Inc.
Price: $715.00

Kimber Classic 45 Gold Match Auto Pistol Same as the Custom Royal except also has Bo-Mar BMCS low-mount adjustable rear sight, fancy walnut grips, tighter tolerances. Comes with one 10-shot and one 8-shot magazine, factory proof target. Introduced 1995. Made in U.S. by Kimber of America, Inc.
Price: $925.00

Kimber Classic 45 Gold Match

L.A.R. GRIZZLY WIN MAG MK I PISTOL Caliber: 357 Mag., 357/45, 10mm, 44 Mag., 45 Win. Mag., 45 ACP, 7-shot magazine. **Barrel:** 5.4″, 6.5″. **Weight:** 51 oz. **Length:** 10½″ overall. **Stocks:** Checkered rubber, non-slip combat-type. **Sights:** Ramped blade front, fully adjustable rear. **Features:** Uses basic Browning/Colt 1911A1 design; interchangeable calibers; beveled magazine well; combat-type flat, checkered rubber mainspring housing; lowered and back-chamfered ejection port; polished feed ramp; throated barrel; solid barrel bushings. Available in satin hard chrome, matte blue, Parkerized finishes. Introduced 1983. From L.A.R. Mfg., Inc.
Price: 45 Win. Mag. $920.00
Price: 357 Mag. $933.00
Price: Conversion units (357 Mag.) $228.00
Price: As above, 45 ACP, 10mm, 45 Win. Mag., 357/45 Win. Mag. $214.00

L.A.R. Girzzly MK I

L.A.R. Grizzly 44 Mag MK IV Similar to the Win. Mag. Mk I except chambered for 44 Magnum, has beavertail grip safety. Matte blue finish only. Has 5.4″ or 6.5″ barrel. Introduced 1991. From L.A.R. Mfg., Inc.
Price: $933.00

L.A.R. Grizzly Win Mag 8″ & 10″ Similar to the standard Grizzly Win Mag except has lengthened slide and either 8″ or 10″ barrel. Available in 45 Win. Mag., 45 ACP, 357/45 Grizzly Win. Mag., 10mm or 357 Magnum. Introduced 1987.
Price: 8″ barrel, 45 ACP, 45 Win. Mag., 357/45 Grizzly Win. Mag. $1,313.00
Price: As above, 10″ $1,375.00
Price: 8″ barrel, 357 Magnum $1,337.50
Price: As above, 10″ $1,400.00

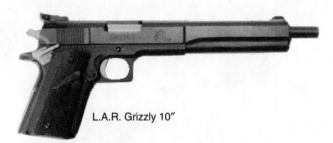

L.A.R. Grizzly 10″

L.A.R. Grizzly 50

L.A.R. Grizzly 50 Mark V Pistol Similar to the Grizzly Win Mag Mark I except chambered for 50 Action Express with 6-shot magazine. Weight, empty, is 56 oz., overall length 10⅝″. Choice of 5.4″ or 6.5″ barrel. Has same features as Mark I, IV pistols. Introduced 1993. From L.A.R. Mfg., Inc.
Price: $1,060.00

Laseraim Series I

LASERAIM ARMS SERIES I AUTO PISTOL Caliber: 10mm Auto, 8-shot, 45 ACP, 7-shot magazine. **Barrel:** 6″, with compensator. **Weight:** 46 oz. **Length:** 9.75″ overall. **Stocks:** Pebble-grained black composite. **Sights:** Blade front, fully adjustable rear. **Features:** Single action; barrel compensator; stainless steel construction; ambidextrous safety-levers; extended slide release; matte black Teflon finish; integral mount for laser sight. Introduced 1993. Made in U.S. by Emerging Technologies, Inc.
Price: Standard, fixed sight $552.95
Price: Standard, Compact (4⅜″ barrel), fixed sight $552.95
Price: Adjustable sight $579.95
Price: Standard, fixed sight, Auto Illusion red dot sight system $649.95
Price: Standard, fixed sight, Laseraim Laser with Hotdot $694.95

Laseraim Arms Series II Auto Pistol Similar to the Series I except without compensator, has matte stainless finish. Standard Series II has 5″ barrel, weighs 43 oz., Compact has 3⅜″ barrel, weighs 37 oz. Blade front sight, rear adjustable for windage or fixed. Introduced 1993. Made in U.S. by Emerging Technologies, Inc.
Price: Standard or Compact (3⅜″ barrel), fixed sight . . . **$399.95**
Price: Adjustable sight, 5″ only **$429.95**
Price: Standard, fixed sight, Auto Illusion red dot sight **$499.95**
Price: Standard, fixed sight, Laseraim Laser **$499.95**

Laseraim Arms Series III Auto Pistol Similar to the Series II except has 5″ barrel only, with dual-port compensator; weighs 43 oz.; overall length is 7⅝″. Choice of fixed or adjustable rear sight. Introduced 1994. Made in U.S. by Emerging Technologies, Inc.
Price: Fixed sight **$533.95**
Price: Adjustable sight **$559.95**
Price: Fixed sight Dream Team Laseraim laser sight . . . **$629.95**

> Consult our Directory pages for the location of firms mentioned.

Llama Max-I

LLAMA MAX-I AUTO PISTOLS **Caliber:** 9mm Para., 9-shot, 45 ACP, 7-shot. **Barrel:** 4¼″ (Compact); 5⅛″ (Government). **Weight:** 34 oz. (Compact); 36 oz. (Government). **Length:** 7⅜″ overall (Compact). **Stocks:** Black rubber. **Sights:** Blade front, rear adjustable for windage; three-dot system. **Features:** Single-action trigger; skeletonized combat-style hammer; steel frame; extended manual and grip safeties. Introduced 1995. Imported from Spain by SGS Importers, International.
Price: 9mm, 9-shot, Government model **$349.95**
Price: As above, Compact model **$349.95**
Price: 45 ACP, 7-shot, Government model **$349.95**
Price: As above, Duo-Tone finish **$366.95**
Price: As above, Compact model **$349.95**

Llama Large Frame

LLAMA IX-O COMPACT FRAME AUTO PISTOL **Caliber:** 45 ACP, 10-shot. **Barrel:** 4¼″. **Weight:** 39 oz. **Stocks:** Black rubber. **Sights:** Blade front, rear adjustable for windage; three-dot system. **Features:** Scaled-down version of the Large Frame gun. Locked breech mechanism; manual and grip safeties. Introduced 1995. Imported from Spain by SGS Importers Int'l., Inc.
Price: Matte finish **$399.95**

LLAMA IX-C LARGE FRAME AUTO PISTOL **Caliber:** 45 ACP, 10-shot. **Barrel:** 5⅛ ″. **Weight:** 41 oz. **Length:** 8½″ overall. **Stocks:** Black rubber. **Sights:** Blade front, rear adjustable for windage; three-dot system. **Features:** Grip and manual safeties, ventilated rib. Imported from Spain by SGS Importers Int'l., Inc.
Price: Matte finish **$399.95**

Llama Small Frame

LLAMA III-A SMALL FRAME AUTO PISTOL **Caliber:** 380 ACP. **Barrel:** 3¹¹/₁₆″. **Weight:** 23 oz. **Length:** 6½″ overall. **Stocks:** Checkered polymer, thumbrest. **Sights:** Fixed front, adjustable notch rear. **Features:** Ventilated rib, manual and grip safeties. Imported from Spain by SGS Importers International, Inc.
Price: Blue **$258.95**
Price: Satin Chrome **$291.95**

LORCIN L9MM AUTO PISTOL **Caliber:** 9mm Para., 10-shot magazine. **Barrel:** 4.5″. **Weight:** 31 oz. **Length:** 7.5″ overall. **Stocks:** Grooved black composition. **Sights:** Fixed; three-dot system. **Features:** Matte black finish; hooked trigger guard; grip safety. Introduced 1994. Made in U.S. by Lorcin Engineering.
Price: **$159.00**

Lorcin L9MM

CAUTION: PRICES SHOWN ARE SUPPLIED BY THE MANUFACTURER OR IMPORTER. CHECK YOUR LOCAL GUNSHOP.

LORCIN L-22 AUTO PISTOL **Caliber:** 22 LR, 9-shot magazine. **Barrel:** 2.5″. **Weight:** 16 oz. **Length:** 5.25″ overall. **Stocks:** Black combat, or pink or pearl. **Sights:** Fixed three-dot system. **Features:** Available in chrome or black Teflon finish. Introduced 1989. From Lorcin Engineering.
Price: About **$89.00**

LORCIN L-25, LT-25 AUTO PISTOLS **Caliber:** 25 ACP, 7-shot magazine. **Barrel:** 2.4″. **Weight:** 14.5 oz. **Length:** 4.8″ overall. **Stocks:** Smooth composition. **Sights:** Fixed. **Features:** Available in choice of finishes: chrome, black Teflon or camouflage. Introduced 1989. From Lorcin Engineering.
Price: L-25 .... **$69.00**
Price: LT-25 .... **$79.00**

Lorcin L-25

LORCIN L-32, L-380 AUTO PISTOLS **Caliber:** 32 ACP, 380 ACP, 7-shot magazine. **Barrel:** 3.5″. **Weight:** 27 oz. **Length:** 6.6″ overall. **Stocks:** Grooved composition. **Sights:** Fixed. **Features:** Black Teflon or chrome finish with black grips. Introduced 1992. From Lorcin Engineering.
Price: L-32 32 ACP **$89.00**
Price: L-380 380 ACP **$100.00**

MITCHELL ARMS SPORT-KING II AUTO PISTOL **Caliber:** 22 LR, 10-shot magazine. **Barrel:** 4.5″, 6.75″. **Weight:** 39 oz. (4.5″ barrel). **Length:** 9″ overall (4.5″ barrel). **Stocks:** Checkered black plastic. **Sights:** Blade front, rear adjustable for windage. **Features:** Military grip; standard trigger; push-button barrel takedown. Stainless steel or blue. Introduced 1992. From Mitchell Arms, Inc.
Price: **$325.00**

Mitchell Sport King II

MITCHELL ARMS ALPHA AUTO PISTOL **Caliber:** 45 ACP, 8- and 10-shot magazine. **Barrel:** 5″. **Weight:** 41 oz. **Length:** 8.5″ overall. **Stocks:** Smooth polymer. **Sights:** Interchangeable blade front, fully adjustable rear or drift adjustable rear. **Features:** Interchangeable trigger modules permit double-action-only, single-action-only or SA/DA fire. Accepts any single-column, 8-shot 1911-style magazine. Frame-mounted decocker/safety; extended ambidextrous safety; extended slide latch; serrated combat hammer; beveled magazine well; heavy bull barrel (no bushing design); extended slide underlug; full-length recoil spring guide system. Introduced 1995. Made in U.S. From Mitchell Arms, Inc.
Price: Blue, fixed sight **$689.00**
Price: Blue, adjustable sight **$725.00**
Price: Stainless, fixed sight **$725.00**
Price: Stainless, adjustable sight **$749.00**

Mitchell Arms Alpha

MITCHELL 45 GOLD SERIES **Caliber:** 45 ACP, 8- or 10-shot magazine. **Barrel:** 5″. **Weight:** 39 oz. **Length:** 8.75″ overall. **Stocks:** Smooth American walnut or checkered black rubber. **Sights:** Interchangeable blade front, drift adjustable combat rear or fully adjustable rear. **Features:** Royal blue or stainless steel. Also available with 10-shot skirted magazine. Bull barrel/slide lockup (no bushing design); full-length guide rod; extended ambidextrous safety; adjustable trigger; beveled magazine well; interchangeable front sight. Introduced 1994. Made in U.S. From Mitchell Arms, Inc.
Price: Blue, drift adjustable sight **$535.00**
Price: As above, stainless **$565.00**
Price: Blue, fully adjustable sight **$575.00**
Price: As above, stainless **$599.00**

Mitchell Wide-Body Gold Series Similar to the Gold Series except comes only with 10-shot magazine (accepts 8- and 13-shot magazines). Blue or stainless steel. Introduced 1994. Made in U.S. From Mitchell Arms, Inc.
Price: Blue, fixed combat sights, black rubber stocks ...**$685.00**
Price: As above, stainless **$710.00**
Price: Blue, adjustable sight, changeable front sight blade,
    smooth walnut stocks **$750.00**
Price: As above, stainless **$750.00**

Mitchell 45 Gold Series

Mitchell American Eagle

MITCHELL ARMS AMERICAN EAGLE AUTO Caliber: 9mm Para., 7-shot magazine. **Barrel:** 4″. **Weight:** 29.6 oz. **Length:** 9.6″ overall. **Stocks:** Checkered walnut. **Sights:** Blade front, fixed rear. **Features:** Recreation of the American Eagle Parabellum pistol in stainless steel. Chamber loaded indicator. Made in U.S. From Mitchell Arms, Inc.
Price: **$695.00**

Mountain Eagle Target

MOUNTAIN EAGLE AUTO PISTOL Caliber: 22 LR, 10-shot magazine. **Barrel:** 6.5″, 8″. **Weight:** 21 oz., 23 oz. **Length:** 10.6″ overall (with 6.5″ barrel). **Stocks:** One-piece impact-resistant polymer in "conventional contour"; checkered panels. **Sights:** Serrated ramp front with interchangeable blades, rear adjustable for windage and elevation; interchangeable blades. **Features:** Injection moulded grip frame, alloy receiver; hybrid composite barrel replicates shape of the Desert Eagle pistol. Flat, smooth trigger. Introduced 1992. From Magnum Research.
Price: Mountain Eagle Compact **$199.00**
Price: Mountain Eagle Standard **$239.00**
Price: Mountain Eagle Target Edition (8″ barrel) **$279.00**

Para-Ordnance P12.45

PARA-ORDNANCE P-SERIES AUTO PISTOLS Caliber: 40 S&W, 45 ACP, 10-shot magazine. **Barrel:** 5″. **Weight:** 28 oz. (alloy frame). **Length:** 8.5″ overall. **Stocks:** Textured composition. **Sights:** Blade front, rear adjustable for windage. High visibility three-dot system. **Features:** Available with alloy, steel or stainless steel frame with black finish (silver or stainless gun). Steel and stainless steel frame guns weigh 38 oz. (P14.45), 35 oz. (P13.45), 33 oz. (P12.45). Grooved match trigger, rounded combat-style hammer. Beveled magazine well. Manual thumb, grip and firing pin lock safeties. Solid barrel bushing. Introduced 1990. Made in Canada by Para-Ordnance.
Price: P14.45E (steel frame) **$745.00**
Price: P14.45R (alloy frame) **$700.00**
Price: P12.45R (3¹/₂″ bbl., 24 oz., alloy frame) **$700.00**
Price: P13.45R (4¹/₄″ barrel, 28 oz., alloy frame) **$700.00**
Price: P12.45E (steel frame) **$745.00**
Price: P16.40E (steel frame) **$745.00**

PHOENIX ARMS MODEL RAVEN AUTO PISTOL Caliber: 25 ACP, 6-shot magazine. **Barrel:** 2⁷/₁₆″. **Weight:** 15 oz. **Length:** 4³/₄″ overall. **Stocks:** Ivory-colored or black slotted plastic. **Sights:** Ramped front, fixed rear. **Features:** Available in blue, nickel or chrome finish. Made in U.S. Available from Phoenix Arms.
Price: **$69.95**

Para-Ordnance P14.45

Para-Ordnance P16.40

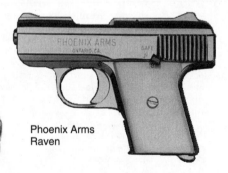

Phoenix Arms
Raven

PHOENIX ARMS HP22, HP25 AUTO PISTOLS **Caliber:** 22 LR, 10-shot (HP22), 25 ACP, 10-shot (HP25). **Barrel:** 3". **Weight:** 20 oz. **Length:** 5½" overall. **Stocks:** Checkered composition. **Sights:** Blade front, adjustable rear. **Features:** Single action, exposed hammer; manual hold-open; button magazine release. Available in satin nickel, polished blue finish. Introduced 1993. Made in U.S. by Phoenix Arms.
Price: $99.95

Phoenix Arms HP22

PSP-25 AUTO PISTOL **Caliber:** 25 ACP, 6-shot magazine. **Barrel:** 2⅛". **Weight:** 9.5 oz. **Length:** 4⅛" overall. **Stocks:** Checkered black plastic. **Sights:** Fixed. **Features:** All steel construction with polished finish. Introduced 1990. Made in the U.S. by PSP.
Price: Blue $249.00
Price: Hard chrome $299.00

ROCKY MOUNTAIN ARMS PATRIOT PISTOL **Caliber:** 223, 10-shot magazine. **Barrel:** 7", with muzzle brake. **Weight:** 5 lbs. **Length:** 20.5" overall. **Stocks:** Black composition. **Sights:** None furnished. **Features:** Milled upper receiver with enhanced Weaver base; milled lower receiver from billet plate; machined aluminum National Match handguard. Finished in DuPont Teflon-S matte black or NATO green. Comes with black nylon case, one magazine. Introduced 1993. From Rocky Mountain Arms, Inc.
Price: With A-2 handle top ....$2,500.00 to $2,800.00
Price: Flat top model ....$3,000.00 to $3,500.00

Phoenix Arms HP25

RUGER P89 AUTOMATIC PISTOL **Caliber:** 9mm Para., 10-shot magazine. **Barrel:** 4.50". **Weight:** 32 oz. **Length:** 7.84" overall. **Stocks:** Grooved black Xenoy composition. **Sights:** Square post front, square notch rear adjustable for windage, both with white dot inserts. **Features:** Double action with ambidextrous slide-mounted safety-levers. Slide is 4140 chrome moly steel or 400-series stainless steel, frame is a lightweight aluminum alloy. Ambidextrous magazine release. Blue or stainless steel. Introduced 1986; stainless introduced 1990.
Price: P89, blue, with extra magazine and magazine loading tool, plastic case $410.00
Price: KP89, stainless, with extra magazine and magazine loading tool, plastic case $452.00

Ruger P89

Ruger P89D Decocker Automatic Pistol Similar to the standard P89 except has ambidextrous decocking levers in place of the regular slide-mounted safety. The decocking levers move the firing pin inside the slide where the hammer can not reach it, while simultaneously blocking the firing pin from forward movement—allows shooter to decock a cocked pistol without manipulating the trigger. Conventional thumb decocking procedures are therefore unnecessary. Blue or stainless steel. Introduced 1990.
Price: P89D, blue with extra magazine and loader, plastic case $410.00
Price: KP89D, stainless, with extra magazine, plastic case $452.00

Ruger KP89D

Ruger P89 Double-Action Only Automatic Pistol Same as the KP89 except operates only in the double-action mode. Has a spurless hammer, gripping grooves on each side of the rear of the slide; no external safety or decocking lever. An internal safety prevents forward movement of the firing pin unless the trigger is pulled. Available in 9mm Para., stainless steel only. Introduced 1991.
Price: With lockable case, extra magazine, magazine loading tool $452.00

Ruger P89 DAO

RUGER P90 AUTOMATIC PISTOL Caliber: 45 ACP, 7-shot magazine. **Barrel:** 4.50″. **Weight:** 33.5 oz. **Length:** 7.87″ overall. **Stocks:** Grooved black Xenoy composition. **Sights:** Square post front, square notch rear adjustable for windage, both with white dot inserts. **Features:** Double action with ambidextrous slide-mounted safety-levers which move the firing pin inside the slide where the hammer can not reach it, while simultaneously blocking the firing pin from forward movement. Stainless steel only. Introduced 1991.
Price: KP90 with lockable case, extra magazine **$488.65**

Ruger KP90

Ruger P90 Decocker Automatic Pistol Similar to the P90 except has a manual decocking system. The ambidextrous decocking levers move the firing pin inside the slide where the hammer can not reach it, while simultaneously blocking the firing pin from forward movement—allows shooter to decock a cocked pistol without manipulating the trigger. Available only in stainless steel. Overall length 7.87″, weight 34 oz. Introduced 1991.
Price: P90D with lockable case, extra magazine, and magazine loading tool **$488.65**

Ruger P93 Compact Automatic Pistol Has 3.9″ barrel, 7.3″ overall length, and weighs 31 oz. The forward third of the slide is tapered and polished to the muzzle. Front of the slide is crowned with a convex curve. Slide has seven finger grooves. Trigger guard bow is higher for better grip. Square post front sight, square notch rear drift adjustable for windage, both with white dot inserts. Slide is 400-series stainless steel, lightweight alloy frame. Available as decocker-only or double action-only. Introduced 1993
Price: KP93DAO (double action only) **$520.00**
Price: KP93 (decocker) **$520.00**

Ruger KP93D

> Consult our Directory pages for the location of firms mentioned.

Ruger KP94 Automatic Pistol Sized midway between the full-size P-Series and the compact P93. Has 4.25″ barrel, 7.5″ overall length and weighs about 33 oz. KP94 is manual safety model; KP94DAO is double-action-only (both 9mm Para., 10-shot magazine); KP94D is decocker-only in 40 S&W with 10-shot magazine. Slide gripping grooves roll over top of slide. KP94 has ambidextrous safety-levers; KP94DAO has no external safety, full-cock hammer position or decocking lever; KP94D has ambidextrous decocking levers. Matte finish stainless slide, barrel, alloy frame. Introduced 1994. Made in U.S. by Sturm, Ruger & Co.
Price: KP94 (9mm), KP944 (40 S&W) **$520.00**
Price: KP94DAO (9mm), KP944DAO (40 S&W) **$520.00**
Price: KP94D (40 S&W) **$520.00**

Ruger KP94

Ruger P94L Automatic Pistol Same as the KP94 except mounts a laser sight in a housing cast integrally with the frame. Allen-head screws control windage and elevation adjustments. Announced 1994. Made in U.S. by Sturm, Ruger & Co.
Price: For law enforcement only ....**NA**

RUGER MARK II STANDARD AUTO PISTOL Caliber: 22 LR, 10-shot magazine. **Barrel:** 4³/₄″ or 6″. **Weight:** 25 oz. (4³/₄″ bbl.). **Length:** 8⁵/₁₆″ (4³/₄″ bbl.). **Stocks:** Checkered plastic. **Sights:** Fixed, wide blade front, square notch rear adjustable for windage. **Features:** Updated design of the original Standard Auto. Has new bolt hold-open latch. 10-shot magazine, magazine catch, safety, trigger and new receiver contours. Introduced 1982.
Price: Blued (MK 4, MK 6) **$252.00**
Price: In stainless steel (KMK 4, KMK 6) **$330.25**

Ruger Mark II Standard

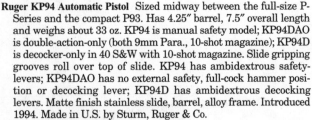

Ruger 22/45 Mark II Pistol Similar to the other 22 Mark II autos except has grip frame of Zytel that matchs the angle and magazine latch of the Model 1911 45 ACP pistol. Available in 4³/₄″ standard and 5¹/₂″ bull barrel. Introduced 1992.
Price: KP4 (4³/₄″ barrel) $280.00
Price: KP512 (5¹/₂″ bull barrel) $330.00
Price: P512 (5¹/₂″ bull barrel, all blue) $237.50

Ruger P512 22/45

SCHUETZEN PISTOL WORKS CREST SERIES PISTOLS Caliber: 45 ACP, 7-shot magazine (standard), 6-shot (4-Star). **Barrel:** 5″ (standard), 4.5″ (4-Star); 416 stainless steel. **Weight:** 39 oz. (standard), 35.7 oz. (4-Star). **Length:** 8.5″ overall (standard). **Stocks:** Checkered walnut. **Sights:** Ramped blade front, LPA adjustable rear. **Features:** Right- or left-hand models available. Long aluminum trigger, full-length recoil spring guide; throated, polished, tuned. Satin stainless steel. Introduced 1993. Made in U.S. by Olympic Arms, Inc.
Price: Right-hand, standard $815.00
Price: Left-hand, standard $1,165.00
Price: Right-hand, 4-Star $875.00
Price: Left-hand, 4-Star $1,135.00

Schuetzen Big Deuce

SCHUETZEN PISTOL WORKS BIG DEUCE PISTOL Caliber: 45 ACP, 7-shot magazine. **Barrel:** 6″; 416 stainless steel. **Weight:** 40.3 oz. **Length:** 9.5″ overall. **Stocks:** Smooth walnut. **Sights:** Ramped blade front, LPA adjustable rear. **Features:** Beavertail grip safety; extended thumb safety and slide release; Commander-style hammer. Throated, polished and tuned. Parkerized matte black slide with satin stainless steel frame. Introduced 1995. Made in U.S. by Olympic Arms, Inc.
Price: $1,035.00

SCHUETZEN PISTOL WORKS GRIFFON PISTOL Caliber: 45 ACP, 10-shot magazine. **Barrel:** 5″; 416 stainless steel. **Weight:** NA. **Length:** 8.5″ overall. **Stocks:** Smooth walnut. **Sights:** Ramped blade front, LPA adjustable rear. **Features:** 10+1 1911 enhanced 45. Beavertail grip safety; long aluminum trigger; full-length recoil spring guide; Commander-style hammer. Throated, polished and tuned. Grip size comparable to standard 1911. Satin stainless steel finish. Announced 1995. Made in U.S. by Olympic Arms, Inc.
Price: ....NA

Schuetzen Enforcer

SCHUETZEN PISTOL WORKS ENFORCER PISTOL Caliber: 45 ACP, 6-shot magazine. **Barrel:** 3.8″; stainless. **Weight:** 36 oz. **Length:** 7.3″ overall. **Stocks:** Smooth walnut with etched black widow spider logo. **Sights:** Ramped blade front, LPA adjustable rear. **Features:** Extended safety, extended slide release; Commander-style hammer; beavertail grip safety; throated, polished, tuned. Parkerized matte black or satin stainless steel finishes. Made in U.S. by Olympic Arms
Price: $825.00

Schuetzen Gun Works Enforcer Carrycomp II Pistol Similar to the Enforcer except has Wil Schueman-designed hybrid compensator system. Introduced 1993. Made in U.S. by Olympic Arms, Inc.
Price: $1,425.00

Seacamp LWS 32

SEECAMP LWS 32 STAINLESS DA AUTO Caliber: 32 ACP Win. Silvertip, 6-shot magazine. **Barrel:** 2″, integral with frame. **Weight:** 10.5 oz. **Length:** 4¹/₈″ overall. **Stocks:** Glass-filled nylon. **Sights:** Smooth, no-snag, contoured slide and barrel top. **Features:** Aircraft quality 17-4 PH stainless steel. Inertia-operated firing pin. Hammer fired double-action only. Hammer automatically follows slide down to safety rest position after each shot—no manual safety needed. Magazine safety disconnector. Polished stainless. Introduced 1985. From L.W. Seecamp.
Price: $375.00

SIG P-210-2 AUTO PISTOL Caliber: 7.65mm or 9mm Para., 8-shot magazine. **Barrel:** 4³/₄″. **Weight:** 31³/₄ oz. (9mm). **Length:** 8¹/₂″ overall. **Stocks:** Checkered black composition. **Sights:** Blade front, rear adjustable for windage. **Features:** Lanyard loop; matte finish. Conversion unit for 22 LR available. Imported from Switzerland by Mandall Shooting Supplies.
Price: P-210-2 Service Pistol $3,500.00

CAUTION: PRICES SHOWN ARE SUPPLIED BY THE MANUFACTURER OR IMPORTER. CHECK YOUR LOCAL GUNSHOP.

8th ANNUAL EDITION **253**

SIG P-210-6 AUTO PISTOL Caliber: 9mm Para., 8-shot magazine. **Barrel:** 4³/₄″. **Weight:** 36.2 oz. **Length:** 8¹/₂″ overall. **Stocks:** Checkered black plastic; walnut optional. **Sights:** Blade front, micro. adjustable rear for windage and elevation. **Features:** Adjustable trigger stop; target trigger; ribbed frontstrap; sand-blasted finish. Conversion unit for 22 LR consists of barrel, recoil spring, slide and magazine. Imported from Switzerland by Mandall Shooting Supplies.
Price: P-210-6 . . . .**$3,700.00**
Price: P-210-5 Target **$3,700.00**

SIG Sauer P220 American

SIG SAUER P220 "AMERICAN" AUTO PISTOL Caliber: 38 Super, 45 ACP, (9-shot in 38 Super, 7 in 45). **Barrel:** 4³/₈″. **Weight:** 28¹/₄ oz. (9mm). **Length:** 7³/₄″ overall. **Stocks:** Checkered black plastic. **Sights:** Blade front, drift adjustable rear for windage. **Features:** Double action. De-cocking lever permits lowering hammer onto locked firing pin. Squared combat-type trigger guard. Slide stays open after last shot. Imported from Germany by SIGARMS, Inc.
Price: "American," blue (side-button magazine release, 45 ACP only) **$805.00**
Price: 45 ACP, blue, Siglite night sights **$905.00**
Price: K-Kote finish **$850.00**
Price: K-Kote, Siglite night sights **$950.00**

SIG Sauer P225

SIG SAUER P225 DA AUTO PISTOL Caliber: 9mm Para., 8-shot magazine. **Barrel:** 3.8″. **Weight:** 26 oz. **Length:** 7³/₃₂″ overall. **Stocks:** Checkered black plastic. **Sights:** Blade front, rear adjustable for windage. Optional Siglite night sights. **Features:** Double action. De-cocking lever permits lowering hammer onto locked firing pin. Square combat-type trigger guard. Shortened, lightened version of P220. Imported from Germany by SIGARMS, Inc.
Price: Blue, SA/DA or DAO **$780.00**
Price: With Siglite night sights, blue, SA/DA or DAO . . .**$880.00**
Price: K-Kote finish **$850.00**
Price: K-Kote with Siglite night sights **$950.00**

SIG Sauer P226

SIG Sauer P226 DA Auto Pistol Similar to the P220 pistol except has 4.4″ barrel, and weighs 26¹/₂ oz. 9mm only. Imported from Germany by SIGARMS, Inc.
Price: Blue **$825.00**
Price: With Siglite night sights **$930.00**
Price: Blue, double-action only **$825.00**
Price: Blue, double-action only, Siglite night sights **$930.00**
Price: K-Kote finish **$875.00**
Price: K-Kote, Siglite night sights **$975.00**
Price: K-Kote, double-action only **$875.00**
Price: K-Kote, double-action only, Siglite night sights . . .**$975.00**

SIG Sauer P228 DA Auto Pistol Similar to the P226 except has 3.86″ barrel, with 7.08″ overall length and 3.35″ height. Chambered for 9mm Para. only, 10-shot magazine. Weight is 29.1 oz. with empty magazine. Introduced 1989. Imported from Germany by SIGARMS, Inc.
Price: Blue **$825.00**
Price: Blue, with Siglite night sights **$930.00**
Price: Blue, double-action only **$825.00**
Price: Blue, double-action only, Siglite night sights **$930.00**
Price: K-Kote finish **$875.00**
Price: K-Kote, Siglite night sights **$975.00**
Price: K-Kote, double-action only **$875.00**
Price: K-Kote, double-action only, Siglite night sights . . .**$975.00**

SIG Sauer P228

SIG Sauer P229 DA Auto Pistol Similar to the P228 except chambered for 9mm Para., 40 S&W, 357 SIG. Has 3.86″ barrel, 7.08″ overall length and 3.35″ height. Weight is 30.5 oz. Introduced 1991. Frame made in Germany, stainless steel slide assembly made in U.S.; pistol assembled in U.S. From SIGARMS, Inc.
Price: Blue **$875.00**
Price: Blue, double-action only **$875.00**
Price: With Siglite night sights **$975.00**

　　　CAUTION: PRICES SHOWN ARE SUPPLIED BY THE MANUFACTURER OR IMPORTER. CHECK YOUR LOCAL GUNSHOP.

SIG SAUER P230 DA AUTO PISTOL **Caliber:** 380 ACP, 7-shot. **Barrel:** 3³/₄″. **Weight:** 16 oz. **Length:** 6¹/₂″ overall. **Stocks:** Checkered black plastic. **Sights:** Blade front, rear adjustable for windage. **Features:** Double action. Same basic action design as P220. Blowback operation, stationary barrel. Introduced 1977. Imported from Germany by SIGARMS, Inc.
Price: Blue $510.00
Price: In stainless steel (P230 SL) $595.00

SIG Sauer P230

SMITH & WESSON MODEL 422, 622 AUTO **Caliber:** 22 LR, 10-shot magazine. **Barrel:** 4¹/₂″, 6″. **Weight:** 22 oz. (4¹/₂″ bbl.). **Length:** 7¹/₂″ overall (4¹/₂″ bbl.). **Stocks:** Checkered simulated woodgrain polymer. **Sights:** Field—serrated ramp front, fixed rear; Target—serrated ramp front, adjustable rear. **Features:** Aluminum frame, steel slide, brushed stainless steel or blue finish; internal hammer. Introduced 1987. Model 2206 introduced 1990.
Price: Blue, 4¹/₂″, 6″, fixed sight $235.00
Price: As above, adjustable sight $290.00
Price: Stainless (Model 622), 4¹/₂″, 6″, fixed sight $284.00
Price: As above, adjustable sight $337.00

Smith & Wesson Model 422

Smith & Wesson Model 2214 Sportsman Auto Similar to the Model 422 except has 3″ barrel, 8-shot magazine; dovetail Patridge front sight with white dot, fixed rear with two white dots; matte blue finish, black composition grips with checkered panels. Overall length 6¹/₈″, weight 18 oz. Introduced 1990.
Price: $269.00
Price: Model 2213 (stainless steel) $314.00

Smith & Wesson Model 2206 Auto Similar to the Model 422/622 except made entirely of stainless steel with non-reflective finish. Weight is 35 oz. with 4¹/₂″ barrel, 39 oz. with 6″ barrel. Introduced 1990.
Price: With fixed sight $327.00
Price: With adjustable sight $385.00

Smith & Wesson Model 2214

Smith & Wesson Model 2206 Target Auto Same as the Model 2206 except 6″ barrel only; Millett Series 100 fully adjustable sight system; Patridge front sight; smooth contoured Herrett walnut target grips with thumbrest; serrated trigger with adjustable stop. Frame is bead-blasted along sighting plane, drilled and tapped for optics mount. Introduced 1994. Made in U.S. by Smith & Wesson.
Price: $433.00

SMITH & WESSON MODEL 909, 910 DA AUTO PISTOLS **Caliber:** 9mm Para., 10-shot magazine. **Barrel:** 4″. **Weight:** 28 oz. **Length:** 7³/₈″ overall. **Stocks:** One-piece Xenoy, wraparound with straight backstrap. **Sights:** Post front with white dot, fixed two-dot rear. **Features:** Alloy frame, blue carbon steel slide. Slide-mounted decocking lever. Introduced 1995.
Price: Model 910 . . . .$467.00
Price: Model 909 (has 9-shot magazine, curved backstrap, 27 oz.) $443.00

Smith & Wesson Model 411 DA Auto Pistol Same as the Model 910 except chambered for 40 S&W, 10-shot magazine. Alloy frame, blue carbon steel slide. Introduced 1994. Made in U.S. by Smith & Wesson.
Price: $525.00

Smith & Wesson Model 910

SMITH & WESSON MODEL 3913/3914 DOUBLE ACTIONS **Caliber:** 9mm Para., 8-shot magazine. **Barrel:** 3¹/₂″. **Weight:** 26 oz. **Length:** 6¹³/₁₆″ overall. **Stocks:** One-piece Delrin wraparound, textured surface. **Sights:** Post front with white dot, Novak LoMount Carry with two dots, adjustable for windage. **Features:** Aluminum alloy frame, stainless slide (M3913) or blue steel slide (M3914). Bobbed hammer with no half-cock notch; smooth .304″ trigger with rounded edges. Straight backstrap. Extra magazine included. Introduced 1989.
Price: Model 3913 . . . .$622.00
Price: Model 3914 . . . .$562.00

CAUTION: PRICES SHOWN ARE SUPPLIED BY THE MANUFACTURER OR IMPORTER. CHECK YOUR LOCAL GUNSHOP.

8th ANNUAL EDITION **255**

Smith & Wesson Model 3913 LadySmith Auto Similar to the standard Model 3913/3914 except has frame that is upswept at the front, rounded trigger guard. Comes in frosted stainless steel with matching gray grips. Grips are ergonomically correct for a woman's hand. Novak LoMount Carry rear sight adjustable for windage, smooth edges for snag resistance. Extra magazine included. Introduced 1990.
Price: **$640.00**

Smith & Wesson Model 3953DA Pistol Same as the Models 3913/3914 except double-action only. Model 3953 has stainless slide with alloy frame. Overall length 7"; weight 25.5 oz. Extra magazine included. Introduced 1990.
Price: **$622.00**

Smith & Wesson 3913 LadySmith

SMITH & WESSON MODEL 4006 DA AUTO Caliber: 40 S&W, 10-shot magazine. **Barrel:** 4". **Weight:** 38.5 oz. **Length:** 7⁷/₈" overall. **Stocks:** Xenoy wraparound with checkered panels. **Sights:** Replaceable post front with white dot, Novak LoMount Carry fixed rear with two white dots, or micro. click adjustable rear with two white dots. **Features:** Stainless steel construction with non-reflective finish. Straight back-strap. Extra magazine included. Introduced 1990.
Price: With adjustable sights **$775.00**
Price: With fixed sight **$745.00**
Price: With fixed night sights **$855.00**

Smith & Wesson Model 4046 DA Pistol Similar to the Model 4006 except is double-action only. Has a semi-bobbed hammer, smooth trigger, 4" barrel; Novak LoMount Carry rear sight, post front with white dot. Overall length is 7¹/₂", weight 28 oz. Extra magazine included. Introduced 1991.
Price: **$745.00**
Price: With fixed night sights **$855.00**

Smith & Wesson 4006

Smith & Wesson Model 4053

SMITH & WESSON MODEL 4013, 4053 AUTOS Caliber: 40 S&W, 8-shot magazine. **Barrel:** 3¹/₂". **Weight:** 26 oz. **Length:** 7" overall. **Stocks:** One-piece Xenoy wraparound with straight backstrap. **Sights:** Post front with white dot, fixed Novak LoMount Carry rear with two white dots. **Features:** Model 4013 is traditional double action; Model 4053 is double-action only; stainless slide on alloy frame. Introduced 1991.
Price: Model 4013 . . . . **$722.00**
Price: Model 4053 . . . . **$722.00**

SMITH & WESSON MODEL 4500 SERIES AUTOS Caliber: 45 ACP, 7-shot (M4516), 8-shot magazine for M4506, 4566/4586. **Barrel:** 3³/₄" (M4516), 5" (M4506). **Weight:** 41 oz. (4506). **Length:** 7¹/₈" overall (4516). **Stocks:** Xenoy one-piece wraparound, arched or straight backstrap on M4506, straight only on M4516. **Sights:** Post front with white dot, adjustable or fixed Novak LoMount Carry on M4506. **Features:** M4506 has serrated hammer spur. Extra magazine included. Contact Smith & Wesson for complete data. Introduced 1989.
Price: Model 4506, fixed sight **$774.00**
Price: Model 4506, adjustable sight **$806.00**
Price: Model 4516, fixed sight **$774.00**
Price: Model 4566 (stainless, 4¹/₄", traditional DA, ambidextrous safety, fixed sight) **$774.00**
Price: Model 4586 (stainless, 4¹/₄", DA only) **$774.00**

Smith & Wesson Model 4506

SMITH & WESSON MODEL 5900 SERIES AUTO PISTOLS Caliber: 9mm Para., 10-shot magazine. **Barrel:** 4″. **Weight:** 28½ to 37½ oz. (fixed sight); 38 oz. (adj. sight). **Length:** 7½″ overall. **Stocks:** Xenoy wraparound with curved backstrap. **Sights:** Post front with white dot, fixed or fully adjustable with two white dots. **Features:** All stainless, stainless and alloy or carbon steel and alloy construction. Smooth .304″ trigger, .260″ serrated hammer. Extra magazine included. Introduced 1989.
Price: Model 5903 (stainless, alloy frame, traditional DA, fixed sight, ambidextrous safety) **$690.00**
Price: Model 5904 (blue, alloy frame, traditional DA, adjustable sight, ambidextrous safety) **$642.00**
Price: Model 5906 (stainless, traditional DA, adjustable sight, ambidextrous safety) **$742.00**
Price: As above, fixed sight **$707.00**
Price: With fixed night sights **$817.00**
Price: Model 5946 (as above, stainless frame and slide) .**$707.00**

Smith & Wesson 5946

Smith & Wesson Model 6904/6906 Double-Action Autos Similar to the Models 5904/5906 except with 3½″ barrel, 10-shot magazine, fixed rear sight, .260″ bobbed hammer. Extra magazine included. Introduced 1989.
Price: Model 6904, blue **$614.00**
Price: Model 6906, stainless **$677.00**
Price: Model 6906 with fixed night sights **$788.00**
Price: Model 6946 (stainless, DA only, fixed sights) **$677.00**

Smith & Wesson 6904

> Consult our Directory pages for the location of firms mentioned.

SMITH & WESSON SIGMA SW380 AUTO PISTOL Caliber: 380 ACP, 6-shot magazine. **Barrel:** 3″. **Weight:** 14 oz. **Length:** 5.8″ overall. **Stocks:** Integral. **Sights:** Fixed groove in the slide. **Features:** Polymer frame; double-action-only trigger mechanism; grooved/serrated front and rear straps; two passive safeties. Introduced 1995. Made in U.S. by Smith & Wesson.
Price: **$308.00**

Smith & Wesson 6906

SMITH & WESSON SIGMA SERIES PISTOLS Caliber: 9mm Para., 40 S&W, 10-shot magazine. **Barrel:** 4.5″. **Weight:** 26 oz. **Length:** 7.4″ overall. **Stocks:** Integral. **Sights:** White dot front, fixed rear; three-dot system. Tritium night sights available. **Features:** Ergonomic polymer frame; low barrel centerline; internal striker firing system; corrosion-resistant slide; Teflon-filled, electroless-nickel coated magazine. Introduced 1994. Made in U.S. by Smith & Wesson.
Price: Model SW9F (9mm Para.) **$593.00**
Price: Model SW40F (40 S&W) **$593.00**
Price: Model Compact, SW9C, SW40C (4″ bbl., 24.4 oz.) **$593.00**
Price: With fixed tritium night sights **$697.00**

Smith & Wesson 6946

Smith & Wesson Sigma

Smith & Wesson Sigma SW380

SPHINX AT-380 AUTO PISTOL Caliber: 380 ACP, 10-shot magazine. **Barrel:** 3.27″. **Weight:** 25 oz. **Length:** 6.03″ overall. **Stocks:** Checkered plastic. **Sights:** Fixed. **Features:** Double-action-only mechanism, Chamber loaded indicator; ambidextrous magazine release and slide latch. Blued slide, bright Palladium frame, or bright Palladium overall. Introduced 1993. Imported from Switzerland by Sphinx USA, Inc.
Price: Two-tone $575.00

Sphinx AT-380

SPHINX AT-2000S DOUBLE-ACTION PISTOL Caliber: 9mm Para., 9x21mm, 40 S&W, 10-shot magazine. **Barrel:** 4.53″. **Weight:** 36.3 oz. **Length:** 8.03″ overall. **Stocks:** Checkered neoprene. **Sights:** Fixed, three-dot system. **Features:** Double-action mechanism changeable to double-action-only. Stainless frame, blued slide. Ambidextrous safety, magazine release, slide latch. Introduced 1993. Imported from Switzerland by Sphinx USA, Inc.
Price: 9mm, two-tone $1,183.00
Price: 9mm, Palladium finish $1,273.00
Price: 40 S&W, two-tone $1,207.00
Price: 40 S&W, Palladium finish $1,297.00

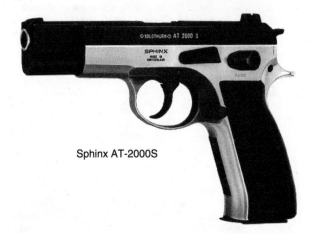

Sphinx AT-2000S

Sphinx AT-2000P, AT-2000PS Auto Pistols Same as the AT-2000S except AT-2000P has shortened frame, 3.74″ barrel, 7.25″ overall length, and weighs 34 oz. Model AT-2000PS has full-size frame. Both have stainless frame with blued slide or bright Palladium finish. Introduced 1993. Imported from Switzerland by Sphinx USA, Inc.
Price: 9mm, two-tone $1,056.00
Price: 9mm, Palladium finish $1,146.00
Price: 40 S&W, two-tone $1,079.00
Price: 40 S&W, Palladium finish $1,169.00

Sphinx AT-2000H Auto Pistol Similar to the AT-2000P except has shorter slide with 3.54″ barrel, shorter frame, 10-shot magazine, with 7″ overall length. Weight is 32.2 oz. Stainless frame with blued slide, or overall bright Palladium finish. Introduced 1993. Imported from Switzerland by Sphinx USA, Inc.
Price: 9mm, two-tone $1,056.00
Price: 9mm, Palladium finish $1,146.00
Price: 40 S&W, two-tone $1,079.00
Price: 40 S&W, Palladium $1,169.00

Sphinx AT-2000P

Sphinx AT2000H

Springfield 1911A1 Mil-spec

SPRINGFIELD INC. 1911A1 AUTO PISTOL Caliber: 9mm Para., 9-shot; 38 Super, 9-shot; 45 ACP, 8-shot. **Barrel:** 5″. **Weight:** 35.6 oz. **Length:** 8⅝″ overall. **Stocks:** Checkered plastic. **Sights:** Fixed three-dot system. **Features:** Beveled magazine well. All forged parts, including frame, barrel, slide. All new production. Introduced 1990. From Springfield Inc.
Price: Basic, 45 ACP, Parkerized $459.00
Price: Standard, 45 ACP, blued $515.00
Price: Basic, 45 ACP, stainless $555.00
Price: Mil-spec (Parkerized), 38 Super $515.00
Price: Lightweight (28.6 oz., matte finish) $515.00
Price: Standard, 9mm, 38 Super, blued $545.00
Price: Standard, 9mm, stainless steel $570.00
Price: Factory Comp, 45 ACP $915.00
Price: As above, 38 Super $949.00

CAUTION: PRICES SHOWN ARE SUPPLIED BY THE MANUFACTURER OR IMPORTER. CHECK YOUR LOCAL GUNSHOP.

Springfield 1911A1 Factory Comp

Springfield Champion Comp

Springfield Champion

Springfield V10 Ultra Compact

Springfield Inc. V10 Ultra Compact Pistol Similar to the 1911A1 Compact except has recoil reducing compensator built into the barrel and slide. Beavertail grip safety, beveled magazine well, "hi-viz" combat sights, Videcki speed trigger, flared ejection port, stainless steel frame, blued slide, match grade barrel, walnut grips. Introduced 1995. From Springfield, Inc.
Price: 45 ACP **$637.00**
Price: Ultra Compact (no compensator), 45 ACP **$549.00**
Price: Ultra Compact MD-1 Lightweight (380 ACP, matte finish) **$449.00**

Springfield Inc. 1911A1 Custom Carry Gun Similar to the standard 1911A1 except has fixed three-dot low profile sights, Videki speed trigger, match barrel and bushing; extended thumb safety, beavertail grip safety; beveled, polished magazine well, polished feed ramp and throated barrel; match Commander hammer and sear, tuned extractor; lowered and flared ejection port; recoil buffer system, full-length spring guide rod; walnut grips. Comes with two magazines with slam pads, plastic carrying case. Available in all popular calibers. Introduced 1992. From Springfield Inc.
Price: **$1,388.00**

Springfield Inc. N.R.A. PPC Pistol Specifically designed to comply with NRA rules for PPC competition. Has custom slide-to-frame fit; polished feed ramp; throated barrel; total internal honing; tuned extractor; recoil buffer system; fully checkered walnut grips; two fitted magazines; factory test target; custom carrying case. Introduced 1995. From Springfield Inc.
Price: **$1,632.00**

> Consult our Directory pages for the location of firms mentioned.

Springfield Inc. 1911A1 Factory Comp Similar to the standard 1911A1 except comes with bushing-type dual-port compensator, adjustable rear sight, extended thumb safety, Videki speed trigger, and beveled magazine well. Checkered walnut grips standard. Available in 38 Super or 45 ACP, blue only. Introduced 1992.
Price: 38 Super **$1,074.00**
Price: 45 ACP **$1,049.00**

Springfield Inc. 1911A1 Champion Pistol Similar to the standard 1911A1 except slide is 4.25". Has low-profile three-dot sight system. Comes with skeletonized hammer and walnut stocks. Available in 45 ACP only; blue or stainless. Introduced 1989.
Price: Blue **$525.00**
Price: Stainless **$565.00**
Price: Blue, comp **$840.00**
Price: Mil-Spec **$459.00**
Price: Champion Comp (single-port compensator) **$840.00**

Springfield Inc. Champion MD-1 Auto Pistol Similar to the 1911A1 Champion except chambered for 380 ACP, 7-shot magazine. Weighs 30 oz., has $3^{1}/_{2}$" barrel, $7^{1}/_{8}$" overall. Three-dot "hi-viz" sights. Blued or Parkerized. Introduced 1995. From Springfield, Inc.
Price: Parkerized **$424.00**
Price: Blued **$429.00**

Springfield Inc. Product Improved 1911A1 Defender Pistol Similar to the 1911A1 Champion except has tapered cone dual-port compensator system, rubberized grips. Has reverse recoil plug, full-length recoil spring guide, serrated frontstrap, extended thumb safety, skeletonized hammer with modified grip safety to match and a Videki speed trigger. Bi-Tone finish. Introduced 1991.
Price: 45 ACP **$958.00**

Springfield Inc. 1911A1 Compact Pistol Similar to the Champion model except has a shortened slide with 4.025" barrel, 7.75" overall length. Magazine capacity is 7 shots. Has Commander hammer, checkered walnut grips. Available in 45 ACP only. Introduced 1989.
Price: Blued **$525.00**
Price: Stainless **$565.00**
Price: Compact Lightweight **$525.00**
Price: Mil-Spec **$459.00**

Springfield High Capacity Factory Comp

Star Firestar

Star Firestar Plus

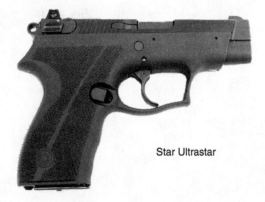

Star Ultrastar

Springfield Inc. 1911A1 High Capacity Pistol Similar to the Standard 1911A1 except available in 45 ACP and 9mm with 10-shot magazine (45 ACP). Has Commander-style hammer, walnut grips, ambidextrous thumb safety, beveled magazine well, plastic carrying case. Introduced 1993. From Springfield, Inc.
Price: 45 ACP **$622.00**
Price: 9mm **$638.00**
Price: 45 ACP Factory Comp **$964.00**
Price: 45 ACP Comp Lightweight, matte finish **$840.00**
Price: 45 ACP Compact, blued **$609.00**
Price: As above, stainless steel **$648.00**

STAR FIRESTAR AUTO PISTOL **Caliber:** 9mm Para., 7-shot; 40 S&W, 6-shot. **Barrel:** 3.39″. **Weight:** 30.35 oz. **Length:** 6.5″ overall. **Stocks:** Checkered rubber. **Sights:** Blade front, fully adjustable rear; three-dot system. **Features:** Low-profile, combat-style sights; ambidextrous safety. Available in blue or weather-resistant Starvel finish. Introduced 1990. Imported from Spain by Interarms.
Price: Blue, 9mm **$469.00**
Price: Starvel finish 9mm **$496.00**
Price: Blue, 40 S&W **$486.00**
Price: Starvel finish, 40 S&W **$513.00**

Star Firestar M45 Auto Pistol Similar to the standard Firestar except chambered for 45 ACP with 6-shot magazine. Has 3.6″ barrel, weighs 35 oz., 6.85″ overall length. Reverse-taper Acculine barrel. Introduced 1992. Imported from Spain by Interarms.
Price: Blue **$516.00**
Price: Starvel finish **$543.00**

Star Firestar Plus Auto Pistol Same as the standard Firestar except has 10-shot magazine in 9mm. Also available in 40 S&W and 45 ACP. Introduced 1994. Imported from Spain by Interarms.
Price: Blue, 9mm **$507.00**
Price: Starvel, 9mm **$533.00**
Price: Blue, 40 S&W **$527.00**
Price: Starvel, 40 S&W **$554.00**
Price: Blue, 45 ACP **$554.00**
Price: Starvel, 45 ACP **$580.00**

STAR ULTRASTAR DOUBLE-ACTION PISTOL **Caliber:** 9mm Para., 9-shot magazine. **Barrel:** 3.57″. **Weight:** 26 oz. **Length:** 7″ overall. **Stocks:** Checkered black polymer. **Sights:** Blade front, rear adjustable for windage; three-dot system. **Features:** Polymer frame with inside steel slide rails; ambidextrous two-position safety (Safe and Decock). Introduced 1994. Imported from Spain by Interarms.
Price: **$547.00**

STOEGER AMERICAN EAGLE LUGER **Caliber:** 9mm Para., 7-shot magazine. **Barrel:** 4″, 6″. **Weight:** 32 oz. **Length:** 9.6″ overall. **Stocks:** Checkered walnut. **Sights:** Blade front, fixed rear. **Features:** Recreation of the American Eagle Luger pistol in stainless steel. Chamber loaded indicator. Introduced 1994. From Stoeger Industries.
Price: **$695.00**
Price: Navy Model, 6″ barrel **$695.00**

Stoeger American Eagle Luger

CAUTION: PRICES SHOWN ARE SUPPLIED BY THE MANUFACTURER OR IMPORTER. CHECK YOUR LOCAL GUNSHOP.

SUNDANCE BOA AUTO PISTOL Caliber: 25 ACP, 7-shot magazine. **Barrel:** 2½″. **Weight:** 16 oz. **Length:** 4⅞″. **Stocks:** Grooved ABS or smooth simulated pearl; optional pink. **Sights:** Fixed. **Features:** Patented grip safety, manual rotary safety; button magazine release; lifetime warranty. Bright chrome or black Teflon finish. Introduced 1991. Made in the U.S. by Sundance Industries, Inc.
Price: **$95.00**

Sundance BOA

SUNDANCE MODEL A-25 AUTO PISTOL Caliber: 25 ACP, 7-shot magazine. **Barrel:** 2.5″. **Weight:** 16 oz. **Length:** 4⅞″ overall. **Stocks:** Grooved black ABS or simulated smooth pearl; optional pink. **Sights:** Fixed. **Features:** Manual rotary safety; button magazine release. Bright chrome or black Teflon finish. Introduced 1989. Made in U.S. by Sundance Industries, Inc.
Price: **$79.95**

Sundance A-25

TAURUS MODEL PT 22/PT 25 AUTO PISTOLS Caliber: 22 LR, 9-shot (PT 22); 25 ACP, 8-shot (PT 25). **Barrel:** 2.75″. **Weight:** 12.3 oz. **Length:** 5.25″ overall. **Stocks:** Smooth Brazilian hardwood. **Sights:** Blade front, fixed rear. **Features:** Double action. Tip-up barrel for loading, cleaning. Blue or stainless. Introduced 1992. Made in U.S. by Taurus International.
Price: 22 LR or 25 ACP **$193.00**
Price: Stainless **$201.00**

Taurus PT 25

TAURUS MODEL PT58 AUTO PISTOL Caliber: 380 ACP, 10-shot magazine. **Barrel:** 4.01″. **Weight:** 30 oz. **Length:** 7.2″ overall. **Stocks:** Brazilian hardwood. **Sights:** Integral blade on slide front, notch rear adjustable for windage. Three-dot system. **Features:** Double action with exposed hammer; inertia firing pin. Introduced 1988. Imported by Taurus International.
Price: Blue **$462.00**
Price: Stainless steel **$526.00**

Taurus PT58

TAURUS MODEL PT 92AF AUTO PISTOL Caliber: 9mm Para., 10-shot magazine. **Barrel:** 4.92″. **Weight:** 34 oz. **Length:** 8.54″ overall. **Stocks:** Brazilian hardwood. **Sights:** Fixed notch rear. Three-dot sight system. **Features:** Double action, exposed hammer, chamber loaded indicator. Inertia firing pin. Imported by Taurus International.
Price: Blue **$511.00**
Price: Blue, Deluxe Shooter's Pak (extra magazine, case)**$542.00**
Price: Stainless steel **$582.00**
Price: Stainless, Deluxe Shooter's Pak (extra magazine, case) **$610.00**

Taurus PT 92AFC Compact Pistol Similar to the PT-92 except has 4.25″ barrel, 10-shot magazine, weighs 31 oz. and is 7.5″ overall. Available in stainless steel, blue or satin nickel. Introduced 1991. Imported by Taurus International.
Price: Blue **$511.00**
Price: Stainless steel **$582.00**

Taurus PT 92

Taurus PT99AF

Taurus PT 99AF Auto Pistol Similar to the PT-92 except has fully adjustable rear sight, smooth Brazilian walnut stocks and is available in stainless steel, polished blue or satin nickel. Introduced 1983.
Price: Blue **$554.00**
Price: Blue, Deluxe Shooter's Pak (extra magazine, case)**$584.00**
Price: Stainless steel **$605.00**
Price: Stainless, Deluxe Shooter's Pak (extra magazine, case) **$659.00**

TAURUS PT 100 AUTO PISTOL Caliber: 40 S&W, 10-shot magazine. **Barrel:** 5″. **Weight:** 34 oz. **Stocks:** Smooth Brazilian hardwood. **Sights:** Fixed front, drift-adjustable rear. Three-dot combat. **Features:** Double action, exposed hammer. Ambidextrous hammer-drop safety; inertia firing pin; chamber loaded indicator. Introduced 1991. Imported by Taurus International.
Price: Blue $522.00
Price: Blue, Deluxe Shooter's Pak (extra magazine, case)$551.00
Price: Stainless $592.00
Price: Stainless, Deluxe Shooter's Pak (extra magazine, case) $622.00

Taurus PT 101

Taurus PT 101 Auto Pistol Same as the PT 100 except has micro-click rear sight adjustable for windage and elevation, three-dot combat-style. Introduced 1991.
Price: Blue $564.00
Price: Blue, Deluxe Shooter's Pak (extra magazine, case)$594.00
Price: Stainless $644.00
Price: Stainless, Deluxe Shooter's Pak (extra magazine, case) $673.00

TAURUS MODEL PT-908 AUTO PISTOL Caliber: 9mm Para., 8-shot magazine. **Barrel:** 3.8″. **Weight:** 30 oz. **Length:** 7.05″ overall. **Stocks:** Checkered black composition. **Sights:** Drift-adjustable front and rear; three-dot combat. **Features:** Double action, exposed hammer; manual ambidextrous hammer-drop; inertia firing pin; chamber loaded indicator. Introduced 1993. Imported by Taurus International.
Price: Blue $511.00
Price: Stainless steel $582.00

Taurus PT-908

TAURUS PT-945 AUTO PISTOL Caliber: 45 ACP, 8-shot magazine. **Barrel:** 4.25″. **Weight:** 29.5 oz. **Length:** 7.48″ overall. **Stocks:** Santoprene II. **Sights:** Drift-adjustable front and rear; three-dot system. **Features:** Double-action mechanism. Has manual ambidextrous hammer drop safety, intercept notch, firing pin block, chamber loaded indicator, last-shot hold-open. Introduced 1995. Imported by Taurus International.
Price: Blue $570.00
Price: Stainless $646.00

Taurus PT 945

WALTHER P-38 AUTO PISTOL Caliber: 9mm Para., 8-shot. **Barrel:** 4^{15}/$_{16}$″. **Weight:** 28 oz. **Length:** 8½″ overall. **Stocks:** Checkered plastic. **Sights:** Fixed. **Features:** Double action; safety blocks firing pin and drops hammer. Matte finish standard, polished blue, engraving and/or plating available. Imported from Germany by Interarms.
Price: $824.00
Price: Engraved models ....**On Request**

Walther P-38

Walther P-5 Auto Pistol Latest Walther design that uses the basic P-38 double-action mechanism. Caliber 9mm Para., barrel length 3½″; weight 28 oz., overall length 7″.
Price: $1,096.00
Price: P-5 Compact $1,096.00

WALTHER PP AUTO PISTOL Caliber: 32 ACP, 380 ACP, 7-shot magazine. **Barrel:** 3.86″. **Weight:** 23½ oz. **Length:** 6.7″ overall. **Stocks:** Checkered plastic. **Sights:** Fixed, white markings. **Features:** Double action; manual safety blocks firing pin and drops hammer; chamber loaded indicator on 32 and 380; extra finger rest magazine provided. Imported from Germany by Interarms.
Price: 32 ....$1,206.00
Price: 380 ....$1,206.00
Price: Engraved models ....**On Request**

Walther PPK American Auto Pistol Similar to Walther PPK/S except weighs 21 oz., has 6-shot capacity. Made in the U.S. Introduced 1986.
Price: Stainless, 380 ACP only $651.00
Price: Blue, 380 ACP only $651.00

Walther PPK/S American Auto Pistol Similar to Walther PP except made entirely in the United States. Has 3.27″ barrel with 6.1″ length overall. Introduced 1980.
Price: 380 ACP only, blue $651.00
Price: As above, stainless $651.00

Walther PPK/S American

WALTHER MODEL TPH AUTO PISTOL Caliber: 22 LR, 25 ACP, 6-shot magazine. **Barrel:** 2¼″. **Weight:** 14 oz. **Length:** 5⅜″ overall. **Stocks:** Checkered black composition. **Sights:** Blade front, rear drift-adjustable for windage. **Features:** Made of stainless steel. Scaled-down version of the Walther PP/PPK series. Made in U.S. Introduced 1987. From Interarms.
Price: Blue or stainless steel, 22 or 25 ....$486.00

Walther TPH

WILDEY AUTOMATIC PISTOL Caliber: 10mm Wildey Mag., 11mm Wildey Mag., 30 Wildey Mag., 357 Peterbuilt, 45 Win. Mag., 475 Wildey Mag., 7-shot magazine. **Barrel:** 5″, 6″, 7″, 8″, 10″, 12″, 14″ (45 Win. Mag.); 8″, 10″, 12″, 14″ (all other cals.). Interchangeable. **Weight:** 64 oz. (5″ barrel). **Length:** 11″ overall (7″ barrel). **Stocks:** Hardwood. **Sights:** Ramp front (interchangeable blades optional), fully adjustable rear. Scope base available. **Features:** Gas-operated action. Made of stainless steel. Has three-lug rotary bolt. Double or single action. Polished and matte finish. Made in U.S. by Wildey, Inc.
Price: ....$1,175.00 to $1,495.00

WILKINSON "SHERRY" AUTO PISTOL Caliber: 22 LR, 8-shot magazine. **Barrel:** 2⅛″. **Weight:** 9¼ oz. **Length:** 4⅜″ overall. **Stocks:** Checkered black plastic. **Sights:** Fixed, groove. **Features:** Cross-bolt safety locks the sear into the hammer. Available in all blue finish or blue slide and trigger with gold frame. Introduced 1985.
Price: $195.00

Wilkinson Sherry

WILKINSON "LINDA" AUTO PISTOL Caliber: 9mm Para. **Barrel:** 8⁵⁄₁₆″. **Weight:** 4 lbs., 13 oz. **Length:** 12¼″ overall. **Stocks:** Checkered black plastic pistol grip, walnut forend. **Sights:** Protected blade front, aperture rear. **Features:** Fires from closed bolt. Semi-auto only. Straight blowback action. Cross-bolt safety. Removable barrel. From Wilkinson Arms.
Price: $533.33

HANDGUNS—COMPETITION HANDGUNS

Includes models suitable for several forms of competition and other sporting purposes.

Auto-Ordnance Competition Model

AUTO-ORDNANCE 1911A1 COMPETITION MODEL Caliber: 45 ACP. **Barrel:** 5″. **Weight:** NA. **Length:** NA. **Stocks:** Black textured rubber wrap-around. **Sights:** Blade front, rear adjustable for windage; three-dot system. **Features:** Machined compensator, combat Commander hammer; flat mainspring housing; low profile magazine funnel; metal form magazine bumper; high-ride beavertail grip safety; full-length recoil spring guide system; extended slide stop, safety and magazine catch; Videcki adjustable speed trigger; extended combat ejector. Introduced 1994. Made in U.S. by Auto-Ordnance Corp.
Price: $615.00

CAUTION: PRICES SHOWN ARE SUPPLIED BY THE MANUFACTURER OR IMPORTER. CHECK YOUR LOCAL GUNSHOP.

8th ANNUAL EDITION **263**

Baer 1911 Ultimate Master

Baer 1911 Bullseye Wadcutter

Benelli MP95E

Bernardelli Model 69

BAER 1911 ULTIMATE MASTER COMBAT PISTOL Caliber: 45 ACP (others available), 10-shot magazine. **Barrel:** 5″; Baer NM. **Weight:** 37 oz. **Length:** 8.5″ overall. **Stocks:** Checkered rosewood. **Sights:** Baer dovetail front, low-mount Bo-Mar rear with hidden leaf. **Features:** Full-house competition gun. Baer forged NM blued steel frame and double serrated slide; Baer triple port, tapered cone compensator; fitted slide to frame; lowered, flared ejection port; Baer reverse recoil plug; full-length guide rod; recoil buff; beveled magazine well; Baer Commander hammer, sear; Baer extended ambidextrous safety, extended ejector, checkered slide stop, beavertail grip safety with pad, extended magazine release button; Baer speed trigger. Made in U.S. by Les Baer Custom, Inc.

Price: Compensated, open sights **$1,996.00**
Price: Uncompensated "Limited" Model **$1,843.00**
Price: Compensated, with Baer optics mount **$2,360.00**

Baer 1911 Ultimate Master "Steel Special" Pistol Similar to the Ultimate Master except chambered for 38 Super with supported chamber (other calibers availoable), lighter slide, bushing-type compensator; two-piece guide rod. Designed for maximum 150 power factor. Comes without sights—scope and mount only. Hard chrome finish. Made in U.S. by Les Baer Custom, Inc.
Price: **$2,570.00**

> Consult our Directory pages for the location of firms mentioned.

BAER 1911 NATIONAL MATCH HARDBALL PISTOL Caliber: 45 ACP, 7-shot magazine. **Barrel:** 5″. **Weight:** 37 oz. **Length:** 8.5″ overall. **Stocks:** Checkered walnut. **Sights:** Baer dovetail front with undercut post, low-mount Bo-Mar rear with hidden leaf. **Features:** Baer NM forged steel frame, double serrated slide and barrel with stainless bushing; slide fitted to frame; Baer match trigger with 4-lb. pull; polished feed ramp, throated barrel; checkered front strap, arched mainspring housing; Baer beveled magazine well; lowered, flared ejection port; tuned extractor; Baer extended ejector, checkered slide stop; recoil buff. Made in U.S. by Les Baer Custom, Inc.
Price: **$1,130.00**

Baer 1911 Bullseye Wadcutter Pistol Similar to the National Match Hardball except designed for wadcutter loads only. Has polished feed ramp and barrel throat; Bo-Mar rib on slide; full-length recoil rod; Baer speed trigger with 3½-lb. pull; Baer deluxe hammer and sear; Baer beavertail grip safety with pad; flat mainspring housing checkered 20 lpi. Blue finish; checkered walnut grips. Made in U.S. by Les Baer Custom, Inc.
Price: **$1,347.00**

Baer 1911 Target Master Pistol Similar to the National Match Hardball except available in 45 ACP and other calibers, has Baer post-style dovetail front sight, flat serrated mainspring housing, standard trigger. Made in U.S. by Les Baer Custom, Inc.
Price: **$1,233.00**

BENELLI MP95E MATCH PISTOL Caliber: 22 LR, 10-shot magazine, or 32 S&W WC, 10-shot magazine. **Barrel:** 4.33″. **Weight:** 38.8 oz. **Length:** 11.81″ overall. **Stocks:** Checkered walnut match type; anatomically shaped. **Sights:** Match type. Blade front, click-adjustable rear for windage and elevation. **Features:** Removable, adjustable trigger. Special internal weight box on subframe below barrel. Cut for scope rails. Introduced 1993. Imported from Italy by European American Armory.
Price: Blue **$550.00**
Price: Chrome **$625.00**
Price: MP90S (competition version of MP95E), 22 LR .**$1,295.00**
Price: As above, 32 S&W **$1,495.00**

BERNARDELLI MODEL 69 TARGET PISTOL Caliber: 22 LR, 10-shot magazine. **Barrel:** 5.9″. **Weight:** 38 oz. **Length:** 9″ overall. **Stocks:** Wrap-around, hand-checkered walnut with thumbrest. **Sights:** Fully adjustable and interchangeable target type. **Features:** Conforms to U.I.T. regulations. Has 7.1″ sight radius, .27″ wide grooved trigger. Manual thumb safety and magazine safety. Introduced 1987. Imported from Italy by Armsport.
Price: **$612.00**

CAUTION: PRICES SHOWN ARE SUPPLIED BY THE MANUFACTURER OR IMPORTER. CHECK YOUR LOCAL GUNSHOP.

COMPETITION HANDGUNS

BERETTA MODEL 89 WOOD SPORT GOLD STANDARD PISTOL
Caliber: 22 LR, 8-shot magazine. **Barrel:** 6″ **Weight:** 41 oz.
Length: 9.5″ overall. **Stocks:** Target-type walnut with thumbrest. **Sights:** Interchangeable blade front, fully adjustable rear.
Features: Single-action target pistol. Matte blue finish. Imported from Italy by Beretta U.S.A.
Price: **$736.00**

Beretta Model 89

BF SINGLE SHOT PISTOL **Caliber:** 22 LR, 357 Mag., 44 Mag., 7-30 Waters, 30-30 Win., 375 Win., 45-70; custom chamberings from 17 Rem. through 45-cal. **Barrel:** 10″, 10.75″, 12″, 15+″. **Weight:** 52 oz. **Length:** NA. **Stocks:** Custom Herrett finger-groove grip and forend. **Sights:** Undercut Patridge front, 1/2-MOA match-quality fully adjustable RPM Iron Sight rear; barrel or receiver mounting. Drilled and tapped for scope mounting. **Features:** Rigid barrel/receiver; falling block action with short lock time; automatic ejection; air-gauged match barrels by Wilson or Douglas; matte black oxide finish standard, electroless nickel optional. Barrel has 11-degree recessed target crown. Introduced 1988. Made in U.S. by E.A. Brown Mfg.
Price: 10″, no sights **$499.95**
Price: 10″, RPM sights **$564.95**
Price: 10.75″, no sights **$529.95**
Price: 10.75″, RPM sights **$594.95**
Price: 12″, no sights **$562.95**
Price: 12″, RPM sights **$643.75**
Price: 15″, no sights **$592.95**
Price: 15″, RPM sights **$675.00**
Price: 10.75″ Ultimate Silhouette (heavy barrel, special forend, RPM rear sight, hooded front, gold-plated trigger) ...**$687.95**

BF Single Shot

BROWNING BUCK MARK SILHOUETTE **Caliber:** 22 LR, 10-shot magazine. **Barrel:** 9⅞″. **Weight:** 53 oz. **Length:** 14″ overall. **Stocks:** Smooth walnut stocks and forend, or finger-groove walnut. **Sights:** Post-type hooded front adjustable for blade width and height; Pro Target rear fully adjustable for windage and elevation. **Features:** Heavy barrel with .900″ diameter; 12½″ sight radius. Special sighting plane forms scope base. Introduced 1987. Made in U.S. From Browning.
Price: **$421.95**

Browning Buck Mark Silhouette

Browning Buck Mark Unlimited Match Same as the Buck Mark Silhouette except has 14″ heavy barrel. Conforms to IHMSA 15″ maximum sight radius rule. Introduced 1991.
Price: **$519.95**

Browning Buck Mark Target 5.5 Same as the Buck Mark Silhouette except has a 5½″ barrel with .900″ diameter. Has hooded sights mounted on a scope base that accepts an optical or reflex sight. Rear sight is a Browning fully adjustable Pro Target, front sight is an adjustable post that customizes to different widths, and can be adjusted for height. Contoured walnut grips with thumbrest, or finger-groove walnut. Matte blue finish. Overall length is 9⅝″, weight is 35½ oz. Has 10-shot magazine. Introduced 1990. From Browning.
Price: **$399.95**
Price: Target 5.5 Gold (as above with gold anodized frame and top rib) **$449.95**
Price: Target 5.5 Nickel (as above with nickel frame and top rib) **$449.95**

Browning Buck Mark Target 5.5

Browning Buck Mark Target 5.5 Nickel

Browning Buck Mark Unlimited

Browning Buck Mark Field 5.5

Browning Buck Mark Field 5.5 Same as the Target 5.5 except has hoodless ramp-style front sight and low profile rear sight. Matte blue finish, contoured or finger-groove walnut stocks. Introduced 1991.
Price: $399.95

Colt Gold Cup National Match

COLT GOLD CUP NATIONAL MATCH MK IV/SERIES 80 Caliber: 45 ACP, 8-shot magazine. **Barrel:** 5″, with new design bushing. **Weight:** 39 oz. **Length:** 8½″. **Stocks:** Checkered rubber composite with silver-plated medallion. **Sights:** Patridge-style front, Colt-Elliason rear adjustable for windage and elevation, sight radius 6¾″. **Features:** Arched or flat housing; wide, grooved trigger with adjustable stop; ribbed-top slide, hand fitted, with improved ejection port.
Price: Blue $937.00
Price: Stainless $1,003.00
Price: Bright stainless $1,073.00
Price: Delta Gold Cup (10mm, stainless) $1,027.00

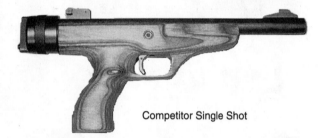

Competitor Single Shot

COMPETITOR SINGLE SHOT PISTOL Caliber: 22 LR through 50 Action Express, including belted magnums. **Barrel:** 14″ standard; 10.5″ silhouette; 16″ optional. **Weight:** About 59 oz. (14″ bbl.). **Length:** 15.12″ overall. **Stocks:** Ambidextrous; synthetic (standard) or laminated or natural wood. **Sights:** Ramp front, adjustable rear. **Features:** Rotary canon-type action cocks on opening; cammed ejector; interchangeable barrels, ejectors. Adjustable single stage trigger, sliding thumb safety and trigger safety. Matte blue finish. Introduced 1988. From Competitor Corp., Inc.
Price: 14″, standard calibers, synthetic grip $379.90
Price: Extra barrels, from $132.95

E.A.A. Witness Gold Team

E.A.A. WITNESS GOLD TEAM AUTO Caliber: 9mm Para., 9x21, 38 Super, 40 S&W, 45 ACP. **Barrel:** 5.1″. **Weight:** 41.6 oz. **Length:** 9.6″ overall. **Stocks:** Checkered walnut, competition style. **Sights:** Square post front, fully adjustable rear. **Features:** Triple-chamber cone compensator; competition SA trigger; extended safety and magazine release; competition hammer; beveled magazine well; beavertail grip. Hand-fitted major components. Hard chrome finish. Match-grade barrel. From E.A.A. Custom Shop. Introduced 1992. From European American Armory.
Price: $2,195.00

E.A.A. Witness Silver Team Auto Similar to the Wittness Gold Team except has double-chamber compensator, oval magazine release, black rubber grips, double-dip blue finish. Comes with Super Sight and drilled and tapped for scope mount. Built for the intermediate competition shooter. Introduced 1992. From European American Armory Custom Shop.
Price: 9mm Para., 9x21, 38 Super, 40 S&W, 45 ACP ...$975.00

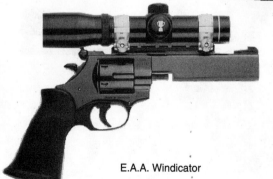

E.A.A. Windicator

E.A.A. WINDICATOR TARGET GRADE REVOLVERS Caliber: 22 LR, 8-shot, 38 Special, 357 Mag., 6-shot. **Barrel:** 6″. **Weight:** 50.2 oz. **Length:** 11.8″ overall. **Stocks:** Walnut, competition style. **Sights:** Blade front with three interchangeable blades, fully adjustable rear. **Features:** Adjustable trigger with trigger stop and trigger shoe; frame drilled and tapped for scope mount; target hammer. Comes with barrel weights, plastic carrying box. Introduced 1991. Imported from Germany by European American Armory.
Price: $299.00

ERMA ER MATCH REVOLVER Caliber: 32 S&W Long, 6-shot. **Barrel:** 6″. **Weight:** 47.3 oz. **Length:** 11.2″ overall. **Stocks:** Stippled walnut, adjustable match-type. **Sights:** Blade front, micrometer rear adjustable for windage and elevation. **Features:** Polished blue finish. Introduced 1989. Imported from Germany by Precision Sales International.
Price: 32 S&W Long $1,248.00

ERMA ESP 85A MATCH PISTOL **Caliber:** 22 LR, 6-shot; 32 S&W, 6-shot magazine. **Barrel:** 6″. **Weight:** 39 oz. **Length:** 10″ overall. **Stocks:** Match-type of stippled walnut; adjustable. **Sights:** Interchangeable blade front, micrometer adjustable rear with interchangeable leaf. **Features:** Five-way adjustable trigger; exposed hammer and separate firing pin block allow unlimited dry firing practice. Blue or matte chrome; right- or left-hand. Introduced 1989. Imported from Germany by Precision Sales International.

Price: 22 LR	$1,695.00
Price: 22 LR, left-hand	$1,735.00
Price: 22 LR, matte chrome	$1,890.00
Price: 32 S&W	$1,790.00
Price: 32 S&W, left-hand	$1,830.00
Price: 32 S&W, matte chrome	$2,095.00
Price: 32 S&W, matte chrome, left-hand	$2,135.00

Erma ESP 85A

Erma ESP Junior Match Pistol Similar to the ESP 85A Match except chambered only for 22 LR, blue finish only. Stippled non-adjustable walnut match grips (adjustable grips optional). Introduced 1995. Imported from Germany by Precision Sales International.

Price: $1,295.00

Erma ESP Junior Match

FAS 607 MATCH PISTOL **Caliber:** 22 LR, 5-shot. **Barrel:** 5.6″. **Weight:** 37 oz. **Length:** 11″ overall. **Stocks:** Walnut wraparound; sizes small, medium or large, or adjustable. **Sights:** Match. Blade front, open notch rear fully adjustable for windage and elevation. Sight radius is 8.66″. **Features:** Line of sight is only ¹¹/₃₂″ above centerline of bore; magazine is inserted from top; adjustable and removable trigger mechanism; single lever takedown. Full 5-year warranty. Imported from Italy by Nygord Precision Products.

Price:	$1,175.00
Price: Model 603 (32 S&W)	$1,175.00

FAS 607 Match

FAS 601 Match Pistol Similar to Model 607 except has different match stocks with adjustable palm shelf, 22 Short only for rapid fire shooting; weighs 40 oz., 5.6″ bbl.; has gas ports through top of barrel and slide to reduce recoil; slightly different trigger and sear mechanisms. Imported from Italy by Nygord Precision Products.

Price: $1,250.00

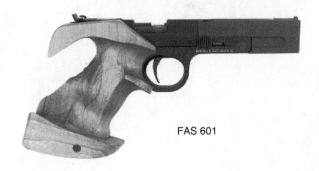

FAS 601

FREEDOM ARMS CASULL MODEL 252 SILHOUETTE **Caliber:** 22 LR, 5-shot cylinder. **Barrel:** 9.95″. **Weight:** 63 oz. **Length:** NA **Stocks:** Black micarta, western style. **Sights:** ⅛″ Patridge front, Iron Sight Gun Works silhouette rear, click adjustable for windage and elevation. **Features:** Stainless steel. Built on the 454 Casull frame. Two-point firing pin, lightened hammer for fast lock time. Trigger pull is 3 to 5 lbs. with pre-set overtravel screw. Introduced 1991. From Freedom Arms.

Price: Silhouette Class	$1,432.00
Price: Extra fitted 22 WMR cylinder	$247.00

Freedom Arms Casull Model 252 Varmint Similar to the Silhouette Class revolver except has 7.5″ barrel, weighs 59 oz., has black and green laminated hardwood grips, and comes with brass bead front sight, express shallow V rear sight with windage and elevation adjustments. Introduced 1991. From Freedom Arms.

Price: Varmint Class	$1,384.00
Price: Extra fitted 22 WMR cylinder	$247.00

Freedom Arms Casull 252 Varmint

GAUCHER GP SILHOUETTE PISTOL **Caliber:** 22 LR, single shot. **Barrel:** 10″. **Weight:** 42.3 oz. **Length:** 15.5″ overall. **Stocks:** Stained hardwood. **Sights:** Hooded post on ramp front, open rear adjustable for windage and elevation. **Features:** Matte chrome barrel, blued bolt and sights. Other barrel lengths available on special order. Introduced 1991. Imported by Mandall Shooting Supplies.

Price: $425.00

CAUTION: PRICES SHOWN ARE SUPPLIED BY THE MANUFACTURER OR IMPORTER. CHECK YOUR LOCAL GUNSHOP.

8th ANNUAL EDITION **267**

GLOCK 17L COMPETITION AUTO Caliber: 9mm Para., 10-shot magazine. **Barrel:** 6.02″. **Weight:** 23.3 oz. **Length:** 8.85″ overall. **Stocks:** Black polymer. **Sights:** Blade front with white dot, fixed or adjustable rear. **Features:** Polymer frame, steel slide; double-action trigger with "Safe Action" system; mechanical firing pin safety, drop safety; simple takedown without tools; locked breech, recoil operated action. Introduced 1989. Imported from Austria by Glock, Inc.
Price: $806.67

GLOCK 24 COMPETITION MODEL PISTOL Caliber: 40 S&W, 10-shot magazine. **Barrel:** 6.02″. **Weight:** 29.5 oz. **Length:** 8.85″ overall. **Stocks:** Black polymer. **Sights:** Blade front with dot, white outline rear adjustable for windage. **Features:** Long-slide competition model available as compensated or non-compensated gun. Factory-installed competition trigger; drop-free magazine. Introduced 1994. Imported from Austria by Glock, Inc.
Price: $806.67

Glock 24 Competition

HAMMERLI MODEL 160/162 FREE PISTOLS Caliber: 22 LR, single shot. **Barrel:** 11.30″. **Weight:** 46.94 oz. **Length:** 17.52″ overall. **Stocks:** Walnut; full match style with adjustable palm shelf. Stippled surfaces. **Sights:** Changeable blade front, open, fully adjustable match rear. **Features:** Model 160 has mechanical set trigger; Model 162 has electronic trigger; both fully adjustable with provisions for dry firing. Introduced 1993. Imported from Switzerland by Hammerli Pistols USA.
Price: Model 160, about $2,034.00
Price: Model 162, about $2,189.00

Hammerli Model 160

HAMMERLI MODEL 208s PISTOL Caliber: 22 LR, 8-shot magazine. **Barrel:** 5.9″. **Weight:** 37.5 oz. **Length:** 10″ overall. **Stocks:** Walnut, target-type with thumbrest. **Sights:** Blade front, open fully adjustable rear. **Features:** Adjustable trigger, including length; interchangeable rear sight elements. Imported from Switzerland by Hammerli Pistols USA, Mandall Shooting Supplies.
Price: About $1,768.00

Hammerli Model 162

Hammerli Model 208s

Hammerli Model 280

Harris-McMillan Wolverine

HAMMERLI MODEL 280 TARGET PISTOL Caliber: 22 LR, 6-shot; 32 S&W Long WC, 5-shot. **Barrel:** 4.5″. **Weight:** 39.1 oz. (32). **Length:** 11.8″ overall. **Stocks:** Walnut match-type with stippling, adjustable palm shelf. **Sights:** Match sights, micrometer adjustable; interchangeable elements. **Features:** Has carbon-reinforced synthetic frame and bolt/barrel housing. Trigger is adjustable for pull weight, take-up weight, let-off, and length, and is interchangeable. Interchangeable metal or carbon fiber counterweights. Sight radius of 8.8″. Comes with barrel weights, spare magazine, loading tool, cleaning rods. Introduced 1990. Imported from Switzerland by Hammerli Pistols USA and Mandall Shooting Supplies.
Price: 22-cal., about $1,558.00
Price: 32-cal., about $1,747.00

HARRIS-McMILLAN WOLVERINE AUTO PISTOL Caliber: 9mm Para., 10mm Auto, 38 Wadcutter, 38 Super, 45 Italian, 45 ACP. **Barrel:** 6″. **Weight:** 45 oz. **Length:** 9.5″ overall. **Stocks:** Pachmayr rubber. **Sights:** Blade front, fully adjustable rear; low profile. **Features:** Integral compensator; round burr-style hammer; extended grip safety; checkered backstrap; skeletonized aluminum match trigger. Many finish options. Announced 1992. Made in U.S. by Harris-McMillan Gunworks, Inc.
Price: Combat or Competition Match $1,700.00

CAUTION: PRICES SHOWN ARE SUPPLIED BY THE MANUFACTURER OR IMPORTER. CHECK YOUR LOCAL GUNSHOP.

High Standard Olympic ISU

High Standard Tournament

High Standard Supermatic Trophy

High Standard Victor

High Standard Supermatic Citation Pistol Same as the Supermatic Trophy except has nickel-plated trigger, slide lock, safety-lever, magazine release, and has slightly heavier trigger pull. Has stippled front grip and backstrap, checkered walnut thumbrest grips, adjustable trigger and sear. Blue finish. Conversion unit for 22 Short available. Reintroduced 1994. From High Standard Mfg. Co., Inc.
Price: $425.00

HARRIS-McMILLAN SIGNATURE JR. LONG RANGE PISTOL
Caliber: Any suitable caliber. **Barrel:** To customer specs. **Weight:** 5 lbs. **Stock:** McMillan fiberglass. **Sights:** None furnished; comes with scope rings. **Features:** Right- or left-hand McMillan benchrest action of titanium or stainless steel; single shot or repeater. Comes with bipod. Introduced 1992. Made in U.S. by Harris-McMillan Gunworks, Inc.
Price: $2,400.00

HIGH STANDARD OLYMPIC ISU PISTOL Caliber: 22 Short, 5-shot magazine. **Barrel:** 6.75"; tapered with integral stabilizer; push-button takedown. **Weight:** 45 oz. **Length:** 10.75" overall. **Stocks:** Checkered walnut. **Sights:** Undercut ramp front, micro-click rear adjustable for windage and elevation. **Features:** Adjustable trigger and sear; stippled front grip and backstrap. Comes with weights and brackets. Reintroduced 1994. From High Standard Mfg. Co., Inc.
Price: $625.00

High Standard Olympic Military Target Pistol Same as the Olympic ISU model except has 5.50" bull barrel with removable stabilizer. High strength aluminum slide, carbon steel frame. Barrel weights and brackets included. Adjustable trigger and sear. Overall blue finish. Reintroduced 1994. From High Standard Mfg. Co., Inc.
Price: $504.00

HIGH STANDARD SUPERMATIC TOURNAMENT PISTOL
Caliber: 22 LR, 10-shot magazine. **Barrel:** 4.5", 5.5"; push-button takedown. **Weight:** 43 oz. **Length:** 8.5" overall. **Stocks:** Black rubber; ambidextrous. **Sights:** Undercut ramp front, micro-click rear adjustable for windage and elevation. **Features:** Slide-mounted rear sight; 5.5" barrel drilled and tapped for scope mount. Blue finish. Reintroduced 1994. From High Standard Mfg. Co., Inc.
Price: $425.00

HIGH STANDARD 10X MODEL TARGET PISTOL Caliber: 22 LR, 10-shot magazine. **Barrel:** 5.5"; push-button takedown. **Weight:** 44 oz. **Length:** 9.5" overall. **Stocks:** Checkered black epoxied walnut; ambidextrous. **Sights:** Undercut ramp front, micro-click rear adjustable for windage and elevation. **Features:** Hand built with select parts. Adjustable trigger and sear; Parkerized finish; stippled front grip and backstrap. Barrel weights optional. Comes with test target, extended warranty. Reintroduced 1994. From High Standard Mfg. Co., Inc.
Price: $790.00

HIGH STANDARD SUPERMATIC TROPHY PISTOL Caliber: 22 LR, 10-shot magazine. **Barrel:** 5.5" or 7.25"; push-button takedown; drilled and tapped for scope mount. **Weight:** 44 oz. **Length:** 9.5" overall. **Stocks:** Checkered walnut with thumbrest. **Sights:** Undercut ramp front, micro-click rear adjustable for windage and elevation. **Features:** Removable muzzle stabilizer; gold-plated trigger, slide lock, safety-lever and magazine release; stippled front grip and backstrap; adjustable trigger and sear. Barrel weights optional. A 22 Short version is available. Reintroduced 1994. From High Standard Mfg. Co., Inc.
Price: $536.00

HIGH STANDARD VICTOR TARGET PISTOL Caliber: 22 LR, 10-shot magazine. **Barrel:** 4.5" or 5.5"; push-button takedown. **Weight:** 46 oz. **Length:** 9.5" overall. **Stocks:** Checkered walnut with thumbrest. **Sights:** Undercut ramp front, micro-click rear adjustable for windage and elevation. **Features:** Full-length aluminum vent rib (steel optional).Gold-plated trigger, slide lock, safety-lever and magazine release; stippled front grip and backstrap; adjustable trigger and sear. Comes with barrel weight. Blue or Parkerized finish. Reintroduced 1994. From High Standard Mfg. Co., Inc.
Price: $532.00

MITCHELL ARMS SHARPSHOOTER II PISTOL Caliber: 22 LR, 10-shot magazine. **Barrel:** 5.5″ bull. **Weight:** 45 oz. **Length:** 10.25″ overall. **Stocks:** Checkered walnut. **Sights:** Ramp front, slide-mounted square notch rear adjustable for windage and elevation. **Features:** Military grip. Slide lock; smooth grip straps; push-button takedown; drilled and tapped for barrel weights. Introduced 1992. From Mitchell Arms, Inc.
Price: Stainless steel, blue or combo $395.00

Mitchell Sharpshooter II

MITCHELL ARMS TROPHY II PISTOL Caliber: 22 LR, 10-shot magazine. **Barrel:** 5.5″ bull, 7.25″ fluted. **Weight:** 44.5 oz. **Length:** 9.75″ overall (5.5″ barrel). **Stocks:** Checkered walnut with thumbrest. **Sights:** Undercut ramp front, click-adjustable frame-mounted rear. **Features:** Grip duplicates feel of military 45; positive action magazine latch; front and rear straps stippled. Trigger adjustable for pull, over-travel; gold-filled roll marks, gold-plated trigger, safety, magazine release; push-button barrel takedown. Introduced 1992. From Mitchell Arms, Inc.
Price: Stainless steel or blue $498.00

Mitchell Arms Citation II Pistol Same as the Trophy II except has nickel-plated trigger, safety and magazine release, and has silver-filled roll marks. Available in satin finish stainless steel or blue. Introduced 1992. From Mitchell Arms, Inc.
Price: $489.00

Mitchell Trophy II

MITCHELL ARMS OLYMPIC II I.S.U. AUTO PISTOL Caliber: 22 Short, 22 LR, 10-shot magazine. **Barrel:** 6.75″ round tapered, with stabilizer. **Weight:** 40 oz. **Length:** 11.25″ overall. **Stocks:** Checkered walnut with thumbrest. **Sights:** Undercut ramp front, frame-mounted click adjustable square notch rear. **Features:** Integral stabilizer with two removable weights. Trigger adjustable for pull and over-travel; blue finish or stainless or combo; stippled front and backstraps; push-button barrel takedown. Announced 1992. From Mitchell Arms.
Price: $599.00

Mitchell Olympic II I.S.U.

MITCHELL VICTOR II AUTO PISTOL Caliber: 22 LR, 10-shot magazine. **Barrel:** 4.5″ vent rib, 5.5″ vent, dovetail or Weaver ribs. **Weight:** 44 oz. **Length:** 9.75″ overall. **Stocks:** Military-type checkered walnut with thumbrest. **Sights:** Blade front, fully adjustable rear mounted on rib. **Features:** Push-button takedown for barrel interchangeability. Bright stainless steel combo or royal blue finish. Introduced 1994. Made in U.S. From Mitchell Arms.
Price: Vent rib, 4.5″ barrel $595.00
Price: Dovetail rib, 5.5″ barrel $650.00
Price: Weaver rib, 5.5″ barrel $675.00
Price: Dual color $675.00

Mitchell Victor II

PARDINI GP RAPID FIRE MATCH PISTOL Caliber: 22 Short, 5-shot magazine. **Barrel:** 4.6″. **Weight:** 43.3 oz. **Length:** 11.6″ overall. **Stocks:** Wrap-around stippled walnut. **Sights:** Interchangeable post front, fully adjustable match rear. **Features:** Model GP Schuman has extended rear sight for longer sight radius. Introduced 1995. Imported from Italy by Nygord Precision Products.
Price: Model GP $995.00
Price: Model GP Schuman $1,395.00

PARDINI K50 FREE PISTOL Caliber: 22 LR, single shot. **Barrel:** 9.8″. **Weight:** 34.6 oz. **Length:** 18.7″ overall. **Stocks:** Wrap-around walnut; adjustable match type. **Sights:** Interchangeable post front, fully adjustable match open rear. **Features:** Removable, adjustable match trigger. Barrel weights mount above the barrel. Introduced 1995. Imported from Italy by Nygord Precision Products.
Price: $995.00

MORINI MODEL 84E FREE PISTOL Caliber: 22 LR, single shot. **Barrel:** 11.4″. **Weight:** 43.7 oz. **Length:** 19.4″ overall. **Stocks:** Adjustable match type with stippled surfaces. **Sights:** Interchangeable blade front, match-type fully adjustable rear. **Features:** Fully adjustable electronic trigger. Introduced 1995. Imported from Switzerland by Nygord Precision Products.
Price: $1,495.00

PARDINI MODEL SP, HP TARGET PISTOLS Caliber: 22 LR, 32 S&W, 5-shot magazine. **Barrel:** 4.7″. **Weight:** 38.9 oz. **Length:** 11.6″ overall. **Stocks:** Adjustable; stippled walnut; match type. **Sights:** Interchangeable blade front, interchangeable, fully adjustable rear. **Features:** Fully adjustable match trigger. Introduced 1995. Imported from Italy by Nygord Precision Products.
Price: Model SP (22 LR) $950.00
Price: Model HP (32 S&W) $1,095.00

Ruger Mark II Target

Ruger Mark II Bull Stainless

Ruger Mark II Bull Blue

Ruger Government Target

Ruger Mark II Government Competition

Schuetzen Matchmaster

RUGER MARK II TARGET MODEL AUTO PISTOL **Caliber:** 22 LR, 10-shot magazine. **Barrel:** 5½", 6⅞". **Weight:** 42 oz. **Length:** 11⅛" overall. **Stocks:** Checkered hard plastic. **Sights:** .125" blade front, micro-click rear, adjustable for windage and elevation. Sight radius 9⅜". **Features:** Introduced 1982.
Price: Blued (MK-514, MK-678) $310.50
Price: Stainless (KMK-514, KMK-678) $389.00

Ruger Mark II Bull Barrel Same gun as the Target Model except has 5½" or 10" heavy barrel (10" meets all IHMSA regulations). Weight with 5½" barrel is 42 oz., with 10" barrel, 51 oz.
Price: Blued (MK-512) $310.50
Price: Blued (MK-10) $294.50
Price: Stainless (KMK-10) $373.00
Price: Stainless (KMK-512) $389.00

Ruger Mark II Government Target Model Same gun as the Mark II Target Model except has 6⅞" barrel, higher sights and is roll marked "Government Target Model" on the right side of the receiver below the rear sight. Identical in all aspects to the military model used for training U.S. armed forces except for markings. Comes with factory test target. Introduced 1987.
Price: Blued (MK-678G) $356.50
Price: Stainless (KMK-678G) $427.25

Ruger Stainless Government Competition Model 22 Pistol Similar to the Mark II Government Target Model stainless pistol except has 6⅞" slab-sided barrel; the receiver top is drilled and tapped for a Ruger scope base adaptor of blued, chrome moly steel; comes with Ruger 1" stainless scope rings with integral bases for mounting a variety of optical sights; has checkered laminated grip panels with right-hand thumbrest. Has blued open sights with 9¼" radius. Overall length is 11⅛", weight 45 oz. Introduced 1991.
Price: KMK-678GC $441.00

SCHUETZEN PISTOL WORKS MATCHMASTER PISTOL **Caliber:** 45 ACP, 7-shot magazine. **Barrel:** 5", 6"; stainless steel. **Weight:** 38 oz. **Length:** 8.5" overall. **Stocks:** Smooth walnut with etched scorpion logo. **Sights:** Ramped blade front, LPA adjustable rear. **Features:** Beavertail grip safety, extended safety, extended slide release, Commander-style hammer; throated, polished, tuned. Finishes: Parkerized matte black, or satin stainless steel. Made in U.S. by Olympic Arms, Inc.
Price: $770.00

Schuetzen Pistol Works Matchmaster Carrycomp I Similar to the Matchmaster except has Wil Schueman-designed hybrid compensator system. Introduced 1993. Made in U.S. by Olympic Arms, Inc.
Price: $1,275.00

SMITH & WESSON MODEL 41 TARGET **Caliber:** 22 LR, 12-shot clip. **Barrel:** 5½", 7". **Weight:** 44 oz. (5½" barrel). **Length:** 9" overall (5½" barrel). **Stocks:** Checkered walnut with modified thumbrest, usable with either hand. **Sights:** ⅛" Patridge on ramp base; micro-click rear adjustable for windage and elevation. **Features:** ⅜" wide, grooved trigger; adjustable trigger stop.
Price: S&W Bright Blue, either barrel **$753.00**

Smith & Wesson Model 41

SPHINX AT-2000C COMPETITOR PISTOL **Caliber:** 9mm Para., 9x21mm, 15-shot, 40 S&W, 11-shot. **Barrel:** 5.31". **Weight:** 40.56 oz. **Length:** 9.84" overall. **Stocks:** Checkered neoprene. **Sights:** Fully adjustable Bo-Mar or Tasco Pro-Point dot sight in Sphinx mount. **Features:** Extended magazine release. Competition slide with dual-port compensated barrel. Two-tone finish only. Introduced 1993. Imported from Switzerland by Sphinx U.S.A., Inc.
Price: With Bo-Mar sights (AT-2000CS) **$1,902.00**
Price: With Tasco Pro-Point and mount **$2,189.00**

Sphinx AT-2000GM Grand Master Pistol Similar to the AT-2000C except has single-action-only trigger mechanism, squared trigger guard, extended beavertail grip, safety and magazine release; notched competition slide for easier cocking. Two-tone finish only. Has dual-port compensated barrel. Available with fully adjustable Bo-Mar sights or Tasco Pro-Point and Sphinx mount. Introduced 1993. Imported from Switzerland by Sphinx U.S.A., Inc.
Price: With Bo-Mar sights (AT-2000GMS) **$2,894.00**
Price: With Tasco Pro-Point and mount (AT-2000GM) **$2,972.00**

Sphinx AT-2000c Competitor

SPRINGFIELD INC. 1911A1 BULLSEYE WADCUTTER PISTOL **Caliber:** 45 ACP. **Barrel:** 5". **Weight:** 45 oz. **Length:** 8.59" overall (5" barrel). **Stocks:** Checkered walnut. **Sights:** Bo-Mar rib with undercut blade front, fully adjustable rear. **Features:** Built for wadcutter loads only. Has full-length recoil spring guide rod, fitted Videki speed trigger with 3.5-lb. pull; match Commander hammer and sear; beavertail grip safety; lowered and flared ejection port; tuned extractor; fitted slide to frame; recoil buffer system; beveled and polished magazine well; checkered front strap and steel mainspring housing (flat housing standard); polished and throated National Match barrel and bushing. Comes with two magazines with slam pads, plastic carrying case, test target. Introduced 1992. From Springfield Inc.
Price: **$1,665.00**

Sphinx AT-2000 GM Grand Master

Springfield Inc. Competition Pistol Similar to the 1911A1 Entry Level Wadcutter Pistol except has brazed, serrated improved ramp front sight; extended ambidextrous thumb safety; match Commander hammer and sear; serrated rear slide; Pachmay flat mainspring housing; extended magazine release; beavertail grip safety; full-length recoil spring guide; Pachmayr wrap-around grips. Comes with two magazines with slam pads, plastic carrying case. Introduced 1992. From Springfield Inc
Price: 45 ACP, blue **$1,598.00**

Springfield Inc. 1911A1 Trophy Match Pistol Similar to the 1911A1 except factory accurized, has 4- to 5½-lb. trigger pull, click adjustable rear sight, match-grade barrel and bushing. Comes with checkered walnut grips. Introduced 1994. From Springfield, Inc.
Price: Blue **$919.00**
Price: Stainless steel **$951.00**

Springfield 1911A1 Trophy Match

Springfield Inc. Expert Pistol Similar to the 1911A1 Trophy Master Competition Pistol except has triple-chamber tapered cone compensator on match barrel with dovetailed front sight; lowered and flared ejection port; fully tuned for reliability. Comes with two magazines, plastic carrying case. Introduced 1992. From Springfield Inc.
Price: 45 ACP, Duotone finish **$1,915.00**
Price: Trophy Master Expert Ltd. **$1,804.00**

CAUTION: PRICES SHOWN ARE SUPPLIED BY THE MANUFACTURER OR IMPORTER. CHECK YOUR LOCAL GUNSHOP.

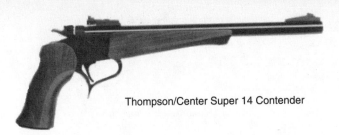

Thompson/Center Super 14 Contender

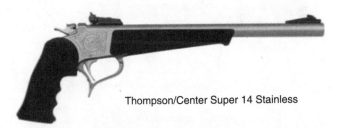

Thompson/Center Super 14 Stainless

Thompson/Center Super 16 Contender

Unique D.E.S. 69U

UNIQUE D.E.S. 69U TARGET PISTOL Caliber: 22 LR, 5-shot magazine. **Barrel:** 5.91″. **Weight:** 35.3 oz. **Length:** 10.5″ overall. **Stocks:** French walnut target-style with thumbrest and adjustable shelf; hand-checkered panels. **Sights:** Ramp front, micro. adj. rear mounted on frame; 8.66″ sight radius. **Features:** Meets U.I.T. standards. Comes with 260-gram barrel weight; 100, 150, 350-gram weights available. Fully adjustable match trigger; dry-firing safety device. Imported from France by Nygord Precision Products.
Price: Right-hand, about $1,250.00
Price: Left-hand, about $1,290.00

WALTHER GSP MATCH PISTOL Caliber: 22 LR, 32 S&W Long (GSP-C), 5-shot magazine. **Barrel:** 4.22″. **Weight:** 44.8 oz. (22 LR), 49.4 oz. (32). **Length:** 11.8″ overall. **Stocks:** Walnut. **Sights:** Post front, match rear adjustable for windage and elevation. **Features:** Available with either 2.2 lb. (1000 gm) or 3 lb. (1360 gm) trigger. Spare magazine, barrel weight, tools supplied. Imported from Germany by Nygord Precision Products.
Price: GSP, with case $1,495.00
Price: GSP-C, with case $1,595.00

Springfield Inc. Distinguished Pistol Has all the features of the 1911A1 Trophy Master Expert except is full-house pistol with Bo-Mar low-mounted adjustable rear sight; full-length recoil spring guide rod and recoil spring retainer; beveled and polished magazine well; walnut grips. Hard chrome finish. Comes with two magazines with slam pads, plastic carrying case. From Springfield Inc.
Price: 45 ACP $2,717.00
Price: Distinguished Limited $2,606.00

Springfield Inc. Basic Competition Pistol Has low-mounted Bo-Mar adjustable rear sight, undercut blade front; match throated barrel and bushing; polished feed ramp; lowered and flared ejection port; fitted Videki speed trigger with tuned 3.5-lb. pull; fitted slide to frame; recoil buffer system; Pachmayr mainspring housing; Pachmayr grips. Comes with two magazines with slam pads, plastic carrying case. Introduced 1992. From Springfield Inc.
Price: 45 ACP, blue, 5″ only $1,439.00

Springfield Inc. 1911A1 N.M. Hardball Pistol Has Bo-Mar adjustable rear sight with undercut front blade; fitted match Videki trigger with 4-lb. pull; fitted slide to frame; throated National Match barrel and bushing, polished feed ramp; recoil buffer system; tuned extractor; Herrett walnut grips. Comes with two magazines, plastic carrying case, test target. Introduced 1992. From Springfield Inc.
Price: 45 ACP, blue $1,485.00

THOMPSON/CENTER SUPER 14 CONTENDER Caliber: 22 LR, 222 Rem., 223 Rem., 7mm TCU, 7-30 Waters, 30-30 Win., 35 Rem., 357 Rem. Maximum, 44 Mag., 10mm Auto, 445 Super Mag., single shot. **Barrel:** 14″. **Weight:** 45 oz. **Length:** 17¼″ overall. **Stocks:** T/C "Competitor Grip" (walnut and rubber). **Sights:** Fully adjustable target-type. **Features:** Break-open action with auto safety. Interchangeable barrels for both rimfire and centerfire calibers. Introduced 1978.
Price: Blued $460.00
Price: Stainless steel $490.00
Price: Extra barrels, blued $217.50
Price: Extra barrels, stainless steel $232.50

Thompson/Center Super 16 Contender Same as the T/C Super 14 Contender except has 16¼″ barrel. Rear sight can be mounted at mid-barrel position (10⅜″ radius) or moved to the rear (using scope mount position) for 14¾″ radius. Overall length is 20¼″. Comes with T/C Competitor Grip of walnut and rubber. Available in 22 LR, 22 WMR, 223 Rem., 7-30 Waters, 30-30 Win., 35 Rem., 44 Mag., 45-70 Gov't. Also available with 16″ vent rib barrel with internal choke, caliber 45 Colt/410 shotshell.
Price: Blue $465.00
Price: Stainless steel $495.00
Price: 45-70 Gov't., blue $470.00
Price: As above, stainless steel $515.00
Price: Super 16 Vent Rib, 45-70, blued $495.00
Price: As above, stainless steel $525.00
Price: Extra 16″ barrel, blued $222.50
Price: As above, stainless steel $237.50
Price: Extra 45-70 barrel, blued $227.50
Price: As above, stainless steel $257.50
Price: Extra Super 16 vent rib barrel, blue $252.50
Price: As above, stainless steel $257.50

UNIQUE D.E.S. 32U TARGET PISTOL Caliber: 32 S&W Long wadcutter. **Barrel:** 5.9″. **Weight:** 40.2 oz. **Stocks:** Anatomically shaped, adjustable stippled French walnut. **Sights:** Blade front, micrometer click rear. **Features:** Trigger adjustable for weight and position; dry firing mechanism; slide stop catch. Optional sleeve weights. Introduced 1990. Imported from France by Nygord Precision Products.
Price: Right-hand, about $1,350.00
Price: Left-hand, about $1,380.00

CAUTION: PRICES SHOWN ARE SUPPLIED BY THE MANUFACTURER OR IMPORTER. CHECK YOUR LOCAL GUNSHOP.

8th ANNUAL EDITION **273**

WESSON FIREARMS MODEL 22 SILHOUETTE REVOLVER

Caliber: 22 LR, 6-shot. **Barrel:** 10″, regular vent or vent heavy. **Weight:** 53 oz. **Stocks:** Combat style. **Sights:** Patridge-style front, .080″ narrow notch rear. **Features:** Single action only. Available in blue or stainless. Introduced 1989. From Wesson Firearms Co., Inc.

Price: Blue, regular vent $474.00
Price: Blue, vent heavy $492.00
Price: Stainless, regular vent $504.00
Price: Stainless, vent heavy $532.00

Wesson Firearms 22 Silhouette

WESSON FIREARMS MODEL 322/7322 TARGET REVOLVER

Caliber: 32-20, 6-shot. **Barrel:** 2.5″, 4″, 6″, 8″, standard, vent, vent heavy. **Weight:** 43 oz. (6″ VH). **Length:** 11.25″ overall. **Stocks:** Checkered walnut. **Sights:** Red ramp interchangeable front, fully adjustable rear. **Features:** Brigh blue or stainless. Introduced 1991. From Wesson Firearms Co., Inc.

Price: 6″, blue $377.00
Price: 6″, stainless $419.00
Price: 8″, vent, blue $429.00
Price: 8″, stainless $472.00
Price: 6″, vent heavy, blue $437.00
Price: 6″, vent heavy, stainless $480.00
Price: 8″, vent heavy, blue $449.00
Price: 8″, vent heavy, stainless $501.00

Wesson Firearms Model 40

WESSON FIREARMS MODEL 40 SILHOUETTE

Caliber: 357 Maximum, 6-shot. **Barrel:** 4″, 6″, 8″, 10″. **Weight:** 64 oz. (8″ bbl.). **Length:** 14.3″ overall (8″ bbl.). **Stocks:** Smooth walnut, target-style. **Sights:** $1/8$″ serrated front, fully adjustable rear. **Features:** Meets criteria for IHMSA competition with 8″ slotted barrel. Blue or stainless steel. Made in U.S. by Wesson Firearms Co., Inc.

Price: Blue, 4″ $502.00
Price: Blue, 6″ $544.00
Price: Blue, 8″ $567.94
Price: Blue, 10″ $597.20
Price: Stainless, 4″ $567.00
Price: Stainless, 6″ $610.00
Price: Stainless, 8″ slotted $645.83
Price: Stainless, 10″ $671.16

Wesson Firearms 45 Pin Gun

WESSON FIREARMS 45 PIN GUN

Caliber: 45 ACP, 6-shot. **Barrel:** 5″ with 1:14″ twist; Taylor two-stage forcing cone; compensated shroud. **Weight:** 54 oz. **Length:** 12.5″ overall. **Stocks:** Finger-groove Hogue Monogrip. **Sights:** Pin front, fully adjustable rear. Has 8.375″ sight radius. **Features:** Based on 44 Magnum frame. Polished blue or brushed stainless steel. Uses half-moon clips with 45 ACP, or 45 Auto Rim ammunition. Introduced 1994. Made in U.S. by Wesson Firearms Co., Inc.

Price: Blue, regular vent $654.00
Price: Blue, vent heavy $663.00
Price: Stainless, regular vent $713.00
Price: Stainless vent heavy $762.00

Wesson 445 Firearms Supermag

Wesson Firearms Model 445 Supermag Revolver

Similar size and weight as the Model 40 revolvers. Chambered for the 445 Supermag cartridge, a longer version of the 44 Magnum. Barrel lengths of 4″, 6″, 8″, 10″. Contact maker for complete price list. Introduced 1989. From Wesson Firearms Co., Inc.

Price: 4″, vent heavy, blue $542.00
Price: As above, stainless $621.00
Price: 8″, vent heavy, blue $597.00
Price: As above, stainless $665.00
Price: 10″, vent heavy, blue $619.00
Price: As above, stainless $687.00
Price: 8″, vent slotted, blue $577.00
Price: As above, stainless $636.00
Price: 10″, vent slotted, blue $601.00
Price: As above, stainless $661.00

> Consult our Directory pages for the location of firms mentioned.

WICHITA CLASSIC SILHOUETTE PISTOL

Caliber: All standard calibers with maximum overall length of 2.800″. **Barrel:** 11¼″. **Weight:** 3 lbs., 15 oz. **Stocks:** AAA American walnut with oil finish, checkered grip. **Sights:** Hooded post front, open adjustable rear. **Features:** Three locking lug bolt, three gas ports; completely adjustable Wichita trigger. Introduced 1981. From Wichita Arms.

Price: $3,450.00

CAUTION: PRICES SHOWN ARE SUPPLIED BY THE MANUFACTURER OR IMPORTER. CHECK YOUR LOCAL GUNSHOP.

WICHITA SILHOUETTE PISTOL Caliber: 308 Win. F.L., 7mm IHMSA, 7mm-308. **Barrel:** 14¹⁵/₁₆″. **Weight:** 4½ lbs. **Length:** 21³/₈″ overall. **Stock:** American walnut with oil finish. Glass bedded. **Sights:** Wichita Multi-Range sight system. **Features:** Comes with left-hand action with right-hand grip. Round receiver and barrel. Fluted bolt, flat bolt handle. Wichita adjustable trigger. Introduced 1979. From Wichita Arms.
Price: Center grip stock **$1,350.00**
Price: As above except with Rear Position Stock and target-type Lightpull trigger **$1,350.00**

Wichita Silhouette

DOUBLE-ACTION REVOLVERS, SERVICE & SPORT

Includes models suitable for hunting and competitive courses for fire, both police and international.

CHARTER BULLDOG PUG REVOLVER Caliber: 44 Spec., 5-shot. **Barrel:** 2½″. **Weight:** 19½ oz. **Length:** 7″ overall. **Stocks:** Checkered walnut Bulldog. **Sights:** Ramp-style front, fixed rear. **Features:** Blue or stainless steel construction. Fully shrouded barrel. Available with Pocket Hammer. Reintroduced 1993. Made in U.S. by Charco, Inc.
Price: Blue **$267.60**
Price: Nickel **$289.51**

Charter Bulldog Pug

CHARTER OFF-DUTY REVOLVER Caliber: 22 LR, 22 WMR, 6-shot, 38 Spec., 5-shot. **Barrel:** 2″. **Weight:** 17 oz. (38 Spec.). **Length:** 6¹/₄″ overall. **Stocks:** Checkered walnut or rubber combat. **Sights:** Ramp-style front, fixed rear. **Features:** Available in blue, stainless or electroless nickel. Fully shrouded barrel. Introduced 1993. Made in U.S. by Charco, Inc.
Price: Blue, 22 or 38 Spec. **$200.48**
Price: Electroless nickel, 22 or 38 Spec. **$239.68**
Price: Blue, DA only **$207.98**
Price: Electroless nickel, DA only **$247.18**

Charter Off-Duty

Charter Lady On Duty Revolver Similar to the Off-Duty except has rosewood-color checkered plastic grips and comes in a lockable plastic case and nightglow trigger lock. Choice of spur, pocket or double-action hammer. Introduced 1995. Made in U.S. by Charco, Inc.
Price: 38 Spec., 5 shot, blue or nickel **$219.28**
Price: 32 S&W, 6 shot, blue or nickel **$219.28**

Charter Magnum Pug Revolver Similar to the Off-Duty except chambered for 357 Mag., has 2.2″ barrel, Bulldog or neoprene combat grips. Weighs 18 oz. Blue finish only. Pocket or spur hammer. Introduced 1995. Made in U.S. by Charco, Inc.
Price: **$273.50**

Charter Magnum Pug

CHARTER POLICE UNDERCOVER REVOLVER Caliber: 32 H&R Mag., 38 Spec., 6-shot. **Barrel:** 2.2″. **Weight:** 16 oz. (38 Spec.). **Length:** 6¹/₄″ overall. **Stocks:** Checkered walnut. **Sights:** Ramp-style front, fixed rear. **Features:** Blue or stainless steel. Fully shrouded barrel. Reintroduced 1993. Made in U.S. by Charco, Inc.
Price: Blue **$237.75**
Price: Electroless nickel **$252.00**

COLT ANACONDA REVOLVER Caliber: 44 Rem. Magnum, 45 Colt, 6-shot. **Barrel:** 4″, 6″, 8″. **Weight:** 53 oz. (6″ barrel). **Length:** 11⁵/₈″ overall. **Stocks:** TP combat style with finger grooves. **Sights:** Red insert front, adjustable white outline rear. **Features:** Stainless steel; full-length ejector rod housing; ventilated barrel rib; offset bolt notches in cylinder; wide spur hammer. Introduced 1990.
Price: **$612.00**
Price: 45 Colt, 6″, 8″ barrel only **$612.00**

Colt Anaconda

COLT DETECTIVE SPECIAL REVOLVER Caliber: 38 Special, 6-shot. **Barrel:** 2″. **Weight:** 22 oz. **Length:** 6⅝″ overall. **Stocks:** Black composition. **Sights:** Fixed. Ramp front, square notch rear. **Features:** Glare-proof sights, grooved trigger, shrouded ejector rod. Colt blue finish. Reintroduced 1993.
Price: **$400.00**

COLT 38 SF-VI REVOLVER Caliber: 38 Special, 6-shot. **Barrel:** 2″. **Weight:** 21 oz. **Length:** 7″ overall. **Stocks:** Checkered black composition. **Sights:** Ramp front, fixed rear. **Features:** Has new lockwork. Made of stainless steel. Introduced 1995. From Colt's Mfg.
Price: . . . .**NA**

Colt Police Positive Revolver Similar to the Detective Special except has 4″ barrel. Blue finish, fixed sight, black composition grips. Introduced 1995. From Colt's Mfg.
Price: **$400.00**

COLT KING COBRA REVOLVER Caliber: 357 Magnum, 6-shot. **Barrel:** 4″, 6″. **Weight:** 42 oz. (4″ bbl.). **Length:** 9″ overall (4″ bbl.). **Stocks:** TP combat style. **Sights:** Red insert ramp front, adjustable white outline rear. **Features:** Full-length contoured ejector rod housing, barrel rib. Introduced 1986.
Price: Stainless **$455.00**

COLT PYTHON REVOLVER Caliber: 357 Magnum (handles all 38 Spec.), 6-shot. **Barrel:** 4″, 6″ or 8″, with ventilated rib. **Weight:** 38 oz. (4″ bbl.). **Length:** 9¼″ (4″ bbl.). **Stocks:** Hogue Monogrip (4″), TP combat style (6″, 8″). **Sights:** ⅛″ ramp front, adjustable notch rear. **Features:** Ventilated rib; grooved, crisp trigger; swing-out cylinder; target hammer.
Price: Royal blue, 4″, 6″, 8″ **$815.00**
Price: Stainless, 4″, 6″, 8″ **$904.00**
Price: Bright stainless, 4″, 6″, 8″ **$935.00**

E.A.A. STANDARD GRADE REVOLVERS Caliber: 22 LR, 22 LR/22 WMR, 8-shot; 38 Special, 6-shot. **Barrel:** 4″, 6″ (22 rimfire); 2″, 4″ (38 Special). **Weight:** 38 oz. (22 rimfire, 4″). **Length:** 8.8″ overall (4″ bbl.). **Stocks:** Rubber with finger grooves. **Sights:** Blade front, fixed or adjustable on rimfires; fixed only on 32, 38. **Features:** Swing-out cylinder; hammer block safety; blue finish. Introduced 1991. Imported from Germany by European American Armory.
Price: 38 Special 2″ **$180.00**
Price: 38 Special, 4″ **$199.00**
Price: 22 LR, 6″ **$199.00**
Price: 22 LR/22 WMR combo, 4″ **$200.00**
Price: As above, 6″ **$200.00**

Colt Detective Special

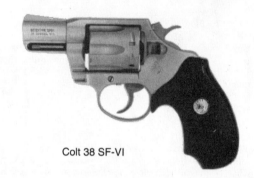

Colt 38 SF-VI

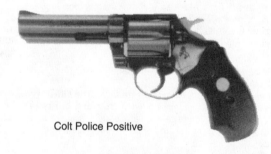

Colt Police Positive

Colt King Cobra

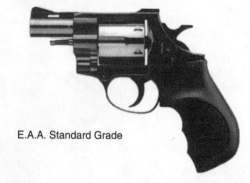

E.A.A. Standard Grade

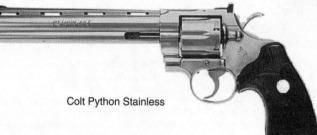

Colt Python Stainless

ERMA ER-777 SPORTING REVOLVER Caliber: 357 Mag., 6-shot. **Barrel:** 5½". **Weight:** 43.3 oz. **Length:** 9½" overall (4" barrel). **Stocks:** Stippled walnut service-type. **Sights:** Interchangeable blade front, micro-adjustable rear for windage and elevation. **Features:** Polished blue finish. Adjustable trigger. Imported from Germany by Precision Sales Int'l. Introduced 1988.
Price: $1,019.00

Erma ER-777

HARRINGTON & RICHARDSON 939 PREMIER REVOLVER Caliber: 22 LR, 9-shot cylinder. **Barrel:** 6" heavy. **Weight:** 36 oz. **Length:** NA. **Stocks:** Walnut-finished hardwood. **Sights:** Blade front, fully adjustable rear. **Features:** Swing-out cylinder with plunger-type ejection; solid barrel rib; high-polish blue finish; double-action mechanism; Western-style grip. Introduced 1995. Made in U.S. by H&R 1871, Inc.
Price: $184.95

HARRINGTON & RICHARDSON 949 WESTERN REVOLVER Caliber: 22 LR, 9-shot cylinder. **Barrel:** 5½", 7½". **Weight:** 36 oz. **Length:** NA. **Stocks:** Walnut-stained hardwood. **Sights:** Blade front, adjustable rear. **Features:** Color case-hardened frame and backstrap, traditional loading gate and ejector rod. Introduced 1994. Made in U.S. by Harrington & Richardson.
Price: About $184.95

Harrington & Richardson 949

HARRINGTON & RICHARDSON SPORTSMAN 999 REVOLVER Caliber: 22 Short, Long, Long Rifle, 9-shot. **Barrel:** 4", 6". **Weight:** 30 oz. (4" barrel). **Length:** 8.5" overall. **Stocks:** Walnut-finished hardwood. **Sights:** Blade front adjustable for elevation, rear adjustable for windage. **Features:** Top-break loading; polished blue finish; automatic shell ejection. Reintroduced 1992. From Harrington & Richardson.
Price: $279.95

Harrington & Richardson Sportsman 999

HERITAGE SENTRY DOUBLE-ACTION REVOLVERS Caliber: 22 LR, 8-shot, 22 WMR, 9mm Para., 38 Spec., 6-shot. **Barrel:** 2", 4". **Weight:** 23 oz. (2" barrel). **Length:** 6¼" overall (2" barrel). **Stocks:** Magnum-style round butt; checkered plastic. **Sights:** Ramp front, fixed rear. **Features:** Pill-pin-type ejection; serrated hammer and trigger. Polished blue or nickel finish. Introduced 1993. Made in U.S. by Heritage Mfg., Inc.
Price: ....$124.95 to $134.95

Heritage Sentry

MANURHIN MR 73 SPORT REVOLVER Caliber: 357 Magnum, 6-shot cylinder. **Barrel:** 6". **Weight:** 37 oz. **Length:** 11.1" overall. **Stocks:** Checkered walnut. **Sights:** Blade front, fully adjustable rear. **Features:** Double action with adjustable trigger. High-polish blue finish, straw-colored hammer and trigger. Comes with extra sight. Introduced 1984. Imported from France by Century International Arms.
Price: About $1,500.00

MITCHELL ARMS GUARDIAN II, III REVOLVERS Caliber: 38 Spec., 6-shot. **Barrel:** 3", 4" (Guardian II); 3", 4", 6" (Guardian III). **Weight:** 32 oz. (3" barrel). **Length:** 8½" overall (3" barrel). **Stocks:** Combat, target; checkered black rubber, walnut. **Sights:** Blade on ramp front, fixed rear (Guardian II); adjustable rear on Guardian III. **Features:** Target hammer; shrouded ejector rod; smooth trigger. Blue only. Introduced 1995. Made in U.S. From Mitchell Arms, Inc.
Price: Guardian II, fixed sight $275.00
Price: Guardian III, adjustable sight $305.00

Mitchell Guardian II

MITCHELL ARMS TITAN II, III REVOLVERS Caliber: 357 Magnum, 6-shot. **Barrel:** 2", 4", 6". **Weight:** 38 oz. (2" barrel). **Length:** 7¾" overall (2" barrel). **Stocks:** Pachmayr black rubber; combat or target. **Sights:** Blade front, fixed rear (Titan II); adjustable rear (Titan III). **Features:** Blue or stainless steel; crane-mounted cylinder release; shrouded ejector rod. Introduced 1995. Made in U.S. From Mitchell Arms, Inc.
Price: Titan II, blue or stainless, fixed sight $339.00
Price: Titan III, blue or stainless, adjustable sight $429.00

Manurhin MR73 Sport Revolver

CAUTION: PRICES SHOWN ARE SUPPLIED BY THE MANUFACTURER OR IMPORTER. CHECK YOUR LOCAL GUNSHOP.

8th ANNUAL EDITION **277**

NEW ENGLAND FIREARMS LADY ULTRA REVOLVER Caliber: 32 H&R Mag., 5-shot. **Barrel:** 3″. **Weight:** 31 oz. **Length:** 7.25″ overall. **Stocks:** Walnut-finished hardwood with NEF medallion. **Sights:** Blade front, fully adjustable rear. **Features:** Swing-out cylinder; polished blue finish. Comes with lockable storage case. Introduced 1992. From New England Firearms Co.
Price: **$165.95**

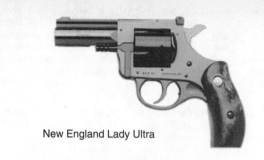

New England Lady Ultra

NEW ENGLAND FIREARMS ULTRA REVOLVER Caliber: 22 LR, 9-shot; 22 WMR, 6-shot. **Barrel:** 4″, 6″. **Weight:** 36 oz. **Length:** 10⅝″ overall (6″ barrel). **Stocks:** Walnut-finished hardwood with NEF medallion. **Sights:** Blade front, fully adjustable rear. **Features:** Blue finish. Bull-style barrel with recessed muzzle, high "Lustre" blue/black finish. Introduced 1989. From New England Firearms.
Price: **$165.95**
Price: Ultra Mag 22 WMR **$165.95**

New England Ultra

NEW ENGLAND FIREARMS STANDARD REVOLVERS Caliber: 22 LR, 9-shot; 32 H&R Mag., 5-shot. **Barrel:** 2½″, 4″. **Weight:** 26 oz. (22 LR, 2½″). **Length:** 8½″ overall (4″ bbl.). **Stocks:** Walnut-finished American hardwood with NEF medallion. **Sights:** Fixed. **Features:** Choice of blue or nickel finish. Introduced 1988. From New England Firearms Co.
Price: 22 LR, 32 H&R Mag., blue **$129.95**
Price: 22 LR, 2½″, 4″, nickel, 32 H&R Mag. 2½″ nickel .**$139.95**

New England Standard

ROSSI LADY ROSSI REVOLVER Caliber: 38 Spec., 5-shot. **Barrel:** 2″, 3″. **Weight:** 21 oz. **Length:** 6.5″ overall (2″ barrel). **Stocks:** Smooth rosewood. **Sights:** Fixed. **Features:** High-polish stainless steel with "Lady Rossi" engraved on frame. Comes with velvet carry bag. Introduced 1995. Imported from Brazil by Interarms.
Price: **$312.00**

Rossi Lady Rossi

ROSSI MODEL 68 REVOLVER Caliber: 38 Spec. **Barrel:** 2″, 3″. **Weight:** 22 oz. **Stocks:** Checkered wood and rubber. **Sights:** Ramp front, low profile adjustable rear. **Features:** All-steel frame, thumb latch operated swing-out cylinder. Introduced 1978. Imported from Brazil by Interarms.
Price: 38, blue, 3″, wood or rubber grips **$234.00**
Price: M68/2 (2″ barrel), wood or rubber grips **$246.00**
Price: 3″, nickel **$238.00**

ROSSI MODEL 515, 518 REVOLVERS Caliber: 22 LR (Model 518), 22 WMR (Model 515), 6-shot. **Barrel:** 4″. **Weight:** 30 oz. **Length:** 9″ overall. **Stocks:** Checkered wood and finger-groove wrap-around rubber. **Sights:** Blade front with red insert, rear adjustable for windage and elevation. **Features:** Small frame; stainless steel construction; solid integral barrel rib. Introduced 1994. Imported from Brazil by Interarms.
Price: Model 518, 22 LR **$281.00**
Price: Model 515, 22 WMR **$296.00**

Rossi Model 518

Rossi Model 68 2″

ROSSI MODEL 88 STAINLESS REVOLVER Caliber: 38 Spec., 5-shot. **Barrel:** 2″, 3″. **Weight:** 22 oz. **Length:** 7.5″ overall. **Stocks:** Checkered wood, service-style, and rubber. **Sights:** Ramp front, square notch rear drift adjustable for windage. **Features:** All metal parts except springs are of 440 stainless steel; matte finish; small frame for concealability. Introduced 1983. Imported from Brazil by Interarms.
Price: 3″ barrel, wood or rubber grips **$265.00**
Price: 2″ barrel, wood or rubber grips **$281.00**

ROSSI MODEL 720 REVOLVER Caliber: 44 Special, 5-shot. **Barrel:** 3″. **Weight:** 27.5 oz. **Length:** 8″ overall. **Stocks:** Checkered rubber, combat style. **Sights:** Red insert front on ramp, fully adjustable rear. **Features:** All stainless steel construction; solid barrel rib; full ejector rod shroud. Introduced 1992. Imported from Brazil by Interarms.
Price: **$320.00**
Price: Model 720C, spurless hammer, DA only **$320.00**

ROSSI MODEL 851 REVOLVER Caliber: 38 Special, 6-shot. **Barrel:** 3″ or 4″. **Weight:** 27.5 oz. (3″ bbl.). **Length:** 8″ overall (3″ bbl.). **Stocks:** Checkered Brazilian hardwood. **Sights:** Blade front with red insert, rear adjustable for windage. **Features:** Medium-size frame; stainless steel construction; ventilated barrel rib. Introduced 1991. Imported from Brazil by Interarms.
Price: **$281.00**

ROSSI MODEL 971 REVOLVER Caliber: 357 Mag., 6-shot. **Barrel:** 2½″, 4″, 6″, heavy. **Weight:** 36 oz. **Length:** 9″ overall. **Stocks:** Checkered Brazilian hardwood. Stainless models have checkered, contoured rubber. **Sights:** Blade front, fully adjustable rear. **Features:** Full-length ejector rod shroud; matted sight rib; target-type trigger, wide checkered hammer spur. Introduced 1988. Imported from Brazil by Interarms.
Price: 4″, stainless **$320.00**
Price: 6″, stainless **$320.00**
Price: 4″, blue **$281.00**
Price: 2½″, stainless **$320.00**

Rossi Model 971 Comp Gun Same as the Model 971 stainless except has 3¼″ barrel with integral compensator. Overall length is 9″, weight 32 oz. Has red insert front sight, fully adjustable rear. Checkered, contoured rubber grips. Introduced 1993. Imported from Brazil by Interarms.
Price: **$320.00**

RUGER GP-100 REVOLVERS Caliber: 38 Special, 357 Magnum, 6-shot. **Barrel:** 3″, 3″ heavy, 4″, 4″ heavy, 6″, 6″ heavy. **Weight:** 3″ barrel—35 oz., 3″ heavy barrel—36 oz., 4″ barrel—37 oz., 4″ heavy barrel—38 oz. **Sights:** Fixed; adjustable on 4″ heavy, 6″, 6″ heavy barrels. **Stocks:** Ruger Santoprene Cushioned Grip with Goncalo Alves inserts. **Features:** Uses action and frame incorporating improvements and features of both the Security-Six and Redhawk revolvers. Full length and short ejector shroud. Satin blue and stainless steel. Available in high-gloss stainless steel finish. Introduced 1988.
Price: GP-141 (357, 4″ heavy, adj. sights, blue) **$425.00**
Price: GP-160 (357, 6″, adj. sights, blue) **$425.00**
Price: GP-161 (357, 6″ heavy, adj. sights, blue) **$425.00**
Price: GPF-331 (357, 3″ heavy), GPF-831 (38 Spec.) **$408.00**
Price: GPF-340 (357, 4″), GPF-840 (38 Spec.) **$408.00**
Price: GPF-341 (357, 4″ heavy), GPF-841 (38 Spec.) **$408.00**
Price: KGP-141 (357, 4″ heavy, adj. sights, stainless) ..**$459.00**
Price: KGP-160 (357, 6″, adj. sights, stainless) **$459.00**
Price: KGP-161 (357, 6″ heavy, adj. sights, stainless) ..**$459.00**
Price: KGPF-330 (357, 3″, stainless), KGPF-830
(38 Spec.) **$442.00**
Price: KGPF-331 (357, 3″ heavy, stainless), KGPF-831 (38
Spec.) **$442.00**
Price: KGPF-340 (357, 4″, stainless), KGPF-840 (38
Spec.) **$442.00**
Price: KGPF-341 (357, 4″ heavy, stainless), KGPF-841
(38 Spec.) **$442.00**

Rossi Model 88 2″

Rossi Model 720C

Rossi Model 851

Rossi Model 971 Comp

Ruger GP-100

CAUTION: PRICES SHOWN ARE SUPPLIED BY THE MANUFACTURER OR IMPORTER. CHECK YOUR LOCAL GUNSHOP.

8th ANNUAL EDITION **279**

Ruger SP101 (KSP-821)

Ruger SP101 DAO

Ruger Redhawk

Ruger Redhawk Blue

Smith & Wesson Model 10

RUGER SP101 REVOLVERS Caliber: 22 LR, 32 H&R Mag., 6-shot, 9mm Para., 38 Special +P, 357 Mag., 5-shot. **Barrel:** 2¼", 3¹/₁₆", 4". **Weight:** 2¼"—25 oz.; 3¹/₁₆"—27 oz. **Sights:** Adjustable on 22, 32, fixed on others. **Stocks:** Ruger Santoprene Cushioned Grip with Xenoy inserts. **Features:** Incorporates improvements and features found in the GP-100 revolvers into a compact, small frame, double-action revolver. Full-length ejector shroud. Stainless steel only. Available with high-polish finish. Introduced 1988.

Price: KSP-821 (2½", 38 Spec.) $428.00
Price: KSP-831 (3¹/₁₆", 38 Spec.) $428.00
Price: KSP-221 (2¼", 22 LR) $428.00
Price: KSP-240 (4", 22 LR) $428.00
Price: KSP-241 (4" heavy bbl., 22 LR) $428.00
Price: KSP-3231 (3¹/₁₆", 32 H&R) $428.00
Price: KSP-921 (2¼", 9mm Para.) $428.00
Price: KSP-931 (3¹/₁₆", 9mm Para.) $428.00
Price: KSP-321 (2¼", 357 Mag.) $428.00
Price: KSP-331 (3¹/₁₆", 357 Mag.) $428.00

Ruger SP101 Double-Action-Only Revolver Similar to the standard SP101 except is double action only with no single-action sear notch. Has spurless hammer for snag-free handling, floating firing pin and Ruger's patented transfer bar safety system. Available with 2¼" barrel in 38 Special +P and 357 Magnum only. Weight is 25½ oz., overall length 7.06". Natural brushed satin or high-polish stainless steel. Introduced 1993.
Price: KSP821L (38 Spec.), KSP321XL (357 Mag.) $428.00

RUGER REDHAWK Caliber: 44 Rem. Mag., 6-shot. **Barrel:** 5½", 7½". **Weight:** About 54 oz. (7½" bbl.). **Length:** 13" overall (7½" barrel). **Stocks:** Square butt Goncalo Alves. **Sights:** Interchangeable Patridge-type front, rear adjustable for windage and elevation. **Features:** Stainless steel, brushed satin finish, or blued ordnance steel. Has a 9½" sight radius. Introduced 1979.
Price: Blued, 44 Mag., 5½", 7½" $475.00
Price: Blued, 44 Mag., 7½", with scope mount, rings ...$512.00
Price: Stainless, 44 Mag., 5½", 7½" $532.00
Price: Stainless, 44 Mag., 7½", with scope mount, rings .$574.00

Ruger Super Redhawk Revolver Similar to the standard Redhawk except has a heavy extended frame with the Ruger Integral Scope Mounting System on the wide topstrap. The wide hammer spur has been lowered for better scope clearance. Incorporates the mechanical design features and improvements of the GP-100. Choice of 7½" or 9½" barrel, both with ramp front sight base with Redhawk-style Interchangeable Insert sight blades, adjustable rear sight. Comes with Ruger "Cushioned Grip" panels of Santoprene with Goncalo Alves wood panels. Satin or high-polished stainless steel. Introduced 1987.
Price: KSRH-7 (7½"), KSRH-9 (9½") $574.00

SMITH & WESSON MODEL 10 M&P REVOLVER Caliber: 38 Special, 6-shot. **Barrel:** 2", 4". **Weight:** 30 oz. **Length:** 9⁵/₁₆" overall. **Stocks:** Uncle Mike's Combat soft rubber; square butt. Wood optional. **Sights:** Fixed, ramp front, square notch rear.
Price: Blue $383.00

Smith & Wesson Model 10 38 M&P Heavy Barrel Same as regular M&P except has heavy 4" ribbed barrel with square butt grips. Weight: **33½ oz.**
Price: Blue $390.00

Ruger Super Redhawk 9½"

SMITH & WESSON MODEL 13 H.B. M&P Caliber: 357 and 38 Special, 6-shot. **Barrel:** 3″ or 4″. **Weight:** 34 oz. **Length:** 9⁵⁄₁₆″ overall (4″ bbl.). **Stocks:** Uncle Mike's soft rubber; wood optional. **Sights:** ⅛″ serrated ramp front, fixed square notch rear. **Features:** Heavy barrel, K-frame, square butt (4″), round butt (3″).
Price: Blue $394.00
Price: Model 65, as above in stainless steel $427.00

Smith & Wesson Model 65

SMITH & WESSON MODEL 14 FULL LUG REVOLVER Caliber: 38 Special, 6-shot. **Barrel:** 6″, full lug. **Weight:** 47 oz. **Length:** 11⅛″ overall. **Stocks:** Hogue soft rubber; wood optional. **Sights:** Pinned Patridge front, adjustable micrometer click rear. **Features:** Has .500″ target hammer, .312″ smooth combat trigger. Polished blue finish. Reintroduced 1991. Limited production.
Price: $465.00

Smith & Wesson Model 14

SMITH & WESSON MODEL 15 COMBAT MASTERPIECE Caliber: 38 Special, 6-shot. **Barrel:** 4″. **Weight:** 32 oz. **Length:** 9⁵⁄₁₆″ (4″ bbl.). **Stocks:** Uncle Mike's Combat soft rubber; wood optional. **Sights:** Front, Baughman Quick Draw on ramp, micro-click rear, adjustable for windage and elevation.
Price: Blued $419.00

SMITH & WESSON MODEL 19 COMBAT MAGNUM Caliber: 357 Magnum and 38 Special, 6-shot. **Barrel:** 2½″, 4″, 6″. **Weight:** 36 oz. **Length:** 9⁹⁄₁₆″ (4″ bbl.). **Stocks:** Uncle Mike's Combat soft rubber; wood optional. **Sights:** Serrated ramp front 2½″ or 4″ bbl., red ramp on 4″, 6″ bbl., micro-click rear adjustable for windage and elevation.
Price: S&W Bright Blue, adj. sights . . . .$416.00 to $430.00

Smith & Wesson Model 629

SMITH & WESSON MODEL 29, 629 REVOLVERS Caliber: 44 Magnum, 6-shot. **Barrel:** 6″, 8⅜″ (Model 29); 4″, 6″, 8⅜″ (Model 629). **Weight:** 47 oz. (6″ bbl.). **Length:** 11⅜″ overall (6″ bbl.). **Stocks:** Soft rubber; wood optional. **Sights:** ⅛″ red ramp front, micro-click rear, adjustable for windage and elevation.
Price: S&W Bright Blue, 6″ $554.00
Price: S&W Bright Blue, 8⅜″ $566.00
Price: Model 629 (stainless steel), 4″ $587.00
Price: Model 629, 6″ $592.00
Price: Model 629, 8⅜″ barrel $606.00

Smith & Wesson Model 629 Classic Revolver Similar to the standard Model 629 except has full-lug 5″, 6½″ or 8⅜″ barrel; chamfered front of cylinder; interchangable red ramp front sight with adjustable white outline rear; Hogue grips with S&W monogram; the frame is drilled and tapped for scope mounting. Factory accurizing and endurance packages. Overall length with 5″ barrel is 10½″; weight is 51 oz. Introduced 1990.
Price: Model 629 Classic (stainless), 5″, 6½″ $629.00
Price: As above, 8⅜″ $650.00

Smith & Wesson Model 629 Classic DX

Smith & Wesson Model 629 Classic DX Revolver Similar to the Classic Hunters except offered only with 6½″ or 8⅜″ full-lug barrel; comes with five front sights: 50-yard red ramp; 50-yard black Patridge; 100-yard black Patridge with gold bead; 50-yard black ramp; and 50-yard black Patridge with white dot. Comes with Hogue combat-style round butt grip. Introduced 1991.
Price: Model 629 Classic DX, 6½″ $811.00
Price: As above, 8⅜″ $838.00

SMITH & WESSON MODEL 36, 37 CHIEFS SPECIAL & AIR-WEIGHT Caliber: 38 Special, 5-shot. **Barrel:** 2″. **Weight:** 19½ oz. (2″ bbl.); 13½ oz. (Airweight). **Length:** 6½″ (2″ bbl. and round butt). **Stocks:** Round butt soft rubber; wood optional. **Sights:** Fixed, serrated ramp front, square notch rear.
Price: Blue, standard Model 36 . . . .$377.00
Price: Blue, Airweight Model 37, 2″ only $412.00
Price: As above, nickel, 2″ only $428.00

Smith & Wesson Model 37

Smith & Wesson Model 60LS

Smith & Weson Model 60 3"

Smith & Wesson Model 649

Smith & Wesson Model 63

Smith & Wesson Model 65LS

Smith & Wesson Model 36LS, 60LS LadySmith Similar to the standard Model 36. Available with 2″ barrel. Comes with smooth, contoured rosewood grips with the S&W monogram. Has a speedloader cutout. Comes in a fitted carry/storage case. Introduced 1989.
Price: Model 36LS **$408.00**
Price: Model 60LS (as above except in stainless) **$461.00**

Smith & Wesson Model 60 Chiefs Special Stainless Same as Model 36 except all stainless construction, 2″ bbl. and round butt only.
Price: Stainless steel **$431.00**

Smith & Wesson Model 60 3″ Full-Lug Revolver Similar to the Model 60 Chief's Special except has 3″ full-lug barrel, adjustable micrometer click black blade rear sight; rubber Uncle Mike's Custom Grade Boot Grip. Overall length 7¹⁄₂″; weight 24¹⁄₂ oz. Introduced 1991.
Price: **$458.00**

SMITH & WESSON MODEL 38 BODYGUARD Caliber: 38 Special, 5-shot. **Barrel:** 2″. **Weight:** 14¹⁄₂ oz. **Length:** 6⁵⁄₁₆″ overall. **Stocks:** Soft rubber; wood optional. **Sights:** Fixed serrated ramp front, square notch rear. **Features:** Alloy frame; internal hammer.
Price: Blue **$444.00**
Price: Nickel **$460.00**

Smith & Wesson Model 49, 649 Bodyguard Revolvers Same as Model 38 except steel construction, weight 20¹⁄₂ oz.
Price: Blued, Model 49 . . . .**$409.00**
Price: Stainless, Model 649 . . . .**$469.00**

SMITH & WESSON MODEL 63 KIT GUN Caliber: 22 LR, 6-shot. **Barrel:** 2″, 4″. **Weight:** 24 oz. (4″ bbl.). **Length:** 8³⁄₈″ (4″ bbl. and round butt). **Stocks:** Round butt soft rubber; wood optional. **Sights:** Red ramp front, micro-click rear adjustable for windage and elevation. **Features:** Stainless steel construction.
Price: 2″ **$458.00**
Price: 4″ **$462.00**

SMITH & WESSON MODEL 64 STAINLESS M&P Caliber: 38 Special, 6-shot. **Barrel:** 2″, 3″, 4″. **Weight:** 34 oz. **Length:** 9⁵⁄₁₆″ overall. **Stocks:** Soft rubber; wood optional. **Sights:** Fixed, ¹⁄₈″ serrated ramp front, square notch rear. **Features:** Satin finished stainless steel, square butt.
Price: 2″ **$415.00**
Price: 3″, 4″ **$423.00**

SMITH & WESSON MODEL 65LS LADYSMITH Caliber: 357 Magnum, 6-shot. **Barrel:** 3″. **Weight:** 31 oz. **Length:** 7.94″ overall. **Stocks:** Rosewood, round butt. **Sights:** Serrated ramp front, fixed notch rear. **Features:** Stainless steel with frosted finish. Smooth combat trigger, service hammer, shrouded ejector rod. Comes with soft case. Introduced 1992.
Price: **$461.00**

SMITH & WESSON MODEL 66 STAINLESS COMBAT MAGNUM Caliber: 357 Magnum and 38 Special, 6-shot. **Barrel:** 2¹⁄₂″, 4″, 6″. **Weight:** 36 oz. (4″ barrel). **Length:** 9⁹⁄₁₆″ overall. **Stocks:** Soft rubber; wood optional. **Sights:** Red ramp front, micro-click rear adjustable for windage and elevation. **Features:** Satin finish stainless steel.
Price: 2¹⁄₂″ **$466.00**
Price: 4″, 6″ **$471.00**

SMITH & WESSON MODEL 67 COMBAT MASTERPIECE Caliber: 38 Special, 6-shot. **Barrel:** 4″. **Weight:** 32 oz. **Length:** 9⁵⁄₁₆″ overall. **Stocks:** Soft rubber; wood optional. **Sights:** Red ramp front, micro-click rear adjustable for windage and elevation. **Features:** Stainless steel with satin finish. Smooth combat trigger, semi-target hammer. Introduced 1994.
Price: **$467.00**

SMITH & WESSON MODEL 586, 686 DISTINGUISHED COMBAT MAGNUMS **Caliber:** 357 Magnum. **Barrel:** 4″, 6″, full shroud. **Weight:** 46 oz. (6″), 41 oz. (4″). **Stocks:** Soft rubber; wood optional. **Sights:** Baughman red ramp front, four-position click-adjustable front, S&W micrometer click rear. Drilled and tapped for scope mount. **Features:** Uses new L-frame, but takes all K-frame grips. Full-length ejector rod shroud. Smooth combat-type trigger, semi-target type hammer. Trigger stop on 6″ models. Also available in stainless as Model 686. Introduced 1981.

Price: Model 586, blue, 4″, from $461.00
Price: Model 586, blue, 6″ $466.00
Price: Model 686, 6″, ported barrel $528.00
Price: Model 686, 8³/₈″ $515.00
Price: Model 686, 2¹/₂″ $481.00

Smith & Wesson Model 625

SMITH & WESSON MODEL 617 FULL LUG REVOLVER **Caliber:** 22 LR, 6-shot. **Barrel:** 4″, 6″, 8³/₈″. **Weight:** 42 oz. (4″ barrel). **Length:** NA. **Stocks:** Soft rubber; wood optional. **Sights:** Patridge front, adjustable rear. Drilled and tapped for scope mount. **Features:** Stainless steel with satin finish; 4″ has .312″ smooth trigger, .375″ semi-target hammer; 6″ has either .312″ combat or .400″ serrated trigger, .375″ semi-target or .500″ target hammer; 8³/₈″ with .400″ serrated trigger, .500″ target hammer. Introduced 1990.

Price: 4″ $460.00
Price: 6″, target hammer, combat trigger $490.00
Price: 8³/₈″ $501.00

Smith & Wesson Model 640

SMITH & WESSON MODEL 625 REVOLVER **Caliber:** 45 ACP, 6-shot. **Barrel:** 5″. **Weight:** 46 oz. **Length:** 11.375″ overall. **Stocks:** Soft rubber; wood optional. **Sights:** Patridge front on ramp, S&W micrometer click rear adjustable for windage and elevation. **Features:** Stainless steel construction with .400″ semi-target hammer, .312″ smooth combat trigger; full lug barrel. Introduced 1989.

Price: $597.00

SMITH & WESSON MODEL 640 CENTENNIAL **Caliber:** 357/38 Special, 5-shot. **Barrel:** 2¹/₈″. **Weight:** 25 oz. **Length:** 6³/₄″ overall. **Stocks:** Uncle Mike's Boot Grip. **Sights:** Serrated ramp front, fixed notch rear. **Features:** Stainless steel version of the original Model 40 but without the grip safety. Fully concealed hammer, snag-proof smooth edges. Introduced 1995 in 357 Magnum.

Price: $469.00
Price: Model 940 (9mm Para.) $474.00

Smith & Wesson Model 651

Smith & Wesson Model 442 Centennial Airweight Similar to the Model 640 Centennial except has alloy frame giving weight of 15.8 oz. Chambered for 38 Special, 2″ carbon steel barrel; carbon steel cylinder; concealed hammer; Uncle Mike's Custom Grade Santoprene grips. Fixed square notch rear sight, serrated ramp front. Introduced 1993.

Price: Blue $427.00
Price: Nickel $442.00

SMITH & WESSON MODEL 651 REVOLVER **Caliber:** 22 WMR, 6-shot cylinder. **Barrel:** 4″. **Weight:** 24¹/₂ oz. **Length:** 8¹¹/₁₆″ overall. **Stocks:** Soft rubber; wood optional. **Sights:** Red ramp front, adjustable micrometer click rear. **Features:** Stainless steel construction with semi-target hammer, smooth combat trigger. Reintroduced 1991. Limited production.

Price: $460.00

Taurus Model 44

SMITH & WESSON MODEL 657 REVOLVER **Caliber:** 41 Magnum, 6-shot. **Barrel:** 6″. **Weight:** 48 oz. **Length:** 11³/₈″ overall. **Stocks:** Soft rubber; wood optional. **Sights:** Pinned ¹/₈″ red ramp front, micro-click rear adjustable for windage and elevation. **Features:** Stainless steel construction.

Price: $528.00

TAURUS MODEL 44 REVOLVER **Caliber:** 44 Magnum, 6-shot. **Barrel:** 4″, 6¹/₂″, 8³/₈″. **Weight:** 44³/₄ oz. (4″ barrel). **Length:** NA. **Stocks:** Checkered Brazilian hardwood. **Sights:** Serrated ramp front, micro-click rear adjustable for windage and elevation. **Features:** Heavy solid rib on 4″, vent rib on 6¹/₂″, 8³/₈″. Compensated barrel. Blued model has color case-hardened hammer and trigger. Introduced 1994. Imported by Taurus International.

Price: Blue, 4″ $439.00
Price: Blue, 6¹/₂″, 8³/₈″ $457.00
Price: Stainless, 4″ $499.00
Price: Stainless, 6¹/₂″, 8³/₈″ $520.00

CAUTION: PRICES SHOWN ARE SUPPLIED BY THE MANUFACTURER OR IMPORTER. CHECK YOUR LOCAL GUNSHOP.

8th ANNUAL EDITION **283**

Taurus Model 66

Taurus Model 80

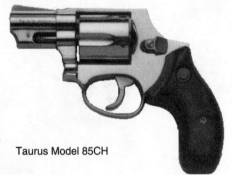

Taurus Model 82 4″

Taurus Model 85CH

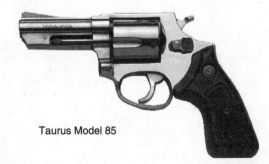

Taurus Model 85

TAURUS MODEL 66 REVOLVER Caliber: 357 Magnum, 6-shot. **Barrel:** 2.5″, 4″, 6″. **Weight:** 35 oz.(4″ barrel). **Stocks:** Checkered Brazilian hardwood. **Sights:** Serrated ramp front, micro-click rear adjustable for windage and elevation. Red ramp front with white outline rear on stainlees models only. **Features:** Wide target-type hammer spur, floating firing pin, heavy barrel with shrouded ejector rod. Introduced 1978. Imported by Taurus International.
Price: Blue, 2.5″, 4″, 6″ **$329.00**
Price: Stainless, 2.5″, 4″, 6″ **$405.00**

Taurus Model 65 Revolver Same as the Model 66 except has fixed rear sight and ramp front. Available with 2.5″ or 4″ barrel only, round butt grip. Imported by Taurus International.
Price: Blue, 2.5″, 4″ **$299.00**
Price: Stainless, 2.5″, 4″ **$369.00**

TAURUS MODEL 80 STANDARD REVOLVER Caliber: 38 Spec., 6-shot. **Barrel:** 3″ or 4″. **Weight:** 30 oz. (4″ bbl.). **Length:** 9¼″ overall (4″ bbl.). **Stocks:** Checkered Brazilian hardwood. **Sights:** Serrated ramp front, square notch rear. **Features:** Imported by Taurus International.
Price: Blue **$260.00**
Price: Stainless **$308.00**

TAURUS MODEL 82 HEAVY BARREL REVOLVER Caliber: 38 Spec., 6-shot. **Barrel:** 3″ or 4″, heavy. **Weight:** 34 oz. (4″ bbl.). **Length:** 9¼″ overall (4″ bbl.). **Stocks:** Checkered Brazilian hardwood. **Sights:** Serrated ramp front, square notch rear. **Features:** Imported by Taurus International.
Price: Blue **$260.00**
Price: Stainless **$308.00**

TAURUS MODEL 83 REVOLVER   Caliber: 38 Spec., 6-shot. **Barrel:** 4″ only, heavy. **Weight:** 34 oz. **Stocks:** Oversize checkered Brazilian hardwood. **Sights:** Ramp front, micro-click rear adjustable for windage and elevation. **Features:** Blue or nickel finish. Introduced 1977. Imported by Taurus International.
Price: Blue **$274.00**
Price: Stainless **$319.00**

TAURUS MODEL 85 REVOLVER   Caliber: 38 Spec., 5-shot. **Barrel:** 2″, 3″. **Weight:** 21 oz. **Stocks:** Checkered Brazilian hardwood. **Sights:** Ramp front, square notch rear. **Features:** Blue, satin nickel finish or stainless steel. Introduced 1980. Imported by Taurus International.
Price: Blue, 2″, 3″ **$284.00**
Price: Stainless steel **$343.00**

Taurus Model 85CH Revolver Same as the Model 85 except has 2″ barrel only and concealed hammer. Smooth Brazilian hardwood stocks. Introduced 1991. Imported by Taurus International.
Price: Blue **$284.00**
Price: Stainless **$343.00**

TAURUS MODEL 94 REVOLVER Caliber: 22 LR, 9-shot cylinder. **Barrel:** 3″, 4″. **Weight:** 25 oz. **Stocks:** Checkered Brazilian hardwood. **Sights:** Serrated ramp front, click-adjustable rear for windage and elevation. **Features:** Floating firing pin, color case-hardened hammer and trigger. Introduced 1989. Imported by Taurus International.
Price: Blue **$303.00**
Price: Stainless **$350.00**

TAURUS MODEL 96 REVOLVER Caliber: 22 LR, 6-shot. **Barrel:** 6″. **Weight:** 34 oz. **Length:** NA. **Stocks:** Checkered Brazilian hardwood. **Sights:** Patridge-type front, micrometer click rear adjustable for windage and elevation. **Features:** Heavy solid barrel rib; target hammer; adjustable target trigger. Blue only. Imported by Taurus International.
Price: **$370.00**

TAURUS MODEL 441/431 REVOLVERS Caliber: 44 Special, 5-shot. **Barrel:** 3″, 4″, 6″. **Weight:** 40.4 oz. (6″ barrel). **Length:** NA. **Stocks:** Checkered Brazilian hardwood. **Sights:** Serrated ramp front, micrometer click rear adjustable for windage and elevation. **Features:** Heavy barrel with solid rib and full-length ejector shroud. Introduced 1992. Imported by Taurus International.
Price: Blue, 3″, 4″, 6″ $307.00
Price: Stainless, 3″, 4″, 6″ $386.00
Price: Model 431 (fixed sights), blue $295.00
Price: Model 431 (fixed sights), stainless $362.00

Taurus Model 441

TAURUS MODEL 605 REVOLVER Caliber: 357 Mag., 5-shot. **Barrel:** 2¼″. **Weight:** 24.5 oz. **Length:** NA. **Stocks:** Finger-groove Santoprene I. **Sights:** Serrated ramp front, fixed notch rear. **Features:** Heavy, solid rib barrel; floating firing pin. Blue or stainless. Introduced 1995. Imported by Taurus International.
Price: Blue $305.00
Price: Stainless $369.00

TAURUS MODEL 607 REVOLVER Caliber: 357 Mag., 7-shot. **Barrel:** 4″, 6½″. **Weight:** 44 oz. **Length:** NA. **Stocks:** Santoprene I with finger grooves. **Sights:** Serrated ramp front, fully adjustable rear. **Features:** Ventilated rib with built-in compensator on 6½″ barrel. Available in blue or stainless. Introduced 1995. Imported by Taurus international.
Price: Blue, 4″ $439.00
Price: Blue, 6½″ $457.00
Price: Stainless, 4″ $499.00
Price: Stainless, 6½″ $520.00

Taurus Model 607

TAURUS MODEL 669 REVOLVER Caliber: 357 Mag., 6-shot. **Barrel:** 4″, 6″. **Weight:** 37 oz., (4″ bbl.). **Stocks:** Checkered Brazilian hardwood. **Sights:** Serrated ramp front, micro-click rear adjustable for windage and elevation. **Features:** Wide target-type hammer, floating firing pin, full-length barrel shroud. Introduced 1988. Imported by Taurus International.
Price: Blue, 4″, 6″ $338.00
Price: Blue, 4″, 6″ compensated $357.00
Price: Stainless, 4″, 6″ $414.00
Price: Stainless, 4″, 6″ compensated $434.00

Taurus Model 689 Revolver Same as the Model 669 except has full-length ventilated barrel rib. Available in blue or stainless steel. Introduced 1990. From Taurus International.
Price: Blue, 4″ or 6″ $352.00
Price: Stainless, 4″ or 6″ $428.00

Taurus Model 669

TAURUS MODEL 941 REVOLVER Caliber: 22 WMR, 8-shot. **Barrel:** 3″, 4″. **Weight:** 27.5 oz. (4″ barrel). **Length:** NA. **Stocks:** Checkered Brazilian hardwood. **Sights:** Serrated ramp front, rear adjustable for windage and elevation. **Features:** Solid rib heavy barrel with full-length ejector rod shroud. Blue or stainless steel. Introduced 1992. Imported by Taurus International.
Price: Blue $326.00
Price: Stainless $378.00

Taurus Model 32M

THUNDER FIVE REVOLVER Caliber: 45 Colt/410 shotshell, 2″ and 3″; 5-shot cylinder. **Barrel:** 2″. **Weight:** 48 oz. **Length:** 9″ overall. **Stocks:** Pachmayr checkered rubber. **Sights:** Fixed. **Features:** Double action with ambidextrous hammer-block safety; squared trigger guard; internal draw bar safety. Made of chrome moly steel, with matte blue finish. Announced 1991. From Holston Ent.
Price: $549.00
Price: Model T-70, 45-70 Gov't. (from Dragun Ent.) $599.00

Wesson Firearms Model 9, 15 & 32M Revolvers Same as Models 8 and 14 except they have adjustable sight. Model 9 chambered for 38 Special, Model 15 for 357 Magnum. Model 32M is chambered for 32 H&R Mag. Same specs and prices as for Model 15 guns. Available in blue or stainless. Contact Wesson Firearms for complete price list.
Price: Model 9-2 or 15-2, 2½″, blue $346.00
Price: As above except in stainless $376.00

WESSON FIREARMS MODEL 8 & MODEL 14 Caliber: 38 Special (Model 8); 357 (Model 14), both 6-shot. **Barrel:** 2½″, 4″, 6″; interchangeable. **Weight:** 30 oz. (2½″). **Length:** 9¼″ overall (4″ bbl.). **Stocks:** Checkered, interchangeable. **Sights:** ⅛″ serrated front, fixed rear. **Features:** Interchangeable barrels and grips; smooth, wide trigger; wide hammer spur with short double-action travel. Available in stainless or Brite blue. Contact Wesson Firearms for complete price list.
Price: Model 8-2, 2½″, blue $274.00
Price: As above except in stainless $319.00

CAUTION: PRICES SHOWN ARE SUPPLIED BY THE MANUFACTURER OR IMPORTER. CHECK YOUR LOCAL GUNSHOP.

8th ANNUAL EDITION **285**

Wesson Firearms FB-44

Wesson Firearms 738P

Wesson Firearms FB15

Wesson Firearms Model 15 Gold Series Similar to the Model 15 except has smoother action to reduce DA pull to 8-10 lbs.; comes with either 6" or 8" vent heavy slotted barrel shroud with bright blue barrel. Shroud is stamped "Gold Series" with the Wesson signature engraved and gold filled. Hammer and trigger are polished bright; rosewood grips. New sights with orange dot Patridge front, white triangle on rear blade. Introduced 1989.
Price: 6" ....**NA**
Price: 8" ....**NA**

WESSON FIREARMS FB44, FB744 REVOLVERS **Caliber:** 44 Magnum, 6-shot. **Barrel:** 4", 5", 6", 8". **Weight:** 50 oz. (4" barrel). **Length:** 9³/₄" overall (4" barrel). **Stocks:** Hogue finger-groove rubber. **Sights:** Interchangeable blade front, fully adjustable rear. **Features:** Fixed, non-vented heavy barrel shrouds, but other features same as other Wesson revolvers. Brushed stainless or polished blue finish. Introduced 1994. Made in U.S. by Wesson Firearms Co., Inc.
Price: FB44-4 (4", blue) **$447.00**
Price: As above, stainless (FB744-4) **$493.00**
Price: FB44-5 (5", blue) **$450.00**
Price: As above, stainless (FB744-5) **$496.00**
Price: FB44-6 (6", blue) **$454.00**
Price: As above, stainless (FB744-6) **$500.00**
Price: FB44-8 (8", blue) **$462.00**
Price: As above, stainless (FB744-8) **$508.00**

WESSON FIREARMS MODEL 22 REVOLVER **Caliber:** 22 LR, 22 WMR, 6-shot. **Barrel:** 2¹/₂", 4", 6", 8"; interchangeable. **Weight:** 36 oz. (2¹/₂"), 44 oz. (6"). **Length:** 9¹/₄" overall (4" barrel). **Stocks:** Checkered; undercover, service or over-size target. **Sights:** ¹/₈" serrated, interchangeable front, white outline rear adjustable for windage and elevation. **Features:** Built on the same frame as the Wesson 357; smooth, wide trigger with over-travel adjustment, wide spur hammer, with short double-action travel. Available in Brite blue or stainless steel. Contact Wesson Firearms for complete price list.
Price: 2¹/₂" bbl., blue **$357.00**
Price: As above, stainless **$400.00**
Price: With 4", vent. rib, blue **$392.00**
Price: As above, stainless **$432.00**
Price: Blue Pistol Pac, 22 LR **$653.00**

WESSON FIREARMS MODEL 41V, 44V, 45V REVOLVERS **Caliber:** 41 Mag., 44 Mag., 45 Colt, 6-shot. **Barrel:** 4", 6", 8", 10"; interchangeable. **Weight:** 48 oz. (4"). **Length:** 12" overall (6" bbl.). **Stocks:** Smooth. **Sights:** ¹/₈" serrated front, white outline rear adjustable for windage and elevation. **Features:** Available in blue or stainless steel. Smooth, wide trigger with adjustable over-travel; wide hammer spur. Available in Pistol Pac set also. Contact Wesson Firearms for complete price list.
Price: 41 Mag., 4", vent **$447.00**
Price: As above except in stainless **$524.00**
Price: 44 Mag., 4", blue **$447.00**
Price: As above except in stainless **$524.00**
Price: 45 Colt, 4", vent **$447.00**
Price: As above except in stainless **$524.00**

WESSON FIREARMS MODEL 738P REVOLVER **Caliber:** 38 Special +P, 5-shot. **Barrel:** 2". **Weight:** 24.6 oz. **Length:** 6.5" overall. **Stocks:** Pauferro wood or rubber. **Sights:** Blade front, fixed notch rear. **Features:** Designed for +P ammunition. Stainless steel construction. Introduced 1992. Made in U.S. by Wesson Firearms Co., Inc.
Price: **$340.00**

WESSON FIREARMS HUNTER SERIES REVOLVERS **Caliber:** 357 Supermag, 41 Mag., 44 Mag., 445 Supermag, 6-shot. **Barrel:** 6", 7¹/₂", depending upon model. **Weight:** About 64 oz. **Length:** 14" overall. **Stocks:** Hogue finger-groove rubber, wood presentation. **Sights:** Blade front, dovetailed Iron Sight Gunworks rear. **Features:** Fixed barrel revolvers. Barrels have 1:18.75" twist, Alan Taylor two-stage forcing cone; non-fluted cylinder; bright blue or satin stainless. Introduced 1994. Made in U.S. by Wesson Firearms Co., Inc.
Price: Open Hunter (open sights, 7¹/₂" barrel), blue **$805.00**
Price: As above, stainless **$849.00**
Price: Compensated Open Hunter (6" compensated barrel, 7" shroud), blue **$837.00**
Price: As above, stainless **$881.00**
Price: Scoped Hunter (7¹/₂" barrel, no sights, comes with scope rings on shroud), blue **$838.00**
Price: As above, stainless **$881.00**
Price: Compensated Scoped Hunter (6" barrel, 7" shroud, scope rings on shroud), blue **$871.00**
Price: As above, stainless **$914.00**

WESSON FIREARMS FB15, FB715 REVOLVERS **Caliber:** 357 Magnum, 6-shot. **Barrel:** 2¹/₂", 4" (Service models), 3", 4", 5", 6" (target models). **Weight:** 40 oz. (4" barrel). **Length:** 9³/₄" overall (4" barrel). **Stocks:** Service style or Hogue rubber. **Sights:** Blade front, adjustable rear (Target); fixed rear on Service. **Features:** Fixed barrels, but other features same as other Wesson revolvers. Service models in brushed stainless, satin blue, Target in brushed stainless or polished blue. Introduced 1993. Made in U.S. by Wesson Firearms Co., Inc.
Price: FB14-2 (Service, 2¹/₂", blue) **$289.00**
Price: As above, 4" **$296.00**
Price: FB714-2 (Service, 2¹/₂", stainless) **$313.00**
Price: As above, 4" **$319.00**
Price: FB15-3 (Target, 3", blue) **$322.00**
Price: As above, 5" **$331.00**
Price: FB715 (Target, 4", stainless) **$354.00**
Price: As above, 6" **$370.00**

Both classic six-shooters and modern adaptations for hunting and sport.

AMERICAN ARMS REGULATOR SINGLE ACTIONS Caliber: 357 Mag. 44-40, 45 Colt. **Barrel:** 4³/₄″, 5¹/₂″, 7¹/₂″. **Weight:** 32 oz. (4³/₄″ barrel) **Length:** 8¹/₆″ overall (4³/₄″ barrel). **Stocks:** Smooth walnut. **Sights:** Blade front, groove rear. **Features:** Blued barrel and cylinder, brass trigger guard and backstrap. Introduced 1992. Imported from Italy by American Arms, Inc.
Price: Regulator, single cylinder $328.00
Price: Regulator, dual cylinder (44-40/44 Spec. or 45 Colt/45 ACP) $374.00
Price: Regulator DLX (all steel) $374.00

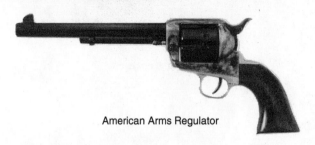

American Arms Regulator

American Arms Buckhorn Single Action Similar to the Regulator single action except chambered for 44 Magnum. Available with 4³/₄″, 6″ or 7¹/₂″ barrel. Overall length 11³/₄″, weight is 44 oz. with 6″ barrel. Introduced 1993. Imported from Italy by American Arms, Inc.
Price: $359.00

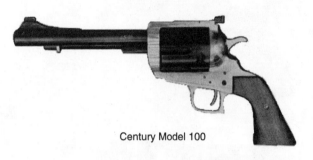

Century Model 100

CENTURY GUN DIST. MODEL 100 SINGLE ACTION Caliber: 30-30, 375 Win., 444 Marlin, 45-70, 50-70. **Barrel:** 6¹/₂″ (standard), 8″, 10″, 12″. **Weight:** 6 lbs. (loaded). **Length:** 15″ overall (8″ bbl.). **Stocks:** Smooth walnut. **Sights:** Ramp front, Millett adjustable square notch rear. **Features:** Highly polished high tensile strength manganese bronze frame, blue cylinder and barrel; coil spring trigger mechanism. Calibers other than 45-70 start at $2,000.00. Contact maker for full price information. Introduced 1975. Made in U.S. From Century Gun Dist., Inc.
Price: 6¹/₂″ barrel, 45-70 ....$1,250.00

CIMARRON U.S. CAVALRY MODEL SINGLE ACTION Caliber: 45 Colt **Barrel:** 7¹/₂″. **Weight:** 42 oz. **Length:** 13¹/₂″ overall. **Stocks:** Walnut. **Sights:** Fixed. **Features:** Has "A.P. Casey" markings; "U.S." plus patent dates on frame, serial number on backstrap, trigger guard, frame and cylinder, "APC" cartouche on left grip; color case-hardened frame and hammer, rest charcoal blue. Exact copy of the original. Imported by Cimarron Arms.
Price: $459.00

Cimarron U.S. Cavalry

Cimarron Artillery Model Single Action Similar to the U.S. Cavalry model except has 5¹/₂″ barrel, weighs 39 oz., and is 11¹/₂″ overall. U.S. markings and cartouche, case-hardened frame and hammer; 45 Colt only.
Price: $459.00

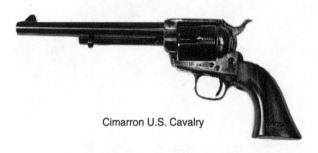

Cimarron Artillery

CIMARRON 1873 PEACEMAKER REPRO Caliber: 38 WCF, 357 Mag., 44 WCF, 44 Spec., 45 Colt. **Barrel:** 4³/₄″, 5¹/₂″, 7¹/₂″. **Weight:** 39 oz. **Length:** 10″ overall (4″ barrel). **Stocks:** Walnut. **Sights:** Blade front, fixed or adjustable rear. **Features:** Uses "old model" blackpowder frame with "Bullseye" ejector or New Model frame. Imported by Cimarron Arms.
Price: Peacemaker Reproduction, 4³/₄″ barrel $429.95
Price: Frontier Six Shooter, 5¹/₂″ barrel $429.95
Price: Single Action Army, 7¹/₂″ barrel $429.95

Cimarron Peacemaker

CIMARRON NEW THUNDERER REVOLVER Caliber: 357 Mag., 44 WCF, 44 Spec., 45 Colt, 6-shot. **Barrel:** 3¹/₂″, 4³/₄″, with ejector. **Weight:** 38 oz. (3¹/₂″ barrel). **Length:** NA. **Stocks:** Hand-checkered walnut. **Sights:** Blade front, notch rear. **Features:** Thunderer grip; color case-hardened frame with balance blued, or nickel finish. Introduced 1993. Imported by Cimarron Arms.
Price: Color case-hardened $439.95
Price: Nickeled $559.95

SINGLE-ACTION REVOLVERS

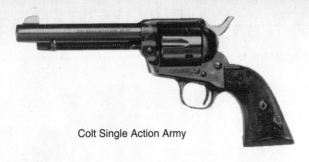

Colt Single Action Army

D-Max Sidewinder

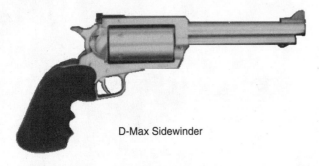

E.A.A. Big Bore Bounty Hunter

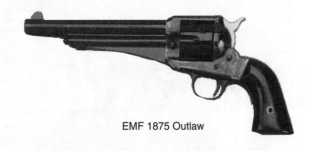

EMF 1875 Outlaw

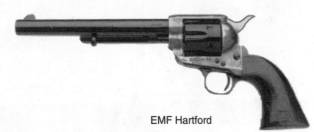

EMF Hartford

COLT SINGLE ACTION ARMY REVOLVER Caliber: 44-40, 45 Colt, 6-shot. **Barrel:** 4³/₄″, 5¹/₂″, 7¹/₂″. **Weight:** 40 oz. (4³/₄″ barrel). **Length:** 10¹/₄″ overall (4³/₄″ barrel). **Stocks:** Black Eagle composite. **Sights:** Blade front, notch rear. **Features:** Available in full nickel finish with nickel grip medallions, or Royal Blue with color case-hardened frame, gold grip medallions. Reintroduced 1992.
Price: $1,213.00

D-MAX SIDEWINDER REVOLVER Caliber: 45 Colt/410 shotshell, 6-shot. **Barrel:** 6.5″ or 7.5″. **Weight:** 57 oz. (6.5″). **Length:** 14.1″ (6.5″ barrel). **Stocks:** Hogue black rubber with finger grooves. **Sights:** Blade on ramp front, fully adjustable rear. **Features:** Stainless steel construction. Has removable choke for firing shotshells. Grooved, wide-spur hammer; transfer bar ignition; satin stainless finish. Introduced 1992. Made in U.S. by D-Max, Inc.
Price: $750.00

E.A.A. BIG BORE BOUNTY HUNTER SA REVOLVERS Caliber: 357 Mag., 44 Mag., 45 Colt, 6-shot. **Barrel:** 4¹/₂″, 7¹/₂″. **Weight:** 2.5 lbs. **Length:** 11″ overall (4⁵/₈″ barrel). **Stocks:** Smooth walnut. **Sights:** Blade front, grooved topstrap rear. **Features:** Transfer bar safety; three position hammer; hammer forged barrel. Introduced 1992. Imported by European American Armory.
Price: Blue $299.00
Price: Color case-hardened frame $310.00

EMF DAKOTA 1875 OUTLAW REVOLVER Caliber: 357, 44-40, 45 Colt. **Barrel:** 7¹/₂″. **Weight:** 46 oz. **Length:** 13¹/₂″ overall. **Stocks:** Smooth walnut. **Sights:** Blade front, fixed groove rear. **Features:** Authentic copy of 1875 Remington with firing pin in hammer; color case-hardened frame, blue cylinder, barrel, steel backstrap and brass trigger guard. Also available in nickel, factory engraved. Imported by E.M.F.
Price: All calibers $465.00
Price: Nickel $550.00
Price: Engraved $600.00
Price: Engraved Nickel $710.00

EMF Dakota 1890 Police Revolver Similar to the 1875 Outlaw except has 5¹/₂″ barrel, weighs 40 oz., with 12¹/₂″ overall length. Has lanyard ring in butt. No web under barrel. Calibers 357, 44-40, 45 Colt. Imported by E.M.F.
Price: All calibers $470.00
Price: Nickel $560.00
Price: Engraved $620.00
Price: Engraved nickel $725.00

EMF HARTFORD SINGLE-ACTION REVOLVERS Caliber: 22 LR, 357 Mag., 32-20, 38-40, 44-40, 44 Spec., 45 Colt. **Barrel:** 4³/₄″, 5¹/₂″, 7¹/₂″. **Weight:** 45 oz. **Length:** 13″ overall (7¹/₂″ barrel). **Stocks:** Smooth walnut. **Sights:** Blade front, fixed rear. **Features:** Identical to the origianl Colts with inspector cartouche on left grip, original patent dates and U.S. markings. All major parts serial numbered using original Colt-style lettering, numbering. Bullseye ejector head and color case-hardening on frame and hammer. Introduced 1990. From E.M.F.
Price: $600.00
Price: Cavalry or Artillery $655.00
Price: Nickel plated $725.00
Price: Engraved, nickel plated $840.00
Price: Pinkerton (bird's-head grip), 45 Colt, 4″ barrel ...$680.00

EMF Dakota New Model Single-Action Revolvers Similar to the standard Dakota except has color case-hardened forged steel frame, black nickel backstrap and trigger guard. Calibers 357 Mag., 44-40, 45 Colt only.
Price: $460.00
Price: Nickel $585.00

EMF 1894 Target Bisley Revolver Similar to the Hartford single-action revolver except has special grip frame and trigger guard, wide spur hammer; available in 45 Colt only, 5¹/₂″ or 7¹/₂″ barrel. Introduced 1995. Imported by EMF.
Price: Blue $680.00
Price: Nickel $805.00

CAUTION: PRICES SHOWN ARE SUPPLIED BY THE MANUFACTURER OR IMPORTER. CHECK YOUR LOCAL GUNSHOP.

SINGLE-ACTION REVOLVERS

FREEDOM ARMS PREMIER 454 CASULL Caliber: 454 Casull with 45 Colt, 45 ACP, 45 Win. Mag. optional cylinders, 5-shot. **Barrel:** 4³/₄″, 6″, 7¹/₂″, 10″. **Weight:** 50 oz. **Length:** 14″ overall (7¹/₂″ bbl.). **Stocks:** Impregnated hardwood. **Sights:** Blade front, notch or adjustable rear. **Features:** All stainless steel construction; sliding bar safety system. Lifetime warranty. Made in U.S. by Freedom Arms, Inc.

Price: Field Grade (matte finish, Pachmayr grips), adjustable
sights, 4³/₄″, 6″, 7¹/₂″, 10″ **$1,263.00**
Price: Field Grade, fixed sights, all barrel lengths **$1,171.00**
Price: Field Grade, 44 Rem. Mag., adjustable sights, all barrel
lengths **$1,216.00**
Price: Premier Grade 454 (brush finish, impregnated hardwood
grips) adjustable sights, 4³/₄″, 6″, 7¹/₂″, 10″ **$1,612.00**
Price: Premier Grade, fixed sights, all barrel lengths ..**$1,507.00**
Price: Premier Grade, 44 Rem. Mag., adjustable sights, all
lengths **$1,564.00**
Price: Fitted 45 ACP, 45 Colt or 45 Win. Mag. cylinder,
add **$247.00**

Freedom 454 Field Grade

Freedom Arms Casull 44 Mag and Model 353 Revolvers Similar to the Premier 454 Casull except chambered for 357 Magnum with 5-shot cylinder; 4³/₄″, 6″, 7¹/₂″ or 9″ barrel. Weighs 59 oz. with 7¹/₂″ barrel. Standard model has adjustable sights, matte finish, Pachmayr grips, 7¹/₂″ or 9″ barrel; Silhouette has 9″ barrel, Patridge front sight, Iron Sight Gun Works Silhouette adjustable rear, Pachmayr grips, trigger over-travel adjustment screw. All stainless steel. Introduced 1992.

Price: Field Grade **$1,216.00**
Price: Premier Grade (brushed finish, impregnated hardwood
grips, Premier Grade sights) **$1,564.00**
Price: Silhouette (9″, 357 Mag., 10″, 44 Mag.) **$1,304.35**

Heritage Rough Rider

Freedom Arms Model 555 Revolver Same as the 454 Casull except chambered for the 50 A.E. (Action Express) cartridge. Offered in Premier and Field Grades with adjustable sights, 4³/₄″, 6″, 7¹/₂″ or 10″ barrel. Introduced 1994. Made in U.S. by Freedom Arms, Inc.

Price: Premier Grade **$1,612.00**
Price: Field Grade **$1,263.00**

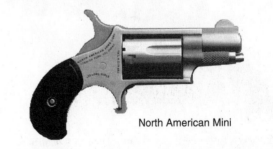

Navy Arms 1873

HERITAGE ROUGH RIDER REVOLVER Caliber: 22 LR, 22 LR/22 WMR combo, 6-shot. **Barrel:** 4³/₄″, 6¹/₂″, 9″. **Weight:** 31 to 38 oz. **Length:** NA **Stocks:** Goncolo Alves. **Sights:** Blade front, fixed rear. **Features:** Hammer block safety. High polish blue or nickel finish. Introduced 1993. Made in U.S. by Heritage Mfg., Inc.

Price: ....**$104.95 to $134.95**
Price: 2″, 3″, 4″, birdshead grip ....**$104.95 to $149.95**

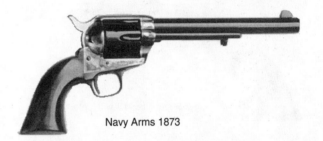

Navy Arms Schofield

NAVY ARMS 1873 SINGLE-ACTION REVOLVER Caliber: 44-40, 45 Colt, 6-shot cylinder. **Barrel:** 3″, 4³/₄″, 5¹/₂″, 7¹/₂″. **Weight:** 36 oz. **Length:** 10³/₄″ overall (5¹/₂″ barrel). **Stocks:** Smooth walnut. **Sights:** Blade front, groove in topstrap rear. **Features:** Blue with color case-hardened frame, or nickel. Introduced 1991. Imported by Navy Arms.

Price: Blue **$390.00**
Price: Nickel **$455.00**
Price: Economy model with brass backstrap and trigger
guard **$345.00**
Price: 1873 U.S. Cavalry Model (7¹/₂″, 45 Colt, arsenal mark-
ings) **$480.00**
Price: 1895 U.S. Artillery Model (as above, 5¹/₂″ barrel) .**$480.00**

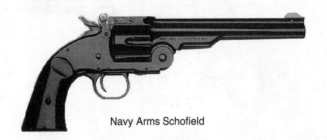

North American Mini

NAVY ARMS 1875 SCHOFIELD REVOLVER Caliber: 44-40, 45 Colt, 6-shot cylinder. **Barrel:** 5″, 7″. **Weight:** 39 oz. **Length:** 10³/₄″ overall (5″ barrel). **Stocks:** Smooth walnut. **Sights:** Blade front, notch rear. **Features:** Replica of Smith & Wesson Model 3 Schofield. Single-action, top-break with automatic ejection. Polished blue finish. Introduced 1994. Imported by Navy Arms.

Price: Wells Fargo (5″ barrel, Wells Fargo markings) ...**$795.00**
Price: U.S. Cavalry model (7″ barrel, military markings) **$795.00**

NORTH AMERICAN MINI-REVOLVERS Caliber: 22 Short, 22 LR, 22 WMR, 5-shot. **Barrel:** 1¹/₈″, 1⁵/₈″. **Weight:** 4 to 6.6 oz. **Length:** 3⁵/₈″ to 6¹/₈″ overall. **Stocks:** Laminated wood. **Sights:** Blade front, notch fixed rear. **Features:** All stainless steel construction. Polished satin and matte finish. Engraved models available. From North American Arms.

Price: 22 Short, 22 LR, 1¹/₈″ barrel **$157.00**
Price: 22 LR, 1⁵/₈″ barrel **$157.00**
Price: 22 WMR, 1⁵/₈″ barrel **$178.00**
Price: 22 WMR, 1¹/₈″ or 1⁵/₈″ barrel with extra 22 LR
cylinder **$210.00**

North American Mini-Master

Ruger Blackhawk

Ruger Super Blackhawk Hunter

Ruger Bisley

Ruger Vaquero

NORTH AMERICAN MINI-MASTER **Caliber:** 22 LR, 22 WMR, 5-shot cylinder. **Barrel:** 4″. **Weight:** 10.7 oz. **Length:** 7.75″ overall. **Stocks:** Checkered hard black rubber. **Sights:** Blade front, white outline rear adjustable for elevation, or fixed. **Features:** Heavy vent barrel; full-size grips. Non-fluted cylinder. Introduced 1989.
Price: Adjustable sight, 22 WMR or 22 LR $279.00
Price: As above with extra WMR/LR cylinder $317.00
Price: Fixed sight, 22 WMR or 22 LR $264.00
Price: As above with extra WMR/LR cylinder $302.00

North American Black Widow Revolver Similar to the Mini-Master except has 2″ Heavy Vent barrel. Built on the 22 WMR frame. Non-fluted cylinder, black rubber grips. Available with either Millett Low Profile fixed sights or Millett sight adjustable for elevation only. Overall length 5⅞″, weight 8.8 oz. From North American Arms.
Price: Adjustable sight, 22 LR or 22 WMR $249.00
Price: As above with extra WMR/LR cylinder $285.00
Price: Fixed sight, 22 LR or 22 WMR $235.00
Price: As above with extra WMR/LR cylinder $270.00

RUGER BLACKHAWK REVOLVER **Caliber:** 30 Carbine, 357 Mag./38 Spec., 41 Mag., 45 Colt, 6-shot. **Barrel:** 4⅝″ or 6½″, either caliber; 7½″ (30 Carbine, 45 Colt only). **Weight:** 42 oz. (6½″ bbl.). **Length:** 12¼″ overall (6½″ bbl.). **Stocks:** American walnut. **Sights:** ⅛″ ramp front, micro-click rear adjustable for windage and elevation. **Features:** Ruger transfer bar safety system, independent firing pin, hardened chrome moly steel frame, music wire springs throughout.
Price: Blue, 30 Carbine (7½″ bbl.), BN31 . . . .$345.00
Price: Blue, 357 Mag. (4⅝″, 6½″), BN34, BN36 . . . .$345.00
Price: Blue, 357/9mm Convertible (4⅝″, 6½″), BN34X, BN36X $365.00
Price: Blue, 41 Mag., 45 Colt (4⅝″, 6½″), BN41, BN42, BN45 . . . .$345.00
Price: Stainless, 357 Mag. (4⅝″, 6½″), KBN34, KBN36 .$428.00
Price: High-gloss stainless, 357 Mag. (4⅝″, 6½″), GKBN34, GKBN36 . . . .$428.00
Price: High-gloss stainless, 45 Colt (4⅝″, 7½″), GKBN44, GKBN45 . . . .$428.00

> Consult our Directory pages for the location of firms mentioned.

Ruger Bisley Single-Action Revolver Similar to standard Blackhawk except the hammer is lower with a smoothly curved, deeply checkered wide spur. The trigger is strongly curved with a wide smooth surface. Longer grip frame has a hand-filling shape. Adjustable rear sight, ramp-style front. Has an unfluted cylinder and roll engraving, adjustable sights. Chambered for 357, 41, 44 Mags. and 45 Colt; 7½″ barrel; overall length of 13″. Introduced 1985.
Price: $415.00

RUGER VAQUERO SINGLE-ACTION REVOLVER **Caliber:** 44-40, 44 Magnum, 45 Colt, 6-shot. **Barrel:** 4⅝″, 5½″, 7½″. **Weight:** 41 oz. **Length:** 13⅜″ overall (7½″ barrel). **Stocks:** Smooth rosewood with Ruger medallion. **Sights:** Blade front, fixed notch rear. **Features:** Uses Ruger's patented transfer bar safety system and loading gate interlock with classic styling. Blued model has color case-hardened finish on the frame, the rest polished and blued. Stainless model has high-gloss polish. Introduced 1993. From Sturm, Ruger & Co.
Price: BNV44 (4⅝″), BNV445 (5½″), BNV45 (7½″), blue $419.00
Price: KBNV44 (4⅝″), KBNV455 (5½″), KBNV45 (7½″), stainless $419.00

RUGER SUPER BLACKHAWK **Caliber:** 44 Magnum, 6-shot. Also fires 44 Spec. **Barrel:** 4⅝″, 5½″, 7½″, 10½″. **Weight:** 48 oz. (7½″ bbl.), 51 oz. (10½″ bbl.). **Length:** 13⅜″ overall (7½″ bbl.). **Stocks:** American walnut. **Sights:** ⅛″ ramp front, micro-click rear adjustable for windage and elevation. **Features:** Ruger transfer bar safety system, non-fluted cylinder, steel grip and cylinder frame, square back trigger guard, wide serrated trigger and wide spur hammer.
Price: Blue (S45N, S47N, S411N) $398.00
Price: Stainless (KS45N, KS47N, KS411N) $435.00
Price: Stainless KS47NH Hunter with scope rings, 7½″ $498.00
Price: High-gloss stainless (4⅝″, 5½″, 7½″), GKS458N, GKS45N, GKS47N $435.00

SINGLE-ACTION REVOLVERS

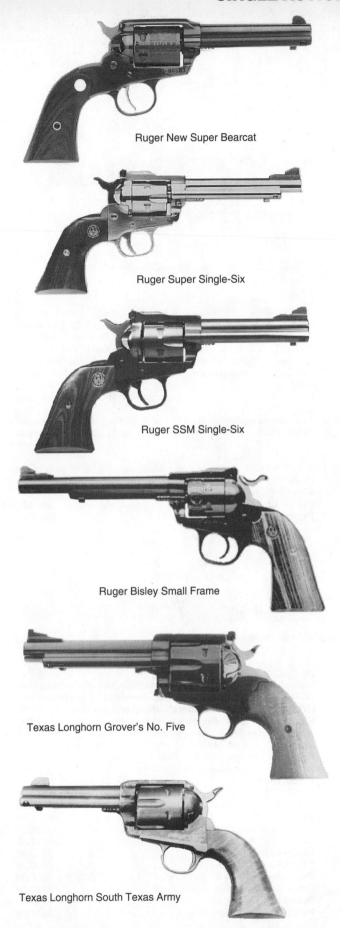

Ruger New Super Bearcat

Ruger Super Single-Six

Ruger SSM Single-Six

Ruger Bisley Small Frame

Texas Longhorn Grover's No. Five

Texas Longhorn South Texas Army

RUGER NEW SUPER BEARCAT SINGLE ACTION **Caliber:** 22 LR/22 WMR, 6-shot. **Barrel:** 4″. **Weight:** 23 oz. **Length:** 8⅞″ overall. **Stocks:** Smooth rosewood with Ruger medallion. **Sights:** Blade front, fixed notch rear. **Features:** Reintroduction of the Ruger Super Bearcat with slightly lengthened frame, Ruger patented transfer bar safety system. Comes with two cylinders. Available in blue or stainless steel. Introduced 1993. From Sturm, Ruger & Co.
Price: SBC4, blue $298.00
Price: KSBC4, stainless $325.00

RUGER SUPER SINGLE-SIX CONVERTIBLE **Caliber:** 22 LR, 6-shot; 22 WMR in extra cylinder. **Barrel:** 4⅝″, 5½″, 6½″, or 9½″ (6-groove). **Weight:** 34½ oz. (6½″ bbl.). **Length:** 11¹³⁄₁₆″ overall (6½″ bbl.). **Stocks:** Smooth American walnut. **Sights:** Improved Patridge front on ramp, fully adjustable rear protected by integral frame ribs; or fixed sight. **Features:** Ruger transfer bar safety system, gate-controlled loading, hardened chrome moly steel frame, wide trigger, music wire springs throughout, independent firing pin.
Price: 4⅝″, 5½″, 6½″, 9½″ barrel, blue, fixed or adjustable sight (5½″, 6½″) $298.00
Price: 5½″, 6½″ bbl. only, high-gloss stainless steel, fixed or adjustable sight $378.00

Ruger SSM Single-Six Revolver Similar to the Super Single-Six revolver except chambered for 32 H&R Magnum (also handles 32 S&W and 32 S&W Long). Weight is about 34 oz. with 6½″ barrel. Barrel lengths: 4⅝″, 5½″, 6½″, 9½″. Introduced 1985.
Price: $298.00

Ruger Bisley Small Frame Revolver Similar to the Single-Six except frame is styled after the classic Bisley "flat-top." Most mechanical parts are unchanged. Hammer is lower and smoothly curved with a deeply checkered spur. Trigger is strongly curved with a wide smooth surface. Longer grip frame designed with a hand-filling shape, and the trigger guard is a large oval. Adjustable dovetail rear sight; front sight base accepts interchangeable square blades of various heights and styles. Has an unfluted cylinder and roll engraving. Weight about 41 oz. Chambered for 22 LR and 32 H&R Mag., 6½″ barrel only. Introduced 1985.
Price: $345.00

TEXAS LONGHORN ARMS GROVER'S IMPROVED NO. FIVE **Caliber:** 44 Magnum, 6-shot. **Barrel:** 5½″. **Weight:** 44 oz. **Length:** NA. **Stocks:** Fancy AAA walnut. **Sights:** Square blade front on ramp, fully adjustable rear. **Features:** Music wire coil spring action with double locking bolt; polished blue finish. Handmade in limited 1,200-gun production. Grip contour, straps, over-sized base pin, lever latch and lockwork identical copies of Elmer Keith design. Lifetime warranty to original owner. Introduced 1988.
Price: $1,195.00

TEXAS LONGHORN ARMS RIGHT-HAND SINGLE ACTION **Caliber:** All centerfire pistol calibers. **Barrel:** 4¾″. **Weight:** NA. **Length:** NA. **Stocks:** One-piece fancy walnut, or any fancy AAA wood. **Sights:** Blade front, grooved topstrap rear. **Features:** Loading gate and ejector housing on left side of gun. Cylinder rotates to the left. All steel construction; color case-hardened frame; high polish blue; music wire coil springs. Lifetime guarantee to original owner. Introduced 1984. From Texas Longhorn Arms.
Price: South Texas Army Limited Edition—handmade, only 1,000 to be produced; "One of One Thousand" engraved on barrel $1,595.00

Texas Longhorn Arms Sesquicentennial Model Revolver Similar to the South Texas Army Model except has ¾-coverage Nimschke-style engraving, antique golden nickel plate finish, one-piece elephant ivory grips. Comes with handmade solid walnut presentation case, factory letter to owner. Limited edition of 150 units. Introduced 1986.
Price: $2,500.00

SINGLE-ACTION REVOLVERS

Texas Longhorn Arms Texas Border Special Similar to the South Texas Army Limited Edition except has 3½″ barrel, bird's-head style grip. Same special features. Introduced 1984.
Price: **$1,595.00**

Texas Longhorn Arms West Texas Flat Top Target Similar to the South Texas Army Limited Edition except choice of barrel length from 7½″ through 15″; flat-top style frame; ⅛″ contoured ramp front sight, old model steel micro-click rear adjustable for windage and elevation. Same special features. Introduced 1984.
Price: **$1,595.00**

Texas Longhorn Arms Cased Set Set contains one each of the Texas Longhorn Right-Hand Single Actions, all in the same caliber, same serial numbers (100, 200, 300, 400, 500, 600, 700, 800, 900). Ten sets to be made (#1000 donated to NRA museum). Comes in hand-tooled leather case. All other specs same as Limited Edition guns. Introduced 1984.
Price: **$5,750.00**
Price: With ¾-coverage "C-style" engraving **$7,650.00**

UBERTI 1890 ARMY OUTLAW REVOLVER Caliber: 357 Mag., 44-40, 45 Colt, 45 Colt/45 ACP convertible, 6-shot. **Barrel:** 5½″, 7½″. **Weight:** 37 oz. **Length:** 12½″ overall. **Stocks:** American walnut. **Sights:** Blade front, groove rear. **Features:** Replica of the 1890 Remington single action. Brass trigger guard, rest is blued. Imported by Uberti USA.
Price: **$410.00**
Price: 45 Colt/45 ACP convertible **$415.00**

UBERTI 1875 SA ARMY OUTLAW REVOLVER Caliber: 357 Mag., 44-40, 45 Colt, 45 Colt/45 ACP convertible, 6-shot. **Barrel:** 5½″, 7½″. **Weight:** 44 oz. **Length:** 13¾″ overall. **Stocks:** Smooth walnut. **Sights:** Blade front, notch rear. **Features:** Replica of the 1875 Remington S.A. Army revolver. Brass trigger guard, color case-hardened frame, rest blued. Imported by Uberti USA.
Price: **$405.00**
Price: 45 Colt/45 ACP convertible **$450.00**

Texas Longhorn Flat Top

Uberti Cattleman

UBERTI 1873 CATTLEMAN SINGLE ACTIONS Caliber: 22 LR/22 WMR, 38 Spec., 357 Mag., 44 Spec., 44-40, 45 Colt/45 ACP, 6-shot. **Barrel:** 4¾″, 5½″, 7½″; 44-40, 45 Colt also with 3″, 4″. **Weight:** 38 oz. (5½″ bbl.). **Length:** 10¾″ overall (5½″ bbl.). **Stocks:** One-piece smooth walnut. **Sights:** Blade front, groove rear; fully adjustable rear available. **Features:** Steel or brass backstrap, trigger guard; color case-hardened frame, blued barrel, cylinder. Imported from Italy by Uberti USA.
Price: Steel backstrap, trigger guard, fixed sights **$410.00**
Price: Brass backstrap, trigger guard, fixed sights **$365.00**

Uberti 1873 Buckhorn Single Action A slightly larger version of the Cattleman revolver. Available in 44 Magnum or 44 Magnum/44-40 convertible, otherwise has same specs.
Price: Steel backstrap, trigger guard, fixed sights **$410.00**
Price: Convertible (two cylinders) **$460.00**

MISCELLANEOUS

Specially adapted single-shot and multi-barrel arms.

American Derringer Model 1

AMERICAN DERRINGER MODEL 1 Caliber: 22 LR, 22 WMR, 30 Carbine, 30 Luger, 30-30 Win., 32 H&R Mag., 32-20, 380 ACP, 38 Super, 38 Spec., 38 Spec. shotshell, 38 Spec. +P, 9mm Para., 357 Mag., 357 Mag./45/410, 357 Maximum, 10mm, 40 S&W, 41 Mag., 38-40, 44-40 Win., 44 Spec., 44 Mag., 45 Colt, 45 Win. Mag., 45 ACP, 45 Colt/410, 45-70 single shot. **Barrel:** 3″. **Weight:** 15½ oz. (38 Spec.). **Length:** 4.82″ overall. **Stocks:** Rosewood, Zebra wood. **Sights:** Blade front. **Features:** Made of stainless steel with high-polish or satin finish. Two-shot capacity. Manual hammer block safety. Introduced 1980. Available in almost any pistol caliber. Contact the factory for complete list of available calibers and prices. From American Derringer Corp.
Price: 22 LR **$245.00**
Price: 38 Spec. **$245.00**
Price: 357 Maximum **$265.00**
Price: 357 Mag. **$257.00**
Price: 9mm, 380, ... **$245.00**
Price: 40 S&W **$257.00**
Price: 44 Spec., ... **$320.00**
Price: 44-40 Win., 45 Colt **$320.00**
Price: 30-30, 41, 44 Mags., 45 Win. Mag. . . . . **$375.00** to **$385.00**
Price: 45-70, single shot **$312.00**
Price: 45 Colt, 410, 2½″ **$320.00**
Price: 45 ACP, 10mm Auto **$257.00**

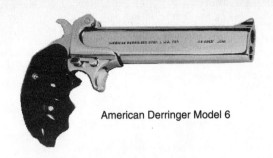

American Derringer Model 6

American Derringer Model 7 Ultra Lightweight Similar to Model 1 except made of high strength aircraft aluminum. Weighs 7½ oz., 4.82″ o.a.l., rosewood stocks. Available in 22 LR, 22 WMR, 32 H&R Mag., 380 ACP, 38 Spec., 44 Spec. Introduced 1986.
Price: 22 LR, WMR $240.00
Price: 38 Spec. $240.00
Price: 380 ACP $240.00
Price: 32 H&R Mag. $240.00
Price: 44 Spec. $500.00

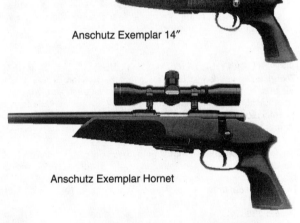

Anschutz Exemplar 14″

Anschutz Exemplar Hornet

Anschutz Exemplar

Davis 22 Derringer

DAVIS DERRINGERS Caliber: 22 LR, 22 WMR, 25 ACP, 32 ACP. **Barrel:** 2.4″. **Weight:** 9.5 oz. **Length:** 4″ overall. **Stocks:** Laminated wood. **Sights:** Blade front, fixed notch rear. **Features:** Choice of black Teflon or chrome finish; spur trigger. Introduced 1986. Made in U.S. by Davis Industries.
Price: $75.00

American Derringer Texas Commemorative A Model 1 Derringer with solid brass frame, stainless steel barrel and rosewood grips. Available in 38 Speical, 44-40 Win., or 45 Colt. Introduced 1987.
Price: 38 Spec. $225.00
Price: 44-40 or 45 Colt $320.00

American Derringer Model 4 Similar to the Model 1 except has 4.1″ barrel, overall length of 6″, and weighs 16½ oz.; chambered for 357 Mag., 357 Maximum, 45-70, 3″ 410-bore shotshells or 45 Colt or 44 Magnum. Made of stainless steel. Manual hammer block safety. Introduced 1985.
Price: 3″ 410/45 Colt $352.00
Price: 3″ 410/45 Colt or 45-70 (Alaskan Survival model) .$387.50
Price: 44 Magnum with oversize grips $422.00
Price: Alaskan Survival model (45-70 upper, 410 or 45 Colt lower) $387.50

American Derringer Model 6 Similar to the Model 1 except has 6″ barrels chambered for 3″ 410 shotshells or 22 WMR, 357 Mag., 45 ACP, 45 Colt; rosewood stocks; 8.2″ o.a.l. and weighs 21 oz. Shoots either round for each barrel. Manual hammer block safety. Introduced 1986.
Price: 22 WMR $300.00
Price: 357 Mag. $310.00
Price: 45 Colt/410 . . . .$362.50
Price: 45 ACP $345.00

American Derringer Model 10 Lightweight Similar to the Model 1 except frame is of aluminum, giving weight of 10 oz. Stainless barrels. Available in 38 Spec., 45 Colt or 45 ACP only. Matte gray finish. Introduced 1989.
Price: 45 Colt $320.00
Price: 45 ACP $257.00
Price: 38 Spec. $240.00

American Derringer Lady Derringer Same as the Model 1 except has tuned action, is fitted with scrimshawed synthetic ivory grips; chambered for 32 H&R Mag. and 38 Spec.; 357 Mag., 45 Colt. Deluxe Grade is highly polished; Deluxe Engraved is engraved in a pattern similar to that used on 1880s derringers. All come in a French fitted jewelry box. Introduced 1991.
Price: 32 H&R Mag. $255.00
Price: 357 Mag. $275.00
Price: 38 Spec. $235.00
Price: 45 Colt $320.00

AMERICAN DERRINGER DA 38 MODEL Caliber: 9mm Para., 38 Spec., 357 Mag., 40 S&W. **Barrel:** 3″. **Weight:** 14.5 oz. **Length:** 4.8″ overall. **Stocks:** Rosewood, walnut or other hardwoods. **Sights:** Fixed. **Features:** Double-action only; two-shots. Manual safety. Made of satin-finished stainless steel and aluminum. Introduced 1989. From American Derringer Corp.
Price: 38 Spec. $300.00
Price: 9mm Para. $325.00
Price: 357 Mag., 40 S&W $350.00

ANSCHUTZ EXEMPLAR BOLT-ACTION PISTOL Caliber: 22 LR, 5-shot; 22 Hornet, 5-shot. **Barrel:** 10″, 14″. **Weight:** 3½ lbs. **Length:** 17″ overall. **Stock:** European walnut with stippled grip and forend. **Sights:** Hooded front on ramp, open notch rear adjustable for windage and elevation. **Features:** Uses Match 64 action with left-hand bolt; Anschutz #5091 two-stage trigger set at 9.85 oz. Receiver grooved for scope mounting; open sights easily removed. The 22 Hornet version uses Match 54 action with left-hand bolt, Anschutz #5099 two-stage trigger set at 19.6 oz. Introduced 1987. Imported from Germany by Precision Sales International.
Price: 22 LR $558.00
Price: 22 LR, left-hand $558.00
Price: 22 LR, 14″ barrel $562.00
Price: 22 Hornet (no sights, 10″ bbl.) $995.00

Davis D-38 Derringer

Feather Guardian Angel

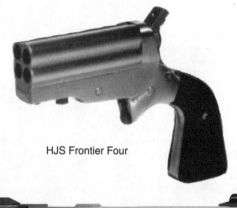

HJS Frontier Four

Gaucher GN1 Silhouette

Magnum Research Lone Eagle

DAVIS LONG-BORE DERRINGERS Caliber: 22 WMR, 32 H&R Mag., 38 Spec., 9mm Para. **Barrel:** 3.5″. **Weight:** 16 oz. **Length:** 5.4″ overall. **Stocks:** Textured black synthetic. **Sights:** Fixed. **Features:** Chrome or black teflon finish. Larger than Davis D-Series models. Introduced 1995. Made in U.S. by Davis Industries.
Price: **$104.00**
Price: Big-Bore models (same calibers but with ³⁄₄″ shorter barrels) **$98.00**

DAVIS D-SERIES DERRINGERS Caliber: 22 WMR, 32 H&R, 38 Special. **Barrel:** 2.75″. **Weight:** 11.5 oz. **Length:** 4.65″ overall. **Stocks:** Textured black synthetic. **Sights:** Blade front, fixed notch rear. **Features:** Alloy frame, steel-lined barrels, steel breech block. Plunger-type safety with integral hammer block. Chrome or black Teflon finish. Introduced 1992. Made in U.S. by Davis Industries.
Price: **$98.00**

Consult our Directory pages for the location of firms mentioned.

FEATHER GUARDIAN ANGEL PISTOL Caliber: 22 LR/22 WMR. **Barrel:** 2″. **Weight:** 12 oz. **Length:** 5″ overall. **Stocks:** Black composition. **Sights:** Fixed. **Features:** Uses a pre-loaded two-shot drop-in "magazine." Stainless steel construction; matte finish. From Feather Industries. Introduced 1988.
Price: **$119.95**

HJS FRONTIER FOUR DERRINGER Caliber: 22 LR. **Barrel:** 2″. **Weight:** 5¹⁄₂ oz. **Length:** 3¹⁵⁄₁₆″ overall. **Stocks:** Brown plastic. **Sights:** None. **Features:** Four barrels fire with rotating firing pin. Stainless steel construction. Introduced 1993. Made in U.S. by HJS Arms, Inc.
Price: **$165.00**

HJS LONE STAR DERRINGER Caliber: 380 ACP. **Barrel:** 2″. **Weight:** 6 oz. **Length:** 3¹⁵⁄₁₆″ overall. **Stocks:** Brown plastic. **Sights:** Groove. **Features:** Stainless steel Construction. Beryllium copper firing pin. Button-rifled barrel. Introduced 1993. Made in U.S. by HJS Arms, Inc.
Price: **$185.00**

HJS Antigua Derringer Same as the Frontier Four except blued barrel, brass frame, brass pivot pins. Brown plastic grips. Introduced 1994. Made in U.S. by HJS Arms, Inc.
Price: **$180.00**

GAUCHER GN1 SILHOUETTE PISTOL Caliber: 22 LR, single shot. **Barrel:** 10″. **Weight:** 2.4 lbs. **Length:** 15.5″ overall. **Stock:** European hardwood. **Sights:** Blade front, open adjustable rear. **Features:** Bolt action, adjustable trigger. Introduced 1990. Imported from France by Mandall Shooting Supplies.
Price: About **$525.00**
Price: Model GP Silhouette **$425.00**

MAGNUM RESEARCH LONE EAGLE SINGLE SHOT PISTOL Caliber: 22 Hornet, 223, 22-250, 243, 7mm BR, 7mm-08, 30-30, 308, 30-06, 357 Max., 35 Rem., 358 Win., 44 Mag., 444 Marlin. **Barrel:** 14″, interchangable. **Weight:** 4lbs., 3 oz. to 4 lbs., 7 oz. **Length:** 15″ overall. **Stocks:** Composition, with thumbrest. **Sights:** None furnished; drilled and tapped for scope mounting and open sights. Open sights optional. **Features:** Cannon-type rotating breech with spring-activated ejector. Ordnance steel with matte blue finish. Cross-bolt safety. External cocking lever on left side of gun. Introduced 1991. Available from Magnum Research, Inc.
Price: Complete pistol **$344.00**
Price: Barreled action only **$254.00**
Price: Scope base **$14.00**
Price: Adjustable open sights **$35.00**

MANDALL/CABANAS PISTOL Caliber: 177, pellet or round ball; single shot. **Barrel:** 9″. **Weight:** 51 oz. **Length:** 19″ overall. **Stock:** Smooth wood with thumbrest. **Sights:** Blade front on ramp, open adjustable rear. **Features:** Fires round ball or pellets with 22 blank cartridge. Automatic safety; muzzlebrake. Imported from Mexico by Mandall Shooting Supplies.
Price: **$139.95**

CAUTION: PRICES SHOWN ARE SUPPLIED BY THE MANUFACTURER OR IMPORTER. CHECK YOUR LOCAL GUNSHOP.

MAXIMUM SINGLE SHOT PISTOL Caliber: 22 LR, 22 Hornet, 22 BR, 22 PPC, 223 Rem., 22-250, 6mm BR, 6mm PPC, 243, 250 Savage, 6.5mm-35M, 270 MAX, 270 Win., 7mm TCU, 7mm BR, 7mm-35, 7mm INT-R, 7mm-08, 7mm Rocket, 7mm Super Mag., 30 Herrett, 30 Carbine, 30-30, 308 Win., 30x39, 32-20, 357 Mag., 357 Maximum, 358 Win., 44 Mag., 454 Casull. **Barrel:** 8³/₄″, 10¹/₂″, 14″. **Weight:** 61 oz. (10¹/₂″ bbl.); 78 oz. (14″ bbl.). **Length:** 15″, 18¹/₂″ overall (with 10¹/₂″ and 14″ bbl., respectively). **Stocks:** Smooth walnut stocks and forend. **Sights:** Ramp front, fully adjustable open rear. **Features:** Falling block action; drilled and tapped for M.O.A. scope mounts; integral grip frame/receiver; adjustable trigger; Douglas barrel (interchangeable). Introduced 1983. Made in U.S. by M.O.A. Corp.
Price: Stainless receiver, blue barrel $653.00
Price: Stainless receiver, stainless barrel $711.00
Price: Extra blued barrel $180.00
Price: Extra stainless barrel $244.00
Price: Scope mount $52.00

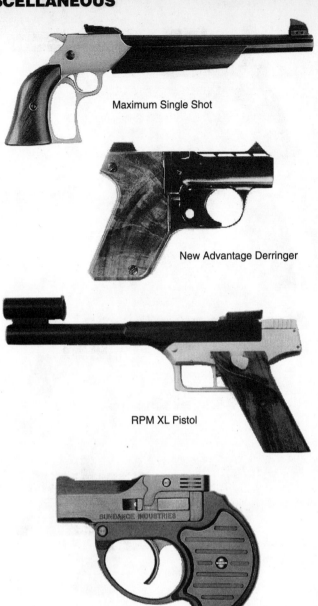

Maximum Single Shot

New Advantage Derringer

RPM XL Pistol

NEW ADVANTAGE ARMS DERRINGER Caliber: 22 LR, 22 WMR, 4-shot. **Barrel:** 2¹/₂″. **Weight:** 15 oz. **Length:** 4¹/₂″ overall. **Stocks:** Smooth walnut. **Sights:** Fixed. **Features:** Double-action mechanism, four barrels, revolving hammer with four firing pins. Rebounding hammer. Blue or stainless. Reintroduced 1989. From New Advantage Arms Corp.
Price: 22 LR, 22 WMR, blue, about $249.99
Price: As above, stainless, about $249.99

RPM XL SINGLE SHOT PISTOL Caliber: 22 LR through 45-70. **Barrel:** 8″, 10³/₄″, 12″, 14″. **Weight:** About 60 oz. **Length:** NA. **Stocks:** Smooth Goncalo Alves with thumb and heel rests. **Sights:** Hooded front with interchangeable post, or Patridge; ISGW rear adjustable for windage and elevation. **Features:** Barrel drilled and tapped for scope mount. Visible cocking indicator. Spring-loaded barrel lock, positive hammer-block safety. Trigger adjustable for weight of pull and over-travel. Contact maker for complete price list. Made in U.S. by RPM.
Price: Hunter model (stainless frame, ⁵/₁₆″ underlug, latch lever and positive extractor) $1,195.00
Price: Silhouette model (chrome-moly frame, blue or hard chrome finish) $857.50
Price: Extra barrel, 8″ through 10³/₄″ $287.50
Price: Muzzle brake $100.00

SUNDANCE POINT BLANK O/U DERRINGER Caliber: 22 LR, 2-shot. **Barrel:** 3″. **Weight:** 8 oz. **Length:** 4.6″ overall. **Stocks:** Grooved composition. **Sights:** Blade front, fixed notch rear. **Features:** Double-action trigger, push-bar safety, automatic chamber selection. Fully enclosed hammer. Matte black finish. Introduced 1994. Made in U.S. by Sundance Industries.
Price: $99.00

Sundance Point Blank

TEXAS ARMORY DEFENDER DERRINGER Caliber: 9mm Para., 357 Mag., 44 Mag., 45 ACP, 45 Colt/410. **Barrel:** 3″. **Weight:** 21 oz. **Length:** 5″ overall. **Stocks:** Smooth wood. **Sights:** Blade front, fixed rear. **Features:** Interchangeable barrels; retracting firing pins; rebounding hammer; cross-bolt safety; removable trigger guard; automatic extractor. Blasted finish stainless steel. Introduced 1993. Made in U.S. by Texas Armory.
Price: $310.00
Price: Extra barrel $100.00

Texas Armory Defender

TEXAS LONGHORN "THE JEZEBEL" PISTOL Caliber: 22 Short, Long, Long Rifle, single shot. **Barrel:** 6″. **Weight:** 15 oz. **Length:** 8″ overall. **Stocks:** One-piece fancy walnut grip (right- or left-hand), walnut forend. **Sights:** Bead front, fixed rear. **Features:** Handmade gun. Top-break action; all stainless steel; automatic hammer block safety; music wire coil springs. Barrel is half-round, half-octagon. Announced 1986. From Texas Longhorn Arms.
Price: About $250.00

THE JUDGE SINGLE SHOT PISTOL Caliber: 22 Hornet, 22 K-Hornet, 218 Bee, 7-30 Waters, 30-30. **Barrel:** 10″ or 16.2″. **Weight:** NA. **Length:** NA. **Stocks:** Walnut. **Sights:** Bead on ramp front, open adjustable rear. **Features:** Break-open design; made of 17-4 stainless steel. Also available as a kit. Introduced 1995. Made in U.S. by Cumberland Mountain Arms.
Price: ....NA

CAUTION: PRICES SHOWN ARE SUPPLIED BY THE MANUFACTURER OR IMPORTER. CHECK YOUR LOCAL GUNSHOP.

8th ANNUAL EDITION **295**

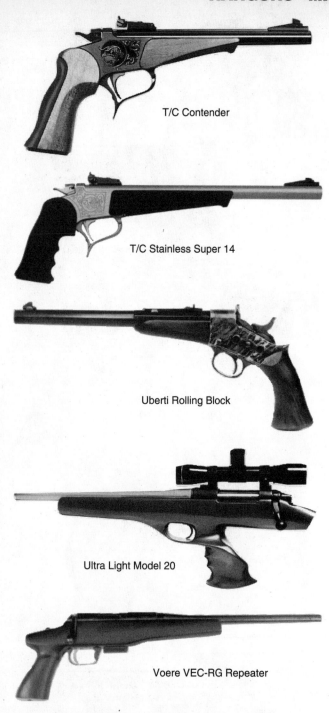

T/C Contender

T/C Stainless Super 14

Uberti Rolling Block

Ultra Light Model 20

Voere VEC-RG Repeater

VOERE VEC-95CG SINGLE SHOT PISTOL Caliber: 5.56mm, 6mm UCC caseless, single shot. **Barrel:** 12″, 14″. **Weight:** 3 lbs. **Length:** NA. **Stock:** Black synthetic; center grip. **Sights:** None furnished. **Features:** Fires caseless ammunition via electronic ignition; two batteries in the grip last about 500 shots. Bolt action has two forward locking lugs. Tang safety. Drilled and tapped for scope mounting. Introduced 1995. Imported from Austria by JagerSport, Ltd.
Price: **$1,495.00**

Voere VEC-RG Repeater Pistol Similar to the VEC-95CG except has rear grip stock and detachable 5-shot magazine. Available with 12″ or 14″ barrel. Introduced 1995. Imported from Austria by JagerSport, Ltd.
Price: **$1,495.00**

THOMPSON/CENTER CONTENDER Caliber: 7mm TCU, 30-30 Win., 22 LR, 22 WMR, 22 Hornet, 223 Rem., 270 Ren, 7-30 Waters, 32-20 Win., 357 Mag., 357 Rem. Max., 44 Mag., 10mm Auto, 445 Super Mag., 45/410, single shot. **Barrel:** 10″, tapered octagon, bull barrel and vent. rib. **Weight:** 43 oz. (10″ bbl.). **Length:** 13¼″ (10″ bbl.). **Stocks:** T/C "Competitor Grip." Right or left hand. **Sights:** Under-cut blade ramp front, rear adjustable for windage and elevation. **Features:** Break-open action with automatic safety. Single-action only. Interchangeable bbls., both caliber (rim & centerfire), and length. Drilled and tapped for scope. Engraved frame. See T/C catalog for exact barrel/caliber availability.
Price: Blued (rimfire cals.) **$450.00**
Price: Blued (centerfire cals.) **$450.00**
Price: Extra bbls. (standard octagon) **$207.50**
Price: 45/410, internal choke bbl. **$227.50**

Thompson/Center Stainless Contender Same as the standard Contender except made of stainless steel with blued sights, black Rynite forend and ambidextrous finger-groove grip with a built-in rubber recoil cushion that has a sealed-in air pocket. Receiver has a different cougar etching. Available with 10″ bull barrel in 22 LR, 22 LR Match, 22 Hornet, 223 Rem., 30-30 Win., 357 Mag., 44 Mag., 45 Colt/410. Introduced 1993.
Price: **$480.00**
Price: 45 Colt/410 . . . .**$485.00**
Price: With 22 LR match chamber **$490.00**

Thompson/Center Stainless Super 14, Super 16 Contender Same as the standard Super 14 and Super 16 except they are made of stainless steel with blued sights. Both models have black Rynite forend and finger-groove, ambidextrous grip with a built-in rubber recoil cushion that has a sealed-in air pocket. Receiver has a different cougar etching. Available in 22 LR, 22 LR Match, 22 Hornet, 223 Rem., 30-30 Win., 35 Rem. (Super 14), 45-70 (Super 16 only), 45 Colt/410. Introduced 1993.
Price: 14″ bull barrel **$490.00**
Price: 16¼″ bull barrel **$495.00**
Price: 45 Colt/410, 14″ **$520.00**
Price: 45 Colt/410, 16″ **$525.00**

Thompson/Center Contender Hunter Package Package contains the Contender pistol in 223, 7-30 Waters, 30-30, 375 Win., 357 Rem. Maximum, 35 Rem., 44 Mag. or 45-70 with 14″ barrel with T/C's Muzzle Tamer, a 2.5x Recoil Proof Long Eye Relief scope with lighted reticle, q.d. sling swivels with a nylon carrying sling. Comes with a suede leather case with foam padding and fleece lining. Introduced 1990. From Thompson/Center Arms.
Price: 14″ barrel **$765.00**

UBERTI ROLLING BLOCK TARGET PISTOL Caliber: 22 LR, 22 WMR, 22 Hornet, 357 Mag., 45 Colt, single shot. **Barrel:** 9⅞″, half-round, half-octagon. **Weight:** 44 oz. **Length:** 14″ overall. **Stocks:** Walnut grip and forend. **Sights:** Blade front, fully adjustable rear. **Features:** Replica of the 1871 rolling block target pistol. Brass trigger guard, color case-hardened frame, blue barrel. Imported by Uberti USA.
Price: **$380.00**

ULTRA LIGHT ARMS MODEL 20 REB HUNTER'S PISTOL Caliber: 22-250 thru 308 Win. standard. Most silhouette calibers and others on request. 5-shot magazine. **Barrel:** 14″, Douglas No. 3. **Weight:** 4 lbs. **Stock:** Composite Kevlar, graphite reinforced. Du Pont Imron paint in green, brown, black and camo. **Sights:** None furnished. Scope mount included. **Features:** Timney adjustable trigger; two-position, three-function safety; benchrest quality action; matte or bright stock and metal finish; right- or left-hand action. Shipped in hard case. Introduced 1987. From Ultra Light Arms.
Price: **$1,600.00**

CAUTION: PRICES SHOWN ARE SUPPLIED BY THE MANUFACTURER OR IMPORTER. CHECK YOUR LOCAL GUNSHOP.

Dixie Charleville

CVA Hawken

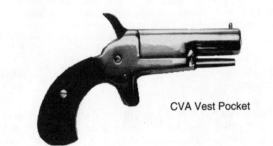

CVA Vest Pocket

Dixie Pennsylvania

Navy Arms Kentucky Flintlock

BLACK WATCH SCOTCH PISTOL Caliber: 577 (.500″ round ball). **Barrel:** 7″, smoothbore. **Weight:** 1½ lbs. **Length:** 12″ overall. **Stock:** Brass. **Sights:** None. **Features:** Faithful reproduction of this military flintlock. From Dixie Gun Works.
Price: **$175.00**

CHARLEVILLE FLINTLOCK PISTOL Caliber: 69 (.680″ round ball). **Barrel:** 7½″. **Weight:** 48 oz. **Length:** 13½″ overall. **Stock:** Walnut. **Sights:** None. **Features:** Brass frame, polished steel barrel, iron belt hook, brass buttcap and backstrap. Replica of original 1777 pistol. Imported by Dixie Gun Works.
Price: **$195.00**

CVA HAWKEN PISTOL Caliber: 50. **Barrel:** 9¾″; ¹⁵/₁₆″ flats. **Weight:** 50 oz. **Length:** 16½″ overall. **Stock:** Select hardwood. **Sights:** Beaded blade front, fully adjustable open rear. **Features:** Color case-hardened lock, polished brass wedge plate, nose cap, ramrod thimble, trigger guard, grip cap. Imported by CVA.
Price: **$139.95**
Price: Kit **$119.95**
Price: With laminated stock **$159.95**

CVA VEST POCKET DERRINGER Caliber: 31. **Barrel:** 2½″, brass. **Weight:** 16 oz. **Stock:** Two-piece walnut. **Features:** All brass frame and barrel. A muzzle-loading version of the Colt No. 3 derringer. Imported by CVA.
Price: Finished **$84.95**

DIXIE PENNSYLVANIA PISTOL Caliber: 44 (.430″ round ball). **Barrel:** 10″ (⅞″ octagon). **Weight:** 2½ lbs. **Stock:** Walnut-stained hardwood. **Sights:** Blade front, open rear drift-adjustable for windage; brass. **Features:** Available in flint only. Brass trigger guard, thimbles, nosecap, wedgeplates; high-luster blue barrel. Imported from Italy by Dixie Gun Works.
Price: Finished **$149.95**
Price: Kit **$119.95**

DIXIE SCREW BARREL PISTOL Caliber: .445″. **Barrel:** 2½″. **Weight:** 8 oz. **Length:** 6½″ overall. **Stock:** Walnut. **Features:** Trigger folds down when hammer is cocked. Close copy of the originals once made in Belgium. Uses No. 11 percussion caps. From Dixie Gun Works.
Price: **$89.00**
Price: Kit **$74.95**

> Consult our Directory pages for the location of firms mentioned.

FRENCH-STYLE DUELING PISTOL Caliber: 44. **Barrel:** 10″. **Weight:** 35 oz. **Length:** 15¾″ overall. **Stock:** Carved walnut. **Sights:** Fixed. **Features:** Comes with velvet-lined case and accessories. Imported by Mandall Shooting Supplies.
Price: **$295.00**

HARPER'S FERRY 1806 PISTOL Caliber: 58 (.570″ round ball). **Barrel:** 10″. **Weight:** 40 oz. **Length:** 16″ overall. **Stock:** Walnut. **Sights:** Fixed. **Features:** Case-hardened lock, brass-mounted browned barrel. Replica of the first U.S. Gov't.-made flintlock pistol. Imported by Navy Arms, Dixie Gun Works.
Price: . . . .**$249.95 to $405.00**
Price: Kit (Dixie) **$199.95**
Price: Cased set (Navy Arms) **$335.00**

KENTUCKY FLINTLOCK PISTOL Caliber: 44, 45. **Barrel:** 10⅛″. **Weight:** 32 oz. **Length:** 15½″ overall. **Stock:** Walnut. **Sights:** Fixed. **Features:** Specifications, including caliber, weight and length may vary with importer. Case-hardened lock, blued barrel; available also as brass barrel flint Model 1821. Imported by Navy Arms (44 only), The Armoury.
Price: . . . .**$145.00 to $225.00**
Price: In kit form, from . . . .**$90.00 to $112.00**
Price: Single cased set (Navy Arms) **$325.00**
Price: Double cased set (Navy Arms) **$550.00**

BLACKPOWDER SINGLE-SHOT PISTOLS—FLINT & PERCUSSION

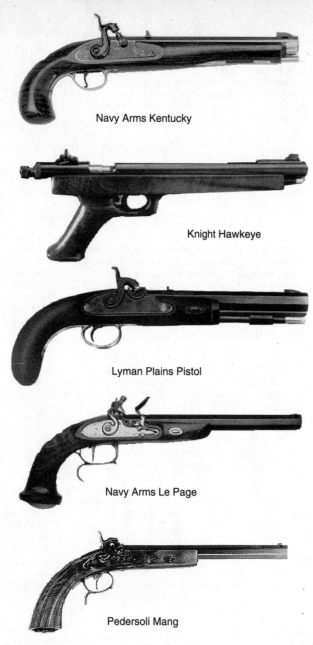

Navy Arms Kentucky

Knight Hawkeye

Lyman Plains Pistol

Navy Arms Le Page

Pedersoli Mang

Dixie Queen Anne

Kentucky Percussion Pistol Similar to flint version but percussion lock. Imported by The Armoury, Navy Arms, CVA (50-cal.).
Price: ....$129.95 to $250.00
Price: Steel barrel (Armoury) $179.00
Price: Single cased set (Navy Arms) $310.00
Price: Double cased set (Navy Arms) $525.00

KNIGHT HAWKEYE PISTOL Caliber: 50. **Barrel:** 12″, 1:20″ twist. **Weight:** 3¼ lbs. **Length:** 20″ overall. **Stock:** Black composite, autumn brown or shadow black laminate. **Sights:** Bead front on ramp, open fully adjustable rear. **Features:** In-line ignitiion design; patented double safety system; removeable breech plug; fully adjustable trigger; receiver drilled and tapped for scope mounting. Made in U.S. by Modern Muzzle Loading, Inc.
Price: Blued $374.95
Price: Stainless $424.50

LE PAGE PERCUSSION DUELING PISTOL Caliber: 45. **Barrel:** 10″, rifled. **Weight:** 40 oz. **Length:** 16″ overall. **Stock:** Walnut, fluted butt. **Sights:** Blade front, notch rear. **Features:** Double-set triggers. Blued barrel; trigger guard and buttcap are polished silver. Imported by Dixie Gun Works.
Price: $259.95

LYMAN PLAINS PISTOL Caliber: 50 or 54. **Barrel:** 8″, 1:30 twist, both calibers. **Weight:** 50 oz. **Length:** 15″ overall. **Stock:** Walnut half-stock. **Sights:** Blade front, square notch rear adjustable for windage. **Features:** Polished brass trigger guard and ramrod tip, color case-hardened coil spring lock, spring-loaded trigger, stainless steel nipple, blackened iron furniture. Hooked patent breech, detachable belt hook. Introduced 1981. From Lyman Products.
Price: Finished $224.95
Price: Kit $179.95

NAVY ARMS LE PAGE DUELING PISTOL Caliber: 44. **Barrel:** 9″, octagon, rifled. **Weight:** 34 oz. **Length:** 15″ overall. **Stock:** European walnut. **Sights:** Adjustable rear. **Features:** Single-set trigger. Polished metal finish. From Navy Arms.
Price: Percussion $500.00
Price: Single cased set, percussion $775.00
Price: Double cased set, percussion $1,300.00
Price: Flintlock, rifled $625.00
Price: Flintlock, smoothbore (45-cal.) $625.00
Price: Flintlock, single cased set $900.00
Price: Flintlock, double cased set $1,575.00

PEDERSOLI MANG TARGET PISTOL Caliber: 38. **Barrel:** 10.5″, octagonal; 1:15″ twist, **Weight:** 2.5 lbs. **Length:** 17.25″ overall. **Stock:** Walnut with fluted grip. **Sights:** Blade front, open rear adjustable for windage. **Features:** Browned barrel, polished breech plug, rest color case-hardened. Imported from Italy by Dixie Gun Works.
Price: $749.00

QUEEN ANNE FLINTLOCK PISTOL Caliber: 50 (.490″ round ball). **Barrel:** 7½″, smoothbore. **Stock:** Walnut. **Sights:** None. **Features:** Browned steel barrel, fluted brass trigger guard, brass mask on butt. Lockplate left in the white. Made by Pedersoli in Italy. Introduced 1983. Imported by Dixie Gun Works.
Price: $189.95
Price: Kit $138.50

THOMPSON/CENTER SCOUT PISTOL Caliber: 45, 50 and 54. **Barrel:** 12″, interchangeable. **Weight:** 4 lbs., 6 oz. **Length:** NA. **Stocks:** American black walnut stocks and forend. **Sights:** Blade on ramp front, fully adjustable Patridge rear. **Features:** Patented in-line ignition system with special vented breech plug. Patented trigger mechanism consists of only two moving parts. Interchangeable barrels. Wide grooved hammer. Brass trigger guard assembly. Introduced 1990. From Thompson/Center.
Price: 45-, 50- or 54-cal. $340.00
Price: Extra barrel, 45-, 50- or 54-cal. $145.00

Thompson/Center Scout

CAUTION: PRICES SHOWN ARE SUPPLIED BY THE MANUFACTURER OR IMPORTER. CHECK YOUR LOCAL GUNSHOP.

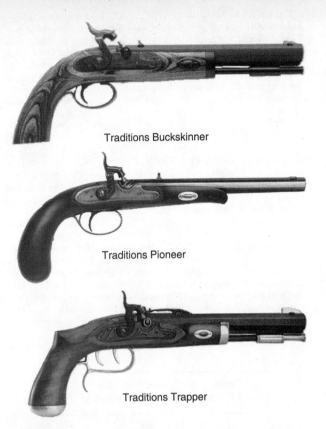

Traditions Buckskinner

Traditions Pioneer

Traditions Trapper

TRADITIONS BUCKSKINNER PISTOL Caliber: 50. **Barrel:** 10″ octagonal, 15/16″ flats. **Weight:** 40 oz. **Length:** 15″ overall. **Stocks:** Stained beech or laminated wood. **Sights:** Blade front, rear adjustable for windage. **Features:** Percussion ignition. Blackened furniture. Imported by Traditions, Inc.
Price: Beech stocks $165.00
Price: Laminated stocks $181.50

TRADITIONS KENTUCKY PISTOL Caliber: 50. **Barrel:** 9¾″; octagon with 7/8″ flats; 1:20″ twist. **Weight:** 40 oz. **Length:** 15½″ overall. **Stock:** Stained beech. **Sights:** Blade front, drift-adjustable rear. **Features:** Birds-head grip; brass thimbles; color case-hardened lock. Percussion only. Introduced 1995. From Traditions.
Price: Finished $142.00
Price: Kit $106.50

TRADITIONS PIONEER PISTOL Caliber: 45. **Barrel:** 9⅝″, 13/16″ flats. **Weight:** 31 oz. **Length:** 15″ overall. **Stock:** Beech. **Sights:** Blade front, fixed rear. **Features:** V-type mainspring; 1:16″ twist. Single trigger. German silver furniture, blackened hardware. From Traditions.
Price: $160.00
Price: Kit $126.50

TRADITIONS TRAPPER PISTOL Caliber: 50. **Barrel:** 9¾″, 7/8″ flats. **Weight:** 2¾ lbs. **Length:** 16″ overall. **Stock:** Beech. **Sights:** Blade front, adjustable rear. **Features:** Double-set triggers; brass buttcap, trigger guard, wedge plate, forend tip, thimble. From Traditions.
Price: Percussion $178.00
Price: Flintlock $198.00
Price: Kit $139.00

WHITE SHOOTING SYSTEMS JAVELINA PISTOL Caliber: 45, 50. **Barrel:** 14″. **Weight:** 5.2 lbs. **Length:** 22″ overall. **Stock:** Black composite; two-hand style. **Sights:** Blade or bead front, fully adjustable rear. **Features:** Has stainless steel action with InstaFire ignition system; match-grade trigger. Drilled and tapped for scope mounting. Announced 1995. From White Shooting Systems, Inc.
Price: $449.00

TRADITIONS WILLIAM PARKER PISTOL Caliber: 50. **Barrel:** 10⅜″, 15/16″ flats; polished steel. **Weight:** 40 oz. **Length:** 17½″ overall. **Stock:** Walnut with checkered grip. **Sights:** Brass blade front, fixed rear. **Features:** Replica dueling pistol with 1:20″ twist, hooked breech. Brass wedge plate, trigger guard, cap guard; separate ramrod. Double-set triggers. Polished steel barrel, lock. Imported by Traditions.
Price: $274.00

BLACKPOWDER REVOLVERS

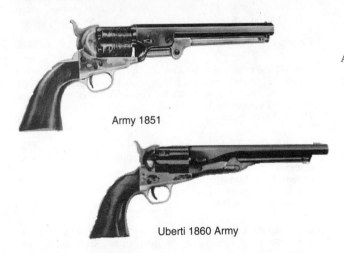

Army 1851

Uberti 1860 Army

ARMY 1851 PERCUSSION REVOLVER Caliber: 44, 6-shot. **Barrel:** 7½″. **Weight:** 45 oz. **Length:** 13″ overall. **Stocks:** Walnut finish. **Sights:** Fixed. **Features:** 44-caliber version of the 1851 Navy. Imported by The Armoury, Armsport.
Price: $129.00

ARMY 1860 PERCUSSION REVOLVER Caliber: 44, 6-shot. **Barrel:** 8″. **Weight:** 40 oz. **Length:** 13⅝″ overall. **Stocks:** Walnut. **Sights:** Fixed. **Features:** Engraved Navy scene on cylinder; brass trigger guard; case-hard~ened frame, loading lever and hammer. Some importers supply pistol cut for detachable shoulder stock, have accessory stock available. Imported by American Arms, Cabela's (1860 Lawman), E.M.F., Navy Arms, The Armoury, Cimarron, Dixie Gun Works (half-fluted cylinder, not roll engraved), Euroarms of America (brass or steel model), Armsport, Traditions (brass or steel), Uberti USA.
Price: About . . . .$92.95 to $300.00
Price: Hartford model, steel frame, German silver trim, car-touches (E.M.F.) $215.00
Price: Single cased set (Navy Arms) $300.00
Price: Double cased set (Navy Arms) $490.00
Price: 1861 Navy: Same as Army except 36-cal., 7½″ bbl., wgt. 41 oz., cut for shoulder stock; round cylinder (fluted avail.), from CVA (brass frame, 44-cal.) . . . .$99.95 to $249.00
Price: Steel frame kit (E.M.F., Navy Arms, Euroarms) . . . .$125.00 to $216.25
Price: Colt Army Police, fluted cylinder, 5½″, 36-caliber. (Cabela's) $124.95

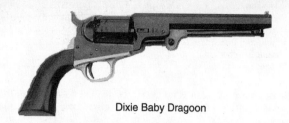

Dixie Baby Dragoon

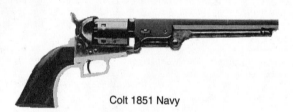

Cabela's Paterson

Colt 1847 Walker

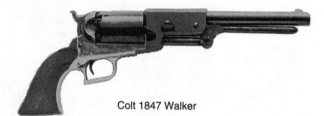

Colt 1851 Navy

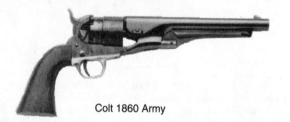

Colt 1860 Army

Colt 1860 "Cavalry Model" Percussion Revolver Similar to the 1860 Army except has fluted cylinder. Color case-hardened frame, hammer, loading lever and plunger; blued barrel, backstrap and cylinder, brass trigger guard. Has four-screw frame cut for optional shoulder stock. From Colt Blackpowder Arms Co.
Price: **$465.00**

COLT THIRD MODEL DRAGOON Caliber: 44. **Barrel:** 7½".
Weight: 66 oz. **Length:** 13¾" overall. **Stocks:** One-piece walnut. **Sights:** Blade front, hammer notch rear. **Features:** Color case-hardened frame, hammer, lever and plunger; round trigger guard; flat mainspring; hammer roller; rectangular bolt cut. From Colt Blackpowder Arms Co.
Price: Three-screw frame with brass grip straps **$487.50**
Price: Four-screw frame with blued steel grip straps, shoulder
  stock cuts, dovetailed folding leaf rear sight **$502.50**

BABY DRAGOON 1848, 1849 POCKET, WELLS FARGO Caliber: 31. **Barrel:** 3", 4", 5", 6"; seven-groove, RH twist. **Weight:** About 21 oz. **Stock:** Varnished walnut. **Sights:** Brass pin front, hammer notch rear. **Features:** No loading lever on Baby Dragoon or Wells Fargo models. Unfluted cylinder with stagecoach holdup scene; cupped cylinder pin; no grease grooves; one safety pin on cylinder and slot in hammer face; straight (flat) mainspring. From Armsport, Dixie Gun Works, Uberti USA, Cabela's, Stone Mountain Arms.
Price: 6" barrel, with loading lever (Dixie Gun Works) . .**$254.00**
Price: 4" (Cabela's, Uberti USA) **$169.95**

CABELA'S PATERSON REVOLVER Caliber: 36, 5-shot cylinder.
Barel: 7½". **Weight:** 24 oz. **Length:** 11½" overall. **Stocks:** One-piece walnut. **Sights:** Fixed. **Features:** Recreation of the 1836 gun. Color case-hardened frame, steel backstrap; roll-engraved cylinder scene. Imported by Cabela's.
Price: **$229.95**

COLT 1847 WALKER PERCUSSION REVOLVER Caliber: 44.
Barrel: 9", 7 groove, right-hand twist. **Weight:** 73 oz. **Stocks:** One-piece walnut. **Sights:** German silver front sight, hammer notch rear. **Features:** Made in U.S. Faithful reproduction of the original gun, including markings. Color case-hardened frame, hammer, loading lever and plunger. Blue steel backstrap, brass square-back trigger guard. Blue barrel, cylinder, trigger and wedge. From Colt Blackpowder Arms Co.
Price: **$442.50**

> Consult our Directory pages for
> the location of firms mentioned.

COLT 1849 POCKET DRAGOON REVOLVER Caliber: 31. **Barrel:** 4". **Weight:** 24 oz. **Length:** 9½" overall. **Stocks:** One-piece walnut. **Sights:** Fixed. Brass pin front, hammer notch rear. **Features:** Color case-hardened frame. No loading lever. Unfluted cylinder with engraved scene. Exact reproduction of original. From Colt Blackpowder Arms Co.
Price: **$390.00**

COLT 1851 NAVY PERCUSSION REVOLVER Caliber: 36. **Barrel:** 7½", octagonal, 7 groove left-hand twist. **Weight:** 40½ oz. **Stocks:** One-piece oiled American walnut. **Sights:** Brass pin front, hammer notch rear. **Features:** Faithful reproduction of the original gun. Color case-hardened frame, loading lever, plunger, hammer and latch. Blue cylinder, trigger, barrel, screws, wedge. Silver-plated brass backstrap and square-back trigger guard. From Colt Blackpowder Arms Co.
Price: **$427.50**

Uberti 1861 Navy Percussion Revolver Similar to 1851 Navy except has round 7½" barrel, rounded trigger guard, German silver blade front sight, "creeping" loading lever. Available with fluted or round cylinder. Imported by Uberti USA.
Price: Steel backstrap, trigger guard, cut for stock **$300.00**

CVA Colt Sheriff's Model Similar to the Uberti 1861 Navy except has 5½" barrel, brass or steel frame, semi-fluted cylinder. In 36-caliber only.
Price: Brass frame, finished **$149.95**
Price: Brass frame (Armsport) **$155.00**
Price: Steel frame (Armsport) **$193.00**

COLT 1860 ARMY PERCUSSION REVOLVER Caliber: 44. **Barrel:** 8", 7 groove, left-hand twist. **Weight:** 42 oz. **Stocks:** One-piece walnut. **Sights:** German silver front sight, hammer notch rear. **Features:** Steel backstrap cut for shoulder stock; brass trigger guard. Cylinder has Navy scene. Color case-hardened frame, hammer, loading lever. Reproduction of original gun with all original markings. From Colt Blackpowder Arms Co.
Price: **$427.50**

CAUTION: PRICES SHOWN ARE SUPPLIED BY THE MANUFACTURER OR IMPORTER. CHECK YOUR LOCAL GUNSHOP.

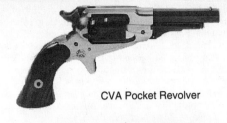

CVA Pocket Revolver

Dixie Third Model Dragoon

Griswold & Gunnison

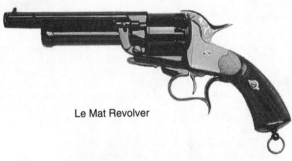

Le Mat Revolver

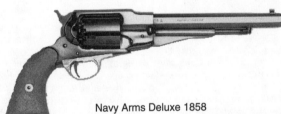

Navy Arms Deluxe 1858

NAVY MODEL 1851 PERCUSSION REVOLVER Caliber: 36, 44, 6-shot. **Barrel:** 7½". **Weight:** 44 oz. **Length:** 13" overall. **Stocks:** Walnut finish. **Sights:** Post front, hammer notch rear. **Features:** Brass backstrap and trigger guard; some have 1st Model square-back trigger guard, engraved cylinder with navy battle scene; case-hardened frame, hammer, loading lever. Imported by American Arms, The Armoury, Cabela's, Navy Arms, E.M.F., Dixie Gun Works, Euroarms of America, Armsport, CVA (36-cal. only), Traditions (44 only), Uberti USA, Stone Mountain Arms.
Price: Brass frame ....$99.95 to $280.00
Price: Steel frame ....$130.00 to $285.00
Price: Kit form ....$110.00 to $123.95
Price: Engraved model (Dixie Gun Works) $139.95
Price: Single cased set, steel frame (Navy Arms) $280.00
Price: Double cased set, steel frame (Navy Arms) $455.00
Price: Confederate Navy (Cabela's) $69.95
Price: Hartford model, steel frame, German silver trim, cartouche (E.M.F.) $190.00

COLT 1861 NAVY PERCUSSION REVOLVER Caliber: 36. **Barrel:** 7½". **Weight:** 42 oz. **Length:** 13⅛" overall. **Stocks:** One-piece walnut. **Sights:** Blade front, hammer notch rear. **Features:** Color case-hardened frame, loading lever, plunger; blued barrel, backstrap, trigger guard; roll-engraved cylinder and barrel. From Colt Blackpowder Arms Co.
Price: $465.00

COLT 1862 POCKET POLICE "TRAPPER MODEL" REVOLVER Caliber: 36. **Barrel:** 3½". **Weight:** 20 oz. **Length:** 8½" overall. **Stocks:** One-piece walnut. **Sights:** Blade front, hammer notch rear. **Features:** Has separate 4⅝" brass ramrod. Color case-hardened frame and hammer; silver-plated backstrap and trigger guard; blued semi-fluted cylinder, blued barrel. From Colt Blackpowder Arms Co.
Price: $442.50

CVA POCKET REVOLVER Caliber: 31, 5-shot. **Barrel:** 4", octagonal. **Weight:** 15 oz. **Length:** 7½" overall. **Stocks:** Two-piece walnut. **Sights:** Post front, grooved topstrap rear. **Features:** Spur trigger, brass frame with blued barrel and cylinder. Introduced 1984. Imported by CVA.
Price: Finished $139.95

DIXIE THIRD MODEL DRAGOON Caliber: 44 (.454" round ball). **Barrel:** 7⅜". **Weight:** 4 lbs., 2½ oz. **Stocks:** One-piece walnut. **Sights:** Brass pin front, hammer notch rear, or adjustable folding leaf rear. **Features:** Cylinder engraved with Indian fight scene. This is the only Dragoon replica with folding leaf sight. Brass backstrap and trigger guard; color case-hardened steel frame, blue-black barrel. Imported by Dixie Gun Works.
Price: $199.95

DIXIE WYATT EARP REVOLVER Caliber: 44. **Barrel:** 12" octagon. **Weight:** 46 oz. **Length:** 18" overall. **Stocks:** Two-piece walnut. **Sights:** Fixed. **Features:** Highly polished brass frame, backstrap and trigger guard; blued barrel and cylinder; case-hardened hammer, trigger and loading lever. Navy-size shoulder stock ($45) will fit with minor fitting. From Dixie Gun Works.
Price: $130.00

GRISWOLD & GUNNISON PERCUSSION REVOLVER Caliber: 36 or 44, 6-shot. **Barrel:** 7½". **Weight:** 44 oz. (36-cal.). **Length:** 13" overall. **Stocks:** Walnut. **Sights:** Fixed. **Features:** Replica of famous Confederate pistol. Brass frame, backstrap and trigger guard; case-hardened loading lever; rebated cylinder (44-cal. only). Rounded Dragoon-type barrel. Imported by Navy Arms as Reb Model 1860.
Price: About $115.00
Price: Single cased set (Navy Arms) $235.00
Price: Double cased set (Navy Arms) $365.00
Price: As above, kit $90.00

LE MAT REVOLVER Caliber: 44/65. **Barrel:** 6¾" (revolver); 4⅞" (single shot). **Weight:** 3 lbs., 7 oz. **Stocks:** Hand-checkered walnut. **Sights:** Post front, hammer notch rear. **Features:** Exact reproduction with all-steel construction; 44-cal. 9-shot cylinder, 65-cal. single barrel; color case-hardened hammer with selector; spur trigger guard; ring at butt; lever-type barrel release. From Navy Arms.
Price: Cavalry model (lanyard ring, spur trigger guard) .$595.00
Price: Army model (round trigger guard, pin-type barrel release) $595.00
Price: Naval-style (thumb selector on hammer) $595.00
Price: Engraved 18th Georgia cased set $795.00
Price: Engraved Beauregard cased set $1,000.00

NAVY ARMS DELUXE 1858 REMINGTON-STYLE REVOLVER Caliber: 44. **Barrel:** 8". **Weight:** 2 lbs., 13 oz. **Stocks:** Smooth walnut. **Sights:** Dovetailed blade front. **Features:** First exact reproduction—correct in size and weight to the original, with progressive rifling; highly polished with blue finish, silver-plated trigger guard. From Navy Arms.
Price: Deluxe model $415.00

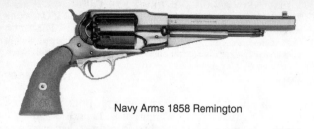

Navy Arms 1858 Remington

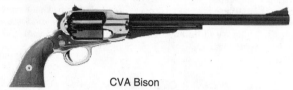

CVA Bison

Uberti 1862 Police

Euroarms Rogers & Spencer

Ruger Old Army

Sheriff Model 1851

RUGER OLD ARMY PERCUSSION REVOLVER Caliber: 45, 6-shot. Uses .457″ dia. lead bullets. **Barrel:** 7½″ (6-groove, 16″ twist). **Weight:** 46 oz. **Length:** 13¾″ overall. **Stocks:** Smooth walnut. **Sights:** Ramp front, rear adjustable for windage and elevation; or fixed (groove). **Features:** Stainless steel; standard size nipples, chrome-moly steel cylinder and frame, same lockwork as in original Super Blackhawk. Also available in stainless steel. Made in USA. From Sturm, Ruger & Co.

Price: Stainless steel (Model KBP-7) $450.00
Price: Blued steel (Model BP-7) $398.00
Price: Stainless steel, fixed sight (KBP-7F) $450.00
Price: Blued steel, fixed sight (BP-7F) $398.00

NEW MODEL 1858 ARMY PERCUSSION REVOLVER Caliber: 36 or 44, 6-shot. **Barrel:** 6½″ or 8″. **Weight:** 38 oz. **Length:** 13½″ overall. **Stocks:** Walnut. **Sights:** Blade front, groove-in-frame rear. **Features:** Replica of Remington Model 1858. Also available from some importers as Army Model Belt Revolver in 36-cal., a shortened and lightened version of the 44. Target Model (Uberti USA, Navy Arms) has fully adjustable target rear sight, target front, 36 or 44. Imported by American Arms, Cabela's, Cimarron, CVA (as 1858 Army, steel or brass frame), Dixie Gun Works, Navy Arms, The Armoury, E.M.F., Euroarms of America (engraved, stainless and plain), Armsport, Traditions (44 only), Uberti USA.

Price: Steel frame, about ....$99.95 to $280.00
Price: Steel frame kit (Euroarms, Navy
  Arms) ....$115.95 to $242.00
Price: Single cased set (Navy Arms) $290.00
Price: Double cased set (Navy Arms) $480.00
Price: Stainless steel Model 1858 (American Arms, Euroarms,
  Uberti USA, Cabela's, Navy Arms, Armsport,
  Traditions) ....$169.95 to $380.00
Price: Target Model, adjustable rear sight (Cabela's, Euroarms,
  Uberti USA, Navy Arms, Stone Mountain
  Arms) ....$95.95 to $399.00
Price: Brass frame (CVA, Cabela's, Traditions,
  Navy Arms) ....$79.95 to $212.95
Price: As above, kit (CVA, Dixie Gun Works,
  Navy Arms) ....$145.00 to $188.95
Price: Buffalo model, 44-cal. (Cabela's) $129.95
Price: Hartford model, steel frame, German silver trim, cartouche (E.M.F.) $215.00

CVA Bison Revolver Similar to the CVA 1858 except has 10¼″ octagonal barrel, 44-caliber, brass frame, two-piece walnut grips, adjustable target rear sight.

Price: Finished $187.95
Price: From Armsport $222.00

POCKET POLICE 1862 PERCUSSION REVOLVER Caliber: 36, 5-shot. **Barrel:** 4½″, 5½″, 6½″, 7½″. **Weight:** 26 oz. **Length:** 12″ overall (6½″ bbl.). **Stocks:** Walnut. **Sights:** Fixed. **Features:** Round tapered barrel; half-fluted and rebated cylinder; case-hard~ened frame, loading lever and hammer; silver or brass trigger guard and backstrap. Imported by CVA (7½″ only), Navy Arms (5½″ only), Uberti USA (5½″, 6½″ only).

Price: About ....$139.95 to $310.00
Price: Single cased set with accessories (Navy Arms) ...$365.00
Price: Hartford model, steel frame, German silver trim, cartouche (E.M.F.) $215.00

ROGERS & SPENCER PERCUSSION REVOLVER Caliber: 44. **Barrel:** 7½″. **Weight:** 47 oz. **Length:** 13¾″ overall. **Stocks:** Walnut. **Sights:** Cone front, integral groove in frame for rear. **Features:** Accurate reproduction of a Civil War design. Solid frame; extra large nipple cut-out on rear of cylinder; loading lever and cylinder easily removed for cleaning. From Euroarms of America (standard blue, engraved, burnished, target models), Navy Arms, Stone Mountain Arms.

Price: ....$160.00 to $289.00
Price: Nickel-plated $215.00
Price: Engraved (Euroarms) $287.00
Price: Kit version ....$245.00-$252.00
Price: Target version (Euroarms, Navy
  Arms) ....$239.00 to $270.00
Price: Burnished London Gray (Euroarms, Navy
  Arms) ....$245.00 to $270.00

SHERIFF MODEL 1851 PERCUSSION REVOLVER Caliber: 36, 44, 6-shot. **Barrel:** 5″. **Weight:** 40 oz. **Length:** 10½″ overall. **Stocks:** Walnut. **Sights:** Fixed. **Features:** Brass backstrap and trigger guard; engraved navy scene; case-hard~ened frame, hammer, loading lever. Imported by E.M.F., Stone Mountain Arms (5½″ barrel).

Price: Steel frame (E.M.F.) $172.00
Price: Brass frame (E.M.F.) $140.00
Price: Steel frame (Stone Mountain Arms) $159.95

BLACKPOWDER REVOLVERS

Navy Arms Spiller & Burr

Texas Paterson

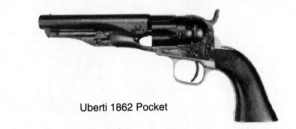

Uberti 1862 Pocket

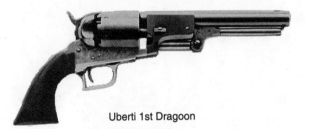

Uberti 1st Dragoon

Uberti 3rd Dragoon

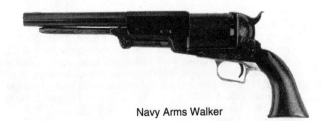

Navy Arms Walker

SPILLER & BURR REVOLVER Caliber: 36 (.375″ round ball).
Barrel: 7″, octagon. **Weight:** 2½ lbs. **Length:** 12½″ overall.
Stocks: Two-piece walnut. **Sights:** Fixed. **Features:**
Reproduction of the C.S.A. revolver. Brass frame and trigger
guard. Also available as a kit. From Cabela's, Dixie Gun Works,
Navy Arms.
Price: . . . .**$89.95 to $199.00**
Price: Kit form **$95.00**
Price: Single cased set (Navy Arms) **$270.00**
Price: Double cased set (Navy Arms) **$430.00**

TEXAS PATERSON 1836 REVOLVER Caliber: 36 (.375″ round
ball). **Barrel:** 7½″. **Weight:** 42 oz. **Stocks:** One-piece walnut.
Sights: Fixed. **Features:** Copy of Sam Colt's first commercially-
made revolving pistol. Has no loading lever but comes with load-
ing tool. From Dixie Gun Works, Navy Arms, Uberti USA.
Price: About . . . .**$325.00 to $395.00**
Price: With loading lever (Uberti USA) **$450.00**
Price: Engraved (Navy Arms) **$465.00**

UBERTI 1862 POCKET NAVY PERCUSSION REVOLVER Caliber:
36, 5-shot. **Barrel:** 5½″, 6½″, octagonal, 7-groove, LH twist.
Weight: 27 oz. (5½″ barrel). **Length:** 10½″ overall (5½″ bbl.).
Stocks: One-piece varnished walnut. **Sights:** Brass pin front,
hammer notch rear. **Features:** Rebated cylinder, hinged loading
lever, brass or silver-plated backstrap and trigger guard, color-
cased frame, hammer, loading lever, plunger and latch, rest blued.
Has original-type markings. From Uberti USA.
Price: With brass backstrap, trigger guard **$310.00**

UBERTI 1st MODEL DRAGOON Caliber: 44. **Barrel:** 7½″, part
round, part octagon. **Weight:** 64 oz. **Stocks:** One-piece walnut.
Sights: German silver blade front, hammer notch rear.
Features: First model has oval bolt cuts in cylinder, square-back
flared trigger guard, V-type mainspring, short trigger. Ranger and
Indian scene roll-engraved on cylinder. Color case-hardened
frame, loading lever, plunger and hammer; blue barrel, cylinder,
trigger and wedge. Available with old-time charcoal blue or standard blue-black finish. Polished brass backstrap and trigger
guard. From Uberti USA.
Price: **$325.00**

> Consult our Directory pages for
> the location of firms mentioned.

Uberti 2nd Model Dragoon Revolver Similar to the 1st Model except
distinguished by rectangular bolt cuts in the cylinder.
Price: **$325.00**

Uberti 3rd Model Dragoon Revolver Similar to the 2nd Model except
for oval trigger guard, long trigger, modifications to the loading
lever and latch. Imported by Uberti USA.
Price: Military model (frame cut for shoulder stock, steel back-
strap) **$330.00**
Price: Civilian (brass backstrap, trigger guard) **$325.00**

WALKER 1847 PERCUSSION REVOLVER Caliber: 44, 6-shot.
Barrel: 9″. **Weight:** 84 oz. **Length:** 15½″ overall. **Stocks:**
Walnut. **Sights:** Fixed. **Features:** Case-hardened frame, load-
ing lever and hammer; iron backstrap; brass trigger guard;
engraved cylinder. Imported by American Arms, Cabela's, CVA,
Navy Arms, Dixie Gun Works, Uberti USA, E.M.F., Cimarron,
Traditions.
Price: About . . . .**$225.00 to $360.00**
Price: Single cased set (Navy Arms) **$405.00**
Price: Deluxe Walker with French fitted case (Navy
Arms) **$505.00**
Price: Hartford model , steel frame, German silver trim, car-
touche (E.M.F.) **$295.00**

AIRROW MODEL A6 AIR PISTOL Caliber: #2512 10.75″ arrow. **Barrel:** 10.75″. **Weight:** 1.75 lbs. **Length:** 16.5″ overall. **Power:** CO_2 or compressed air. **Stocks:** Checkered composition. **Sights:** Bead front, fully adjustable Williams rear. **Features:** Velocity to 375 fps. Pneumatic air trigger. Floating barrel. All aircraft aluminum and stainless steel construction; Mil-spec materials and finishes. Announced 1993. From Swivel Machine Works, Inc.
Price: About **$597.00**

Airrow Model A6

BEEMAN P1 MAGNUM AIR PISTOL Caliber: 177, 5mm, single shot. **Barrel:** 8.4″. **Weight:** 2.5 lbs. **Length:** 11″ overall. **Power:** Top lever cocking; spring-piston. **Stocks:** Checkered walnut. **Sights:** Blade front, square notch rear with click micrometer adjustments for windage and elevation. Grooved for scope mounting. **Features:** Dual power for 177 and 20-cal.: low setting gives 350-400 fps; high setting 500-600 fps. Rearward expanding mainspring simulates firearm recoil. All Colt 45 auto grips fit gun. Dry-firing feature for practice. Optional wooden shoulder stock. Introduced 1985. Imported by Beeman.
Price: 177, 5mm **$395.00**

Beeman P2 Match Air Pistol Similar to the Beeman P1 Magnum except shoots only 177 pellets; completely recoilless single-stroke pnuematic action. Weighs 2.2 lbs. Choice of thumbrest match grips or standard style. Introduced 1990.
Price: 177, 5mm, standard grip **$435.00**
Price: 177, match grip **$465.00**

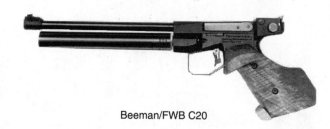

Beeman P1

BEEMAN/FEINWERKBAU C20 CO_2 PISTOL Caliber: 177, single shot. **Barrel:** 10.1″, 12-groove rifling. **Weight:** 2.5 lbs. **Length:** 16″ overall. **Power:** Special CO_2 cylinder. **Stock:** Stippled walnut with adjustable palm shelf. **Sights:** Blade front, open rear adjustable for windage and elevation. Notch size adjustable for width. Interchangeable front blades. **Features:** Fully adjustable trigger; can be set for dry firing. Separate gas chamber for uniform power. Cylinders interchangeable even when full. Short-barrel model also available. Introduced 1988. Imported by Beeman.
Price: Right-hand, regular or Mini **$1,160.00**
Price: Left-hand **$1,225.00**

Beeman/FWB C20

BEEMAN/FEINWERKBAU C25 CO_2 PISTOL Caliber: 177, single shot. **Barrel:** 10.1″; 12-groove rifling. **Weight:** 2.5 lbs. **Length:** 16.5″ overall. **Power:** Vertical interchangeable CO_2 bottles. **Stocks:** Stippled walnut with adjustable palm shelf. **Sights:** Blade front, rear micrometer adjustable. Notch size adjustable for width; interchangeable front blades. **Features:** Fully adjustable trigger; can be set for dry firing. Has special vertical CO_2 cylinder and weight rail for balance. Short-barrel model (C25 Mini) also available. Introduced 1992. Imported by Beeman.
Price: Right-hand **$1,325.00**
Price: Left-hand **$1,375.00**
Price: C25 Mini **$1,325.00**

BEEMAN/FWB C55 CO_2 RAPID FIRE PISTOL Caliber: 177, single shot or 5-shot magazines. **Barrel:** 7.3″. **Weight:** 2.5 lbs. **Length:** 15″ overall. **Power:** Special CO_2 cylinder. **Stocks:** Anatomical, adjustable. **Sights:** Interchangeable front, fully adjustable open micro-click rear with adjustable notch size. **Features:** Velocity 510 fps. Has 11.75″ sight radius. Built-in muzzle brake. Introduced 1993. Imported by Beeman Precision Airguns.
Price: Right-hand **$1,630.00**
Price: Left-hand **$1,700.00**

BEEMAN/FEINWERKBAU 65 MKII AIR PISTOL Caliber: 177, single shot. **Barrel:** 6.1″, removable bbl. wgt. available. **Weight:** 42 oz. **Length:** 13.3″ overall. **Power:** Spring, sidelever cocking. **Stocks:** Walnut, stippled thumbrest; adjustable or fixed. **Sights:** Front, interchangeable post element system, open rear, click adjustable for windage and elevation and for sighting notch width. Scope mount available. **Features:** New shorter barrel for better balance and control. Cocking effort 9 lbs. Two-stage trigger, four adjustments. Quiet firing, 525 fps. Programs instantly for recoil or recoilless operation. Permanently lubricated. Steel piston ring. Imported by Beeman.
Price: Right-hand **$1,140.00**
Price: Left-hand **$1,185.00**

BEEMAN/FEINWERKBAU 102 PISTOL Caliber: 177, single shot. **Barrel:** 10.1″, 12-groove rifling. **Weight:** 2.5 lbs. **Length:** 16.5″ overall. **Power:** Single-stroke pneumatic, underlever cocking. **Stocks:** Stippled walnut with adjustable palm shelf. **Sights:** Blade front, open rear adjustable for windage and elevation. Notch size adjustable for width. Interchangeable front blades. **Features:** Velocity 460 fps. Fully adjustable trigger. Cocking effort 12 lbs. Introduced 1988. Imported by Beeman.
Price: Right-hand **$1,410.00**
Price: Left-hand **$1,460.00**

CAUTION: PRICES SHOWN ARE SUPPLIED BY THE MANUFACTURER OR IMPORTER. CHECK YOUR LOCAL GUNSHOP.

BEEMAN/FWB P30 MATCH AIR PISTOL Caliber: 177, single shot. **Barrel:** $10^{5/16}''$, with muzzle brake. **Weight:** 2.4 lbs. **Length:** 16.5″ overall. **Power:** Pre-charged pneumatic. **Stocks:** Stippled walnut; adjustable match type. **Sights:** Undercut blade front, fully adjustable match rear. **Features:** Velocity to 525 fps; up to 200 shots per CO_2 cartridge. Fully adjustable trigger; built-in muzzle brake. Introduced 1995. Imported from Germany by Beeman.
Price: Right-hand $1,410.00
Price: Left-hand $1,460.00

Beeman/Feinwekbau 102

BEEMAN HW70A AIR PISTOL Caliber: 177, single shot. **Barrel:** $6^{1/4}''$, rifled. **Weight:** 38 oz. **Length:** $12^{3/4}''$ overall. **Power:** Spring, barrel cocking. **Stocks:** Plastic, with thumbrest. **Sights:** Hooded post front, square notch rear adjustable for windage and elevation. Comes with scope base. **Features:** Adjustable trigger, 24-lb. cocking effort, 410 fps MV; automatic barrel safety. Imported by Beeman.
Price: $205.00

BEEMAN/WEBLEY NEMESIS AIR PISTOL Caliber: 177, single shot. **Barrel:** 7″. **Weight:** 2.2 lbs. **Length:** 9.8″ overall. **Power:** Single-stroke pneumatic. **Stocks:** Checkered black composition. **Sights:** Blade on ramp front, fully adjustable rear. Integral scope rail. **Features:** Velocity to 400 fps. Adjustable two-stage trigger, manual safety. Recoilless action. Introduced 1995. Imported from England by Beeman.
Price: $180.00

Beeman/Webley Nemesis

BEEMAN/WEBLEY TEMPEST AIR PISTOL Caliber: 177, 22, single shot. **Barrel:** $6^{7/8}''$. **Weight:** 32 oz. **Length:** 8.9″ overall. **Power:** Spring-piston, break barrel. **Stocks:** Checkered black plastic with thumbrest. **Sights:** Blade front, adjustable rear. **Features:** Velocity to 500 fps (177), 400 fps (22). Aluminum frame; black epoxy finish; manual safety. Imported from England by Beeman.
Price: $190.00

Beeman/Webley Tempest

Beeman/Webley Hurricane Air Pistol Similar to the Tempest except has extended frame in the rear for a click-adjustable rear sight; hooded front sight; comes with scope mount. Imported from England by Beeman.
Price: $215.00

BENJAMIN SHERIDAN CO_2 PELLET PISTOLS Caliber: 177, 20, 22, single shot. **Barrel:** $6^{3/8}''$, rifled brass. **Weight:** 29 oz. **Length:** 9.8″ overall. **Power:** 12-gram CO_2 cylinder. **Stocks:** Walnut. **Sights:** High ramp front, fully adjustable notch rear. **Features:** Velocity to 500 fps. Turn-bolt action with cross-bolt safety. Gives about 40 shots per CO_2 cylinder. Black or nickel finish. Made in U.S. by Benjamin Sheridan Co.
Price: Black finish, EB17 (177), EB20 (20), EB22 (22), about $97.25
Price: Nickel finish, E17 (177), E20 (20), E22 (22), about $110.50

Benjamin Sheridan CO_2

BENJAMIN SHERIDAN PNEUMATIC PELLET PISTOLS Caliber: 177, 20, 22, single shot. **Barrel:** $9^{3/8}''$, rifled brass. **Weight:** 38 oz. **Length:** $13^{1/8}''$ overall. **Power:** Underlever pnuematic, hand pumped. **Stocks:** Walnut stocks and pump handle. **Sights:** High ramp front, fully adjustable notch rear. **Features:** Velocity to 525 fps (variable). Bolt action with cross-bolt safety. Choice of black or nickel finish. Made in U.S. by Benjamin Sheridan Co.
Price: Black finish, HB17 (177), HB20 (20), HB22 (22), about $106.00
Price: Nickel finish, H17 (177), H20 (20), H22 (22), about $112.75

BRNO TAU-7 CO_2 MATCH PISTOL Caliber: 177. **Barrel:** 10.24″. **Weight:** 37 oz. **Length:** 15.75″ overall. **Power:** 12.5-gram CO_2 cartridge. **Stocks:** Stippled hardwood with adjustable palm rest. **Sights:** Blade front, open fully adjustable rear. **Features:** Comes with extra seals and counterweight. Blue finish. Imported by Century International Arms, Great Lakes Airguns.
Price: About $326.50

CROSMAN AUTO AIR II PISTOL Caliber: BB, 17-shot magazine, 177 pellet, single shot. **Barrel:** $8^{5/8}''$ steel, smoothbore. **Weight:** 13 oz. **Length:** $10^{3/4}''$ overall. **Power:** CO_2 Powerlet. **Stocks:** Grooved plastic. **Sights:** Blade front, adjustable rear; highlighted system. **Features:** Velocity to 480 fps (BBs), 430 fps (pellets). Semi-automatic action with BBs, single shot with pellets. Silvered finish. Introduced 1991. From Crosman.
Price: About $29.00

CROSMAN MODEL 357 AIR PISTOL Caliber: 177, 6- and 10-shot pellet clips. **Barrel:** 4″ (Model 357-4), 6″ (Model 357-6), rifled steel; 8″ (Model 357-8), rifled brass. **Weight:** 32 oz. (6″). **Length:** $11^{3/8}''$ overall (357-6). **Power:** CO_2 Powerlet. **Stocks:** Checkered wood-grain plastic. **Sights:** Ramp front, fully adjustable rear. **Features:** Average 430 fps (Model 357-6). Break-open barrel for easy loading. Single or double action. Vent. rib barrel. Wide, smooth trigger. Two cylinders come with each gun. Model 357-8 has matte gray finish, black grips. From Crosman.
Price: 4″ or 6″, about $46.50
Price: 8″, about $53.25
Price: Model 1357 (same gun as above, except shoots BBs, has 6-shot clip), about $46.50

Crosman Model 1322

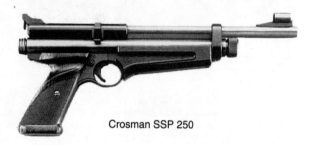

Crosman SSP 250

Daisy Model 91

Daisy Model 288

CROSMAN MODEL 1008 REPEAT AIR Caliber: 177, 8-shot pellet clip **Barrel:** 4.25″, rifled steel. **Weight:** 17 oz. **Length:** 8.625″ overall. **Power:** CO_2 Powerlet. **Stocks:** Checkered plastic. **Sights:** Post front, adjustable rear. **Features:** Velocity about 430 fps. Break-open barrel for easy loading; single or double semi-automatic action; two 8-shot clips included. Optional carrying case available. Introduced 1992. From Crosman.
Price: About $45.00
Price: With case, about $55.00
Price: Model 1008SB (silver and black finish), about $47.00

CROSMAN MODEL 1322, 1377 AIR PISTOLS Caliber: 177 (M1377), 22 (M1322), single shot. **Barrel:** 8″, rifled steel. **Weight:** 39 oz. **Length:** 13⅝″. **Power:** Hand pumped. **Sights:** Blade front, rear adjustable for windage and elevation. **Features:** Moulded plastic grip, hand size pump forearm. Cross-bolt safety. Model 1377 also shoots BBs. From Crosman.
Price: About $53.00

CROSMAN MODEL SSP 250 PISTOL Caliber: 177, 20, 22, single shot. **Barrel:** 9⅞″, rifled steel. **Weight:** 3 lbs., 1 oz. **Length:** 14″ overall. **Power:** CO_2 Powerlet. **Stocks:** Composition; black, with checkering. **Sights:** Hooded front, fully adjustable rear. **Features:** Velocity about 560 fps. Interchangeable accessory barrels. Two-stage trigger. High/low power settings. From Crosman.
Price: About $52.00

DAISY MODEL 91 MATCH PISTOL Caliber: 177, single shot. **Barrel:** 10.25″, rifled steel. **Weight:** 2.5 lbs. **Length:** 16.5″ overall. **Power:** CO_2, 12-gram cylinder. **Stocks:** Stippled hardwood; anatomically shaped and adjustable. **Sights:** Blade and ramp front, changeable-width rear notch with full micrometer adjustments. **Features:** Velocity to 476 fps. Gives 55 shots per cylinder. Fully adjustable trigger. Imported by Daisy Mfg. Co.
Price: About $670.00

DAISY MODEL 288 AIR PISTOL Caliber: 177 pellets, 24-shot. **Barrel:** Smoothbore steel. **Weight:** .8 lb. **Length:** 12.1″ overall. **Power:** Single stroke spring-air. **Stocks:** Moulded resin with checkering and thumbrest. **Sights:** Blade and ramp front, open fixed rear. **Features:** Velocity to 215 fps. Cross-bolt trigger block safety. Black finish. From Daisy Mfg. Co.
Price: About $26.00

DAISY MODEL 500 RAVEN AIR PISTOL Caliber: 177 pellets, single shot. **Barrel:** Rifled steel. **Weight:** 36 oz. **Length:** 8.5″ overall. **Power:** CO_2. **Stocks:** Moulded plastic with checkering. **Sights:** Blade front, fixed rear. **Features:** Velocity up to 500 fps. Hammer-block safety. Resembles semi-auto centerfire pistol. Barrel tips up for loading. Introduced 1993. From Daisy Mfg. Co.
Price: About $65.00

DAISY/POWER LINE 44 REVOLVER Caliber: 177 pellets, 6-shot. **Barrel:** 6″, rifled steel; interchangeable 4″ and 8″. **Weight:** 2.7 lbs. **Power:** CO_2. **Stocks:** Moulded plastic with checkering. **Sights:** Blade on ramp front, fully adjustable notch rear. **Features:** Velocity up to 400 fps. Replica of 44 Magnum revolver. Has swingout cylinder and interchangeable barrels. Introduced 1987. From Daisy Mfg. Co.
Price: $70.00

DAISY/POWER LINE 93 PISTOL Caliber: 177, BB, 15-shot clip. **Barrel:** 5″, steel. **Weight:** 17 oz. **Length:** NA. **Power:** CO_2. **Stocks:** Checkered plastic. **Sights:** Fixed. **Features:** Velocity to 400 fps. Semi-automatic repeater. Manual lever-type trigger-block safety. Introduced 1991. From Daisy Mfg. Co.
Price: About $80.00
Price: Model 693 (nickel-chrome plated), about $85.00

DAISY/POWERLINE 400 BB PISTOL Caliber: BB, 20-shot magazine. **Barrel:** Smoothbore steel. **Weight:** 1.4 lbs. **Length:** 10.7″ overall. **Power:** 12-gram CO_2. **Stocks:** Moulded black checkered plastic. **Sights:** Blade front, fixed open rear. **Features:** Velocity to 420 fps. Blowback slide cycles automatically on firing. Rotary trigger block safety. Introduced 1994. From Daisy Mfg. Co.
Price: About $83.00

Daisy/Power Line 747 Pistol Similar to the 717 pistol except has a 12-groove rifled steel barrel by Lothar Walther, and adjustable trigger pull weight. Velocity of 360 fps. Manual cross-bolt safety.
Price: About $160.00

DAISY/POWER LINE 45 AIR PISTOL Caliber: 177, 13-shot clip. **Barrel:** 5″, rifled steel. **Weight:** 1.25 lbs. **Length:** 8.5″ overall. **Power:** CO_2. **Stocks:** Checkered plastic. **Sights:** Fixed. **Features:** Velocity 400 fps. Semi-automatic repeater with double-action trigger. Manually operated lever-type trigger block safety; magazine safety. Introduced 1990. From Daisy Mfg. Co.
Price: About $80.00
Price: Model 645 (nickel-chrome plated), about $85.00

CAUTION: PRICES SHOWN ARE SUPPLIED BY THE MANUFACTURER OR IMPORTER. CHECK YOUR LOCAL GUNSHOP.

Daisy/Power Line Match 777

Daisy/Power Line 1140

Hammerli Model 480

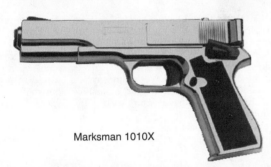

Marksman 1010X

DAISY/POWER LINE 717 PELLET PISTOL Caliber: 177, single shot. **Barrel:** 9.61″. **Weight:** 2.8 lbs. **Length:** 13½″ overall. **Stocks:** Moulded wood-grain plastic, with thumbrest. **Sights:** Blade and ramp front, micro-adjustable notch rear. **Features:** Single pump pneumatic pistol. Rifled steel barrel. Cross-bolt trigger block. Muzzle velocity 385 fps. From Daisy Mfg. Co. Introduced 1979.
Price: About **$80.00**

DAISY/POWER LINE MATCH 777 PELLET PISTOL Caliber: 177, single shot. **Barrel:** 9.61″ rifled steel by Lothar Walther. **Weight:** 32 oz. **Length:** 13½″ overall. **Power:** Sidelever, single-pump pneumatic. **Stocks:** Smooth hardwood, fully contoured with palm and thumbrest. **Sights:** Blade and ramp front, match-grade open rear with adjustable width notch, micro. click adjustments. **Features:** Adjustable trigger; manual cross-bolt safety. MV of 385 fps. Comes with cleaning kit, adjustment tool and pellets. From Daisy Mfg. Co.
Price: About **$335.00**

DAISY/POWER LINE 1140 PELLET PISTOL Caliber: 177, single shot. **Barrel:** Rifled steel. **Weight:** 1.3 lbs. **Length:** 11.7″ overall. **Power:** Single-stroke barrel cocking. **Stocks:** Checkered resin. **Sights:** Hooded post front, open adjustable rear. **Features:** Velocity to 325 fps. Made of black lightweight engineering resin. Introduced 1995. From Daisy.
Price: About **$45.50**

DAISY/POWER LINE CO_2 1200 PISTOL Caliber: BB, 177. **Barrel:** 10½″, smooth. **Weight:** 1.6 lbs. **Length:** 11.1″ overall. **Power:** Daisy CO_2 cylinder. **Stocks:** Contoured, checkered moulded wood-grain plastic. **Sights:** Blade ramp front, fully adjustable square notch rear. **Features:** 60-shot BB reservoir, gravity feed. Cross-bolt safety. Velocity of 420-450 fps for more than 100 shots. From Daisy Mfg. Co.
Price: About **$37.50**

DAISY/POWERLINE 1700 AIR PISTOL Caliber: 177 BB, 60-shot magazine. **Barrel:** Smoothbore steel. **Weight:** 1.4 lbs. **Length:** 11.2″ overall. **Power:** CO_2 pistol. **Stocks:** Moulded checkered plastic. **Sights:** Blade front, adjustable rear. **Features:** Velocity to 420 fps. Cross-bolt trigger block safety; matte finish. Has ⅜″ dovetail mount for scope or point sight. Introduced 1994. From Daisy Mfg. Co.
Price: About **$40.00**

"GAT" AIR PISTOL Caliber: 177, single shot. **Barrel:** 7½″ cocked, 9½″ extended. **Weight:** 22 oz. **Power:** Spring-piston. **Stocks:** Cast checkered metal. **Sights:** Fixed. **Features:** Shoots pellets, corks or darts. Matte black finish. Imported from England by Stone Enterprises, Inc.
Price: **$21.95**

HAMMERLI 480 COMPETITION AIR PISTOL Caliber: 177, single shot. **Barrel:** 9.8″. **Weight:** 37 oz. **Length:** 16.5″ overall. **Power:** Air or CO_2. **Stocks:** Walnut with 7-degree rake adjustment. Stippled grip area. **Sights:** Undercut blade front, fully adjustable open match rear. **Features:** Under-barrel cannister charges with air or CO_2 for power supply; gives 320 shots per filling. Trigger adjustable for position. Introduced 1994. Imported from Switzerland by Hammerli Pistols USA.
Price: **$1,353.00**

MARKSMAN 1010 REPEATER PISTOL Caliber: 177, 18-shot repeater. **Barrel:** 2½″, smoothbore. **Weight:** 24 oz. **Length:** 8¼″ overall. **Power:** Spring. **Features:** Velocity to 200 fps. Thumb safety. Black finish. Uses BBs, darts or pellets. Repeats with BBs only. From Marksman Products.
Price: Matte black finish **$25.50**
Price: Model 1010X (as above except nickel-plated) **$33.50**

MARKSMAN 1015 SPECIAL EDITION AIR PISTOL Caliber: 177, 24-shot repeater. **Barrel:** 3.8″, rifled. **Weight:** 22 oz. **Length:** 10.3″ overall. **Power:** Spring-air. **Stocks:** Checkered brown composition. **Sights:** Fixed. **Features:** Velocity about 230 fps. Skeletonized trigger, extended barrel with "ported compensator." Shoots BBs, pellets, darts or bolts. From Marksman Products.
Price: **$31.75**

MORINI 162E MATCH AIR PISTOL Caliber: 177, single shot. **Barrel:** 9.4″. **Weight:** 32 oz. **Length:** 16.1″ overall. **Power:** Pre-charged CO_2. **Stocks:** Adjustable match type. **Sights:** Interchangeable blade front, fully adjustable match-type rear. **Features:** Power mechanism shuts down when pressure drops to a pre-set level. Adjustable electronic trigger. Introduced 1995. Imported from Switzerland by Nygord Precision Products.
Price: **$950.00**

PARDINI K58 MATCH AIR PISTOL Caliber: 177, single shot. **Barrel:** 9.0″. **Weight:** 37.7 oz. **Length:** 15.5″ overall. **Power:** Pre-charged compressed air; single-stroke cocking. **Stocks:** Adjustable match type; stippled walnut. **Sights:** Interchangeable post front, fully adjustable match rear. **Features:** Fully adjustable trigger. Introduced 1995. Imported from Italy by Nygord Precision Products.
Price: **$650.00**
Price: K60 model (CO_2 . . . .**$650.00**

Record Jumbo

RWS/Diana Model 5G

RWS/Diana Model 6G

RWS/Diana Model 6M

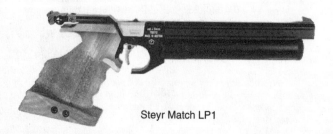

Steyr Match LP1

RECORD JUMBO DELUXE AIR PISTOL Caliber: 177, single shot. **Barrel:** 6″, rifled. **Weight:** 1.9 lbs. **Length:** 7.25″ overall. **Power:** Spring-air, lateral cocking lever. **Stocks:** Smooth walnut. **Sights:** Blade front, fully adjustable open rear. **Features:** Velocity to 322 fps. Thumb safety. Grip magazine compartment for extra pellet storage. Introduced 1983. Imported from Germany by Great Lakes Airguns.
Price: $113.50

RWS/DIANA MODEL 5G AIR PISTOL Caliber: 177, single shot. **Barrel:** 7″. **Weight:** 2³/₄ lbs. **Length:** 16″ overall. **Power:** Spring-air, barrel cocking. **Stocks:** Plastic, thumbrest design. **Sights:** Tunnel front, micro-click open rear. **Features:** Velocity of 410 fps. Two-stage trigger with automatic safety. Imported from Germany by Dynamit Nobel-RWS, Inc.
Price: $225.00

RWS/DIANA MODEL 6M MATCH AIR PISTOL Caliber: 177, single shot. **Barrel:** 7″. **Weight:** 3 lbs. **Length:** 16″ overall. **Power:** Spring-air, barrel cocking. **Stocks:** Walnut-finished hardwood with thumbrest. **Sights:** Adjustable front, micro. click open rear. **Features:** Velocity of 410 fps. Recoilless double piston system, movable barrel shroud to protect from sight during cocking. Imported from Germany by Dynamit Nobel-RWS, Inc.
Price: Right-hand $525.00
Price: Left-hand $560.00

RWS/Diana Model 6G Air Pistols Similar to the Model 6M except does not have the movable barrel shroud. Has click micrometer rear sight, two-stage adjustable trigger, interchangeable tunnel front sight. Available in right- or left-hand models.
Price: Right-hand $395.00
Price: Left-hand $425.00

STEYR CO₂ MATCH LP1 PISTOL Caliber: 177, single shot. **Barrel:** 9″. **Weight:** 38.7 oz. **Length:** 15.3″ overall. **Power:** Pre-compressed CO₂ cylinders. **Stocks:** Fully adjustable Morini match with palm shelf; stippled walnut. **Sights:** Interchangeable blade in 4mm, 4.5mm or 5mm widths, fully adjustable open rear with interchangeable 3.5mm or 4mm leaves. **Features:** Velocity about 500 fps. Adjustable trigger, adjustable sight radius from 12.4″ to 13.2″. Imported from Austria by Nygord Precision Products.
Price: About $1,095.00
Price: LP1C (compensated) $1,150.00

STEYR LP5 MATCH PISTOL Caliber: 177, 5-shot magazine. **Barrel:** NA. **Weight:** 40.2 oz. **Length:** 13.39″ overall. **Power:** Pre-compressed CO₂ cylinders. **Stocks:** Adjustable Morini match with palm shelf; stippled walnut. **Sights:** Movable 2.5mm blade front; 2-3mm interchangeable in .2mm increments; fully adjustable open match rear. **Features:** Velocity about 500 fps. Fully adjustable trigger; has dry-fire feature. Barrel and grip weights available. Introduced 1993. Imported from Austria by Nygord Precision Products.
Price: About $1,250.00

STEYR LP5C MATCH AIR PISTOL Caliber: 177, 5-shot magazine. **Barrel:** NA. **Weight:** 40.7 oz. **Length:** 15.2″ overall. **Power:** Pre-charged air cylinder. **Stocks:** Adjustable match type. **Sights:** Interchangeable blade front, fully adjustable match rear. **Features:** Adjustable sight radius; fully adjustable trigger. Has barrel compensator. Introduced 1995. Imported from Austria by Nygord Precision Products.
Price: $1,325.00

WALTHER CPM-1 CO₂ MATCH PISTOL Caliber: 177, single shot. **Barrel:** 8.66″. **Weight:** NA. **Length:** 15.1″ overall. **Power:** CO₂. **Stocks:** Orthopaedic target type. **Sights:** Undercut blade front, open match rear fully adjustable for windage and elevation. **Features:** Adjustable velocity; matte finish. Introduced 1995. Imported from Germany by Nygord Precision Products.
Price: $950.00

CAUTION: PRICES SHOWN ARE SUPPLIED BY THE MANUFACTURER OR IMPORTER. CHECK YOUR LOCAL GUNSHOP.

METALLIC SIGHTS

Handgun Sights

BO-MAR DELUXE BMCS Gives ³/₈″ windage and elevation adjustment at 50 yards on Colt Gov't 45; sight radius under 7″. For GM and Commander models only. Uses existing dovetail slot. Has shield-type rear blade.
Price: $65.95
Price: BMCS-2 (for GM and 9mm) $65.95
Price: Flat bottom $65.95
Price: BMGC (for Colt Gold Cup), angled serrated blade, rear $65.95
Price: BMGC front sight $12.00
Price: BMCZ-75 (for CZ-75, TZ-75, P-9 and most clones.
Works with factory front $65.95
BO-MAR FRONT SIGHTS Dovetail style for S&W 4506, 4516, 1076; undercut style (.250″, .280″, ⁵/₁₆″ high); Fast Draw style (.210″, .250″, .230″ high).
Price $12.00
BO-MAR BMU XP-100/T/C CONTENDER No gunsmithing required; has .080″ notch.
Price: $77.00
BO-MAR BMML For muzzleloaders; has .062″ notch, flat bottom.
Price: $65.95
Price: With ³/₈″ dovetail $65.95
BO-MAR RUGER "P" ADJUSTABLE SIGHT Replaces factory front and rear sights.
Price: Rear sight $65.95
Price: Front sight $12.00

Bo-Mar BMSW
(photo: Brownells, Inc.)

BO-MAR BMR Fully adjustable rear sight for Ruger MKI, MKII Bull barrel autos.
Price: Rear $65.95
Price: Undercut front sight $12.00
BO-MAR BMSW SMITH & WESSON SIGHTS Replace the S&W Novak-style fixed sights. A .385″ high front sight and minor machining required. For models 4506, 4516, 1076; all 9mms with 5³/₄″ and 6³/₁₆″ radius.
Price: $65.95
Price: .385″ front sight $12.00
Price: BM-645 rear sight (for S&W 645, 745), uses factory front ...$65.95
Price: BMSW-52 rear sight (for Model 52), fits factory dovetail, uses factory front $65.95
BO-MAR LOW PROFILE RIB & ACCURACY TUNER Streamlined rib with front and rear sights; 7¹/₈″ sight radius. Brings sight line closer to the bore than standard or extended sight and ramp. Weight 5 oz. Made for Colt Gov't 45, Super 38, and Gold Cup 45 and 38.
Price: $123.00
BO-MAR COMBAT RIB For S&W Model 19 revolver with 4″ barrel. Sight radius 5³/₄″, weight 5¹/₂ oz.
Price: $110.00
BO-MAR HUNTER REAR SIGHT Replacement rear sight in two models—S&W K and L frames use 2³/₄″ Bo-Mar base with ⁷/₁₆″ overhang, has two screw holes; S&W N frame has 3″ base, three screw holes. A .200″ taller front blade is required.
Price: $79.00
BO-MAR WINGED RIB For S&W 4″ and 6″ length barrels—K-38, M10, HB 14 and 19. Weight for the 6″ model is about 7¹/₄ oz.
Price: $123.00
BO-MAR COVER-UP RIB Adjustable rear sight, winged front guards. Fits right over revolver's original front sight. For S&W 4″ M-10HB, M-13, M-58, M-64 & 65, Ruger 4″ models SDA-34, SDA-84, SS-34, SS-84, GF-34, GF-84.
Price: $117.00
C-MORE SIGHTS Replacement front sight blades offered in two types and five styles. Made of Du Pont Acetal, they come in a set of five high-contrast colors: blue, green, pink, red and yellow. Easy to install. Patridge style for Colt Python (all barrels), Ruger Super Blackhawk (7¹/₂″), Ruger Blackhawk (4⁵/₈″); ramp style for Python (all barrels), Blackhawk (4⁵/₈″), Super Blackhawk (7¹/₂″ and 10¹/₂″). From C-More Systems.
Price: Per set $19.95
MMC COMBAT FIXED REAR SIGHT (Colt 1911-Type Pistols) This veteran MMC sight is well known to those who prefer a true combat sight for "carry" guns. Steel construction for long service. Choose from a wide variety of front sights.
Price: Combat Fixed Rear, plain $18.45
Price: As above, white outline $23.65
Price: Combat Front Sight for above, six styles, from $5.15

MMC M/85 ADJUSTABLE REAR SIGHT Designed to be compatible with the Ruger P-85 front sight. Fully adjustable for windage and elevation.
Price: M/85 Adjustable Rear Sight, plain $52.45
Price: As above, white outline $57.70
MMC STANDARD ADJUSTABLE REAR SIGHT Available for Colt 1911 type, Ruger Standard Auto, and now for S&W 469 and 659 pistols. No front sight change is necessary, as this sight will work with the original factory front sight.
Price: Standard Adjustable Rear Sight, plain leaf $46.05
Price: Standard Adjustable Rear Sight, white outline ...$51.15
MMC MINI-SIGHT Miniature size for carrying, fully adjustable, for maximum accuracy with your pocket auto. MMC's Mini-Sight will work with the factory front sight. No machining is necessary; easy installation. Available for Walther PP, PPK, and PPK/S pistols. Will also fit fixed sight Browning Hi-Power (P-35).
Price: Mini-Sight, plain $58.45
Price: Mini-Sight, white bar $63.45
MEPROLIGHT TRITIUM NIGHT SIGHTS Replacement sight assemblies for use in low-light conditions. Available for rifles, shotguns, handguns and bows. **TRU-DOT** models carry a 12-year warranty on the useable illumination, while non-TRU-DOT have a 5-year warranty. Contact Hesco, Inc. for complete details.
Price: Shotgun bead sight $22.95
Price: AR-15/M-16 front sight only $34.95
Price: AR-15/M-16 sight sets, Rem. rifle sights $89.95
Price: TRU-DOT fixed sight sets $94.95
Price: TRU-DOT adjustable sight sets, pistols $139.95
Price: TRU-DOT adjustable sights for Python, King Cobra, Taurus 669, Ruger GP-100 ....$124.95
Price: H&K MP5, SR9 front sight only $49.95
Price: H&K MP5, SR9 sight sets $94.95

Bo-Mar BMCG Gold Cup

Bo-Mar "P" Series
(photo: Brownells, Inc.)

MMC Mini-Sight
(photo: Brownells, Inc.)

MILLETT 3-DOT SYSTEM SIGHTS The 3-Dot System sights use a single white dot on the front blade and two dots flanking the rear notch. Fronts available in Dual-Crimp and Wide Stake-On styles, as well as special applications. Adjustable rear sight available for most popular auto pistols and revolvers.
Price: Front, from $16.00
Price: Adjustable rear ....$55.60 to $56.80
MILLETT REVOLVER FRONT SIGHTS All-steel replacement front sights with either white or orange bar. Easy to install. For Ruger GP-100, Redhawk, Security-Six, Police-Six, Speed-Six, Colt Trooper, Diamondback, King Cobra, Peacemaker, Python, Dan Wesson 22 and 15-2.
Price: ....$13.60 to $16.00
MILLETT DUAL-CRIMP FRONT SIGHTS Replacement front sight for automatic pistols. Dual-Crimp uses an all-steel two-point hollow rivet system. Available in eight heights and four styles. Has a skirted base that covers the front sight pad. Easily installed with the Millett Installation Tool Set. Available in Blaze Orange Bar, White Bar, Serrated Ramp, Plain Post.
Price: $16.00

MILLETT STAKE-ON FRONT SIGHT Replacement front sight for automatic pistols. Stake-On sights have skirted base that covers the front sight pad. Easily installed with the Millet Installation Tool Set. Available in seven heights and four styles—Blaze Orange Bar, White Bar, Serrated Ramp, Plain Post.
Price: **$16.00**

OMEGA OUTLINE SIGHT BLADES Replacement rear sight blades for Colt and Ruger single-action guns and the Interarms Virginian Dragoon. Standard Outline available in gold or white notch outline on blue metal. From Omega Sales, Inc.
Price: **$8.95**

OMEGA MAVERICK SIGHT BLADES Replacement "peep-sight" blades for Colt, Ruger SAs, Virginian Dragoon. Three models available—No. 1, Plain; No. 2, Single Bar; No. 3, Double Bar Rangefinder. From Omega Sales, Inc.
Price: Each **$6.95**

P-T TRITIUM NIGHT SIGHTS Self-luminous tritium sights for most popular handguns, Colt AR-15, H&K rifles and shotguns. Replacement handgun sight sets available in 3-Dot style (green/green, green/yellow, green/orange) with bold outlines around inserts; Bar-Dot available in green/green with or without white outline rear sight. Functional life exceeds 15 years. From Innovative Weaponry, Inc.
Price: Handgun sight sets **$99.95**
Price: Rifle sight sets **$99.95**
Price: Rifle, front only **$49.95**
Price: Shotgun, front only **$49.95**

TRIJICON NIGHT SIGHTS Three-dot night sight system uses tritium inserts in the front and rear sights. Tritium "lamps" are mounted in silicone rubber inside a metal cylinder. A polished crystal sapphire provides protection and clarity. Inlaid white outlines provide 3-dot aiming in daylight also. Available for most popular handguns with fixed or adjustable sights. From Trijicon, Inc.
Price: . . . .**$19.95 to $175.00**

Millett Dual Crimp (top), Stake-On front sights

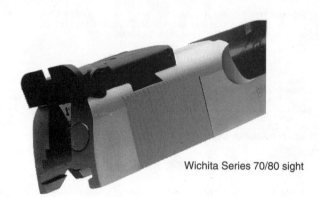

Wichita Series 70/80 sight

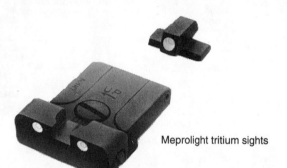

Meprolight tritium sights

Trijicon three-dot fixed

Trijicon three-dot adjustable

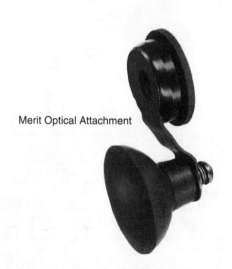

Merit Optical Attachment

THOMPSON/CENTER SILHOUETTE SIGHTS Replacement front and rear sights for the T/C Contender. Front sight has three interchangeable blades. Rear sight has three notch widths. Rear sight can be used with existing soldered front sights.
Price: Front sight **$34.10**
Price: Rear sight **$88.00**

WICHITA SERIES 70/80 SIGHT Provides click windage and elevation adjustments with precise repeatability of settings. Sight blade is grooved and angled back at the top to reduce glare. Available in Low Mount Combat or Low Mount Target styles for Colt 45s and their copies, S&W 645, Hi-Power, CZ 75 and others.
Price: Rear sight, target or combat **$71.45**
Price: Front sight, Patridge or ramp **$12.00**

WICHITA GRAND MASTER DELUXE RIBS Ventilated rib has wings machined into it for better sight acquisition and is relieved for Mag-Na-Porting. Milled to accept Weaver see-thru-style rings. Made of stainless or blued steel; front and rear sights blued. Has Wichita Multi-Range rear sight system, adjustable front sight. Made for revolvers with 6" barrel.
Price: Model 301S, 301B (adj. sight K frames with custom bbl. of 1" to 1.032" dia. L and N frame with 1.062" to 1.100" dia. bbl.) **$160.00**
Price: Model 303S, 303B (adj. sight K, L, N frames with factory barrel) . .**$160.00**

Sight Attachments

MERIT IRIS SHUTTER DISC Eleven clicks give 12 different apertures. No. 3 Disc and Master, primarily target types, 0.22" to .125"; No. 4, 1/2" dia. hunting type, .025" to .155". Available for all popular sights. The Master Deluxe, with flexible rubber light shield, is particularly adapted to extension, scope height, and tang sights. All Merit Deluxe models have internal click springs; are hand fitted to minimum tolerance.
Price: Master Deluxe **$63.00**
Price: No. 3 Disc **$52.00**
Price: No. 4 Hunting Disc **$45.00**

MERIT LENS DISC Similar to Merit Iris Shutter (Model 3 or Master), but incorporates provision for mounting prescription lens integrally. Lens may be obtained locally from your optician. Sight disc is 7/16" wide (Model 3), or 3/4" wide (Master). Model 3 Target.
Price: **$65.00**
Price: Master Deluxe **$75.00**

MERIT OPTICAL ATTACHMENT For revolver and pistol shooters, instantly attached by rubber suction cup to regular or shooting glasses. Any aperture .020" to .156".
Price: Deluxe (swings aside) **$63.00**

Maker and Model	Magn.	Field at 100 Yds. (feet)	Eye Relief (in.)	Length (in.)	Tube Dia. (in.)	W&E Adjustments	Weight (ozs.)	Price	Other Data
AAL OPTICS									[1]Ultra Dot sights include rings, battery, polarized filter, and 5-year warranty. All models available in black or satin finish. [2]Illuminated red dot has eleven brightness settings. Shock-proof aluminum tube. [3]Fiber optic red dot has five brightness settings. Shock-proof polymer tube. From AAL Optics.
Ultra-Dot Sights[1]									
Ultra-Dot 25[2]	1	—	—	5.1	1	Int.	3.9	139.00	
Ultra-Dot 30[2]	1	—	—	5.1	30mm	Int.	4.0	149.00	
Ultra Dot Patriot[3]	1	—	—	5.1	1	Int.	2.9	119.00	
ADCO									[1]Multi-Color Dot system changes from red to green. [2]For airguns, paintball, rimfires. Uses common lithium wafer battery. [3]Comes with standard dovetail mount. [4]3/8" dovetail mount; poly body; adj. intensity diode. All come with extension tube for mounting. Black or matte nickel finish. Optional 2x booster available. Five year warranty. From ADCO Sales.
MiRAGE Ranger 1"	0	—	—	5.2	1	Int.	4.5	159.00	
MiRAGE Ranger 30mm	0	—	—	5.5	30mm	Int.	5.5	169.00	
MiRAGE Sportsman[1]	0	—	—	5.2	1	Int.	4.5	219.00	
MiRAGE Competitor[1]	0	—	—	5.5	30mm	Int.	5.5	249.00	
IMP Sight[2]	0	—	—	4.5	—	Int.	2	19.95	
Square Shooter[3]	0	—	—	5.0	—	Int.	5	118.00	
MiRAGE Eclipse[1]	0	—	—	5.5	30mm	Int.	5.3	219.00	
MiRAGE Champ Red Dot	0	—	—	4.5	—	Int.	2	39.95	
AIMPOINT									Illuminates red dot in field of view. Noparallax (dot does not need to be centered). Unlimited field of view and eye relief. On/off, adj. intensity. Dot covers 3" @ 100 yds. Mounts avail. for all sights and scopes. [1]Comes with 30mm rings, lens cloth. [2]Requires 1" rings. Black or stainless finish. 3x scope attachment (for rifles only), **$129.95**. [3]Projects red dot of visible laser light onto target. Black finish (LSR-2B) or stainless (LSR-2S); or comes with rings and accessories. Optional toggle switch, **$34.95**. Lithium battery life up to 15 hours. [4]Black finish (AP 5000-B) or stainless (AP 5000-S); avail. with regular 3-min. or 10-min. Mag Dot as B2 or S2. [5]For Beretta, Browning, Colt Gov't., Desert Eagle, Glock, Ruger, SIG-Sauer, S&W. [6]For Colt, S&W. From Aimpoint.
Comp	0	—	—	4.6	30mm	Int.	4.3	308.00	
Series 5000[4]	0	—	—	5.75	30mm	Int.	5.8	277.00	
Series 3000 Universal[2]	0	—	—	5.5	1	Int.	5.5	232.00	
Series 5000/2x[1]	2	—	—	7	30mm	Int.	9	367.00	
Laserdot[3]	—	—	—	3.5	1	Int.	4.0	319.95	
Autolaser[5]	—	—	—	3.75	1	Int.	4.3	351.00	
Revolver Laser[6]	—	—	—	3.5	1	Int.	3.6	339.00	
APPLIED LASER SYSTEMS									[1]Output power 5mW; also MA-35, power less than 3mW, **$350.00**; [2]for HK USP; 5mW; also HK USP 635nm (3mW), **$350.00**; [3]also SP 89/MP5 635nm (3mW), **$350.00**; [4]5mW power. Mounts avail. for Browning Hi-Power, S&W, Colt 1911, Beretta 92F, Glock, SIG-Sauer, Ruger P-85 MkII, Firestor. From Applied Laser Systems.
MiniAimer MA-3[1]	—	—	—	1.36	—	Int.	.88	246.00	
Custom MiniAimer[2]	—	—	—	1.74	—	Int.	1.6	298.00	
Custom MiniAimer[3]	—	—	—	2.08	—	Int.	1.2	298.00	
T2 Custom Aimer[4]	—	—	—	2.8	—	Int.	2.2	198.00	
AR-15 Custom Aimer[4]	—	—	—	2.0	—	Int.	3.0	279.00	
Custom Glock Mini Laser[4]	—	—	—	.75	—	Int.	.8	385.00	
ARMSON O.E.G.									Shows red dot aiming point. No batteries needed. Standard model fits 1" ring mounts (not incl.). Other models available for many popular shotguns, para-military rifles and carbines. From Trijicon, Inc.
Standard	0	—	—	5 1/8	1	Int.	4.3	175.00	
22 Day/Night	0	—	—	3 3/4	—	Int.	3.0	146.00	
Colt Pistol	0	—	—	3 3/4	—	Int.	3.0	209.00	
BAUSCH & LOMB									[1]Also in silver finish, **$318.95**. [2]Also in silver finish, **$428.95** Contact Bausch & Lomb Sports Optics Div. for details.
Elite 3000 Handgun									
30-2028G[1]	2	23	9-26	8.4	1	Int.	6.9	299.95	
30-2632G[2]	2-6	10-4	20	9.0	1	Int.	10.0	409.95	
BEEMAN									All scopes have 5-point reticle, all glass, fully coated lenses. [1]Includes mount. [2]Also as 66RL with lighted color reticle, **$355.00**. [3]Also as SS-2L 3x with color 4pt. reticle. Imported by Beeman
Blue Ribbon SS-3[1]	1.5-4	42-25	3	5.8	7/8	Int.	8.5	300.00	
Blue Ribbon 66R[2]	2-7	62-16	3	11.4	1	Int.	14.9	315.00	
Blue Ribbon SS-2[1,3]	4	25	3.5	7.0	1.4	Int.	13.7	305.00	
Blue Ribbon 25 Pistol	2	19	10-24	9.1	1	Int.	7.4	155.00	
B-SQUARE									[1]Blue finish; stainless, **$209.95**. T-slot mount; cord or integral switch. [2]Blue finish; stainless, **$259.95**. T-slot mount; cord or integral switch. Uses common A76 batteries. [3]High intensity 635 beam, **$349.95** (blue), **$359.95** (stainless). Dimensions 1.1"x1.1"x.6". From B-Square.
BSL-1[1]	—	—	—	2.75	.75	Int.	2.25	199.95	
Mini-Laser[2,3]	—	—	—	1.1	—	Int.	2.9	239.95	
BURRIS									All scopes avail. in Plex reticle. Steel-on-steel click adjustments. [1]Dot reticle on some models. [2]Matte satin finish. [3]Available with parallax adjustment (standard on 10x, 12x, 4-12x, 6-12x, 6-18x, 6x HBR and 3-12x Signature). [4]Silver matte finish extra. [5]Target knobs extra, standard on silhouette models, LER and XER with P.A., 6x HBR. [6]Available with Posi-Lock. LER=Long Eye Relief; IER=Intermediate Eye Relief; XER=Extra Eye Relief. Partial listing shown, contact maker for complete data. From Burris.
Handgun									
1 1/2-4x LER[1,4,6]	1.6-3.	16-11	11-25	10 1/4	1	Int.	11	342.00	
2-7x LER[2,3,4,6]	2-6.5	21-7	7-27	9.5	1	Int.	12.6	334.00	
3-9x LER[3,4,6]	3.4-8.4	12-5	22-14	11	1	Int.	14	376.00	
1x LER[1]	1.1	27	10-24	8 3/4	1	Int.	6.8	212.00	
2x LER[3,4,5]	1.7	21	10-24	8 3/4	1	Int.	6.8	219.00	
3x LER[3,5]	2.7	17	10-20	8 7/8	1	Int.	6.8	236.00	
4x LER[1,3,4,5,6]	3.7	11	10-22	9 5/8	1	Int.	9.0	245.00	
7x IER[1,3,4,5]	6.5	6.5	10-16	11 1/4	1	Int.	10	307.00	
10x IER[1,3,5]	9.5	4	8-12	13 1/2	1	Int.	14	363.00	

Maker and Model	Magn.	Field at 100 Yds. (feet)	Eye Relief (in.)	Length (in.)	Tube Dia. (in.)	W&E Adjustments	Weight (ozs.)	Price	Other Data
BUSHNELL									[1]Also silver finish, **$204.95**. [2]Also silver finish, **$257.95**. **Only selected models shown.** Contact Bausch & Lomb Sports Optics Div. for details.
Trophy Handgun									
73-0232[1]	2	20	9-26	8.7	1	Int.	7.7	189.95	
73-2632[2]	2-6	21-7	9-26	9.1	1	Int.	9.6	244.95	
INTERAIMS									Intended for handguns. Comes with rings. Dot size less than 1½" @ 100 yds. Waterproof. Battery life 50-10,000 hours. Black or nickel finish. 2x booster, 1" or 30mm, **$139.00** Imported by Stoeger.
One V	0	—	—	4.5	1	Int.	4	159.95	
One V 30	0	—	—	4.5	30mm	Int.	4	176.95	
KILHAM									Unlimited eye relief; internal click adjustments; crosshair reticle. Fits Thompson/Center rail mounts, for S&W K, N, Ruger Blackhawk, Super, Super Single-Six, Contender.
Hutson Handgunner II	1.7	8	—	5½	7/8	Int.	5.1	119.95	
Hutson Handgunner	3	8	10-12	6	7/8	Int.	5.3	119.95	
LASERAIM									[1]300-yd. range; 15-hr. batt. [2]Red dot laser; fits Weaver-style mounts; also LA2XM with Hotdot, **$269.95**. [3]300-yd. range; 2" dot at 100 yds.; rechargeable Nicad battery. [4]1.5-mile range; 1" dot at 100 yds.; 20+ hrs. batt. life. [5]1.5-mile range; 1" dot at 100 yds.; rechargeable Nicad battery (comes with in-field charger); [6]Black or satin finish. With mount, **$169.00**. [7]Fits any pistol magazine without bumper pad; Hotdot model (LA18), **$319.00** [8]Laser mounts in revolver grip (included); Hotdot model (LA20), **$292.00**. [9]Rings included; 6-MOA dot, seven brightness settings. [10]Ext. tube, polarizing filter incl.; 4-MOA dot, seven brightness settings. [11]Auto. brightness control; 30mm lens; fits std. Weaver base, no rings required. [12]Fits std. Weaver base, no rings required; 6-MOA dot; seven brightness settings. All have w&e adj.; black or satin silver finish. From Emerging Technologies, Inc.
LA8[1]	—	—	—	2.94	.74	Int.	NA	139.00	
LA2X Dualdot[2]	—	—	—	NA	30mm	Int.	NA	319.00	
LA5[3]	—	—	—	2	.75	Int.	1.2	236.00	
LA10 Hotdot[4]	—	—	—	3.87	.75	Int.	NA	396.00	
LA11 Hotdot[5]	—	—	—	2.75	.75	Int.	NA	292.00	
LA14	—	—	—	NA	NA	Int.	NA	314.00	
LA16 Hotdot Mighty Sight[6]	—	—	—	1.5	NA	Int.	1.5	140.00	
LA17 Clip Sight[7]	—	—	—	1.5	NA	Int.	2.0	278.00	
LA19 Grip Sight[8]	—	—	—	1.5	NA	Int.	NA	244.00	
Red Dot Sights									
LA94 Illusion II[9]	—	—	—	6.0	30mm	Int.	6.0	111.00	
LA99 Illusion[10]	—	—	—	5.5	1	Int.	5.0	138.00	
LA930 Auto Illusion[11]	—	—	—	4.75	—	Int.	5.75	181.00	
LA9750 Grand Illusion[12]	—	—	—	5.5	50mm	Int.	7.0	236.00	
LASER DEVICES									Projects high intensity beam of laser light onto target as an aiming point. Adj. for w. & e. [1]Diode laser system. From Laser Devices, Inc.
He Ne FA-6	—	—	—	6.2	—	Int.	11	229.50	
He Ne FA-9	—	—	—	12	—	Int.	16	299.00	
He Ne FA-9P	—	—	—	9	—	Int.	14	299.00	
FA-4[1]	—	—	—	4.5	—	Int.	3.5	299.00	
LASERSIGHT									Projects a highly visible beam of concentrated laser light onto the target. Adjustable for w.& e. Visible up to 500 yds. at night. For handguns, rifles, shotguns. Uses two standard 9V batteries. From Imatronic Lasersight.
LS45	0	—	—	7.5	—	Int.	8.5	245.00	
LS25	0	—	—	6	3/4	Int.	3.5	270.00	
LS55	0	—	—	7	1	Int.	7	299.00	
LEUPOLD									Constantly centered reticles, choice of Duplex, tapered CPC, Leupold Dot, Crosshair and Dot. CPC and Dot reticles extra. [1]2x and 4x scopes have from 12"-24" of eye relief and are suitable for handguns, top ejection arms and muzzleloaders. [2]Battery life 60 min.; dot size .625" @ 25 yds. Black matte finish Partial listing shown. **Contact Leupold for complete details.**
M8-2X EER[1]	1.7	21.2	12-24	7.9	1	Int.	6.0	264.30	
M8-2X EER Silver[1]	1.7	21.2	12-24	7.9	1	Int.	6.0	285.70	
M8-4X EER[1]	3.7	9	12-24	8.4	1	Int.	7.0	357.10	
M8-4X EER Silver[1]	3.7	9	12-24	8.4	1	Int.	7.0	357.10	
Vari-X 2.5-8 EER	2.5-8.0	13-4.3	11.7-12	9.7	1	Int.	10.9	514.30	
Laser									
LaserLight[2]	—	—	—	1.18	NA	Int.	.5	266.10	
MILLETT									Full coated lenses; parallax-free; three lenses; 30mm has 10-min. dot, 1-Inch has 3-min. dot. Black or silver finish. From Millett Sights.
Red Dot 1 Inch	1	36.65	—	NA	1	Int.	NA	189.95	
Red Dot 30mm	1	58	—	NA	30mm	Int.	NA	289.95	
NIKON									Super multi-coated lenses and blackening of all internal metal parts for maximum light gathering capability; positive ¼-MOA; fogproof; waterproof; shockproof; luster and matte finish. From Nikon, Inc.
1.5-4.5x24 EER	1.5-4.4	13.7-5.8	24-18	8.9	1	Int.	9.3	352.00	
2x20 EER	2	22	26.4	8.1	1	Int.	6.3	213.00	
PENTAX									[1]Glossy finish; satin chrome, **$260.00**. [2]Glossy finish; satin chrome, **$380.00**. [3]Glossy finish; satin chrome, **$390.00**. Imported by Pentax Corp.
Pistol									
2x[1]	2	21	10-24	8.8	1	Int.	6.8	230.00	
1.5-4x[2]	1.5-4	16-11	11-25, 11-18	10.0	1	Int.	11.0	350.00	
2.5-7x[3]	2.5-7	12-7.5	11-28, 9-14	12.0	1	Int.	12.5	370.00	
REDFIELD									4-Plex reticle is standard. [1]Magnum proof. Specially designed for magnum and auto pistols. Uses Double Dovetail mounts. Also in nickel-plated finish, 2x, **$239.95**, 4x, **$239.95**, 2½-7x, **$322.95**, 2½-7x matte black, **$322.95**. All Golden Five Star scopes come with Butler Creek flip-up lens covers. **Contact Redfield for full data.**
Handgun Scopes									
Golden Five Star 2x[1]	2	24	9.5-20	7.88	1	Int.	6	223.95	
Golden Five Star 4x[1]	4	75	13-19	8.63	1	Int.	6.1	223.95	
Golden Five Star 2½-7x[1]	2½-7	11-3.75	11-26	9.4	1	Int.	9.3	303.95	
SIGHTRON									[1]Black finish; also stainless. [2]3 MOA dot; also with 5 or 10 MOA dot. [3]Variable 3, 5, 10 MOA dot; black finish; also stainless. Electronic Red Dot scopes come with ring mounts, front and rear extension tubes, polarizing filter, battery, haze filter caps, wrench. Pistol scopes have aluminum tubes, Exac Trak adjustments. Lifetime warranty. From Sightron, Inc.
Electronic Red Dot									
S33-3[1,2]	1	58	—	5.15	33mm	Int.	5.43	279.99	
S33-30[3]	1	58	—	5.74	33mm	Int.	6.27	369.99	
Pistol Scopes									
SII 1x28P[1]	1	30	9.0-24.0	9.44	1	Int.	8.46	197.99	
SII 2x28P[1]	2	16-10	9.0-24.0	9.56	1	Int.	8.28	196.99	

HANDGUN SCOPES

Maker and Model	Magn.	Field at 100 Yds. (feet)	Eye Relief (in.)	Length (in.)	Tube Dia. (in.)	W&E Adjust-ments	Weight (ozs.)	Price	Other Data
SIMMONS									[1]Black or silver matte. [6]Black polish. **Only selected models shown.** Contact Simmons Outdoor Corp. for complete details.
Master Red Dot									
51004[1]	1	40	—	5.25	30mm	Int.	4.8	269.95	
Gold Medal Handgun									
22002[2]	2.5-7	9.7-4.0	8.9-19.4	9.25	1	Int.	9.0	329.95	
22004[2]	2	3.9	8.6-19.5	7.3	1	Int.	7.4	229.95	
22006[2]	4	8.9	9.8-18.7	9	1	Int.	8.8	269.95	
SWIFT									All Swift scopes have Quadraplex reticles and are fogproof and waterproof. [1]Available in black or silver finish—same price. From Swift Instruments.
Pistol Scopes									
661 4x32	4	90	10-22	9.2	1	Int.	9.5	115.00	
662 2.5x32	2.5	14.3	9-22	8.9	1	Int.	9.3	110.00	
663 2x20[1]	2	18.3	9-21	7.2	1	Int.	8.4	115.00	
TASCO									[1]Electronic dot reticle with rheostat; coated optics; adj. for windage and elevation; waterproof, shockproof, fogproof; Lithium battery; 3x power booster avail.; matte black or matte aluminum finish; dot or T-3 reticle. [2]Also matte aluminum finish. [3]Also with crosshair reticle. [4]Dot size 1.5" at 100 yds.; waterproof. [5]Black matte or stainless finish. [6]Available with 5-min. or 10-min. dot. [7]Available with 10, 15, 20-min. dot. **Contact Tasco for details on complete line.**
World Class Pistol									
PWC2x22[2]	2	25	11-20	8.75	1	Int.	7.3	288.00	
PWC4x28[2]	4	8	12-19	9.45	1	Int.	7.9	340.00	
P1.254x28	1.25-4	23-9	15-23	9.25	1	Int.	8.2	339.00	
Propoint									
PDP2[1,2,6]	1	40	—	5	30mm	Int.	5	267.00	
PDP3[1,2,6]	1	52	—	5	30mm	Int.	5	367.00	
PDP4[5,7]	1	82	—	—	45mm	Int.	6.1	458.00	
PB1[3]	3	35	3	5.5	30mm	Int.	6.0	183.00	
PB3	2	30	—	1.25	30mm	Int.	2.6	214.00	
LaserPoint LP2[4]	—	—	—	2	5/8	Int.	.75	374.00	
THOMPSON/CENTER RECOIL PROOF PISTOL SCOPES									[1]Black finish; silver, **$224.00.** [2]Rail mount. [3]Black finish; silver, **$330.00.** [4]Black; silver, **$254.00.** [5]Lighted reticle, black, rail mount; std. mount, **$290.00;** silver, std., **$300.** [6]Lighted reticle, black. [7]Red dot scope. From Thompson/Center.
Pistol Scopes									
8356[1]	2	22.1	10.5-26.4	7⅘	1	Int.	6.4	220.00	
8312[2]	2.5	15	9-21	7⅖	1	Int.	6.6	210.00	
8315[3]	2.5-7	15-5	8-21, 8-11	9¼	1	Int.	9.2	300.00	
8352[4]	4	22.1	10.5-26.4	7⅘	1	Int.	6.4	250.00	
8320[5]	2.5	15	9-21	7⅖	1	Int.	8.2	300.00	
8326[6]	2.5-7	15-5	8-21, 8-11	9¼	1	Int.	10.5	360.00	
8650[7]	1	40	—	5¼	30mm	Int.	4.8	238.00	
WEAVER									Micro-Trac adjustment system with ¼-minute clicks on all models. All have Dual-X reticle. One-piece aluminum tube, satin finish, nitrogen filled, multi-coated lenses, waterproof. [1]4 MOA red dot; also with 12 MOA dot; comes with Weaver q.d. rings. [2]Variable 4, 8, 12 MOA red dot; comes with Weaver q.d. rings. [3]4 MOA, 12 MOA, variable 4, 8, 12 MOA (**$364.86.** [4]Stainless finish, **$207.71.** [5]Stainless finish, **$218.64.** [6]Stainless finish, **$263.83.** From Weaver.
Qwik-Point									
QP30[1]	1	12.6	—	5.39	30mm	Int.	5.3	224.57	
QP33[2]	1	14.4	—	5.74	33mm	Int.	6.3	364.11	
QP45[3]	1	21.8	—	4.8	45mm	Int.	8.46	282.09	
Handgun									
2x28[4]	2	21	4-29	8.5	1	Int.	6.7	196.80	
4x28[5]	4	18	11.5-18	8.5	1	Int.	6.7	207.71	
1.5-4x20[6]	1.5-4	13.5-5.8	12-24, 10.5-17	8.6	1	Int.	8.1	252.91	
WILLIAMS									[1]Matte or glossy black finish. TNT models. From Williams Gunsight Co.
Twilight Crosshair TNT	1½-5	57¾-21	3½	10¾	1	Int.	10	221.37	
Twilight Crosshair TNT	2½	32	3¾	11¼	1	Int.	8½	156.66	
Guideline II									
1.5-5x[1]	1.5-5	57¾-21	3.5	10¾	1	Int.	10	286.01	

Hunting scopes in general are furnished with a choice of reticle—crosshairs, post with crosshairs, tapered or blunt post, or dot crosshairs, etc. The great majority of target and varmint scopes have medium or fine crosshairs but post or dot reticles may be ordered. W—Windage E—Elevation MOA—Minute of angle or 1" (approx.) at 100 yards, etc.

Burris 1-4x XER Fullfield.

Swift Model 663

Thompson/Center 8356

Weaver Qwik-Point 1x 33mm.

CAUTION: PRICES SHOWN ARE SUPPLIED BY THE MANUFACTURER OR IMPORTER. CHECK YOUR LOCAL GUNSHOP.

8th ANNUAL EDITION **313**

HANDGUN SCOPE MOUNTS

Maker, Model, Type	Adjust.	Scopes	Price
AIMPOINT	No	1"	$49.95-89.95
Laser Mounts[1]	No	1", 30mm	51.95

Mounts/rings for all Aimpoint sights and 1" scopes. For many popular revolvers, auto pistols, shotguns, military-style rifles/carbines, sporting rifles. Most require no gunsmithing. [1]Mounts Aimpoint Laser-dot below barrel; many popular handguns, military-style rifles. Contact Aimpoint.

Maker, Model, Type	Adjust.	Scopes	Price
AIMTECH			
Handguns			
AMT Auto Mag II, III	No	1"	56.99-64.95
Auto Mag IV	No	1"	64.95
Astra revolvers	No	1"	63.25
Beretta/Taurus auto	No	1"	63.25
Browning Buck Mark/Challenger II	No	1"	56.99
Browning Hi-Power	No	1"	63.25
Glock 17, 17L, 19, 22, 23	No	1"	63.25
Govt. 45 Auto	No	1"	63.25
Rossi revolvers	No	1"	63.25
Ruger Mk I, Mk II	No	1"	49.95
S&W K,L,N frame	No	1"	63.25
S&W Model 41 Target	No	1"	63.25
S&W Model 52 Target	No	1"	63.25
S&W 45, 9mm autos	No	1"	56.99
S&W 422/622/2206	No	1"	56.99
Taurus revolvers	No	1"	63.25
TZ/CZ/P9 9mm	No	1"	63.25

Mount scopes, lasers, electronic sights using Weaver-style base. All mounts allow use of iron sights; no gunsmithing. Available in satin black or satin stainless finish. **Partial listing shown.** Contact maker for full details. From L&S Technologies, Inc.

Maker, Model, Type	Adjust.	Scopes	Price
B-SQUARE			
Pistols			
Beretta/Taurus 92/99[5]	—	1"	69.95
Browning Buck Mark[5]	No	1"	49.95
Colt 45 Auto	E only	1"	69.95
Colt Python/MkIV, 4",6",8"[1,5]	E	1"	59.95
Dan Wesson Clamp-On[2,5]	E	1"	59.95
Ruger 22 Auto Mono-Mount[3]	No	1"	59.95
Ruger Single-Six[4]	No	1"	59.95
Ruger Blackhawk, Super B'hwk[6]	W&E	1"	59.95
Ruger GP-100[7]	No	1"	59.95
Ruger Redhawk[6]	W&E	1"	59.95
S&W 422/2206[7]	No	1"	59.95
Taurus 66[7]	No	1"	59.95
S&W K, L, N frame[2,5]	No	1"	59.95
T/C Contender (Dovetail Base)	W&E	1"	39.95
BSL Laser Mounts			
Scope Tube Clamp[9,10,11]	No	—	39.95
45 Auto[9,10,11]	No	—	39.95
SIG P226[9,10,11]	No	—	39.95
Beretta 92F/Taurus PT99[9,10,11]	No	—	39.95
Colt King Cobra, Python, MkV[9,10,11]	No	—	39.95
S&W L Frame[10,11]	No	—	39.95
Browning HP[7,10,11]	No	—	39.95
Glock	No	—	39.95
Star Firestar[9,10,11]	No	—	39.95
Rossi small frame revolver[9,10,11]	No	—	39.95
Taurus 85 revolver[9,10,11]	No	—	39.95

[1]Clamp-on, blue finish; stainless finish **$59.95.** [2]Blue finish; stainless finish **$59.95.** [3]Clamp-on; blue; stainless finish **$59.95.** [4]Dovetail; stainless finish **$59.95.** [5]Weaver-style rings. Rings not included with Weaver-type bases; stainless finish add $10. [6]Blue; stainless **$69.95.** [7]Blue; stainless finish **$69.95.** [8]Receiver mounts. [9]Stainless finish add $10. [10]Under-barrel mount, no gunsmithing. [11]Used with B-Square BSL-1 Laser Sight only. Mounts for many shotguns, airguns, military and law enforcement guns also available. **Partial listing of mounts shown here.** Contact B-Square for more data.

Maker, Model, Type	Adjust.	Scopes	Price
BURRIS			
L.E.R. (LU) Mount Bases[1]	W only	1" split rings	25.00-66.00
L.E.R. No Drill-No Tap Bases[1,2,3]	W only	1" split rings	46.00-52.00

[1]Universal dovetail; accept Burris, Universal, Redfield, Leupold rings. For Dan Wesson, S&W, Virginian, Ruger Blackhawk, Win. 94. [2]Selected rings and bases available with matte Safari or silver finish. [3]For S&W K,L,N frames, Colt Python, Dan Wesson with 6" or longer barrels. From Burris.

Maker, Model, Type	Adjust.	Scopes	Price
CONETROL			
Pistol Bases, 2 or 3-ring[1]	W only	1" scopes	—

[1]For XP-100, T/C Contender, Colt SAA, Ruger Blackhawk, S&W. Three-ring mount available for T/C Contender and other pistols in Conetrol's three grades. From Conetrol

Maker, Model, Type	Adjust.	Scopes	Price
IRONSIGHTER			
Ironsighter Handguns[1]	No	1" split rings	33.95-58.95

[1]For 1" dia. extended eye relief scopes. Some models in stainless finish. From Ironsighter Co.

Maker, Model, Type	Adjust.	Scopes	Price
KRIS MOUNTS			
One Piece (T)	No	1", 26mm split rings	12.98

Blackhawk revolver. Mounts have oval hole to permit use of iron sights. From Kris Mounts.

Maker, Model, Type	Adjust.	Scopes	Price
LASERAIM	No	Laser Aim	29.00-69.00

Mounts Laser Aim above or below barrel. Avail. for most popular handguns, rifles, shotguns, including militaries. From Emerging Technologies, Inc.

Maker, Model, Type	Adjust.	Scopes	Price
LASERSIGHT	No	LS45 only	29.95-149.00

For the LS45 Lasersight. Allows LS45 to be mounted alongside any 1" scope. Universal adapter attaches to any full-length Weaver-type base. For most popular military-type rifles, Mossberg, Rem. shotguns, Python, Desert Eagle, S&W N frame, Colt 45ACP. From Imatronic Lasersight.

Maker, Model, Type	Adjust.	Scopes	Price
LEUPOLD			
STD Handgun mounts[1]	No	—	56.00

[1]Base and two rings; Casull, Ruger, S&W, T/C; add $5.00 for silver finish. From Leupold.

Maker, Model, Type	Adjust.	Scopes	Price
MILLETT			
Handgun Bases, Rings[1]	—	1"	34.60-69.15

[1]Two and three-ring sets for Colt Python, Trooper, Diamondback, Peacekeeper, Dan Wesson, Ruger Redhawk, Super Redhawk. From Millett Sights.

Maker, Model, Type	Adjust.	Scopes	Price
OAKSHORE			
Handguns			
Browning Buck Mark	No	1"	29.00
Colt Cobra, Diamondback, Python, 1911	No	1"	38.00-52.00
Ruger 22 Auto, GP100	No	1"	33.00-49.00
S&W N Frame	No	1"	45.00-60.00
S&W 422	No	1"	35.00-38.00

See Through offered in some models. Black or silver finish; 1" rings also avail. for 3/8" grooved receivers (See Through). From Oakshore Electronic Sights, Inc.

Maker, Model, Type	Adjust.	Scopes	Price
REDFIELD			
Three-Ring Pistol System SMP[1]	No	1" split rings (three)	56.95-62.95

[1]Used with MP scopes for: S&W K, L or N frame, XP-100, T/C Contender, Ruger receivers.

Maker, Model, Type	Adjust.	Scopes	Price
SSK INDUSTRIES			
T'SOB	No	1"	65.00-145.00
Quick Detachable	No	1"	From 160.00

Custom installation using from two to four rings (included). For T/C Contender, most 22 auto pistols, Ruger and other S.A. revolvers, Ruger, Dan Wesson, S&W, Colt DA revolvers. Black or white finish. Uses Kimber rings in two- or three-ring sets. In blue or SSK Khrome. For T/C Contender or most popular revolvers. Standard, non-detachable model also available, from **$65.00.**

Maker, Model, Type	Adjust.	Scopes	Price
TASCO			
Handgun Revolver	No	1"	33.50-58.00
Handgun Competition	No	1"	103.00
Bases	Yes	—	24.00-61.00

Handgun bases have w&e adj. From Tasco.

Maker, Model, Type	Adjust.	Scopes	Price
THOMPSON/CENTER			
Contender 97411[1]	No	2½, 4 RP	17.00
Duo-Ring Mount[2]	No	1"	57.20
Weaver-Style Rings[3]	No	1"	25.00-37.00
Quick Release System[4]	No	1"	Rings 48.00 Base 24.50

[1]T/C rail mount scopes; all Contenders except vent. rib. [2]Attaches directly to T/C Contender bbl., no drilling/tapping; blue or stainless. [3]Medium and high; blue or silver finish. [4]For Contender pistol, Carbine, Scout, all M/L long guns. From Thompson/Center.

Maker, Model, Type	Adjust.	Scopes	Price
WEAVER			
Mount Base System[1]			
Blue Finish	No	1"	75.00
Stainless Finish	No	1"	105.00

[1]No drilling, tapping. For Colt Python, Trooper, 357, Officer's Model, Ruger Blackhawk & Super, Mini-14, Security-Six, 22 auto pistols, Single-Six 22, Redhawk, Blackhawk SRM 357, S&W current K, L with adj. sights. From Weaver.

CAUTION: PRICES SHOW ARE SUPPLIED BY THE MANUFACTURER OR IMPORTER. CHECK YOUR LOCAL GUNSHOP.

Thompson/Center Weaver-Style

Laseraim

B-Square Beretta 92

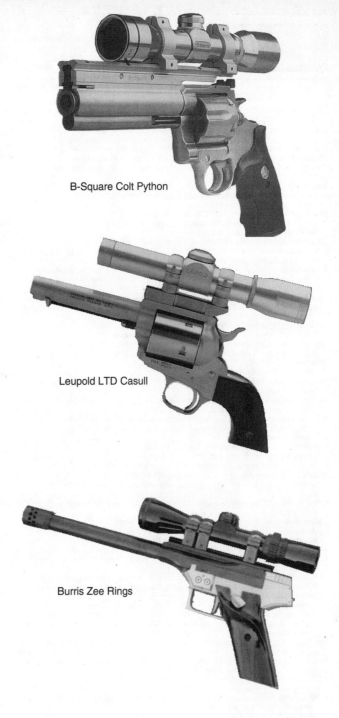

B-Square Colt Python

Leupold LTD Casull

Burris Zee Rings

Maker, Model, Type	Adjust.	Scopes	Price
WEIGAND			
1911 PDP4[1]	No	40mm, PDP4	69.95
1911 General Purpose[2]	No	—	59.95
Ruger Mark II[3]	No	—	49.95
3rd Generation[4]	No	—	99.95
Pro Ringless[5]	No	30mm	99.95
Stabilizer I Ringless[6,7]	No	30mm	99.95
Revolver Mount[8]	No	—	35.50

[1]For Tasco PDP4 and similar 40mm sights. [2]Weaver rail; takes any standard rings. [3]No drilling, tapping. [4]For M1911; grooved top for Weaver-style rings; requires drilling, tapping. [5]Two-piece design; for M1911, P9/EA-9, CZ-75 copies; integral rings; silver alum. finish. [6]Three-piece design; fits M1911, P9/EA-9, TZ, CZ-75 copies; silver alum. finish. [7]Stabilizer II —more forward position; for M1911, McCormick frames. [8]Frame mount. From Weigand Combat Handguns, Inc.

Maker, Model, Type	Adjust.	Scopes	Price
WILLIAMS			
Guideline Handgun[1]	No	1" split rings.	61.75

[1]No drilling, tapping required; heat treated alloy. For Ruger MkII Bull Barrel (**$61.75**); Streamline Top Mount for T/C Contender (**$41.15**). From Williams Gunsight Co.

NOTES

(S)—Side Mount (T)—Top Mount; 22mm=.866"; 25.4mm=1.024"; 26.5mm=1.045"; 30mm=1.81"

PERIODICAL PUBLICATIONS

AAFTA News (M) 5911 Cherokee Ave., Tampa, FL 33604. Official newsletter of the American Airgun Field Target Assn.

Action Pursuit Games Magazine (M) CFW Enterprises, Inc., 4201 W. Vanowen Pl., Burbank, CA 91505 818-845-2656. $2.95 single copy U.S., $3.50 Canada. Editor: Jessica Sparks, 818-845-2656. World's leading magazine of paintball sports.

Air Gunner Magazine 4 The Courtyard, Denmark St., Wokingham, Berkshire RG11 2AZ, England/011-44-734-771677. $U.S. $44 for 1 yr. Leading monthly airgun magazine in U.K.

Airgun Ads Box 33, Hamilton, MT 59840/406-363-3805. $35 1 yr. (for first mailing; $20 for second mailing; $35 for Canada and foreign orders.) Monthly tabloid with extensive For Sale and Wanted airgun listings.

The Airgun Letter Gapp, Inc., 4614 Woodland Rd., Ellicott City, MD 41042-6329/410-730-5496. $18 U.S., $21 Canada, $24 Mexico and $30 other foreign orders, 1 yr. Monthly newsletter for airgun users and collectors.

Airgun World 4 The Courtyard, Denmark St., Wokingham, Berkshire RG11 2AZ, England/011-44-734-771677. Call for subscription rates. Oldest monthly airgun magazine in the U.K., now a sister publication to *Air Gunner*.

Alaska Magazine Alaska Publishing Properties Inc., 808 E St., Suite 200, Anchorage, AK 99501. $24.00 yr. Hunting, Fishing and Life on the Last Frontier articles of Alaska and western Canada. Outdoors Editor, Ken Marsh.

American Firearms Industry Nat'l. Assn. of Federally Licensed Firearms Dealers, 2455 E. Sunrise Blvd., Suite 916, Ft. Lauderdale, FL 33304. $25.00 yr. For firearms retailers, distributors and manufacturers.

American Handgunner 591 Camino de la Reina, Suite 200, San Diego, CA 92108. $16.75 yr. Articles for handgun enthusiasts, competitors, police and hunters.

American Hunter (M) National Rifle Assn., 11250 Waples Mill Rd., Fairfax, VA 22030 (Same address for both.) Publications Div. $35.00 yr. Wide scope of hunting articles.

American Survival Guide McMullen and Yee Publishing, Inc., 774 S. Placentia Ave., Placentia, CA 92670-6846. 12 issues $19.95/714-572-2255; FAX: 714-572-1864.

American West American West Management Corp., 7000 E. Tanque Verde Rd., Suite #30, Tucson, AZ 85715. $15.00 yr.

Arms Collecting (Q) Museum Restoration Service, P.O. Box 70, Alexandria Bay, NY 13607-0070. $22.00 yr.; $62.00 3 yrs.; $112.00 5 yrs.

Australian Shooters Journal Sporting Shooters' Assn. of Australia, Inc., P.O. Box 2066, Kent Town SA 5071, Australia. $45.00 yr. locally; $55.00 yr. overseas surface mail only. Hunting and shooting articles.

The Backwoodsman Magazine P.O. Box 627, Westcliffe, CO 81252. $15.00 for 6 issues per yr.; $28.00 for 2 yrs.; sample copy $2.50. Subjects include muzzle-loading, woodslore, primitive survival, trapping, homesteading, blackpowder cartridge guns, 19th century how-to.

Black Powder Times P.O. Box 1131, Stanwood, WA 98292. $15.00 yr.; add $2 per year for Canada, $5 per year other foreign. Tabloid newspaper for blackpowder activities; test reports.

Caliber GFI-Verlag, Theodor-Heuss Ring 62, 50668 Köln, Germany. For hunters, target shooters and reloaders.

Cartridge Journal (M) Robert Mellichamp, 907 Shirkmere, Houston, TX 77008/713-869-0558. Dues $12 for U.S. and Canadian members (includes the newsletter); 6 issues.

The Cast Bullet*(M) Official journal of The Cast Bullet Assn. Director of Membership, 4103 Foxcraft Dr., Traverse City, MI 49684. Annual membership dues $14, includes 6 issues.

Combat Handguns* Harris Publications, Inc., 1115 Broadway, New York, NY 10010. Single copy $2.95 U.S.A.; $3.25 Canada.

The Derringer Peanut (M) The National Association of Derringer Collectors, P.O. Box 20572, San Jose, CA 95160. A newsletter dedicated to developing the best derringer information. Write for details.

Deutsches Waffen Journal Journal-Verlag Schwend GmbH, Postfach 100340, D-74523 Schwäbisch Hall, Germany/0791-404-500; FAX:0791-404-505 and 404-424. DM97. 7 yr. (interior); DM120.30 (abroad), postage included. Antique and modern arms and equipment. German text.

The Engraver (M) (Q) P.O. Box 4365, Estes Park, CO 80517. Mike Dubber, editor. The journal of firearms engraving.

The Field King's Reach Tower, Stamford St., London SE1 9LS England. £35.00 sterling U.S. (approx. $70.00) yr. Hunting and shooting articles, and all country sports.

Field & Stream Times Mirror Magazines, Two Park Ave., New York, NY 10016. $11.94 yr. Monthly shooting column. Articles on hunting and fishing.

FIRE Euro-Editions, Boulevard Lambermont 140, B1030 Brussels, Belgium. Belg. Franc 2100 for 6 issues. Arms, shooting, ammunition. French text.

Fur-Fish-Game A.R. Harding Pub. Co., 2878 E. Main St., Columbus, OH 43209. $15.95 yr. "Gun Rack" column by Don Zutz.

The Gottlieb-Tartaro Report Second Amendment Foundation, James Madison Bldg., 12500 NE 10th Pl., Bellevue, WA 98005/206-454-7012;Fax:206-451-3959. $30 for 12 issues. An insiders guide for gun owners.

Gray's Sporting Journal Gray's Sporting Journal, Inc., P.O. Box 1207, Augusta, GA 30903. $35.95 per yr. for 6 consecutive issues. Hunting and fishing journals. Expeditions and Guides Book (Annual Travel Guide).

Gun List 700 E. State St., Iola, WI 54990. $27.95 yr. (26 issues); $52.00 2 yrs. (52 issues). Indexed market publication for firearms collectors and active shooters; guns, supplies and services.

Gun News Digest (Q) Second Amendment Fdn., P.O. Box 488, Station C, Buffalo, NY 14209/716-885-6408; Fax:716-884-4471. $10 U.S.; $20 foreign.

The Gun Report World Wide Gun Report, Inc., Box 38, Aledo, IL 61231-0038. $33.00 yr. For the antique and collectable gun dealer and collector.

Gunmaker (M) (Q) ACGG, P.O. Box 812, Burlington, IA 52601-0812. The journal of custom gunmaking.

The Gunrunner Div. of Kexco Publ. Co. Ltd., Box 565G, Lethbridge, Alb., Canada T1J 3Z4. $23.00 yr. Monthly newspaper, listing everything from antiques to artillery.

Gun Show Calendar (Q) 700 E. State St., Iola, WI 54990. $12.95 yr. (4 issues). Gun shows listed.

Gun Tests 11 Commerce Blvd., Palm Coast, FL 32142. The consumer resource for the serious shooter. Write for information.

Gun Trade News The Street, West Raynham, Falkenham NR21 7EZ, England/01328/838755; Fax:01328-838523. Britain's only "trade only" magazine exclusive to the gun trade.

Gun Week† Second Amendment Foundation, P.O. Box 488, Station C, Buffalo, NY 14209. $32.00 yr. U.S. and possessions; $40.00 yr. other countries. Tabloid paper on guns, hunting, shooting and collecting (50 issues).

Gun Week's Gun and Ammo Guide Second Amendment Foundation, James Madison Bldg., 12500 NE 10th Pl., Bellevue, WA 98005. $5.95 Annual (1st issue forthcoming).

Gun World Gallant/Charger Publications, Inc., 34249 Camino Capistrano, Capistrano Beach, CA 92624. $20.00 yr. For the hunting, reloading and shooting enthusiast.

Guns & Ammo Petersen Publishing Co., 6420 Wilshire Blvd., Los Angeles, CA 90048. $21.94 yr. Guns, shooting, and technical articles.

Guns Guns Magazine, P.O. Box 85201, San Diego, CA 92138. $19.95 yr.; $34.95 2 yrs.; $46.95 3 yrs. In-depth articles on a wide range of guns, shooting equipment and related accessories for gun collectors, hunters and shooters.

Guns and Gear Creative Arts, Inc., 4901 Northwest 17th Way, Fort Lauderdale, FL 33309/305-772-2788; FAX: 305-351-0484. Single copy $4.95. Covering all aspects of the shooting sports.

Guns Review Ravenhill Publishing Co. Ltd., Box 35, Standard House, Bonhill St., London EC 2A 4DA, England. £20.00 sterling (approx. U.S. $38 USA & Canada) yr. For collectors and shooters.

H.A.C.S. Newsletter (M) Harry Moon, Pres., P.O. Box 50117, South Slope RPO, Burnaby BC, V5J 5G3, Canada/604-936-9141. $15 p. yr. Canada; $17.00 outside Canada. Official newsletter of The Historical Arms Collectors of B.C. (Canada).

Handgunning* PJS Publications, News Plaza, P.O. Box 1790, Peoria, IL 61656. Cover price $3.95; subscriptions $19.98 for 6 issues. Premier journal for multi-sport handgunners: hunting, reloading, law enforcement, practical pistol and target shooting, and home defense.

Handgun Times Creative Arts, Inc., 4901 NW 17th Way, Fort Lauderdale, FL 33309/305-772-2788; FAX: 305-351-0484. Single copy $4.95. Technical evaluations, detailed information and testing by handgun experts.

Handloader* Wolfe Publishing Co., 6471 Airpark Dr., Prescott, AZ 86301. $22.00 yr. The journal of ammunition reloading.

Hunting Horizons Wolfe Publishing Co., 6471 Airpark Dr., Prescott, AZ 86301. $6.95 Annual. Dedicated to the finest pursuit of the hunt.

The Insider Gun News The Gunpress Publishing Co., 1347 Webster St. NE, Washington, DC 20017. Editor, John D. Aquilino. $50.00 yr. (12 issues). Newsletter by former NRA communications director.

INSIGHTS* NRA, 11250 Waples Mill Rd., Fairfax, VA 22030. Editor, John E. Robbins. $15.00 yr., which includes NRA junior membership; $10.00 for adult subscriptions (12 issues). Plenty of details for the young hunter and target shooter; emphasizes gun safety, marksmanship training, hunting skills.

International Shooting Sport*/UIT Journal International Shooting Union (UIT), Bavariaring 21, D-80336 Munich, Germany. Europe: (Deutsche Mark) DM44.00 yr., 2 yrs. DM83.00; outside Europe: DM50.00 yr., 2 yrs. DM95.00 (air mail postage included.) For international sport shooting.

Internationales Waffen-Magazin Habegger-Verlag Zürich, Postfach 9230, CH-8036 Zürich, Switzerland. SF 102.00 (approx. U.S. $82.00) surface mail for 10 issues. Modern and antique arms, self-defense. German text; English summary of contents.

The Journal of the Arms & Armour Society (M) E.J.B. Greenwood (Hon. Sec.), Field House, Upper Dicker, Hailsham, East Sussex, BN27 3PY, England. £15.00 surface mail; £20.00 airmail sterling only yr. Articles for the historian and collector.

Journal of the Historical Breechloading Smallarms Assn. Published annually. Imperial War Museum, Lambeth Road, London SE1 6HZ, England. $13.00 yr. Articles for the collector plus mailings of short articles on specific arms, reprints, newsletters, etc.; a surcharge is made for airmail.

Law and Order Law and Order Magazine, 1000 Skokie Blvd., Wilmette, IL 60091. $20.00 yr. Articles for law enforcement professionals.

Man At Arms* P.O. Box 460, Lincoln, RI 02865. $27.00 yr., $52.00 2 yrs. plus $8.00 for foreign subscribers. The N.R.A. magazine of arms collecting-investing, with excellent articles for the collector of antique arms and militaria.

MAN/MAGNUM S.A. Man (Pty) Ltd., P.O. Box 35204, Northway, Durban 4065, Republic of South Africa. SA Rand 125.00 for 12 issues. Africa's only publication on hunting, shooting, firearms, bushcraft, knives, etc.

Muzzle Blasts (M) National Muzzle Loading Rifle Assn., P.O. Box 67, Friendship, IN 47021. $30.00 yr. annual membership. For the blackpowder shooter.

Muzzleloader Magazine* Rebel Publishing Co., Inc., Dept. Gun, Route 5, Box 347-M, Texarkana, TX 75501. $16.00 U.S.; $19.00 U.S. for foreign subscribers a yr. The publication for blackpowder shooters.

National Defense (M)* American Defense Preparedness Assn., Two Colonial Place, Suite 400, 2101 Wilson Blvd., Arlington, VA 22201-3061/703-522-1820; FAX: 703-522-1885. $35.00 yr. Articles on both military and civil defense field, including weapons, materials technology, management.

National Rifle Assn. Journal (British) (Q) Natl. Rifle Assn. (BR.), Bisley Camp, Brookwood, Woking, Surrey, England. GU24, OPB. £22.00 Sterling including postage.

New Zealand GUNS* Waitekauri Publishing, P.O. 45, Waikino 3060, New Zealand. $NZ90.00 (6 issues) yr. Covers the hunting and firearms scene in New Zealand.

North American Hunter* (M) P.O. Box 3401, Minnetonka, MN 55343. $18.00 yr. (7 issues). Articles on all types of North American hunting.

Outdoor Life Times Mirror Magazines, Two Park Ave., New York, NY 10016. Special 1-yr. subscription, $11.97. Extensive coverage of hunting and shooting. Shooting column by Jim Carmichel.

La Passion des Courteaux (Q) Phenix Editions, 25 rue Mademoiselle, 75015 Paris, France. French text.

Paintball Consumer Reports 14573-C Jefferson Davis Highway, Woodridge, VA 22191/703-491-6199. $19.95 1 yr. U.S., $27.95 foreign. Product testing for the paintball industry.

PERIODICAL PUBLICATIONS

Paintball Games International Magazine Aceville Publications, Castle House, 97 High St., Colchester, Essex, England CO1 1TH/011-44-206-564840. Write for subscription rates. Leading magazine in the U.K. covering competitive paintball activities.

Paintball Hotline† American Paintball Media and Marketing, 15507 S. Normandie Ave. #487, Gardena, CA 90247/310-323-1021. $50 U.S. 1 yr. $75 Mexico and Canada, $125 other foreign orders. Weekly newsletter that tracks inside industry news.

Paintball News PBN Publishing, P.O. Box 1608, 24 Henniker St., Hillsboro, NH 03244/603-464-6080. $35 U.S. 1 yr. Bi-weekly newspaper covering new product reviews and industry features.

Paintball Players Bible* American Paintball Media and Marketing, 15507 S. Normandie Ave. #487, Gardena, CA 90247/310-323-1021. $12.95 U.S. 1 yr., $19.95 foreign. Profiles of guns and accessories.

Paintball Sports (Q) Paintball Publications, Inc., 540 Main St., Mount Kisco, NY 10549/941-241-7400. $24.75 U.S. 1 yr., $32.75 foreign. Covering the competitive paintball scene.

Petersen's HUNTING Magazine Petersen Publishing Co., 6420 Wilshire Blvd., Los Angeles, CA 90048. $19.94 yr.; Canada $29.34 yr.; foreign countries $29.94 yr. Hunting articles for all game; test reports.

P.I. Magazine America's Private Investigation Journal, 755 Bronx Dr., Toledo, OH 43609. Chuck Klein, firearms editor with column about handguns.

Pirsch BLV Verlagsgesellschaft mbH, Postfach 400320, 80703 Munich, Germany/089-12704-0; Fax:089-12705-354. German text.

Point Blank Citizens Committee for the Right to Keep and Bear Arms (sent to contributors), Liberty Park, 12500 NE 10th Pl., Bellevue, WA 98005

POINTBLANK (M) Natl. Firearms Assn., Box 4384 Stn. C, Calgary, AB T2T 5N2, Canada. Official publication of the NFA.

The Police Marksman* 6000 E. Shirley Lane, Montgomery, AL 36117. $17.95 yr. For law enforcement personnel.

Police Times (M) Membership Records, 3801 Biscayne Blvd., Miami, FL 33137/305-573-0070.

Safari Magazine, 4800 W. Gates Pass Rd., Tucson, AZ 85745/602-620-1220. $30.00 (6 times). The journal of big game hunting, published by Safari Club International. Also publish Safari Times, a monthly newspaper, included in price of $30.00 field membership.

Second Amendment Reporter Second Amendment Foundation, James Madison Bldg., 12500 NE 10th Pl., Bellevue, WA 98005. $15.00 yr. (non-contributors).

Shooting Industry Publisher's Dev. Corp., 591 Camino de la Reina, Suite 200, San Diego, CA 92108. $50.00 yr. To the trade $25.00.

Shooting Sports USA National Rifle Assn. of America, 11250 Waples Mill Road, Fairfax, VA 22030. Annual subscriptions for NRA members are $5 for classified shooters and $10 for non-classified shooters. Non-NRA member subscriptions are $15. Covering events, techniques and personalities in competitive shooting.

The Shooting Times & Country Magazine (England)† IPC Magazines Ltd., King's Reach Tower, Stamford St, 1 London SE1 9LS, England/0171-261-6180; Fax:0171-261-7179. £65 (approx. $98.00) yr.; £79 yr. overseas (52 issues). Game shooting, wild fowling, hunting, game fishing and firearms articles. Britain's best selling field sports magazine.

Shooting Times PJS Publications, News Plaza, P.O. Box 1790, Peoria, IL 61656/309-682-6626. $21.98 yr. Guns, shooting, reloading; articles on every gun activity.

The Shotgun News‡ Snell Publishing Co., Box 669, Hastings, NE 68902. $22.00 yr.; all other countries $110.00 yr. Sample copy $4.00. Gun ads of all kinds.

SHOT Business Flintlock Ridge Office Center, 11 Mile Hill Rd., Newtown, CT 06470-2359/203-426-1320; FAX: 203-426-1087. For the shooting, hunting and outdoor trade retailer.

The Sixgunner (M) Handgun Hunters International, P.O. Box 357, MAG, Bloomingdale, OH 43910

Soldier of Fortune Subscription Dept., P.O. Box 348, Mt. Morris, IL 61054. $24.95 yr.; $34.95 Canada; $45.95 foreign.

SPG Lubricants/BP Cartridge (Q) SPG Lubricant, P.O. Box 761, Livingston, MT 59047. $15 yr. For the blackpowder cartridge enthusiast.

Sporting Goods Business Miller Freeman, Inc., 1515 Broadway, New York, NY 10036. Trade journal.

Sporting Goods Dealer Two Park Ave., New York, NY 10016. $100.00 yr. Sporting goods trade journal.

TACARMI Via E. De Amicis, 25; 20123 Milano, Italy. $100.00 yr. approx. Antique and modern guns. (Italian text.)

The U.S. Handgunner* (M) U.S. Revolver Assn., 40 Larchmont Ave., Taunton, MA 02780. $10.00 yr. General handgun and competition articles. Bi-monthly sent to members.

U.S. Airgun Magazine (Q) 2603 Rollingbrook, Benton, AR 72015/501-778-2615. Cover the sport from hunting, 10-meter, field target and collecting. Write for details.

Waffenmarkt-Intern GFI-Verlag, Theodor-Heuss-Ring 62, 50668 Köln, Germany. Only for gunsmiths, licensed firearms dealers and their suppliers in Germany, Austria and Switzerland.

Women & Guns P.O. Box 488, Sta. C, Buffalo, NY 14209. $24.00 yr. U.S.; (12 issues). Only magazine edited by and for women gun owners.

World War II* Empire Press, Inc., 602 King St., Suite 300, Leesburg, VA 22075. Annual subscriptions $16.95 U.S.; $22.95 Canada and overseas. The title says it—WWII; good articles, ads, etc.

---

*Published bi-monthly †Published weekly ‡Published three times per month. All others are published monthly.
M=Membership requirements; write for details. Q-Published Quarterly.

ARMS ASSOCIATIONS

UNITED STATES

ALABAMA

Alabama Gun Collectors Assn. Secretary, P.O. Box 70965, Tuscaloosa, AL 35407

ALASKA

Alaska Gun Collectors Assn., Inc. C.W. Floyd, Pres., 5240 Little Tree, Anchorage, AK 99507

ARIZONA

Arizona Arms Assn. Don DeBusk, President, 4837 Bryce Ave., Glendale, AZ 85301

CALIFORNIA

California Cartridge Collectors Assn. Rick Montgomery, 1729 Christina, Stockton, CA 95204

Greater Calif. Arms & Collectors Assn. Donald L. Bullock, 8291 Carburton St., Long Beach, CA 90808-3302

Los Angeles Gun Ctg. Collectors Assn. F.H. Ruffra, 20810 Amie Ave., Apt. #9, Torrance, CA 90503

Stock Gun Players Assn. 6038 Appian Way, Long Beach, CA, 90803

COLORADO

Colorado Gun Collectors Assn. L.E.(Bud) Greenwald, 2553 S. Quitman St., Denver, CO 80219/303-935-3850

Rocky Mountain Cartridge Collectors Assn. George Blakslee, 15072 E. Mississippi Ave. #1, Aurora, CO 80012

CONNECTICUT

Ye Connecticut Gun Guild, Inc. Dick Fraser, P.O. Box 425, Windsor, CT 06095

FLORIDA

Unified Sportsmen of Florida P.O. Box 6565, Tallahassee, FL 32314

GEORGIA

Georgia Arms Collectors Assn., Inc. Michael Kindberg, President, P.O. Box 277, Alpharetta, GA 30239-0277

ILLINOIS

Mississippi Valley Gun & Cartridge Coll. Assn. Bob Filbert, P.O. Box 61, Port Byron, IL 61275/309-523-2593

Sauk Trail Gun Collectors Gordell M. Matson, P.O. Box 1113, Milan, IL 61264

Wabash Valley Gun Collectors Assn., Inc. Roger L. Dorsett, 2601 Willow Rd., Urbana, IL 61801/217-284-7302

INDIANA

Indiana State Rifle & Pistol Assn. Thos. Glancy, P.O. Box 552, Chesterton, IN 46304

Southern Indiana Gun Collectors Assn., Inc. Sheila McClary, 309 W. Monroe St., Boonville, IN 47601/812-897-3742

IOWA

Beaver Creek Plainsmen Inc. Steve Murphy, Secy., P.O. Box 298, Bondurant, IA 50035

Central States Gun Collectors Assn. Avery Giles, 1104 S. 1st Ave., Marshtown, IA 50158

KANSAS

Kansas Cartridge Collectors Assn. Bob Linder, Box 84, Plainville, KS 67663

KENTUCKY

Kentuckiana Arms Collectors Assn. Charles Billips, President, Box 1776, Louisville, KY 40201

Kentucky Gun Collectors Assn., Inc. Ruth Johnson, Box 64, Owensboro, KY 42302/502-729-4197

LOUISIANA

Washitaw River Renegades Sandra Rushing, P.O. Box 256, Main St., Grayson, LA 71435

MARYLAND

Baltimore Antique Arms Assn. Mr. Cillo, 1034 Main St., Darlington, MD 21304

MASSACHUSETTS

Bay Colony Weapons Collectors, Inc. John Brandt, Box 111, Hingham, MA 02043

Massachusetts Arms Collectors Bruce E. Skinner, P.O. Box 31, No. Carver, MA 02355/508-866-5259

MICHIGAN

Association for the Study and Research of .22 Caliber Rimfire Cartridges George Kass, 4512 Nakoma Dr., Okemos, MI 48864

MINNESOTA

Sioux Empire Cartridge Collectors Assn. Bob Cameron, 14597 Glendale Ave. SE, Prior Lake, MN 55372

MISSISSIPPI

Mississippi Gun Collectors Assn. Jack E. Swinney, P.O. Box 16323, Hattiesburg, MS 39402

MISSOURI

Greater St. Louis Cartridge Collectors Assn. Don MacChesney, 145 East Maple, Kirkwood, MO 63122

Mineral Belt Gun Collectors Assn. D.F. Saunders, 1110 Cleveland Ave., Monett, MO 65708

Missouri Valley Arms Collectors Assn., Inc. L.P Brammer II, Membership Secy., P.O. Box 33033, Kansas City, MO 64114

MONTANA

Montana Arms Collectors Assn. Lewis E. Yearout, 308 Riverview Dr. East, Great Falls, MT 59404

NEBRASKA

Nebraska Cartridge Collectors Club Gary Muckel, 6531 Carlsbad Dr., Lincoln, NE 68510

ARMS ASSOCIATIONS

NEW HAMPSHIRE
New Hampshire Arms Collectors, Inc. Frank H. Galeucia, Rt. 28, Box 44, Windham, NH 03087

NEW JERSEY
Jersey Shore Antique Arms Collectors Joe Sisia, P.O. Box 100, Bayville, NJ 08721-1950
New Jersey Arms Collectors Club, Inc. Angus Laidlaw, President, 230 Valley Rd., Montclair, NJ 07042/201-746-0939

NEW YORK
Iroquois Arms Collectors Assn. Bonnie Robinson, Show Secy., P.O. Box 142, Ransomville, NY 14131/716-791-4096
Mid-State Arms Coll. & Shooters Club Jack Ackerman, 24 S. Mountain Terr., Binghamton, NY 13903

NORTH CAROLINA
North Carolina Gun Collectors Assn. Jerry Ledford, 3231-7th St. Dr. NE, Hickory, NC 28601

OHIO
Ohio Gun Collectors Assn. P.O. Box 9007, Maumee, OH 43537-9007/419-897-0861; Fax:419-897-0860
The Stark Gun Collectors, Inc. William I. Gann, 5666 Waynesburg Dr., Waynesburg, OH 44688

OKLAHOMA
Indian Territory Gun Collector's Assn. P.O. Box 4491, Tulsa, OK 74159/918-745-9141

OREGON
Oregon Arms Collectors Assn., Inc. Phil Bailey, P.O. Box 13000-A, Portland, OR 97213
Oregon Cartridge Collectors Assn. Gale Stockton, 52 N.W. 2nd, Gresham, OR 97030

PENNSYLVANIA
Presque Isle Gun Collectors Assn. James Welch, 156 E. 37 St., Erie, PA 16504

SOUTH CAROLINA
Belton Gun Club, Inc. J.K. Phillips, 195 Phillips Dr., Belton, SC 29627
Gun Owners of South Carolina Membership Div.: William Strozier, Secretary, P.O. Box 70, Johns Island, SC 29457-0070/803-762-3240; Fax:803-795-0711

SOUTH DAKOTA
Dakota Territory Gun Coll. Assn., Inc. Curt Carter, Castlewood, SD 57223

TENNESSEE
Smoky Mountain Gun Coll. Assn., Inc. Hugh W. Yabro, President, P.O. Box 23225, Knoxville, TN 37933
Tennessee Gun Collectors Assn., Inc. M.H. Parks, 3556 Pleasant Valley Rd., Nashville, TN 37204-3419

TEXAS
Houston Gun Collectors Assn., Inc. P.O. Box 741429, Houston, TX 77274-1429
Texas Cartridge Collectors Assn., Inc. Robert Mellichamp, Memb. Contact, 907 Shirkmere, Houston, TX 77008/713-869-0558
Texas Gun Collectors Assn. Bob Eder, Pres., P.O. Box 12067/915-584-8183

WASHINGTON
Association of Cartridge Collectors on the Pacific Northwest Robert Jardin, 14214 Meadowlark Drive KPN, Gig Harbor, WA 98329
Washington Arms Collectors, Inc. J. Dennis Cook, P.O. Box 7335, Tacoma, WA 98407/206-752-2268

WISCONSIN
Great Lakes Arms Collectors Assn., Inc. Edward C. Warnke, 2913 Woodridge Lane, Waukesha, WI 53188
Wisconsin Gun Collectors Assn., Inc. Lulita Zellmer, P.O. Box 181, Sussex, WI 53089

WYOMING
Wyoming Weapons Collectors P.O. Box 284, Laramie, WY 82070/307-745-4652 or 745-9530

NATIONAL ORGANIZATIONS
American Airgun Field Target Assn. 5911 Cherokee Ave., Tampa, FL 33604
American Custom Gunmakers Guild Jan Billeb, Exec. Director, P.O. Box 812, Burlington, IA 52601-0812/319-752-6114 (Phone or Fax)
American Defense Preparedness Assn. Two Colonial Place, 2101 Wilson Blvd., Suite 400, Arlington, VA 22201-3061
American Paintball League P.O. Box 3561, Johnson City, TN 37602/800-541-9169
American Pistolsmiths Guild Alex B. Hamilton, Pres., 1449 Blue Crest Lane, San Antonio, TX 78232/210-494-3063
American Police Pistol & Rifle Assn. 3801 Biscayne Blvd., Miami, FL 33137

American Society of Arms Collectors George E. Weatherly, P.O. Box 2567, Waxahachie, TX 75165
American Tactical Shooting Assn. (A.T.S.A.) c/o Charles A. Davis. P.O. Box 12265, Silver Spring, MD 20908/301-924-1373; Fax:301-924-3854
Association of Firearm and Toolmark Examiners Eugenia A. Bell, Secy., 7857 Esterel Dr., LaJolla, CA 92037; Membership Secy., Andrew B. Hart, 80 Mountain View Ave., Rensselaer, NY 12144
Boone & Crockett Club 250 Station Dr., Missoula, MT 59801-2753
Browning Collectors Assn. Bobbie Hamit, P.O. Box 526, Aurora, NE 68818/402-694-6602
The Cast Bullet Assn., Inc. Ralland J. Fortier, Membership Director, 4103 Foxcraft Dr., Traverse City, MI 49684
Citizens Committee for the Right to Keep and Bear Arms Natl. Hq., Liberty Park, 12500 NE Tenth Pl., Bellevue, WA 98005
Colt Collectors Assn. 25000 Highland Way, Los Gatos, CA 95030
Firearms Coalition Box 6537, Silver Spring, MD 20906/301-871-3006
Firearms Engravers Guild of America Robert Evans, Secy., 332 Vine St., Oregon City, OR 97045
Golden Eagle Collectors Assn. Chris Showler, 11144 Slate Creek Rd., Grass Valley, CA 95945
Gun Owners of America 8001 Forbes Place, Suite 102, Springfield, VA 22151/703-321-8585
Handgun Hunters International J.D. Jones, Director, P.O. Box 357 MAG, Bloomingdale, OH 43910
Harrington & Richardson Gun Coll. Assn. George L. Cardet, 330 S.W. 27th Ave., Suite 603, Miami, FL 33135
Hopkins & Allen Arms & Memorabilia Society (HAAMS) 1309 Pamela Circle, Delphos, OH 45833
International Ammunition Association, Inc. 8 Hillock Lane, Chadds Ford, PA 19317/610-358-1258; Fax:610-358-1560
International Blackpowder Hunting Assn. P.O. Box 1180, Glenrock, WY 82637/307-436-9817
IHMSA (Intl. Handgun Metallic Silhouette Assn.) Frank Scotto, P.O. Box 5038, Meriden, CT 06450
International Handloader Assn. 6471 Airpark Dr., Prescott, AZ 86301
International Paintball Field Operators Assn. 15507 S. Normandie Ave. #487, Gardena, CA 90247/310-323-1021
IPPA (International Paintball Players Assn.) P.O. Box 26669, San Diego, CA 92196-0669/619-695-8882; Fax:619-695-6909
Jews for the Preservation of Firearms Ownership (JPFO) 501(c)(3) 2872 S. Wentworth Ave., Milwaukee, WI 53207/414-769-0760; Fax:414-483-8435
Miniature Arms Collectors/Makers Society, Ltd. Ralph Koebbeman, Pres., 4910 Kilburn Ave., Rockford, IL 61101/815-964-2569
National Association of Buckskinners (NAB) Tim Pray, P.O. Box 29307, Thornton, CO 80602
The National Association of Derringer Collectors P.O. Box 20572, San Jose, CA 95160
National Assn. of Federally Licensed Firearms Dealers Andrew Molchan, 2455 E. Sunrise, Ft. Lauderdale, FL 33304
National Association to Keep and Bear Arms P.O. Box 78336, Seattle, WA 98178
National Automatic Pistol Collectors Assn. Tom Knox, P.O. Box 15738, Tower Grove Station, St. Louis, MO 63163
National Firearms Assn. P.O. Box 160038, Austin, TX 78716/403-439-1094; FAX: 403-439-4091
National Professional Paintball League (NPPL) 540 Main St., Mount Kisco, NY 10549/914-241-7400
National Reloading Manufacturers Assn. One Centerpointe Dr., Suite 300, Lake Oswego, OR 97035
National Rifle Assn. of America 11250 Waples Mill Rd., Fairfax, VA 22030
National Shooting Sports Foundation, Inc. Robert T. Delfay, President, Flintlock Ridge Office Center, 11 Mile Hill Rd., Newtown, CT 06470-2359/203-426-1320; FAX: 203-426-1087
North American Hunting Club P.O. Box 3401, Minnetonka, MN 55343
North American Paintball Referees Association (NAPRA) 584 Cestaric Dr., Milpitas, CA 95035
North-South Skirmish Assn., Inc. Stevan F. Meserve, Exec. Secretary, 507 N. Brighton Court, Sterling, VA 20164-3919
Remington Society of America Leon W. Wier Jr., President, 8268 Lone Feather Ln., Las Vegas, NV 89123
Ruger Collector's Assn., Inc. P.O. Box 240, Greens Farms, CT 06436
Safari Club International Philip DeLone, Executive Dir., 4800 W. Gates Pass Rd., Tucson, AZ 85745/602-620-1220
Second Amendment Foundation James Madison Building, 12500 NE 10th Pl., Bellevue, WA 98005
Smith & Wesson Collectors Assn. George Linne, 2711 Miami St., St. Louis, MO 63118
Sporting Arms & Ammunition Manufacturers Institute (SAAMI) Flintlock Ridge Office Center, 11 Mile Hill Rd., Newtown, CT 06470-2359/203-426-1320; FAX: 203-426-1087
The Thompson/Center Assn. Joe Wright, President, Box 792, Northboro, MA 01532/508-845-6960
U.S. Practical Shooting Assn./IPSC Marilyn Stanford, P.O. Box 811, Sedro Woolley, WA 98284/360-855-2245
U.S. Revolver Assn. Brian J. Barer, 40 Larchmont Ave., Taunton, MA 02780/508-824-4836
U.S. Shooting Team U.S. Olympic Shooting Center, One Olympic Plaza, Colorado Springs, CO 80909/719-578-4670
The Wildcatters P.O. Box 170, Greenville, WI 54942
Winchester Arms Collectors Assn. Richard Berg, Executive Secy., P.O. Box 6754, Great Falls, MT 59406

The Women's Shooting Sports Foundation (WSSF) 1505 Highway 6 South, Suite 101, Houston, TX 77077

ARGENTINA
Association Argentina de Colleccionistas de Armes y Municiones Castilla de Correas No. 28, Succursal I B, 1401 Buenos Aires, Republica Argentina

AUSTRALIA
The Arms Collector's Guild of Queensland Inc. Ian Skennerton, P.O. Box 433, Ashmore City 4214, Queensland, Australia
Australian Cartridge Collectors Assn., Inc. Bob Bennett, 126 Landscape Dr., E. Doncaster 3109, Victoria, Ausrtalia
Sporting Shooters Assn. of Australia, Inc. P.O. Box 2066, Kent Town, SA 5071, Australia

CANADA

ALBERTA
Canadian Historical Arms Society P.O. Box 901, Edmonton, Alb., Canada T5J 2L8
National Firearms Assn. Natl. Hq: P.O. Box 1779, Edmonton, Alb., Canada T5J 2P1

BRITISH COLUMBIA
The Historical Arms Collectors of B.C. (Canada) Harry Moon, Pres., P.O. Box 50117, South Slope RPO, Burnaby, BC V5J 5G3, Canada/604-936-9141

ONTARIO
Association of Canadian Cartridge Collectors Monica Wright, RR 1, Millgrove, ON, LOR IVO, Canada
Tri-County Antique Arms Fair P.O. Box 122, RR #1, North Lancaster Ont., Canada K0C 1Z0

EUROPE

BELGIUM
European Catridge Researchers Assn. Graham Irving, 21 Rue Schaltin, 49 Spa, Belgium

CZECHOSLOVAKIA
Spolecnost Pro Studium Naboju JUDr. Jaroslav Bubak, Sovetske Armady 1439, 26601 Beroun 2, Czechoslovakia

DENMARK
Aquila Patronsamler Club (Danish Cartridge Collectors Club) Sten Elgaard Moler, Ulriksdalsvej 7, 4840 Nr. Alslev, Denmark

ENGLAND
Arms and Armour Society E.J.B. Greenwood, Field House, Upper Dicker, Hailsham, East Sussex, BN27 3PY, England
Dutch Paintball Federation Aceville Publ., Castle House 97 High Street, Colchester, Essex C01 1TH, England/011-44-206-564840
European Paintball Sports Foundation c/o Aceville Publ., Castle House 97 High St., Colchester, Essex, C01 1TH, England
Historical Breechloading Smallarms Assn. D.J. Penn M.A., Imperial War Museum, Lambeth Rd., London SE 1 6HZ, England. Journal and newsletter are $13 a yr., plus surcharge for airmail.
United Kingdom Cartridge Club Ian Southgate, 20 Millfield, Elmley Castle, Nr. Pershore, Worcestershire, WR10 3HR, England

FRANCE
Syndicat National de l'Arquebuserie du Commerce de l'Arme Historique B.P. No. 3, 78110 Le Vesinet, France

GERMANY
Bund Deutscher Sportschützen e.v. (BDS) Borsigallee 10, 53125 Bonn 1, Germany
Deutscher Schützenbund Lahnstrasse 120, 65195 Wiesbaden, Germany

SPAIN
Asociacion Espanola de Colleccionistas de Cartuchos Francisco Carreras Morate, Rio Tajuna 5 II B, Alcala de Henares, Madrid, Spain

SWEDEN
Scandinavian Ammunition Research Assn. Box 107, 77622 Hedemora, Sweden

NEW ZEALAND
New Zealand Cartridge Collectors Club Terry Castle, 70 Tiraumea Dr., Pakuranga, Auckland, New Zealand
New Zealand Deerstalkers Assn. Michael Watt, P.O. Box 6514, Wellington, New Zealand

SOUTH AFRICA
Historical Firearms Soc. of South Africa P.O. Box 145, 7725 Newlands, Republic of South Africa
Republic of South Africa Cartridge Collectors Assn. Arno Klee, 20 Eugene St., Malanshof Randburg 2194, Republic of South Africa
SAGA (S.A. Gunowners' Assn.) P.O. Box 35203, Northway 4065, Republic of South Africa

HANDGUNNER'S LIBRARY

*New Book

ABC's of Reloading, 5th Edition, by Dean A. Grennell, DBI Books, Inc., Northbrook, IL, 1993. 288 pp., illus. Paper covers. $19.95.
The definitive guide to every facet of cartridge and shotshell reloading.

***Advanced Master Handgunning,** by Charles Stephens, Paladin Press, Boulder, CO., 1994. 72 pp., illus. Paper covers. $10.00.
Secrets and surefire techniques for winning handgun competitions.

Advanced Muzzleloader's Guide, by Toby Bridges, Stoeger Publishing Co., So. Hackensack, NJ, 1985. 256 pp., illus. Paper covers. $14.95.
The complete guide to muzzle-loading rifles, pistols and shotguns—flintlock and percussion.

Air Gun Digest, 3rd Edition, by J.I. Galan, DBI Books, Inc., Northbrook, IL, 1995. 258 pp., illus. Paper covers. $18.95
Everything from A to Z on air gun history, trends and technology.

The American Cartridge, by Charles R. Suydam, Borden Publishing Co., Alhambra, CA, 1986. 184 pp., illus. $18.00.
An illustrated study of the rimfire cartridge in the United States.

America's Great Gunmakers, by Wayne van Zwoll, Stoeger Publishing Co., So. Hackensack, NJ, 1992. 288 pp., illus. Paper covers. $16.95.
Traces the evolution of guns and ammunition in America, the men who formed the companies that produced them.

Ammunition Making, by George E. Frost, National Rifle Association of America, Washington, D.C., 1990. 160 pp., illus. Paper covers. $17.95.
Perspective of "an insider" with half a century's experience in ammunition manufacturing operations.

***Antique Guns, the Collector's Guide, 2nd Edition,** edited by John Traister, Stoeger Publishing Co., S. Hackensack, NJ, 1994. 320 pp., illus. Paper covers. $19.95.
Covers a vast spectrum of pre-1900 firearms: those manufactured by U.S. gunmakers as well as Canadian, French, German, Belgian, Spanish and other foreign firms.

Armed and Female, by Paxton Quigley, E.P. Dutton, New York, NY, 1989. 237 pp., illus. $16.95.
The first complete book on the arming of the American woman.

Arms & Accoutrements of the Mounted Police 1873-1973, by Roger F. Phillips and Donald J. Klancher, Museum Restoration Service, Ont., Canada, 1982. 224 pp., illus. $49.95.
A definitive history of the revolvers, rifles, machine guns, cannons, ammunition, swords, etc. used by the NWMP, the RNWMP and the RCMP during the first 100 years of the Force.

The Art of Engraving, by James B. Meek, F. Brownell & Son, Montezuma, IA, 1973. 196 pp., illus. $33.95.
A complete, authoritative, imaginative and detailed study in training for gun engraving.

Artistry in Arms, The R. W. Norton Gallery, Shreveport, LA, 1970. 42 pp., illus. Paper covers. $9.95.
The art of gunsmithing and engraving.

Artistry in Arms: The Guns of Smith & Wesson, by Roy G. Jinks, Smith & Wesson, Springfield, MA, 1991. 85 pp., illus. Paper covers. $19.95.
Catalog of the Smith & Wesson International Museum Tour 1991-1995.

Astra Automatic Pistols, by Leonardo M. Antaris, FIRAC Publishing Co., Sterling, CO, 1989. 248 pp., illus. $45.00.
Charts, tables, serial ranges, etc. The definitive work on Astra pistols.

Barrels & Actions, by Harold Hoffman, H&P Publishers, San Angelo, TX, 1990. 309 pp., illus. Sprial bound. $25.95.
A manual on barrel making.

Basic Handloading, by George C. Nonte, Jr., Outdoor Life Books, New York, NY, 1982. 192 pp., illus. Paper covers. $6.95.
How to produce high-quality ammunition using the safest, most efficient methods.

Beretta Automatic Pistols, by J.B. Wood, Stackpole Books, Harrisburg, PA, 1985. 192 pp., illus. $24.95.
Only English-language book devoted to the Beretta line. Includes all important models.

Black Powder Guide, 2nd Edition, by George C. Nonte, Jr., Stoeger Publishing Co., So. Hackensack, NJ, 1991. 288 pp., illus. Paper covers. $14.95.
How-to instructions for selection, repair and maintenance of muzzleloaders, making your own bullets, restoring and refinishing, shooting techniques.

Black Powder Hobby Gunsmithing, by Sam Fadala and Dale Storey, DBI Books, Inc., Northbrook, IL., 1994. 256 pp., illus. Paper covers. $17.95.
A how-to guide for gunsmithing blackpowder pistols, rifles and shotguns.

***Blackpowder Loading Manual, 3rd Edition,** edited by Sam Fadala, DBI Books, Inc., Northbrook, IL, 1995. 368 pp., illus. Paper covers. $19.95.
Revised and expanded edition of this landmark blackpowder loading book. Covers hundreds of loads for most of the popular blackpowder rifles, handguns and shotguns.

The Blackpowder Notebook, by Sam Fadala, Wolfe Publishing Co., Prescott, AZ, 1994. 212 pp., illus. $22.50.
This book will help improve scores and obtain accuracy and reliability.

Blacksmith Guide to Ruger Flat-top & Super Blackhawks, by H.W. Ross, Jr., Blacksmith Corp., Chino Valley, AZ, 1990. 96 pp., illus. Paper covers. $9.95.
A key source on the extensively collected Ruger Blackhawk revolvers.

Blue Steel and Gun Leather, by John Bianchi, Beinfeld Publishing, Inc., No. Hollywood, CA, 1978. 200 pp., illus. $19.95.
A complete and comprehensive review of holster uses plus available products on today's market.

British Small Arms Ammunition, 1864-1938, by Peter Labett, Armory Publications, Oceanside, CA, 1994. 352 pp., illus. $75.00.
The military side of the story illustrating the rifles, carbines, machine guns, revolvers and automatic pistols and their ammunition, experimental and adopted, from 577 Snider to modern times.

British Small Arms of World War 2, by Ian D. Skennerton, I.D.S.A. Books, Piqua, OH, 1988. 110 pp., 37 illus. $25.00.

Browning Dates of Manufacture, compiled by George Madis, Art and Reference House, Brownsboro, TX, 1989. 48 pp. $5.00.
Gives the date codes and product codes for all models from 1824 to the present.

Browning Hi-Power Pistols, Desert Publications, Cornville, AZ, 1982. 20 pp., illus. Paper covers. $9.95.
Covers all facets of the various military and civilian models of the Browning Hi-Power pistol.

***Browning Sporting Arms of Distinction 1903-1992,** by Matt Eastman, Matt Eastman Publications, Fitzgerald, GA, 1995. 450 pp., illus. $49.95.
The most recognized publication on Browning sporting arms ever written; covers all models.

The Bullet Swage Manual. MDSU/I, by Ted Smith, Corbin Manufacturing and Supply Co., White City, OR, 1988. 45 pp., illus. Paper covers. $10.00.
A book that fills the need for information on bullet swaging.

Burning Powder, compiled by Major D.B. Wesson, Wolfe Publishing Company, Prescott, AZ, 1992. 110 pp. Soft cover. $10.95.
A rare booklet from 1932 for Smith & Wesson collectors.

***Canadian Military Handguns 1855-1985,** by Clive M. Law, Museum Restoration Service, Bloomfield, Ont. Canada, 1994. 130pp., illus. $40.00.
A long-awaited and important history for arms historians and pistol collectors.

Cartridge Case Measurements, by Dr. Arthur J. Mack, Amrex Enterprises, Vienna, VA, 1990. 300 pp., illus. Paper covers. $49.95.
Lists over 5000 cartridges of all kinds. Gives basic measurements (rim, head, shoulder, neck, length, plus bullet diameter) in both English and Metric. Hundreds of experimental and wildcats.

Cartridges of the World, 7th Edition, by Frank Barnes, edited by Mike Bussard, DBI Books, Inc., Northbrook, IL, 1993. 464 pp., illus. Paper covers. $23.95.
Completely revised edition of the general purpose reference work for which collectors, police, scientists and laymen reach first for answers to cartridge identification questions.

Cast Bullets, by Col. E. H. Harrison, A publication of the National Rifle Association of America, Washington, DC, 1979. 144 pp., illus. Paper covers. $12.95.
An authoritative guide to bullet casting techniques and ballistics.

Civil War Pistols, by John D. McAulay, Andrew Mowbray Inc., Lincoln, RI, 1992. 166 pp., illus. $38.50.
A survey of the handguns used during the American Civil War.

Colt Automatic Pistols, by Donald B. Bady, Borden Publ. Co., Alhambra, CA, 1974, 368 pp., illus. $19.95.
Complete information on every automatic marked with Colt's name.

The Colt Double Action Revolvers: A Shop Manual, Volume 1, by Jerry Kuhnhausen, VSP Publishers, McCall, ID, 1988. 224 pp., illus. Paper covers. $24.95.
Covers D, E, and I frames.

The Colt Double Action Revolvers: A Shop Manual, Volume 2, by Jerry Kuhnhausen, VSP Publishers, McCall, ID, 1988. 156 pp., illus. Paper covers. $18.95.
Covers J, V, and AA models.

The Colt .45 Auto Pistol, compiled from U.S. War Dept. Technical Manuals, and reprinted by Desert Publications, Cornville, AZ, 1978. 80 pp., illus. Paper covers. $9.95.
Covers mechanical training, manual of arms, disassembly, repair and replacement of parts.

The Colt .45 Automatic Shop Manual, by Jerry Kuhnhausen, VSP Publishers, McCall, ID, 1987. 200 pp., illus. Paper covers. $22.95.
Covers repairing, accurizing, trigger/sear work, action tuning, springs, bushings, rebarreling, and custom .45 modification.

Colt 45 Service Pistol Models of 1911 and 1911A1, by Charles W. Clawson, Charles W. Clawson, Fort Wayne, IN, 1991. 429 pp., illus. $65.00.
Complete military history, development and production 1900 through 1945 plus foreign pistols, gallery pistols, revolvers, cartridge development, and much more.

Colt Heritage, by R.L. Wilson, Simon & Schuster, 1979. 358 pp., illus. $75.00.
The official history of Colt firearms 1836 to the present.

Colt Peacemaker British Model, by Keith Cochran, Cochran Publishing Co., Rapid City, SD, 1989. 160 pp., illus. $35.00.
Covers those revolvers Colt squeezed in while completing a large order of revolvers for the U.S. Cavalry in early 1874, to cased target revolvers used in the pistol competitions at Bisley Commons in the 1890s.

Colt Peacemaker Encyclopedia, by Keith Cochran, Keith Cochran, Rapid City, SD, 1986. 434 pp., illus. $65.00.
A must book for the Peacemaker collector.

Colt Peacemaker Encyclopedia, Volume 2, by Keith Cochran, Cochran Publishing Co., SD, 1992. 416 pp., illus. $60.00.
Included in this volume are extensive notes on engraved, inscribed, historical and noted revolvers, as well as those revolvers used by outlaws, lawmen, movie and television stars.

***Colt Percussion Accoutrements 1834-1873,** by Robin Rapley, Robin Rapley, Newport Beach, CA, 1994. 432 pp., illus. Paper covers. $39.95.
The complete collector's guide to the identification of Colt percussion accoutrements; including Colt conversions and their values.

Colt Revolvers and the Tower of London, by Joseph G. Rosa, Royal Armouries of the Tower of London, London, England, 1988. 72 pp., illus. Soft covers. $15.00.
Details the story of Colt in London through the early cartridge period.

Colt Revolvers and the U.S. Navy 1865-1889, by C. Kenneth Moore, Dorrance and Co., Bryn Mawr, PA, 1987. 140 pp., illus. $29.95.
The Navy's use of all Colt handguns and other revolvers during this era of change.

Colt Single Action Army Revolvers and the London Agency, by C. Kenneth Moore, Andrew Mowbray Publishers, Lincoln, RI, 1990. 144 pp., illus. $35.00.
This work chronicles the relationship between the London Agency and the Hartford home office.

The Colt U.S. General Officers' Pistols, by Horace Greeley IV, Andrew Mowbray Inc., Lincoln, RI, 1990. 199 pp., illus. $38.00.
These unique weapons, issued as a badge of rank to General Officers in the U.S. Army from WWII onward, remain personal artifacts of military leaders who carried them. Includes serial numbers and dates of issue.

Colt's Dates of Manufacture 1837-1978, by R.L. Wilson, published by Maurie Albert, Coburg, Australia; N.A. distributor I.D.S.A. Books, Hamilton, OH, 1983. 61 pp. $10.00.
An invaluable pocket guide to the dates of manufacture of Colt firearms up to 1978.

Colt's 100th Anniversary Firearms Manual 1836-1936: A Century of Achievement, Wolfe Publishing Co., Prescott, AZ, 1992. 100 pp., illus. Paper covers. $12.95.
Originally published by the Colt Patent Firearms Co., this booklet covers the history, manufacturing procedures and the guns of the first 100 years of the genius of Samuel Colt.

The Colt Whitneyville-Walker Pistol, by Lt. Col. Robert D. Whittington, Brownlee Books, Hooks, TX, 1984. 96 pp., illus. Limited edition. $20.00.
A study of the pistol and associated characters 1846-1851.

Combat Handgunnery, 3rd Edition, The Gun Digest Book of, by Chuck Karwan, DBI Books, Inc., Northbrook, IL, 1992. 256 pp., illus. Paper covers. $16.95.
Looks at real world combat handgunnery from three different perspectives—military, police and civilian.

Combat Pistols, by Terry Gander, Sterling Publishing Co., Inc., 1991. Paper covers. $9.95.
Pistols are shown close-up, with detailed specifications, muzzle velocity, rate of fire, ammunition, etc.

***Combat Raceguns,** by J.M. Ramos, Paladin Press, Boulder, CO, 1994. 168 pp., illus. Paper covers. $25.00.
Build precision combat raceguns with the best compensators, frames, controls, sights and accessories.

Competitive Shooting, by A.A. Yuryev, introduction by Gary L. Anderson, NRA Books, The National Rifle Assoc. of America, Wash., DC, 1985. 399 pp., illus. $29.95.
A unique encyclopedia of competitive rifle and pistol shooting.

The Complete Black Powder Handbook, Revised Edition, by Sam Fadala, DBI Books, Inc., Northbrook, IL, 1990. 320 pp., illus. Soft covers. $18.95.
Expanded and refreshed edition of the definitive book on the subject of blackpowder.

The Complete Book of Combat Handgunning, by Chuck Taylor, Desert Publications, Cornville, AZ, 1982. 168 pp., illus. Paper covers. $16.95.
Covers virtually every aspect of combat handgunning.

Complete Book of Shooting: Rifles, Shotguns, Handguns, by Jack O'Connor, Stackpole Books, Harrisburg, PA, 1983. 392 pp., illus. $24.95.
A thorough guide to each area of the sport, appealing to those with a new or ongoing interest in shooting.

***Complete Guide to Guns & Shooting,** by John Malloy, DBI Books, Inc., Northbrook, IL, 1995. 256 pp., illus. Paper covers. $18.95.
What every shooter and gun owner should know about firearms, ammunition, shooting techniques, safety, collecting and much more.

***The Complete Guide to U.S. Infantry Weapons of World War Two,** by Bruce Canfield, Andrew Mowbray, Publisher, Lincoln, RI, 1995. 303 pp., illus. $35.00.
A definitive work on the weapons used by the United States Armed Forces in WWII.

The Complete Handloader for Rifles, Handguns and Shotguns, by John Wootters, Stackpole Books, Harrisburg, PA, 1988. 214 pp., $29.95.
Loading-bench know-how.

The Complete Metal Finishing Book, by Harold Hoffman, H&P Publishers, San Angelo, TX, 1992. 364 pp., illus. Paper covers. $28.95.
Instructions for the different metal finishing operations that the normal craftsman or shop will use.

Compliments of Col. Ruger: A Study of Factory Engraved Single Action Revolvers, by John C. Dougan, Taylor Publishing Co., El Paso, TX, 1992. 238 pp., illus. $46.50.
Clearly detailed black and white photographs and a precise text present an accurate history of the Sturm, Ruger & Co. single-action revolver engraving project.

Confederate Revolvers, by William A. Gary, Taylor Publishing Co., Dallas, TX, 1987. 174 pp., illus. $49.95.
Comprehensive work on the rarest of Confederate weapons.

***Cowboy Action Shooting,** by Charly Gullett, Wolfe Publishing Co., Prescott, AZ, 1995. 400 pp., illus. Paper covers. $24.50.
The fastest growing of the shooting sports is comprehensively covered in this text—the guns, loads, tactics and the fun and flavor of this Old West era competition.

Cowboy Collectibles and Western Memorabilia, by Bob Bell and Edward Vebell, Schiffer Publishing, Atglen, PA, 1992. 160 pp., illus. Paper covers. $29.95.
The exciting era of the cowboy and the wild west collectibles including rifles, pistols, gun rigs, etc.

***The Custom Government Model Pistol,** by Layne Simpson, Wolfe Publishing Co., Prescott, AZ, 1994. 639 pp., illus. Paper covers. $24.50.
The book about one of the world's greatest firearms and the things pistolsmiths do to make it even greater.

The CZ-75 Family: The Ultimate Combat Handgun, by J.M. Ramos, Paladin Press, Boulder, CO, 1990. 100 pp., illus. Soft covers. $16.00.
Early- and late-model CZ-75s, as well as the many newest additions to the Czech pistol family.

The Deringer in America, Volume 1, The Percussion Period, by R.L. Wilson and L.D. Eberhart, Andrew Mowbray Inc., Lincoln, RI, 1985. 271 pp., illus. $48.00.
A long awaited book on the American percussion deringer.

The Deringer in America, Volume 2, The Cartridge Period, by L.D. Eberhart and R.L. Wilson, Andrew Mowbray Inc., Publishers, Lincoln, RI, 1993. 284 pp., illus. $65.00.
Comprehensive coverage of cartridge deringers organized alphabetically by maker. Includes all types of deringers known by the authors to have been offered to the American market.

Encyclopedia of Modern Firearms, Vol. 1, compiled and publ. by Bob Brownell, Montezuma, IA, 1959. 1057 pp. plus index, illus. $60.00. Dist. By Bob Brownell, Montezuma, IA 50171.
Massive accumulation of basic information of nearly all modern arms pertaining to "parts and assembly." Replete with arms photographs, exploded drawings, manufacturers' lists of parts, etc.

Encyclopedia of Ruger Rimfire Semi-Automatic Pistols: 1949-1992, by Chad Hiddleson, Krause Publications, Iola, WI, 1993. 250 pp., illus. $29.95.
Covers all physical aspects of Ruger 22-caliber pistols including important features such as boxes, grips, muzzle-brakes, instruction manuals, serial numbers, etc.

***Encyclopedia of Ruger Semi-Automatic Rimfire Pistols 1949-1992,** by Chad Hiddleson, Krause Publications, Iola, WI, 1994. 304 pp., illus. $29.95.
This book is a compilation of years of research, outstanding photographs and technical data on Ruger.

English Pistols: The Armories of H.M. Tower of London Collection, by Howard L. Blackmore, Arms and Armour Press, London, England, 1985. 64 pp., illus. Soft covers. $14.95.
All the pistols described and pictured are from this famed collection.

Experiments of a Handgunner, by Walter Roper, Wolfe Publishing Co., Prescott, AZ, 1989. 202 pp., illus. $37.00.
A limited edition reprint. A listing of experiments with functioning parts of handguns, with targets, stocks, rests, handloading, etc.

Exploded Handgun Drawings, The Gun Digest Book of, edited by Harold A. Murtz, DBI Books, Inc., Northbrook, IL. 1992. 512 pp., illus. Paper covers. $20.95.
Exploded or isometric drawings for 494 of the most popular handguns.

***The Farnam Method of Defensive Handgunning,** by John S. Farnam, DTI, Inc., Seattle, WA, 1994. 191 pp., illus. Paper covers. $13.95.
A book intended to not only educate the new shooter, but also to serve as a guide and textbook for his and his instructor's training courses.

Fast and Fancy Revolver Shooting, by Ed. McGivern, Anniversary Edition, Winchester Press, Piscataway, NJ, 1984. 484 pp., illus. $18.95.
Packed with handgun lore and solid information by the acknowledged dean of revolver shooters.

'51 Colt Navies, by Nathan L. Swayze, The Gun Room Press, Highland Park, NJ, 1993. 243 pp., illus. $59.95.
The Model 1851 Colt Navy, its variations and markings.

Firearms Assembly/Disassembly, Part I: Automatic Pistols, Revised Edition, The Gun Digest Book of, by J.B. Wood, DBI Books, Inc., Northbrook, IL, 1990. 480 pp., illus. Paper covers. $18.95.
Covers 58 popular autoloading pistols plus nearly 200 variants of those models integrated into the text and completely cross-referenced in the index.

Firearms Assembly/Disassembly Part II: Revolvers, Revised Edition, The Gun Digest Book of, by J.B. Wood, DBI Books, Inc., Northbrook, IL, 1990. 480 pp., illus. Paper covers. $18.95.
Covers 49 popular revolvers plus 130 variants. The most comprehensive and professional presentation available to either hobbyist or gunsmith.

Firearms Assembly/Disassembly Part VI: Law Enforcement Weapons, The Gun Digest Book of, by J.B. Wood, DBI Books, Inc., Northbrook, IL, 1981. 288 pp., illus. Paper covers. $16.95.
Step-by-step instructions on how to completely dismantle and reassemble the most commonly used firearms found in law enforcement arsenals.

Firearms Assembly 4: The NRA Guide to Pistols and Revolvers, NRA Books, Wash., DC, 1980. 253 pp., illus. Paper covers. $13.95.
Text and illustrations explaining the takedown of 124 pistol and revolver models, domestic and foreign.

Firearms Bluing and Browning, By R.H. Angier, Stackpole Books, Harrisburg, PA. 151 pp., illus. $18.95.
A world master gunsmith reveals his secrets of building, repairing and renewing a gun, quite literally, lock, stock and barrel. A useful, concise text on chemical coloring methods for the gunsmith and mechanic.

***Firearms Disassembly—With Exploded Views,** by John A. Karns & John E. Traister, Stoeger Publishing Co., S. Hackensack, NJ, 1995. 320 pp., illus. Paper covers. $19.95.
Provides the dos and don'ts of firearms disassembly.

Firearms Engraving as Decorative Art, by Dr. Fredric A. Harris, Barbara R. Harris, Seattle, WA, 1989. 172 pp., illus. $115.00.
The origin of American firearms engraving motifs in the decorative art of the Middle East.

Firearms Pressure Factors, by Dr. Lloyd Brownell, Wolfe Publishing Co., Prescott, AZ, 1990. 200 pp., illus. $14.00.
Devoted entirely to firearms and pressure. Contains chapters on secondary explosion effect, modern pressure measuring techniques in revolvers and rifles, and Dr. Brownell's series on pressure factors.

***Firing Back,** by Clayton E. Cramer, Krause Publications, Iola, WI, 1995. 208 pp., Paper covers. $9.95.
Proposes answers and arguments to counter the popular anti-gun sentiments.

First Book of Gunsmithing, by John E. Traister, Stackpole Books, Harrisburg, PA, 1981. 192 pp., illus. $18.95.
Beginner's guide to gun care, repair and modification.

Flayderman's Guide to Antique American Firearms...and Their Values, 6th Edition, by Norm Flayderman, DBI Books, Inc., Northbrook, IL, 1994. 624 pp., illus. Paper covers. $29.95.
Updated edition of this bible of the antique gun field.

.45 ACP Super Guns, by J.M. Ramos, Paladin Press, Boulder, CO, 1991. 144 pp., illus. Paper covers. $24.00.
Modified .45 automatic pistols for competition, hunting and personal defense.

The .45, The Gun Digest Book of, by Dean A. Grennell, DBI Books, Inc., Northbrook, IL, 1989. 256 pp., illus. Paper covers. $16.95.
Definitive work on one of America's favorite calibers.

From the Kingdom of Lilliput: The Miniature Firearms of David Kucer, by K. Corey Keeble and **The Making of Miniatures,** by David Kucer, Museum Restoration Service, Ontario, Canada, 1994. 51 pp., illus, $25.00.
An overview of the subject with an outline by the artist on the way he makes a miniature firearm.

German Military Rifles and Machine Pistols, 1871-1945, by Hans Dieter Gotz, Schiffer Publishing Co., West Chester, PA, 1990. 245 pp., illus. $35.00.
Development of the modern German weapons and their ammunition including experimental types.

German Pistols and Holsters 1934-1945, Vol. 2, by Robert Whittington, Brownlee Books, Hooks, TX, 1990. 312 pp., illus. $55.00.
This volume addresses pistols only: military (Heer, Luftwaffe, Kriegsmarine & Waffen-SS), captured, commercial, police, NSDAP and government.

German Pistols and Holsters, 1934-1945, Volume 4, by Lt. Col. Robert D. Whittington, 3rd, U.S.A.R., Brownlee Books, Hooks, TX, 1991. 208 pp. $30.00.
Pistols and holsters issued in 412 selected armed forces, army and Waffen-SS units including information on personnel, other weapons and transportation.

Glock: The New Wave in Combat Handguns, by Peter Alan Kasler, Paladin Press, Boulder, CO, 1993. 304 pp., illus. $25.00.
Kasler debunks the myths that surround what is a most innovative handgun.

***The Golden Age of Remington,** by Robert W.D. Ball, Krause publications, Iola, WI, 1995. 208 pp., illus. $29.95.
For Remington collectors or firearms historians, this book provides a pictorial history of Remington through World War I. Includes value guide.

Good Friends, Good Guns, Good Whiskey: The Selected Works of Skeeter Skelton, by Skeeter Skelton, PJS Publications, Peoria, IL, 1989. 347 pp. $21.95.
A guidebook to the world of Skeeter Skelton.

Great Combat Handguns, by Leroy Thompson and Rene Smeets, Sterling Publishing Co., New York, NY, 1993. 256 pp., illus. $29.95.
Revised and newly designed edition of the successful classic in handgun use and reference.

Great Shooters of the World, by Sam Fadala, Stoeger Publishing Co., So. Hackensack, NJ, 1991. 288 pp., illus. Paper covers. $18.95.
An overview of the men and women who have forged the history of firearms over the past 150 years.

Guerrilla Warfare Weapons, by Terry Gander, Sterling Publishing Co., Inc., 1990. 128 pp., illus. Paper covers. $9.95.
The latest and most sophisticated armaments of the modern underground fighter's armory.

Guide to Ruger Single Action Revolvers Production Dates, 1953-73, by John C. Dougan, Blacksmith Corp., Chino Valley, AZ, 1991. 22 pp., illus. Paper covers. $9.95.
A unique pocket-sized handbook providing production information for the popular Ruger single-action revolvers manufactured during the first 20 years.

Gun Collecting, by Geoffrey Boothroyd, Sportsman's Press, London, 1989. 208 pp., illus. $29.95.
The most comprehensive list of 19th century British gunmakers and gunsmiths ever published.

Gun Collector's Digest, 5th Edition, edited by Joseph J. Schroeder, DBI Books, Inc., Northbrook, IL, 1989. 224 pp., illus. Paper covers. $16.95.
The latest edition of this sought-after series.

***Gun Digest, 1996, 50th Anniversary Edition,** edited by Ken Warner, DBI Books, Inc., Northbrook, IL, 1995. 592 pp., illus. Paper covers. $24.95.
The *1996 Gun Digest* celebrates the 50th edition of the world's best-selling gun book. Features include 15 pages of four-color, showcasing all 50 *Gun Digest* covers plus a reprint of selected articles and catalog offerings from the very first 1944 *Gun Digest. Gun Digest* is the only one to make the *USA Today* list of best-selling sports books.

Gun Digest Treasury, 7th Edition, edited by Harold A. Murtz, DBI Books, Inc., Northbrook, IL, 1994. 320 pp., illus. Paper covers. $16.95.
Some of the most interesting articles to have appeared in *Gun Digest* over its first 45 years.

***Gun Notes,** by Elmer Keith, Safari Press, Huntington Beach, CA, 1995. 280 pp., illus. $24.95.
A collection of Elmer Keith's most interesting columns and feature stories that appeared in *Guns and Ammo* magazine from 1961 to the late 1970s.

Gunshot Injuries: How They Are Inflicted, Their Complications and Treatment, by Col. Louis A. La Garde, 2nd revised edition, Lancer Militaria, Mt. Ida, AR, 1991. 480 pp., illus. $34.95.
A classic work which was the standard textbook on the subject at the time of WWI.

Gunsmith Kinks, by F.R. (Bob) Brownell, F. Brownell & Son, Montezuma, IA, 1st ed., 1969. 496 pp., well illus. $18.95.
A widely useful accumulation of shop kinks, short cuts, techniques and pertinent comments by practicing gunsmiths from all over the world.

Gunsmith Kinks 2, by Bob Brownell, F. Brownell & Son, Publishers, Montezuma, IA, 1983. 496 pp., illus. $18.95.
A collection of gunsmithing knowledge, shop kinks, new and old techniques, shortcuts and know-how.

Gunsmith Kinks 3, edited by Frank Brownell, Brownells Inc., Montezuma, IA, 1993. 504 pp., illus. $19.95.
Tricks, knacks and "kinks" by professional gunsmiths and gun tinkerers.

***Gunsmiths of Illinois,** by Curtis L. Johnson, George Shumway Publishers, York, PA, 1995. 160 pp., illus. $50.00.
Genealogical information is provided for nearly one thousand gunsmiths. Contains hundreds of illustrations of rifles and other guns, of handmade origin, from Illinois.

Gun Talk, edited by Dave Moreton, Winchester Press, Piscataway, NJ, 1973. 256 pp., illus. $9.95.
A treasury of original writing by the top gun writers and editors in America.

Gun Tools, Their History and Identification, by James B. Shaffer, Lee A. Rutledge and R. Stephen Dorsey, Collector's Library, Eugene, OR, 1992. 375 pp., illus. $32.00.
Written history of foreign and domestic gun tools from the flintlock period to WWII.

***Gun Trader's Guide, 18th Edition,** published by Stoeger Publishing Co., S. Hackensack, NJ, 1995. 575 pp., illus. Paper covers. $19.95.
Complete, fully illustrated guide to identification of modern firearms along with current market values.

***Guns Illustrated 1996, 28th Edition,** edited by Harold A. Murtz, DBI Books, Inc., Northbrook, IL, 1996. 352 pp., illus. Paper covers. $22.95.
Truly the journal of Gun Buffs, this all new edition consists of articles of interest to every shooter as well as a complete catalog of all U.S. and imported firearms with latest specs and prices.

Guns of the Wild West, by George Markham, Sterling Publishing Co., New York, NY, 1993. 160 pp., illus. Paper covers. $19.95.
Firearms of the American Frontier, 1849-1917.

The Gunfighter, Man or Myth? by Joseph G. Rosa, Oklahoma Press, Norman, OK, 1969. 229 pp., illus. (including weapons). Paper covers. $14.95.
A well-documented work on gunfights and gunfighters of the West and elsewhere.

Gunproof Your Children/Handgun Primer, by Massad Ayoob, Police Bookshelf, Concord, NH, 1989. Paper covers. $4.95.
Two books in one. The first, keeping children safe from unauthorized guns in their hands; the second, a compact introduction to handgun safety.

Guns & Shooting: A Selected Bibliography, by Ray Riling, Ray Riling Arms Books Co., Phila., PA, 1982. 434 pp., illus. Limited, numbered edition. $75.
A limited edition of this, the only modern listing of books devoted to guns and shooting.

Guns, Loads, and Hunting Tips, by Bob Hagel, Wolfe Publishing Co., Prescott, AZ, 1986. 509 pp., illus. $19.95.
A large hardcover book packed with shooting, hunting and handloading wisdom.

Guns of the First World War, Rifle, Handguns and Ammunition from the Text Book of Small Arms, 1909, edited by John Walter, Presidio Press, Novato, CA, 1991. $30.00.
Details of the Austro-Hung. Mann., French Lebels, German Mausers, U.S. Springfields, etc.

Gunsmithing, by Roy F. Dunlap, Stackpole Books, Harrisburg, PA, 1990. 742 pp., illus. $29.95.
A manual of firearm design, construction, alteration and remodeling. For amateur and professional gunsmiths and users of modern firearms.

Gunsmithing at Home, by John E. Traister, Stoeger Publishing Co., So. Hackensack, NJ, 1985. 256 pp., illus. Paper covers. $14.95.
Over 25 chapters of explicit information on every aspect of gunsmithing.

The Gunsmith's Manual, by J.P. Stelle and Wm. B. Harrison, The Gun Room Press, Highland Park, NJ, 1982. 376 pp., illus. $19.95.
For the gunsmith in all branches of the trade.

***Home Gunsmithing the Colt Single Action Revolvers,** by Loren W. Smith, Ray Riling Arms Books, Co., Phila., PA, 1995. 119 pp., illus. $24.95.
Affords the Colt Single Action owner detailed, pertinent information on the operating and servicing of this famous and historic handgun.

Handbook of Bullet Swaging No. 7, by David R. Corbin, Corbin Manufacturing and Supply Co., White City, OR, 1986. 199 pp., illus. Paper covers. $10.00.
This handbook explains the most precise method of making quality bullets.

Handbook for Shooters and Reloaders, by P.O. Ackley, Salt Lake City, UT, 1970, (Vol. I), 567 pp., illus. (Vol. II), a new printing with specific new material. 495 pp., illus. $17.00 each.

Handbook of Metallic Cartridge Reloading, by Edward Matunas, Winchester Press, Piscataway, NJ, 1981. 272 pp., illus. $19.95.
Up-to-date, comprehensive loading tables prepared by four major powder manufacturers.

***Hand Cannons: The World's Most Powerful Handguns,** by Duncan Long, Paladin Press, Boulder, CO, 1995. 208 pp., illus. Paper covers. $20.00.
Long describes and evaluates each powerful gun according to their features.

The Handgun, by Geoffrey Boothroyd, David and Charles, North Pomfret, VT, 1989. 566 pp., illus. $60.00.
Every chapter deals with an important period in handgun history from the 14th century to the present.

***Handgun Digest, 3rd Edition,** edited by Chris Christian, DBI Books, Inc., Northbrook, IL, 1995. 256 pp., illus. Paper covers. $18.95.
Full coverage of all aspects of handguns and handgunning.

Handgun Reloading, The Gun Digest Book of, by Dean A. Grennell and Wiley M. Clapp, DBI Books, Inc., Northbrook, IL, 1987. 256 pp., illus. Paper covers. $16.95.
Detailed discussions of all aspects of reloading for handguns, from basic to complex. New loading data.

***Handguns '96, 8th Edition,** edited by Ray Ordorica, DBI Books, Inc., Northbrook, IL, 1996. 352 pp., illus. Paper covers. $19.95.
Hal Swiggett, Jeff Cooper, Neal Knox, Wiley Clapp, Bill Jordan, Paxton Quigley and other top handgun experts cover what's new in the world of handguns and handgunning.

***Handloader's Digest 1996, 15th Edition,** edited by Bob Bell, DBI Books, Inc., Northbrook, IL, 1995. 480 pp., illus. Paper covers. $23.95.
Top writers in the field contribute helpful information on techniques and components. Greatly expanded and fully indexed catalog of all currently available tools, accessories and components for metallic, blackpowder cartridge, shotshell reloading and swaging.

Handloader's Guide, by Stanley W. Trzoniec, Stoeger Publishing Co., So. Hackensack, NJ, 1985. 256 pp., illus. Paper covers. $14.95.
The complete step-by-step fully illustrated guide to handloading ammunition.

Handloader's Manual of Cartridge Conversions, by John J. Donnelly, Stoeger Publishing Co., So. Hackensack, NJ, 1986. Unpaginated. $49.95.
From 14 Jones to 70-150 Winchester in English and American cartridges, and from 4.85 U.K. to 15.2x28R Gevelot in metric cartridges. Over 900 cartridges described in detail.

Handloading, by Bill Davis, Jr., NRA Books, Wash., D.C., 1980. 400 pp., illus. Paper covers. $15.95.
A complete update and expansion of the NRA Handloader's Guide.

Hatcher's Notebook, by S. Julian Hatcher, Stackpole Books, Harrisburg, PA, 1992. 488 pp., illus. $29.95.
A reference work for shooters, gunsmiths, ballisticians, historians, hunters and collectors.

"Hell, I Was There!," by Elmer Keith, Petersen Publishing Co., Los Angeles, CA, 1979. 308 pp., illus. $24.95.
Adventures of a Montana cowboy who gained world fame as a big game hunter.

High Standard: A Collector's Guide to the Hamden & Hartford Target Pistols, by Tom Dance, Andrew Mowbray, Inc., Lincoln, RI, 1991. 192 pp., illus. Paper covers. $24.00.
From Citation to Supermatic, all of the production models and specials made from 1951 to 1984.

High Standard Automatic Pistols 1932-1950, by Charles E. Petty, The Gunroom Press, Highland Park, NJ, 1989. 124 pp., illus. $19.95.
A definitive source of information for the collector of High Standard arms.

Historic Pistols: The American Martial Flintlock 1760-1845, by Samuel E. Smith and Edwin W. Bitter, The Gun Room Press, Highland Park, NJ, 1986. 353 pp., illus. $45.00.
Covers over 70 makers and 163 models of American martial arms.

Historical Hartford Hardware, by William W. Dalrymple, Colt Collector Press, Rapid City, SD, 1976. 42 pp., illus. Paper covers. $10.00.
Historically associated Colt revolvers.

The History and Development of Small Arms Ammunition, Volume 1, by George A. Hoyem, Armory Publications, Oceanside, CA, 1991. 230 pp., illus. $60.00.
Military musket, rifle, carbine and primitive machine gun cartridges of the 18th and 19th centuries, together with the firearms that chambered them.

The History and Development of Small Arms Ammunition, Volume 2, by George A. Hoyem, Armory Publications, Oceanside, CA, 1991. 303 pp., illus. $60.00.
Covers the blackpowder military centerfire rifle, carbine, machine gun and volley gun ammunition used in 28 nations and dominions, together with the firearms that chambered them.

The History and Development of Small Arms Ammunition (British Sporting Rifle) Volume 3, by George A. Hoyem, Armory Publications, Oceanside, CA, 1991. 300 pp., illus. $60.00.
British sporting rifle cartridges that run from the 4-bore through the .600 Nitro to the .297/.230 Morris.

The History of Smith and Wesson, by Roy G. Jinks, Willowbrook Enterprises, Springfield, MA, 1988. 290 pp., illus. $27.95.
Revised 10th Anniversary edition of the definite book on S&W firearms.

***Hodgdon Data Manual No. 26,** Hodgdon Powder Co., Shawnee Mission, KS, 1993. 797 pp. $22.95.
Includes Hercules, Winchester and Dupont powders; data on cartridge cases; loads; silhouette; shotshell; pyrodex and blackpowder; conversion factors; weight equivalents, etc.

The Home Guide to Cartridge Conversions, by Maj. George C. Nonte Jr., The Gun Room Press, Highland Park, NJ, 1976. 404 pp., illus. $24.95.
Revised and updated version of Nonte's definitive work on the alteration of cartridge cases for use in guns for which they were not intended.

Hornady Handbook of Cartridge Reloading, 4th Edition, Vol. I and II, Hornady Mfg. Co., Grand Island, NE, 1991. 1200 pp., illus. $28.50.
New edition of this famous reloading handbook. Latest loads, ballistic information, etc.

Hornady Handbook of Cartridge Reloading, Abridged Edition, Hornady Mfg. Co., Grand Island, NE, 1991. $19.95.
Ballistic data for 25 of the most popular cartridges.

Hornady Load Notes, Hornady Mfg. Co., Grand Island, NE, 1991. $4.95.
Complete load data and ballistics for a single caliber. Eight pistol 9mm-45ACP; 16 rifle, 222-45-70.

How to Become a Master Handgunner: The Mechanics of X-Count Shooting, by Charles Stephens, Paladin Press, Boulder, CO, 1993. 64 pp., illus. Paper covers. $10.00.
A simple formula for success to the handgunner who strives to master the technique of shooting accurately.

How to Buy and Sell Used Guns, by John Traister, Stoeger Publishing Co., So. Hackensack, NJ, 1984. 192 pp., illus. Paper covers. $10.95.
A new guide to buying and selling guns.

Hunting for Handgunners, by Larry Kelly and J.D. Jones, DBI Books, Inc., Northbrook, IL, 1990. 256 pp., illus. Paper covers. $16.95.
Covers the entire spectrum of hunting with handguns in an amusing, easy-flowing manner that combines entertainment with solid information.

The Ideal Handbook of Useful Information for Shooters, No. 15, originally published by Ideal Manufacturing Co., reprinted by Wolfe Publishing Co., Prescott, AZ, 1991. 142 pp., illus. Paper covers. $10.95.
A facsimile reprint of one of the early Ideal Handbooks.

Il Grande Libro Delle Incision (Modern Engravings Real Book), by Marco E. Nobili, Editrice Il Volo, Milano, Italy, 1992. 399 pp., illus. $95.00.
The best existing expressions of engravings on guns, knives and other items. Text in English and Italian.

***Illustrated Encyclopedia of Handguns,** by A.B. Zhuk, Stackpole Books, Mechanicsburg, PA, 1994. 256 pp., illus. $49.95.
Identifies more than 2,000 military and commercial pistols and revolvers with details of more than 100 popular handgun cartridges.

***The Illustrated Reference of Cartridge Dimensions,** edited by Dave Scovill, Wolfe Publishing Co., Prescott, AZ, 1994. 343 pp., illus. Paper covers. $19.00
A comprehensive volume with over 300 cartridges. Standard and metric dimensions have been taken from SAAMI drawings and/or fired cartridges.

Illustrations of United States Military Arms 1776-1903 and Their Inspector's Marks, compiled by Turner Kirkland, Pioneer Press, Union City, TN, 1988. 37 pp., illus. Paper covers. $4.95.
Reprinted from the 1949 Bannerman catalog. Valuable information for both the collector.

Instinct Combat Shooting, by Chuck Klein, Chuck Klein, The Goose Creek, IN, 1989. 49 pp., illus. Paper covers. $12.00.
Defensive handgunning for police.

An Introduction to the Civil War Small Arms, by Earl J. Coates and Dean S. Thomas, Thomas Publishing Co., Gettysburg, PA, 1990. 96 pp., illus. Paper covers. $10.00.
The small arms carried by the individual soldier during the Civil War.

Iver Johnson's Arms & Cycle Works Handguns, 1871-1964, by W.E. "Bill" Goforth, Blacksmith Corp., Chino Valley, AZ, 1991. 160 pp., illus. Paper covers. $14.95.
Covers all of the famous Iver Johnson handguns from the early solid-frame pistols and revolvers to optional accessories, special orders and patents.

James Reid and His Catskill Knuckledusters, by Taylor Brown, Andrew Mowbray Publishers, Lincoln, RI, 1990. 288 pp., illus. $24.95.
A detailed history of James Reid, his factory, and the pistols which he manufactured there.

***Jane's Infantry Weapons, 21st Edition, 1995-96,** Jane's Information Group, Alexandria, VA, 1995. 750 pp., illus. $265.00.
Complete coverage on over 1,700 weapons and accessories from nearly 300 manufacturers in 69 countries.

Japanese Handguns, by Frederick E. Leithe, Borden Publishing Co., Alhambra, CA, 1985. 160 pp., illus. $22.95.
An identification guide to all models and variations of Japanese handguns.

Know Your Broomhandle Mausers, by R.J. Berger, Blacksmith Corp., Southport, CT, 1985. 96 pp., illus. Paper covers. $9.95.
An interesting story on the big Mauser pistol and its variations.

Know Your Czechoslovakian Pistols, by R.J. Berger, Blacksmith Corp., Chino Valley, AZ, 1989. 96 pp., illus. Soft covers. $9.95.
A comprehensive reference which presents the fascinating story of Czech pistols.

Know Your 45 Auto Pistols—Models 1911 & A1, by E.J. Hoffschmidt, Blacksmith Corp., Southport, CT, 1974. 58 pp., illus. Paper covers. $9.95.
A concise history of the gun with a wide variety of types and copies.

Know Your Walther P.38 Pistols, by E.J. Hoffschmidt, Blacksmith Corp., Southport, CT, 1974. 77 pp., illus. Paper covers. $9.95.
Covers the Walther models Armee, M.P., H.P., P.38—history and variations.

Know Your Walther PP & PPK Pistols, by E.J. Hoffschmidt, Blacksmith Corp., Southport, CT, 1975. 87 pp., illus. Paper covers. $9.95.
A concise history of the guns with a guide to the variety and types.

The Krieghoff Parabellum, by Randall Gibson, Midland, TX, 1988. 279 pp., illus. $40.00.
A comprehensive text pertaining to the Lugers manufactured by H. Krieghoff Waffenfabrik.

Lugers at Random, by Charles Kenyon, Jr., Handgun Press, Glenview, IL, 1990. 420 pp., illus. $49.95.
A new printing of this classic, comprehensive reference for all Luger collectors.

Lyman Black Powder Handbook, ed. by C. Kenneth Ramage, Lyman Products for Shooters, Middlefield, CT, 1975. 239 pp., illus. Paper covers. $14.95.
Comprehensive load information for the modern blackpowder shooter.

Lyman Cast Bullet Handbook, 3rd Edition, edited by C. Kenneth Ramage, Lyman Publications, Middlefield, CT, 1980. 416 pp., illus. Paper covers. $19.95.
5000 tested cast bullet loads and 19 pages of trajectory and wind drift tables for cast bullets.

Lyman Pistol & Revolver Handbook, edited by C. Kenneth Ramage, Lyman Publications, Middlefield, CT, 1978. 280 pp., illus. Paper covers. $14.95.
An extensive reference of load and trajectory data for the handgun.

Lyman Reloading Handbook No. 47, edited by Edward A. Matunas, Lyman Publications, Middlefield, CT, 1992. 480 pp., illus. Paper covers. $23.00.
"The world's most comprehensive reloading manual." Complete "How to Reload" information. Expanded data section with all the newest rifle and pistol calibers.

Making Loading Dies and Bullet Molds, by Harold Hoffman, H&P Publishing, San Angelo, TX, 1993. 230 pp., illus. Paper covers. $22.95.
A good book for learning tool and die making.

The Manufacture of Gunflints, by Sydney B.J. Skertchly, facsimile reprint with new introduction by Seymour de Lotbiniere, Museum Restoration Service, Ontario, Canada, 1984. 90 pp., illus. $24.50.
Limited edition reprinting of the very scarce London edition of 1879.

Master Tips, by J. Winokur, Potshot Press, Pacific Palisades, CA, 1985. 96 pp., illus. Paper covers. $11.95.
Basics of practical shooting.

Mauser Rifles and Pistols, by Walter H.B. Smith, Wolfe Publishing Co., Prescott, AZ, 1990. 234 pp., illus. $30.00.
A handbook covering Mauser history and the amrs Mauser manufactured.

The Mauser Self-Loading Pistol, by Belford & Dunlap, Borden Publ. Co., Alhambra, CA. Over 200 pp., 300 illus., large format. $24.95.
The long-awaited book on the "Broom Handles," covering their inception in 1894 to the end of production. Complete and in detail: pocket pistols, Chinese and Spanish copies, etc.

Metallic Cartridge Reloading, 2nd Edition, by Edward A. Matunas, DBI Books, Inc., Northbrook, IL., 1988. 320 pp., illus. Paper covers. $18.95.
A true reloading manual with a wealth of invaluable technical data provided by a recognized expert.

Metallic Silhouette Shooting, 2nd Edition, The Gun Digest Book of, by Elgin Gates, DBI Books, Inc., Northbrook, IL, 1988. 256 pp., illus. Paper covers. $18.95.
All about the rapidly growing sport. With a history and rules of the International Handgun Metallic Silhouette Association.

***Military Handguns of France 1858-1958,** by Eugene Medlin and Jean Huon, Excalibur Publications, Latham, NY, 1994. 124 pp., illus. Paper covers. $24.95.
The first book in English providing students of arms with a thorough history of French military handguns.

Military Pistols of Japan, by Fred L. Honeycutt, Jr., Julin Books, Palm Beach Gardens, FL, 1991. 168 pp., illus. $34.00.
Covers every aspect of military pistol production in Japan through WWII.

Military Small Arms of the 20th Century, 6th Edition, by Ian V. Hogg, DBI Books, Inc., Northbrook, IL, 1991. 352 pp., illus. Paper covers. $20.95.
Fully revised and updated edition of the standard reference in its field.

Modern American Pistols and Revolvers, by A.C. Gould, Wolfe Publishing Co., Prescott, AZ, 1988. 222 pp., illus. $37.00.
A limited edition reprint. The development of those arms as well as the manner of shooting them.

***Modern Beretta Firearms,** by Gene Gangarosa, Jr., Stoeger Publishing Co., S. Hackensack, NJ, 1994. 288 pp., illus. Paper covers. $16.95.
Traces all models of modern Beretta pistols, rifles, machine guns and combat shotguns.

***Modern Guns Identification and Values, 10th Edition,** by Steven and Russell Quertermous, Collector Books, Paducah, KY, 1994. 496 pp., illus. Paper covers. $12.95.
Over 2,500 models of rifles, handguns and shotguns from 1900 to the present are described and prices given for NRA excellent and very good.

Modern Gun Values, The Gun Digest Book of, 9th Edition, Edited by Jack Lewis, DBI Books, Inc., Northbrook, IL., illus. Paper covers. $20.95.
Updated and expanded edition of the book that has become the standard for valuing modern firearms.

Modern Handloading, by Maj. Geo. C. Nonte, Winchester Press, Piscataway, NJ, 1972. 416 pp., illus. $15.00.
Covers all aspects of metallic and shotshell ammunition loading, plus more loads than any book in print.

Modern Law Enforcement Weapons & Tactics, 2nd Edition, by Tom Ferguson, DBI Books, Inc., Northbrook, IL, 1991. 256 pp., illus. Paper covers. $18.95.
An in-depth look at the weapons and equipment used by law enforcement agencies of today.

Modern Practical Ballistics, by Art Pejsa, Pejsa Ballistics, Minneapolis, MN, 1990. 150 pp., illus. $24.95.
Covers all aspects of ballistics and new, simplified methods.

***Modern Small Arms,** by Ian Hogg, Book Sales, Edison, NJ, 1995. 160 pp., illus. $17.98.
Encyclopedia coverage of more than 150 of the most sought after small arms produced today.

The Modern Technique of the Pistol, by Gregory Boyce Morrison, Gunsite Press, Paulden, AZ, 1991. 153 pp., illus. $45.00.
The theory of effective defensive use of modern handguns.

The Navy Luger, by Joachim Gortz and John Walter, Handgun Press, Glenview, IL, 1988. 128 pp., illus. $24.95.
The 9mm Pistole 1904 and the Imperial German Navy. A concise illustrated history.

L.D. Nimschke Firearms Engraver, by R.L. Wilson, R&R Books, Livonia, NY, 1992. 108 pp., illus. $100.00.
The personal work record of one of the 19th century America's foremost engravers. Augmented by a comprehensive text, photographs of deluxe-engraved firearms, and detailed indexes.

The NRA Gunsmithing Guide—Updated, by Ken Raynor and Brad Fenton, National Rifle Association, Wash., DC, 1984. 336 pp., illus. Paper covers. $15.95.
Material includes chapters and articles on all facets of the gunsmithing art.

9mm Handguns, 2nd Edition, The Gun Digest Book of, edited by Steve Comus, DBI Books, Inc., Northbrook, IL, 1993. 256 pp., illus. Paper covers. $17.95.
Covers the 9mmP cartridge and the guns that have been made for it.

9mm Parabellum; The History & Developement of the World's 9mm Pistols & Ammunition, by Klaus-Peter Konig and Martin Hugo, Schiffer Publishing Ltd., Atglen, PA, 1993. 304 pp., illus. $39.95.
Detailed history of 9mm weapons from Belguim, Italy, Germany, Israel, France, USA, Czechoslovakia, Hungary, Poland, Brazil, Finland and Spain.

***1996 Shooter's Bible, No. 87,** edited by William S. Jarrett, Stoeger Publishing Co., S. Hackensack, NJ, 1995. 576 pp., illus. Paper covers. $21.95.
Contains specifications, photos and retail prices of handguns, rifles, shotguns and blackpowder arms currently manufactured by major U.S. and foreign gunmakers.

No Second Place Winner, by Wm. H. Jordan, publ. by the author, Shreveport, LA (Box 4072), 1962. 114 pp., illus. $15.95.
Guns and gear of the peace officer, ably discussed by a U.S. Border Patrolman for over 30 years, and a first-class shooter with handgun, rifle, etc.

Nosler Reloading Manual No. 3, edited by Gail Root, Nosler Bullets, Inc., Bend, OR, 1989. 516 pp., illus. $21.95.
All-new book. New format including featured articles and cartridge introductions by well-known shooters, gun writers and editors.

***The 100 Greatest Combat Pistols,** by Timothy J. Mullin, Paladin Press, Boulder, CO, 1994. 409 pp., illus. Paper covers. $40.00.
Hands-on tests and evaluations of handguns from around the world.

HANDGUNNER'S LIBRARY

The P-08 Parabellum Luger Automatic Pistol, edited by J. David McFarland, Desert Publications, Cornville, AZ, 1982. 20 pp., illus. Paper covers. $10.00.
Covers every facet of the Luger, plus a listing of all known Luger models.

P-38 Automatic Pistol, by Gene Gangarosa, Jr., Stoeger Publishing Co., S. Hackensack, NJ, 1993. 272 pp., illus. Paper covers. $16.95
This book traces the origins and development of the P-38, including the momentous political forces of the World War II era that caused its near demise and, later, its rebirth.

Packing Iron, by Richard C. Rattenbury, Zon International Publishing, Millwood, NY, 1993. 216 pp., illus. $45.00.
The best book yet produced on pistol holsters and rifle scabbards. Over 300 variations of holster and scabbards are illustrated in large, clear plates.

Paterson Colt Pistol Variations, by R.L. Wilson and R. Phillips, Jackson Arms Co., Dallas, TX, 1979. 250 pp., illus. $35.00.
A book about the different models and barrel lengths in the Paterson Colt story.

Pin Shooting: A Complete Guide, by Mitchell A. Ota, Wolfe Publishing Co., Prescott, AZ, 1992. 145 pp., illus. Paper covers. $14.95.
Traces the sport from its humble origins to today's thoroughly enjoyable social event, including the mammoth eight-day Second Chance Pin Shoot in Michigan.

Pistol & Revolver Guide, 3rd Ed., by George C. Nonte, Stoeger Publ. Co., So. Hackensack, NJ, 1975. 224 pp., illus. Paper covers. $11.95.
The standard reference work on military and sporting handguns.

Pistol Guide, by George C. Nonte, Jr., Stoeger Publishing Co., So. Hackensack, NJ, 1991. 280 pp., illus. Paper covers. $13.95.
Covers handling and marksmanship, care and maintenance, pistol ammunition, how to buy a used gun, military pistols, air pistols and repairs.

Pistols of the World, 3rd Edition, by Ian Hogg and John Weeks, DBI Books, Inc., Northbrook, IL, 1992. 320 pp., illus. Paper covers. $20.95.
A totally revised edition of one of the leading studies of small arms.

Pistolsmithing, The Gun Digest Book of, by Jack Mitchell, DBI Books, Inc., Northbrook, IL, 1980. 256 pp., illus. Paper covers. $15.95.
An expert's guide to the operation of each of the handgun actions with all the major functions of pistolsmithing explained.

Pistolsmithing, by George C. Nonte, Jr., Stackpole Books, Harrisburg, PA, 1974. 560 pp., illus. $29.95.
A single source reference to handgun maintenance, repair, and modification at home, unequaled in value.

The Pitman Notes on U.S. Martial Small Arms and Ammunition, 1776-1933, Volume 2, Revolvers and Automatic Pistols, by Brig. Gen. John Pitman, Thomas Publications, Gettysburg, PA, 1990. 192 pp., illus. $29.95.
A most important primary source of information on United States military small arms and ammunition.

Police Handgun Manual, by Bill Clede, Stackpole Books, Inc., Harrisburg, PA, 1985. 128 pp., illus. $18.95.
How to get street-smart survival habits.

Powerhouse Pistols—The Colt 1911 and Browning Hi-Power Source Book, by Duncan Long, Paladin Press, Boulder, CO, 1989. 152 pp., illus. Soft covers. $19.95.
Discusses internal mechanisms, outward design, test-firing results, maintenance and accessories.

Practical Gunsmithing, by Edward A. Matunas, Stackpole Books, Harrisburg, PA, 1989. 352 pp., illus. $31.95.
A complete guide to maintaining, repairing, and improving firearms.

Precision Handloading, by John Withers, Stoeger Publishing Co., So. Hackensack, NJ, 1985. 224 pp., illus. Paper covers. $14.95.
An entirely new approach to handloading ammunition.

Propellant Profiles New and Expanded, 3rd Edition, Wolfe Publishing Co., Prescott, AZ, 1991. Paper covers. $16.95.
Reloading manual for rifles and pistols.

E.C. Prudhomme, Master Gun Engraver, A Retrospective Exhibition: 1946-1973, intro. by John T. Amber, The R. W. Norton Art Gallery, Shreveport, LA, 1973. 32 pp., illus. Paper covers. $9.95.
Examples of master gun engravings by Jack Prudhomme.

The Rare and Valuable Antique Arms, by James E. Serven, Pioneer Press, Union City, TN, 1976. 106 pp., illus. Paper covers. $4.95.
A guide to the collector in deciding which direction his collecting should go, investment value, historic interest, mechanical ingenuity, high art or personal preference.

Reloader's Guide, 3rd Edition, by R.A. Steindler, Stoeger Publishing Co., So. Hackensack, NJ, 1984. 224 pp., illus. Paper covers. $11.95.
Complete, fully illustrated step-by-step guide to handloading ammunition.

Report of Board on Tests of Revolvers and Automatic Pistols, From the Annual Report of the Chief of Ordnance, 1907. Reprinted by J.C. Tillinghast, Marlow, NH, 1969. 34 pp., 7 plates, paper covers. $9.95.
A comparison of handguns, including Luger, Savage, Colt, Webley-Fosbery and other makes.

Revolver Guide, by George C. Nonte, Jr., Stoeger Publishing Co., So. Hackensack, NJ, 1991. 288 pp., illus. Paper covers. $10.95.
A detailed and practical encyclopedia of the revolver, the most common handgun to be found.

Revolvers of the British Services 1854-1954, by W.H.J. Chamberlain and A.W.F. Taylerson, Museum Restoration Service, Ottawa, Canada, 1989. 80 pp., illus. $27.50.
Covers the types issued among many of the United Kingdom's naval, land or air services.

Ruger, edited by Joseph Roberts, Jr., the National Rifle Association of America, Washington, D.C., 1991. 109 pp. illus. Paper covers. $14.95.
The story of Bill Ruger's indelible imprint in the history of sporting firearms.

Ruger Automatic Pistols and Single Action Revolvers, by Hugo A. Lueders, edited by Don Findley, Blacksmith Corp., Chino Valley, AZ, 1993. 79 pp., illus. Paper covers. $14.95.
The definitive work on Ruger automatic pistols and single action revolvers.

Ruger Double Action Revolvers, Vol. 1, Shop Manual, by Jerry Kuhnhausen, VSP Publishers, McCall, ID, 1989. 176 pp., illus. Soft covers. $18.95.
Covers the Ruger Six series of revolvers: Security-Six, Service-Six, and Speed-Six. Includes step-by-step function checks, disassembly, inspection, repairs, rebuilding, reassembly, and custom work.

The Ruger "P" Family of Handguns, by Duncan Long, Desert Publications, El Dorado, AZ, 1993. 128 pp., illus. Paper covers. $14.95.
A full-fledged documentary on a remarkable series of Sturm Ruger handguns.

The Ruger .22 Automatic Pistol, Standard/Mark I/Mark II Series, by Duncan Long, Paladin Press, Boulder, CO, 1989. 168 pp., illus. Paper covers. $12.00.
The definitive book about the pistol that has served more than 1 million owners so well.

Sam Colt's Own Record 1847, by John Parsons, Wolfe Publishing Co., Prescott, AZ, 1992. 167 pp., illus. $24.50.
Chronologically presented, the correspondence published here completes the account of the manufacture, in 1847, of the Walker Model Colt revolver.

The Semiautomatic Pistols in Police Service and Self Defense, by Massad Ayoob, Police Bookshelf, Concord, NH, 1990. 25 pp., illus. Soft covers. $9.95.
This is the first quantitative, documented look at actual police experience with 9mm and 45 police service automatics.

The Sharpshooter—How to Stand and Shoot Handgun Metallic Silhouettes, by Charles Stephens, Yucca Tree Press, Las Cruces, NM, 1993. 86 pp., illus. Paper covers. $10.00.
A narration of some of the author's early experiences in silhouette shooting, plus how-to information.

Shoot a Handgun, by Dave Arnold, PVA Books, Canyon County, CA, 1983. 144 pp., illus. Paper covers. $12.95.
A complete manual of simplified handgun instruction.

Shoot to Win, by John Shaw, Blacksmith Corp., Southport, CT, 1985. 160 pp., illus. Paper covers. $15.50.
The lessons taught here are of interest and value to all handgun shooters.

Shooter's Bible, 1940, Stoeger Arms Corp., Stoeger, Inc., So. Hackensack, NJ, 1990. 512 pp., illus. Soft covers. $16.95.
Reprint of the Stoeger Arms Corp. catalog No. 33 of 1940.

Shooting, by J.H. FitzGerald, Wolfe Publishing Co., Prescott, AZ, 1993. 421 pp., illus. $29.00.
A classic book and reference for anyone interested in pistol and revolver shooting.

Shooting, by Edward A. Matunas, Stackpole Books, Harrisburg, PA, 1986. 416 pp., illus. $31.95.
How to become an expert marksman with rifle, shotgun, handgun, muzzle loader and bow.

Sierra Handgun Manual, 3rd Edition, edited by Kenneth Ramage, Sierra Bullets, Santa Fe Springs, CA, 1990. 704 pp., illus. 3-ring binder. $19.95.
New listings for XP-100 and Contender pistols and TCU cartridges...part of a new single shot section. Covers the latest loads for 10mm Auto, 455 Super Mag, and Accurate powders.

***Sig/Sauer Handguns,** by Duncan Long, Desert Publications, El Dorado, AZ, 1995. 150 pp., illus. Paper covers. $16.95.
The history of Sig/Sauer handguns, including Sig, Sig-Hammerli and Sig/Sauer variants.

Simeon North: First Official Pistol Maker of the United States, by S. North and R. North, The Gun Room Press, Highland Park, NJ, 1972. 207 pp., illus. $15.95.
Reprint of the rare first edition.

Sixgun Cartridges and Loads, by Elmer Keith, The Gun Room Press, Highland Park, NJ, 1986. 151 pp., illus. $24.95.
A manual covering the selection, uses and loading of the most suitable and popular revolver cartridges. Originally published in 1936. Reprint.

Sixguns, by Elmer Keith, Wolfe Publishing Company, Prescott, AZ, 1992. 336 pp. Hardcover. $34.95.
The history, selection, repair, care, loading, and use of the one-hand firearm.

Skeeter Skelton on Handguns, by Skeeter Skelton, PJS Publications, Peoria, IL, 1980. 122 pp., illus. Soft covers. $5.00.
A treasury of facts, fiction and fables.

Small Arms: Pistols & Rifles, by Ian V. Hogg, Greenhill Books, London, England, 1994. 160 pp., illus. $19.95.
An in-depth description of small arms, focusing on pistols and rifles, with detailed information about all small arms used by the world's armed forces.

***Smith & Wesson's Automatics,** by Larry Combs, Desert Publications, El Dorado, AZ, 1994. 143 pp., illus. Paper covers. $27.95.
A must for every S&W auto owner or prospective owner.

***Smith & Wesson Handguns,** by Roy McHenry and Walter Roper, Wolfe Publishing Co., Prescott, AZ, 1994. 233 pp., illus. $32.00.
The bible on Smith & Wesson handguns.

The S&W Revolver: A Shop Manual, by Jerry Kuhnhausen, VSP Publishers, McCall, ID, 1987. 152 pp., illus. Paper covers.
Covers accurizing, trigger jobs, action tuning, rebarreling, barrel setback, forcing cone angles, polishing and rebluing.

Southern Derringers of the Mississippi Valley, by Turner Kirkland, Pioneer Press, Tenn., 1971. 80 pp., illus., paper covers. $10.00.
A guide for the collector, and a much-needed study.

Soviet Russian Postwar Military Pistols and Cartridges, by Fred A. Datig, Handgun Press, Glenview, IL, 1988. 152 pp., illus. $29.95.
Definitive sourcebook covers the development and adoption of the Makarov, Stechkin and the new PSM pistols. Also included is coverage on Russian clandestine weapons and pistol cartridges.

Soviet Russian Tokarev "TT" Pistols and Cartridges 1929-1953, by Fred Datig, Graphic Publishers, Santa Ana, CA, 1993. 168 pp., illus. $39.95.
Details of rare arms and their accessories with a complete bibliography and index.

Speer Reloading Manual Number 12, edited by members of the Speer research staff, Omark Industries, Lewiston, ID, 1987. 621 pp., illus. $18.95.

***Standard Catalog of Firearms, 5th Edition,** by Ned Schwing and Herbert Houze, Krause Publications, Iola, WI, 1995. 900 pp., illus. Paper covers. $27.95.
Over 12,000 antique and modern firearm prices and 3,000 photographs.

Stevens Pistols & Pocket Rifles, by K.L. Cope, Museum Restoration Service, Alexandria Bay, NY, 1992. 114 pp., illus. $24.50.
This is the story of the guns, the man who designed them and the company which he founded.

The Street Smart Gun Book, by John Farnam, Police Bookshelf, Concord, NH, 1986. 45 pp., illus. Paper covers. $11.95.
Weapon selection, defensive shooting techniques, and gunfight-winning tactics from one of the world's leading authorities.

Stress Fire, Vol. 1: Stress Fighting for Police, by Massad Ayoob, Police Bookshelf, Concord, NH, 1984. 149 pp., illus. Paper covers. $9.95.
Gunfighting for police, advanced tactics and techniques.

Successful Pistol Shooting, by Frank and Paul Leatherdale, The Crowood Press, Ramsbury, England, 1988. 144 pp., illus. $34.95.
Easy-to-follow instructions to achieve better results and gain enjoyment from leisure and competitive shooting.

Survival Guns, by Mel Tappan, Desert Publications, El Dorado, AZ, 1993. 456 pp., illus. Paper covers. $21.95.
Discusses in a frank and forthright manner which handguns, rifles and shotguns to buy for personal defense and securing food, and the ones to avoid.

Survival Gunsmithing, by J.B. Wood, Desert Publications, Cornville, AZ, 1986. 92 pp., illus. Paper covers. $9.95.
A guide to repair and maintenance of the most popular rifles, shotguns and handguns.

***System Mauser—2nd Edition: An Illustrated History of the 1896 Self-Loading Pistol,** by John W. Breathed, Jr. and Joseph J. Schrieder, Jr., Handgun Press, Glenview, IL, 1995. Illus. $49.95.
Newly revised and enlarged edition of the definitive work on this famous German handgun.

Textbook of Automatic Pistols, by R.K. Wilson, Wolfe Publishing Co., Prescott, AZ, 1990. 349 pp., illus. $54.00.
Reprint of the 1943 classic being a treatise on the history, development and functioning of modern military self-loading pistols.

The .380 Enfield No. 2 Revolver, by Mark Stamps and Ian Skennerton, I.D.S.A. Books, Piqua, OH, 1993. 124 pp., 80 illus. Paper covers. $19.95.

Triggernometry, by Eugene Cunningham, Caxton Printers Ltd., Caldwell, ID, 1970. 441 pp., illus. $17.95.
A classic study of famous outlaws and lawmen of the West—their stature as human beings, their exploits and skills in handling firearms. A reprint.

U.S. Military Small Arms 1816-1865, by Robert M. Reilly, The Gun Room Press, Highland Park, NJ, 1983. 270 pp., illus. $39.95.
Covers every known type of primary and secondary martial firearms used by Federal forces.

U.S. Naval Handguns, 1808-1911, by Fredrick R. Winter, Andrew Mowbray Publishers, Lincoln, RI, 1990. 128 pp., illus. $26.00.
The story of U.S. Naval Handguns spans an entire century—included are sections on each of the important naval handguns within the period.

Variations of the Smooth Bore H&R Handy Gun, by Eric M. Larson, Eric M. Larson, Takoma Park, MD, 1993. 63 pp., illus. Paper covers. $10.00.
A pocket guide to the identification of the variations of the H&R Handy Gun.

Walther Models PP and PPK, 1929-1945, by James L. Rankin, assisted by Gary Green, James L. Rankin, Coral Gables, FL, 1974. 142 pp., illus. $35.00.
Complete coverage on the subject as to finish, proofmarks and Nazi Party inscriptions.

Walther P-38 Pistol, by Maj. George Nonte, Desert Publications, Cornville, AZ, 1982. 100 pp., illus. Paper covers. $11.95.
Complete volume on one of the most famous handguns to come out of WWII. All models covered.

Walther Volume II, Engraved, Presentation and Standard Models, by James L. Rankin, J.L. Rankin, Coral Gables, FL, 1977. 112 pp., illus. $35.00.
The new Walther book on embellished versions and standard models.

Walther, Volume III, 1908-1980, by James L. Rankin, Coral Gables, FL, 1981. 226 pp., illus. $35.00.
Covers all models of Walther handguns from 1908 to date, includes holsters, grips and magazines.

Webley Revolvers, by Gordon Bruce and Christien Reinhart, Stocker-Schmid, Zurich, Switzerland, 1988. 256 pp., illus. $69.50.
A revised edition of Dowell's "Webley Story."

Webley & Scott Automatic Pistols, by Gordon Bruch, Stocker-Schmid Publishing Co., Dietikon, Switzerland, 1992. 256 pp., illus. $69.95.
The fundamental representation of the history and development of all Webley & Scott automatic pistols.

***Weimar and Early Lugers,** by Jan C. Still, Jan C. Still, Douglas, AK, 1994. 312 pp., illus.
Volume 5 of the series *The Pistol of Germany and Here Allies in Two World Wars.*

Why Not Load Your Own?, by Col. T. Whelen, A. S. Barnes, New York, 1957, 4th ed., rev. 237 pp., illus. $20.00.
A basic reference on handloading, describing each step, materials and equipment. Includes loads.

Wildcat Cartridges, Volume I, Wolfe Publishing Company, Prescott, AZ, 1992. 125 pp. Soft cover. $16.95.
From *Handloader* magazine, the more popular and famous wildcats are profiled.

Wildcat Cartridges, Volume II, compiled from *Handloader* and *Rifle* magazine articles written by featured authors, Wolfe Publishing Co., Prescott, AZ, 1992. 971 pp., illus. Paper covers. $34.95.
This volume details rifle and handtgun cartridges from the 14-221 to the 460 Van Horn. A comprehensive work containing loading tables and commentary.

You Can't Miss, by John Shaw and Michael Bane, John Shaw, Memphis, TN, 1983. 152 pp., illus. Paper covers. $12.95.
The secrets of a successful combat shooter; how to better defensive shooting skills.

HANDGUNS 96

DIRECTORY
OF THE
HANDGUNNER'S TRADE

PRODUCT DIRECTORY

AMMUNITION, COMMERCIAL

Ace Custom 45's
American Ammunition
Beeline Custom Bullets
Black Hills Ammunition, Inc.
Blammo Ammo
Blount, Inc.
BulletMakers Workshop, The
California Magnum
CBC
Cherokee Gun Accessories
Cor-Bon Bullet & Ammo Co.
C.W. Cartridge Co.
Daisy Mfg. Co.
Delta Frangible Ammunition, LLC
Denver Bullets, Inc.
Diana
DKT, Inc.
Dynamit Nobel-RWS, Inc.
Eley Ltd.
Elite Ammunition
Federal Cartridge Co.
Fiocchi of America, Inc.
FN Herstal
Gamo
GDL Enterprises
Glaser Safety Slug, Inc.
Goldcoast Reloaders, Inc.
Grand Falls Bullets, Inc.
Hansen & Co.
Hansen Cartridge Co.
Hirtenberger Aktiengesellschaft
Hornady Mfg. Co.
ICI-America
IMI
Jones, J.D.
Kent Cartridge Mfg. Co. Ltd.
KJM Fabritek, Inc.
Lomont Precision Bullets
M&D Munitions Ltd.

Magnum Research, Inc.
MagSafe Ammo Co.
Maionchi-L.M.I.
Markell, Inc.
Men—Metallwerk Elisenhuette, GmbH
Milstor Corp.
Moreton/Fordyce Enterprises
Mullins Ammo
Naval Ordnance Works
NECO
Neutralizer Police Munitions
New England Ammunition Co.
Oklahoma Ammunition Co.
Old Western Scrounger, Inc.
Omark Industries
PMC/Eldorado Cartridge Corp.
Pony Express Reloaders
Precision Delta Corp.
Pro Load Ammunition, Inc.
Rocky Fork Enterprises
Rucker Ammunition Co.
RWS
Shooting Components Marketing
Southern Ammunition Co., Inc.
Speer Products
SSK Industries
Star Reloading Co., Inc.
Talon Mfg. Co., Inc.
Tapco, Inc.
3-D Ammunition & Bullets
USAC
Victory USA
Voere-KGH m.b.H.
Vortek Products
Widener's Reloading & Shooting Supply,
  Inc.
Winchester Div., Olin Corp.
Yukon Arms Classic Ammunition
Zero Ammunition Co., Inc.

AMMUNITION, CUSTOM

Accuracy Unlimited (Littleton, CO)
AFSCO Ammunition
Allred Bullet Co.
American Derringer Corp.
Ballistica Maximus North
Bear Arms
Berger Bullets
Bertram Bullet Co.
Black Hills Ammunition, Inc.
Brynin, Milton
BulletMakers Workshop, The
CBC
CHAA, Ltd.
Champlin Firearms, Inc.
Christman Jr., David
Country Armourer, The
Custom Tackle and Ammo
C.W. Cartridge Co.
Dead Eye's Sport Center
DKT, Inc.
Elite Ammunition
Elko Arms
Ellis Sport Shop, E.W.
Epps "Orillia" Ltd., Ellwood
Estate Cartridge, Inc.
Fitz Pistol Grip Co.
Freedom Arms, Inc.
Gammog, Gregory B. Gally
Gonzalez Guns, Ramon B.
"Gramps" Antique Cartridges
Grand Falls Bullets, Inc.
Granite Custom Bullets
Heidenstrom Bullets
Hirtenberger Aktiengesellschaft
Hoelscher, Virgil
Horizons Unlimited
Hornady Mfg. Co.

Jackalope Gun Shop
Jensen Bullets
Jensen's Custom Ammunition
Jensen's Firearms Academy
Jett & Co., Inc.
Jones, J.D.
Kaswer Custom, Inc.
Keeler, R.H.
Kent Cartridge Mfg. Co. Ltd.
KJM Fabritek, Inc.
Kortz, Dr. L.
KLA Enterprises
Lindsley Arms Cartridge Co.
Lomont Precision Bullets
MagSafe Ammo Co.
Marple & Associates, Dick
McMurdo, Lynn
Men-Metallwerk Elisenhuette, GmbH
Monte Kristo Pistol Grip Co.
Moreton/Fordyce Enterprises
Mullins Ammo
Naval Ordnance Works
NECO
Northern Precision Custom Swaged Bullets
Old Western Scrounger, Inc.
Oklahoma Ammunition Company
Parts & Surplus
Personal Protection Systems
Precision Delta Corp.
Precision Munitions, Inc.
Professional Hunter Supplies
Sanders Custom Gun Service
Sandia Die & Cartridge Co.
Specialty Gunsmithing
Spence, George W.
Spencer's Custom Guns
SSK Industries

Star Custom Bullets
State Arms Gun Co.
Stewart's Gunsmithing
Swift Bullet Co.
Talon Mfg. Co., Inc.
3-D Ammunition & Bullets

3-Ten Corp.
Vulpes Ventures, Inc.
Warren Muzzleloading Co., Inc.
Weaver Arms Corp.
Westley Richards & Co.
Worthy Products, Inc.

AMMUNITION, FOREIGN

AFSCO Ammunition
Ammunition Consulting Services, Inc.
Armscorp USA, Inc.
Bertram Bullet Co.
B-West Imports, Inc.
BulletMakers Workshop, The
CBC
Century International Arms, Inc.
Diana
DKT, Inc.
Dynamit Nobel-RWS, Inc.
Fiocchi of America, Inc.
Forgett Jr., Valmore J.
Gamo
"Gramps" Antique Cartridges
Hirtenberger Aktiengesellschaft
Hornady Mfg. Co.
IMI
IMI Services USA, Inc.
Jackalope Gun Shop
JagerSport, Ltd.

Kassnar
K.B.I., Inc.
Magnum Research, Inc.
MAGTECH Recreational Products, Inc.
Maionchi-L.M.I.
Merkuria Ltd.
Monte Kristo Pistol Grip Co.
New England Arms Co.
Oklahoma Ammunition Co.
Old Western Scrounger, Inc.
Paragon Sales & Services, Inc.
Precision Delta Corp.
R.E.T. Enterprises
Rocky Fork Enterprises
RWS
Southern Ammunition Co., Inc.
Spence, George W.
SwaroSports, Inc.
Talon Mfg. Co., Inc.
T.F.C. S.p.A.
USA Sporting Inc.

AMMUNITION COMPONENTS—BULLETS, POWDER, PRIMERS, CASES

Acadian Ballistic Specialties
Accuracy Unlimited (Littleton, CO)
Accurate Arms Co., Inc.
Action Bullets, Inc.
Alaska Bullet Works
Alpha LaFranck Enterprises
American Products Co.
Ames Metal Products Co.
Arco
Atlantic Rose
Azone
Ballard Built
Banaczkowski Bullets
Barnes Bullets, Inc.
Beartooth Bullets
Beeline Custom Bullets
Bell Reloading, Inc.
Bergman & Williams
Berry's Bullets
Bertram Bullet Co.
Black Belt Bullets
Black Hills Shooters Supply
Black Mountain Bullets
Blackhawk East
Blount, Inc.
Blue Point
Briese Bullet Co., Inc.
Brown Co., E. Arthur
Brownells, Inc.
BRP, Inc.
Buck Stix
Buckeye Custom Bullets
Buckskin Bullet Co.
Buffalo Bullet Co., Inc.
Buffalo Rock Shooters Supply
Bullet, Inc.
Bullet Meister Bullets
Bullet Mills
Bullseye Bullets
Bull-X, Inc.
Butler Enterprises
Buzztail Brass
Canyon Cartridge Corp.
Carnahan Bullets
Carroll Bullets
Cascade Bullet Co., Inc.
CCI

Champion's Choice, Inc.
Cheddite France, S.A.
CheVron Bullets
Circle M Custom Bullets
C.J. Ballistics, Inc.
Clark Custom Guns, Inc.
Classic Brass
Competitor Corp., Inc.
Complete Handloader, The
Corbin, Inc.
Cor-Bon Bullet & Ammo Co.
Crawford Co., Inc., R.M.
Creative Cartridge Co.
Cummings Bullets
Curtis Gun Shop
Custom Bullets by Hoffman
Cutsinger Bench Rest Bullets
D&J Bullet Co. & Custom Gun Shop, Inc.
Diamondback Supply
Dillon Precision
DKT, Inc.
Dohring Bullets
Double A Ltd.
DuPont
Eagle Flight
Federal Cartridge Co.
Finch Custom Bullets
Forkin, Ben
Foy Custom Bullets
Freedom Arms, Inc.
Fusilier Bullets
G&C Bullet Co., Inc.
Gehmann, Walter
GOEX, Inc.
Golden Bear Bullets
Gonic Bullet Works
Gonzalez Guns, Ramon B.
Gotz Bullets
"Gramps" Antique Cartridges
Granite Custom Bullets
Grayback Wildcats
Green Bay Bullets
Grier's Hard Cast Bullets
Gun City
Guns
Hardin Specialty Dist.
Harrison Bullets

Haselbauer Products, Jerry
Heidenstrom Bullets
Hercules, Inc.
HH Engineering
Hirtenberger Aktiengesellschaft
Hobson Precision Mfg. Co.
Hodgdon Powder Co., Inc.
Hornady Mfg. Co.
Huntington Die Specialties
IMI
IMI Services USA, Inc.
IMR Powder Co.
J-4, Inc.
J&D Components
J&L Superior Bullets
Jensen's Firearms Academy
Jester Bullets
Jones, J.D.
Ka Pu Kapili
Kasmarsik Bullets
Kaswer Custom, Inc.
Keith's Bullets
Ken's Kustom Kartridge
Kent Cartridge Mfg. Co. Ltd.
KJM Fabritek, Inc.
KLA Enterprises
Kodiak Custom Bullets
Lapua Ltd.
Lathrop's, Inc.
Legend Products Corp.
Liberty Shooting Supplies
Lightfield Ammunition Corp., The Slug Group
Lindsley Arms Cartridge Co.
Littleton, J.F.
Lomont Precision Bullets
M&D Munitions Ltd.
Magnus Bullets
Maine Custom Bullets
Maionchi-L.M.I.
Marchmon Bullets
Master Class Bullets
McMurdo, Lynn
MEC, Inc.
Men-Metallwerk Elisenhuette, GmbH
Merkuria Ltd.
Michael's Antiques
Miller Enterprises, Inc., R.P.
MI-TE Bullets
MoLoc Bullets
Montana Precision Swaging
Mt. Baldy Bullet Co.
Murmur Corp.
Mushroom Express Bullet Co.
Nagel's Bullets
National Bullet Co.
Naval Ordnance Works
Necromancer Industries, Inc.
Norma
North American Shooting Systems
North Devon Firearms Services
Northern Precision Custom Swaged Bullets
Nosler, Inc.
Oklahoma Ammunition Co.
Old Wagon Bullets
Old Western Scrounger, Inc.
Omark Industries
Ordnance Works, The
Pace Marketing, Inc.

Page Custom Bullets
Paragon Sales & Services, Inc.
Patrick Bullets
Penn Bullets
Petro-Explo, Inc.
Phillippi Custom Bullets, Justin
Pinetree Bullets
Pomeroy, Robert
Powder Valley Services
Precision Components
Precision Components and Guns
Precision Delta Corp.
Precision Munitions, Inc.
Prescott Projectile Co.
Price Bullets, Patrick W.
Professional Hunter Supplies
Rainier Ballistics Corp.
Ranger Products
Red Cedar Precision Mfg.
Redwood Bullet Works
Reloading Specialties, Inc.
Renner Co., R.J.
Radical Concepts
R.M. Precision, Inc.
Robinson H.V. Bullets
Rolston, Inc., Fred W.
Rucker Ammunition Co.
Scharch Mfg., Inc.
Schmidtman Custom Ammunition
Schroeder Bullets
Scot Powder
Shappy Bullets
Shooting Components Marketing
SOS Products Co.
Specialty Gunsmithing
Speer Products
Spencer's Custom Guns
Stanley Bullets
Stark's Bullet Mfg.
Stewart's Gunsmithing
Swift Bullet Co.
Talon Mfg. Co., Inc.
Taracorp Industries
TCCI
TCSR
T.F.C. S.p.A.
Thompson Precision
3-D Ammunition & Bullets
TMI Products
True Flight Bullet Co.
USAC
Vann Custom Bullets
VihtaVuori Oy
VihtaVuori Oy/Kaltron-Pettibone
Vincent's Shop
Walters, John
Western Nevada West Coast Bullets
Widener's Reloading & Shooting Supply
Williams Bullet Co., J.R.
Winchester Div., Olin Corp.
Winkle Bullets
Worthy Products, Inc.
Wosenitz VHP, Inc.
Wyant Bullets
Wyoming Custom Bullets
Zero Ammunition Co., Inc.
Zonie Bullets

ANTIQUE ARMS DEALERS

Ad Hominem
Ahlman Guns
Antique American Firearms
Antique Arms Co.
Aplan Antiques & Art, James O.
Bear Mountain Gun & Tool
Boggs, Wm.
Buckskin Machine Works
Bustani Appraisers, Leo
Cannon's Guns
Carlson, Douglas R.
Chadick's Ltd.
Champlin Firearms, Inc.
Chuck's Gun Shop
Classic Guns, Inc.
Cole's Gun Works
Cullity Restoration, Daniel
D&D Gunsmiths, Ltd.
Delhi Gun House
Dixon Muzzleloading Shop, Inc.
Dyson & Son Ltd., Peter
Ed's Gun House
Enguix Import-Export
Epps "Orillia" Ltd., Ellwood
Fagan & Co., William
Fish, Marshall F.

Flayderman & Co., N.
Forgett Jr., Valmore J.
Forty Five Ranch Enterprises
Frielich Police Equipment
Fulmer's Antique Firearms, Chet
Galazan Shotgun Mfg. Co.
Glass, Herb
Goergen's Gun Shop, Inc.
Golden Age Arms Co.
Goodwin, Fred
Gun Room, The
Gun Room Press, The
Gun Works, The
Guncraft Sports, Inc.
Hansen & Co.
Hunkeler, A.
Johns, Bill
Kelley's
Ledbetter Airguns, Riley
LeFever Arms Co., Inc.
Lock's Philadelphia Gun Exchange
Log Cabin Sport Shop
Martin's Gun Shop
Mathews & Son, Inc., George E.
McKinney, R.P.
Mendez, John A.

Montana Outfitters
Museum of Historical Arms, Inc.
Muzzleloaders Etcetera, Inc.
Navy Arms Co.
N.C. Ordnance Co.
New England Arms Co.
New Orleans Arms Co.
Pioneer Guns
Pony Express Sport Shop, Inc.
P.S.M.G. Gun Co.
Retting, Inc., Martin B.
S&S Firearms
Sarco, Inc.

APPRAISERS—GUNS, ETC.

Accuracy Gun Shop
Ad Hominem
Ahlman Guns
Ammunition Consulting Services, Inc.
Amodei, Jim
Antique Arms Co.
Armoury, Inc., The
Arundel Arms & Ammunition, Inc., A.
Behlert Precision
Billings Gunsmiths, Inc.
Blue Book Publications, Inc.
Bustani Appraisers, Leo
Butterfield & Butterfield
Camilli, Lou
Cannon's Guns
Chadick's Ltd.
Champlin Firearms, Inc.
Christie's East
Clark Custom Guns, Inc.
Clark Firearms Engraving
Classic Guns, Inc.
Clements' Custom Leathercraft, Chas
Cole's Gun Works
Colonial Repair
Corry, John
Cullity Restoration, Daniel
Custom Tackle and Ammo
D&D Gunsmiths, Ltd.
DGR Custom Rifles
Dixon Muzzleloading Shop, Inc.
D.O.C. Specialists, Inc.
Duane's Gun Repair
Ed's Gun House
Ellis Sport Shop, E.W.
Enguix Import-Export
Epps "Orillia" Ltd., Ellwood
Fagan & Co., William
Fish, Marshall F.
Flayderman & Co., Inc., N.
Forgett, Valmore J., Jr.
Forty Five Ranch Enterprises
Fredrick Gun Shop
Frontier Arms Co., Inc.
Goergen's Gun Shop, Inc.
Golden Age Arms Co.
Gonzalez Guns, Ramon B.
Goodwin, Fred
Greenwald, Leon E. "Bud"
Griffin & Howe, Inc.
Groenewold, John
Gun Room Press, The
Gun Shop, The
Gun Works, The
Guncraft Sports, Inc.
Guns
Hammans, Charles E.
HandiCrafts Unltd.
Hank's Gun Shop
Hansen & Co.
Hughes, Steven Dodd
Irwin, Campbell H.
Jensen's Custom Ammunition
Jonas Appraisers—Taxidermy Animals, Jack

Scott Fine Guns, Inc., Thad
Semmer, Charles
Silver Ridge Gun Shop
Starnes Gunmaker, Ken
Steves House of Guns
Stott's Creek Armory, Inc.
Strawbridge, Victor W.
Track of the Wolf, Inc.
Vic's Gun Refinishing
Vintage Arms, Inc.
Wiest, M.C.
Wood, Frank
Yearout, Lewis E.

Kelley's
Ledbetter Airguns, Riley
Lee's Red Ramps
LeFever Arms Co., Inc.
Lock's Philadelphia Gun Exchange
Mac's .45 Shop
Madis, George
Marple & Associates, Dick
Martin's Gun Shop
Mathews & Son, Inc., George E.
McCann's Machine & Gun Shop
McGowen Rifle Barrels
Montana Outfitters
Mowrey's Guns & Gunsmithing
Museum of Historical Arms, Inc.
Muzzleloaders Etcetera, Inc.
Navy Arms Co.
N.C. Ordnance Co.
Old Western Scrounger, Inc.
Orvis Co., The
Parke-Bernet
Pasadena Gun Center
Pentheny de Pentheny
Peterson Gun Shop, Inc., A.W.
Pettinger Books, Gerald
Pioneer Guns
Pony Express Sport Shop, Inc.
P.S.M.G. Gun Co.
R.E.T. Enterprises
Retting, Inc., Martin B.
Richards, John
Richards Classic Oil Finish
S&S Firearms
Safari Outfitters Ltd.
Sarco, Inc.
Scott Fine Guns, Inc., Thad
Shell Shack
Silver Ridge Gun Shop
Sipes Gun Shop
S.K. Guns, Inc.
Sotheby's
Starnes Gunmaker, Ken
Steger, James R.
Stott's Creek Armory, Inc.
Stratco, Inc.
Strawbridge, Victor W.
Thurston Sports, Inc.
Ulrich, Doc & Bud
Unick's Gunsmithing
Vic's Gun Refinishing
Walker Arms Co., Inc.
Wayne Firearms for Collectors and Investors, James
Wells Custom Gunsmith, R.A.
Wessinger Custom Guns & Engraving
Whildin & Sons Ltd., E.H.
Whitestone Lumber Corp.
Wiest, M.C.
Williams Shootin' Iron Service
Wood, Frank
Yankee Gunsmith
Yearout, Lewis E.

AUCTIONEERS—GUNS, ETC.

Ammunition Consulting Services, Inc.
Butterfield & Butterfield
Christie's East
Enguix Import-Export
Fagan & Co., William

Kelley's
"Little John's" Antique Arms
Parke-Bernet
Sotheby's

BOOKS (Publishers and Dealers)

American Handgunner Magazine
Armory Publications
Arms & Armour Press
Ballistic Products, Inc.
Barnes Bullets, Inc.
Blackhawk East

Blackhawk West
Blacksmith Corp.
Blacktail Mountain Books
Blue Book Publications, Inc.
Brown Co., E. Arthur
Brownell's, Inc.

PRODUCT DIRECTORY

Calibre Press, Inc.
Colonial Repair
Colorado Sutlers Arsenal
Corbin, Inc.
DBI Books, Inc.
Faith Associates, Inc.
Flores Publications, Inc., J.
Golden Age Arms Co.
"Gramps" Antique Cartridges
Gun City
Gun Hunter Books
Gun Parts Corp., The
Gun Room Press, The
Gun Works, The
Guncraft Sports, Inc.
Gunnerman Books
Guns, (Div. of D.C. Engineering, Inc.)
GUNS Magazine
Gunsite Training Center
H&P Publishing
Handgun Press
Harris Publications
Hodgdon Powder Co., Inc.
Home Shop Machinist, The
Hornady Mfg. Co.
Hungry Horse Books
Ironside International Publishers, Inc.
Krause Publications, Inc.
Lane Publishing
Lapua Ltd.
Lethal Force Institute
Lyman Products Corp.
Madis, David
Magma Engineering Co.
MarMik Inc.

Martin Bookseller, J.
MI-TE Bullets
Mountain South
New Win Publishing, Inc.
Old Western Scrounger, Inc.
Outdoorsman's Bookstore, The
Pejsa Ballistics
Petersen Publishing Co.
Pettinger Books, Gerald
Police Bookshelf
Precision Shooting, Inc.
Reloading Specialties, Inc.
R.G.-G., Inc.
Rutgers Book Center
S&S Firearms
Safari Press, Inc.
Saunders Gun & Machine Shop
Shootin' Accessories, Ltd.
Sinclair International, Inc.
Stackpole Books
Stoeger Publishing Co.
"Su-Press-On," Inc.
Tapco, Inc.
Thomas, Charles C.
Track of the Wolf, Inc.
Trafalgar Square
Trotman, Ken
VSP Publishers
WAMCO—New Mexico
Wiest, M.C.
Wilderness Sound Products Ltd.
Williams Gun Sight Co.
Wolfe Publishing Co.
Wolf's Western Traders

BULLET AND CASE LUBRICANTS

Bear Reloaders
Blackhawk West
Blount, Inc.
Brass-Tech Industries
Break-Free, Inc.
Brown Co., E. Arthur
Camp-Cap Products
C-H Tool & Die Corp.
Chem-Pak, Inc.
Cooper-Woodward
Corbin, Inc.
Dillon Precision Prods., Inc.
Eezox, Inc.
Elkhorn Bullets
E-Z-Way Systems
Forster Products
4-D Custom Die Co.
GAR
Green Bay Bullets
Guardsman Products
HEBB Resources
Hollywood Engineering
Hornady Mfg. Co.
Imperial

Javelina Products
Lee Precision, Inc.
Lithi Bee Bullet Lube
M&N Bullet Lube
Magma Engineering Co.
Micro-Lube
MI-TE Bullets
Monte Kristo Pistol Grip Co.
NECO
Old Western Scrounger, Inc.
Paco's
RCBS
Reardon Products
Redding Reloading Equipment
Rooster Laboratories
Shay's Gunsmithing
Small Custom Mould & Bullet Co.
SPG Lubricants
Tamarack Products, Inc.
Warren Muzzleloading Co., Inc.
Widener's Reloading & Shooting
   Supply, Inc.
Young Country Arms

BULLET SWAGE DIES AND TOOLS

Berger Bullets
Blount, Inc.
Bruno Shooters Supply
Brynin, Milton
Bullet Swaging Supply, Inc.
Camdex, Inc.
C-H Tool & Die Corp.
Corbin, Inc.
4-D Custom Die Co.
Holland's

Hollywood Engineering
King & Co.
LAP Systems Groups, N.A.
Monte Kristo Pistol Grip Co.
Necromancer Industries, Inc.
Niemi Engineering, W.B.
North Devon Firearms Services
Rorschach Precision Products
Speer Products
Sport Flite Manufacturing Co.

CARTRIDGES FOR COLLECTORS

Ad Hominem
Alpha 1 Drop Zone
Ammunition Consulting Services, Inc.
Buck Stix
Cameron's
Campbell, Dick
Cole's Gun Works
Colonial Repair
Delhi Gun House
Duffy, Charles E.
Ed's Gun House
Eichelberger Bullets, Wm.
Enguix Import-Export
Epps "Orillia" Ltd., Ellwood
Forty Five Ranch Enterprises
Goergen's Gun Shop, Inc.
"Gramps" Antique Cartridges

Gun Parts Corp., The
Hank's Gun Shop
Idaho Ammunition Service
Michael's Antiques
Montana Outfitters
Monte Kristo Pistol Grip Co.
Old Western Scrounger, Inc.
Pasadena Gun Center
Rifle Works & Armory
San Francisco Gun Exchange
Samco Global Arms, Inc.
SOS Products Co.
Sportsmen's Exchange & Western Gun
   Traders, Inc.
Ward & Van Valkenburg
Yearout, Lewis E.

CHRONOGRAPHS AND PRESSURE TOOLS

Brown Co., E. Arthur
Canons Delcour
Chronotech
Competition Electronics, Inc.
Custom Chronograph, Inc.
D&H Precision Tooling
Firearms Supplies Inc.
Hornady Mfg. Co.
Kent Cartridge Mfg. Co. Ltd.

Oehler Research, Inc.
Old Western Scrounger, Inc.
Pace Marketing, Inc.
P.A.C.T., Inc.
Shooting Chrony, Inc.
SKAN A.R.
Stratco, Inc.
Tepeco

CLEANING AND REFINISHING SUPPLIES

AC Dyna-tite Corp.
Acculube II, Inc.
Accupro Gun Care
Accuracy Products, S.A.
ADCO International
American Gas & Chemical Co., Ltd.
American Import Co., The/Export Division
Answer Products Co.
Armoloy Co. of Ft. Worth
Atlantic Mills, Inc.
Barnes Bullets, Inc.
Belltown, Ltd.
Beretta, Dr. Franco
Bill's Gun Repair
Birchwood Casey
Blount, Inc.
Blue and Gray Products, Inc.
Break-Free, Inc.
Bridgers Best
Brown Co., E. Arthur
Bruno Shooters Supply
Carroll Bullets
Chem-Pak, Inc.
Chopie Mfg., Inc.
Clenzoil Corp.
Corbin, Inc.
Crane & Crane Ltd.
Creedmoor Sports, Inc.
CRL, Inc.
Custom Products
D&H Prods. Co., Inc.
Dangler, Homer L.
Dara-Nes, Inc.
Deepeeka Exports Pvt. Ltd.
Dever Co., Jack
Dewey Mfg. Co., Inc., J.
Du-Lite Corp.
Dutchman's Firearms, Inc., The
Dykstra, Doug
E&L Mfg., Inc.
Eezox, Inc.
Ekol Leather Care
Faith Associates, Inc.
Firearms Supplies Inc.
Flaig's
Flitz International Ltd.
Flouramics, Inc.
Forster Products
Frontier Products Co.
G96 Products Co., Inc.
G.B.C. Industries, Inc.
Goddard, Allen
Golden Age Arms Co.
Gozon Corp.
Guardsman Products
Gun Works, The
Heatbath Corp.
Hoppe's Div.
Hornady Mfg. Co.
Hydrosorbent Products
Iosso Products
Jackalope Gun Shop
Jantz Supply
J-B Bore Cleaner
Johnston Bros.
Kent Cartridge Mfg. Co. Ltd.
Kesselring Gun Shop

Kleen-Bore, Inc.
Laurel Mountain Forge
Lee Supplies, Mark
LEM Gun Specialties, Inc.
List Precision Engineering
LPS Laboratories, Inc.
Marble Arms
Micro Sight Co.
Minute Man High Tech. Ind.
Mountain View Sports, Inc.
MTM Molded Products Co., Inc.
Muscle Products Corp.
Nesci Enterprises, Inc.
Old Western Scrounger, Inc.
Old World Oil Products
Omark Industries
Original Mink Oil, Inc.
Outers Laboratories, Div. of Blount
Ox-Yoke Originals, Inc.
P&M Sales and Service
Pace Marketing, Inc.
Pachmayr Ltd.
Parker Gun Finishes
Pendleton Royal
Precision Reloading, Inc.
Prolix
Pro-Shot Products, Inc.
R&S Industries Corp.
Radiator Specialty Co.
Richards, John
Richards Classic Oil Finish
Rickard, Inc., Pete
RIG Products Co.
Rod Guide Co.
Rooster Laboratories
Rusteprufe Laboratories
Rusty Duck Premium Gun Care
   Products
Saunders Gun & Machine Shop
Sharp Shooter, Inc.
Shiloh Creek
Shooter's Choice
Shootin' Accessories, Ltd.
Sinclair International, Inc.
Speer Products
Spencer's Custom Guns
Starr Trading Co., Jedediah
Stoney Point Products, Inc.
Svon Corp.
Tag Distributors
Tapco, Inc.
TDP Industries, Inc.
Tetra Gun Lubricants
Texas Platers Supply Co.
T.F.C. S.p.A.
Track of the Wolf, Inc.
United States Products Co.
Van Gorden & Son, Inc., C.S.
Venco Industries, Inc.
Warren Muzzleloading Co., Inc.
WD-40 Co.
Whitestone Lumber Corp.
Williams Shootin' Iron Service
Willow Bend
World of Targets
Young Country Arms
Z-Coat Industrial Coatings, Inc.

COMPUTER SOFTWARE—BALLISTICS

Action Target, Inc.
AmBr Software Group Ltd.
Arms, Peripheral Data Systems
Ballistic Engineering & Software, Inc.
Ballistic Program Co., Inc., The
Barnes Bullets, Inc.
Beartooth Bullets
Blackwell, W.
Blount, Inc.
Canons Delcour
Corbin, Inc.

Country Armourer, The
Data Tech Software Systems
Exe, Inc.
FlashTek, Inc.
Ford, Jack
JBM Software
Jensen Bullets
J.I.T. Ltd.
JWH = Software
Kent Cartridge Mfg. Co. Ltd.
Load From A Disk

Magma Engineering Co.
Maionchi-L.M.I.
P.A.C.T., Inc.
PC Bullet/ADC, Inc.
Pejsa Ballistics
Starnes Gunmaker, Ken
Tioga Engineering Co., Inc.

CUSTOM METALSMITHS

Adair Custom Shop, Bill
Ahlman Guns
Aldis Gunsmithing & Shooting Supply
Allen, Richard L.
Amrine's Gun Shop
Answer Products Co.
Arundel Arms & Ammunition, Inc., A.
Baer Custom, Inc., Les
Bansner's Gunsmithing Specialties
Baron Technology
Bear Mountain Gun & Tool
Behlert Precision
Beitzinger, George
Benchmark Guns
Bengtson Arms Co., L.
Biesen, Al
Billingsley & Brownell
Brace, Larry D.
Brian, C.T.
Briganti & Co., A.
Broad Creek Rifle Works
Brockmans Custom Gunsmithing
Broughton Rifle Barrels
Brown Precision, Inc.
Buckhorn Gun Works
Bull Mountain Rifle Co.
Bullberry Barrel Works, Ltd.
C&J Enterprises, Inc.
Campbell, Dick
Carter's Gun Shop
Checkmate Refinishing
Classic Guns, Inc.
Colonial Repair
Costa, David
Craftguard
Crandall Tool & Machine Co.
Cullity Restoration, Daniel
Custom Gun Products
Custom Gunsmiths
Custom Shop, The
D&D Gunsmiths, Ltd.
D&H Precision Tooling
Desert Industries, Inc.
Dever Co., Jack
Dietz Gun Shop & Range, Inc.
Duncan's Gunworks, Inc.
Erhardt, Dennis
Fisher, Jerry A.
Forster, Larry L.
Francesca, Inc.
Frank Custom Gun Service, Ron
Fullmer, Geo. M.
Goodwin, Fred
Gordie's Gun Shop
Graybill's Gun Shop
Green, Roger M.
Griffin & Howe, Inc.
Gun Shop, The
Guns
Gunsite Training Center
Gunsmithing Ltd.
Hallberg Gunsmith, Fritz
Hamilton, Alex B.
Harold's Custom Gun Shop, Inc.
Hecht, Hubert J.
Heilmann, Stephen
Heppler's Machining
Highline Machine Co.
Hiptmayer, Armurier
Hiptmayer, Klaus
Hoag, James W.
Hoelscher, Virgil
Holland's
Hollis Gun Shop
Hyper-Single, Inc.
Intermountain Arms & Tackle
Island Pond Gun Shop
Ivanoff, Thomas G.
J&S Heat Treat
Jamison's Forge Works
Jeffredo Gunsight
Johnston, James
Ken's Gun Specialties
Kilham & Co.
Klein Custom Guns, Don
Kleinendorst, K.W.
Kopp, Terry K.
LaFrance Specialties
Lampert, Ron
Lawson Co., Harry
List Precision Engineering
Lock's Philadelphia Gun Exchange
Mac's .45 Shop
Mains Enterprises, Inc.
Makinson, Nicholas
Marek, George
Martin's Gun Shop
McCament, Jay
McCann's Machine & Gun Shop
McFarland, Stan
McKinney, R.P.
Mid-America Recreation, Inc.
Morrison Custom Rifles, J.W.
Morrow, Bud
Mullis Guncraft
Nettestad Gun Works
Newman Gunshop
Nicholson Custom
Noreen, Peter H.
North American Shooting Systems
North Fork Custom Gunsmithing
Olson, Vic
Ozark Gun Works
Pace Marketing, Inc.
Pagel Gun Works, Inc.
Parker Gun Finishes
Pasadena Gun Center
Penrod Precision
Precision Metal Finishing
Precise Metalsmithing Enterprises
Precision Metal Finishing, John Westrom
Precision Specialties
Rice, Keith
R.M. Precision, Inc.
Robar Co.'s, Inc., The
Rocky Mountain Arms, Inc.
Sanders Custom Gun Service
Silver Ridge Gun Shop
Sipes Gun Shop
S.K. Guns, Inc.
Skeoch, Brian R.
Snapp's Gunshop
Spencer's Custom Guns
Sportsmatch Ltd.
Sportsmen's Exchange & Western Gun
    Traders, Inc.
Starnes Gunmaker, Ken
Steffens, Ron
Stiles Custom Guns
Stott's Creek Armory, Inc.
Strawbridge, Victor W.
Szweda, Robert
Taylor & Robbins
Ten-Ring Precision, Inc.
Thompson, Randall
Time Precision, Inc.
Tom's Gun Repair
T.S.W. Conversions, Inc.
Unick's Gunsmithing
Van Horn, Gil
Van Patten, J.W.
Vic's Gun Refinishing
Von Minden Gunsmithing Services
Vorhes, David
Wardell Precision Handguns Ltd.
Werth, T.W.
Wessinger Custom Guns & Engraving
West, Robert G.
Western Design
Westrom, John
White Rock Tool & Die
Wiebe, Duane
Williams Gun Sight Co.
Williams Shootin' Iron Service
Williamson Precision Gunsmithing
Wilson's Gun Shop
Winter, Robert M.
Wise Guns, Dale
Wisner's Gun Shop, Inc.
Wood, Frank

ENGRAVERS, ENGRAVING TOOLS

Adair Custom Shop, Bill
Adams, John J.
Adams Jr., John J.
Ahlman Guns

Alfano, Sam
Allard, Gary
Allen, Richard L.
Altamont Co.
American Pioneer Video
Anthony and George Ltd.
Baron Technology
Bates Engraving, Billy
Bell Originals, Inc., Sid
Bleile, C. Roger
Boessler, Erich
Bone Engraving, Ralph
Bratcher, Dan
Brgoch, Frank
Brooker, Dennis
Burgess, Byron
CAM Enterprises
Churchill, Winston
Clark Firearms Engraving
Collings, Ronald
Creek Side Metal & Woodcrafters
Cullity Restoration, Daniel
Cupp, Custom Engraver, Alana
Davidson, Jere
Delorge, Ed
Dixon Muzzleloading Shop, Inc.
Dolbare, Elizabeth
Drain, Mark
Dubber, Michael W.
Dyson & Son Ltd., Peter
EMF Co., Inc.
Engraving Artistry
Evans Engraving, Robert
Fanzoj GmbH
Firearms Engraver's Guild of America
Flannery Engraving Co., Jeff W.
Floatstone Mfg. Co.
Fountain Products
Francolini, Leonard
Frank Custom Gun Service, Ron
Frank Knives
French, J.R.
Gene's Custom Guns
George, Tim
Glimm, Jerome C.
Golden Age Arms Co.
Gournet, Geoffroy
Grant, Howard V.
Griffin & Howe, Inc.
GRS Corp., Glendo
Gun Room, The
Guns
Gurney, F.R.
Gwinnell, Bryson J.
Hale, Peter
Hand Engravers Supply Co.
Hands Engraving, Barry Lee
Harris Hand Engraving, Paul A.
Harris-McMillan Gunworks
Harwood, Jack O.
Hendricks, Frank E.
Herrett's Stocks, Inc.
Hiptmayer, Heidemarie
Horst, Alan K.
Ingle, Ralph W.
Johns, Bill
Kamyk Engraving Co., Steve
Kehr, Roger
Kelly, Lance
Klingler Woodcarving
Koevenig's Engraving Service

Kudlas, John M.
LaFrance Specialties
Lebeau-Courally
LeFever Arms Co., Inc.
Leibowitz, Leonard
Letschnig, Franz
Lindsay, Steve
Little Trees Ramble
Lutz Engraving, Ron
Mains Enterprises, Inc.
Marek, George
Master Engravers, Inc.
McCombs, Leo
McDonald, Dennis
McKenzie, Lynton
Mele, Frank
Mid-America Recreation, Inc.
Mittermeier, Inc., Frank
Montgomery Community College
Moschetti, Mitchell R.
Mountain States Engraving
Nelson, Gary K.
New Orleans Arms Co.
New Orleans Jewelers Supply Co.
NgraveR Co., The
Oker's Engraving
Old Dominion Engravers
P&S Gun Service
Palmgren Steel Products
Pedersen, C.R.
Pedersen, Rex C.
Pilgrim Pewter, Inc.
Pilkington, Scott
Piquette, Paul R.
Potts, Wayne E.
Rabeno, Martin
Reed, Dave
Reno, Wayne
Riggs, Jim
Roberts, J.J.
Rohner, Hans
Rohner, John
Rosser, Bob
Rundell's Gun Shop
Runge, Robert P.
Sampson, Roger
Schiffman, Mike
Sheffield Knifemakers Supply
Sherwood, George
Sinclair, W.P.
Singletary, Kent
Skaggs, R.E.
Smith & Wesson
Smith, Mark A.
Smith, Ron
Theis, Terry
Thiewes, George W.
Thirion Hand Engraving, Denise
Valade, Robert B.
Vest, John
Viramontez, Ray
Vorhes, David
Wagoner, Vernon G.
Wallace, Terry
Warenski, Julie
Warren, Kenneth W.
Welch, Sam
Wells, Rachel
Wessinger Custom Guns & Engraving
Willig Custom Engraving, Claus

GAME CALLS

Adventure Game Calls
Arkansas Mallard Duck Calls
Ashby Turkey Calls
Blakemore Game Calls, Jim
Bostick Wildlife Calls, Inc.
Carter's Wildlife Calls, Inc., Garth
Cedar Hill Game Calls, Inc.
Crawford Co., Inc., R.M.
D&H Prods. Co., Inc.
D-Boone Ent., Inc.
Deepeeka Exports Pvt. Ltd.
Dr. O's Products Ltd.
Duck Call Specialists
Faulhaber Wildlocker
Faulk's Game Call Co., Inc.
Flow-Rite of Tennessee, Inc.
Green Head Game Call Co.
Hally Caller
Haydel's Game Calls, Inc.
Herter's Manufacturing, Inc.
Hunter's Specialties, Inc.
Keowee Game Calls
Kingyon, Paul L.

Knight & Hale Game Calls
Lohman Mfg. Co., Inc.
Mallardtone Game Calls
Marsh, Johnny
Moss Double Tone, Inc.
Mountain Hollow Game Calls
Oakman Turkey Calls
Olt Co., Philip S.
Penn's Woods Products, Inc.
Primos, Inc.
Quaker Boy, Inc.
Rickard, Inc., Pete
Robbins Scent, Inc.
Rocky Mountain Wildlife Products
Salter Calls, Inc., Eddie
Savana Sports, Inc.
Sceery Co., E.J.
Scobey Duck & Goose Calls, Glynn
Scruggs' Game Calls, Stanley
Sports Innovations, Inc.
Stewart Game Calls, Inc., Johnny
Sure-Shot Game Calls, Inc.
Tanglefree Industries

Tink's & Ben Lee Hunting Products
Tink's Safariland Hunting Corp.
Wellington Outdoors

Wilderness Sound Products Ltd.
Woods Wise Products
Wyant's Outdoor Products, Inc.

Trooper Walsh
UltraSport Arms, Inc.
Venom Arms Co.
Walther GmbH, Carl
Webley and Scott Ltd.

Weihrauch KG, Hermann
Whiscombe
Wright's Hardwood Gunstock Blanks
World Class Airguns

GUN PARTS, U.S. AND FOREIGN

ABS Co. Inc./Lothar Walther
Accuracy Gun Shop
Ad Hominem
Ahlman Guns
American Bullets
Amherst Arms
Armscorp USA, Inc.
Badger Shooters Supply, Inc.
Bear Mountain Gun & Tool
Beauchamp & Son, Inc.
Behlert Precision
Billings Gunsmiths, Inc.
Bob's Gun Shop
Boyds' Gunstock Industries, Inc.
Briese Bullet Co., Inc.
Bushmaster Firearms
C&J Enterprises, Inc.
Caspian Arms Ltd.
Century International Arms, Inc.
Clark Custom Guns, Inc.
Cole's Gun Works
Colonial Repair
Cylinder & Slide, Inc.
Defense Moulding Enterprises
Delta Arms Ltd.
DGR Custom Rifles
Dibble, Derek A.
Duane's Gun Repair
Duffy, Charles E.
Dyson & Son Ltd., Peter
Elliott Inc., G.W.
EMF Co., Inc.
Enguix Import-Export
Fabian Bros. Sporting Goods, Inc.
FAPA Corp.
Fleming Firearms
Flintlocks, Etc.
Forrest, Inc., Tom
Forster Products
Galati International
Goodwin, Fred
Groenewold, John
Gun Parts Corp., The
Gun Shop, The
Guns
Gun-Tec
High Performance International
High Standard Mfg. Co., Inc.
Irwin, Campbell H.
I.S.S.
Johnson Gunsmithing, Inc., Neal G.
K&T Co.
K.K. Arms Co.
Krico/Kriegeskorte GmbH, A.
Laughridge, William R.
Liberty Antique Gunworks
List Precision Engineering
Lodewick, Walter H.

Mac's .45 Shop
Markell, Inc.
Martin's Gun Shop
Martz, John V.
McCann's Machine & Gun Shop
McCormick Corp., Chip
Merkuria Ltd.
Morrow, Bud
Nu-Line Guns, Inc.
Olympic Arms
Pace Marketing, Inc.
Pachmayr Ltd.
Parts & Surplus
Peacemaker Specialists
Pennsylvania Gun Parts
Perazone, Brian
Peterson Gun Shop, Inc., A.W.
Precision Small Arms
Quality Firearms of Idaho, Inc.
Ranch Products
Randco UK
Retting, Inc., Martin B.
R.M. Precision, Inc.
S&S Firearms
Sarco, Inc.
Scherer
Shockley, Harold H.
Silver Ridge Gun Shop
Sipes Gun Shop
Smires, C.L.
Smith & Wesson
Southern Ammunition Co., Inc.
Southern Armory, The
Sportsmen's Exchange & Western Gun
    Traders, Inc.
Springfield, Inc.
Springfield Sporters, Inc.
Starnes Gunmaker, Ken
"Su-Press-On," Inc.
Swampfire Shop, The
Tapco, Inc.
Track of the Wolf, Inc.
Tradewinds, Inc.
T.S.W. Conversions, Inc.
Twin Pine Armory
USA Sporting Inc.
Vintage Arms, Inc.
Vintage Industries, Inc.
Volquartsen Custom Ltd.
Walker Arms Co., Inc.
Weaver's Gun Shop
Westfield Engineering
Wilson's Gun Shop
Wise Guns, Dale
Wisner's Gun Shop, Inc.
Wolff Co., W.C.
Wood, Mel

GUNS, AIR

Air Rifle Specialists
Air Venture
Air Werks International
Airgun Repair Centre
Airguns-R-Us
Airrow
Beeman Precision Airguns
Benjamin/Sheridan Co.
Brass Eagle, Inc.
Brocock Ltd.
BSA Guns Ltd.
Champion's Choice, Inc.
Component Concepts, Inc.
Crawford Co., Inc., R.M.
Creedmoor Sports, Inc.
Crosman Airguns
Crosman Products of Canada Ltd.
Daisy Mfg. Co.
Daystate Arms
Diana
Dynamit Nobel-RWS, Inc.
Frankonia Jagd
FWB
Gamo
GFR Corp.
Great Lakes Airguns
GZ Paintball Sports Products
Hebard Guns, Gil
Hofmann & Co.
Howa Machinery, Ltd.

Labanu, Inc.
List Precision Engineering
Mac-1 Distributors
Marksman Products
Maryland Paintball Supply
MCS, Inc.
Merkuria Ltd.
Mo's Competitor Supplies
National Survival Game, Inc.
Nationwide Airgun Repairs
P&S Gun Service
Pardini Armi Srl
Park Rifle Co., Inc.
Precision Airgun Sales, Inc.
Precision Sales Int'l, Inc.
Ripley Rifles
Rutten
RWS
Savana Sports, Inc.
S.G.S. Sporting Guns Srl
Shanghai Airguns, Ltd.
SKAN A.R.
Smart Parts
Sportsman Airguns, Inc.
Sportsmatch Ltd.
Stone Enterprises Ltd.
Swivel Machine Works, Inc.
Tapco, Inc.
Theoben Engineering
Tippman Pneumatics, Inc.

GUNS, FOREIGN—IMPORTERS (Manufacturers)

Air Rifle Specialists (BSA Guns Ltd.;
    Theoben Engineering)
Air Venture (airguns)
Air Werks International (Park Rifle Co.,
    Ltd.; Rutten)
Airguns-R-Us (Brocock Ltd.; Falcon
    Pneumatic Systems)
American Arms, Inc. (Uberti, Aldo;
    blackpowder arms)
Armoury, Inc., The (blackpowder)
Beeman Precision Airguns (Beeman
    Precision Airguns; Feinwerkbau;
    FWB; Webley & Scott Ltd.; Weihrauch
    KG, Hermann)
Beretta U.S.A. Corp. (Beretta Firearms,
    Pietro)
Browning Arms Co. (Browning Arms
    Co.)
B-West Imports, Inc.
Cabela's (Pedersoli, Davide & C.;
    blackpowder arms)
Century International Arms, Inc.
    (Famas; FEG; Norinco)
Cimarron Arms (Uberti, Aldo;
    blackpowder arms)
CVA (blackpowder arms)
Daisy Mfg. Co. (Daisy Mfg. Co.; Gamo)
Dixie Gun Works, Inc. (Pedersoli,
    Davide & C.; Uberti, Aldo;
    blackpowder arms)
Dynamit Nobel-RWS, Inc. (Brenneke
    KG, Wilhelm; Diana; Gamo; Norma
    Precision AB; RWS)
EMF Co., Inc. (Dakota; Pedersoli,
    Davide & C.; San Marco; Uberti, Aldo;
    blackpowder arms)
Euroarms of America, Inc. (blackpowder
    arms)
Forgett Jr., Valmore J. (Navy Arms Co.;
    Uberti, Aldo)
Glock, Inc. (Glock GmbH)
Great Lakes Airguns (Sharp)
Hammerli USA (Hammerli Ltd.)
Harris-McMillan Gunworks (Peters Stahl
    GmbH)
Heckler & Koch, Inc. (Benelli Armi
    S.p.A.; Heckler & Koch, GmbH)

Interarms (Helwan; Interarms; Star
    Bonifacio Echeverria S.A.; Walther
    GmbH, Carl)
JägerSport, Ltd. (Voere-KGH m.b.H.)
J.O. Arms Inc. (KSN Industries, Ltd.)
K.B.I., Inc. (FEG; Kassnar; K.B.I., Inc.)
K-Sports Imports, Inc.
Mac-1 Distributors (Venom Arms Co.)
Magnum Research, Inc. (CZ; IMI)
Mandall Shooting Supplies, Inc.
    (Cabanas; Erma Werke GmbH;
    Hammerli Ltd.; Korth; Morini; SIG;
    blackpowder arms)
Marksman Products (Marksman
    Products)
MCS, Inc. (Pardini Armi Srl)
Nationwide Sports Distributors, Inc.
    (Daewoo Precision Industries Ltd.)
Navy Arms Co. (Uberti, Aldo;
    blackpowder and cartridge arms)
Nygord Precision Products (Morini;
    Pardini Armi Srl; Steyr; TOZ;
    Unique/M.A.P.F.)
Olympic Arms (Peters Stahl GmbH)
Para-Ordnance, Inc. (Para-Ordnance
    Mfg., Inc.)
Precision Sales International, Inc. (Erma
    Werke GmbH)
SGS Importers International, Inc. (Llama
    Gabilondo Y Cia)
Sigarms, Inc. (SIG-Sauer)
Sile Distributors (Benelli Armi S.p.A.;
    Marocchi F.lli S.p.A.)
Specialty Shooters Supply, Inc. (JSL
    Ltd.)
Sphinx USA Inc. (Sphinx Engineering
    SA)
Springfield, Inc. (Springfield, Inc.)
Stone Enterprises Ltd. (airguns)
Swarovski Optik North America Ltd.
Taurus Firearms, Inc. (Taurus
    International Firearms)
Taylor's & Co., Inc. (Armi Sport; I.A.B.;
    Uberti, Aldo; blackpowder arms)
Uberti USA, Inc. (blackpowder arms)
Vintage Arms, Inc.

GUNS, FOREIGN—MANUFACTURERS (Importers)

Beeman Precision Airguns (Beeman
    Precision Airguns)
Benelli Armi S.p.A. (Heckler & Koch,
    Inc.; Sile Distributors, Inc.)
Beretta Firearms, Pietro (Beretta U.S.A.
    Corp.)
Bersa S.A., Gonzales Castillo
Bondini Paolo (blackpowder arms)
Browning Arms Co. (Browning Arms Co.)
BSA Guns Ltd.
Cabanas (Mandall Shooting Supplies,
    Inc.)
CVA (blackpowder arms)
CZ (Magnum Research, Inc.)
Daewoo Precision Industries Ltd.
    (Nationwide Sports Distributors, Inc.)
Daisy Mfg. Co. (Daisy Mfg. Co.)
Diana (Dynamit Nobel-RWS, Inc.)
Erma Werke GmbH (Mandall Shooting
    Supplies, Inc.; Precision Sales
    International, Inc.)
Falcon Pneumatic Systems
    (Airguns-R-Us)
FEG (Century International Arms, Inc.;
    K.B.I., Inc.)
FN Herstal
FWB (Beeman Precision Airguns)
Gamo (Daisy Mfg. Co.; Dynamit
    Nobel-RWS, Inc.)
Glock GmbH (Glock, Inc.)
Hammerli Ltd. (Hammerli USA)
Heckler & Koch, GmbH (Heckler &
    Koch, Inc.)
I.A.B. (Taylor's & Co., Inc.)
IMI (Magnum Research, Inc.)
J.O. Arms & Ammunition Co. (J.O. Arms
    & Ammunition Co.)
JSL Ltd. (Specialty Shooters Supply, Inc.)
Kassnar (K.B.I., Inc.)

K.B.I., Inc. (K.B.I., Inc.)
Korth (Mandall Shooting Supplies, Inc.)
KSN Industries, Ltd. (J.O. Arms Inc.)
Llama Gabilondo Y Cia (SGS Importers
    International, Inc.)
Marksman Products (Marksman
    Products)
Mitchell Arms, Inc. (Mitchell Arms, Inc.)
Morini (Mandall Shooting Supplies;
    Nygord Precision Products)
Navy Arms Co. (Forgett Jr., Valmore J.;
    Navy Arms Co.)
Norinco (Century International Arms,
    Inc.)
Para-Ordnance Mfg., Inc.
    (Para-Ordnance, Inc.)
Pardini Armi Srl. (MCS, Inc.; Nygord
    Precision Products)
Peters Stahl GmbH (Harris-McMillan
    Gunworks; Olympic Arms)
RWS (Dynamit Nobel-RWS, Inc.)
Sharp (Great Lakes Airguns)
SIG (Mandall Shooting Supplies, Inc.)
SIG-Sauer (Sigarms, Inc.)
Sphinx Engineering SA (Sphinx USA
    Inc.)
Springfield, Inc. (Springfield, Inc.)
Taurus International Firearms (Taurus
    Firearms, Inc.)
TOZ (Nygord Precision Products)
Uberti, Aldo (American Arms, Inc.;
    Cimarron Arms; Dixie Gun Works,
    Inc.; EMF Co., Inc.; Forgett Jr.,
    Valmore J.; Navy Arms Co.; Taylor's
    & Co., Inc.)
Unique/M.A.P.F. (Nygord Precision
    Products)
Venom Arms Co. (Mac-1 Distributors;
    Trooper Walsh)

Voere-KGH m.b.H. (JägerSport, Ltd.)
Webley & Scott Ltd. (Beeman Precision
 Airguns)

Weihrauch KG, Hermann (Beeman
 Precision Airguns)

GUNS, U.S.-MADE

Accu-Tek
Airrow
American Arms & Ordnance, Inc.
American Arms, Inc.
American Derringer Corp.
AMT
Auto-Ordnance Corp.
Baer Custom, Inc., Les
Barrett Firearms Mfg., Inc.
Beretta U.S.A. Corp.
Braverman, R.J.
Brolin Arms
Brown Co., E. Arthur
Browning Arms Co. (Parts & Service)
Bryco Arms
Bushmaster Firearms
Calico Light Weapon Systems
Century Gun Dist., Inc.
CHARCO
Charter Arms
Colt's Mfg. Co., Inc.
Competitor Corp., Inc.
Coonan Arms
CVA
Davis Industries
Desert Industries, Inc.
D-Max, Inc.
Emerging Technologies, Inc.
Essex Arms
Feather Industries, Inc.
Freedom Arms, Inc.
H&R 1871, Inc.
Harris-McMillan Gunworks
High Standard Mfg. Co., Inc.
Hi-Point Firearms
HJS Arms, Inc.
Holston Ent. Inc.

Intratec
Ithaca Aquisition Corp./Ithaca Gun
Jennings Firearms Inc.
Kahr Arms
Kel-Tec CNC Industries, Inc.
Kimber of America, Inc.
Kimel Industries
Knight's Mfg. Co.
L.A.R. Manufacturing, Inc.
Laseraim, Inc.
Lorcin Engineering Co., Inc.
Magnum Research, Inc.
Mitchell Arms, Inc.
MKS Supply, Inc.
M.O.A. Corp.
New Advantage Arms Corp.
New England Firearms
North American Arms, Inc.
Olympic Arms, Inc.
Phoenix Arms
Precision Small Arms
Rocky Mountain Arms, Inc.
Seecamp Co., Inc., L.W.
Smith & Wesson
Springfield, Inc.
Sturm, Ruger & Co., Inc.
Sundance Industries, Inc.
Swivel Machine Works, Inc.
Taurus Firearms, Inc.
Texas Armory
Texas Longhorn Arms, Inc.
Thompson/Center Arms
Ultra Light Arms, Inc.
Wichita Arms, Inc.
Wildey, Inc.
Wilkinson Arms

GUNS AND GUN PARTS, REPLICA AND ANTIQUE

Ahlman Guns
Armi San Paolo
Bear Mountain Gun & Tool
Beauchamp & Son, Inc.
Bill's Gun Repair
Bob's Gun Shop
Buckskin Machine Works
Burgess & Son Gunsmiths, R.W.
C&J Enterprises, Inc.
Cache La Poudre Rifleworks
Campbell, Dick
Century International Arms, Inc.
Cogar's Gunsmithing
Cole's Gun Works
Colonial Repair
Curly Maple Stock Blanks
Dangler, Homer L.
Day & Sons, Inc., Leonard
Delhi Gun House
Delta Arms Ltd.
Dilliott Gunsmithing, Inc.
Dixon Muzzleloading Shop, Inc.
Dyson & Son Ltd., Peter
Ed's Gun House
EMF Co., Inc.
Enguix Import-Export
Flintlocks, Etc.
Forgett, Valmore J., Jr.
Forster Products
Franchi S.p.A., Luigi
Frank Custom Gun Service, Ron
Golden Age Arms Co.
Goodwin, Fred
Groenewold, John
Gun Parts Corp., The
Gun Works, The
Guns
Gun-Tec

Hunkeler, A.
Liberty Antique Gunworks
List Precision Engineering
Log Cabin Sport Shop
Lucas, Edw. E.
Martin's Gun Shop
McCann's Muzzle-Gun Works
McKinney, R.P.
Mountain State Muzzleloading Supplies
Munsch Gunsmithing, Tommy
Museum of Historical Arms, Inc.
Neumann GmbH
Newman Gunshop
Parker Gun Finishes
Pasadena Gun Center
PEM's Mfg. Co.
P.M. Enterprises, Inc.
Pony Express Sport Shop, Inc.
Precise Metalsmithing Enterprises
Quality Firearms of Idaho, Inc.
Radical Concepts
Randco UK
Retting, Inc., Martin B.
S&S Firearms
Sarco, Inc.
Silver Ridge Gun Shop
Sipes Gun Shop
Sklany, Steve
Starr Trading Co., Jedediah
Stott's Creek Armory, Inc.
Taylor's & Co., Inc.
Tiger-Hunt
Track of the Wolf, Inc.
Uberti USA, Inc.
Vintage Industries, Inc.
Weisz Parts
Wescombe

GUNS, SURPLUS—PARTS AND AMMUNITION

Armscorp USA, Inc.
Arundel Arms & Ammunition, Inc., A.
Aztec International Ltd.
Badger Shooters Supply, Inc.
Ballistica Maximus North
Bohemia Arms Co.
Bondini Paolo
Braun, M.
Century International Arms, Inc.
Chuck's Gun Shop

Cole's Gun Works
Combat Military Ordnance Ltd.
Delta Arms Ltd.
Fleming Firearms
Forgett, Valmore J., Jr.
Forrest, Inc., Tom
Fulton Armory
Garcia National Gun Traders, Inc.
Goodwin, Fred
"Gramps" Antique Cartridges

Gun Parts Corp., The
Hank's Gun Shop
KLA Enterprises
Mathews & Son, Inc., George E.
Moreton/Fordyce Enterprises
Navy Arms Co.
Nevada Pistol Academy Inc.
Newman Gunshop
Nu-Line Guns, Inc.
Oil Rod and Gun Shop
Old Western Scrounger, Inc.
Paragon Sales & Services, Inc.
Parts & Surplus
Pasadena Gun Center
Quality Firearms of Idaho, Inc.
Retting, Inc., Martin B.

Samco Global Arms, Inc.
Sanders Custom Gun Service
Sarco, Inc.
Silver Ridge Gun Shop
Sipes Gun Shop
Southern Ammunition Co., Inc.
Southern Armory, The
Sportsmen's Exchange & Western Gun
 Traders, Inc.
Springfield Sporters, Inc.
Starnes Gunmaker, Ken
T.F.C. S.p.A.
Thurston Sports, Inc.
Westfield Engineering
Whitestone Lumber Corp.

GUNSMITH SCHOOLS

Bull Mountain Rifle Co.
Colorado School of Trades
Cylinder & Slide, Inc.
Lassen Community College,
 Gunsmithing Dept.
Laughridge, William R.
Modern Gun Repair School
Montgomery Community College
Murray State College
North American Correspondence Schools
Nowlin Custom Mfg.

NRI Gunsmith School
Pennsylvania Gunsmith School
Piedmont Community College
Pine Technical College
Professional Gunsmiths of America, Inc.
Southeastern Community College
Spencer's Custom Guns
Trinidad State Junior College
 Gunsmithing Dept.
Weigand Combat Handguns, Inc.
Wessinger Custom Guns & Engraving

GUNSMITH SUPPLIES, TOOLS, SERVICES

Actions by "T"
Aldis Gunsmithing & Shooting Supply
Alley Supply Co.
Aro-Tek, Ltd.
Baer Custom, Inc., Les
Bald Eagle Precision Machine Co.
Bear Mountain Gun & Tool
Behlert Precision
Bengtson Arms Co., L.
Biesen, Al
Biesen, Roger
Billingsley & Brownell
Birchwood Laboratories, Inc.
Blue Ridge Machinery & Tools, Inc.
Bowen Classic Arms Corp.
Boyds' Gunstock Industries, Inc.
Break-Free, Inc.
Brownells, Inc.
B-Square Co., Inc.
Bull Mountain Rifle Co.
Carbide Checkering Tools
Chapman Manufacturing Co.
Chem-Pak, Inc.
Choate Machine & Tool Co., Inc.
Chopie Mfg., Inc.
Chuck's Gun Shop
Clark Custom Guns, Inc.
Colonial Arms, Inc.
Conetrol Scope Mounts
Corbin, Inc.
Craig Custom Ltd.
Cumberland Arms
Custom Checkering Service
Custom Gun Products
D&J Bullet Co. & Custom Gun Shop, Inc.
Decker Shooting Products
Dem-Bart Checkering Tools, Inc.
Dilliott Gunsmithing, Inc.
Dremel Mfg. Co.
Duffy, Charles E.
Du-Lite Corp.
Dutchman's Firearms, Inc., The
Dyson & Son Ltd., Peter
Echols & Co., D'Arcy
EGW Evolution Gun Works
Faith Associates, Inc.
Fisher, Jerry A.
Forgreens Tool Mfg., Inc.
Forster, Kathy
Forster Products
Frazier Brothers Enterprises
G.B.C. Industries, Inc.
Grace Metal Products, Inc.
Greider Precision
Gunline Tools
Guns
Gunsite Training Center
Gun-Tec
Half Moon Rifle Shop
Henriksen Tool Co., Inc.
Hoelscher, Virgil
Holland's
Iosso Products
Ivanoff, Thomas G.

Jacobson, Teddy
Jantz Supply
Jarvis Gunsmithing, Inc.
JBM Software
JGS Precision Tool Mfg.
Kasenit Co., Inc.
Kimball, Gary
Kleinendorst, K.W.
Kmount
Korzinek Riflesmith, J.
Kwik Mount Corp.
LaBounty Precision Reboring
LaRocca Gun Works, Inc.
Lea Mfg. Co.
Lee's Red Ramps
Lee Supplies, Mark
List Precision Engineering
Lortone, Inc.
Marsh, Mike
Menck, Thomas W.
Metalife Industries
Metaloy Inc.
Michael's Antiques
Millett Sights
MMC
Morrow, Bud
N&J Sales
Nitex, Inc.
Nowlin Custom Mfg.
Ole Frontier Gunsmith Shop
Pace Marketing, Inc.
Palmgren Steel Products
Palsa Outdoor Products
PanaVise Products, Inc.
PEM's Mfg. Co.
Perazone, Brian
Power Custom, Inc.
Practical Tools, Inc.
Precision Metal Finishing
Precision Specialties
Reardon Products
Rice, Keith
Roto Carve
Ruvel & Co., Inc.
Scott, McDougall & Associates
Sharp Shooter, Inc.
Shooter's Choice
Sinclair International, Inc.
S.K. Guns, Inc.
Smith Abrasives, Inc.
Starrett Co., L.S.
Stoney Point Products, Inc.
Stuart Products, Inc.
Sullivan, David S.
Sure Shot of LA, Inc.
Talley, Dave
TDP Industries, Inc.
Texas Platers Supply
Time Precision, Inc.
Tom's Gun Repair
Track of the Wolf, Inc.
Trulock Tool
Turnbull Restoration, Doug
Venco Industries, Inc.

Vintage Industries, Inc.
Washita Mountain Whetstone Co.
Weaver's Gun Shop
Weigand Combat Handguns, Inc.
Wessinger Custom Guns & Engraving
Westfield Engineering
Westrom, John
Westwind Rifles, Inc.
White Rock Tool & Die

Wilcox All-Pro Tools & Supply
Will-Burt Co.
Williams Gun Sight Co.
Willow Bend
Wilson's Gun Shop
Wise Guns, Dale
World of Targets
Wright's Hardwood Gunstock Blanks

HANDGUN ACCESSORIES

Ace Custom 45's
ADCO International
Adventurer's Outpost
Aimtech Mount Systems
Ajax Custom Grips, Inc.
American Derringer Corp.
Armite Laboratories
Aro-Tek, Ltd.
Astra Sport, S.A.
Auto-Ordnance Corp.
Baer Custom, Inc., Les
Bagmaster Mfg., Inc.
Bar-Sto Precision Machine
Baumannize Custom
Behlert Precision
Black Sheep Brand
Blue and Gray Products, Inc.
Bob's Gun Shop
Boonie Packer Products
Bowen Classic Arms Corp.
Broken Gun Ranch
Brown Products, Inc., Ed
Brownells, Inc.
Bucheimer, J.M.
Bushmaster Firearms
Butler Creek Corp.
C3 Systems
Centaur Systems, Inc.
Central Specialties Ltd.
Clark Custom Guns, Inc.
Cobra Gunskin
Conetrol Scope Mounts
Craig Custom Ltd.
CRL, Inc.
Dade Screw Machine Products
Delhi Gun House
Doskocil Mfg. Co., Inc
EGW Evolution Gun Works
Faith Associates, Inc.
Feather Industries, Inc.
Feminine Protection, Inc.
Ferris Firearms
Fleming Firearms
Forgett Jr., Valmore J.
Frielich Police Equipment
Glock, Inc.
GML Products, Inc.
Greider Precision
Gremmel Enterprises
Gun Parts Corp., The
Gun-Alert
Guncraft Sports, Inc.
Gunfitters, The
Gun-Ho Sports Cases
Gunsite Training Center
Haselbauer Products, Jerry
Hebard Guns, Gil
Heinie Specialty Products
Hill Speed Leather, Ernie
H.K.S. Products
Hoppe's Div.
Hunter Co., Inc.
Jarvis Gunsmithing, Inc.
Jeffredo Gunsight
Jett & Co., Inc.
John's Custom Leather
Jones, J.D.
J.P. Enterprises, Inc.
Jumbo Sports Products
K&K Ammo Wrist Band

KeeCo Impressions
Keller Co., The
King's Gun Works
L&S Technologies Inc.
Lakewood Products, Inc.
LaRocca Gun Works, Inc.
Lee's Red Ramps
Lem Sports, Inc.
Loch Leven Industries
Lohman Mfg. Co., Inc.
Mac's .45 Shop
Magnolia Sports, Inc.
Magnum Research, Inc.
Marble Arms
Markell Inc.
Masen Co., Inc., John
Master Products, Inc.
McCann's Machine & Gun Shop
McCormick Corp., Chip
MEC-Gar S.R.L.
Menck, Thomas W.
Merkuria Ltd.
Michaels of Oregon Co.
Millett Sights
MTM Molded Products Co., Inc.
Mustra's Custom Guns, Inc., Carl
Noble Co., Jim
No-Sho Mfg. Co.
Nowlin Custom Mfg.
Owen, Harry
Ox-Yoke Originals, Inc.
Pace Marketing, Inc.
Pardini Armi Srl
PAST Sporting Goods, Inc.
Peacemaker Specialists
Pendleton Royal
Power Custom, Inc.
Practical Tools, Inc.
Protector Mfg. Co., Inc., The
Protektor Model
Ranch Products
Round Edge, Inc.
Safariland Ltd., Inc.
Scott, McDougall & Associates
Sinclair International, Inc.
Slings 'N Things, Inc.
Smith & Wesson
Sonderman, Robert
Southwind Sanctions
Sport Specialties
SSK Industries
Starnes Gunmaker, Ken
"Su-Press-On," Inc.
TacTell, Inc.
Tapco, Inc.
Tarnham Supply
T.F.C. S.p.A.
Thompson/Center Arms
TMI Products
Triple-K Mfg. Co.
Tyler Mfg.-Dist., Melvin
Uncle Mike's
Vintage Industries, Inc.
Volquartsen Custom Ltd.
Weigand Combat Handguns, Inc.
Wessinger Custom Guns & Engraving
Western Design
Whitestone Lumber Corp.
Wichita Arms, Inc.

HANDGUN GRIPS

Ace Custom 45's
Ahrends, Kim
Ajax Custom Grips, Inc.
Altamont Co.
American Derringer Corp.
American Gripcraft
Aro-Tek, Ltd.
Art Jewel Enterprises Ltd.
Baer Custom, Inc., Les
Barami Corp.
Bear Hug Grips, Inc.
Bell Originals, Inc., Sid

Bob's Gun Shop
Boone's Custom Ivory Grips, Inc.
Brooks Tactical Systems
Brown Products, Inc., Ed
CAM Enterprises
Clark Custom Guns, Inc.
Cobra Gunskin
Cole-Grip
Colonial Repair
Curtis Gun Shop
Custom Firearms
Dayson Arms Ltd.

Desert Industries, Inc.
Eagle Mfg. & Engineering
EMF Co., Inc.
Eyears Insurance
Ferris Firearms
Fisher Custom Firearms
Fitz Pistol Grip Co.
Forrest, Inc., Tom
Gunsite Training Center
Herrett's Stocks, Inc.
Hogue Grips
J.P. Enterprises, Inc.
KeeCo Impressions
Lett Custom Grips
Linebaugh Custom Sixguns & Rifle Works
Mac's .45 Shop
Masen Co., Inc., John
McCann's Machine & Gun Shop
Michaels of Oregon Co.
Millett Sights

Monte Kristo Pistol Grip Co.
N.C. Ordnance Co.
Newell, Robert H.
Pardini Armi Srl
Peacemaker Specialists
Pilgrim Pewter, Inc.
Reiswig, Wallace E.
Rosenberg & Sons, Jack A.
Roy's Custom Grips
Savana Sports, Inc.
Sile Distributors, Inc.
Smith & Wesson
Spegel, Craig
Taurus Firearms, Inc.
Tyler Mfg.-Dist., Melvin
Uncle Mike's
Vintage Industries, Inc.
Volquartsen Custom Ltd.
Wayland Precision Wood Products
Wichita Arms, Inc.

HEARING PROTECTORS

Blount, Inc.
Brown Co., E. Arthur
Browning Arms Co.
Clark Co., Inc., David
Clark Custom Guns, Inc.
Cobra Gunskin
CRL, Inc.
E-A-R, Inc.
Faith Associates, Inc.
Firearms Supplies Inc.
Fitz Pistol Grip Co.
Flents Products Co., Inc.
Gonzalez Guns, Ramon B.

Hoppe's Div.
Kesselring Gun Shop
Marble Arms
North Specialty Products
Paterson Gunsmithing
Peltor, Inc.
RCBS
R.E.T. Enterprises
Safesport Manufacturing Co.
Silencio/Safety Direct
Smith & Wesson
Tyler Mfg.-Dist., Melvin
Willson Safety Prods. Div.

HOLSTERS AND LEATHER GOODS

A&B Industries, Inc.
Action Products, Inc.
Aker Leather Products
Alessi Holsters, Inc.
Alley Supply Co.
American Import Co., The/Export
    Division
American Sales & Kirkpatrick
Arratoonian, Andy
Bagmaster Mfg., Inc.
Baker's Leather Goods, Roy
Bandcor Industries
Bang-Bang Boutique
Barami Corp.
Bear Hug Grips, Inc.
Bianchi International, Inc.
Black Sheep Brand
Blocker's Holsters, Inc., Ted
Brauer Bros. Mfg. Co.
Brown, H.R.
Browning Arms Co.
Bucheimer, J.M.
Bushmaster Hunting & Fishing
Bushwacker Backpack & Supply Co.
Carvajal Belts & Holsters
Cathey Enterprises, Inc.
Chace Leather Products
Cimarron Arms
Clark Custom Guns, Inc.
Clements' Custom Leathercraft, Chas
Cobra Gunskin
Cobra Sport
Colonial Repair
Counter Assault
CRDC Laser Systems Group
Crawford Co., Inc., R.M.
Creedmoor Sports, Inc.
Davis Leather Co., G. Wm.
Delhi Gun House
DeSantis Holster & Leather Goods, Inc.
Easy Pull Outlaw Products
Ekol Leather Care
El Dorado Leather
El Paso Saddlery Co.
EMF Co., Inc.
Epps "Orillia" Ltd., Ellwood
Eutaw Co., Inc., The
F&A Inc.
Faust, Inc., T.G.
Ferdinand, Inc.
Firearms Supplies Inc.
Flores Publications, Inc., J.
Fobus International Ltd.
Forgett Jr., Valmore J.
Fury Cutlery
Gage Manufacturing
Galati International
GALCO International Ltd.

Glock, Inc.
GML Products, Inc.
Gonzalez Guns, Ramon B.
Gould & Goodrich
Gun Leather Limited
Gun Works, The
Gunfitters, The
Gunsite Training Center
Gusty Winds Corp.
Hafner Creations, Inc.
HandiCrafts Unltd.
Hebard Guns, Gil
Hellweg Ltd.
Henigson & Associates, Steve
High North Products, Inc.
Hill Speed Leather, Ernie
Holster Shop, The
Horseshoe Leather Products
Hoyt Holster Co., Inc.
Hume, Don
Hunter Co., Inc.
John's Custom Leather
Joy Enterprises
Jumbo Sports Products
Kane Products, Inc.
Keller Co., The
Kirkpatrick Leather Co.
Kolpin Mfg., Inc.
Korth
Kramer Handgun Leather, Inc.
L.A.R. Manufacturing, Inc.
Law Concealment Systems, Inc.
Lawrence Leather Co.
Leather Arsenal
Lone Star Gunleather
Magnolia Sports, Inc.
Markell, Inc.
Michaels of Oregon Co.
Minute Man High Tech. Ind.
Mixson Corp.
Nelson Combat Leather, Bruce
Noble Co., Jim
No-Sho Mfg. Co.
Null Holsters Ltd., K.L.
Ojala Holsters, Arvo
Oklahoma Leather Products, Inc.
Old West Reproductions, Inc.
Pace Marketing, Inc.
Pathfinder Sports Leather
Protektor Model
PWL Gunleather
Renegade
Ringler Custom Leather Co.
Rybka Custom Leather Equipment, Thad
Safariland Ltd., Inc.
Safety Speed Holster, Inc.
Savana Sports, Inc.
Schulz Industries

Second Chance Body Armor
Shoemaker & Sons, Inc., Tex
Silhouette Leathers
Smith Saddlery, Jesse W.
Southwind Sanctions
Sparks, Milt
Stalker, Inc.
Strong Holster Co.
Stuart, V. Pat
Tabler Marketing
Texas Longhorn Arms, Inc.

Top-Line USA Inc.
Torel, Inc.
Triple-K Mfg. Co., Inc.
Tyler Mfg.-Dist., Melvin
Uncle Mike's
Venus Industries
Viking Leathercraft, Inc.
Walt's Custom Leather
Whinnery, Walt
Whitestone Lumber Corp.
Wild Bill's Originals

LABELS, BOXES, CARTRIDGE HOLDERS

Accuracy Products, S.A.
Ballistic Products, Inc.
Berry's Mfg. Inc.
Brown Co., E. Arthur
Cabinet Mountain Outfitters Scents &
    Lures
Corbin, Inc.
Crane & Crane Ltd.
Del Rey Products
DeSantis Holster & Leather Goods, Inc.
Dyson & Son Ltd., Peter
Fitz Pistol Grip Co.
Flambeau Products Corp.
Galati International

J&J Products Co.
King & Co.
Kolpin Mfg., Inc.
Lakewood Products, Inc.
Loadmaster
Michaels of Oregon Co.
Midway Arms, Inc.
Monte Kristo Pistol Grip Co.
MTM Molded Products Co., Inc.
Noble Co., Jim
Pendleton Royal
Scharch Mfg., Inc.
Sinclair International, Inc.
Uncle Mike's

LOAD TESTING AND PRODUCT TESTING,
(Chronographing, Ballistic Studies)

Ammunition Consulting Services, Inc.
Ballistic Research
Briese Bullet Co., Inc.
Bustani Appraisers, Leo
Clerke Co., J.A.
D&H Precision Tooling
Dead Eye's Sport Center
Defense Training International, Inc.
DGR Custom Rifles
Duane's Gun Repair
Farr Studio, Inc.
Hank's Gun Shop
Hensler, Jerry
High North Products, Inc.
High Performance International
Hoelscher, Virgil
Jackalope Gun Shop
Jensen Bullets
Jones, J.D.
Jurras, L.E.

Lomont Precision Bullets
Maionchi-L.M.I.
Master Class Bullets
McMurdo, Lynn
Moreton/Fordyce Enterprises
Multiplex International
Neutralizer Police Munitions
Newman Gunshop
Nowlin Custom Mfg.
Oil Rod and Gun Shop
Ransom International Corp.
R.I.S. Co., Inc.
Rupert's Gun Shop
Spencer's Custom Guns
SSK Industries
Whildin & Sons Ltd., E.H.
White Laboratory, Inc., H.P.
Whitestone Lumber Corp.
X-Spand Target Systems

MUZZLE-LOADING GUNS, BARRELS AND EQUIPMENT

ABS Co. Inc./Lothar Walther
Accuracy Unlimited (Littleton, CO)
Ackerman & Co.
Adkins, Luther
Allen Manufacturing
American Bullets
Anderson Manufacturing Co., Inc.
Armi San Paolo
Armoury, Inc., The
Beauchamp & Son, Inc.
Beaver Lodge
Bentley, John
Birdsong & Associates, W.E.
Blackhawk East
Blackhawk West
Blount, Inc.
Blue and Gray Products, Inc.
Boyds' Gunstock Industries, Inc.
Bridgers Best
Buckskin Machine Works
Buffalo Bullet Co., Inc.
Burgess & Son Gunsmiths, R.W.
Butler Creek Corp.
Cache La Poudre Rifleworks
California Sights
Camas Hot Springs Mfg.
Cash Manufacturing Co., Inc.
CenterMark
Chambers Flintlocks, Ltd., Jim
Chopie Mfg., Inc.
Cimarron Arms
Cogar's Gunsmithing
Colonial Repair
Colt Blackpowder Arms Co.
Cousin Bob's Mountain Products
Cumberland Arms
Cumberland Knife & Gun Works
Curly Maple Stock Blanks
CVA
Dangler, Homer L.
Day & Sons, Inc., Leonard
deHaas Barrels

Delhi Gun House
Dewey Mfg. Co., Inc., J.
DGS, Inc.
Dilliott Gunsmithing, Inc.
Dixie Gun Works
Dyson & Son Ltd., Peter
Eades' Muzzleloader Builders' Supply,
    Don
EMF Co., Inc.
Euroarms of America, Inc.
Eutaw Co., Inc., The
Fautheree, Andy
Feken, Dennis
Fellowes, Ted
Flintlocks, Etc.
Forster Products
Fort Hill Gunstocks
Frontier
GOEX, Inc.
Golden Age Arms Co.
Gun Works, The
Hege Jagd-u. Sporthandels, GmbH
Hoppe's Div.
Hornady Mfg. Co.
House of Muskets, Inc., The
Hunkeler, A.
Jamison's Forge Works
Jones Co., Dale
JSL (Hereford) Ltd.
K&M Industries, Inc.
Kennedy Firearms
L&R Lock Co.
Legend Products Corp.
Lite Tek International
Log Cabin Sport Shop
Lutz Engraving, Ron
Lyman
McCann's Muzzle-Gun Works
Michaels of Oregon Co.
MMP
Modern MuzzleLoading, Inc.
Montana Precision Swaging

MSC Industrial Supply Co.
Mt. Alto Outdoor Products
Mushroom Express Bullet Co.
Muzzleloaders Etcetera, Inc.
Navy Arms Co.
North Star West
October Country
Oklahoma Leather Products, Inc.
Olson, Myron
Orion Rifle Barrel Co.
Ox-Yoke Originals, Inc.
Pedersoli, Davide & C.
Pioneer Arms Co.
R.E. Davis
Rusty Duck Premium Gun Care Products
R.V.I.
S&B Industries
S&S Firearms
Selsi Co., Inc.
Shooter's Choice
Sile Distributors
Single Shot, Inc.
Slings 'N Things, Inc.
Southern Bloomer Mfg. Co.
SPG Lubricants

Starr Trading Co., Jedediah
Stone Mountain Arms
Storey, Dale A.
Sturm, Ruger & Co., Inc.
TDP Industries, Inc.
Tennessee Valley Mfg.
Thompson Bullet Lube Co.
Thompson/Center Arms
Thunder Mountain Arms
Tiger-Hunt
Time Precision, Inc.
Track of the Wolf, Inc.
Traditions, Inc.
Treso, Inc.
UFA, Inc.
Uberti, Aldo
Upper Missouri Trading Co.
Venco Industries, Inc.
Warren Muzzleloading Co., Inc.
Wescombe
White Owl Enterprises
Williams Gun Sight Co.
Woodworker's Supply
Wright's Hardwood Gunstock Blanks
Young Country Arms

PISTOLSMITHS

Accuracy Gun Shop
Accuracy Unlimited (Glendale, AZ)
Accurate Plating & Weaponry, Inc.
Ace Custom 45's
Ackley Rifle Barrels, P.O.
Actions by "T"
Adair Custom Shop, Bill
Ahlman Guns
Ahrends, Kim
Aldis Gunsmithing & Shooting Supply
Alpha Precision, Inc.
Alpine's Precision Gunsmithing & Indoor
    Shooting Range
Amodei, Jim
Armament Gunsmithing Co., Inc.
AWC Systems Technology
Baer Custom, Inc., Les
Bain & Davis, Inc.
Baity's Custom Gunworks
Banks, Ed
Bar-Sto Precision Machine
Bear Arms
Behlert Precision
Bellm Contenders
Bengtson Arms Co., L.
Bowen Classic Arms Corp.
Brian, C.T.
Broken Gun Ranch
Campbell, Dick
Cannon's Guns
Caraville Manufacturing
Cellini, Inc., Vito Francesca
Clark Custom Guns, Inc.
Colonial Repair
Corkys Gun Clinic
Costa, David
Craig Custom Ltd.
Curtis Custom Shop
Custom Firearms
Custom Gunsmiths
D&L Sports
Davis Service Center, Bill
D.O.C. Specialists, Inc.
Ellicott Arms, Inc./Woods Pistolsmithing
EMF Co., Inc.
Ferris Firearms
Fisher Custom Firearms
Francesca, Inc.
Frielich Police Equipment
Garthwaite, Jim
Giron, Robert E.
Greider Precision
Guncraft Sports, Inc.
Gunsite Gunsmithy
Gunsite Training Center
Gunsmithing Ltd.
Hamilton, Keith
Hank's Gun Shop
Hanson's Gun Center, Dick
Hardison, Charles
Harris-McMillan Gunworks
Hebard Guns, Gil
Heinie Specialty Products
High Bridge Arms, Inc.
Highline Machine Co.
Hoag, James W.
Intermountain Arms & Tackle, Inc.
Irwin, Campbell H.
Island Pond Gun Shop

Ivanoff, Thomas G.
Jacobson, Teddy
Jarvis Gunsmithing, Inc.
Jensen's Custom Ammunition
Johnston, James
Jones, J.D.
J.P. Enterprises, Inc.
Jungkind, Reeves C.
K-D, Inc.
Ken's Gun Specialties
Kilham & Co.
Kimball, Gary
Kleinendorst, K.W.
Kopp, Terry K.
La Clinique du .45
LaRocca Gun Works, Inc.
Lawson, John G.
Lee's Red Ramps
Leckie Professional Gunsmithing
Linebaugh Custom Sixguns & Rifle Works
List Precision Engineering
Lock's Philadelphia Gun Exchange
Long, George F.
Mac's .45 Shop
Mahony, Philip Bruce
Marent, Rudolf
Marvel, Alan
Mathews & Son, Inc., George E.
Maxi-Mount
McCann's Machine & Gun Shop
MCS, Inc.
Mid-America Recreation, Inc.
Middlebrooks Custom Shop
Miller Custom
Mitchell's Accuracy Shop
MJK Gunsmithing, Inc.
Mo's Competitor Supplies
Mullis Guncraft
Mustra's Custom Guns, Inc., Carl
Nastoff's 45 Shop, Inc., Steve
North Fork Custom Gunsmithing
Novak's Inc.
Nowlin Custom Mfg.
Oglesby & Oglesby Gunmakers, Inc.
Pace Marketing, Inc.
Pardini Armi Srl
Paris, Frank J.
Pasadena Gun Center
Peacemaker Specialists
PEM's Mfg. Co.
Performance Specialists
Peterson Gun Shop, Inc., A.W.
Pierce Pistols
Plaxco, J. Michael
Precision Specialties
Randco UK
Ries, Chuck
Rim Pac Sports, Inc.
Robar Co.'s, Inc., The
Rogers Gunsmithing, Bob
Sanders Custom Gun Service
Scott, McDougall & Associates
Seecamp Co., Inc., L.W.
Shell Shack
Shooter Shop, The
Shooters Supply
Sight Shop, The
Sipes Gun Shop
S.K. Guns, Inc.

Smith & Wesson
Spokhandguns, Inc.
Springfield, Inc.
SSK Industries
Starnes, Ken
Steger, James R.
Strawbridge, Victor W.
Swampfire Shop, The
Swenson's 45 Shop, A.D.
Thompson, Randall
300 Gunsmith Service, Inc.
Thurston Sports, Inc.
Tom's Gun Repair

T.S.W. Conversions, Inc.
Ulrich, Doc & Bud
Unick's Gunsmithing
Vic's Gun Refinishing
Volquartsen Custom Ltd.
Walker Arms Co., Inc.
Walters Industries
Wardell Precision Handguns Ltd.
Weigand Combat Handguns, Inc.
Wessinger Custom Guns & Engraving
Williams Gun Sight Co.
Williamson Precision Gunsmithing
Wilson's Gun Shop

REBORING AND RERIFLING

Ackley Rifle Barrels, P.O.
Bauska Barrels
Bellm Contenders
Blackstar Barrel Accurizing
Flaig's
H&S Liner Service
Ivanoff, Thomas G.
Jackalope Gun Shop
K-D, Inc.
Kopp, Terry K.
LaBounty Precision Reboring
Matco, Inc.
Mid-America Recreation, Inc.
Morrow, Bud
Pence Precision Barrels

Redman's Rifling & Reboring
Rice, Keith
Ridgetop Sporting Goods
Schumakers Gun Shop, William
Shaw, Inc., E.R.
Siegrist Gun Shop
Sonora Rifle Barrel Co.
Starnes Gunmaker, Ken
300 Gunsmith Service, Inc.
Tom's Gun Repair
Van Patten, J.W.
Wessinger Custom Guns & Engraving
West, Robert G.
White Rock Tool & Die

RELOADING TOOLS AND ACCESSORIES

AC Dyna-tite Corp.
Acadian Ballistic Specialties
Accuracy Components Co.
Action Bullets, Inc.
Advance Car Mover Co., Rowell Div.
Alpha LaFranck Enterprises
American Products Co.
Ammo Load, Inc.
Armfield Custom Bullets
Bald Eagle Precision Machine Co.
Ballard Built
Ballistic Products, Inc.
Ballisti-Cast, Inc.
Barlett, J.
Bear Reloaders
Beeline Custom Bullets
Belltown, Ltd.
Ben's Machines
Berry's Mfg. Inc.
Blackhawk East
Blount, Inc.
Brass-Tech Industries
Break-Free, Inc.
Brobst, Jim
Brown Co., E. Arthur
BRP, Inc. High Performance Cast Bullets
Brynin, Milton
B-Square Co., Inc.
Buck Stix
Bull Mountain Rifle Co.
Bullet Mills
Bullet Swaging Supply, Inc.
Bullseye Bullets
C&D Special Products
Camdex, Inc.
Canyon Cartridge Corp.
Carbide Die & Mfg. Co., Inc.
Carroll Bullets
Case Sorting System
CCI
C-H Tool & Die Corp.
Chem-Pak, Inc.
CheVron Case Master
Clark Custom Guns, Inc.
Clymer Manufacturing Co., Inc.
Coats, Mrs. Lester
Colorado Shooter's Supply
Competitor Corp., Inc.
CONKKO
Cook Engineering Service
Corbin, Inc.
Crouse's Country Cover
Curtis Gun Shop
Davis, Don
Davis Products, Mike
D.C.C. Enterprises
Denver Instrument Co.
Dever Co., Jack
Dewey Mfg. Co., Inc., J.
Dillon Precision Prods., Inc.
Double A Ltd.
Dutchman's Firearms, Inc., The
E&L Mfg., Inc.

Eagan, Donald V.
Eezox, Inc.
Engineered Accessories
Essex Metals
F&A Inc.
Federal Cartridge Co.
Feken, Dennis
Ferguson, Bill
Fisher Enterprises
Fish-N-Hunt, Inc.
Fitz Pistol Grip Co.
Flambeau Products Corp.
Forgett Jr., Valmore J.
Forgreens Tool Mfg., Inc.
Forster Products
4-D Custom Die Co.
Fremont Tool Works
Fusilier Bullets
G&C Bullet Co., Inc.
Gage Manufacturing
Gehmann, Walter
Goddard, Allen
GOEX, Inc.
Gonzalez Guns, Ramon B.
"Gramps" Antique Cartridges
Graphics Direct
Graves Co.
Green, Arthur S.
Greenwood Precision
Grizzly Bullets
Gun Works, The
Guns
Hanned Line, The
Hanned Precision
Hardin Specialty Dist.
Harrell's Precision
Harris Enterprises
Harrison Bullets
Haselbauer Products, Jerry
Haydon Shooters' Supply, Russ
Heidenstrom Bullets
Hensley & Gibbs
Hirtenberger Aktiengesellschaft
Hoch Custom Bullet Moulds
Hoehn Sales, Inc.
Hoelscher, Virgil
Hollywood Engineering
Hondo Industries
Hornady Mfg. Co.
Howell Machine
Huntington Die Specialties
IMI Services USA, Inc.
INTEC International, Inc.
Iosso Products
J&D Components
J&L Superior Bullets
Jantz Supply
Javelina Products
JGS Precision Tool Mfg.
JLK Bullets
Jonad Corp.
Jones Moulds, Paul
K&M Services

K&S Mfg. Inc.
Kapro Mfg. Co., Inc.
Kent Cartridge Mfg. Co. Ltd.
King & Co.
KLA Enterprises
LAP Systems Group, N.A.
Lathrop's, Inc.
LBT
Lee Precision, Inc.
Legend Products Corp.
Liberty Metals
Liberty Shooting Supplies
Lindsley Arms Cartridge Co.
Littleton, J.F.
Lortone, Inc.
Loweth Firearms, Richard
Luch Metal Merchants, Barbara
Lyman Instant Targets, Inc.
Lyman Products Corp.
MA Systems
Magma Engineering Co.
Magnus Bullets
Mag-Pack Corp.
MarMik Inc.
Master Class Bullets
Match Prep
McKillen & Heyer, Inc.
MCRW Associates Shooting Supplies
MCS, Inc.
MEC, Inc.
Midway Arms, Inc.
Miller Engineering
MI-TE Bullets
MKL Service Co.
MMP
Mo's Competitor Supplies
MoLoc Bullets
Montana Precision Swaging
Monte Kristo Pistol Grip Co.
Mt. Baldy Bullet Co.
MTM Molded Products Co., Inc.
Naval Ordnance Works
Necromancer Industries, Inc.
NEI Handtools, Inc.
Niemi Engineering, W.B.
Noble Co., Jim
North American Shooting Systems
North Devon Firearms Services
October Country
OK Weber, Inc.
Old West Bullet Moulds
Old Western Scrounger, Inc.
Omark Industries
Pace Marketing, Inc.
Paco's
Pedersoli, Davide & C.
Peerless Alloy, Inc.
Pend Oreille Sport Shop
Petro-Explo, Inc.
Pinetree Bullets
Plum City Ballistic Range
Policlips North America
Pomeroy, Robert
Ponsness/Warren
Powder Valley Services
Precision Castings & Equipment, Inc.
Precision Components
Precision Reloading, Inc.
Prime Reloading
Prolix
Pro-Shot Products, Inc.
Protector Mfg. Co., Inc., The
Quinetics Corp.
R&D Engineering & Manufacturing
Ransom International Corp.
Rapine Bullet Mould Mfg. Co.
Raytech
RCBS
R.D.P. Tool Co., Inc.

Redding Reloading Equipment
R.E.I.
Reloading Specialties, Inc.
Rice, Keith
Riebe Co., W.J.
RIG Products
R.I.S. Co., Inc.
R.M. Precision, Inc.
Roberts Products
Rochester Lead Works, Inc.
Rolston, Inc., Fred W.
Rooster Laboratories
Rorschach Precision Products
Rosenthal, Brad and Sallie
Rucker Ammunition Co.
SAECO
Sandia Die & Cartridge Co.
Saunders Gun & Machine Shop
Saville Iron Co.
Scharch Mfg., Inc.
Scot Powder Co. of Ohio, Inc.
Scott, Dwight
Shiloh Creek
Shooting Components Marketing
Sierra Bullets
Sierra Specialty Prod. Co.
Silver Eagle Machining
Simmons, Jerry
Sinclair International, Inc.
Skip's Machine
S.L.A.P. Industries
Small Custom Mould & Bullet Co.
SOS Products Co.
Speer Products
Spencer's Custom Guns
Sport Flite Manufacturing Co.
Sportsman Supply Co.
Stalwart Corp.
Star Machine Works
Stillwell, Robert
Stoney Point Products, Inc.
Talon Mfg. Co., Inc.
Tamarack Products, Inc.
Taracorp Industries
TCSR
Tetra Gun Lubricants
Thompson Bullet Lube Co.
Timber Heirloom Products
Time Precision, Inc.
TMI Products
Trammco, Inc.
Tru-Square Metal Prods., Inc.
TTM
Tyler Scott, Inc.
Varner's Service
Vega Tool Co.
VibraShine, Inc.
Vibra-Tek Co.
VihtaVuori Oy
VihtaVuori Oy/Kaltron-Pettibone
Von Minden Gunsmithing Services
Walters, John
Webster Scale Mfg. Co.
Welsh, Bud
Werner, Carl
Westfield Engineering
White Rock Tool & Die
Whitestone Lumber Corp.
Whitetail Design & Engineering Ltd.
Widener's Reloading & Shooting Supply
William's Gun Shop, Ben
Wilson, Inc., L.E.
Wise Guns, Dale
Wolf's Western Traders
Woodleigh
Yesteryear Armory & Supply
Young Country Arms
Zero Ammunition Co., Inc.

SCOPES, MOUNTS, ACCESSORIES, OPTICAL EQUIPMENT

Accuracy Innovations, Inc.
Ace Custom 45's
ADCO International
Adventurer's Outpost
Aimpoint, Inc.
Aimtech Mount Systems
Air Venture
Ajax Custom Grips, Inc.
Alley Supply Co.
American Import Co. The/Export Division
Anderson Manufacturing Co., Inc.
Apel GmbH, Ernst
Applied Laser Systems, Inc.
A.R.M.S., Inc.
Armscorp USA, Inc.

Aro-Tek, Ltd.
Baer Custom, Inc., Les
Barrett Firearms Mfg., Inc.
Bausch & Lomb, Inc.
Beaver Park Products, Inc.
Blount, Inc.
Bohemia Arms Co.
Brown Co., E. Arthur
Brownells, Inc.
Browning Arms Co.
Brunton U.S.A.
B-Square Co., Inc.
Bull Mountain Rifle Co.
Bullberry Barrel Works, Ltd.
Burris

Bushnell
Butler Creek Corp.
California Grip
Celestron International
Center Lock Scope Rings
Champion's Choice, Inc.
Clark Custom Guns, Inc.
Clearview Mfg. Co., Inc.
Combat Military Ordnance Ltd.
Compass Industries, Inc.
Concept Development Corp.
Conetrol Scope Mounts
CRDC Laser Systems Group
Creedmoor Sports, Inc.
Custom Quality Products, Inc.
D&H Prods. Co., Inc.
D.C.C. Enterprises
Del-Sports, Inc.
DHB Products
Eagle International, Inc.
Eagle Mfg. & Engineering
Edmund Scientific Co.
Ednar, Inc.
Eggleston, Jere D.
Emerging Technologies, Inc.
Europtik Ltd.
Excaliber Enterprises
Faith Associates, Inc.
Farr Studio, Inc.
Feather Industries, Inc.
Firearms Supplies Inc.
Forster Products
From Jena
Fujinon, Inc.
Galati International
G.G. & G.
Gonzalez Guns, Ramon B.
GSI, Inc.
Guns, (Div. of D.C. Engineering, Inc.)
Guns, Gear & Gadgets, L.L.C.
Gunsite Training Center
Hakko Co. Ltd.
Hammerli USA
Harris-McMillan Gunworks
Hermann Leather Co., H.J.
Hertel & Reuss
Hiptmayer, Armurier
Holland's
House of Muskets, Inc., The
Ironsighter Co.
Jackalope Gun Shop
JagerSport, Ltd.
Jeffredo Gunsight
Jenco Sales, Inc.
Jewell, Arnold W.
Johnson Gunsmithing, Inc., Neal G.
Jones, J.D.
JSL (Hereford) Ltd.
Kahles USA
KDF, Inc.
Kelbly, Inc.
Keng's Firearms Specialty, Inc.
Kesselring Gun Shop
Kmount
Kowa Optimed, Inc.
Kris Mounts
KVH Industries, Inc.
Kwik Mount Corp.
L&S Technologies, Inc.
LaFrance Specialties
Laser Devices, Inc.
Laseraim
LaserMax
Lectro Science, Inc.
Lee Co., T.K.
Leica USA, Inc.
Leupold & Stevens, Inc.
Lightforce USA
List Precision Engineering
Lite Tek International
Lohman Mfg. Co., Inc.
Mac's .45 Shop
Maxi-Mount

McCann's Machine & Gun Shop
McMillan Optical Gunsight Co.
MDS
Meier Works
Merit Corp.
Michaels of Oregon Co.
Military Armament Corp.
Millett Sights
Mirador Optical Corp.
MWG Co.
New Democracy, Inc.
Nikon, Inc.
Nowlin Custom Mfg.
Oakshore Electronic Sights, Inc.
Old Western Scrounger, Inc.
Olympic Optical Co.
Orchard Park Enterprise
Outdoor Connection, Inc., The
Pace Marketing, Inc.
Parsons Optical Mfg. Co.
PECAR Herbert Schwarz, GmbH
Peltor, Inc.
PEM's Mfg. Co.
Pentax Corp.
Pilkington Gun Co.
Precise Metalsmithing Enterprises
Precision Sport Optics
Premier Reticles
Ranch Products
Randolph Engineering, Inc.
Ranging, Inc.
Redfield, Inc.
Rice, Keith
Rocky Mountain High Sports Glasses
S&K Mfg. Co.
Sanders Custom Gun Service
Saunders Gun & Machine Shop
Scope Control Inc.
ScopLevel
Seattle Binocular & Scope Repair Co.
Selsi Co., Inc.
Sightron, Inc.
Silencio/Safety Direct
Simmons Enterprises, Ernie
Simmons Outdoor Corp.
Sinclair International, Inc.
Six Enterprises
SKAN A.R.
Speer Products
Spencer's Custom Guns
Sportsmatch Ltd.
Springfield, Inc.
SSK Industries
Sure Shot of LA, Inc.
SwaroSports, Inc.
Swarovski Optik North America Ltd.
Swift Instruments, Inc.
Talley, Dave
Tank's Rifle Shop
Tapco, Inc.
Tasco Sales, Inc.
Tele-Optics
Thompson/Center Arms
Time Precision, Inc.
Uncle Mike's
Unertl Optical Co., Inc., John
United Binocular Co.
United States Optics Technologies, Inc.
Volquartsen Custom Ltd.
Warne Manufacturing Co.
Warren Muzzleloading Co., Inc.
WASP Shooting Systems
Weaver Products
Weaver Scope Repair Service
Weigand Combat Handguns, Inc.
Wessinger Custom Guns & Engraving
Western Design
Westfield Engineering
White Rock Tool & Die
Wichita Arms, Inc.
Williams Gun Sight Co.
Zeiss Optical, Carl

SHOOTING/TRAINING SCHOOLS

Accuracy Gun Shop
Alpine Precision Gunsmithing & Indoor
  Shooting Range
American Small Arms Academy
Auto Arms
Bob's Tactical Indoor Shooting Range &
  Gun Shop
Chapman Academy of Practical Shooting
Chelsea Gun Club of New York City, Inc.
Clark Custom Guns, Inc.
CQB Training

Daisy Mfg. Co.
Defense Training International, Inc.
Dowtin Gunworks
Executive Protection Institute
Firearm Training Center, The
Firearms Academy of Seattle
G.H. Enterprises Ltd.
Gunfitters, The
Gunsite Training Center
InSights Training Center, Inc.
International Shootists, Inc.

Jensen's Custom Ammunition
Jensen's Firearms Acadamy
J.P. Enterprises, Inc.
McMurdo, Lynn
Mendez, John A.
Nevada Pistol Academy Inc.
North Mountain Pines Training Center
Pace Marketing, Inc.
Pacific Pistolcraft
Quigley's Personal Protection Strategies,
  Paxton
Robar Co.'s, Inc., The

SAFE
Scott, McDougall & Associates
Shooter's World
Shooting Gallery, The
Smith & Wesson
Specialty Gunsmithing
Spencer's Custom Guns
Starlight Training Center, Inc.
Tactical Defense Institute
300 Gunsmith Service, Inc.
Western Missouri Shooters Alliance
Yavapai Firearms Academy Ltd.

SIGHTS, METALLIC

Alpec Team, Inc.
Andela Tool & Machine, Inc.
Aro-Tek, Ltd.
Baer Custom, Inc., Les
Bob's Gun Shop
Bo-Mar Tool & Mfg. Co.
Bond Custom Firearms
Bowen Classic Arms Corp.
Bradley Gunsight Co.
Brown Co., E. Arthur
Bullberry Barrel Works, Ltd.
California Sights
Champion's Choice, Inc.
C-More Systems
Colonial Repair
CRL, Inc.
DHB Products
Engineered Accessories
Evans Gunsmithing
Fautheree, Andy
Gun Doctor, The
Guns, (Div. of D.C. Engineering, Inc.)
Gunsite Training Center
Heinie Specialty Products
Hesco-Meprolight
House of Muskets, Inc., The
Innovative Weaponry, Inc.
Jackalope Gun Shop
Lee's Red Ramps
List Precision Engineering
Lofland, James W.
L.P.A. Snc

Lyman Instant Targets, Inc.
Lyman Products Corp.
Mac's .45 Shop
Mag-Na-Port International, Inc.
Marble Arms
MCS, Inc.
Meadow Industries
MEC-Gar S.R.L.
Meier Works
Meprolight
Merit Corp.
Mid-America Recreation, Inc.
Millett Sights
MMC
Mo's Competitor Supplies
Novak's Inc.
Oakshore Electronic Sights, Inc.
Pace Marketing, Inc.
Pachmayr Ltd.
PEM's Mfg. Co.
P.M. Enterprises, Inc.
Robar Co.'s, Inc., The
RPM
Starnes Gunmaker, Ken
Talley, Dave
Tank's Rifle Shop
Tapco, Inc.
T.F.C. S.p.A.
Time Precision, Inc.
WASP Shooting Systems
Wichita Arms, Inc.
Williams Gun Sight Co.

TARGETS AND BULLET TRAPS

Action Target, Inc.
American Target
American Whitetail Target Systems
A-Tech Corp.
Barsotti, Bruce
Birchwood Laboratories, Inc.
Blount, Inc.
Blue and Gray Products, Inc.
Caswell International Corp.
Champion's Choice, Inc.
Cunningham Co., Eaton
Curtis Gun Shop
Dapkus Co., Inc., J.G.
Datumtech Corp.
Dayson Arms Ltd.
D.C.C. Enterprises
Detroit-Armor Corp.
Diamond Mfg. Co.
Enguix Import-Export
Epps "Orillia" Ltd., Ellwood
Freeman Animal Targets
G.H. Enterprises Ltd.
Gozon Corp.
Gun Parts Corp., The
Hiti-Schuch, Atelier Wilma
Hornady Mfg. Co.
Hunterjohn
Jackalope Gun Shop

JWH = Software
Kennebec Journal
Kleen-Bore, Inc.
Littler Sales Co.
Lyman Instant Targets, Inc.
Lyman Products Corp.
Marksman Products
MSR Targets
National Target Co.
N.B.B., Inc.
North American Shooting Systems
Nu-Teck
Outers Laboratories
Ox-Yoke Originals, Inc.
PlumFire Press, Inc.
Red Star Target Co.
Rockwood Corp., Speedwell Div.
Rocky Mountain Target Co.
Schaefer Shooting Sports
Seligman Shooting Products
Shooters Supply
Shoot-N-C Inc.
Stoney Baroque Shooters Supply
Thompson Target Technology
Trius Products, Inc.
World of Targets
X-Spand Target Systems
Zriny's Metal Targets

TRIGGERS, RELATED EQUIPMENT

Actions by "T"
B&D Trading Co., Inc.
Baer Custom, Inc., Les
Bob's Gun Shop
Bond Custom Firearms
Boyds' Gunstock Industries, Inc.
Bull Mountain Rifle Co.
Clark Custom Guns, Inc.
Cycle Dynamics, Inc.
Electronic Trigger Systems, Inc.
Eversull Co., Inc., K.
Guns, (Div. of D.C. Engineering, Inc.)
Hoelscher, Virgil
Holland's
Jackalope Gun Shop
Jacobson, Teddy

Jewell, Arnold W.
J.P. Enterprises, Inc.
List Precision Engineering
Mahony, Philip Bruce
Master Lock Co.
Mid-America Recreation, Inc.
Pace Marketing, Inc.
PEM's Mfg. Co.
Penrod Precision
Perazone, Brian
S&B Industries
Tarnham Supply
Tennessee Valley Mfg.
Time Precision, Inc.
Tyler Mfg.-Dist., Melvin

MANUFACTURERS' DIRECTORY

A

A&B Industries, Inc. (See Top-Line USA, Inc.)

AC Dyna-tite Corp., 155 Kelly St., P.O. Box 0984, Elk Grove Village, IL 60007/708-593-5566; FAX: 708-593-1304

Acadian Ballistic Specialties, P.O. Box 61, Covington, LA 70434

Acculube II, Inc., 4366 Shackleford Rd., Norcross, GA 30093-2912

Accupro Gun Care, 15512-109 Ave., Surrey, BC U3R 7E8, CANADA/604-583-7807

Accuracy Components Co., P.O. Box 60034, Renton, WA 98058/206-255-4577

Accuracy Gun Shop, 7818 Wilkerson Ct., San Diego, CA 92111/619-282-8500

Accuracy Innovations, Inc., P.O. Box 376, New Paris, PA 15554/814-839-4517; FAX: 814-839-2601

Accuracy Products, S.A., 14 rue de Lawsanne, Brussels, 1060 BELGIUM/32-2-539-34-42; FAX: 32-2-539-39-60

Accuracy Unlimited, 7479 S. DePew St., Littleton, CO 80123

Accuracy Unlimited, 16036 N. 49 Ave., Glendale, AZ 85306/602-978-9089

Accurate Arms Co., Inc., Rt. 1, Box 167, McEwen, TN 37101/615-729-4207, 800-416-3006; FAX 615-729-4217

Accurate Plating & Weaponry, Inc., 1937 Calumet St., Clearwater, FL 34625/813-449-9112

Accu-Tek, 4525 Carter Ct., Chino, CA 91710/909-627-2404; FAX: 909-627-7817

Ace Custom 45's, 1880½ Upper Turtle Creek Rd., Kerrville, TX 78028/210-257-4290; FAX: 210-257-5724

Ackerman & Co., 16 Cortez St., Westfield, MA 01085/413-568-8008

Ackley Rifle Barrels, P.O. (See Bellm Contenders)

Action Bullets, Inc., 1811 W. 13th Ave., Denver, CO 80204/303-595-9636; FAX: 303-893-9161

Action Products, Inc., 22 N. Mulberry St., Hagerstown, MD 21740/301-797-1414; FAX: 301-733-2073

Action Target, Inc., P.O. Box 636, Provo, UT 84603/801-377-8033; FAX: 801-377-8096

Actions by "T", Teddy Jacobson, 16315 Redwood Forest Ct., Sugar Land, TX 77478/713-277-4008

Ad Hominem, RR 3, Orillia, Ont. L3V 6H3, CANADA/705-689-5303

Adair Custom Shop, Bill, 2886 Westridge, Carrollton, TX 75006

Adams, John J., 87 Acorn Rd., Dennis, MA 02638/508-385-7971

Adams, John J., 87 Acorn Rd., Dennis, MA 02638/508-385-7971

ADCO International, 10 Cedar St., Unit 17, Woburn, MA 01801/617-935-1799; FAX: 617-935-1011

Adkins, Luther, 1292 E. McKay Rd., Shelbyville, IN 46176-9353/317-392-3795

Advance Car Mover Co., Rowell Div., P.O. Box 1, 240 N. Depot St., Juneau, WI 53039/414-386-4464; FAX: 414-386-4416

Adventure Game Calls, R.D. #1, Leonard Rd., Spencer, NY 14883/607-589-4611

Adventurer's Outpost, P.O. Box 70, Cottonwood, AZ 86326/800-762-7471; FAX: 602-634-8781

AFSCO Ammunition, 731 W. Third St., P.O. Box L, Owen, WI 54460/715-229-2516

Ahlman Guns, Rt. 1, Box 20, Morristown, MN 55052/507-685-4243; FAX: 507-685-4247

Ahrends, Kim, Custom Firearms, Box 203, Clarion, IA 50525/515-532-3449

Aimpoint, Inc., 580 Herndon Parkway, Suite 500, Herndon, VA 22070/703-471-6828; FAX: 703-689-0575

Aimtech Mount Systems, P.O. Box 223, 101 Inwood Acres, Thomasville, GA 31799/912-226-4313; FAX: 912-227-0222

Air Rifle Specialists, 311 East Water St., Elmira, NY 14901/607-734-7340; FAX: 607-733-3261

Air Venture, 9752 E. Flower St., Bellflower, CA 90706/310-867-6355

Air Werks International, 403 W. 24th St., Norfolk, VA 23517-1204/800-247-9375

Airgun Repair Centre, 3227 Garden Meadows, Lawrenceburg, IN 47025/812-637-1463; FAX: 812-637-1463

Airguns-R-Us, 300 S. Campbell, Columbia, TN 38401

Airrow (See Swivel Machine Works, Inc.)

Ajax Custom Grips, Inc., Div. of A. Jack Rosenberg & Sons, 9130 Viscount Row, Dallas, TX 75247/214-630-8890; FAX: 214-630-4942

Aker Leather Products, 2248 Main St., Suite 6, Chula Vista, CA 91911/619-

423-5182; FAX: 619-423-1363

Alaska Bullet Works, P.O. Box 54, Douglas, AK 99824/907-789-3834

Aldis Gunsmithing & Shooting Supply, 502 S. Montezuma St., Prescott, AZ 86303/602-445-6723; FAX: 602-445-6763

Alessi Holsters, Inc., 2465 Niagara Falls Blvd., Amherst, NY 14228-3527/716-691-5615

Alfano, Sam, 36180 Henry Gaines Rd., Pearl River, LA 70452/504-863-3364; FAX: 504-863-7715

Allard, Gary, Creek Side Metal & Woodcrafters, Fishers Hill, VA 22626/703-465-3903

Allen, Richard L., 339 Grove Ave., Prescott, AZ 86301/602-778-1237

Allen Mfg., 6449 Hodgson Rd., Circle Pines, MN 55014/612-429-8231

Alley Supply Co., P.O. Box 848, Gardnerville, NV 89410/702-782-3800

Allred Bullet Co., 932 Evergreen Drive, Logan, UT 84321/801-752-6983

Alpec Team, Inc., 201 Ricken Backer Cir., Livermore, CA 94550/510-606-8245; FAX: 510-606-4279

Alpha 1 Drop Zone, 2121 N. Tyler, Wichita, KS 67212/316-729-0800

Alpha LaFranck Enterprises, P.O. Box 81072, Lincoln, NE 68501/402-466-3193

Alpha Precision, Inc., 2765-B Preston Rd. NE, Good Hope, GA 30641/404-267-6163

Alpine's Precision Gunsmithing & Indoor Shooting Range, 2401 Government Way, Coeur d'Alene, ID 83814/208-765-3559; FAX: 208-765-3559

Altamont Co., 901 N. Church St., P.O. Box 309, Thomasboro, IL 61878/217-643-3125, 800-626-5774; FAX: 217-643-7973

AmBr Software Group Ltd., The, P.O. Box 301, Reistertown, MD 21136-0301/410-526-4106; FAX: 410-526-7212

American Ammunition, 3545 NW 71st St., Miami, FL 33147/305-835-7400; FAX: 305-694-0037

American Arms & Ordnance, Inc., P.O. Box 2691, 1303 S. College Ave., Bryan, TX 77805/409-822-4983

American Arms, Inc., 715 Armour Rd., N. Kansas City, MO 64116/816-474-3161; FAX: 816-474-1225

American Derringer Corp., 127 N. Lacy Dr., Waco, TX 76705/800-642-7817, 817-799-9111; FAX: 817-799-7935

American Gas & Chemical Co., Ltd., 220 Pegasus Ave., Northvale, NJ 07647/201-767-7300

American Gripcraft, 3230 S. Dodge #2, Tucson, AZ 85713/602-790-1222

American Handgunner Magazine, 591 Camino de la Reina, Suite 200, San Diego, CA 92108/619-297-5350; FAX: 619-297-5353

American Import Co., The/Export Division, 1453 Mission St., San Francisco, CA 94103/415-863-1506; FAX: 415-863-0939

American Pioneer Video, P.O. Box 50049, Bowling Green, KY 42102-2649/800-743-4675

American Products Co., 14729 Spring Valley Road, Morrison, IL 61270/815-772-3336; FAX: 815-772-7921

American Sales & Kirkpatrick, P.O. Box 677, Laredo, TX 78042/210-723-6893; FAX: 210-725-0672

American Small Arms Academy, P.O. Box 12111, Prescott, AZ 86304/602-778-5623

American Target, 1328 S. Jason St., Denver, CO 80223/303-733-0433; FAX: 303-777-0311

American Whitetail Target Systems, P.O. Box 41, 106 S. Church St., Tennyson, IN 47637/812-567-4527

Ames Metal Products Co., 4324 S. Western Blvd., Chicago, IL/312-523-3230; FAX: 312-523-3854

Amherst Arms, P.O. Box 1457, Englewood, FL 34295/813-475-2020

Ammo Load, Inc., 1560 E. Edinger, Suite G, Santa Ana, CA 92705/714-558-8858; FAX: 714-569-0319

Ammunition Consulting Services, Inc., P.O. Box 701084, San Antonio, TX 78270-1084/201-646-9624; FAX: 210-646-0141

Amodei, Jim (See D.O.C. Specialists, Inc.)

Amrine's Gun Shop, 937 La Luna, Ojai, CA 93023/805-646-2376

Andela Tool & Machine, Inc., RD3, Box 246, Richfield Springs, NY 13439

Anderson Manufacturing Co., Inc., P.O. Box 2640, 2741 N. Crosby Rd., Oak Harbor, WA 98277/360-675-7300; FAX: 360-675-3939

Answer Products Co., 1519 Westbury Drive, Davison, MI 48423/810-653-2911

Anthony and George Ltd., Rt. 1, P.O. Box 45, Evington, VA 24550/804-821-8117

Antique American Firearms (See Carlson, Douglas R.)

Antique Arms Co., 1110 Cleveland Ave., Monett, MO 65708/417-235-6501

Apel GmbH, Ernst, Am Kirschberg 3, D-97218 Gerbrunn, GERMANY/0 (931) 70 71 91

Aplan Antiques & Art, James O., HC 80, Box 793-25, Piedmont, SD 57769/605-347-5016

Applied Laser Systems, Inc., 2160 NW Vine St., Grants Pass, OR 97526/503-479-0484; FAX: 503-476-5105

Arco, 3590 S. State Rd. 7, Suite 31, Miramar, FL 33023/305-989-9782; FAX: 305-962-8377

Arkansas Mallard Duck Calls, Rt. Box 182, England, AR 72046/501-842-3597

Armament Gunsmithing Co., Inc., 525 Rt. 22, Hillside, NJ 07205/908-686-0960

Armfield Custom Bullets, 4775 Caroline Drive, San Diego, CA 92115/619-582-7188; FAX: 619-287-3238

Armi San Paolo, via Europa 172-A, I-25062 Concesio, 030-2751725 (BS) ITALY

Armite Laboratories, 1845 Randolph St., Los Angeles, CA 90001/213-587-7768; FAX: 213-587-5075

Armoloy Co. of Ft. Worth, 204 E. Daggett St., Fort Worth, TX 76104/817-332-5604; FAX: 817-335-6517

Armory Publications, P.O. Box 4206, Oceanside, CA 92052-4206/619-757-3930; FAX: 619-722-4108

Armoury, Inc., The, Rt. 202, Box 2340, New Preston, CT 06777/203-868-0001

Arms & Armour Press, Villiers House, 41-47 Strand, London WC2N 5JE ENGLAND/071-839-4900; FAX: 071-839-1804

A.R.M.S., Inc., 230 W. Center St., West Bridgewater, MA 02379-1620/508-584-7816; FAX: 508-588-8045

Arms, Peripheral Data Systems, P.O. Box 1526, Lake Oswego, OR 97035/800-366-5559, 503-697-0533; FAX: 503-697-3337

Aro-Tek, Ltd., 206 Frontage Rd. North, Suite C, Pacific, WA 98047/206-351-2984; FAX: 206-833-4483

Arundel Arms & Ammunition, Inc., A., 24 Defense St., Annapolis, MD 21401/301-224-8683

Arratoonian, Andy (See Horseshoe Leather Products)

Art Jewel Enterprises Ltd., Eagle Business Ctr., 460 Randy Rd., Carol Stream, IL 60188/708-260-0400

Arundel Arms & Ammunition, Inc., A., 24 Defense St., Annapolis, MD 21401/301-224-8683

Ashby Turkey Calls, HCR 5, Box 345, Houston, MO 65483/417-967-3787

Astra Sport, S.A., Apartado 3, 48300 Guernica, Espagne, SPAIN/34-4-6250100; FAX: 34-4-6255186 (U.S. importer—E.A.A. Corp.)

A-Tech Corp., P.O. Box 1281, Cottage Grove, OR 97424

Atlantic Mills, Inc., 1325 Washington Ave., Asbury Park, NJ 07712/800-242-7374

Atlantic Rose, P.O. Box 1305, Union, NJ 07083

Auto Arms, 738 Clearview, San Antonio, TX 78228/512-434-5450

Auto-Ordnance Corp., Williams Lane, West Hurley, NY 12491/914-679-4190; FAX: 914-679-2698

AWC Systems Technology, P.O. Box 41938, Phoenix, AZ 85080-1938/602-780-1050

A Zone Bullets, 2039 Walter Rd., Billings, MT 59105/800-252-3111; 406-248-1961

Aztec International Ltd., P.O. Box 1384, Clarkesville, GA 30523/706-754-7263

B

B&D Trading Co., Inc., 3935 Fair Hill Rd., Fair Oaks, CA 95628/800-334-3790, 916-967-9366; FAX: 916-967-4873

Badger Shooters Supply, Inc., 202 N. Harding, Owen, WI 54460/715-229-2101; FAX: 715-229-2332

Baer Custom, Inc., Les, 29601 34th Ave., Hillsdale, IL 61257/309-658-2716; FAX: 309-658-2610

Bagmaster Mfg., Inc., 2731 Sutton Ave., St. Louis, MO 63143/314-781-8002; FAX: 314-781-3363

Bain & Davis, Inc., 307 E. Valley Blvd., San Gabriel, CA 91776-3522/818-573-4241, 213-283-7449

Baity's Custom Gunworks, 414 2nd St., N. Wilkesboro, NC 28659/919-667-8785

Baker's Leather Goods, Roy, P.O. Box 893, Magnolia, AR 71753/501-234-0344

Bald Eagle Precision Machine Co., 101 Allison St., Lock Haven, PA 17745/717-748-6772; FAX: 717-748-4443

Ballard Built, P.O. Box 1443, Kingsville, TX 78364/512-592-0853

Ballistic Engineering & Software, Inc., 185 N. Park Blvd., Suite 330, Lake Orion, MI 48362/313-391-1074

Ballistic Products, Inc., 20015 75th Ave. North, Corcoran, MN 55340-9456/612-494-9237; FAX: 612-494-9236

Ballistic Program Co., Inc., The, 2417 N. Patterson St., Thomasville, GA 31792/912-228-5739, 800-368-0835

Ballistic Research, 1108 W. May Ave., McHenry, IL 60050/815-385-0037

Ballistica Maximus North, 107 College Park Plaza, Johnstown, PA 15904/814-266-8380

Ballisti-Cast, Inc., Box 383, Parshall, ND 58770/701-862-3324; FAX: 701-862-3331

Banaczkowski Bullets, 56 Victoria Dr., Mount Barker, S.A. 5251 AUSTRALIA

Bandcor Industries, Div. of Man-Sew Corp., 6108 Sherwin Dr., Port Richey, FL 34668/813-848-0432

Bang-Bang Boutique (See Holster Shop, The)

Banks, Ed, 2762 Hwy. 41 N., Ft. Valley, GA 31030/912-987-4665

Bansner's Gunsmithing Specialties, 261 East Main St. Box VH, Adamstown, PA 19501/800-368-2379; FAX: 717-484-0523

Barami Corp., 6689 Orchard Lake Rd. No. 148, West Bloomfield, MI 48322/810-738-0462; FAX: 810-855-4084

Barlett, J., 6641 Kaiser Ave., Fontana, CA 92336-3265

Barnes Bullets, Inc., P.O. Box 215, American Fork, UT 84003/801-756-4222, 800-574-9200; FAX: 801-756-2465

Baron Technology, 62 Spring Hill Rd., Trumbull, CT 06611/203-452-0515; FAX: 203-452-0663

Barrett Firearms Manufacturer, Inc., P.O. Box 1077, Murfreesboro, TN 37133/615-896-2938; FAX: 615-896-7313

Bar-Sto Precision Machine, 73377 Sullivan Rd., P.O. Box 1838, Twentynine Palms, CA 92277/619-367-2747; FAX: 619-367-2407

Bates Engraving, Billy, 2302 Winthrop Dr., Decatur, AL 35603/205-355-3690

Baumannize Custom, 4784 Sunrise Hwy., Bohemia, NY 11716/800-472-4387; FAX: 516-567-0001

Bausch & Lomb, Inc., 42 East Ave., Rochester, NY 14603/913-752-3433, 800-828-5423; FAX: 913-752-3489

Bauska Barrels, 105 9th Ave. W., Kalispell, MT 59901/406-752-7706

Bear Arms, 121 Rhodes St., Jackson, SC 29831/803-471-9859

Bear Hug Grips, Inc., 17230 County Rd. 338, Buena Vista, CO 81211/800-232-7710

Bear Mountain Gun & Tool, 120 N. Plymouth, New Plymouth, ID 83655/208-278-5221; FAX: 208-278-5221

Bear Reloaders, P.O. Box 1613, Akron, OH 44309-1613/216-920-1811

Beartooth Bullets, P.O. Box 491, Dept. HLD, Dover, ID 83825-0491/208-448-1865

Beauchamp & Son, Inc. 160 Rossiter Rd., Richmond, MA 01254/413-698-3822; FAX: 413-698-3866

Beaver Lodge (See Fellowes, Ted)

Beaver Park Products, Inc., 840 J St., Penrose, CO 81240/719-372-6744

Beeline Custom Bullets, P.O. Box 85, Yarmouth, Nova Scotia CANADA B5A 4B1/902-648-3494; FAX: 902-648-0253

Beeman Precision Airguns, 5454 Argosy Dr., Huntington Beach, CA 92649/714-890-4800; FAX: 714-890-4808

Behlert Precision, P.O. Box 288, 7067 Easton Rd., Pipersville, PA 18947/215-766-8681; FAX: 215-766-8681

Beitzinger, George, 116-20 Atlantic Ave., Richmond Hill, NY 11419/718-847-7661

Bell Originals, Inc., Sid, 7776 Shackham Rd., Tully, NY 13159-9333/607-842-6431

Bell Reloading, Inc., 1725 Harlin Lane Rd., Villa Rica, GA 30180

Bellm Contenders, P.O. Ackley Rifle Barrels, P.O. Box 459, Cleveland, UT 84518/801-653-2530

Belltown, Ltd., 11 Camps Rd., Kent, CT 06757/203-354-5750

Ben's Machines, 1151 S. Cedar Ridge, Duncanville, TX 75137/214-780-1807; FAX: 214-780-0316

Benchmark Guns, 12593 S. Ave. 5 East, Yuma, AZ 85365

Benelli Armi, S.p.A., Via della Stazione, 61029 Urbino, ITALY/39-722-328633; FAX: 39-722-327427 (U.S. importers—E.A.A. Corp.; Heckler & Koch, Inc.; Sile Distributors)

Bengtson Arms Co., L., 6345-B E. Akron St., Mesa, AZ 85205/602-981-6375

Benjamin/Sheridan Co., Crossman, Rts. 5 and 20, E. Bloomfield, NY 14443/716-657-6161; FAX: 716-657-5405

Bentley, John, 128-D Watson Dr., Turtle Creek, PA 15145

Beretta Firearms, Pietro, 25063 Gardone V.T., ITALY (U.S. importer—Beretta U.S.A. Corp.)

Beretta U.S.A. Corp., 17601 Beretta Drive, Accokeek, MD 20607/301-283-2191; FAX: 301-283-0435

Berger Bullets, Ltd., 5342 W. Camelback Rd., Suite 500, Glendale, AZ 85301/602-842-4001; FAX: 602-934-9083

Bergman & Williams, 2450 Losee Rd., Suite F, Las Vegas, NV 89030/702-642-1901; FAX: 702-642-1540

Bernardelli S.p.A., Vincenzo, 125 Via Matteotti, P.O. Box 74, Gardone V.T., Brescia ITALY, 25063/39-30-8912851-2-3; FAX: 39-30-8910249 (U.S. importer—Armsport, Inc.)

Berry's Bullets, Div. of Berry's Mfg., Inc., 401 N. 3050 E., St. George, UT 84770-9004

Berry's Mfg., Inc., 401 North 3050 East St., St. George, UT 84770/801-634-1682; FAX: 801-634-1683

Bersa S.A., Gonzales Castillo 312, 1704 Ramos Mejia, ARGENTINA/541-656-2377; FAX: 541-656-2093 (U.S. importer—Eagle Imports, Inc.)

Bertram Bullet Co., P.O. Box 313, Seymour, Victoria 3660, AUSTRALIA/61-57-922912; FAX: 61-57-991650

Bianchi International, Inc., 100 Calle Cortez, Temecula, CA 92590/909-676-5621; FAX: 909-676-6777

Biesen, Al, 5021 Rosewood, Spokane, WA 99208/509-328-9340

Biesen, Roger, 5021 W. Rosewood, Spokane, WA 99208/509-328-9340

Bill's Gun Repair, 1007 Burlington St., Mendota, IL 61342/815-539-5786

Billings Gunsmiths, Inc., 1940 Grand Ave., Billings, MT 59102/406-652-3104

MANUFACTURERS' DIRECTORY

Billingsley & Brownell, P.O. Box 25, Dayton, WY 82836/307-655-9344

Birdsong & Assoc., W.E., 4832 Windermere, Jackson, MS 39206/601-366-8270

Black Belt Bullets, Big Bore Express Ltd., 7154 W. State St., Suite 200, Boise, ID 83703

Black Hills Ammunition, Inc., P.O. Box 3090, Rapid City, SD 57709-3090/605-348-5150; FAX: 605-348-9827

Black Hills Shooters Supply, P.O. Box 4220, Rapid City, SD 57709/800-289-2506

Black Mountain Bullets, Rt. 7, Box 297, Warrenton, VA 22186/703-347-1199

Black Sheep Brand, 3220 W. Gentry Parkway, Tyler, TX 75702/903-592-3853; FAX: 903-592-0527

Blackhawk East, Box 2274, Loves Park, IL 61131

Blackhawk West, Box 285, Hiawatha, KS 66434

Blacksmith Corp., 830 N. Road No. 1 E., P.O. Box 1752, Chino Valley, AZ 86323/602-636-4456; FAX: 602-636-4457

BlackStar Barrel Accurizing, 11609 N. Galayda St., Houston, TX 77086/713-448-5300; FAX: 713-448-7298

Blacktail Mountain Books, 42 First Ave. W., Kalispell, MT 59901/406-257-5573

Blackwell, W. (See Load From a Disk)

Blakemore Game Calls, Jim, Rt. 2, Box 544, Cape Girardeau, MO 63701

Blammo Ammo, P.O. Box 1677, Seneca, SC 29679/803-882-1768

Bleile, C. Roger, 5040 Ralph Ave., Cincinnati, OH 45238/513-251-0249

Blocker's Holsters, Inc., Ted, 5360 NE 112, Portland, OR 97220/503-254-9950

Blount, Inc., Sporting Equipment Div., 2299 Snake River Ave., P.O. Box 856, Lewiston, ID 83501/800-627-3640, 208-746-2351; FAX: 208-746-2915

Blue and Gray Products, Inc. (See Ox-Yoke Originals, Inc.)

Blue Book Publications, Inc., One Appletree Square, Minneapolis, MN 55425/800-877-4867, 612-854-5229; FAX: 612-853-1486

Blue Point, P.O. Box 722, Marrena, NY 13662

Blue Ridge Machinery & Tools, Inc., P.O. Box 536-GD, Hurricane, WV 25526/800-872-6500; FAX: 304-562-5311

Bob's Gun Shop, P.O. Box 200, Royal, AR 71968/501-767-1970

Bob's Tactical Indoor Shooting Range & Gun Shop, 122 Lafayette Rd., Salisbury, MA 01952/508-465-5561

Boessler, Erich, Am Vogeltal 3, 97702 Munnerstadt, GERMANY/9733-9443

Boggs, Wm., 1816 Riverside Dr. #C, Columbus, OH 43212/614-486-6965

Bo-Mar Tool & Mfg. Co., Rt. 12, Box 405, Longview, TX 75605/903-759-4784; FAX: 903-759-9141

Bond Custom Firearms, 8954 N. Lewis Ln., Bloomington, IN 47408/812-332-4519

Bondini Paolo, Via Sorrento, 345, San Carlo di Cesena, ITALY I-47020/0547 663 240; FAX: 0547 663 780

Bone Engraving, Ralph, 718 N. Atlanta, Owasso, OK 74055/918-272-9745

Boone's Custom Ivory Grips, Inc., 562 Coyote Rd., Brinnon, WA 98320/206-796-4330

Boonie Packer Products, P.O. Box 12204, Salem, OR 97309/800-477-3244, 503-581-3244; FAX: 503-581-3191

Bostick Wildlife Calls, Inc., P.O. Box 728, Estill, SC 29918/803-625-2210, 803-625-4512

Bowen Classic Arms Corp., P.O. Box 67, Louisville, TN 37777/615-984-3583

Boyds' Gunstock Industries, Inc., 3rd & Main, P.O. Box 305, Geddes, SD 57342/605-337-2125; FAX: 605-337-3363

Brace, Larry D., 771 Blackfoot Ave., Eugene, OR 97404/503-688-1278

Bradley Gunsight Co., P.O. Box 140, Plymouth, VT 05056/203-589-0531; FAX: 203-582-6294

Brass Eagle, Inc., 7050A Bramalea Rd., Unit 19, Mississauga, Ont. L4Z 1C7, CANADA/416-848-4844

Brass-Tech Industries, P.O. Box 521-v, Wharton, NJ 07885/201-366-8540

Bratcher, Dan, 311 Belle Air Pl., Carthage, MO 64836/417-358-1518

Brauer Bros. Mfg. Co., 2020 Delman Blvd., St. Louis, MO 63103/314-231-2864; FAX: 314-249-4952

Braun, M., 32, rue Notre-Dame, 2440 LUXEMBURG

Braverman Corp., R.J., 88 Parade Rd., Meridith, NH 03293/800-736-4867

Break-Free, Inc., P.O. Box 25020, Santa Ana, CA 92799/714-953-1900; FAX: 714-953-0402

Brgoch, Frank, 1580 S. 1500 East, Bountiful, UT 84010/801-295-1885

Brian, C.T., Pistolsmith, P.O. Box 308, Rocky Ford, CO 81067/719-254-3849

Bridgers Best, P.O. Box 1410, Berthoud, CO 80513

Briese Bullet Co., Inc., RR1, Box 108, Tappen, ND 58487/701-327-4578; FAX: 701-327-4579

Briganti & Co., A., 475 Rt. 32, Highland Mills, NY 10930/914-928-9573

Broad Creek Rifle Works, 120 Horsey Ave., Laurel, DE 19956/302-875-5446

Brobst, Jim, 299 Poplar St., Hamburg, PA 19526/215-562-2103

Brockman's Custom Gunsmithing, P.O. Box 357, Goodling, ID 83330/208-934-5050

Broken Gun Ranch, 10739 126 Rd., Spearville, KS 67876/316-385-2587; FAX: 316-385-2597

Brolin Arms, 2755 Thompson Creek Rd., Pomona, CA 91767/909-392-2345; FAX: 909-392-2354

Brooker, Dennis, Rt. 1, Box 12A, Derby, IA 50068/515-533-2103

Brooks Tactical Systems, 279-A Shorewood Ct., Fox Island, WA 98333/800-410-4747; FAX: 206-572-6797

Brown, H.R. (See Silhouette Leathers)

Brown Co., E. Arthur, 3404 Pawnee Dr., Alexandria, MN 56308/612-762-8847

Brown Precision, Inc., 7786 Molinos Ave., Los Molinos, CA 96055/916-384-2506; FAX: 916-384-1638

Brown Products, Inc., Ed, Rt. 2, Box 2922, Perry, MO 63462/314-565-3261; FAX: 565-2791

Brownells, Inc., 200 S. Front St., Montezuma, IA 50171/515-623-5401; FAX: 515-623-3896

Browning Arms Co. (Parts & Service), 3005 Arnold Tenbrook Rd., Arnold, MO 63010-9406/314-287-6800; FAX: 314-287-9751

Browning Arms Co.(Gen. Offices), One Browning Place, Morgan, UT 84050/801-876-2711; FAX: 801-876-3331

BRP, Inc. High Performance Cast Bullets, 1210 Alexander Rd., Colorado Springs, CO 80909/719-633-0658

Bruno Shooters Supply, 106 N. Wyoming St., Hazleton, PA 18201/717-455-2211; FAX: 717-455-2211

Brunton U.S.A., 620 E. Monroe Ave., Riverton, WY 82501/307-856-6559; FAX: 307-856-1840

Bryco Arms (See U.S. distributor—Jennings Firearms, Inc.)

Brynin, Milton, P.O. Box 383, Yonkers, NY 10710/914-779-4333

BSA Guns Ltd., Armoury Rd. Small Heath, Birmingham, ENGLAND B11 2PX/011-021-772-8543; FAX: 011-021-773-0845

B-Square Company, Inc., P.O. Box 11281, 2708 St. Louis Ave., Ft. Worth, TX 76110/817-923-0964, 800-433-2909; FAX: 817-926-7012

Bucheimer, J.M., Jumbo Sports Products, 721 N. 20th St., St. Louis, MO 63103/314-241-1020

Buck Stix—SOS Products Co., Box 3, Neenah, WI 54956

Buckeye Custom Bullets, 6490 Stewart Rd., Elida, OH 45807/419-641-4463

Buckhorn Gun Works, 115 E. North St., Rapid City, SD 57701/605-341-2277

Buckskin Bullet Co., P.O. Box 245, Cedar City, UT 84721/801-586-3286

Buckskin Machine Works, A. Hunkeler, 3235 S. 358th St., Auburn, WA 98001/206-927-5412

Buffalo Bullet Co., Inc., 12637 Los Nietos Rd., Unit A, Santa Fe Springs, CA 90670/310-944-0322; FAX: 310-944-5054

Buffalo Rock Shooters Supply, R.R. 1, Ottawa, IL 61350/815-433-2471

Bull Mountain Rifle Co., 6327 Golden West Terrace, Billings, MT 59106/406-656-0778

Bullberry Barrel Works, Ltd., 2430 W. Bullberry Ln. 67-5, Hurricane, UT 84737/801-635-9866

Bullet Mills, P.O. Box 102, Port Carbon, PA 17965/717-622-0657

Bullet Swaging Supply, Inc., P.O. Box 1056, 303 McMillan Rd, West Monroe, LA 71291/318-387-7257; FAX: 318-387-7779

Bullet, Inc., 3745 Hiram Alworth Rd., Dallas, GA 30132

BulletMakers Workshop, The, RFD 1 Box 1755, Brooks, ME 04921

Bullseye Bullets, 1610 State Road 60, No. 12, Valrico, FL 33594/813-654-6563

Bull-X, Inc., P.O. Box 182, 520 N. Main., Farmer City, IL 61842/309-928-2574, 800-248-3845 orders only; FAX: 309-928-2130

Burgess, Byron, P.O. Box 6853, Los Osos, CA 93412/805-534-1304

Burgess & Son Gunsmiths, R.W., P.O. Box 3364, Warner Robins, GA 31099/912-328-7487

Burris Co., Inc., P.O. Box 1747, 331 E. 8th St., Greeley, CO 80631/303-356-1670; FAX: 303-356-8702

Bushmaster Hunting & Fishing, 451 Alliance Ave., Toronto, Ont. M6N 2J1 CANADA/416-763-4040; FAX: 416-763-0623

Bushnell (See Bausch & Lomb)

Bushwacker Backpack & Supply Co. (See Counter Assault)

Bustani Appraisers, Leo, P.O. Box 8125, W. Palm Beach, FL 33407/305-622-2710

Butler Creek Corp., 290 Arden Dr., Belgrade, MT 59714/800-423-8327, 406-388-1356; FAX: 406-388-7204

Butler Enterprises, 834 Oberting Rd., Lawrenceburg, IN 47025/812-537-3584

Butterfield & Butterfield, 220 San Bruno Ave., San Francisco, CA 94103/415-861-7500

Buzztail Brass, 5306 Bryant Ave., Klamath Falls, OR 97603-5020/503-884-1072

B-West Imports, Inc., 2425 N. Huachuca Dr., Tucson, AZ 85745-1201/602-628-1990; FAX: 602-628-3602

C

C3 Systems, 678 Killingly St., Johnston, RI 02919

C&D Special Products (Claybuster), 309 Sequoya Dr., Hopkinsville, KY 42240/800-922-6287, 800-284-1746, 502-885-8088; FAX: 502-885-1951

C&J Enterprises, Inc., 7101 Jurupa Ave., No. 12, Riverside, CA 92504/909-689-7758

Cabanas (See U.S. importer—Mandall Shooting Supplies, Inc.)

Cabela's, 812-13th Ave., Sidney, NE 69160/308-254-6644; FAX: 308-254-6669

Cabinet Mtn. Outfitters Scents & Lures, P.O. Box 766, Plains, MT 59859/406-826-3970

Cache La Poudre Rifleworks, 140 N. College, Ft. Collins, CO 80524/303-482-6913

Calibre Press, Inc., 666 Dundee Rd., Suite 1607, Northbrook, IL 60062-2760/800-323-0037; FAX: 708-498-6869

Calico Light Weapon Systems, 405 E. 19th St., Bakersfield, CA 93305/805-323-1327; FAX: 805-323-7844

California Grip, 1323 Miami Ave., Clovis, CA 93612/209-299-1316

California Magnum, 20746 Dearborn St., Chatsworth, CA 91313/818-341-7302; FAX: 818-341-7304

California Sights (See Fautheree, Andy)

CAM Enterprises, 5090 Iron Springs Rd., Box 2, Prescott, AZ 86301/602-776-9640

Camas Hot Springs Mfg., P.O. Box 639, Hot Springs, MT 59845/406-741-3756

Camdex, Inc., 2330 Alger, Troy, MI 48083/810-528-2300; FAX: 810-528-0989

Cameron's, 16690 W. 11th Ave., Golden, CO 80401/303-279-7365; FAX: 303-628-5413

Camilli, Lou, 4700 Oahu Dr. NE, Albuquerque, NM 87111/505-293-5259

Campbell, Dick, 20,000 Silver Ranch Road, Conifer, CO 80433/303-697-0150

Camp-Cap Products, P.O. Box 173, Chesterfield, MO 63006/314-532-4340

Cannon's Guns, Box 1036, 320 Main St., Polson, MT 59860/406-887-2048

Canons Delcour, Rue J.B. Cools, B-4040 Herstal, BELGIUM/+32.(0)41.40.13.40; FAX: +32(0)412.40.22.88

Canyon Cartridge Corp., P.O. Box 152, Albertson, NY 11507/FAX: 516-294-8946

Caraville Manufacturing, P.O. Box 4545, Thousand Oaks, CA 91359/805-499-1234

Carbide Checkering Tools, P.O. Box 77, 200 Lyons Hill Rd., Athol, MA 01331/508-249-9241

Carbide Die & Mfg. Co., Inc., 15615 E. Arrow Hwy., Irwindale, CA 91706/818-337-2518

Carlson, Douglas R., Antique American Firearms, P.O. Box 71035, Dept. GD, Des Moines, IA 50325/515-224-6552

Carnahan Bullets, 17645 110th Ave. SE, Renton, WA 98055

Carroll Bullets (See Precision Reloading, Inc.)

Carter's Gun Shop, 225 G St., Penrose, CO 81240/719-372-6240

Carter's Wildlife Calls, Inc., Garth, P.O. Box 821, Cedar City, UT 84720/801-586-7639

Carvajal Belts & Holsters, 422 Chestnut, San Antonio, TX 78202/210-222-1634

Cascade Bullet Co., Inc., 2355 South 6th St., Klamath Falls, OR 97601/503-884-9316

Case Sorting System, 12695 Cobblestone Creek Rd., Poway, CA 92064/619-486-9340

Cash Mfg. Co., Inc., P.O. Box 130, 201 S. Klein Dr., Waunakee, WI 53597-0130/608-849-5664; FAX: 608-849-5664

Caspian Arms Ltd., 14 North Main St., Hardwick, VT 05843/802-472-6454; FAX: 802-472-6709

Caswell International Corp., 1221 Marshall St. NE, Minneapolis, MN 55413-1055/612-379-2000; FAX: 612-379-2367

Cathey Enterprises, Inc., P.O. Box 2202, Brownwood, TX 76804/915-643-2553; FAX: 915-643-3653

CCI, Div. of Blount, Inc., 2299 Snake River Ave., P.O. Box 856, Lewiston, ID 83501/800-627-3640, 208-746-2351; FAX: 208-746-2915

Cedar Hill Game Calls, Inc., Rt. 2 Box 236, Downsville, LA 71234/318-982-5632; FAX: 318-368-2245

Celestron International, P.O. Box 3578, 2835 Columbia St., Torrance, CA 90503/310-328-9560; FAX: 310-212-5835

Centaur Systems, Inc., 1602 Foothill Rd., Kalispell, MT 59901/406-755-8609; FAX: 406-755-8609

Center Lock Scope Rings, 9901 France Ct., Lakeville, MN 55044/612-461-2114

CenterMark, P.O. Box 4066, Parnassus Station, New Kensington, PA 15068/412-335-1319

Central Specialties Ltd., 1122 Silver Lake Road, Cary, IL 60013/708-639-3900; FAX: 708-639-3972

Century Gun Dist., Inc., 1467 Jason Rd., Greenfield, IN 46140/317-462-4524

Century International Arms, Inc., P.O. Box 714, St. Albans, VT 05478-0714/802-527-1252; FAX: 802-527-0470

C-H Tool & Die Corp. (See 4-D Custom Die Co.)

CHAA, Ltd., P.O. Box 565, Howell, MI 48844/800-677-8737; FAX: 313-894-6930

Chace Leather Products, 507 Alden St., Fall River, MA 02722/508-678-7556; FAX: 508-675-9666

Chadick's Ltd., P.O. Box 100, Terrell, TX 75160/214-563-7577

Chambers Flintlocks Ltd., Jim, Rt. 1, Box 513-A, Candler, NC 28715/704-667-8361

Champlin Firearms, Inc., P.O. Box 3191, Woodring Airport, Enid, OK 73701/405-237-7388; FAX: 405-242-6922

Chapman Academy of Practical Shooting, 4350 Academy Rd., Hallsville, MO 65255/314-696-5544; FAX: 314-696-2266

Chapman Manufacturing Co., 471 New Haven Rd., P.O. Box 250, Durham, CT 06422/203-349-9228; FAX: 203-349-0084

CHARCO, 26 Beaver St., Ansonia, CT 06401/203-735-4686; 203-735-6569

Charter Arms (See CHARCO)

Checkmate Refinishing, 370 Champion Dr., Brooksville, FL 34601/904-799-5774

Cheddite France, S.A., 99, Route de Lyon, F-26500 Bourg-les-Valence, FRANCE/33-75-56-4545; FAX: 33-75-56-3587

Chelsea Gun Club of New York City, Inc., 237 Ovington Ave., Apt. D53, Brooklyn, NY 11209/718-836-9422, 718-833-2704

Chem-Pak, Inc., 11 Oates Ave., P.O. Box 1685, Winchester, VA 22604/800-336-9828, 703-667-1341; FAX: 703-722-3993

Cherokee Gun Accessories (See Glaser Safety Slug, Inc.)

CheVron Bullets, RR1, Ottawa, IL 61350/815-433-2471

CheVron Case Master (See CheVron Bullets)

Choate Machine & Tool Co., Inc., P.O. Box 218, 116 Lovers Ln., Bald Knob, AR 72010/501-724-6193, 800-972-6390; FAX: 501-724-5873

Chopie Mfg., Inc., 700 Copeland Ave., LaCrosse, WI 54603/608-784-0926

Christie's East, 219 E. 67th St., New York, NY 10021/212-606-0400

Christman Jr., David, 937 Lee Hedrick Rd., Colville, WA 99114/509-684-5686 days; 509-684-3314 evenings

Chronotech, 1655 Siamet Rd. Unit 6, Mississauga, Ont. L4W 1Z4 CANADA/905-625-5200; FAX: 905-625-5190

Chuck's Gun Shop, P.O. Box 597, Waldo, FL 32694/904-468-2264

Churchill, Winston, Twenty Mile Stream Rd., RFD P.O. Box 29B, Proctorsville, VT 05153/802-226-7772

Cimarron Arms, P.O. Box 906, Fredericksburg, TX 78624-0906/210-997-9090; FAX: 210-997-0802

Circle M Custom Bullets, 29 Avenida de Silva, Abilene, TX 79602-7509/915-698-3106

C.J. Ballistics, Inc., P.O. Box 132, Acme, WA 98220/206-595-5001

Clark Co., Inc., David, P.O. Box 15054, Worcester, MA 01615-0054/508-756-6216; FAX: 508-753-5827

Clark Custom Guns, Inc., P.O. Box 530, 11462 Keatchie Rd., Keithville, LA 71047/318-925-0836; FAX: 318-925-9425

Clark Firearms Engraving, P.O. Box 80746, San Marino, CA 91118/818-287-1652

Classic Brass, 14 Grove St., Plympton, MA 02367/FAX: 617-585-5673

Classic Guns, Inc., Frank S. Wood, 3230 Medlock Bridge Rd., Suite 110, Norcross, GA 30092/404-242-7944

Clearview Mfg. Co., Inc., 413 S. Oakley St., Fordyce, AR 71742/501-352-8557; FAX: 501-352-8557

Clements' Custom Leathercraft, Chas, 1741 Dallas St., Aurora, CO 80010-2018/303-364-0403

Clenzoil Corp., P.O. Box 80226, Sta. C, Canton, OH 44708-0226/216-833-9758

Clerke Co., J.A., P.O. Box 627, Pearblossom, CA 93553-0627/805-945-0713

Clymer Manufacturing Co., Inc., 1645 W. Hamlin Rd., Rochester Hills, MI 48309-1530/810-853-5555, 810-853-5627; FAX: 810-853-1530

C-More Systems, P.O. Box 1750, 7553 Gary Rd., Manassas, VA 22110/703-361-2663; FAX: 703-361-5881

Coats, Mrs. Lester, 300 Luman Rd., Space 125, Phoenix, OR 97535/503-535-1611

Cobra Gunskin, 133-30 32nd Ave., Flushing, NY 11354/718-762-8181; FAX: 718-762-0890

Cobra Sport s.r.l., Via Caduti Nei Lager No. 1, 56020 San Romano, Montopoli v/Arno (Pi), ITALY/0039-571-450490; FAX: 0039-571-450492

Cogar's Gunsmithing, P.O. Box 755, Houghton Lake, MI 48629/517-422-4591

Cole's Gun Works, Old Bank Building, Rt. 4, Box 250, Moyock, NC 27958/919-435-2345

Cole-Grip, 16135 Cohasset St., Van Nuys, CA 91406/818-782-4424

Collings, Ronald, 1006 Cielta Linda, Vista, CA 92083

Colonial Arms, Inc., P.O. Box 636, Selma, AL 36702-0636/334-872-9455; FAX: 334-872-9540

Colonial Repair, P.O. Box 372, Hyde Park, MA 02136-9998/617-469-4951

Colorado School of Trades, 1575 Hoyt St., Lakewood, CO 80215/800-234-4594; FAX: 303-233-4723

Colorado Shooter's Supply, 1163 W. Paradise Way, Fruita, CO 81521/303-858-9191

Colorado Sutlers Arsenal, 365 S. Moore, Lurewood, CO 80226/303-985-2983

Colt Blackpowder Arms Co., 5 Centre Market Place, New York, NY 10013/212-925-2159; FAX: 212-966-4986

Colt's Mfg. Co., Inc., P.O. Box 1868, Hartford, CT 06144-1868/800-962-COLT, 203-236-6311; FAX: 203-244-1449

Combat Military Ordnance Ltd., 3900 Hopkins St., Savannah, GA 31405/912-238-1900; FAX: 912-236-7570

Compass Industries, Inc., 104 East 25th St., New York, NY 10010/212-473-2614, 800-221-9904; FAX: 212-353-0826

Competition Electronics, Inc., 3469 Precision Dr., Rockford, IL 61109/815-874-8001; FAX: 815-874-8181

Competitor Corp., Inc., P.O. Box 244, 293 Townsend Rd., West Groton, MA 01472/508-448-3521; FAX: 508-448-6691

Complete Handloader, The, P.O. Box 5264, Arvada, CO 80005/303-460-9489

Component Concepts, Inc., 10240 SW Nimbus Ave., Suite L-8, Portland, OR 97223/503-684-9262; FAX: 503-620-4285

Concept Development Corp., 14715 N. 78th Way, Suite 300, Scottsdale, AZ 85260/800-472-4405; FAX: 602-948-7560

Conetrol Scope Mounts, 10225 Hwy. 123 South, Seguin, TX 78155/210-379-3030, 800-CONETROL

CONKKO, P.O. Box 40, Broomall, PA 19008/215-356-0711

Cook Engineering Service, 891 Highbury Rd., Vermont VICT 3133 AUSTRALIA

Cooper-Woodward, 3800 Pelican Rd., Helena, MT 59601/406-458-3800

Corbin, Inc., 600 Industrial Circle, P.O. Box 2659, White City, OR 97503/503-826-5211; FAX: 503-826-8669

Cor-Bon Bullet & Ammo Co., 1311 Industry Rd., Sturgis, SD 57785/800-626-7266; FAX: 800-923-2666

Corkys Gun Clinic, 4401 Hot Springs Dr., Greeley, CO 80634/303-330-0516

Corry, John, 861 Princeton Ct., Neshanic Station, NJ 08853/908-369-8019

Costa, David, Island Pond Gun Shop, P.O. Box 428, Cross St., Island Pond, VT 05846/802-723-4546

Counter Assault, Box 4721, Missoula, MT 59806/406-728-6241; FAX: 406-728-8800

Country Armourer, The, P.O. Box .308, Ashby, MA 01431-0308/508-386-7590; FAX: 508-386-7789

Cousin Bob's Mountain Products, 7119 Ohio River Blvd., Ben Avon, PA 15202/412-766-5114; FAX: 412-766-5114

CQB Training, P.O. Box 1739, Manchester, MO 63011

Craftguard, 3624 Logan Ave., Waterloo, IA 50703/319-232-2959

Craig Custom Ltd., Research & Development, 629 E. 10th, Hutchinson, KS 67501/316-669-0601

Crandall Tool & Machine Co., 1545 N. Mitchell St., P.O. Box 569, Cadillac, MI 49601/616-775-5562

Crane & Crane Ltd., 105 N. Edison Way #6, Reno, NV 89502-2355/702-856-1516; FAX: 702-856-1616

Crawford Co., Inc., R.M., P.O. Box 277, Everett, PA 15537/814-652-6536; FAX: 814-652-9526

CRDC Laser Systems Group, 3972 Barranca Parkway, Ste. J-484, Irvine, CA 92714/714-586-1295; FAX: 714-831-4823

Creative Cartridge Co., 56 Morgan Rd., Canton, CT 06019/203-693-2529

Creedmoor Sports, Inc., P.O. Box 1040, Oceanside, CA 92051/619-757-5529

Creek Side Metal & Woodcrafters, Fishers Hill, VA 22626/703-465-3903

CRL, Inc., 420 Industrial Park, P.O. Box 111, Gladstone, MI 49837/906-428-3710; FAX: 906-428-3711

Crosman Airguns, Rts. 5 and 20, E. Bloomfield, NY 14443/716-657-6161; FAX: 716-657-5405

Crosman Products of Canada Ltd., 1173 N. Service Rd. West, Oakville, Ontario, L6M 2V9 CANADA/905-827-1822

Crouse's Country Cover, P.O. Box 160, Storrs, CT 06268/203-429-4715

Cullity Restoration, Daniel, 209 Old County Rd., East Sandwich, MA 02537/508-888-1147

Cumberland Arms, Rt. l, Box 1150 Shafer Rd., Blantons Chapel, Manchester, TN 37355/800-797-8414

Cumberland Knife & Gun Works, 5661 Bragg Blvd., Fayetteville, NC 28303/919-867-0009

Cummings Bullets, 1417 Esperanza Way, Escondido, CA 92027

Cunningham Co., Eaton, 607 Superior St., Kansas City, MO 64106/816-842-2600

Cupp, Alana, Custom Engraver, P.O. Box 207, Annabella, UT 84711/801-896-4834

Curly Maple Stock Blanks (See Tiger-Hunt)

Curtis Custom Shop, RR1, Box 193A, Wallingford, KY 41093/703-659-4265

Curtis Gun Shop, Dept. ST, 119 W. College, Bozeman, MT 59715/406-587-4934

Custom Bullets by Hoffman, 2604 Peconic Ave., Seaford, NY 11783

Custom Checkering Service, Kathy Forster, 2124 SE Yamhill St., Portland, OR 97214/503-236-5874

Custom Chronograph, Inc., 5305 Reese Hill Rd., Sumas, WA 98295/360-988-7801

Custom Gun Products, 5021 W. Rosewood, Spokane, WA 99208/509-328-9340

Custom Gunsmiths, 4303 Friar Lane, Colorado Springs, CO 80907/719-599-3366

Custom Quality Products, Inc., 345 W. Girard Ave., P.O. Box 71129, Madison Heights, MI 48071/810-585-1616; FAX: 810-585-0644

Custom Shop, The, 890 Cochrane Crescent, Peterborough, Ont. K9H 5N3 CANADA/705-742-6693

Custom Tackle and Ammo, P.O. Box 1886, Farmington, NM 87499/505-632-3539

Cutsinger Bench Rest Bullets, RR 8, Box 161-A, Shelbyville, IN 46176/317-729-5360

CVA, 5988 Peachtree Corners East, Norcross, GA 30071/800-251-9412; FAX: 404-242-8546

C.W. Cartridge Co., 71 Hackensack St., Wood Ridge, NJ 07075

C.W. Cartridge Co., 242 Highland Ave., Kearney, NJ 07032/201-998-1030

Cycle Dynamics, Inc., 74 Garden St., Feeding Hills, MA 01030/413-786-0141

Cylinder & Slide, Inc., William R. Laughridge, 245 E. 4th St., Fremont, NE 68025/402-721-4277; FAX: 402-721-0263

CZ (See U.S. importer—Magnum Research, Inc.)

D

D&D Gunsmiths, Ltd., 363 E. Elmwood, Troy, MI 48083/313-583-1512

D&H Precision Tooling, 7522 Barnard Mill Rd., Ringwood, IL 60072/815-653-4011

D&H Prods. Co., Inc., 465 Denny Rd., Valencia, PA 16059/412-898-2840, 800-776-0281; FAX: 412-898-2013

D&J Bullet Co. & Custom Gun Shop, Inc., 426 Ferry St., Russell, KY 41169/606-836-2663; FAX: 606-836-2663

D&L Sports, P.O. Box 651, Gillette, WY 82717/307-686-4008

Dade Screw Machine Products, 2319 NW 7th Ave., Miami, FL 33127/305-573-5050

Daewoo Precision Industries Ltd., 34-3 Yeoeuido-Dong, Yeongdeungoo-GU, 15th Fl., Seoul, KOREA (U.S. importer—Nationwide Sports Distributors)

Daisy Mfg. Co., P.O. Box 220, Rogers, AR 72757/501-636-1200; FAX: 501-636-1601

Dangler, Homer L., Box 254, Addison, MI 49220/517-547-6745

Dapkus Co., Inc., J.G., P.O. Box 293, Durham, CT 06422

Dara-Nes, Inc. (See Nesci Enterprises, Inc.)

Data Tech Software Systems, 19312 East Eldorado Drive, Aurora, CO 80013

Datumtech Corp., 2275 Wehrle Dr., Buffalo, NY 14221

Davidson, Jere, Rt. 1, Box 132, Rustburg, VA 24588/804-821-3637

Davis, Don, 1619 Heights, Katy, TX 77493/713-391-3090

Davis Co., R.E., 3450 Pleasantville NE, Pleasantville, OH 43148/614-654-9990

Davis Industries, 15150 Sierra Bonita Ln., Chino, CA 91710/909-597-4726; FAX: 909-393-9771

Davis Leather Co., G. Wm., 3990 Valley Blvd., Unit D, Walnut, CA 91789/909-598-5620

Davis Products, Mike, 643 Loop Dr., Moses Lake, WA 98837/509-765-6178, 509-766-7281 orders only

Davis Service Center, Bill, 7221 Florin Mall Dr., Sacramento, CA 95823/916-393-4867

Day & Sons, Inc., Leonard, P.O. Box 122, Flagg Hill Rd., Heath, MA 01346/413-337-8369

Dayson Arms Ltd., P.O. Box 532, Vincennes, IN 47591/812-882-8680; FAX: 812-882-8680

Daystate Arms Ltd., Newcastle Street, Stone, Staffs, ST 15 8UJ ENGLAND/011-0785-812473

DBI Books, Inc., 4092 Commercial Ave., Northbrook, IL 60062/708-272-6310; FAX: 708-272-2051

D-Boone Ent., Inc., 5900 Colwyn Dr., Harrisburg, PA 17109

D.C.C. Enterprises, 259 Wynburn Ave., Athens, GA 30601

Dead Eye's Sport Center, RD 1, Box 147B, Shickshinny, PA 18655/717-256-7432

Decker Shooting Products, 1729 Laguna Ave., Schofield, WI 54476/715-359-5873

Deepeeka Exports Pvt. Ltd., D-78, Saket, Meerut-250-006, INDIA/011-91-121-512889, 011-91-121-545363; FAX: 011-91-121-542988, 011-91-121-511599

Defense Moulding Enterprises, 16781 Daisey Ave., Fountain Valley, CA 92708/714-842-5062

Defense Training International, Inc., 749 S. Lemay, Ste. A3-337, Ft. Collins, CO 80524/303-482-2520; FAX: 303-482-0548

deHaas Barrels, RR #3, Box 77, Ridgeway, MO 64481/816-872-6308

Del Rey Products, P.O. Box 91561, Los Angeles, CA 90009/213-823-0494

Delhi Gun House, 1374 Kashmere Gate, Delhi, INDIA 110 006/(011)237375+239116; FAX: 91-11-2917344

Delorge, Ed, 2231 Hwy. 308, Thibodaux, LA 70301/504-447-1633

Del-Sports, Inc., Box 685, Main St., Margaretville, NY 12455/914-586-4103; FAX: 914-586-4105

Delta Arms Ltd., P.O. Box 1000, Delta, VT 84624-1000

Delta Frangible Ammunition, LLC, 1111 Jefferson Davis Hwy., Suite 508, Arlington, VA 22202/703-416-4928; FAX: 703-416-4934

Dem-Bart Checkering Tools, Inc., 6807 Bickford Ave., Old Hwy. #2, Snohomish, WA 98290/206-568-7356; FAX: 206-568-3134

Denver Bullets, Inc., 1811 W. 13th Ave., Denver, CO 80204/303-893-3146; FAX: 303-893-9161

Denver Instrument Co., 6542 Fig St., Arvada, CO 80004/800-321-1135, 303-431-7255; FAX: 303-423-4831

DeSantis Holster & Leather Goods, Inc., P.O. Box 2039, 149 Denton Ave., New Hyde Park, NY 11040-0701/516-354-8000; FAX: 516-354-7501

Desert Industries, Inc., P.O. Box 93443, Las Vegas, NV 89193-3443/702-597-1066; FAX: 702-871-9452

Detroit-Armor Corp., 720 Industrial Dr. No. 112, Cary, IL 60013/708-639-7666; FAX: 708-639-7694

Dever Co., Jack, 8590 NW 90, Oklahoma City, OK 73132/405-721-6393

Dewey Mfg. Co., Inc., J., P.O. Box 2014, Southbury, CT 06488/203-264-3064; FAX: 203-598-3119

DGR Custom Rifles, RR1, Box 8A, Tappen, ND 58487/701-327-8135

DGS, Inc., Dale A. Storey, 1117 E. 12th, Casper, WY 82601/307-237-2414

DHB Products, P.O. Box 3092, Alexandria, VA 22302/703-836-2648

Diamond Mfg. Co., P.O. Box 174, Wyoming, PA 18644/800-233-9601

Diamondback Supply, 2431 Juan Tabo, Suite 163, Albuquerque, NM 87112/505-237-0068

Diana (See U.S. importer—Dynamit Nobel-RWS, Inc.)

Dibble, Derek A., 555 John Downey Dr., New Britain, CT 06051/203-224-2630

Dietz Gun Shop & Range, Inc., 421 Range Rd., New Braunfels, TX 78132/210-885-4662

Dilliott Gunsmithing, Inc., 657 Scarlett Rd., Dandridge, TN 37725/615-397-9204

Dillon Precision Products, Inc., 8009 East Dillon's Way, Scottsdale, AZ 85260/602-948-8009, 800-762-3845; FAX: 602-998-2786

Dixie Gun Works, Inc., Hwy. 51 South, Union City, TN 38261/901-885-0561, order 800-238-6785; FAX: 901-885-0440

Dixon Muzzleloading Shop, Inc., RD 1, Box 175, Kempton, PA 19529/610-756-6271

DKT, Inc., 14623 Vera Drive, Union, MI 49130-9744/616-641-7120; FAX: 616-641-2015

D-Max, Inc., RR1, Box 473, Bagley, MN 56621/218-785-2278

D.O.C. Specialists, Inc.; Doc & Bud Ulrich, Jim Amodei, 2209 S. Central Ave., Cicero, IL 60650/708-652-3606; FAX: 708-652-2516

Dohring Bullets, 100 W. 8 Mile Rd., Ferndale, MI 48220

Dolbare, Elizabeth, 39 Dahlia, Casper, WY 82604/307-266-5924

Doskocil Mfg. Co., Inc., P.O. Box 1246, 4209 Barnett, Arlington, TX 76017/817-467-5116; FAX: 817-472-9810

Double A Ltd., Dept. ST, Box 11306, Minneapolis, MN 55411

Dowtin Gunworks, Rt. 4, Box 930A, Flagstaff, AZ 86001/602-779-1898

Dr. O's Products Ltd., P.O. Box 111, Niverville, NY 12130/518-784-3333; FAX: 518-784-2800

Drain, Mark, SE 3211 Kamilche Point Rd., Shelton, WA 98584/206-426-5452

Dremel Mfg. Co., 4915-21st St., Racine, WI 53406

Duane's Gun Repair (See DGR Custom Rifles)

Dubber, Michael W., P.O. Box 312, Evansville, IN 47702/812-424-9000; FAX: 812-424-6551

Duck Call Specialists, P.O. Box 124, Jerseyville, IL 62052/618-498-9855

Duffy, Charles E., Williams Lane, West Hurley, NY 12491/914-679-2997

Du-Lite Corp., 171 River Rd., Middletown, CT 06457/203-347-2505; FAX: 203-347-9404

Duncan's Gun Works, Inc., 1619 Grand Ave., San Marcos, CA 92069/619-727-0515

DuPont (See IMR Powder Co.)

Dutchman's Firearms, Inc., The, 4143 Taylor Blvd., Louisville, KY 40215/502-366-0555

Dykstra, Doug, 411 N. Darling, Fremont, MI 49412/616-924-3950

Dynamit Nobel-RWS, Inc., 81 Ruckman Rd., Closter, NJ 07624/201-767-7971; FAX: 201-767-1589

Dyson & Son Ltd., Peter, 29-31 Church St., Honley, Huddersfield, W. Yorkshire HDL7 2AH, ENGLAND/0484-661062; FAX: 0484 663709

E

E&L Mfg., Inc., 4177 Riddle by Pass Rd., Riddle, OR 97469/503-874-2137; FAX: 503-874-3107

Eades' Muzzleloader Builders' Supply, Don, 201-J Beasley Dr., Franklin, TN 37064/615-791-1731

Eagan, Donald V., P.O. Box 196, Benton, PA 17814/717-925-6134

Eagle Flight, 925 Lakeville St., Suite 123-H, Petauma, CA 94952

Eagle International, Inc., 5195 W. 58th Ave., Suite 300, Arvada, CO 80002/303-426-8100; FAX: 303-426-5475

Eagle Mfg. & Engineering, 2648 Keen Dr., San Diego, CA 92139/619-479-4402; FAX: 619-472-5585

E-A-R, Inc., Div. of Cabot Safety Corp., 5457 W. 79th St., Indianapolis, IN 46268/800-327-3431; FAX: 800-488-8007

Easy Pull Outlaw Products, 316 1st St. East, Polson, MT 59860/406-883-6822

Echols & Co., D'Arcy, 164 W. 580 S., Providence, UT 84332/801-753-2367

Ed's Gun House, Rt. 1, Box 62, Minnesota City, MN 55959/507-689-2925

Edmund Scientific Co., 101 E. Gloucester Pike, Barrington, NJ 08033/609-543-6250

Ednar, Inc., 2-4-8 Kayabacho, Nihonbashi, Chuo-ku, Tokyo, JAPAN 103/81(Japan)-3-3667-1651; FAX: 81-3-3661-8113

Eezox, Inc., P.O. Box 772, Waterford, CT 06385-0772/203-447-8282, 800-462-3331; FAX: 203-447-3484

Eggleston, Jere D., 400 Saluda Ave., Columbia, SC 29205/803-799-3402

EGW Evolution Gun Works, 4050 B-8 Skyron Dr., Doylestown, PA 18901/215-348-9892; FAX: 215-348-1056

Eichelberger Bullets, Wm., 158 Crossfield Rd., King of Prussia, PA 19406

Ekol Leather Care, P.O. Box 2652, West Lafayette, IN 47906/317-463-2250; FAX: 317-463-7004

El Dorado Leather, P.O. Box 2603, Tucson, AZ 85702/602-623-0606; FAX: 602-623-0606

El Paso Saddlery Co., P.O. Box 27194, El Paso, TX 79926/915-544-2233; FAX: 915-544-2535

Electronic Trigger Systems, Inc., P.O. Box 13, 230 Main St. S., Hector, MN 55342/612-848-2760

Eley Ltd., P.O. Box 705, Witton, Birmingham, B6 7UT, ENGLAND/021-356-8899; FAX: 021-331-4173

Elite Ammunition, P.O. Box 3251, Oakbrook, IL 60522/708-366-9006

Elkhorn Bullets, P.O. Box 5293, Central Point, OR 97502/503-826-7440

Elko Arms, Dr. L. Kortz, 28 rue Ecole Moderne, B-7060 Soignies, BELGIUM/(32)67-33-29-34

Ellicott Arms, Inc./Woods Pistolsmithing, 3840 Dahlgren Ct., Ellicott City, MD 21042/410-465-7979

Elliott Inc., G.W., 514 Burnside Ave., East Hartford, CT 06108/203-289-5741; FAX: 203-289-3137

Ellis Sport Shop, E.W., RD 1, Route 9N, P.O. Box 315, Corinth, NY 12822/518-654-6444

Emerging Technologies, Inc., 721 Main St., Little Rock, AR 72201/501-375-2227; FAX: 501-372-1445

EMF Co., Inc., 1900 E. Warner Ave. Suite 1-D, Santa Ana, CA 92705/714-261-6611; FAX: 714-756-0133

Engineered Accessories, 1307 W. Wabash Ave., Effingham, IL 62401/217-347-7700; FAX: 217-347-7737

Engraving Artistry, 36 Alto Road, RFD #2, Burlington, CT 06013/203-673-6837

Enguix Import-Export, Alpujarras 58, Alzira, Valencia, SPAIN 46600/(96) 241 43 95; FAX: (96) (241 43 95) 240 21 53

Epps "Orillia" Ltd., Ellwood, RR 3, Hwy. 11 North, Orillia, Ont. L3V 6H3, CANADA/705-689-5333

Erhardt, Dennis, 3280 Green Meadow Dr., Helena, MT 59601/406-442-4533

Erma Werke GmbH, Johan Ziegler St., 13/15/FeldiglSt., D-8060 Dachau, GERMANY (U.S. importers—Mandall Shooting Supplies, Inc.; Precision Sales International, Inc.)

Essex Arms, P.O. Box 345, Island Pond, VT 05846/802-723-4313

Essex Metals, 1000 Brighton St., Union, NJ 07083/800-282-8369

Estate Cartridge, Inc., 2778 FM 830, Willis, TX 77078/409-856-7277; FAX: 409-856-5486

Euroarms of America, Inc., 208 E. Piccadilly St., Winchester, VA 22601/703-662-1863; FAX: 703-662-4464

Europtik Ltd., P.O. Box 319, Dunmore, PA 18512/717-347-6049; FAX: 717-969-4330

Eutaw Co., Inc., The, P.O. Box 608, U.S. Hwy. 176 West, Holly Hill, SC 29059/803-496-3341

Evans Engraving, Robert, 332 Vine St., Oregon City, OR 97045/503-656-5693

Evans Gunsmithing, 47532 School St., Oakridge, OR 97463/503-782-4432

Eversull Co., Inc., K., 1 Tracemont, Boyce, LA 71409/318-793-8728; FAX: 318-793-5483

Excaliber Enterprises, P.O. Box 400, Fogelsville, PA 18051-0400/610-391-9106; FAX: 610-391-9223

Exe, Inc., 18830 Partridge Circle, Eden Prairie, MN 55346/612-944-7662

Executive Protection Institute, Rt. 2, Box 3645, Berryville, VA 22611/703-955-1128

Eyears Insurance, 4926 Annhurst Rd., Columbus, OH 43228-1341

E-Z-Way Systems, Box 4310, Newark, OH 43058-4310/614-345-6645, 800-848-2072; FAX: 614-345-6600

F

F&A Inc., 50 Elm St., Richfield Springs, NY 13439/315-858-1470; FAX: 315-858-2969

Fabian Bros. Sporting Goods, Inc., 1510 Morena Blvd., Suite "G", San Diego, CA 92110/619-275-0816; FAX: 619-276-8733

Fagan & Co., William, 22952 15 Mile Rd., Mt. Clemens, MI 48043/313-465-4637; FAX: 313-792-6996

Faith Associates, Inc., 1139 S. Greenville Hwy., Hendersonville, NC 28739/704-692-1916; FAX: 704-697-6827

Falcon Pneumatic Systems (See U.S. importer—Airguns-R-Us)

Fanzoj GmbH, Griesgasse 1, 9170 Ferlach, AUSTRIA 9170/(43) 04227-2283; FAX: (43) 04227-2867

FAPA Corp., P.O. Box 1439, New London, NH 03257/603-735-5652; FAX: 603-735-5154

Farr Studio, Inc., 1231 Robinhood Rd., Greeneville, TN 37743/615-638-8825

Faulhaber Wildlocker, Dipl.-Ing. Norbert Wittasek, Seilergasse 2, A-1010 Wien, AUSTRIA

Faulk's Game Call Co., Inc., 616 18th St., Lake Charles, LA 70601/318-436-9726

Faust, Inc., T.G., 544 Minor St., Reading, PA 19602/610-375-8549; FAX: 610-375-4488

Fautheree, Andy, P.O. Box 4607, Pagosa Springs, CO 81157/303-731-5003

Feather Industries, Inc., 37600 Liberty Dr., Trinidad, CO 81082/719-846-2699; FAX: 719-846-2644

Federal Cartridge Co., 900 Ehlen Dr., Anoka, MN 55303/612-323-2300; FAX: 612-323-2506

FEG, Budapest, Soroksariut 158, H-1095 HUNGARY (U.S. importers—Century International Arms, Inc.; K.B.I., Inc.)

Feken, Dennis, Rt. 2 Box 124, Perry, OK 73077/405-336-5611

Fellowes, Ted, Beaver Lodge, 9245 16th Ave. SW, Seattle, WA 98106/206-763-1698

Feminine Protection, Inc., 10514 Shady Trail, Dallas, TX 75220/214-351-4500; FAX: 214-352-4686

Ferdinand, Inc., P.O. Box 5, 201 Main St., Harrison, ID 83833/208-689-3012, 800-522-6010 (U.S.A.), 800-258-5266 (Canada); FAX: 208-689-3142

Ferguson, Bill, P.O. Box 1238, Sierra Vista, AZ 85636/520-458-5321; FAX: 520-458-9125

Ferris Firearms, 30115 U.S. Hwy. 281 North, Suite 158, Bulverde, TX 78163/210-980-4811

Finch Custom Bullets, 40204 La Rochelle, Prairieville, LA 70769

Firearm Training Center, The, 9555 Blandville Rd., West Paducah, KY 42086/502-554-5886

Firearms Academy of Seattle, P.O. Box 2814, Kirkland, WA 98083/206-820-4853

Firearms Engraver's Guild of America, 332 Vine St., Oregon City, OR 97045/503-656-5693

Firearms Supplies Inc., 514 Quincy St., Hancock, MI 49930/906-482-1673; FAX: 906-482-3822

Fish, Marshall F., Rt. 22 N., P.O. Box 2439, Westport, NY 12993/518-962-4897

Fisher, Jerry A., 535 Crane Mt. Rd., Big Fork, MT 59911/406-837-2722

Fisher Custom Firearms, 2199 S. Kittredge Way, Aurora, CO 80013/303-755-3710

Fisher Enterprises, 655 Main Street #305, Edmonds, WA 98020/206-776-4365

Fish-N-Hunt, Inc., 5651 Beechnut St., Houston, TX 77096-1021/713-777-3285; FAX: 713-777-9884

Fitz Pistol Grip Co., P.O. Box 610, Douglas City, CA 96024/916-623-4019

Flaig's, 2200 Evergreen Rd., Millvale, PA 15209/412-821-1717

Flambeau Products Corp., 15981 Valplast Rd., Middlefield, OH 44062/216-632-1631; FAX: 216-632-1581

Flannery Engraving Co., Jeff W., 11034 Riddles Run Rd., Union, KY 41091/606-384-3127

FlashTek, Inc., 714 Indian Hills Dr., Moscow, ID 83843/208-882-6892; FAX: 208-882-7275

Flayderman & Co., N., Inc., P.O. Box 2446, Ft. Lauderdale, FL 33303/305-761-8855

Fleming Firearms, 9525-J East 51st St., Tulsa, OK 74145/918-665-3624

Flents Products Co., Inc., P.O. Box 2109, Norwalk, CT 06852/203-866-2581; FAX: 203-854-9322

Flintlocks, Etc. (See Beauchamp & Son, Inc.)

Flitz International Ltd., 821 Mohr Ave., Waterford, WI 53185/414-534-5898; FAX: 414-534-2991

Floatstone Mfg. Co., 106 Powder Mill Rd., P.O. Box 765, Canton, CT 06019/203-693-1977

Flores Publications, Inc., J., P.O. Box 830131, Miami, FL 33283/305-559-4652

Flouramics, Inc., 18 Industrial Ave., Mahwah, NJ 07430/800-922-0075, 201-825-7035

Flow-Rite of Tennessee, Inc., 107 Allen St., P.O. Box 196, Bruceton, TN 38317/901-586-2271; FAX: 901-586-2300

FN Herstal, Voie de Liege 33, Herstal 4040, BELGIUM/(32)41.40.82.83; FAX: (32)41.40.86.79

Fobus International Ltd., Kfar Hess, ISRAEL 40692/972-9-911716; FAX: 972-9-911716

Ford, Jack, 1430 Elkwood, Missouri City, TX 77489/713-499-9984

Forgett Jr., Valmore J., 689 Bergen Blvd., Ridgefield, NJ 07657/201-945-2500; FAX: 201-945-6859

Forgreens Tool Mfg., Inc., P.O. Box 990, 723 Austin St., Robert Lee, TX 76945/915-453-2800

Forkin, Ben, 20 E. Tamarack St., Bozeman, MT 59715-2913

Forrest, Inc., Tom, P.O. Box 326, Lakeside, CA 92040/619-561-5800; FAX: 619-561-0227

Forster, Larry L., P.O. Box 212, 220 First St. NE, Gwinner, ND 58040-0212/701-678-2475

Forster Products, 82 E. Lanark Ave., Lanark, IL 61046/815-493-6360; FAX: 815-493-2371

Fort Hill Gunstocks, 12807 Fort Hill Rd., Hillsboro, OH 45133/513-466-2763

Forty Five Ranch Enterprises, Box 1080, Miami, OK 74355-1080/918-542-5875

Fountain Products, 492 Prospect Ave., West Springfield, MA 01089/413-781-4651; FAX: 413-733-8217

4-D Custom Die Co., 711 N. Sandusky St., P.O. Box 889, Mt. Vernon, OH 43050-0889/614-397-7214; FAX: 614-397-6600

Foy Custom Bullets, 104 Wells Ave., Daleville, AL 36322

Francesca, Inc., 3115 Old Ranch Rd., San Antonio, TX 78217/512-826-2584; FAX: 512-826-8211

Francolini, Leonard, 106 Powder Mill Rd., P.O. Box 765, Canton, CT 06019/203-693-1977

Frank Custom Gun Service, Ron, 7131 Richland Rd., Ft. Worth, TX 76118/817-284-4426; FAX: 817-284-9300

Frank Knives, Box 984, Whitefish, MT 59937/406-862-2681; FAX: 406-862-2681

Frankonia Jagd, Hofmann & Co., D-97064 Wurzburg, GERMANY/09302-200; FAX: 09302-20200

Frazier Brothers Enterprises, 1118 N. Main St., Franklin, IN 46131/317-736-4000; FAX: 317-736-4000

Fredrick Gun Shop, 10 Elson Dr., Riverside, RI 02915/401-433-2805

Freedom Arms, Inc., P.O. Box 1776, Freedom, WY 83120/307-883-2468, 800-833-4432 (orders only); FAX: 307-883-2005

Freeman Animal Targets, 2559 W. Morris St., Plainsfield, IN 46168/317-271-5314; FAX: 317-271-9106

Fremont Tool Works, 1214 Prairie, Ford, KS 67842/316-369-2327

French, J.R., 1712 Creek Ridge Ct., Irving, TX 75060/214-254-2654

Frielich Police Equipment, 211 East 21st St., New York, NY 10010/212-254-3045

From Jena, Europtik Ltd., P.O. Box 319, Dunmore, PA 18512/717-347-6049, 800-873-5362; FAX: 717-969-4330

Frontier Arms Co., Inc., 401 W. Rio Santa Cruz, Green Valley, AZ 85614-3932

Frontier Products Co., 164 E. Longview Ave., Columbus, OH 43202/614-262-9357

Fujinon, Inc., 10 High Point Dr., Wayne, NJ 07470/201-633-5600; FAX: 201-633-5216

Fullmer, Geo. M., 2499 Mavis St., Oakland, CA 94601/510-533-4193

Fulmer's Antique Firearms, Chet, P.O. Box 792, Rt. 2 Buffalo Lake, Detroit Lakes, MN 56501/218-847-7712

Fulton Armory, 8725 Bollman Place No. 1, Savage, MD 20763/301-490-9485; FAX: 301-490-9547

Fury Cutlery, 801 Broad Ave., Ridgefield, NJ 07657/201-943-5920; FAX: 201-943-1579

Fusilier Bullets, 10010 N. 6000 W., Highland, UT 84003/801-756-6813

FWB, Neckarstrasse 43, 78727 Oberndorf a. N., GERMANY/07423-814-0; FAX: 07423-814-89 (U.S. importer—Beeman Precision Airguns)

G

G96 Products Co., Inc., River St. Station, P.O. Box 1684, Paterson, NJ 07544/201-684-4050; FAX: 201-684-3848

G&C Bullet Co., Inc., 8835 Thornton Rd., Stockton, CA 95209/209-477-6479; FAX: 209-477-2813

Gage Manufacturing, 663 W. 7th St., San Pedro, CA 90731

Galati International, P.O. Box 326, Catawissa, MO 63015/314-257-4837; FAX: 314-257-2268

Galazan, Div. of Connecticut Shotgun Mfg. Co., P.O. Box 622, 35 Woodland St., New Britain, CT 06051-0622/203-225-6581; FAX: 203-832-8707

GALCO International Ltd., 2019 W. Quail Ave., Phoenix, AZ 85027/602-258-8295; FAX: 602-582-6854

Gammog, Gregory B. Gally, 14608 Old Gunpowder Rd., Laurel, MD 20707-3131/301-725-3838

Gamo (See U.S. importers—Daisy Mfg. Co.; Dynamit Nobel-RWS, Inc.)

GAR, 139 Park Lane, Wayne, NJ 07470/201-256-7641

Garcia National Gun Traders, Inc., 225 SW 22nd Ave., Miami, FL 33135/305-642-2355

Garthwaite, Jim, Rt. 2, Box 310, Watsontown, PA 17777/717-538-1566

Gaucher Armes, S.A., 46, rue Desjoyaux, 42000 Saint-Etienne, FRANCE/77 33 38 92; FAX: 767 41 95 72

G.B.C. Industries, Inc., P.O. Box 1602, Spring, TX 77373/713-350-9690; FAX: 713-350-0601

GDL Enterprises, 409 Le Gardeur, Slidell, LA 70460/504-649-0693

Gehmann, Walter (See Huntington Die Specialties)

Gene's Custom Guns, P.O. Box 10534, White Bear Lake, MN 55110/612-429-5105

George, Tim, Rt. 1, P.O. Box 45, Evington, VA 24550/804-821-8117

GFR Corp., P.O. Box 430, Andover, NH 03216/603-735-5300

G.G. & G., 3602 E. 42nd Stravenue, Tucson, AZ 85713/602-748-7167; FAX: 602-748-7583

G.H. Enterprises Ltd., Bag 10, Okotoks, Alberta T0L 1T0 CANADA/403-938-6070

Giron, Robert E., 1328 Pocono St., Pittsburgh, PA 15218/412-731-6041

Glaser Safety Slug, Inc., P.O. Box 8223, Foster City, CA 94404/800-221-3489, 415-345-7677; FAX: 415-345-8217

Glass, Herb, P.O. Box 25, Bullville, NY 10915/914-361-3021

Glimm, Jerome C., 19 S. Maryland, Conrad, MT 59425/406-278-3574

Glock, Inc., 6000 Highlands Parkway, Smyrna, GA 30082/404-432-1202; FAX: 404-433-8719

Glock GmbH, P.O. Box 50, A-2232 Deutsch Wagram, AUSTRIA (U.S. importer—Glock, Inc.)

GML Products, Inc., 394 Laredo Dr., Birmingham, AL 35226/205-979-4867

Goddard, Allen, 716 Medford Ave., Hayward, CA 94541/510-276-6830

Goergen's Gun Shop, Inc., Rt. 2, Box 182BB, Austin, MN 55912/507-433-9280

GOEX, Inc., 1002 Springbrook Ave., Moosic, PA 18507/717-457-6724; FAX: 717-457-1130

Goldcoast Reloaders, Inc., 2421 NE 4th Ave., Pompano Beach, FL 33064/305-783-4849

Golden Age Arms Co., 115 E. High St., Ashley, OH 43003/614-747-2488

Golden Bear Bullets, 3065 Fairfax Ave., San Jose, CA 95148/408-238-9515

Gonic Bullet Works, P.O. Box 7365, Gonic, NH 03339

Gonzalez Guns, Ramon B., P.O. Box 370, Monticello, NY 12701/914-794-4515

Goodwin, Fred, Silver Ridge Gun Shop, Sherman Mills, ME 04776/207-365-4451

Gordie's Gun Shop, 1401 Fulton St., Streator, IL 61364/815-672-7202

Gotz Bullets, 7313 Rogers St., Rockford, IL 61111

Gould & Goodrich, P.O. Box 1479, Lillington, NC 27546/910-893-2071; FAX: 910-893-4742

Gournet, Geoffroy, 820 Paxinosa Ave., Easton, PA 18042/215-559-0710

Gozon, Corp., U.S.A., P.O. Box 6278, 152 Bittercreek Dr., Folson, CA 95763/916-983-2020; FAX: 916-983-9500

Grace Metal Products, Inc., P.O. Box 67, Elk Rapids, MI 49629/616-264-8133

"Gramps" Antique Cartridges, Box 341, Washago, Ont. L0K 2B0 CANADA/705-689-5348

Grand Falls Bullets, Inc., P.O. Box 720, 803 Arnold Wallen Way, Stockton, MO 65785/816-229-0112

Granite Custom Bullets, Box 190, Philipsburg, MT 59858/406-859-3245

Grant, Howard V., Hiawatha 15, Woodruff, WI 54568/715-356-7146

Graphics Direct, P.O. Box 372421, Reseda, CA 91337-2421/818-344-9002

Graves Co., 1800 Andrews Av., Pompano Beach, FL 33069/800-327-9103; FAX: 305-960-0301

Grayback Wildcats, 5306 Bryant Ave., Klamath Falls, OR 97603/503-884-1072

Graybill's Gun Shop, 1035 Ironville Pike, Columbia, PA 17512/717-684-2739

Great Lakes Airguns, 6175 S. Park Ave., Hamburg, NY 14075/716-648-6666; FAX: 716-648-5279

Green, Arthur S., 485 S. Robertson Blvd., Beverly Hills, CA 90211/310-274-1283

Green, Roger M., P.O. Box 984, 435 E. Birch, Glenrock, WY 82637/307-436-9804

Green Bay Bullets, 1638 Hazelwood Dr., Sobieski, WI 54171/414-826-7760

Green Head Game Call Co., RR 1, Box 33, Lacon, IL 61540/309-246-2155

Greenwald, Leon E. "Bud", 2553 S. Quitman St., Denver, CO 80219/303-935-3850

Greenwood Precision, P.O. Box 468, Nixa, MO 65714-0468/417-725-2330

Greider Precision, 431 Santa Marina Ct., Escondido, CA 92029/619-480-8892

Gremmel Enterprises, 271 Sterling Dr., Eugene, OR 97404/503-688-3319

Grier's Hard Cast Bullets, 1107 11th St., LaGrande, OR 97850/503-963-8796

Griffin & Howe, Inc., 33 Claremont Rd., Bernardsville, NJ 07924/908-766-2287; FAX: 908-766-1068

Grizzly Bullets, 322 Green Mountain Rd., Trout Creek, MT 59874/406-847-2627

Groenewold, John, P.O. Box 830, Mundelein, IL 60060/708-566-2365

GRS Corp., Glendo, P.O. Box 1153, 900 Overlander St., Emporia, KS 66801/316-343-1084, 800-835-3519

Guardsman Products, 411 N. Darling, Fremont, MI 49412/616-924-3950

Gun City, 212 W. Main Ave., Bismarck, ND 58501/701-223-2304

Gun Doctor, The, 435 East Maple, Roselle, IL 60172/708-894-0668

Gun Hunter Books, Div. of Gun Hunter Trading Co., 5075 Heisig St., Beaumont, TX 77705/409-835-3006

Gun Leather Limited, 116 Lipscomb, Ft. Worth, TX 76104/817-334-0225; 800-247-0609

Gun Parts Corp., The, 226 Williams Lane, West Hurley, NY 12491/914-679-2417; FAX: 914-679-5849

Gun Room, The, 1121 Burlington, Muncie, IN 47302/317-282-9073; FAX: 317-282-9073

Gun Room Press, The, 127 Raritan Ave., Highland Park, NJ 08904/908-545-4344; FAX: 908-545-6686

Gun Shop, The, 5550 S. 900 East, Salt Lake City, UT 84117/801-263-3633

Gun Works, The, 236 Main St., Springfield, OR 97477/503-741-4118

Gun-Alert, Master Products, Inc., 1010 N. Maclay Ave., San Fernando, CA 91340/818-365-0864; FAX: 818-365-1308

Guncraft Sports, Inc., 10737 Dutchtown Rd., Knoxville, TN 37932/615-966-4545; FAX: 615-966-4500

Gunfitters, The, P.O. 426, Cambridge, WI 53523-0426/608-764-8128

Gun-Ho Sports Cases, 110 E. 10th St., St. Paul, MN 55101/612-224-9491

Gunline Tools, P.O. Box 478, Placentia, CA 92670/714-528-5252; FAX: 714-572-4128

Gunnerman Books, P.O. Box 214292, Auburn Hills, MI 48321/810-879-2779

Guns, 81 E. Streetsboro St., Hudson, OH 44236/216-650-4563

Guns, Div. of D.C. Engineering, Inc., 8633 Southfield Fwy., Detroit, MI 48228/313-271-7111, 800-886-7623 (orders only); FAX: 313-271-7112

Guns, Gear & Gadgets, L.L.C., P.O. Box 35722, Tucson, AZ 85240-5222/602-747-9578; FAX: 602-747-9715

GUNS Magazine, 591 Camino de la Reina, Suite 200, San Diego, CA 92108/619-297-5350; FAX: 619-297-5353

Gunsite Gunsmithy, P.O. Box 451, Paulden, AZ 86334/602-636-4565; FAX: 602-636-1236

Gunsmithing Ltd., 57 Unquowa Rd., Fairfield, CT 06430/203-254-0436

Gun-Tec, P.O. Box 8125, W. Palm Beach, FL 33407

Gurney, F.R., Box 13, Sooke, BC V0S 1N0 CANADA/604-642-5282

Gusty Winds Corp., 2950 Bear St., Suite 120, Costa Mesa, CA 92626/714-536-3587

Gwinnell, Bryson J., P.O. Box 248C, Maple Hill Rd., Rochester, VT 05767/802-767-3664

GZ Paintball Sports Products, P.O. Box 430, Andover, NH 03216/603-735-5300; FAX: 603-735-5154

H

H&P Publishing, 7174 Hoffman Rd., San Angelo, TX 76905/915-655-5953

H&R 1871, Inc., 60 Industrial Rowe, Gardner, MA 01440/508-632-9393; FAX: 508-632-2300

H&S Liner Service, 515 E. 8th, Odessa, TX 79761/915-332-1021

Hafner Creations, Inc., P.O. Box 1987, Lake City, FL 32055/904-755-6481; FAX: 904-755-6595

Hakko Co. Ltd., 5F Daini-Tsunemi Bldg., 1-13-12, Narimasu, Itabashiku Tokyo 175, JAPAN/03-5997-7870; FAX: 81-3-5997-7840

Hale, Peter, 800 E. Canyon Rd., Spanish Fork, UT 84660/801-798-8215

Half Moon Rifle Shop, 490 Halfmoon Rd., Columbia Falls, MT 59912/406-892-4409

Hallberg Gunsmith, Fritz, 33 S. Main, Payette, ID 83661

Hally Caller, 443 Wells Rd., Doylestown, PA 18901/215-345-6354

Hamilton, Alex B. (See Ten-Ring Precision, Inc.)

Hamilton, Keith, P.O. Box 871, Gridley, CA 95948/916-846-2316

Hammans, Charles E., P.O. Box 788, 2022 McCracken, Stuttgart, AR 72106/501-673-1388

Hammerli Ltd., Seonerstrasse 37, CH-5600 Lenzburg, SWITZERLAND/064-50 11 44; FAX: 064-51 38 27 (U.S. importer—Hammerli USA)

Hammerli USA, 19296 Oak Grove Circle, Groveland, CA 95321/209-962-5311; FAX: 209-962-5931

Hand Engravers Supply Co., 601 Springfield Dr., Albany, GA 31707/912-432-9683

Handgun Press, P.O. Box 406, Glenview, IL 60025/708-657-6500; FAX: 708-724-8831

HandiCrafts Unltd. (See Clements' Custom Leathercraft, Chas)

Hands Engraving, Barry Lee, 26192 E. Shore Route, Bigfork, MT 59911/406-837-0035

Hank's Gun Shop, Box 370, 50 West 100 South, Monroe, UT 84754/801-527-4456

Hanned Line, The, P.O. Box 2387, Cupertino, CA 95015-2387

Hanned Precision (See Hanned Line, The)

Hansen & Co. (See Hansen Cartridge Co.)

Hansen Cartridge Co., 244-246 Old Post Rd., Southport, CT 06490/203-259-6222, 203-259-7337; FAX: 203-254-3832

Hanson's Gun Center, Dick, 233 Everett Dr., Colorado Springs, CO 80911

Hardin Specialty Dist., P.O. Box 338, Radcliff, KY 40159-0338/502-351-6649

Hardison, Charles, P.O. Box 356, 200 W. Baseline Rd., Lafayette, CO 80026-0356/303-666-5171

Harold's Custom Gun Shop, Inc., Broughton Rifle Barrels, Rt. 1, Box 447, Big Spring, TX 79720/915-394-4430

Harrell's Precision, 5756 Hickory Dr., Salem, VA 24133/703-380-2683

Harris Enterprises, P.O. Box 105, Bly, OR 97622/503-353-2625

Harris Hand Engraving, Paul A., 10630 Janet Lee, San Antonio, TX 78230/512-391-5121

Harris Publications, 1115 Broadway, New York, NY 10010/212-807-7100; FAX: 212-627-4678

Harris-McMillan Gunworks, 302 W. Melinda Lane, Phoenix, AZ 85027/602-582-9627; FAX: 602-582-5178

Harrison Bullets, 6437 E. Hobart St., Mesa, AZ 85205

Harwood, Jack O., 1191 S. Pendlebury Lane, Blackfoot, ID 83221/208-785-5368

Haselbauer Products, Jerry, P.O. Box 27629, Tucson, AZ 85726/602-792-1075

Haydel's Game Calls, Inc., 5018 Hazel Jones Rd., Bossier City, LA 71111/318-746-3586, 800-HAYDELS; FAX: 318-746-3711

Haydon Shooters' Supply, Russ, 15018 Goodrich Dr. NW, Gig Harbor, WA 98329/206-857-7557

Heatbath Corp., P.O. Box 2978, Springfield, MA 01101/413-543-3381

Hebard Guns, Gil, 125-129 Public Square, Knoxville, IL 61448

HEBB Resources, P.O. Box 999, Mead, WA 99021-09996/509-466-1292

Hecht, Hubert J., Waffen-Hecht, P.O. Box 2635, Fair Oaks, CA 95628/916-966-1020

Heckler & Koch, Inc., 21480 Pacific Blvd., Sterling, VA 20166-8903/703-450-1900; FAX: 703-450-8160

Heckler & Koch GmbH, Postfach 1329, D-7238 Oberndorf, Neckar, GERMANY (U.S. importer—Heckler & Koch, Inc.)

Hege Jagd-u. Sporthandels, GmbH, P.O. Box 101461, W-7770 Ueberlingen a. Bodensee, GERMANY

Heidenstrom Bullets, Urds GT 1 Heroya, 3900 Porsgrunn, NORWAY

Heilmann, Stephen, P.O. Box 657, Grass Valley, CA 95945/916-272-8758

Heinie Specialty Products, 323 W. Franklin St., Havana, IL 62644/309-543-4535; FAX: 309-543-2521

Hellweg Ltd., 40356 Oak Park Way, Suite H, Oakhurst, CA 93644/209-683-3030; FAX: 209-683-3422

Helwan (See U.S. importer—Interarms)

Hendricks, Frank E., Master Engravers, Inc., HC03, Box 434, Dripping Springs, TX 78620/512-858-7828

Henigson & Associates, Steve, 2049 Kerwood Ave., Los Angeles, CA 90025/213-305-8288

Henriksen Tool Co., Inc., 8515 Wagner Creek Rd., Talent, OR 97540/503-535-2309

Hensler, Jerry, 6614 Country Field, San Antonio, TX 78240/210-690-7491

Hensley & Gibbs, Box 10, Murphy, OR 97533/503-862-2341

Heppler's Machining, 2240 Calle Del Mundo, Santa Clara, CA 95054/408-748-9166; FAX: 408-988-7711

Hercules, Inc., Hercules Plaza, 1313 N Market St., Wilmington, DE 19894/800-276-9337, 302-594-5000; FAX: 302-594-5305

Hermann Leather Co., H.J., Rt. 1, P.O. Box 525, Skiatook, OK 74070/918-396-1226

Herrett's Stocks, Inc., P.O. Box 741, Twin Falls, ID 83303/208-733-1498

Hertel & Reuss, Werk für Optik und Feinmechanik GmbH, Quellhofstrabe 67, 34 127 Kassel, GERMANY/0561-83006; FAX: 0561-893308

Herter's Manufacturing, Inc., 111 E. Burnett St., P.O. Box 518, Beaver Dam, WI 53916/414-887-1765; FAX: 414-887-8444

Hesco-Meprolight, 2821 Greenville Rd., LaGrange, GA 30240/706-884-7967; FAX: 706-882-4683

HH Engineering, Box 642, Dept. HD, Narberth, PA 19072-0642

High Bridge Arms, Inc., 3185 Mission St., San Francisco, CA 94110/415-282-8358

High North Products, Inc., P.O. Box 2, Antigo, WI 54409/715-627-2331

High Performance International, 5734 W. Florist Ave., Milwaukee, WI 53218/414-466-9040

High Standard Mfg. Co., Inc., 264 Whitney St., Hartford, CT 06105-2270/203-586-8220; FAX: 203-231-0411

Highline Machine Co., 654 Lela Place, Grand Junction, CO 81504/303-434-4971

Hill Speed Leather, Ernie, 4507 N. 195th Ave., Litchfield Park, AZ 85340/602-853-9222; FAX: 602-853-9235

Hi-Point Firearms, 5990 Philadelphia Dr., Dayton, OH 45415/513-275-4991; FAX: 513-275-4991

Hiptmayer, Armurier, RR 112 #750, P.O. Box 136, Eastman, Quebec J0E 1P0, CANADA/514-297-2492

Hiptmayer, Heidemarie, RR 112 #750, P.O. Box 136, Eastman, Quebec J0E 1P0, CANADA/514-297-2492

Hiptmayer, Klaus, RR 112 #750, P.O. Box 136, Eastman, Quebec J0E 1P0, CANADA/514-297-2492

Hirtenberger Aktiengesellschaft, Leobersdorferstrasse 31, A-2552 Hirtenberg, AUSTRIA/43(0)2256 81184; FAX: 43(0)2256 81807

Hiti-Schuch, Atelier Wilma, A-8863 Predlitz, Pirming Y1 AUSTRIA/0353418278

HJS Arms, Inc., P.O. Box 3711, Brownsville, TX 78523-3711/800-453-2767, 210-542-2767

H.K.S. Products, 7841 Founion Dr., Florence, KY 41042/606-342-7841, 800-354-9814; FAX: 606-342-5865

Hoag, James W., 8523 Canoga Ave., Suite C, Canoga Park, CA 91304/818-998-1510

Hobson Precision Manufacturing Co., Rt. 1, Box 220-C, Brent, AL 35034/205-926-4662

Hoch Custom Bullet Moulds (See Colorado Shooter's Supply)

Hodgdon Powder Co., Inc., P.O. Box 2932, 6231 Robinson, Shawnee Mission, KS 66202/913-362-9455; FAX: 913-362-1307

Hoehn Sales, Inc., 75 Greensburg Ct., St. Charles, MO 63304/314-441-4231

Hoelscher, Virgil, 11047 Pope Ave., Lynwood, CA 90262/310-631-8545

Hogue Grips, P.O. Box 1138, Paso Robles, CA 93447/800-438-4747, 805-239-1440; FAX: 805-239-2553

Holland's, Box 69, Powers, OR 97466/503-439-5155; FAX: 503-439-5155

Hollis Gun Shop, 917 Rex St., Carlsbad, NM 88220/505-885-3782

Hollywood Engineering, 10642 Arminta St., Sun Valley, CA 91352/818-842-8376

Holster Shop, The, 720 N. Flagler Dr., Ft. Lauderdale, FL 33304/305-463-7910; FAX: 305-761-1483

Holston Ent., Inc., P.O. Box 493, Piney Flats, TN 37686

Home Shop Machinist, The, Village Press Publications, P.O. Box 1810, Traverse City, MI 49685/800-447-7367; FAX: 616-946-3289

Hondo Ind., 510 S. 52nd St.,#104, Tempe, AZ 85281

Hoppe's Div., Penguin Industries, Inc., Airport Industrial Mall, Coatesville, PA 19320/610-384-6000

Horizons Unlimited, P.O. Box 426, Warm Springs, GA 31830/706-655-3603; FAX: 706-655-3603

Hornady Mfg. Co., P.O. Box 1848, Grand Island, NE 68802/800-338-3220, 308-382-1390; FAX: 308-382-5761

Horseshoe Leather Products, Andy Arratoonian, The Cottage Sharow, Ripon HG4 5BP ENGLAND/0765-605858

Horst, Alan K., 3221 2nd Ave. N., Great Falls, MT 59401/406-454-1831

House of Muskets, Inc., The, P.O. Box 4640, Pagosa Springs, CO 81157/303-731-2295

Howell Machine, 815½ D St., Lewiston, ID 83501/208-743-7418

Hoyt Holster Co., Inc., P.O. Box 69, Coupeville, WA 98239-0069/360-678-6640; FAX: 360-678-6549

Hughes, Steven Dodd, P.O. Box 11455, Eugene, OR 97440/503-485-8869

Hume, Don, P.O. Box 351, Miami, OK 74355/918-542-6604

Hungry Horse Books, 4605 Hwy. 93 South, Whitefish, MT 59937/406-862-7997

Hunkeler, A. (See Buckskin Machine Works)

Hunter Co., Inc., 3300 W. 71st Ave., Westminster, CO 80030/303-427-4626; FAX: 303-428-3980

Hunter's Specialties, Inc., 6000 Huntington Ct. NE, Cedar Rapids, IA 52402-1268/319-395-0321; FAX: 319-395-0326

Hunterjohn, P.O. Box 477, St. Louis, MO 63166/314-531-7250

Huntington Die Specialties, 601 Oro Dam Blvd., Oroville, CA 95965/916-534-1210; FAX: 916-534-1212

Hydrosorbent Products, P.O. Box 437, Ashley Falls, MA 01222/413-229-2967; FAX: 413-229-8743

Hyper-Single, Inc., 520 E. Beaver, Jenks, OK 74037/918-299-2391

I

I.A.B. (See U.S. importer—Taylor's & Co., Inc.)

ICI-America, P.O. Box 751, Wilmington, DE 19897/302-575-3000

Idaho Ammunition Service, 2816 Mayfair Dr., Lewiston, ID 83501/208-743-0270; FAX: 208-743-4930

IMI, P.O. Box 1044, Ramat Hasharon 47100, ISRAEL/972-3-5485222 (U.S. importer—Magnum Research, Inc.)

IMI Services USA, Inc., 2 Wisconsin Circle, Suite 420, Chevy Chase, MD 20815/301-215-4800; FAX: 301-657-1446

Imperial (See E-Z-Way Systems)

IMR Powder Co., 1080 Military Turnpike, Suite 2, Plattsburgh, NY 12901/518-563-2253; FAX: 518-563-6916

Ingle, Ralph W., 4 Missing Link, Rossville, GA 30741/404-866-5589

Innovative Weaponry, Inc., 337 Eubank NE, Albuquerque, NM 87123/800-334-3573, 505-296-4645; FAX: 505-271-2633

InSights Training Center, Inc., 240 NW Gilman Blvd., Issaquah, WA 98027/206-391-4834

INTEC International, Inc., P.O. Box 5708, Scottsdale, AZ 85261/602-483-1708

Interarms, 10 Prince St., Alexandria, VA 22314/703-548-1400; FAX: 703-549-7826

Intermountain Arms & Tackle, Inc., 105 E. Idaho St., Meridian, ID 83642/208-888-4911; FAX: 208-888-4381

International Shootists, Inc., P.O. Box 5354, Mission Hills, CA 91345/818-891-1723

Intratec, 12405 SW 130th St., Miami, FL 33186/305-232-1821; FAX: 305-253-7207

Iosso Products, 1485 Lively Blvd., Elk Grove Village, IL 60007/708-437-8400; FAX: 708-437-8478

Ironside International Publishers, Inc., P.O. Box 55, 800 Slaters Lane, Alexandria, VA 22313/703-684-6111; FAX: 703-683-5486

Ironsighter Co., 5555 Treadwell St., Wayne, MI 48184/313-326-8731; FAX: 313-326-3378

Irwin, Campbell H., 140 Hartland Blvd., East Hartland, CT 06027/203-653-3901

I.S.S., P.O. Box 185234, Ft. Worth, TX 76181/817-595-2090

Ivanoff, Thomas G. (See Tom's Gun Repair)

J

J-4, Inc., 1700 Via Burton, Anaheim, CA 92806/714-254-8315; FAX: 714-956-4421

J&D Components, 75 East 350 North, Orem, UT 84057-4719/801-225-7007

J&J Products, Inc., 9240 Whitmore, El Monte, CA 91731/818-571-5228, 800-927-8361; FAX: 818-571-8704

J&L Superior Bullets (See Huntington Die Specialties)

J&S Heat Treat, 803 S. 16th St., Blue Springs, MO 64015/816-229-2149; FAX: 816-228-1135

Jackalope Gun Shop, 1048 S. 5th St., Douglas, WY 82633/307-358-3441

JagerSport, Ltd., One Wholesale Way, Cranston, RI 02920/800-962-4867, 401-944-9682; FAX: 401-946-2587

Jamison's Forge Works, 4527 Rd. 6.5 NE, Moses Lake, WA 98837/509-762-2659

Jantz Supply, P.O. Box 584-GD, Davis, OK 73030/405-369-2316; FAX: 405-369-3082

Jarvis Gunsmithing, Inc., 1123 Cherry Orchard Lane, Hamilton, MT 59840/406-961-4392

Javelina Products, P.O. Box 337, San Bernardino, CA 92402/714-882-5847; FAX: 714-434-6937

J-B Bore Cleaner, 299 Poplar St., Hamburg, PA 19526/610-562-2103

JBM, P.O. Box 3648, University Park, NM 88003

Jeffredo Gunsight, P.O. Box 669, San Marcos, CA 92079/619-728-2695

Jenco Sales, Inc., P.O. Box 1000, Manchaca, TX 78652/800-531-5301; FAX: 800-263-2373

Jennings Firearms, Inc., 17692 Cowan, Irvine, CA 92714/714-252-7621; FAX: 714-252-7626

Jensen Bullets, 86 North, 400 West, Blackfoot, ID 83221/208-785-5590

Jensen's Custom Ammunition, 5146 E. Pima, Tucson, AZ 85712/602-325-3346; FAX: 602-322-5704

Jensen's Firearms Academy, 1280 W. Prince, Tucson, AZ 85705/602-293-8516

Jester Bullets, Rt. 1 Box 27, Orienta, OK 73737

Jett & Co., Inc., 104 W. Water St., Litchfield, IL 62056-2464/217-324-3779

Jewell, Arnold W., 1490 Whitewater Rd., New Braunfels, TX 78132/210-620-0971

JGS Precision Tool Mfg., 1141 S. Summer Rd., Coos Bay, OR 97420/503-267-4331; FAX:503-267-5996

J.I.T., Ltd., P.O. Box 230, Freedom, WY 83120/708-494-0937

JLK Bullets, 414 Turner Rd., Dover, AR 72837/501-331-4194

J.O. Arms Inc., 5709 Hartsdale, Houston, TX 77036/713-789-0745; FAX: 713-789-7513

John's Custom Leather, 523 S. Liberty St., Blairsville, PA 15717/412-459-6802

Johns, Bill, 1412 Lisa Rae, Round Rock, TX 78664/512-255-8246

Johnson's Gunsmithing, Inc., Neal, 208 W. Buchanan St., Suite B, Colorado Springs, CO 80907/800-284-8671 (orders), 719-632-3795; FAX: 719-632-3493

Johnston Bros., 1889 Rt. 9, Unit 22, Toms River, NJ 08755/800-257-2595; FAX: 800-257-2534

Johnston, James (See North Fork Custom Gunsmithing)

Jonad Corp., 2091 Lakeland Ave., Lakewood, OH 44107/216-226-3161

Jonas Appraisals & Taxidermy, Jack, 1675 S. Birch, Suite 506, Denver, CO 80222/303-757-7347

Jones, J.D. (See SSK Industries)

Jones Co., Dale, 680 Hoffman Draw, Kila, MT 59920/406-755-4684

Jones Moulds, Paul, 4901 Telegraph Rd., Los Angeles, CA 90022/213-262-1510

Joy Enterprises (See Fury Cutlery)

J.P. Enterprises, Inc., P.O. Box 26324, Shoreview, MN 55126/612-486-9064; FAX: 612-482-0970

JSL (Hereford) Ltd., 35 Church St., Hereford HR1 2LR ENGLAND/0432-355416; FAX: 0432-355242 (U.S. importer—Specialty Shooters Supply, Inc.)

Jumbo Sports Products (See Bucheimer, J.M.)

Jungkind, Reeves C., 5001 Buckskin Pass, Austin, TX 78745-2841/512-442-1094

Jurras, L.E., P.O. Box 680, Washington, IN 47501/812-254-7698

JWH: Software, 6947 Haggerty Rd., Hillsboro, OH 45133/513-393-2402

K

K&K Ammo Wrist Band, R.D. #1, P.O. Box 448-CA18, Lewistown, PA 17044/717-242-2329

K&M Industries, Inc., Box 66, 510 S. Main, Troy, ID 83871/208-835-2281; FAX: 208-835-5211

K&M Services, 5430 Salmon Run Rd., Dover, PA 17315/717-764-1461

K&S Mfg., 2611 Hwy. 40 East, Inglis, FL 34449/904-447-3571

K&T Co., Div. of T&S Industries, Inc., 1027 Skyview Dr., W. Carrollton, OH 45449/513-859-8414

Ka Pu Kapili, P.O. Box 745, Honokaa, HI 96727/808-776-1644; FAX: 808-776-1731

Kahles U.S.A., P.O. Box 81071, Warwick, RI 02888/800-752-4537; FAX: 401-946-2587

Kahr Arms, P.O. Box 220, 630 Route 303, Blauvelt, NY 10913/914-353-5996; FAX: 914-353-7833

Kamyk Engraving Co., Steve, 9 Grandview Dr., Westfield, MA 01085-1810/413-568-0457

Kane Products, Inc., 5572 Brecksville Rd., Cleveland, OH 44131/216-524-9962

Kapro Mfg. Co., Inc. (See R.E.I.)

Kasenit Co., Inc., 13 Park Ave., Highland Mills, NY 10930/914-928-9595; FAX: 914-928-7292

Kasmarsik Bullets, 152 Crstler Rd., Chehalis, WA 98532

Kassnar (See U.S. importer—K.B.I., Inc.)

Kaswer Custom, Inc., 13 Surrey Drive, Brookfield, CT 06804/203-775-0564; FAX: 203-775-6872

K.B.I., Inc., P.O. Box 5440, Harrisburg, PA 17110-0440/717-540-8518; FAX: 717-540-8567

K-D, Inc., Box 459, 585 North, Highway 155, Cleveland, UT 84518/801-653-2530

KDF, Inc., 2485 Hwy. 46 N., Seguin, TX 78155/210-379-8141; FAX: 210-379-5420

KeeCo Impressions, Inc., 346 Wood Ave., North Brunswick, NJ 08902/800-468-0546

Keeler, R.H., 817 "N" St., Port Angeles, WA 98362/206-457-4702

Kehr, Roger, 2131 Agate Ct. SE, Lacy, WA 98503/360-456-0831

Keith's Bullets, 942 Twisted Oak, Algonquin, IL 60102/708-658-3520

Kelbly, Inc., 7222 Dalton Fox Lake Rd., North Lawrence, OH 44666/216-683-4674; FAX: 216-683-7349

Keller Co., The, 4215 McEwen Rd., Dallas, TX 75244/214-770-8585

Kelley's, P.O. Box 125, Woburn, MA 01801/617-935-3389

Kelly, Lance, 1723 Willow Oak Dr., Edgewater, FL 32132/904-423-4933

Kel-Tec CNC Industries, Inc., P.O. Box 3427, Cocoa, FL 32924/407-631-0068; FAX: 407-631-1169

Ken's Gun Specialties, Rt. 1, Box 147, Lakeview, AR 72642/501-431-5606

Ken's Kustom Kartridges, 331 Jacobs Rd., Hubbard, OH 44425/216-534-4595

Kennebec Journal, 274 Western Ave., Augusta, ME 04330/207-622-6288

Kennedy Firearms, 10 N. Market St., Muncy, PA 17756/717-546-6695

Kent Cartridge Mfg. Co. Ltd., Unit 16, Branbridges Industrial Estate, East Peckham, Tonbridge, Kent, TN12 5HF ENGLAND/622-872255; FAX: 622-872645

Keowee Game Calls, 608 Hwy. 25 North, Travelers Rest, SC 29690/803-834-7204

Kesselring Gun Shop, 400 Hwy. 99 North, Burlington, WA 98233/206-724-3113; FAX: 206-724-7003

Kilham & Co., Main St., P.O. Box 37, Lyme, NH 03768/603-795-4112

Kimball, Gary, 1526 N. Circle Dr., Colorado Springs, CO 80909/719-634-1274

Kimber of America, Inc., 9039 SE Jannsen Rd., Clackamas, OR 97015/503-656-1704, 800-880-2418; FAX: 503-656-5357

Kimel Industries, 3800 Old Monroe Rd., P.O. Box 335, Matthews, NC 28105/800-438-9288; FAX: 704-821-6339

King & Co., P.O. Box 1242, Bloomington, IL 61701/309-473-3964

King's Gun Works, 1837 W. Glenoaks Blvd., Glendale, CA 91201/818-956-6010; FAX: 818-548-8606

Kingyon, Paul L., 607 N. 5th St., Burlington, IA 52601/319-752-4465

Kirkpatrick Leather Co., 1910 San Bernardo, Laredo, TX 78040/210-723-6631; FAX: 210-725-0672

KJM Fabritek, Inc., P.O. Box 162, Marietta, GA 30061/404-426-8251

K.K. Arms Co., Star Route Box 671, Kerrville, TX 78028/210-257-4718; FAX: 210-257-4891

KLA Enterprises, P.O. Box 2028, Eaton Park, FL 33840/813-682-2829; FAX: 813-682-2829

Kleen-Bore, Inc., 16 Industrial Pkwy., Easthampton, MA 01027/413-527-0300; FAX: 413-527-2522

Klein Custom Guns, Don, 433 Murray Park Dr., Ripon, WI 54971/414-748-2931

Kleinendorst, K.W., RR #1, Box 1500, Hop Bottom, PA 18824/717-289-4687

Klingler Woodcarving, P.O. Box 141, Thistle Hill, Cabot, VT 05647/802-426-3811

Kmount, P.O. Box 19422, Louisville, KY 40259/502-239-5447

Knight & Hale Game Calls, Box 468 Industrial Park, Cadiz, KY 42211/502-924-1755; FAX: 502-924-1763

Knight's Mfg. Co., 7750 9th St. SW, Vero Beach, FL 32968/407-562-5697; FAX: 407-569-2955

Kodiak Custom Bullets, 8261 Henry Circle, Anchorage, AK 99507/907-349-2282

Koevenig's Engraving Service, Box 55 Rabbit Gulch, Hill City, SD 57745

Kolpin Mfg., Inc., P.O. Box 107, 205 Depot St., Fox Lake, WI 53933/414-928-3118; FAX: 414-928-3687

Kopp, Terry K., Route 1, Box 224F, Lexington, MO 64067/816-259-2636

Korzinek Riflesmith, J., RD #2, Box 73D, Canton, PA 17724/717-673-8512

Kowa Optimed, Inc., 20001 S. Vermont Ave., Torrance, CA 90502/310-327-1913; FAX: 310-327-4177

Kramer Handgun Leather, P.O. Box 112154, Tacoma, WA 98411/206-564-6652; FAX: 206-564-1214

Krause Publications, Inc., 700 E. State St., Iola, WI 54990/715-445-2214; FAX: 715-445-4087

Kris Mounts, 108 Lehigh St., Johnstown, PA 15905/814-539-9751

KSN Industries, Ltd. (See U.S. importer—J.O. Arms Inc.)

K-Sports Imports, Inc., 2755 Thompson Creek Rd., Pomona, CA 91767/909-392-2345; FAX: 909-392-2354

Kudlas, John M., 622 14th St. SE, Rochester, MN 55904/507-288-5579

Kulis Freeze Dry Taxidermy, 725 Broadway Ave., Bedford, OH 44146/216-232-8352; FAX: 216-232-7305

KVH Industries, Inc., 110 Enterprise Center, Middletown, RI 02842/401-847-3327; FAX: 401-849-0045

Kwik Mount Corp., P.O. Box 19422, Louisville, KY 40259/502-239-5447

L

L&R Lock Co., 1137 Pocalla Rd., Sumter, SC 29150/803-775-6127

L&S Technologies, Inc. (See Aimtech Mount Systems)

La Clinique du .45, 1432 Rougemont, Chambly, Quebec, J3L 2L8 CANADA/514-658-1144

Labanu, Inc., 2201-F Fifth Ave., Ronkonkoma, NY 11779/516-467-6197; FAX: 516-981-4112

LaBounty Precision Reboring, P.O. Box 186, 7968 Silver Lk. Rd., Maple Falls, WA 98266/306-599-2047

LaFrance Specialties, P.O. Box 178211, San Diego, CA 92177-8211/619-293-3373

Lakewood Products, Inc., 275 June St., P.O. Box 230, Berlin, WI 54923/800-US-BUILT; FAX: 414-361-5058

Lampert, Ron, Rt. 1, Box 177, Guthrie, MN 56461/218-854-7345

Lane Publishing, P.O. Box 759, Hot Springs, AR 71902/501-525-7514; FAX: 501-525-7519

LAP Systems Groups, N.A., P.O. Box 162, Marietta, GA 30061

L.A.R. Mfg., Inc., 4133 W. Farm Rd., West Jordan, UT 84088/801-280-3505; FAX: 801-280-1972

LaRocca Gun Works, Inc., 51 Union Place, Worcester, MA 01608/508-754-2887; FAX: 508-754-2887

Laser Devices, Inc., 2 Harris Ct. A-4, Monterey, CA 93940/408-373-0701; FAX: 408-373-0903

Laseraim, Inc. (See Emerging Technologies, Inc.)

LaserMax, 3495 Winton Place, Bldg. B, Rochester, NY 14623/716-272-5420; FAX: 716-272-5427

Lassen Community College, Gunsmithing Dept., P.O. Box 3000, Hwy. 139, Susanville, CA 96130/916-257-6181 ext. 109 or 200; FAX: 916-257-8964

Lathrop's, Inc., 5146 E. Pima, Tucson, AZ 85712/602-881-0226, 800-875-4867

Laurel Mountain Forge, P.O. Box 224, Romeo, MI 48065/810-749-5742

Law Concealment Systems, Inc., P.O. Box 3952, Wilmington, NC 28406/919-791-6656, 800-373-0116 orders

Lawrence Leather Co., P.O. Box 1479, Lillington, NC 27546/910-893-2071; FAX: 910-893-4742

Lawson, John G. (See Sight Shop, The)

Lawson Co., Harry, 3328 North Richey Blvd., Tucson, AZ 85716/520-326-1117

LBT, HCR 62, Box 145, Moyie Springs, ID 83845/208-267-3588

Lea Mfg. Co., 237 E. Aurora St., Waterbury, CT 06720/203-753-5116

Leather Arsenal, 27549 Middleton Rd., Middleton, ID 83644/208-585-6212

Leckie Professional Gunsmithing, 546 Quarry Rd., Ottsville, PA 18942/215-847-8594

Lectro Science, Inc., 6410 W. Ridge Rd., Erie, PA 16506/814-833-6487; FAX: 814-833-0447

Ledbetter Airguns, Riley, 1804 E. Sprague St., Winston Salem, NC 27107-3521/919-784-0676

Lee Co., T.K., One Independence Plaza, Suite 520, Birmingham, AL 35209/205-913-5222

Lee Precision, Inc., 4275 Hwy. U, Hartford, WI 53027/414-673-3075

Lee's Red Ramps, 4 Kristine Ln., Silver City, NM 88061/505-538-8529

Lee Supplies, Mark, 9901 France Ct., Lakeville, MN 55044/612-461-2114

LeFever Arms Co., Inc., 6234 Stokes, Lee Center Rd., Lee Center, NY 13363/315-337-6722; FAX: 315-337-1543

Legend Products Corp., 1555 E. Flamingo Rd., Suite 404, Las Vegas, NV 89119/702-228-1808, 702-796-5778; FAX: 702-228-7484

Leibowitz, Leonard, 1205 Murrayhill Ave., Pittsburgh, PA 15217/412-361-5455

Leica USA, Inc., 156 Ludlow Ave., Northvale, NJ 07647/201-767-7500; FAX: 201-767-8666

LEM Gun Specialties, Inc., P.O. Box 2855, Peachtree City, GA 30269-2024

Lem Sports, Inc., P.O. Box 2107, Aurora, IL 60506/815-286-7421, 800-688-8801 (orders only)

Lethal Force Institute (See Police Bookshelf)

Letschnig, Franz, RR 1, Martintown, Ont. K0C 1SO, CANADA/613-528-4843

Lett Custom Grips, 672 Currier Rd., Hopkinton, NH 03229

Leupold & Stevens, Inc., P.O. Box 688, Beaverton, OR 97075/503-646-9171; FAX: 503-526-1455

Liberty Antique Gunworks, 19 Key St., P.O. Box 183, Eastport, ME 04631/207-853-4116

Liberty Metals, 2233 East 16th St., Los Angeles, CA 90021/213-581-9171; FAX: 213-581-9351

Liberty Shooting Supplies, P.O. Box 357, Hillsboro, OR 97123/503-640-5518

Lightfield Ammunition Corp., The Slug Group, P.O. Box 376, New Paris, PA 15554/814-839-4517; FAX: 814-839-2601

Lightforce U.S.A., Inc., P.O. Box 488, Vaughan, WA 98394/206-876-3225; FAX: 206-876-3249

Lindsay, Steve, RR 2 Cedar Hills, Kearney, NE 68847/308-236-7885

Lindsley Arms Cartridge Co., P.O. Box 757, 20 College Hill Rd., Henniker, NH 03242/603-428-3127

Linebaugh Custom Sixguns, Route 2, Box 100, Maryville, MO 64468/816-562-3031

List Precision Engineering, Unit 1, Ingley Works, 13 River Road, Barking, Essex ENGLAND 1G11 0HE/011-081-594-1686

Lite Tek International, 133-30 32nd Ave., Flushing, NY 11354/718-463-0650; FAX: 718-762-0890

Lithi Bee Bullet Lube, 1885 Dyson St., Muskegon, MI 49442/616-726-3400

"Little John's" Antique Arms, 1740 W. Laveta, Orange, CA 92668

Littler Sales Co., 20815 W. Chicago, Detroit, MI 48228/313-273-6888; FAX: 313-273-1099

Littleton, J.F., 275 Pinedale Ave., Oroville, CA 95966/916-533-6084

Llama Gabilondo Y Cia, Apartado 290, E-01080, Victoria, SPAIN (U.S. importer—SGS Importers International, Inc.)

Load From A Disk, 9826 Sagedale, Houston, TX 77089/713-484-0935

Loadmaster, P.O. Box 1209, Warminster, Wilts. BA12 9XJ ENGLAND/01044 1985 218544; FAX: 01044 1985 214111

Loch Leven Industries, P.O. Box 2751, Santa Rosa, CA 95405/707-573-8735; FAX: 707-573-0369

Lock's Philadelphia Gun Exchange, 6700 Rowland Ave., Philadelphia, PA 19149/215-332-6225; FAX: 215-332-4800

Lodewick, Walter H., 2816 NE Halsey St., Portland, OR 97232/503-284-2554

Lofland, James W., 2275 Larkin Rd., Boothwyn, PA 19061/610-485-0391

Log Cabin Sport Shop, 8010 Lafayette Rd., Lodi, OH 44254/216-948-1082

Lohman Mfg. Co., Inc., 4500 Doniphan Dr., P.O. Box 220, Neosho, MO 64850/417-451-4438; FAX: 417-451-2576

Lomont Precision Bullets, 4236 W. 700 South, Poneto, IN 46781/219-694-6792; FAX: 219-694-6797

Lone Star Gunleather, 1301 Brushy Bend Dr., Round Rock, TX 78681/512-255-1805

Long, George F., 1500 Rogue River Hwy., Ste. F, Grants Pass, OR 97527/503-476-7552

Lorcin Engineering Co., Inc., 10427 San Sevaine Way, Ste. A, Mira Loma, CA 91752/909-360-1406; FAX: 909-360-0623

Lortone, Inc., 2856 NW Market St., Seattle, WA 98107/206-789-3100

Loweth, Richard, 29 Hedgegrow Lane, Kirby Muxloe, Leics. LE9 9BN ENGLAND

L.P.A. Snc, Via Alfieri 26, Gardone V.T., Brescia, ITALY 25063/30-891-14-81; FAX: 30-891-09-51

LPS Laboratories, Inc., 4647 Hugh Howell Rd., P.O. Box 3050, Tucker, GA 30084/404-934-7800

Lucas, Edward E., 32 Garfield Ave., East Brunswick, NJ 08816/201-251-5526

Luch Metal Merchants, Barbara, 48861 West Rd., Wixon, MI 48393/800-876-5337

Lutz Engraving, Ron, E. 1998 Smokey Valley Rd., Scandinavia, WI 54977/715-467-2674

Lyman Instant Targets, Inc. (See Lyman Products Corp.)

Lyman Products Corp., Rt. 147, Middlefield, CT 06455/203-349-3421, 800-22-LYMAN; FAX: 203-349-3586

M

M&D Munitions Ltd., 127 Verdi St., Farmingdale, NY 11735/800-878-2788, 516-752-1038; FAX: 516-752-1905

M&N Bullet Lube, P.O. Box 495, 151 NE Jefferson St., Madras, OR 97741/503-255-3750

MA Systems, P.O. Box 1143, Chouteau, OK 74337/918-479-6378

Mac's .45 Shop, P.O. Box 2028, Seal Beach, CA 90740/310-438-5046

Mac-1 Distributors, 13974 Van Ness Ave., Gardena, CA 90249/310-327-3582

Madis, David, 2453 West Five Mile Pkwy., Dallas, TX 75233/214-330-7168

Madis, George, P.O. Box 545, Brownsboro, TX 75756

Magma Engineering Co., P.O. Box 161, 20955 E. Ocotillo Rd., Queen Creek, AZ 85242/602-987-9008; FAX: 602-987-0148

Mag-Na-Port International, Inc., 41302 Executive Dr., Harrison Twp., MI 48045-1306/810-469-6727; FAX: 810-469-0425

Magnolia Sports, Inc., 211 W. Main, Magnolia, AR 71753/501-234-8410, 800-530-7816; FAX: 501-234-8117

Magnum Research, Inc., 7110 University Ave. NE, Minneapolis, MN 55432/612-574-1868; FAX: 612-574-0109

Magnus Bullets, P.O. Box 239, Toney, AL 35773/205-828-5089; FAX: 205-828-7756

Mag-Pack Corp., P.O. Box 846, Chesterland, OH 44026

MagSafe Ammo Co., 2725 Friendly Grove Rd NE, Olympia, WA 98506/206-357-6383

Mahony, Philip Bruce, 67 White Hollow Rd., Lime Rock, CT 06039-2418/203-435-9341

Maine Custom Bullets, RFD 1, Box 1755, Brooks, ME 04921

Mains Enterprises, Inc., 3111 S. Valley View Blvd., Suite B120, Las Vegas, NV 89102-7790/702-876-6278; FAX: 702-876-1269

Maionchi-L.M.I., Via Di Coselli-Zona Industriale Di Guamo, Lucca, ITALY 55060/011 39-583 94291

Makinson, Nicholas, RR 3, Komoka, Ont. N0L 1R0 CANADA/519-471-5462

Mallardtone Game Calls, 2901 16th St., Moline, IL 61265/309-762-8089

Mandall Shooting Supplies, Inc., 3616 N. Scottsdale Rd., Scottsdale, AZ 85252/602-945-2553; FAX: 602-949-0734

Marble Arms (See CRL, Inc.)

Marchmon Bullets, 8191 Woodland Shore Dr., Brighton, MI 48116

Marek, George, 55 Arnold St., Westfield, MA 01085/413-562-5673

Marent, Rudolf, 9711 Tiltree St., Houston, TX 77075/713-946-7028

Markell, Inc., 422 Larkfield Center #235, Santa Rosa, CA 95403/707-573-0792; FAX: 707-573-9867

Marksman Products, 5482 Argosy Dr., Huntington Beach, CA 92649/714-898-7535, 800-822-8005; FAX: 714-372-3041

Marmik Inc., 2116 S. Woodland Ave., Michigan City, IN 46361-7508/219-872-7231

Marple & Associates, Dick, 21 Dartmouth St., Hooksett, NH 03106/603-627-1837; FAX: 603-641-4837

Marsh, Johnny, 1007 Drummond Dr., Nashville, TN 37211/615-833-3259

Marsh, Mike, Croft Cottage, Main St., Elton, Derbyshire DE4 2BY, ENGLAND/0629 650 669

Martin Bookseller, J., P.O. Drawer AP, Beckley, WV 25802/304-255-4073; FAX: 304-255-4077

Martin's Gun Shop, 937 S. Sheridan Blvd., Lakewood, CO 80226/303-922-2184

Martz, John V., 8060 Lakeview Lane, Lincoln, CA 95648/916-645-2250

Marvel, Alan, 3922 Madonna Rd., Jarretsville, MD 21084/301-557-6545

Maryland Paintball Supply, 8507 Harford Rd., Parkville, MD 21234/410-882-5607

Masen Co., Inc., John, P.O. Box 5050, Suite 165, Lewisville, TX 75057/817-430-8732; FAX: 817-430-1715

Master Class Bullets, 4209-D West 6th, Eugene, OR 97402/503-687-1263, 800-883-1263

Master Engravers, Inc. (See Hendricks, Frank E.)

Master Lock Co., 2600 N. 32nd St., Milwaukee, WI 53245/414-444-2800

Master Products, Inc. (See Gun-Alert/Master Products, Inc.)

Match Prep, P.O. Box 155, Tehachapi, CA 93581/805-822-5383

Matco, Inc., 1003-2nd St., N. Manchester, IN 46962/219-982-8282

Mathews & Son, Inc., George E., 10224 S. Paramount Blvd., Downey, CA 90241/310-862-6719; FAX: 310-862-6719

Mauser Werke Oberndorf Waffensysteme GmbH, Postfach 1349, 78722 Oberndorf/N. GERMANY (U.S. importer—Gibbs Rifle Co., Inc.)

Maxi-Mount, P.O. Box 291, Willoughby Hills, OH 44094-0291/216-585-1329

McCament, Jay, 1730-134th St. Ct. S., Tacoma, WA 98444/206-531-8832

McCann's Machine & Gun Shop, P.O. Box 641, Spanaway, WA 98387/206-537-6919; FAX: 206-537-6993

McCann's Muzzle-Gun Works, 14 Walton Dr., New Hope, PA 18938/215-862-2728

McCombs, Leo, 1862 White Cemetery Road, Patriot, OH 45658/614-256-1714

McCormick Corp., Chip, 1825 Fortview Rd., Ste. 115, Austin, TX 78704/800-328-CHIP, 512-462-0004; FAX: 512-462-0009

McDonald, Dennis, 8359 Brady St., Peosta, IA 52068/319-556-7940

McFarland, Stan, 2221 Idella Ct., Grand Junction, CO 81505/303-243-4704

McGowen Rifle Barrels, 5961 Spruce Lane, St. Anne, IL 60964/815-937-9816; FAX: 815-937-4024

McKenzie, Lynton, 6940 N. Alvernon Way, Tucson, AZ 85718/520-299-5090

McKillen & Heyer, Inc., 35535 Euclid Ave. Suite 11, Willoughby, OH 44094/216-942-2044

McKinney, R.P. (See Schuetzen Gun Service)

McMillan Optical Gunsight Co., 28638 N. 42nd St., Cave Creek, AZ 85331/602-585-7868; FAX: 602-585-7872

McMurdo, Lynn (See Specialty Gunsmithing)

MCRW Associates Shooting Supplies, R.R. #1 Box 1425, Sweet Valley, PA 18656/717-864-3967; FAX: 717-864-2669

MCS, Inc., 34 Delmar Dr., Brookfield, CT 06804/203-775-1013; FAX: 203-775-9462

MDS, P.O. Box 1441, Brandon, FL 33509-1441/813-653-1180; FAX: 813-684-5953

Meadow Industries, P.O. Box 754, Locust Grove, VA 22508/703-972-2175; FAX: 703-972-2175

MEC, Inc., 715 South St., Mayville, WI 53050/414-387-4500; FAX: 414-387-5802

Meier Works, P.O. Box 423, Tijeras, NM 87059/505-281-3783

Mele, Frank, 201 S. Wellow Ave., Cookeville, TN 38501/615-526-4860

Menck, Thomas W., 5703 S. 77th St., Ralston, NE 68127-4201

Mendez, John A., P.O. Box 620984, Orlando, FL 32862/407-282-2178

Men-Metallwerk Elisenhuette, GmbH, P.O. Box 1263, D-56372 Nassau/Lahn, GERMANY/2604-7819

Meprolight (See Hesco-Meprolight)

Merkuria Ltd., Argentinska 38, 17005 Praha 7, CZECH REPUBLIC/422-875117; FAX: 422-809152

Metalife Industries, Box 53 Mong Ave., Reno, PA 16343/814-436-7747; FAX: 814-676-5662

Metaloy Inc., Rt. 5, Box 595, Berryville, AR 72616/501-545-3611

Michael's Antiques, Box 591, Waldoboro, ME 04572

Michaels of Oregon Co., P.O. Box 13010, Portland, OR 97213/503-255-6890; FAX: 503-255-0746

Micro Sight Co., 242 Harbor Blvd., Belmont, CA 94002/415-591-0769; FAX: 415-591-7531

Micro-Lube, Rt. 2, P.O. Box 201, Deming, NM 88030/505-546-9116

Mid-America Recreation, Inc., 1328 5th Ave., Moline, IA 52807/309-764-5089; FAX: 309-764-2722

Middlebrooks Custom Shop, 7366 Colonial Trail East, Surry, VA 23883/804-357-0881; FAX: 804-365-0442

Midway Arms, Inc., 5875 W. Van Horn Tavern Rd., Columbia, MO 65203/800-243-3220, 314-445-6363; FAX: 314-446-1018

Military Armament Corp., P.O. Box 120, Mt. Zion Rd., Lingleville, TX 76461/817-965-3253

Miller Custom, 210 E. Julia, Clinton, IL 61727/217-935-9362

Miller Engineering, R&D Engineering & Manufacturing, P.O. Box 6342, Virginia Beach, VA 23456/804-468-1402

Miller Enterprises, R.P., Inc., 1557 E. Main St., P.O. Box 234, Brownsburg, IN 46112/317-852-8187

Millett Sights, 16131 Gothard St., Huntington Beach, CA 92647/714-842-5575, 800-645-5388; FAX: 714-843-5707

Milstor Corp., 80-975 E. Valley Pkwy. C-7, Indio, CA 92201/619-775-9998; FAX: 619-772-4990

Minute Man High Tech Industries, 3005B 6th Ave., Tacoma, WA 98406/800-233-2734

Mirador Optical Corp., P.O. Box 11614, Marina Del Rey, CA 90295-7614/310-821-5587; FAX: 310-305-0386

Mitchell Arms, Inc. 3433 W. Harvard St., Santa Ana, CA 92704/714-957-5711; FAX: 714-957-5732

Mitchell's Accuracy Shop, 68 Greenridge Dr., Stafford, VA 22554/703-659-0165

MI-TE Bullets, R.R. 1 Box 230, Ellsworth, KS 67439/913-472-4575

Mittermeier, Inc., Frank, P.O. Box 2G, 3577 E. Tremont Ave., Bronx, NY 10465/718-828-3843

Mixson Corp., 7435 W. 19th Ct., Hialeah, FL 33014/305-821-5190, 800-327-0078; FAX: 305-558-9318

MJK Gunsmithing, Inc., 417 N. Huber Ct., E. Wenatchee, WA 98802/509-884-7683

MKL Service Co., 610 S. Troy St., P.O. Box D, Royal Oak, MI 48068/810-548-5453

MKS Supply, Inc., 174 S. Mulberry St., Mansfield, OH 44902/419-522-8330; FAX: 513-522-8330

MMC, 606 Grace Ave., Ft. Worth, TX 76111/817-831-0837

MMP, Rt. 6, Box 384, Harrison, AR 72601/501-741-5019; FAX: 501-741-3104

Mo's Competitor Supplies (See MCS, Inc.)

M.O.A. Corp., 2451 Old Camden Pike, Eaton, OH 45320/513-456-3669

Modern Gun Repair School, 2538 N. 8th St., P.O. Box 5338, Dept. GNX96, Phoenix, AZ 85010/602-990-8346

Modern MuzzleLoading, Inc., 234 Airport Rd., P.O. Box 130, Centerville, IA 52544/515-856-2626; FAX: 515-856-2628

MoLoc Bullets, P.O. Box 2810, Turlock, CA 95381-2810/209-632-1644

Montana Armory, Inc. 100 Centennial Dr., Big Timber, MT 59011/406-932-4353

Montana Outfitters, Lewis E. Yearout, 308 Riverview Dr. E., Great Falls, MT 59404/406-761-0859

Montana Precision Swaging, P.O. Box 4746, Butte, MT 59702/406-782-7502

Monte Kristo Pistol Grip Co., P.O. Box 85, Whiskeytown, CA 96095/916-623-4019

Montgomery Community College, P.O. Box 787, Troy, NC 27371/919-572-3691

Moreton/Fordyce Enterprises, P.O. Box 940, Saylorsburg, PA 18353/717-992-5742; FAX: 717-992-8775

Morini (See U.S. importers—Mandall Shooting Shpplies, Inc.; Nygord Precision Products)

Morrison Custom Rifles, J.W., 4015 W. Sharon, Phoenix, AZ 85029/602-978-3754

Morrow, Bud, 11 Hillside Lane, Sheridan, WY 82801-9729/307-674-8360

Moschetti, Mitchell R., P.O. Box 27065, Denver, CO 80227/303-733-9593

Moss Double Tone, Inc., P.O. Box 1112, 2101 S. Kentucky, Sedalia, MO 65301/816-827-0827

Mountain Hollow Game Calls, Box 121, Cascade, MD 21719/301-241-3282

Mountain South, P.O. Box 381, Barnwell, SC 29812/FAX: 803-259-3227

Mountain State Muzzleloading Supplies, Box 154-1, Rt. 2, Williamstown, WV 26187/304-375-7842; FAX: 304-375-3737

Mountain States Engraving, Kenneth W. Warren, P.O. Box 2842, Wenatchee, WA 98802/509-663-6123

Mountain View Sports, Inc., Box 188, Troy, NH 03465/603-357-9690; FAX: 603-357-9691

Mowrey's Guns & Gunsmithing, RR1, Box 82, Canajoharie, NY 13317/518-673-3483

MSC Industrial Supply Co., 151 Sunnyside Blvd., Plainview, NY 11803-9915/516-349-0330

MSR Targets, P.O. Box 1042, West Covina, CA 91793/818-331-7840

Mt. Alto Outdoor Products, Rt. 735, Howardsville, VA 24562

Mt. Baldy Bullet Co., 12981 Old Hill City Rd., Keystone, SD 57751-6623/605-666-4725

MTM Molded Products Co., Inc., 3370 Obco Ct., Dayton, OH 45414/513-890-7461; FAX: 513-890-1747

Mullins Ammo, Rt. 2, Box 304K, Clintwood, VA 24228/703-926-6772

Mullis Guncraft, 3523 Lawyers Road E., Monroe, NC 28110/704-283-6683

Multiplex International, 26 S. Main St., Concord, NH 03301/FAX: 603-796-2223

Munsch Gunsmithing, Tommy, Rt. 2, P.O. Box 248, Little Falls, MN 56345/612-632-6695

Murmur Corp., 2823 N. Westmoreland Ave., Dallas, TX 75222/214-630-5400

Murray State College, 100 Faculty Dr., Tishomingo, OK 73460/405-371-2371 ext. 238, 800-342-0698

Muscle Products Corp., 112 Fennell Dr., Butler, PA 16001/800-227-7049, 412-283-0567; FAX: 412-283-8310

Museum of Historical Arms Inc., 2750 Coral Way, Suite 204, Miami, FL 33145/305-444-9199

Mushroom Express Bullet Co., 601 W. 6th St., Greenfield, IN 46140/317-462-6332

Mustra's Custom Guns, Inc., Carl, 1002 Pennsylvania Ave., Palm Harbor, FL 34683/813-785-1403

Muzzleloaders Etcetera, Inc., 9901 Lyndale Ave. S., Bloomington, MN 55420/612-884-1161

MWG Co., P.O. Box 971202, Miami, FL 33197/800-428-9394, 305-253-8393; FAX: 305-232-1247

N

N&J Sales, Lime Kiln Rd., Northford, CT 06472/203-484-0247

Nagel's Bullets, 9 Wilburn, Baytown, TX 77520

Nastoff's 45 Shop, Inc., Steve, 12288 Mahoning Ave., P.O. Box 446, North Jackson, OH 44451/216-538-2977

National Bullet Co., 1585 E. 361 St., Eastlake, OH 44095/216-951-1854; FAX: 216-951-7761

National Survival Game, Inc., P.O. Box 1439, New London, NH 03257/603-735-6165; FAX: 603-735-5154

National Target Co., 4690 Wyaconda Rd., Rockville, MD 20852/800-827-7060, 301-770-7060; FAX: 301-770-7892

Nationwide Airgun Repairs (See Airgun Repair Centre)

Nationwide Sports Distributors, Inc., 70 James Way, Southampton, PA 18966/215-322-2050, 800-355-3006; FAX: 702-358-2093

Naval Ordnance Works, Rt. 2, Box 919, Sheperdstown, WV 25443/304-876-0998

Navy Arms Co., 689 Bergen Blvd., Ridgefield, NJ 07657/201-945-2500; FAX: 201-945-6859

N.B.B., Inc., 24 Elliot Rd., Sterling, MA 01564/508-422-7538, 800-942-9444

N.C. Ordnance Co., P.O. Box 3254, Wilson, NC 27895/919-237-2440; FAX: 919-243-0927

NECO, 1316-67th St., Emeryville, CA 94608/510-450-0420

Necromancer Industries, Inc., 14 Communications Way, West Newton, PA 15089/412-872-8722

NEI Handtools, Inc., 51583 Columbia River Hwy., Scappoose, OR 97056/503-543-6776; FAX: 503-543-6799

Nelson, Gary K., 975 Terrace Dr., Oakdale, CA 95361/209-847-4590

Nelson Combat Leather, Bruce, P.O. Box 8691 CRB, Tucson, AZ 85738

Nesci Enterprises, Inc., P.O. Box 119, Summit St., East Hampton, CT 06424/203-267-2588

Nettestad Gun Works, RR 1, Box 160, Pelican Rapids, MN 56572/218-863-4301

Neumann GmbH, Am Galgenberg 6, 90575 Langenzenn, GERMANY/09101/8258; FAX: 09101/6356

Neutralizer Police Munitions, 5029 Middle Rd., Horseheads, NY 14845-9568/607-739-8362; FAX: 607-594-3900

Nevada Pistol Academy Inc., 4610 Blue Diamond Rd., Las Vegas, NV 89139/702-897-1100

New Advantage Arms Corp., 2843 N. Alvernon Way, Tucson, AZ 85712/602-881-7444; FAX: 602-323-0949

New Democracy, Inc., 751 W. Lamar Blvd., Suite 102, Arlington, TX 76012-2010

New England Ammunition Co., 1771 Post Rd. East, Suite 223, Westport, CT 06880/203-254-8048

New England Firearms, 60 Industrial Rowe, Gardner, MA 01440/508-632-9393; FAX: 508-632-2300

New Orleans Arms Co., 5001 Treasure St., New Orleans, LA 70186/504-944-3371

New Orleans Jewelers Supply Co., 206 Charters St., New Orleans, LA 70130/504-523-3839; FAX: 504-523-3836

New Win Publishing, Inc., Box 5159, Clinton, NJ 08809/201-735-9701; FAX: 201-735-9703

Newell, Robert H., 55 Coyote, Los Alamos, NM 87544/505-662-7135

Newman Gunshop, 119 Miller Rd., Agency, IA 52530/515-937-5775

NgraveR Co., The, 67 Wawecus Hill Rd., Bozrah, CT 06334/203-823-1533

Nicholson Custom, Rt. 1, Box 176-3, Sedalia, MO 65301/816-826-8746

Niemi Engineering, W.B., Box 126 Center Road, Greensboro, VT 05841/802-533-7180 days, 802-533-7141 evenings

Nikon, Inc., 1300 Walt Whitman Rd., Melville, NY 11747/516-547-8623; FAX: 516-547-0309

Nitex, Inc., P.O. Box 1706, Uvalde, TX 78801/512-278-8843

Noble Co., Jim, 1305 Columbia St., Vancouver, WA 98660/206-695-1309

Noreen, Peter H., 5075 Buena Vista Dr., Belgrade, MT 59714/406-586-7383

Norinco, 7A, Yun Tan N Beijing, CHINA (U.S. importers—Century International Arms, Inc.; Interarms)

North American Correspondence Schools, The Gun Pro School, Oak & Pawney St., Scranton, PA 18515/717-342-7701

North American Shooting Systems, P.O. Box 306, Osoyoos, B.C. V0H 1V0 CANADA/604-495-3131; FAX: 604-495-2816

North Devon Firearms Services, 3 North St., Braunton, EX33 1AJ ENGLAND/01271 813624; FAX: 01271 813624

North Fork Custom Gunsmithing, James Johnston, 428 Del Rio Rd., Roseburg, OR 97470/503-673-4467

North Mountain Pine Training Center (See Executive Protection Institute)

North Specialty Products, 2664-B Saturn St., Brea, CA 92621/714-524-1665

North Star West, P.O. Box 488, Glencoe, CA 95232/209-293-7010

Northern Precision Custom Swaged Bullets, 329 S. James St., Carthage, NY 13619/315-493-1711

No-Sho Mfg. Co., 10727 Glenfield Ct., Houston, TX 77096/713-723-5332

Nosler, Inc., P.O. Box 671, Bend, OR 97709/800-285-3701, 503-382-3921; FAX: 503-388-4667

Novak's, Inc., 1206½ 30th St., P.O. Box 4045, Parkersburg, WV 26101/304-485-9295; FAX: 304-428-6722

Nowlin Custom Mfg., Rt. 1, Box 308, Claremore, OK 74017/918-342-0689; FAX: 918-342-0624

NRI Gunsmith School, 4401 Connecticut Ave. NW, Washington, D.C. 20008

Nu-Line Guns, Inc., 1053 Caulks Hill Rd., Harvester, MO 63304/314-441-4500; FAX: 314-447-5018

Null Holsters Ltd., K.L., 161 School St. NW, Hill City Station, Resaca, GA 30735/706-625-5643; FAX: 706-625-9392

Nu-Teck, 30 Industrial Park Rd., Box 37, Centerbrook, CT 06409/203-767-3573; FAX: 203-767-9137

Nygord Precision Products, P.O. Box 8394, La Crescenta, CA 91224/818-352-3027; FAX: 818-352-3378

O

Oakman Turkey Calls, RD 1, Box 825, Harrisonville, PA 17228/717-485-4620

Oakshore Electronic Sights, Inc., P.O. Box 4470, Ocala, FL 32678-4470/904-629-7112; FAX: 904-629-1433

October Country, P.O. Box 969, Dept. GD, Hayden Lake, ID 83835/208-772-2068; FAX: 208-772-2068

Oehler Research, Inc., P.O. Box 9135, Austin, TX 78766/512-327-6900, 800-531-5125

Oglesby & Oglesby Gunmakers, Inc., RR #5, Springfield, IL 62707/217-487-7100

Oil Rod and Gun Shop, 69 Oak St., East Douglas, MA 01516/508-476-3687

Ojala Holsters, Arvo, P.O. Box 98, N. Hollywood, CA 91603/503-669-1404

OK Weber, Inc., P.O. Box 7485, Eugene, OR 97401/503-747-0458; FAX: 503-747-5927

Oker's Engraving, 365 Bell Rd., P.O. Box 126, Shawnee, CO 80475/303-838-6042

Oklahoma Ammunition Co., 4310 W. Rogers Blvd., Skiatook, OK 74070/918-396-3187; FAX: 918-396-4270

Oklahoma Leather Products, Inc., 500 26th NW, Miami, OK 74354/918-542-6651; FAX: 918-542-6653

Old Dominion Engravers, 100 Progress Drive, Lynchburg, VA 24502/804-237-4450

Old Wagon Bullets, 32 Old Wagon Rd., Wilton, CT 06897

Old West Bullet Moulds, P.O. Box 519, Flora Vista, NM 87415/505-334-6970

Old West Reproductions, Inc., 446 Florence S. Loop, Florence, MT 59833/406-273-2615

Old Western Scrounger, Inc., 12924 Hwy. A-l2, Montague, CA 96064/916-459-5445; FAX: 916-459-3944

Old World Oil Products, 3827 Queen Ave. N., Minneapolis, MN 55412/612-522-5037

Ole Frontier Gunsmith Shop, 2617 Hwy. 29 S., Cantonment, FL 32533/904-477-8074

Olson, Myron, 989 W. Kemp, Watertown, SD 57201/605-886-9787

Olson, Vic, 5002 Countryside Dr., Imperial, MO 63052/314-296-8086

Olt Co., Philip S., P.O. Box 550, 12662 Fifth St., Pekin, IL 61554/309-348-3633; FAX: 309-348-3300

Olympic Arms, Inc., 620-626 Old Pacific Hwy. SE, Olympia, WA 98513/360-459-3471; FAX: 360-491-3447

Olympic Optical Co., P.O. Box 752377, Memphis, TN 38175-2377/901-794-3890, 800-238-7120; FAX: 901-794-0676, 800-748-1669

Omark Industries, Div. of Blount, Inc., 2299 Snake River Ave., P.O. Box 856, Lewiston, ID 83501/800-627-3640, 208-746-2351

Orchard Park Enterprise, P.O. Box 563, Orchard Park, NY 14227/616-656-0356

Ordnance Works, The, 2969 Pidgeon Point Road, Eureka, CA 95501/707-443-3252

Original Mink Oil, Inc., 10652 NE Holman, Portland, OR 97220/503-255-2814, 800-547-5895; FAX: 503-255-2487

Orion Rifle Barrel Co., RR2, 137 Cobler Village, Kalispell, MT 59901/406-257-5649

Outdoor Connection, Inc., The, 201 Cotton Dr., P.O. Box 7751, Waco, TX 76714-7751/800-533-6076; 817-772-5575; FAX: 817-776-3553

Outdoorsman's Bookstore, The, Llangorse, Brecon, Powys LD3 7UE, U.K./44-1874-658-660; FAX: 44-1874-658-650

Outers Laboratories, Div. of Blount, Inc., Route 2, P.O. Box 39, Onalaska, WI 54650/608-781-5800; FAX: 608-781-0368

Owen, Harry, Sport Specialties, 100 N. Citrus Ave. #412, W. Covina, CA 91791-1614/818-968-5806

Ox-Yoke Originals, Inc., 34 Main St., Milo, ME 04463/800-231-8313, 207-943-7351; FAX: 207-943-2416

Ozark Gun Works, 11830 Cemetery Rd., Rogers, AR 72756/501-631-6944; FAX: 501-631-6944

P

P&M Sales and Service, 5724 Gainsborough Pl., Oak Forest, IL 60452/708-687-7149

P&S Gun Service, 2138 Old Shepardsville Rd., Louisville, KY 40218/502-456-9346

Pace Marketing, Inc., P.O. Box 2039, Stuart, FL 34995/407-223-2189; FAX: 407-286-9547

Pacific Pistolcraft, 1810 E. Columbia Ave., Tacoma, WA 98404/206-474-5465

Paco's (See Small Custom Mould & Bullet Co.)

P.A.C.T., Inc., P.O. Box 531525, Grand Prairie, TX 75053/214-641-0049

Page Custom Bullets, P.O. Box 25, Port Moresby Papua, NEW GUINEA

Pagel Gun Works, Inc., 1407 4th St. NW, Grand Rapids, MN 55744/218-326-3003

Palmgren Steel Products, 8383 S. Chicago Ave., Chicago, IL 60617/312-721-9675; FAX: 312-721-9739

Palsa Outdoor Products, P.O. Box 81336, Lincoln, NE 68501/402-488-5288, 800-456-9281; FAX: 402-488-2321

PanaVise Products, Inc., 1485 Southern Way, Sparks, NV 89431/702-353-2900; FAX: 702-353-2929

Para-Ordnance, Inc., 1919 NE 45th St., Ft. Lauderdale, FL 33308

Para-Ordnance Mfg., Inc., 3411 McNicoll Ave., Unit 14, Scarborough, Ont. M1V 2V6, CANADA/416-297-7855; FAX: 416-297-1289 (U.S. importer—Para-Ordnance, Inc.)

Paragon Sales & Services, Inc., P.O. Box 2022, Joliet, IL 60434/815-725-9212; FAX: 815-725-8974

Pardini Armi Srl, Via Italica 154, 55043 Lido Di Camaiore Lu, ITALY/584-90121; FAX: 584-90122 (U.S. importers—MCS, Inc.; Nygord Precision Products)

Paris, Frank J., 17417 Pershing St., Livonia, MI 48152-3822

Parke-Bernet (See Sotheby's)

Parker, Mark D., 1240 Florida Ave. #7, Longmont, CO 80501/303-772-0214

Parker Gun Finishes, 9337 Smokey Row Rd., Strawberry Plains, TN 37871/615-933-3286

Parsons Optical Mfg. Co., P.O. Box 192, Ross, OH 45061/513-867-0820; FAX: 513-867-8380

Parts & Surplus, P.O. Box 22074, Memphis, TN 38122/901-683-4007

Pasadena Gun Center, 206 E. Shaw, Pasadena, TX 77506/713-472-0417; FAX: 713-472-1322

PAST Sporting Goods, Inc., P.O. Box 1035, Columbia, MO 65205/314-445-9200; FAX: 314-446-6606

Paterson Gunsmithing, 438 Main St., Paterson, NJ 07502/201-345-4100

Pathfinder Sports Leather, 2920 E. Chambers St., Phoenix, AZ 85040/602-276-0016

Patrick Bullets, P.O. Box 172, Warwick QSLD 4370 AUSTRALIA

PC Bullet/ADC, Inc., 32654 Coal Creek Rd., Scappoose, OR 97056-2601/503-543-5088; FAX: 503-543-5990

Peacemaker Specialists, P.O. Box 157, Whitmore, CA 96096/916-472-3438

PECAR Herbert Schwarz, GmbH, Kreuzbergstrasse 6, 10965 Berlin, GERMANY/004930-785-7383; FAX: 004930-785-1934

Pedersen, C.R., 2717 S. Pere Marquette Hwy., Ludington, MI 49431/616-843-2061

Pedersen, Rex C., 2717 S. Pere Marquette Hwy., Ludington, MI 49431/616-843-2061

Peerless Alloy, Inc., 1445 Osage St., Denver, CO 80204/303-825-6394, 800-253-1278

Pejsa Ballistics, 2120 Kenwood Pkwy., Minneapolis, MN 55405/612-374-3337; FAX: 612-374-3337

Peltor, Inc., 41 Commercial Way, E. Providence, RI 02914/401-438-4800; FAX: 401-434-1708, 800-EAR-FAX1

PEM's Mfg. Co., 5063 Waterloo Rd., Atwater, OH 44201/216-947-3721

Pence Precision Barrels, 7567 E. 900 S., S. Whitley, IN 46787/219-839-4745

Pend Oreille Sport Shop, 3100 Hwy. 200 East, Sandpoint, ID 83864/208-263-2412

Pendleton Royal, 4/7 Highgate St., Birmingham, ENGLAND B12 0X5/44 121 440 3060; FAX: 44 121 446 4165

Penn Bullets, P.O. Box 756, Indianola, PA 15051

Penn's Woods Products, Inc., 19 W. Pittsburgh St., Delmont, PA 15626/412-468-8311; FAX: 412-468-8975

Pennsylvania Gun Parts, 1701 Mud Run Rd., York Springs, PA 17372/717-259-8010

Pennsylvania Gunsmith School, 812 Ohio River Blvd., Avalon, Pittsburgh, PA 15202/412-766-1812

Penrod Precision, 312 College Ave., P.O. Box 307, N. Manchester, IN 46962/219-982-8385

Pentax Corp., 35 Inverness Dr. E., Englewood, CO 80112/303-799-8000; FAX: 303-790-1131

Pentheny de Pentheny, 2352 Baggett Ct., Santa Rosa, CA 95401/707-573-1390; FAX: 707-573-1390

Perazone, Brian, Cold Spring Rd., Roxbury, NY 12474/607-326-4088

Performance Specialists, 308 Eanes School Rd., Austin, TX 78746/512-327-0119

Personal Protection Systems, RD #5, Box 5027-A, Moscow, PA 18444/717-842-1766

Peters Stahl GmbH, Stettiner Strasse 42, D-33106 Paderborn, GERMANY/05251-750025; FAX: 05251-75611 (U.S. importers—Harris-McMillan Gunworks; Olympic Arms)

Petersen Publishing Co., 6420 Wilshire Blvd., Los Angeles, CA 90048/213-782-2000; FAX: 213-782-2867

Peterson Gun Shop, Inc., A.W., 4255 W. Old U.S. 441, Mt. Dora, FL 32757-3299/904-383-4258

Petro-Explo, Inc., 7650 U.S. Hwy. 287, Suite 100, Arlington, TX 76017/817-478-8888

Pettinger Books, Gerald, Rt. 2, Box 125, Russell, IA 50238/515-535-2239

Phillippi Custom Bullets, Justin, P.O. Box 773, Ligonier, PA 15658/412-238-9671

Phoenix Arms, 1420 S. Archibald Ave., Ontario, CA 91761/909-947-4843; FAX: 909-947-6798

Piedmont Community College, P.O. Box 1197, Roxboro, NC 27573/910-599-1181

Pierce Pistols, 2326 E. Hwy. 34, Newnan, GA 30263/404-253-8192

Pilgrim Pewter, Inc. (See Bell Originals Inc., Sid)

Pilkington, Scott, Little Trees Ramble, P.O. Box 97, Monteagle, TN 37356/615-924-3475; FAX: 615-924-3489

Pilkington Gun Co., P.O. Box 1296, Muskogee, OK 74402/918-683-9418

Pine Technical College, 1100 4th St., Pine City, MN 55063/800-521-7463; FAX: 612-629-6766

Pinetree Bullets, 133 Skeena St., Kitimat BC, CANADA V8C 1Z1/604-632-3768; FAX: 604-632-3768

Pioneer Arms Co., 355 Lawrence Rd., Broomall, PA 19008/215-356-5203

Pioneer Guns, 5228 Montgomery Rd., Norwood, OH 45212/513-631-4871

Piquette, Paul R., 80 Bradford Dr., Feeding Hills, MA 01030/413-781-8300, Ext. 682

Plaxco, J. Michael, Rt. 1, P.O. Box 203, Roland, AR 72135/501-868-9787

Plum City Ballistic Range, N2162 80th St., Plum City, WI 54761-8622/715-647-2539

PlumFire Press, Inc., 30-A Grove Ave., Patchogue, NY 11772-4112/800-695-7246; FAX:516-758-4071

P.M. Enterprises, Inc., 146 Curtis Hill Rd., Chehalis, WA 98532/206-748-3743; FAX: 206-748-1802

PMC/Eldorado Cartridge Corp., P.O. Box 62508, 12801 U.S. Hwy. 95 S., Boulder City, NV 89005/702-294-0025; FAX: 702-294-0121

Police Bookshelf, P.O. Box 122, Concord, NH 03301/603-224-6814; FAX: 603-226-3554

Policlips North America, 59 Douglas Crescent, Toronto, Ont. CANADA M4W 2E6/800-229-5089, 416-924-0383; FAX: 416-924-4375

Pomeroy, Robert, RR1, Box 50, E. Corinth, ME 04427/207-285-7721

Ponsness/Warren, P.O. Box 8, Rathdrum, ID 83858/208-687-2231; FAX: 208-687-2233

Pony Express Reloaders, 608 E. Co. Rd. D, Suite #3, St. Paul, MN 55117/612-483-9406; FAX: 612-483-9884

Pony Express Sport Shop, Inc., 16606 Schoenborn St., North Hills, CA 91343/818-895-1231

Potts, Wayne E., 912 Poplar St., Denver, CO 80220/303-355-5462

Powder Valley Services, Rt. 1, Box 100, Dexter, KS 67038/316-876-5418

Power Custom, Inc., RR 2, P.O. Box 756AB, Gravois Mills, MO 65037/314-372-5684

Practical Tools, Inc., Div. Behlert Precision, 7067 Easton Rd., P.O. Box 133, Pipersville, PA 18947/215-766-7301; FAX: 215-766-8681

Precise Metalsmithing Enterprises, 146 Curtis Hill Rd., Chehalis, WA 98532/206-748-3743; FAX: 206-748-8102

Precision Airgun Sales, Inc., 5139 Warrensville Center Rd., Maple Hts., OH 44137-1906/216-587-5005

Precision Castings & Equipment, Inc., P.O. Box 326, Jasper, IN 47547-0135/812-634-9167

Precision Components and Guns, Rt. 55, P.O. Box 337, Pawling, NY 12564/914-855-3040

Precision Components, 3177 Sunrise Lake, Milford, PA 18337/717-686-4414

Precision Delta Corp., P.O. Box 128, Ruleville, MS 38771/601-756-2810; FAX: 601-756-2590

Precision Metal Finishing, John Westrom, P.O. Box 3186, Des Moines, IA 50316/515-288-8680; FAX: 515-244-3925

Precision Munitions, Inc., P.O. Box 326, Jasper, IN 47547

Precision Reloading, Inc., P.O. Box 122, Stafford Springs, CT 06076/203-684-7979; FAX: 203-684-6788

Precision Sales International, Inc., P.O. Box 1776, Westfield, MA 01086/413-562-5055; FAX: 413-562-5056

Precision Shooting, Inc., 222 McKee St., Manchester, CT 06040/203-645-8776; FAX: 203-643-8215

Precision Small Arms, 155 Carlton Rd., Charlottesville, VA 22902/804-293-6124; FAX: 804-295-0780

Precision Specialties, 131 Hendom Dr., Feeding Hills, MA 01030/413-786-3365; FAX: 413-786-3365

Precision Sport Optics, 15571 Producer Lane, Unit G, Huntington Beach, CA 92649/714-891-1309; FAX: 714-892-6920

Premier Reticles, 920 Breckinridge Lane, Winchester, VA 22601-6707

Prescott Projectile Co., 1808 Meadowbrook Road, Prescott, AZ 86303

Price Bullets, Patrick W., 16520 Worthley Drive, San Lorenzo, CA 94580/510-278-1547

Prime Reloading, 30 Chiswick End, Meldreth, Royston SG8 6LZ UK/0763-260636

Primos, Inc., P.O. Box 12785, Jackson, MS 39236-2785/601-366-1288; FAX: 601-362-3274

Pro Load Ammunition, Inc., 5180 E. Seltice Way, Post Falls, ID 83854/208-773-9444; FAX: 208-773-9441

Professional Gunsmiths of America, Inc., Route 1, Box 224F, Lexington, MO 64067/816-259-2636

Professional Hunter Supplies (See Star Custom Bullets)

Prolix, P.O. Box 1348, Victorville, CA 92393/800-248-LUBE, 619-243-3129; FAX: 619-241-0148

Pro-Shot Products, Inc., P.O. Box 763, Taylorville, IL 62568/217-824-9133; FAX: 217-824-8861

Protector Mfg. Co., Inc., The, 443 Ashwood Place, Boca Raton, FL 33431/407-394-6011

Protektor Model, 1-11 Bridge St., Galeton, PA 16922/814-435-2442

P.S.M.G. Gun Co., 10 Park Ave., Arlington, MA 02174/617-646-8845; FAX: 617-646-2133

PWL Gunleather, P.O. Box 450432, Atlanta, GA 31145/404-822-1640; FAX: 404-822-1704

Q

Quaker Boy, Inc., 5455 Webster Rd., Orchard Parks, NY 14127/716-662-3979; FAX: 716-662-9426

Quality Firearms of Idaho, Inc., 114 13th Ave. S., Nampa, ID 83651/208-466-1631

Quigley's Personal Protection Strategies, Paxton, 9903 Santa Monica Blvd., #300, Beverly Hills, CA 90212/310-281-1762

Quinetics Corp., 5731 Kenwick, P.O. Box 13237, San Antonio, TX 78238/512-684-8561; FAX: 512-684-2912

R

R&S Industries Corp., 8255 Brentwood Industrial Dr., St. Louis, MO 63144/314-781-5400

Rabeno, Martin, 92 Spook Hole Rd., Ellenville, NY 12428/914-647-4567

Radiator Specialty Co., 1900 Wilkinson Blvd., P.O. Box 34689, Charlotte, NC 28234/800-438-6947; FAX: 800-421-9525

Radical Concepts, P.O. Box 1473, Lake Grove, OR 97035/503-636-6686

Rainier Ballistics Corp., 4500 15th St. East, Tacoma, WA 98424/800-638-8722, 206-922-7589; FAX: 206-922-7854

Ranch Products, P.O. Box 145, Malinta, OH 43535/313-277-3118; FAX: 313-565-8536

Randco UK, 286 Gipsy Rd., Welling, Kent DA16 1JJ, ENGLAND/44 81 303 4118

Randolph Engineering, Inc., 26 Thomas Patten Dr., Randolph, MA 02368/800-541-1405; FAX: 800-RANDOLPH

Ranger Products, 2623 Grand Blvd., Suite 209, Holiday, FL 34609/813-942-4652, 800-407-7007; FAX: 813-942-6221

Ranging, Inc., Routes 5 & 20, East Bloomfield, NY 14443/716-657-6161; FAX: 716-657-5405

Ransom International Corp., P.O. Box 3845, 1040-A Sandretto Dr., Prescott, AZ 86302/602-778-7899; FAX: 602-778-7993

Rapine Bullet Mould Mfg. Co., 9503 Landis Lane, East Greenville, PA 18041/215-679-5413; FAX: 215-679-9795

Raytech, Div. of Lyman Products Corp., Rt. 32 Stafford Ind. Park, Box 6, Stafford Springs, CT 06076/203-684-4273; FAX: 203-684-7938

RCBS, Div. of Blount, Inc., 605 Oro Dam Blvd., Oroville, CA 95965/800-533-5000, 916-533-5191; FAX: 916-533-1647

R.D.P. Tool Co., Inc., 49162 McCoy Ave., East Liverpool, OH 43920/216-385-5129

Reardon Products, P.O. Box 126, Morrison, IL 61270/815-772-3155

Red Cedar Precision Mfg., W. 485 Spruce Dr., Brodhead, WI 53520/608-897-8416

Red Star Target Co., 4519 Brisebois Dr. NW, Calgary AB T2L 2G3 CANADA/403-289-7939; FAX: 403-289-3275

Redding Reloading Equipment, 1089 Starr Rd., Cortland, NY 13045/607-753-3331; FAX: 607-756-8445

Redfield, Inc., 5800 E. Jewell Ave., Denver, CO 80227/303-757-6411; FAX: 303-756-2338

Redman's Rifling & Reboring, Rt. 3, Box 330A, Omak, WA 98841/509-826-5512

Redwood Bullet Works, 3559 Bay Rd., Redwood City, CA 94063/415-367-6741

Reed, Dave, Rt. 1, Box 374, Minnesota City, MN 55959/507-689-2944

R.E.I., P.O. Box 88, Tallevast, FL 34270/813-755-0085

Reiswig, Wallace E., Claro Walnut Gunstock Co., 1235 Stanley Ave., Chico, CA 95928/916-342-5188

Reloading Specialties, Inc., Box 1130, Pine Island, MN 55463/507-356-8500; FAX: 507-356-8800

Renegade, P.O. Box 31546, Phoenix, AZ 85046/602-482-6777; FAX: 602-482-1952

Renner Co., R.J., P.O. Box 10731, Canoga Park, CA 91309/818-700-8131

Reno, Wayne, 2808 Stagestop Rd., Jefferson, CO 80456/719-836-3452

R.E.T. Enterprises, 2608 S. Chestnut, Broken Arrow, OK 74012/918-251-GUNS; FAX: 918-251-0587

Retting, Inc., Martin B., 11029 Washington, Culver City, CA 90232/213-837-2412

R.G.-G., Inc., P.O. Box 1261, Conifer, CO 80433-1261/303-697-4154; FAX: 303-697-4154

Rice, Keith (See White Rock Tool & Die)

Richards, John, Richards Classic Oil Finish, Rt. 2, Box 325, Bedford, KY 40006/502-255-7222

Rickard, Inc., Pete, RD 1, Box 292, Cobleskill, NY 12043/800-282-5663; FAX: 518-234-2454

Ridgetop Sporting Goods, P.O. Box 306, 42907 Hilligoss Ln. East, Eatonville, WA 98328/206-832-6422

Riebe Co., W.J., 3434 Tucker Rd., Boise, ID 83703

Ries, Chuck, 415 Ridgecrest Dr., Grants Pass, OR 97527/503-476-5623

Rifle Works & Armory, 707 N 12 St., Cody, WY 82414/307-587-4914

RIG Products, 87 Coney Island Dr., Sparks, NV 89431-6334/702-331-5666; FAX: 702-331-5669

Riggs, Jim, 206 Azalea, Boerne, TX 78006/210-249-8567

Rim Pac Sports, Inc., 1034 N. Soldano Ave., Azusa, CA 91702-2135

Ringler Custom Leather Co., P.O. Box 206, Cody, WY 82414/307-645-3255

Ripley Rifles, 42 Fletcher Street, Ripley, Derbyshire, DE5 3LP ENGLAND/011-0773-748353

R.I.S. Co., Inc., 718 Timberlake Circle, Richardson, TX 75080/214-235-0933

R.M. Precision, Inc., Attn. Greg F. Smith Marketing, P.O. Box 210, LaVerkin, UT 84745/801-635-4656; FAX: 801-635-4430

Robar Co.'s, Inc., The, 21438 N. 7th Ave., Suite B, Phoenix, AZ 85027/602-581-2648; FAX: 602-582-0059

Robbins Scent, Inc., P.O. Box 779, Connellsville, PA 15425/412-628-2529; FAX: 412-628-9598

Roberts, J.J., 7808 Lake Dr., Manassas, VA 22111/703-330-0448

Roberts Products, 25238 SE 32nd, Issaquah, WA 98027/206-392-8172

Robinson H.V. Bullets, 3145 Church St., Zachary, LA 70791/504-654-4029

Rochester Lead Works, 76 Anderson Ave., Rochester, NY 14607/716-442-8500

Rockwood Corp., Speedwell Division, 136 Lincoln Blvd., Middlesex, NJ 08846/908-560-7171

Rocky Fork Enterprises, P.O. Box 427, 878 Battle Rd., Nolensville, TN 37135/615-941-1307

Rocky Mountain Arms, Inc., 600 S. Sunset, Unit C, Longmont, CO 80501/303-768-8522; FAX: 303-678-8766

Rocky Mountain High Sports Glasses, 8121 N. Central Park Ave., Skokie, IL 60076/708-679-1012; FAX: 708-679-0184

Rocky Mountain Target Co., 3 Aloe Way, Leesburg, FL 34788/904-365-9598

Rocky Mountain Wildlife Products, P.O. Box 999, La Porte, CO 80535/303-484-2768; FAX: 303-223-9389

Rod Guide Co., Box 1149, Forsyth, MO 65653/800-952-2774

Rogers Gunsmithing, Bob, P.O. Box 305, 344 S. Walnut St., Franklin Grove, IL 61031/815-456-2685; FAX: 815-288-7142

Rohner, Hans, 1148 Twin Sisters Ranch Rd., Nederland, CO 80466-9600

Rohner, John, 710 Sunshine Canyon, Boulder, CO 80302/303-444-3841

Rolston, Inc., Fred W., 210 E. Cummins St., Tecumseh, MI 49286/517-423-6002, 800-314-9061 (orders only); FAX: 517-423-6002

Rooster Laboratories, P.O. Box 412514, Kansas City, MO 64141/816-474-1622; FAX: 816-474-1307

Rorschach Precision Products, P.O. Box 151613, Irving, TX 75015/214-790-3487

Rosenberg & Sons, Jack A., 12229 Cox Lane, Dallas, TX 75234/214-241-6302

Rosenthal, Brad and Sallie, 19303 Ossenfort Ct., St. Louis, MO 63038/314-273-5159; FAX: 314-273-5149

Rosser, Bob, 1824 29th Ave., Suite 24, Birmingham, AL 35209/205-870-4422

Roto Carve, 2754 Garden Ave., Janesville, IA 50647

Round Edge, Inc., P.O. Box 723, Lansdale, PA 19446/215-361-0859

Roy's Custom Grips, Rt. 3, Box 174-E, Lynchburg, VA 24504/804-993-3470

RPM, 15481 N. Twin Lakes Dr., Tucson, AZ 85737/602-825-1233; FAX: 602-825-3333

Rucker Ammunition Co., P.O. Box 479, Terrell, TX 75160

Rundell's Gun Shop, 6198 Frances Rd., Clio, MI 48420/313-687-0559

Runge, Robert P., 94 Grove St., Ilion, NY 13357/315-894-3036

Rupert's Gun Shop, 2202 Dick Rd., Suite B, Fenwick, MI 48834/517-248-3252

Rusteprufe Laboratories, 1319 Jefferson Ave., Sparta, WI 54656/608-269-4144

Rusty Duck Premium Gun Care Products, 7785 Foundation Dr., Suite 6, Florence, KY 41042/606-342-5553; FAX: 606-342-5556

Rutgers Book Center, 127 Raritan Ave., Highland Park, NJ 08904/908-545-4344; FAX: 908-545-6686

Ruvel & Co., Inc., 4128-30 W. Belmont Ave., Chicago, IL 60641/312-286-9494

R.V.I., P.O. Box 8019-56, Blaine, WA 98230/206-595-2933

RWS (See U.S. importer—Dynamit Nobel-RWS, Inc.)

Rybka Custom Leather Equipment, Thad, 134 Havilah Hill, Odenville, AL 35120

S

S&B Industries, 11238 McKinley Rd., Montrose, MI 48457/810-639-5491

S&K Mfg. Co., P.O. Box 247, Pittsfield, PA 16340/814-563-7808; FAX: 814-563-7808

S&S Firearms, 74-11 Myrtle Ave., Glendale, NY 11385/718-497-1100; FAX: 718-497-1105

SAECO (See Redding Reloading Equipment)

Safari Outfitters Ltd., 71 Ethan Allan Hwy., Ridgefield, CT 06877/203-544-9505

Safari Press, Inc., 15621 Chemical Lane B, Huntington Beach, CA 92649/714-894-9080; FAX: 714-894-4949

Safariland Ltd., Inc., 3120 E. Mission Blvd., P.O. Box 51478, Ontario, CA 91761/909-923-7300; FAX: 909-923-7400

SAFE, P.O. Box 864, Post Falls, ID 83854/208-773-3624

Safesport Manufacturing Co., 1100 W. 45th Ave., Denver, CO 80211/303-433-6506, 800-433-6506; FAX: 303-433-4112

Safety Speed Holster, Inc., 910 S. Vail Ave., Montebello, CA 90640/213-723-4140; FAX: 213-726-6973

Salter Calls, Inc., Eddie, Hwy. 31 South-Brewton Industrial Park, Brewton, AL 36426/205-867-2584; FAX: 206-867-9005

Samco Global Arms, Inc., 6995 NW 43rd St., Miami, FL 33166/305-593-9782

Sampson, Roger, 430 N. Grove, Mora, MN 55051/612-679-4868

San Francisco Gun Exchange, 124 Second St., San Francisco, CA 94105/415-982-6097

Sanders Custom Gun Service, 2358 Tyler Ln., Louisville, KY 40205/502-454-3338

Sandia Die & Cartridge Co., 37 Atancacio Rd. NE, Albuquerque, NM 87123/505-298-5729

Saunders Gun & Machine Shop, R.R. #2, Delhi Road, Manchester, IA 52057

Savana Sports, Inc., 5763 Ferrier St., Montreal, Quebec, CANADA/514-739-1753; FAX: 514-739-1755

Saville Iron Co. (See Greenwood Precision)

Sceery Co., E.J., 2308 Cedros Circle, Sante Fe, NM 87505/505-983-2125

Schaefer Shooting Sports, 1923 Grand Ave., Baldwin, NY 11510/516-379-4900; FAX: 516-379-6701

Scharch Mfg., Inc., 10325 Co. Rd. 120, Unit C, Salida, CO 81201/719-539-7242; FAX: 719-539-3021

Scherer, Box 250, Ewing, VA 24240/615-733-2615; FAX: 615-733-2073

Schiffman, Mike, 8233 S. Crystal Springs, McCammon, ID 83250/208-254-9114

Schmidtman Custom Ammunition, 6 Gilbert Court, Cotati, CA 94931

Schroeder Bullets, 1421 Thermal Ave., San Diego, CA 92154/619-423-3523

Schulz Industries, 16247 Minnesota Ave., Paramount, CA 90723/213-439-5903

Schumakers Gun Shop, William, 512 Prouty Corner Lp. #A, Colville, WA 99114/509-684-4848

Scobey Duck & Goose Calls, Glynn, Rt. 3, Box 37, Newbern, TN 38059/901-643-6241

Scope Control, Inc., 5775 Co. Rd. 23 SE, Alexandria, MN 56308/612-762-7295

ScopLevel, 151 Lindbergh Ave., Suite H, Livermore, CA 94550/510-449-5052; FAX: 510-373-0861

Scot Powder, Rt.1 Box 167, McEwen, TN 37101/800-416-3006; FAX: 615-729-4211

Scot Powder Co. of Ohio, Inc., Box GD96, Only, TN 37140/615-729-4207, 800-416-3006; FAX: 615-729-4217

Scott, Dwight, 23089 Englehardt St., Clair Shores, MI 48080/313-779-4735

Scott Fine Guns, Inc., Thad, P.O. Box 412, Indianola, MS 38751/601-887-5929

Scott, McDougall & Associates, 7950 Redwood Dr., Cotati, CA 94931/707-546-2264; FAX: 707-795-1911

Scruggs' Game Calls, Stanley, Rt. 1, Hwy. 661, Cullen, VA 23934/804-542-4241, 800-323-4828

Seattle Binocular & Scope Repair Co., P.O. Box 46094, Seattle, WA 98146/206-932-3733

Second Chance Body Armor, P.O. Box 578, Central Lake, MI 49622/616-544-5721; FAX: 616-544-9824

Seecamp Co., Inc., L.W., P.O. Box 255, New Haven, CT 06502/203-877-3429

Seligman Shooting Products, Box 133, Seligman, AZ 86337/602-422-3607

Selsi Co., Inc., 40 Veterans Blvd., Carlstadt, NJ 07072-0497/201-935-0388; FAX: 201-935-5851

Semmer, Charles, 7885 Cyd Dr., Denver, CO 80221/303-429-6947

SGS Importers International, Inc., 1750 Brielle Ave., Unit B1, Wanamassa, NJ 07712/908-493-0302; FAX: 908-493-0301

S.G.S. Sporting Guns Srl., Via Della Resistenza, 37, 20090 Buccinasco (MI) ITALY/2-45702446; FAX: 2-45702464

Shappy Bullets, 76 Milldale Ave., Plantsville, CT 06479/203-621-3704

Sharp (See U.S. importer—Great Lakes Airguns)

Sharp Shooter, Inc., P.O. Box 21362, St. Paul, MN 55121/612-452-4687

Shaw, Inc., E.R. (See Small Arms Mfg. Co.)

Shay's Gunsmithing, 931 Marvin Ave., Lebanon, PA 17042

Sheffield Knifemakers Supply, P.O. Box 141, Deland, FL 32721/904-775-6453; FAX: 904-774-5754

Shell Shack, 113 E. Main, Laurel, MT 59044/406-628-8986

Sherwood, George, 46 N. River Dr., Roseburg, OR 97470/503-672-3159

Shiloh Creek, Box 357, Cottleville, MO 63338/314-447-2900; FAX: 314-447-2900

Shockley, Harold H., 204 E. Farmington Rd., Hanna City, IL 61536/309-565-4524

Shoemaker & Sons, Inc., Tex, 714 W. Cienega Ave., San Dimas, CA 91750/714-592-2071; FAX: 714-592-2378

Shooter's Choice, 16770 Hilltop Park Place, Chagrin Falls, OH 44023/216-543-8808; FAX: 216-543-8811

Shooter Shop, The, 221 N. Main, Butte, MT 59701/406-723-3842

Shooter's World, 3828 N. 28th Ave., Phoenix, AZ 85017/602-266-0170

Shooters Supply, 1120 Tieton Dr., Yakima, WA 98902/509-452-1181

Shootin' Accessories, Ltd., P.O. Box 6810, Auburn, CA 95604/916-889-2220

Shooting Chrony, Inc., 3269 Niagara Falls Blvd., N. Tonawanda, NY 14120/905-276-6292; FAX: 416-276-6295

Shooting Components Marketing, P.O. Box 1069, Englewood, CO 80150/303-987-2543; FAX: 303-989-3508

Shooting Gallery, The, 8070 Southern Blvd., Boardman, OH 44512/216-726-7788

Shoot-N-C Inc., 8951 Bonita Beach Rd., Bonita Springs, FL 33923/813-498-9221

Siegrist Gun Shop, 8754 Turtle Road, Whittemore, MI 48770

Sierra Bullets, 1400 W. Henry St., Sedalia, MO 65301/816-827-6300; FAX: 816-827-6300

Sierra Specialty Prod. Co., 1344 Oakhurst Ave., Los Altos, CA 94024

SIG, CH-8212 Neuhausen, SWITZERLAND (U.S. importer—Mandall Shooting Supplies, Inc.)

Sigarms, Inc., Corporate Park, Exeter, NH 03833/603-772-2302; FAX: 603-772-9082

Sight Shop, The, John G. Lawson, 1802 E. Columbia Ave., Tacoma, WA 98404/206-474-5465

Sightron, Inc., 11701 NW 102nd Rd., Suite 21, Medley, FL 33178/305-863-6767; FAX: 305-863-6652

SIG-Sauer (See U.S. importer—Sigarms, Inc.)

Sile Distributors, Inc., 7 Centre Market Pl., New York, NY 10013/212-925-4111; FAX: 212-925-3149

Silencio/Safety Direct, 56 Coney Island Dr., Sparks, NV 89431/800-648-1812, 702-354-4451; FAX: 702-359-1074

Silhouette Leathers, P.O. Box 1161, Gunnison, CO 81230/303-641-6639

Silver Eagle Machining, 18007 N. 69th Ave., Glendale, AZ 85308

Silver Ridge Gun Shop (See Goodwin, Fred)

Simmons, Jerry, 715 Middlebury St., Goshen, IN 46526/219-533-8546

Simmons Enterprises, Ernie, 709 East Elizabethtown Rd., Manheim, PA 17545/717-664-4040

Simmons Outdoor Corp., P.O. Box 217, Heflin, AL 36264/205-463-5500; FAX: 205-463-5510

Sinclair, W.P., Box 1209, Warminster, Wiltshire BA12 9XJ, ENGLAND/01044-1985-218544; FAX: 01044-1985-214111

Sinclair International, Inc., 2330 Wayne Haven St., Fort Wayne, IN 46803/219-493-1858; FAX: 219-493-2530

Single Shot, Inc. (See Montana Armory, Inc.)

Singletary, Kent, 7516 W. Sells, Phoenix, AZ 85033/602-849-5917

Sipes Gun Shop, 7415 Asher Ave., Little Rock, AR 72204/501-565-8480

Six Enterprises, 320-D Turtle Creek Ct., San Jose, CA 95125/408-999-0201; FAX: 408-999-0216

S.K. Guns, Inc., 3041A Main Ave., Fargo, ND 58103/701-293-4867; FAX: 701-232-0001

Skaggs, R.E., P.O. Box 555, Hamilton, IN 46742/219-488-3755

SKAN A.R., 4 St. Catherines Road, Long Melford, Suffolk, CO10 9JU ENGLAND/011-0787-312942

Skeoch, Brian R., P.O. Box 279, Glenrock, WY 82637/307-436-9655; FAX: 307-436-9034

Skip's Machine, 364 29 Road, Grand Junction, CO 81501/303-245-5417

Sklany, Steve, 566 Birch Grove Dr., Kalispell, MT 59901/406-755-4257

S.L.A.P. Industries, P.O. Box 1121, Parklands 2121, SOUTH AFRICA/27-11-788-0030; FAX: 27-11-788-0030

Slings 'N Things, Inc., 8909 Bedford Circle, Suite 11, Omaha, NE 68134/402-571-6954; FAX: 402-571-7082

Small Custom Mould & Bullet Co., Box 17211, Tucson, AZ 85731

Smart Parts, 1203 Spring St., Latrobe, PA 15650/412-539-2660; FAX: 412-539-2298

Smires, C.L., 28269 Old Schoolhouse Rd., Columbus, NJ 08022/609-298-3158

Smith & Wesson, 2100 Roosevelt Ave., Springfield, MA 01102/413-781-8300; FAX: 413-731-8980

Smith, Mark A., P.O. Box 182, Sinclair, WY 82334/307-324-7929

Smith, Ron, 5869 Straley, Ft. Worth, TX 76114/817-732-6768

Smith Abrasives, Inc., 1700 Sleepy Valley Rd., P.O. Box 5095, Hot Springs, AR 71902-5095/501-321-2244; FAX: 501-321-9232

Smith Saddlery, Jesse W., 3601 E. Boone Ave., Spokane, WA 99202-4501/509-325-0622

Snapp's Gunshop, 6911 E. Washington Rd., Clare, MI 48617/517-386-9226

Sonderman, Robert, 735 Kenton Dr., Charleston, IL 61920/217-345-5429

Sonora Rifle Barrel Co., 14396 D. Tuolumne Rd., Sonora, CA 95370/209-532-4139

SOS Products Co. (See Buck Stix—SOS Products Co.)

Sotheby's, 1334 York Ave. at 72nd St., New York, NY 10021

Southeastern Community College, 1015 S. Gear Ave., West Burlington, IA 52655/319-752-2731

Southern Ammunition Co., Inc., Rt. 1, Box 6B, Latta, SC 29565/803-752-7751; FAX: 803-752-2022

Southern Armory, The, Rt. 2, Box 134, Woodlawn, VA 24381/703-238-1343; FAX: 703-238-1453

Southern Bloomer Mfg. Co., P.O. Box 1621, Bristol, TN 37620/615-878-6660; FAX: 615-878-8761

Southwind Sanctions, P.O. Box 445, Aledo, TX 76008/817-441-8917

Sparks, Milt, 605 E. 44th St. No. 2, Boise, ID 83714-4800

Specialty Gunsmithing, Lynn McMurdo, P.O. Box 404, Afton, WY 83110/307-886-5535

Specialty Shooters Supply, Inc., 3325 Griffin Rd., Suite 9mm, Fort Lauderdale, FL 33317

Speer Products, Div. of Blount, Inc., P.O. Box 856, Lewiston, ID 83501/208-746-2351; FAX: 208-746-2915

Spegel, Craig, P.O. Box 3108, Bay City, OR 97107/503-377-2697

Spence, George W., 115 Locust St., Steele, MO 63877/314-695-4926

Spencer's Custom Guns, Rt. 1, Box 546, Scottsville, VA 24590/804-293-6836

SPG Lubricants, Box 761-H, Livingston, MT 59047

Sphinx Engineering SA, Ch. des Grandes-Vies 2, CH-2900 Porrentruy, SWITZERLAND/41 66 66 73 81; FAX: 41 66 66 30 90 (U.S. importer—Sphinx USA Inc.)

Sphinx USA Inc., 998 N. Colony, Meriden, CT 06450/203-238-1399; FAX: 203-238-1375

Spokhandguns, Inc., 1206 Fig St., Benton City, WA 99320/509-588-5255

Sport Flite Manufacturing Co., P.O. Box 1082, Bloomfield Hills, MI 48303/810-647-3747

Sport Specialties (See Owen, Harry)

Sports Innovations, Inc., P.O. Box 5181, 8505 Jacksboro Hwy., Wichita Falls, TX 76307/817-723-6015

Sportsman Supply Co., 714 East Eastwood, P.O. Box 650, Marshall, MO 65340/816-886-9393

Sportsmatch Ltd., 16 Summer St., Leighton Buzzard, Bedfordshire, LU7 8HT ENGLAND/0525-381638; FAX: 0525-851236

Sportsmen's Exchange & Western Gun Traders, Inc., 560 S. "C" St., Oxnard, CA 93030/805-483-1917

Springfield, Inc., 420 W. Main St., Geneseo, IL 61254/309-944-5631; FAX: 309-944-3676

Springfield Sporters, Inc., RD 1, Penn Run, PA 15765/412-254-2626; FAX: 412-254-9173

SSK Industries, 721 Woodvue Lane, Wintersville, OH 43952/614-264-0176; FAX: 614-264-2257

Stackpole Books, 5067 Ritter Rd., Mechanicsburg, PA 17055-6921/717-234-5041; FAX: 717-234-1359

Stalker, Inc., P.O. Box 21, Fishermans Wharf Rd., Malakoff, TX 75148/903-489-1010

Stalwart Corporation, P.O. Box 357, Pocatello, ID 83204/208-232-7899; FAX: 208-232-0815

Stanley Bullets, 2085 Heatheridge Ln., Reno, NV 89509

Star Bonifacio Echeverria S.A., Torrekva 3, Eibar, SPAIN 20600/43-107340; FAX: 43-101524 (U.S. importer—Interarms)

Star Custom Bullets, P.O. Box 608, 468 Main St., Ferndale, CA 95536/707-786-9140; FAX: 707-786-9117

Star Machine Works, 418 10th Ave., San Diego, CA 92101/619-232-3216

Star Reloading Co., Inc., 5520 Rock Hampton Ct., Indianapolis, IN 46268/317-872-5840

Stark's Bullet Mfg., 2580 Monroe St., Eugene, OR 97405

Starlight Training Center, Inc., Rt. 1, P.O. Box 88, Bronaugh, MO 64728/417-843-3555

Starnes Gunmaker, Ken, 32900 SW Laurelview Rd., Hillsboro, OR 97123/503-628-0705

Starr Trading Co., Jedediah, P.O. Box 2007, Farmington Hills, MI 48333/810-683-4343; FAX: 810-683-3282

Starrett Co., L.S., 121 Crescent St., Athol, MA 01331/617-249-3551

State Arms Gun Co., 815 S. Division St., Waunakee, WI 53597/608-849-5800

Steffens, Ron, 18396 Mariposa Creek Rd., Willits, CA 95490/707-485-0873

Steger, James R., 1131 Dorsey Pl., Plainfield, NJ 07062

Steves House of Guns, Rt. 1, Minnesota City, MN 55959/507-689-2573

Stewart Game Calls, Inc., Johnny, P.O. Box 7954, 5100 Fort Ave., Waco, TX 76714/817-772-3261; FAX: 817-772-3670

Stewart's Gunsmithing, P.O. Box 5854, Pietersburg North 0750, Transvaal, SOUTH AFRICA/01521-89401

Stiles Custom Guns, RD3, Box 1605, Homer City, PA 15748/412-479-9945; 412-479-8666

Stillwell, Robert, 421 Judith Ann Dr., Schertz, TX 78154

Stoeger Industries, 5 Mansard Ct., Wayne, NJ 07470/201-872-9500; 800-631-0722; FAX: 201-872-0722

Stoeger Publishing Co. (See Stoeger Industries)

Stone Enterprises Ltd., Rt. 609, P.O. Box 335, Wicomico Church, VA 22579/804-580-5114; FAX: 804-580-8421

Stone Mountain Arms, 5988 Peachtree Corners E., Norcross, GA 30071/800-251-9412

Stoney Baroque Shooters Supply, John Richards, Rt. 2, Box 325, Bedford, KY 40006/502-255-7222

Stoney Point Products, Inc., 124 Stoney Point Rd., P.O. Box 5, Courtland, MN 56021-0005/507-354-3360; FAX: 507-354-7236

Storey, Dale A. (See DGS, Inc.)

Stott's Creek Armory, Inc., RR1, Box 70, Morgantown, IN 46160/317-878-5489

Stratco, Inc., 200 E. Center St., Kalispell, MT 59901/406-755-4034; FAX: 406-257-4753

Strawbridge, Victor W., 6 Pineview Dr., Dover, NH 03820/603-742-0013

Strong Holster Co., 105 Maplewood Ave., Gloucester, MA 01930/508-281-3300; FAX: 508-281-6321

Stuart, V. Pat, Rt.1, Box 447-S, Greenville, VA 24440/804-556-3845

Stuart Products, Inc., P.O. Box 1587, Easley, SC 29641/803-859-9360

Sturm, Ruger & Co., Inc., Lacey Place, Southport, CT 06490/203-259-4537; FAX: 203-259-2167

Sundance Industries, Inc., 25163 W. Avenue Stanford, Valencia, CA 91355/805-257-4807

"Su-Press-On," Inc., P.O. Box 09161, Detroit, MI 48209/313-842-4222 7:30-11p.m. Mon-Thurs.

Sure Shot of LA, Inc., 103 Coachman Dr., Houma, LA 70360/504-876-6709

Sure-Shot Game Calls, Inc., P.O. Box 816, 6835 Capitol, Groves, TX 77619/409-962-1636; FAX: 409-962-5465

Svon Corp., 280 Eliot St., Ashland, MA 01721/508-881-8852

Swampfire Shop, The (See Peterson Gun Shop, Inc., A.W.)

SwaroSports, Inc. (See JagerSport, Ltd.)

Swarovski Optik North America Ltd., One Wholesale Way, Cranston, RI 02920/401-942-3380, 800-426-3089; FAX: 401-946-2587

Swenson's 45 Shop, A.D., P.O. Box 606, Fallbrook, CA 92028

Swift Bullet Co., P.O. Box 27, 201 Main St., Quinter, KS 67752/913-754-3959; FAX: 913-754-2359

Swift Instruments, Inc., 952 Dorchester Ave., Boston, MA 02125/617-436-2960; FAX: 617-436-3232

Swivel Machine Works, Inc., 167 Cherry St., Suite 286, Milford, CT 06460/203-926-1840; FAX: 203-874-9212

Szweda, Robert (See RMS Custom Gunsmithing)

T

Tabler Marketing, 2554 Lincoln Blvd., Suite 555, Marina Del Rey, CA 90291/818-755-4565; FAX: 818-831-3441

TacTell, Inc., P.O. Box 5654, Maryville, TN 37802/615-982-7855; FAX: 615-558-8294

Tactical Defense Institute, 574 Miami Bluff Ct., Loveland, OH 45140/513-677-8229

Tag Distributors, 1331 Penna. Ave., Emmaus, PA 18049/610-966-3839

Talley, Dave, P.O. Box 821, Glenrock, WY 82637/307-436-8724, 307-436-9315

Talon Mfg. Co., Inc., 575 Bevans Industrial Ln., Paw Paw, WV 25434/304-947-7440; FAX: 304-947-7447

Tamarack Products, Inc., P.O. Box 625, Wauconda, IL 60084/708-526-9333; FAX: 708-526-9353

Tanfoglio S.r.l., Fratelli, via Valtrompia 39, 41, 25068 Gardone V.T., Brescia, ITALY/30-8910361; FAX: 30-8910183 (U.S. importer—E.A.A. Corp.)

Tanglefree Industries, 1261 Heavenly Dr., Martinez, CA 94553/800-982-4868; FAX: 510-825-3874

Tank's Rifle Shop, P.O. Box 474, Fremont, NE 68025/402-727-1317; FAX: 402-721-2573

Tapco, Inc., 3615 Kennesaw N. Ind. Pkwy., Kennesaw, GA 30144/800-554-1445 (orders); FAX: 404-425-1510

Taracorp Industries, Inc., 1200 Sixteenth St., Granite City, IL 62040/618-451-4400

Tarnham Supply, 431 High St., Boscawen, NH 03303

Tasco Sales, Inc., 7600 NW 26th St., Miami, FL 33156/305-591-3670; FAX: 305-592-5895

Taurus Firearms, Inc., 16175 NW 49th Ave., Miami, FL 33014/305-624-1115; FAX: 305-623-7506

Taurus International Firearms (See U.S. importer—Taurus Firearms, Inc.)

Taylor & Robbins, P.O. Box 164, Rixford, PA 16745/814-966-3233

Taylor's & Co., Inc., 304 Lenoir Dr., Winchester, VA 22603/703-722-2017; FAX: 703-722-2018

TCCI, P.O. Box 302, Phoenix, AZ 85001/602-237-3823; FAX: 602-237-3858

TCSR, 3998 Hoffman Rd., White Bear Lake, MN 55110-4626/800-328-5323; FAX: 612-429-0526

TDP Industries, Inc., 603 Airport Blvd., Doylestown, PA 18901/215-345-8687; FAX: 215-345-6057

Tele-Optics, 5514 W. Lawrence Ave., Chicago, IL 60630/312-283-7757; FAX: 312-283-7757

Ten-Ring Precision, Inc., Alex B. Hamilton, 1449 Blue Crest Lane, San Antonio, TX 78232/210-494-3063; FAX: 210-494-3066

Tennessee Valley Mfg., P.O. Box 1175, Corinth, MS 38834/601-286-5014

Tepeco, P.O. Box 342, Friendswood, TX 77546/713-482-2702

Tetra Gun Lubricants, 1812 Margaret Ave., Annapolis, MD 21401/410-268-6451; FAX: 410-268-8377

Texas Armory, P.O. Box 154906, Waco, TX 76715/817-867-6972

Texas Longhorn Arms, Inc., 5959 W. Loop South, Suite 424, Bellaire, TX 77401/713-341-0775; FAX: 713-660-0493

Texas Platers Supply Co., 2453 W. Five Mile Parkway, Dallas, TX 75233/214-330-7168

Theis, Terry, P.O. Box 535, Fredericksburg, TX 78624/210-997-6778

Theoben Engineering, Stephenson Road, St. Ives, Huntingdon, Cambs., PE17 4WJ ENGLAND/011-0480-461718

Thiewes, George W., 14329 W. Parada Dr., Sun City West, AZ 85375

Thirion Hand Engraving, Denise, P.O. Box 408, Graton, CA 95444/707-829-1876

Thomas, Charles C., 2600 S. First St., Springfield, IL 62794/217-789-8980; FAX: 217-789-9130

Thompson, Randall (See Highline Machine Co.)

Thompson Bullet Lube Co., P.O. Box 472343, Garland, TX 75047-2343/214-271-8063; FAX: 214-840-6743

Thompson Precision, 110 Mary St., P.O. Box 251, Warren, IL 61087/815-745-3625

Thompson Target Technology, 618 Roslyn Ave., SW, Canton, OH 44710/216-453-7707; FAX: 216-478-4723

Thompson/Center Arms, P.O. Box 5002, Rochester, NH 03867/603-332-2394; FAX: 603-332-5133

3-D Ammunition & Bullets, 112 W. Plum St., P.O. Box J, Doniphan, NE 68832/402-845-2285, 800-255-6712; FAX: 402-845-6546

300 Gunsmith Service, Inc., at Cherry Creek State Park Shooting Center, 12500 E. Belleview Ave., Englewood, CO 80111/303-690-3300

3-Ten Corp., P.O. Box 269, Feeding Hills, MA 01030/413-789-2086

Thunder Mountain Arms, P.O. Box 593, Oak Harbor, WA 98277/206-679-4657; FAX: 206-675-1114

Thurston Sports, Inc., RD 3 Donovan Rd., Auburn, NY 13021/315-253-0966

Tiger-Hunt, Box 379, Beaverdale, PA 15921/814-472-5161

Timber Heirloom Products, 618 Roslyn Ave. SW, Canton, OH 44710/216-453-7707; FAX: 216-478-4723

Time Precision, Inc., 640 Federal Rd., Brookfield, CT 06804/203-775-8343

Tink's Safariland Hunting Corp., P.O. Box 244, 1140 Monticello Rd., Madison, GA 30650/706-342-4915; FAX: 706-342-7568

Tinks & Ben Lee Hunting Products (See Wellington Outdoors)

Tioga Engineering Co., Inc., P.O. Box 913, 13 Cone St., Wellsboro, PA 16901/717-724-3533, 717-662-3347

Tippman Pneumatics, Inc., 3518 Adams Center Rd., Fort Wayne, IN 46806/219-749-6022; FAX: 219-749-6619

TMI Products, 930 S. Plumer Ave., Tucson, AZ 85719/602-792-1075; FAX: 602-792-0093

Tom's Gun Repair, Thomas G. Ivanoff, 76-6 Rt. Southfork Rd., Cody, WY 82414/307-587-6949

Top-Line USA, Inc., 7920-28 Hamilton Ave., Cincinnati, OH 45231/513-522-2992, 800-346-6699; FAX: 513-522-0916

Torel, Inc., 1708 N. South St., P.O. Box 592, Yoakum, TX 77995/512-293-2341; FAX: 512-293-3413

TOZ (See U.S. importer—Nygord Precision Products)

Track of the Wolf, Inc., P.O. Box 6, Osseo, MN 55369-0006/612-424-2500; FAX: 612-424-9860

Traditions, Inc., P.O. Box 235, Deep River, CT 06417/203-526-9555; FAX: 203-526-4564

Trafalgar Square, P.O. Box 257, N. Pomfret, VT 05053/802-457-1911

Trammco, 839 Gold Run Rd., Boulder, CO 80302

Treso, Inc., P.O. Box 4640, Pagosa Springs, CO 81157/303-731-2295

Trinidad State Junior College, Gunsmithing Dept., 600 Prospect St., Trinidad, CO 81082/719-846-5631; FAX: 719-846-5667

Triple-K Mfg. Co., Inc., 2222 Commercial St., San Diego, CA 92113/619-232-2066; FAX: 619-232-7675

Trius Products, Inc., P.O. Box 25, 221 S. Miami Ave., Cleves, OH 45002/513-941-5682; FAX: 513-941-7970

Trotman, Ken, 135 Ditton Walk, Unit 11, Cambridge CB5 8PY, ENGLAND/01223-211030; FAX: 01223-212317

True Flight Bullet Co., 5581 Roosevelt St., Whitehall, PA 18052/FAX: 610-262-7806

Trulock Tool, Broad St., Whigham, GA 31797/912-762-4678

Tru-Square Metal Prods., Inc., 640 First St. SW, P.O. Box 585, Auburn, WA 98071/206-833-2310; FAX: 206-833-2349

T.S.W. Conversions, Inc., E. 115 Crain Rd., Paramus, NJ 07650-4017/201-265-1618

TTM, 1550 Solomon Rd., Santa Maria, CA 93455/805-934-1281

Turnbull Restoration, Doug, 6426 County Rd. 30, Bloomfield, NY 14469/716-657-6338

Twin Pine Armory, P.O. Box 58, Hwy. 6, Adna, WA 98522/206-748-4590; FAX: 206-748-7011

Tyler Mfg.-Dist., Melvin, 1326 W. Britton Rd., Oklahoma City, OK 73114/405-842-8044

Tyler Scott, Inc., 313 Rugby Ave., Terrace Park, OH 45174/513-831-7603; FAX: 513-831-7417

U

Uberti, Aldo, Casella Postale 43, I-25063 Gardone V.T., ITALY (U.S. importers—American Arms, Inc.; Cape Outfitters; Cimarron Arms; Dixie Gun Works; EMF Co., Inc.; Forgett Jr., Valmore J.; Navy Arms Co; Taylor's & Co., Inc.)

Uberti USA, Inc., 362 Limerock Rd., P.O. Box 509, Lakeville, CT 06039/203-435-8068; FAX: 203-435-8146

UFA, Inc., 7655 East Evans Rd., Suite 2, Scottsdale, AZ 85260/602-998-3941, 800-616-2776; FAX: 602-922-0148

Ulrich, Doc & Bud (See D.O.C. Specialists, Inc.)

Ultra Light Arms, Inc., P.O. Box 1270, 214 Price St., Granville, WV 26505/304-599-5687; FAX: 304-599-5687

UltraSport Arms, Inc., 1955 Norwood Ct., Racine, WI 53403/414-554-3237; FAX: 414-554-9731

Uncle Mike's (See Michaels of Oregon Co.)

Unertl Optical Co., Inc., John, 308 Clay Ave., P.O. Box 818, Mars, PA 16046-0818/412-625-3810

Unick's Gunsmithing, 5005 Center Rd., Lowellville, OH 44436/216-536-8015

Unique/M.A.P.F., 10, Les Allees, 64700 Hendaye, FRANCE 64700/33-59 20 71 93 (U.S. importer—Nygord Precision Products)

United Binocular Co., 9043 S. Western Ave., Chicago, IL 60620

United States Optics Technologies, Inc., 5900 Dale St., Buena Park, CA 90621/714-994-4901; FAX: 714-994-4904

United States Products Co., 518 Melwood Ave., Pittsburgh, PA 15213/412-621-2130

Upper Missouri Trading Co., 304 Harold St., Crofton, NE 68730/402-388-4844

USAC, 4500-15th St. East, Tacoma, WA 98424/206-922-7589

V

Valade Engraving, Robert, 931 3rd Ave., Seaside, OR 97138/503-738-7672

Van Gorden & Son, Inc., C.S., 1815 Main St., Bloomer, WI 54724/715-568-2612

Van Horn, Gil, P.O. Box 207, Llano, CA 93544

Van Patten, J.W., P.O. Box 145, Foster Hill, Milford, PA 18337/717-296-7069

Vann Custom Bullets, 330 Grandview Ave., Novato, CA 94947

Varner's Service, 102 Shaffer Rd., Antwerp, OH 45813/419-258-8631

Vega Tool Co., c/o T.R. Ross, 4865 Tanglewood Ct., Boulder, CO 80301/303-530-0174

Venco Industries, Inc. (See Shooter's Choice)

Venom Arms Co., Unit 1, Gun Garrel Industrial Centre, Hayseech, Cradley Heath, West Midlands B64 7JZ ENGLAND/011-021-501-3794 (U.S. importers—Mac-1 Distributors, Trooper Walsh)

Venus Industries, P.O. Box 246, Sialkot-1, PAKISTAN/FAX: 92 432 85579

Vest, John, P.O. Box 1552, Susanville, CA 96130/916-257-7228

VibraShine, Inc., Rt. 1, Box 64, Mt. Olive, MS 39119/601-733-5614; FAX: 601-733-2226

Vibra-Tek Co., 1844 Arroya Rd., Colorado Springs, CO 80906/719-634-8611; FAX: 719-634-6886

Vic's Gun Refinishing, 6 Pineview Dr., Dover, NH 03820-6422/603-742-0013

Victory USA, P.O. Box 1021, Pine Bush, NY 12566/914-744-2060; FAX: 914-744-5181

VihtaVuori Oy, FIN-41330 Vihtavuori, FINLAND/358-41-3779211; FAX: 358-41-3771643

VihtaVuori Oy/Kaltron-Pettibone, 1241 Ellis St., Bensenville, IL 60106/708-350-1116; FAX: 708-350-1606

Viking Leathercraft, Inc., 1579A Jayken Way, Chula Vista, CA 91911/800-262-6666; FAX: 619-429-8268

Vincent's Shop, 210 Antoinette, Fairbanks, AK 99701

Vintage Arms, Inc., 6003 Saddle Horse, Fairfax, VA 22030/703-968-0779; FAX: 703-968-0780

Vintage Industries, Inc., 781 Big Tree Dr., Longwood, FL 32750/407-831-8949; FAX: 407-831-5346

Viramontez, Ray, 601 Springfield Dr., Albany, GA 31707/912-432-9683

Voere-KGH m.b.H., P.O. Box 416, A-6333 Kufstein, Tirol, AUSTRIA/0043-5372-62547; FAX: 0043-5372-65752 (U.S. importers—JagerSport, Ltd.)

Volquartsen Custom Ltd., RR 1, Box 33A, P.O. Box 271, Carroll, IA 51401/712-792-4238; FAX: 712-792-2542

Von Minden Gunsmithing Services, 2403 SW 39 Terrace, Cape Coral, FL 33914/813-542-8946

Vorhes, David, 3042 Beecham St., Napa, CA 94558/707-226-9116

Vortek Products, P.O. Box 871181, Canton, MI 48187

VSP Publishers, P.O. Box 887, McCall, ID 83638/208-634-4104

Vulpes Ventures, Inc., Fox Cartridge Division, P.O. Box 1363, Bolingbrook, IL 60440-7363/708-759-1229

W

Wagoner, Vernon G., 2325 E. Encanto, Mesa, AZ 85213/602-835-1307

Walker Arms Co., Inc., 499 County Rd. 820, Selma, AL 36701/334-872-6231

Wallace, Terry, 385 San Marino, Vallejo, CA 94589/707-642-7041

Walt's Custom Leather, Walt Whinnery, 1947 Meadow Creek Dr., Louisville, KY 40218/502-458-4361

Walters, John, 500 N. Avery Dr., Moore, OK 73160/405-799-0376

Walters Industries, 6226 Park Lane, Dallas, TX 75225/214-691-6973

Walther GmbH, Carl, B.P. 4325, D-89033 Ulm, GERMANY (U.S. importer—Interarms)

WAMCO—New Mexico, P.O. Box 205, Peralta, NM 87042-0205/505-869-0826

Ward & Van Valkenburg, 114 32nd Ave. N., Fargo, ND 58102/701-232-2351

Wardell Precision Handguns Ltd., 48851 N. Fig Springs Rd., New River, AZ 85027-8513/602-465-7995

Warenski, Julie, 590 E. 500 N., Richfield, UT 84701/801-896-5319; FAX: 801-896-5319

Warne Manufacturing Co., 9039 SE Jannsen Rd., Clackamas, OR 97015/503-657-5590, 800-683-5590; FAX: 503-657-5695

Warren Muzzleloading Co., Inc., Hwy. 21 North, P.O. Box 100, Ozone, AR 72854/501-292-3268

Washita Mountain Whetstone Co., P.O. Box 378, Lake Hamilton, AR 71951/501-525-3914

WASP Shooting Systems, Rt. 1, Box 147, Lakeview, AR 72642/501-431-5606

Wayland Precision Wood Products, P.O. Box 1142, Mill Valley, CA 94942/415-381-3543; FAX: 415-389-1611

Wayne Firearms for Collectors and Investors, James, 2608 N. Laurent, Victoria, TX 77901/512-578-1258; FAX: 512-578-3559

WD-40 Co., 1061 Cudahy Pl., San Diego, CA 92110/619-275-1400; FAX: 619-275-5823

Weaver Arms Corp., P.O. Box 8, Dexter, MO 63841/314-568-3101

Weaver's Gun Shop, P.O. Box 8, Dexter, MO 63841/314-568-3101

Weaver Products, Div. of Blount, Inc., P.O. Box 39, Onalaska, WI 54650/800-635-7656, 608-781-5800; FAX: 608-781-0368

Weaver Scope Repair Service, 1121 Larry Mahan Dr., Suite B, El Paso, TX 79925/915-593-1005

Webley and Scott Ltd., Frankley Industrial Park, Tay Rd., Rubery, Rednal, Birmingham B45 0PA, ENGLAND/011-021-453-1864; FAX: 021-457-7846 (U.S. importer—Beeman Precision Airguns)

Webster Scale Mfg. Co., P.O. Box 188, Sebring, FL 33870/813-385-6362

Weigand Combat Handguns, Inc., P.O. Box 239, Crestwood Industrial Park, Mountain Top, PA 18707/717-474-9804; FAX: 717-474-9987

Weihrauch KG, Hermann, Industriestrasse 11, 8744 Mellrichstadt, GERMANY/09776-497-498 (U.S. importers—Beeman Precision Airguns; E.A.A. Corp.)

Weisz Parts, P.O. Box 20038, Columbus, OH 43220-0038/614-45-70-500; FAX: 614-846-8585

Welch, Sam, CVSR 2110, Moab, UT 84532/801-259-8131

Wellington Outdoors, P.O. Box 244, 1140 Monticello Rd., Madison, GA 30650/706-342-4915; FAX: 706-342-7568

Wells, Rachel, 110 N. Summit St., Prescott, AZ 86301/602-445-3655

Wells Custom Gunsmith, R.A., 3452 1st Ave., Racine, WI 53402/414-639-5223

Welsh, Bud, 80 New Road, E. Amherst, NY 14051/716-688-6344

Werner, Carl, P.O. Box 492, Littleton, CO 80160

Werth, T.W., 1203 Woodlawn Rd., Lincoln, IL 62656/217-732-1300

Wescombe, P.O. Box 488, Glencoe, CA 95232/209-293-7010

Wessinger Custom Guns & Engraving, 268 Limestone Rd., Chapin, SC 29036/803-345-5677

West, Robert G., 3973 Pam St., Eugene, OR 97402/503-344-3700

Western Design, 1629 Via Monserate, Fallbrook, CA 92028/619-723-9279

Western Missouri Shooters Alliance, P.O. Box 11144, Kansas City, MO 64119/816-597-3950; FAX: 816-229-7350

Western Nevada West Coast Bullets, 2307 W. Washington St., Carson City, NV 89703/702-246-3941; FAX: 702-246-0836

Westfield Engineering, 6823 Watcher St., Commerce, CA 90040/FAX: 213-928-8270

Westwind Rifles, Inc., David S. Sullivan, P.O. Box 261, 640 Briggs St., Erie, CO 80516/303-828-3823

Whildin & Sons Ltd., E.H., RR2, Box 119, Tamaqua, PA 18252/717-668-6743; FAX: 717-668-6745

White Laboratory, Inc., H.P., 3114 Scarboro Rd., Street, MD 21154/410-838-6550; FAX: 410-838-2802

White Owl Enterprises, 2583 Flag Rd., Abilene, KS 67410/913-263-2613; FAX: 913-263-2613

White Rock Tool & Die, 6400 N. Brighton Ave., Kansas City, MO 64119/816-454-0478

Whitestone Lumber Corp., 148-02 14th Ave., Whitestone, NY 11357/718-746-4400; FAX: 718-767-1748

Whitetail Design & Engineering Ltd., 9421 E. Mannsiding Rd., Clare, MI 48617/517-386-3932

Wichita Arms, Inc., 923 E. Gilbert, P.O. Box 11371, Wichita, KS 67211/316-265-0661; FAX: 316-265-0760

Widener's Reloading & Shooting Supply, Inc., P.O. Box 3009 CRS, Johnson City, TN 37602/615-282-6786; FAX: 615-282-6651

Wiebe, Duane, 3715 S. Browns Lake Dr. 103, Burlington, WI 53105-7931

Wiest, M.C., 10737 Dutchtown Rd., Knoxville, TN 37932/615-966-4545

Wilcox All-Pro Tools & Supply, RR 1, Montezuma, IA 50171/515-623-3138

Wild Bill's Originals, P.O. Box 13037, Burton, WA 98013/206-463-5738

Wilderness Sound Products Ltd., 4015 Main St. #A, Springfield, OR 97478/503-741-0263, 800-437-0006; FAX: 503-741-7648

Wildey, Inc., P.O. Box 475, Brookfield, CT 06804/203-355-9000; FAX: 203-354-7759

Wilkinson Arms, 26884 Pearl Rd., Parma, ID 83660/208-722-6771; FAX: 208-722-5197

Will-Burt Co., 169 S. Main, Orrville, OH 44667

William's Gun Shop, Ben, 1151 S. Cedar Ridge, Duncanville, TX 75137/214-780-1807

Williams Bullet Co., J.R., 2008 Tucker Rd., Perry, GA 31069/912-987-0274

Williams Gun Sight Co., 7389 Lapeer Rd., Box 329, Davison, MI 48423/810-653-2131, 800-530-9028; FAX: 810-658-2140

Williams Shootin' Iron Service, The Lynx-Line, 8857 Bennett Hill Rd., Central Lake, MI 49622/616-544-6615

Williamson Precision Gunsmithing, 117 W. Pipeline, Hurst, TX 76053/817-285-0064; FAX: 817-285-0064

Willig Custom Engraving, Claus, D-97422 Schweinfurt, Siedlerweg 17, GERMANY/01149-9721-41446; FAX: 01149-9721-44413

Willow Bend, P.O. Box 203, Chelmsford, MA 01824/508-256-8508; FAX: 508-256-9765

Willson Safety Prods. Div., P.O. Box 622, Reading, PA 19603-0622/610-376-6161; FAX: 610-371-7725

Wilson, Inc., L.E., Box 324, 404 Pioneer Ave., Cashmere, WA 98815/509-782-1328

Wilson's Gun Shop, Box 578, Rt. 3, Berryville, AR 72616/501-545-3618; FAX: 501-545-3310

Winchester Div., Olin Corp., 427 N. Shamrock, E. Alton, IL 62024/618-258-3566; FAX: 618-258-3599

Winkle Bullets, R.R. 1 Box 316, Heyworth, IL 61745

Winter, Robert M., P.O. Box 484, Menno, SD 57045/605-387-5322

Wise Guns, Dale, 333 W. Olmos Dr., San Antonio, TX 78212/210-828-3388

Wisner's Gun Shop, Inc., 287 NW Chehalis Ave., Chehalis, WA 98532/206-748-8942; FAX: 206-748-7011

Wolf's Western Traders, 40 E. Works, No. 3F, Sheridan, WY 82801/307-674-5352

Wolfe Publishing Co., 6471 Airpark Dr., Prescott, AZ 86301/602-445-7810, 800-899-7810; FAX: 602-778-5124

Wolff Co., W.C., P.O. Box I, Newtown Square, PA 19073/610-359-9600, 800-545-0077

Wood, Frank (See Classic Guns, Inc.)

Wood, Mel, P.O. Box 1255, Sierra Vista, AZ 85636/602-455-5541

Woodleigh (See Huntington Die Specialties)

Woods Wise Products, P.O. Box 681552, 2200 Bowman Rd., Franklin, TN 37068/800-735-8182; FAX: 615-726-2637

Woodworker's Supply, 1108 North Glenn Rd., Casper, WY 82601/307-237-5354

World Class Airguns, 2736 Morningstar Dr., Indianapolis, IN 46229/317-897-5548

World of Targets (See Birchwood Casey)

World Trek, Inc., P.O. Box 11670, Pueblo, CO 81001-0670/719-546-2121; FAX: 719-543-6886

Worthy Products, Inc., RR 1, P.O. Box 213, Martville, NY 13111/315-324-5298

Wosenitz VHP, Inc., Box 741, Dania, FL 33004/305-923-3748; FAX: 305-925-2217

Wright's Hardwood Gunstock Blanks, 8540 SE Kane Rd., Gresham, OR 97080/503-666-1705

Wyant Bullets, Gen. Del., Swan Lake, MT 59911

Wyant's Outdoor Products, Inc., P.O. Box B, Broadway, VA 22815

Wyoming Custom Bullets, 1626 21st St., Cody, WY 82414

X,Y

X-Spand Target Systems, 26-10th St. SE, Medicine Hat, AB T1A 1P7 CANADA/403-526-7997; FAX: 403-528-2362

Yankee Gunsmith, 2901 Deer Flat Dr., Copperas Cove, TX 76522/817-547-8433

Yavapai Firearms Academy Ltd., P.O. Box 27290, Prescott Valley, AZ 86312/520-772-8262

Yearout, Lewis E. (See Montana Outfitters)

Yesteryear Armory & Supply, P.O. Box 408, Carthage, TN 37030

Young Country Arms, P.O. Box 3615, Simi Valley, CA 93093

Yukon Arms Classic Ammunition, 1916 Brooks, Suite 223, Missoula, MT 59801

Z

Z-Coat Industrial Coatings, Inc., 3375 U.S. Hwy. 98 S. No. A, Lakeland, FL 33803-8365/813-665-1734

Zeiss Optical, Carl, 1015 Commerce St., Petersburg, VA 23803/804-861-0033; FAX: 804-733-4024

Zero Ammunition Co., Inc., 1601 22nd St. SE, P.O. Box 1188, Cullman, AL 35056-1188/800-545-9376; FAX: 205-739-4683

Zonie Bullets, 790 N. Lake Havasu Ave., Suite 26, Lake Havasu City, AZ 86403

Zriny's Metal Targets, P.O. Box 78, South Newbury, NH 03272/603-428-3127